Collective Behavior

Ralph H. Turner   UNIVERSITY OF CALIFORNIA, LOS ANGELES

Lewis M. Killian   FLORIDA STATE UNIVERSITY, TALLAHASSEE

Collective Behavior

Englewood Cliffs, N. J.
PRENTICE-HALL, INC.

PRENTICE-HALL SOCIOLOGY SERIES

Herbert Blumer, editor

Library of Congress
Catalog Card Number: 57–7843

First printing .... May, 1957
Second printing .... July, 1958
Third printing .... December, 1959
Fourth printing .... January, 1961

Printed in the United States of America

14066–C

Preface

EARLY IN THE PREPARATION of this book, it became clear that, without an extended statement of the field of collective behavior, any selection and ordering of readings we might make would seem a hodgepodge to most readers. The readings are of quite diverse types, ranging from the speculative to the historical and to the strictly quantitative. They have been drawn from a variety of disciplines in conformity with our conviction that no field has any monopoly on the contributions to the area. In the absence of any but Blumer's brief, though admirable, statement, and LaPiere's interesting but unconventional work, it also seemed desirable to bring together as much of a comprehensive survey of the field as was practicable. Consequently, although retaining primary emphasis upon the readings, we have tried to write as complete a textual statement as space would allow. Our discussion aims more at assembling existing ideas than at innovation. We have, however, included our own ideas and organization at numerous points where we felt they might add to prevailing treatment.

Our ultimate hope for this book, then, is that it may provide a baseline, however uneven, from which better maps of the field of collective behavior may be developed.

Since we have drawn upon many disciplines, our treatment may seem incomplete or quixotic to those who do not follow our conception of collective behavior. For example, we have selected excerpts from the vast literature on public opinion with a view to clarifying the public as a functioning collectivity. Consequently, we have hardly noted the majority of literature in this field, which concerns the psychological dynamics of individual attitudes and opinions. Similarly, our treatment of social movements omits the discussions of political parties usual when movements are viewed from the standpoint of political sociology. At the same time, our purpose requires that we seek generalizations applicable to phenomena frequently not viewed together. We look, for example, for principles common to

v

political, religious, and minority movements, for uniformities of crowd behavior in economic, political, religious, racial, and recreational contexts. We are forced to examine the public in close connection with the diffuse crowd, since their distinction as collectivities is merely an ideal-typical one. In thus disregarding conventional grouping of materials from other standpoints, we hope we have made some beginning toward their organized treatment as collective behavior.

We are indebted to the many authors and publishers whose materials appear in our book. We hope that the condensations sometimes made have not distorted what remains of the original papers. In the interest of readability we have eliminated footnotes from selections when they were repetitions of references given elsewhere in the book, when they were peripheral to the main point of the selection, and when they gave credit for ideas that are fairly widely diffused among workers in this field.

To our many friends who have steadily encouraged us to complete this work, we extend our warmest appreciation. In the choice of selections we have had the competent advice of David G. Farrelly, C. Joseph Clawson, Walter Goldschmidt, and J. Fred Weston. Walter Staaks advised us on translation. In many of the tasks of securing permissions and manuscript work, Christine Turner has assisted greatly. Sheldon Messinger and Samuel J. Surace are among our many students who have been valuable critics.

The ideas in the book reflect most directly the tradition established by Robert E. Park and Ernest W. Burgess, and subsequently extended by Herbert Blumer. Chief among our teachers whose ideas appear unacknowledged throughout the text are Everett Hughes, Hans Gerth, E. S. Bogardus, and Melvin J. Vincent. The influence of our colleague, Muzafer Sherif, will be evident to any who know his work. Our treatment of rumor owes much to Tamotsu Shibutani's as yet unpublished ideas on this subject.

Our greatest debt is to Herbert Blumer. As our teacher, his contribution to our thought has received only token acknowledgment in footnotes. As our editor, he has reviewed our work with painstaking care. As author of the definitive statement on collective behavior, he has consistently encouraged us to retain in this book our disagreements and departures from his own analysis.

Ralph H. Turner

Lewis M. Killian

to   CHRISTINE   and   KAY

Contents

ix

PART THREE: *The diffuse collectivity*

PART FOUR: *The social movement*

PART FIVE: *Social consequences of collective behavior*

Part 1

THE NATURE AND EMERGENCE
OF COLLECTIVE BEHAVIOR

The field of collective behavior

*T*HE SUBJECT MATTER of sociology, simply stated, is the human group. Scientific analysis is made possible by the existence of certain regularities in group life. A major portion of sociology is the examination of groups and group life in terms of social organization and the normative order, of the group and its culture. The emphasis is placed on the static, orderly, well-structured aspects of group life and on orderly change.

Just as evident as the regular, predictable phases of man's social behavior are instances in which change rather than stability, uncertainty rather than predictability, disorganization rather than stable structure, are characteristic. Sometimes men act as members of short-lived, loosely-knit, disorderly collectivities which we call crowds. The behavior of a rioting mob, a screaming audience, or an ecstatic religious congregation is markedly different from that of either an enduring informal group or a large, formal organization. Predictions about men's daily behavior can usually be made from knowledge of the culture of a group, but at times the members follow bizarre fads which arise suddenly and disappear before they can become a part of the culture. Many problems of a society are dealt with in a traditional manner, through the functioning of institutions. At times, however, problems arise for which tradition provides no clear-cut solution. An issue is created and a public arises. Public opinion is formed and reformed, often with startling shifts, until the issue disappears. The major norms of a society as embodied in its institutions persist for long periods in spite of varying degrees of dissatisfaction with them. But periodically social movements develop which culminate in institutional change and cultural revision. Some of the more spectacular of these movements are popularly termed "revolutions."

Crowds, mass behavior, the behavior of publics, social movements—these, rather than the more stable and predictable phases of group life, are the subject

3

matter of "collective behavior." The limitation of the term "collective behavior" to phenomena of this type alone is somewhat arbitrary, for all human social life is "collective" in that it involves shared understandings. But by agreement the term "collectivity" can be used to refer to that kind of group characterized by the spontaneous development of norms and organization which contradict or reinterpret the norms and organization of the society. Collective behavior is the study of the behavior of collectivities.

LINES OF DEVELOPMENT IN COLLECTIVE BEHAVIOR

Early interest in collective behavior. Collective behavior as a clearly delimited field of study is still relatively new. Interest in the subjects it includes goes back, however, to before the beginnings of sociology. General sociology and collective behavior both stem from observations about group influence over the individual. The writings of the founders of sociology, Comte, Spencer, and their students, represented a revolt against individualistic explanations of human social behavior based on "reason" or "sensations." These philosopher-sociologists felt that a new science was needed because psychology, as they knew it, did not seem adequate to explain human social behavior. Comte contended that the family, not the individual, was the true social unit, and that the mind could develop only in a social state. His writings stimulated interest in the group and in social interaction, particularly among French scholars.

The most outstanding of these early writers was Emile Durkheim, who strongly influenced the development of both collective behavior and general sociology. In his development of the concepts "social facts" and "collective representations," he underlined the importance of the group factor in human behavior. His approach was interactional, in that he believed collective representations, or culture, to be derived from a fusion of individual minds in association, not merely from the imitation of one individual by others. Individual "representations" or ideas are, according to Durkheim, altered and transformed in the process of "psychosocial synthesis" that goes on in a group. Hence a collective representation constitutes a "different thing," which cannot be explained in terms of individual mental processes.

Because of his emphasis on the reality of the group and its products, Durkheim is often classified as a "group mind theorist," having some sort of mystical conception of the group as a superindividual entity with an existence entirely separate from that of the individuals composing it. To a considerable degree this is a misconception arising out of overliteralistic word translations. The fact that men's thoughts are shaped into a cultural uniformity which stems from their own uncritical assumption that the framework of their thought has an independent existence outside of themselves was a crucial discovery in the understanding of group behavior. Even though his ideas were misunderstood, Durkheim succeeded in calling attention to the power of the group to bring forth social products which could not be explained through the analysis of individual physiological and psychological process. His ideas gave a clear definition of the province of sociology as a separate science.

Another writer who, influenced by Comte, turned his attention to social processes and group influence on the individual was Gabriel Tarde. In his attempts to explain human social behavior, Tarde relied upon the process of imitation. He emphasized the diffusion of common forms of behavior in a society through the universal tendency of humans to imitate one another. He adumbrated modern theories of collective behavior in his analysis of various forms of imitation, such as "custom imitation" and "fashion imitation," and in his differentiation between the crowd and the public, as representing compact and diffuse collectivities. Yet Tarde's theory of social behavior was still essentially individualistic, in contrast to Durkheim's theories. The innovations that became "socialized" through imitation were still the products of individual minds. The interaction of individuals in the group served only to spread these individual products, and in no way did it produce them.

For all the influence that they later had on the field of collective behavior, neither Tarde, Durkheim, nor any of the other writers of this period were specifically concerned with collective behavior as a distinct form occurring under specifiable conditions. Rather, they sought to develop a general theory of social action. Their approach had a social-psychological slant which was not evident in the development of sociological theory in England and Germany, but which later reappeared in the emergence of collective behavior as a distinct field of study.

Gustave LeBon is often identified as the founder of collective behavior. He spoke of "the psychology of the crowd" and treated the crowd as the prototype of all group behavior. Thus LeBon had the same broad interest in the group and its influence on the individual as did other sociologists of his day. His subject was social behavior, but he approached it through his theory of "the mind of the crowd." Hence he had no hesitation about applying the "principles of crowd psychology" to the behavior of a wide variety of groups which would not today be classed as crowds, from parliamentary assemblies to entire nations.

LeBon's characterization of "the crowd" as marked by impulsive, uninhibited behavior, contagion, and suggestibility remains an apt one. His descriptions of the behavior of crowds were graphic and highly accurate. His conclusion that "in the crowd, the old is destroyed so that it may be replaced by the new" is a telling assessment of the significance of many instances of crowd behavior for the process of social change. He remained vague, indeed mystical, on the question of how and under what conditions collective behavior emerges. Under "certain circumstances," which LeBon failed to describe, individuals are "transformed" into a crowd, with a "sort of collective mind" being formed. Although he indicated that there are "successive degrees of organization of crowds," LeBon dealt only with what he called "such crowds as have attained to the phase of complete organization." Furthermore, his analysis of the psychological state of the individuals comprising a crowd asserts that they are each experiencing the same emotions and engaging in the same kind of response to a single, compelling source of suggestion. While each reinforces the response of the other, there is no interaction based on differential participation.

These early French writers all were intensely aware of the influence of the group on the individual, as reflected in the persistent, constraining power of tradition. At the time, they were concerned with the fact that these group influences change, sometimes quite suddenly and radically. Regarding culture as essentially a group product, they sought the explanation for its changes in the group. The historical drama of the French Revolution, with the contrast between the solid tradition of the Ancient Regime and the rapid, drastic changes of the Revolutionary Era, no doubt forced them into awareness of both the static and the dynamic aspects of the influence of the group on the individual.

The emergence of collective behavior as a field. As sociology developed in England and America, the static aspects of social influences received more and more emphasis. The evolutionary approach of Spencer, reflected in the *laissez-faire* social science theories of William Graham Sumner, largely dominated American sociology during most of its early development. Culture, regarded as social heritage changing in accordance with its own laws (such as the mechanism of "cultural cumulation"), came to occupy a pre-eminent position in sociological analysis. Emphasis was placed on the notion that man's social behavior was "culturally determined" or "culturally conditioned," while the remaking of culture through collective behavior received relatively little emphasis. The essentially anthropological concepts of cultural accumulation, cultural diffusion, and cultural lag came to dominate theories of social change, and the social-psychological aspects of social change were neglected.

Hence, early in the history of sociology as a discipline, collective behavior was relegated to a peripheral and somewhat inferior position as a special field of sociology. It dealt, in a rather tentative fashion, with types of social behavior which could not be accounted for by the culturally-prescribed patterns of society. Instances of collective behavior seem to have been regarded as aberrations from the main current of cultural continuity, worthy of little study and of only passing reference.

A few American sociologists with a social-psychological orientation kept interest in the field alive. E. A. Ross devoted a large portion of his pioneer volume in social psychology to phenomena that would today be classified as collective behavior: the crowd, the mob, fads, fashions, the public, and mass movements. Influenced strongly by Tarde, he invoked suggestion, or imitation, as the principal mechanism accounting for both "planes"—stable, traditional social influences—and "currents"—dynamic, changing influences.

Writing not long after Ross, the psychologist William McDougall sought to explain the rapid spread of a common emotion through a crowd and the intensification of this emotion as it spreads. Although he wrote a book entitled *The Group Mind,* he rejected a "collective consciousness" as an explanation. In accordance with his general emphasis on instincts as motives, he concluded that the excesses of the crowd are the results of the expression of the primary emotions and coarser sentiments. These primary impulses are expressed in the crowd rather than in more highly organized groups for two reasons, he believed. One is the loss of self-consciousness which the individual experiences in "the collective mental state." The other is a diminution of the sense of personal responsibility and the relaxation of ordinary attitudes of self-criticism and self-restraint.

During the early history of social psychology, Floyd Allport attempted to construct a social psychology based strictly on the principles of behaviorism and completely avoiding the "group mind" fallacy. He applied these principles to collective behavior, denying that any new forms of behavior emerge in the collectivity. Crowd behavior is merely the sum of individual reactions. Identity of reaction means that all members are exposed to the same stimulus. The crowd itself intensifies the reactions of each individual because of the stimulation of seeing others respond in the same way. Allport summed up his theory of collective behavior in the declaration, "The individual in the crowd behaves just as he would behave alone, only more so."

Robert E. Park and Ernest W. Burgess, in their *Introduction to the Science of Sociology,* defined the field of collective behavior and introduced some of its most enduring concepts. Under the heading "collective behavior" they discussed the crowd, the public, sects, and mass movements. They identified "social unrest" as the most elementary form of collective behavior and the condition out of which other forms develop. They used the term "social contagion" to designate the relatively rapid spread of a cultural trait. Pointing out that LeBon failed to distinguish between the crowd and the public, they identified the public as a type of collectivity in which interaction takes the form of discussion. To explain social contagion in the crowd they introduced the concept "milling." It was they, too, who suggested one of the earliest classifications of crowds, as being either "acting" or "expressive."

These early efforts by Park and Burgess to define and delineate the field of collective behavior as a part of sociology were carried on by Herbert Blumer. Blumer gave collective behavior its clearest definition, both as a type of behavior and as a division of sociology. As a separate division of sociology, he said, it is the study of that collective behavior which arises spontaneously and is not due to pre-established understandings or traditions. Blumer also underlined the significance of this field of study when he declared, "The student of collective behavior seeks to understand the way in which a new social order arises, for the appearance of a new social order is equivalent to the emergence of new forms of collective behavior."

Blumer outlined the mechanisms of collective behavior and the forms of elementary collective grouping—the crowd, the mass, and the public. He also proposed a classification of social movements—general, specific, and expressive—and analyzed social movements in terms of stages of development. Although Blumer's analysis of collective behavior constituted a preliminary outline of the field rather than a definitive treatment, his hypotheses have been widely used as a basic for the treatment of the subject in sociology textbooks.

Interest in the influence of the group on the individual constitutes the central, most continuous line of development leading to the present field of collective behavior. What is now termed collective behavior has, however, over a long period of time, been studied by students with other theoretical interests. Hence the field as presently constituted represents the convergence of several lines of development.

The study of the abnormal. One of the most relevant areas of interest has been the psychological study of the abnormal. The impulsive, irrational behavior of the psychotic readily suggests an analogy to the violent, often antisocial, behavior of the crowd. The suggestibility of the patient under hypnosis invites comparison to the suggestibility of the supposedly "normal" members of the crowd or the mass. Since the earliest days of the scientific study of psychopathology, attempts have been made to explain collective behavior by pointing out its similarities to individual psychopathology. One of the earliest analogies was drawn by the psychologist Boris Sidis, who was interested in the phenomenon of "the subconscious," particularly as this "portion" of the mind was made evident in hypnosis. Finding in the "subconscious self" of the individual the impulsiveness, fickleness, passion, and suggestibility which he observed in the crowd, he concluded that a crowd is a collection of individuals under the control of the subconscious. The unity of the crowd was to be explained by the fact that the subconscious self is both gregarious and suggestible. Paradoxically, Sidis explained both institutionalized social behavior and emergent collective behavior as resulting from suggestion. He was particularly concerned with mass behavior. The "civilization of society," he believed, restricts individuality more and more, so that the civilized individual becomes "an automaton, a mere puppet." Hence, "the very organization of society keeps up the disaggregation of consciousness."

The father of psychoanalytic theory, Sigmund Freud, turned his attention to collective behavior in *Group Psychology and the Analysis of the Ego*. Freud suggested that the crowd, presenting the individual with uniform, compelling suggestions as to what was right, became a temporary substitute for the superego and thus controlled his behavior. The crowd or the mass became, so to speak, a collective father-figure.

The most direct and systematic application of psychoanalytic theory to collective behavior was made by Everett Dean Martin, particularly in *The Behavior of Crowds*. Like LeBon and many other writers, Martin ignored the difference between compact and diffuse collectivities. To him, the crowd was not a particular kind of collectivity; it was a mental condition which could "occur simultaneously to people in any gathering or association." This condition he described as a simultaneous release of repressed impulses. This ascendancy of the unconscious in an assemblage may occur when mutual concessions to their socially forbidden impulses are made by a number of individuals who, at the same time, disguise these impulses as respectable, moral sentiments. Martin's approach assumes an initial homogeneity in the members of the crowd, stemming from the fact that they all have the same unconscious impulses, repressed in all by the social. The gist of his conception of collective behavior is contained in his assertion that the crowd consists of "people going crazy together." This is the point of departure for his analysis of the characteristics of crowd behavior by analogy to the psychotic individual, particularly the paranoiac.

A more recent application of psychoanalytic theory to collective behavior is that of E. A. Strecker, in *Beyond the Clinical Frontiers*. His approach is very similar to that of Martin, regarding crowd behavior as an attempt of a group to escape reality in the same manner that a psychotic individual does. Strecker extends this type of reasoning to differentiate between types of social movements. Moderate reform movements are not classified as "social movements" by Strecker; he regards them as the plans of "intelligent minorities." Social movements are forms of crowd behavior, for they "promise unreality disguised as utopias," thus representing the dominance of the primitive and emotional unconscious rather than intelligence.

Certain themes are characteristic of treatments of collective behavior as part of the study of the abnormal. One is the distinction between consciousness and the unconscious, collective behavior being regarded as a form dominated by the latter. This is usually followed by the conclusion that collective behavior results from the simultaneous release in a number of individuals of impulses that are unconscious, repressed, and socially unacceptable. In such writings there is the more or less explicit premise that collective behavior is pathological and socially undesirable. Hence most of these writings express concern over the evils of a "crowd-minded," "mob," or "mass" society, and any behavior of which the author disapproves tends to be classed as "crowd behavior."

Epidemics and crazes in history. An even older line of development is the interest, particularly of historians, in bizarre behavior often referred to as "mental epidemics." Long before social psychologists arose to analyze the causes and mechanisms of such behavior, historians were recording detailed descriptions. The epidemic of religious dances in the 15th and 16th centuries inspired many historical accounts, the most notable being J. F. C. Hecker's *Dancing Mania of the Middle Ages.* The speculative booms of the 17th and 18th centuries, such as the tulip mania in Holland and the "Mississippi Bubble" in France, attracted similar attention. Many of the "epidemics" of this period were graphically described in a book by Charles Mackay, first published in 1841. The frenzied behavior of religious crowds during the Great Revival on the American Frontier, in the first half of the 19th century, as well as the unusual behavior of some religious sects, such as the Shakers, has long intrigued observers. Every century has brought forth instances of bizarre mass behavior which defied logical explanation and stimulated interest in this aspect of collective behavior. Unfortunately, even the more recent examples, such as the Florida Land Boom, the "chain letter" and "pyramid club" fads, college "panty-raids," and the James Dean cult, have been described far more than they have been studied.

The operations of political democracy. Finally, the interest in collective behavior can be traced back through many areas of political theory. With the decline of the absolutism of monarchy, the rise of national states, and the increasing significance of the printed word, philosophers and, later, social scientists began to ask questions about the nature of society, its leaders, the state, and the process of government. During the 18th and 19th centuries the succession of political crises and the continuing controversies about the nature of man and society stimulated interest in many fields which are today relevant to the subject of collective behavior.

As political democracy and representative government came to replace the despotism of kings, one reaction was the evaluation of the role of the leader. This was not simply a revival of the classic argument about the "divine right of kings"; it was a logical, albeit biased, analysis of the role of the individual leader in the functioning of society. Thomas Carlyle's theories of the importance of "the hero" to social order and progress represent one such evaluation. Disgusted by the disorganization accompanying the Industrial Revolution and despairing of the ability of "the common man" to rule wisely, he extolled the virtues of the benevolent despot. A much more objective, less moralistic analysis of leadership is found in the writings of Max Weber. Weber did not regard the leader as the primary instrument of social order and social change. He was concerned with broad social forces and with social structure, symbolized by bureaucracy. He was an acute analyst of both the statics and the dynamics of social life. On the one hand, he perceived that great social systems, such as feudalism, break up and give way to new systems despite the weight of tradition behind them. It was in this connection, the break with tradition and the emergence of new forms, that he devoted his attention to the role of the charismatic leader. In his concept of the "routinization of charisma," however, he expressed the notion that the revolutionary changes of today become institutionalized and constitute the traditions of tomorrow, and that the vigorous, unconventional leadership of the charismatic leader becomes formalized in bureaucracy.

The recurrent breaking up of old forms and the institutionalizing of the new was noted by Vilfredo Pareto in his theory of "the circulation of elites." Although he dealt with classes rather than with individual leaders, Pareto also saw that the static aspects of society, represented by the decadent rentier class, are the end products of the dynamic process of social change initiated over and over by the speculators.

As representative democracy grew and public discussion through the press increased, there was a growth of interest in the public and public opinion. Although public-opinion polling is a relatively recent development, the study of the behavior of publics has a longer history. One of the earliest and most significant attempts to apply social-psychological principles to this important type of collective behavior was that of Walter Bagehot, in *Physics and Politics*. Bagehot is best known for his phrase, "the cake of custom," which suggests that he was most impressed by the binding power of tradition. Actually the focus of his attention was on the breaking up of "the cake of custom" which he observed in his time. He postulated three stages in the emergence of socialized man—"the stage of no polity," "the stage of fixed polity," and "the stage of flexible polity," which he called "the age of discussion." It was during the second stage that rigid custom prevailed, but Bagehot believed that civilized countries had entered the third stage, in which "the cake of custom" was broken by discussion, encouraging diversity, tolerance, intelligence, and choice. He emphasized the unconscious copying of models of behavior presented by the group and by great men as explanation of the formation of public opinion and the spread of fashion. It has been said of Bagehot that "he marks the beginning of the psychological approach to politics."

Another early writer who directed his attention to public opinion and the operation of political democracy was Graham Wallas. Well before it became commonplace for social scientists to recognize that the change from a small, stable community to a mass, urban society demands a new basis for consensus, Wallas pointed out that it is difficult for the voter to have an intelligent opinion on complex practical problems when he is part of one of "our vast delocalized urban populations." He argued that because of the lack of a personal network of communication in a mass society and, more basically, because of the irrational element in human nature itself, irrational factors in politics must receive more intelligent analysis. In line with this contention, he analyzed the bases on which he believed public opinion was formed, including the effects of propaganda, the use of personal contacts by candidates, and the creation of political parties by the use of symbols rather than logical arguments.

Wallas' analysis of the operation of representative democracy in a mass society foreshadowed the writings a few years later of Walter Lippmann, in *Public Opinion* and *The Phantom Public,* and of John Dewey, in *The Public and Its Problems.* Both of these writers conceived of the public as a collectivity attempting to reach consensus on issues about which the individual member could not have adequate knowledge and for which tradition provided no clear-cut solutions. Public opinion was a process of collective behavior, taking place in the interaction of individuals struggling with a common, complex problem in a relatively unstructured situation.

With the development of methods of attitude measurement and opinion polling, this conception of the public and the nature of public opinion ceased to guide most of the analyses of public opinion. Preoccupation with the technique of public-opinion measurement and the prediction of election results led to a conception of public opinion as simply the sum of opinions regarding any issue, as expressed by a number of discrete individuals at a given moment in time. The tentative, emergent nature of public opinion was overlooked in the search for correlations between the personal characteristics of the subjects and their opinions of the moment.

Not only the smooth, orderly workings of democracy, but the disruptions of political systems by revolutions, violent or bloodless, have stimulated interest in collective behavior. Largely out of this line of development grew the current segment of collective behavior concerned with social movements. The earliest writings of this type were not scientific, but were partisan works concerned with philosophical justification of programs of reform and the analysis of how these programs could be put into effect. The essays of the revolutionary philosophers of the 17th and 18th centuries were followed by more detailed blueprints for revolution in the 19th century. The French syndicalist, George Sorel, addressed himself directly to the question of how social change took place. In *Reflections on Violence* he proposed that "the myth," even though impossible of attainment, was essential to the unification and inspiration of a revolutionary movement. In his role as revolutionary, rather than as economist or prophet, Karl Marx suggested ways in which dissatisfaction with the existing order could be crystallized and the revolution of the dispossessed classes organized. Later, Lenin provided even more detailed and explicit suggestions for the tactics of a revolutionary movement. Like the French Revolution, the Russian Revolution became the subject of numerous historical accounts, such as Trotsky's *History of the Russian Revolution*.

After World War I, the unrest which found one of its expressions in fascism inspired many analyses of mass society, its discontents, and its political movements. One of the most notable of these analyses was José Ortega y Gasset's *Revolt of the Masses*. In the United States, the political and religious movements which sprang up, especially during the depression years, focused attention on social movements and led to many historical accounts as well as to such analyses as Hadley Cantril's *Psychology of Social Movements*.

From this review of the converging lines of development of interest in collective behavior, it is evident that even though the field is relatively new, there is a long history of interest in the subjects that it includes. It is also evident that the systematic, empirical study of the phenomena of collective behavior has lagged far behind the interest of historians, journalists, and philosophers. Opportunities to study the various forms of collective behavior have long been abundant. What has been lacking is a set of theoretical propositions founded on actual observation of collective behavior rather than on analogies to individual behavior. A similar need exists for systematic, controlled observation of instances of collective behavior which offer themselves for study, to replace the uncontrolled, often biased descriptions which prevail.

DEFINITION OF COLLECTIVE BEHAVIOR

We are now prepared to attempt a definition of collective behavior as the field is understood at the present time. First, collective behavior refers to the characteristics of *groups* rather than of separate individuals. For example, individuals may panic, but only group panic is an instance of collective behavior.

As a group, a collectivity is more than simply a number of individuals. A group always consists of people who are in interaction and whose interaction is affected by some sense that they constitute a unit. This latter sense is most universally expressed in the members' concern to define the "group's opinions" and what the "group expects" of its members. Thus, the operation of some kind of group norms is a crucial feature of interaction. When we say that collective behavior concerns groups we are referring to the study of individuals interacting in such manner as to acknowledge and create social norms.

But collective behavior is not merely identical with the study of groups. A contrast is generally drawn between collective behavior and organizational behavior. Organizational behavior is the behavior of groups which are governed by established rules of procedure which have behind them the force of tradition. Even in the case of a new organization, there is generally a concern to find operating rules that have sanction in the larger culture, such as Robert's *Rules of Order,* and any action once taken becomes an incipient tradition through the principle of observing precedent. Collectivities, or the groups within which collective behavior takes place, are not guided in a straightforward fashion by the culture of the society. While a collectivity has members, it lacks defined procedures both for selecting and for identifying members. While it has leaders, it lacks defined procedures for selecting and identifying leaders. The members are those who happen to be participating and the leaders are those who are being followed by the members. While the collectivity is oriented toward an object of attention and arrives at some shared objective, these are not defined in any formal sense in advance, and no defined procedures exist whereby decisions are to be reached. While the collectivity has norms governing the interaction of its members and punishes those who violate these norms, there are no established procedures for arriving at these norms, for identifying what are the norms of the group, or for disciplining the nonconformist member. Thus the collectivity is a group governed by emergent or spontaneous norms rather than formalized norms.

Collective behavior may be even more sharply contrasted with institutional behavior. Institutional behavior characterizes groups which are envisaged in and guided by the culture of the larger society. Accordingly, institutional behavior refers to activities which are necessary to the conduct of society's business, which support the norms of the larger society. Collective behavior, on the other hand, develops norms which are not envisaged in the larger society and may even modify or oppose these broader norms.

The relation of collective behavior to certain other areas—such as small groups, the study of informal groups in industry and in other formal associations, and social psychology—is somewhat more complex. Groups may be classified by different criteria. The area of collective behavior is based upon a classification of groups according to the nature of the social norms which govern them. The field of small groups is based upon a classification of groups according to size. The two systems of classification overlap, so that collective behavior may be found in both small and large groups, and small groups may exhibit collective behavior or organizational behavior.

So-called "informal groups" may have certain of the features of collective behavior. Generally, however, they have a continuity of membership and leadership and norms which limits the incidence of collective behavior. Furthermore, they are usually studied from the standpoint of their effect upon formally organized associations within which they operate. Thus interest is not concentrated upon the collective behavior aspects of informal groups. However, it appears again that there is an overlapping between the study of collective behavior and that of informal groups, because their isolation as areas of subject matter is based upon two somewhat different dimensions of classification.

Finally, collective behavior is to be distinguished from social psychology. In collective behavior the absence of tradition-imposed stability leaves more room for group patterns to be shaped by the attitudes of individual members than in regularly organized groups. Consequently the examination of collective behavior must have considerable reliance upon the methods and generalizations of social psychology. However, the individual rather than the group is the center of attention in social psychology. While the study of collective behavior acknowledges that the group is composed of interacting individuals, the collectivity rather than the individual is the ultimate center of interest.

RECURRING ISSUES IN COLLECTIVE BEHAVIOR (*collectively not individuality*)

Collective behavior is not yet an area in which generalizations can be presented in precise form and with the backing of experimental or quantitative evidence. There is no dearth of ideas derived from historical analysis and from the impressionistic examination of cases. But few steps have yet been taken toward the verification of these ideas through more rigorous procedures. Consequently, collective behavior abounds with as yet unresolved issues which must not be prejudged.

Among the issues, however, there are some which rest on semantic confusion, obvious oversimplification, or sheer dogmatism. These issues are used to assign students to "schools of thought" which can be dealt with by name-calling. Such issues impede communication that might lend to discovery of convergences of thought, and by requiring that each person "show his colors" they prevent each faction from modifying its viewpoint to take account of valid observations by the other. Likewise, these pseudo-issues divert attention from the many issues of very real importance.

By eliminating certain major pseudo-issues, and by trying to state other issues in their essential terms, it may be possible to avoid from the start some of the false leads found in the literature. With this objective in mind, we shall examine briefly three groups of issues. First, we shall attempt to separate semantic from empirical questions in the so-called "group mind" problem. Second, we shall consider the justification for describing collective behavior in terms of irrationality or emotional behavior, and for the use of such terms as "emotional contagion." And finally, we shall examine tension theory, as a sort of skeletal psychological framework often employed in the analysis of collective behavior.

The "group mind" issue. A great deal of heat has been generated as to whether there is a "group mind," whether the group is something other than the sum of individual responses, and similar questions. These issues have received unusual attention in the area of collective behavior, where the studies of individual and group behavior tend to merge. Accusations of "group mind fallacy" and "individualistic fallacy" have been freely hurled. Some of the confusion lies in the fact that not one but several questions are actually involved. By looking at some of these questions separately we may be able to eliminate spurious issues and clarify the legitimate points of disagreement.

The first question is how to describe group activity. A group is both many individuals acting and a totality. Groups tend to impress observers more strongly as wholes, with the result that descriptions usually are cast in terms of the group acting and reacting rather than the separate members. We hear that the mob attacked its victim or the public favored a particular course of action. There are dangers in this prevalent way of describing group behavior. In the first place it is often a serious oversimplification. By thinking in these terms we may be blinded to any diversity of individual behavior or differing degrees of individual conviction backing up the apparent behavior of the group.

In the second place, the description of group behavior as the actions of a total unit often leads us to think of the group through analogies derived from individual behavior. Here we find the tendency to attribute to the group a mind, a conscience, a sense of responsibility, a lack of self-control, a sense of self-esteem, etc. A shift in crowd behavior is the crowd "changing its mind," as if a group could change its mind in the same sense as an individual does. These tendencies to personify the group are accentuated in those spectacular instances of crowd behavior which arouse our indignation and make us seek something which can be an object of moral blame.

In order to escape these fallacies, some investigators insist that only the behavior of individuals can be described. But this solution is not without danger. In its most naive form it becomes a mere semantic sleight-of-hand whereby the action of the group is restated as applying to each of its members. Thus we may be told that the members of the crowd attacked their victim. The same danger of overlooking complexity applies here as in group description. And the danger of thinking by analogy between individual and group remains, but in changed form. The tendency is to impute to the individual members of the group the motives and attitudes that would explain the action of the total group—if it had been the action of an individual. Thus the explanation of war is sought by imputing hostile attitudes to the members of the warring nations. Because individuals usually fight each other only when they feel hatred toward one another, it is assumed that war eventuates from the hatred which members of the warring nations feel toward one another. Modern research on war has demonstrated clearly that this is not so, but the pattern of thinking continues to be applied to group behavior in many ways.

Even when these fallacies are assiduously avoided, the simple description of individual actions is likely to be both inefficient and incomplete. Where something more than an aggregation exists, some division of labor inevitably arises and individual behavior is patterned into roles which in some way or another complement one another in furthering some kind of group objective. In a lynching, the individuals who bring ropes are not necessarily interested in ropes per se; those who threaten the sheriff who appears on the scene are not distinguished by their hatred of sheriffs. In each instance these are tasks that fall into place as part of the total objective of lynching, and what one man does is determined in part by what others have left to be done. Specifying the general end and pattern of behavior in the group may be more useful than detailed accounts of individual behavior and will most certainly provide the necessary orientation for interpreting the latter.

There is a place for both group and individual types of description when the respective sets of fallacies can be avoided. Neither the group nor the individual descriptive approach is inherently more error-free than the other. Each type of description completes the other. Which will be given priority depends on the purpose at hand. Groups as wholes have effects on society and they tend to be perceived as wholes. To the degree to which we are interested in society, then, individual description will be subordinated to group description. When groups are of interest only as contexts for the study of individual psychological processes, group description will be subordinated, but not omitted.

A second question involved in the group-versus-individual issue concerns whether the individual in the group acts differently from the way in which he would act if not in the group. Answers have ranged from one extreme view that the group suffuses its members with attitudes and motives which have no counterparts in their individual psyches to the opposing view that the group is no more than several individuals with common purposes doing what each as an individual would be doing anyway. Actually, neither answer has often been given in extreme form. The individualists have admitted that division of labor takes place and that the intensity of behavior may be heightened by the presence of like-minded persons, while contending that the behavior remains an expression of attitudes which were present in the individual originally. The group mind advocates have often meant only that there is a decision-making process which takes place on a group basis, reaching conclusions which would not have eventuated from individual decision-making.

Many of the discrepancies between these points of view vanish when certain observations are made. First, a person seldom has only a single clear-cut attitude on any given matter. The typical American is both for and against granting Negroes equality with whites; the typical laborer conceives of himself as both opposed to and identified with his employer. Not all attitudes on a given question are equally well recognized by the individual. In the extreme case of "repression" the actor possesses attitudes which affect his behavior but which he would vigorously disclaim. Consequently, any individual can find attitudinal support for a variety of courses of action regarding any particular object. In a group situation certain attitudes are elicited and reinforced, so that individuals act in accordance with attitudes which would not necessarily have become dominant had they been acting purely as individuals.

Second, action is a consequence not merely of attitudes toward the object in question, but of attitudes toward the group, toward the self, and many others.

A man who fears a crowd may conform to a course of action that is not in accordance with any of his attitudes toward the object in question. A man who conceives of himself as a leader may sense a direction in which the group decision is going and actively espouse it in order to retain leadership quite apart from his private attitudes toward that course of action.

For these reasons it is entirely appropriate and not in the least mystical to speak of collective decision-making, with group decisions and group action which could never have been predicted simply by any summing of individual attitudes on the matter at hand. At the same time, the attitudes of the individuals, both toward the object in question and toward matters which become indirectly involved, do make decisions in certain directions easier to obtain than decisions in other directions, and will render other potential decisions impossible. Thus both the processes of group decision-making and individual attitudes must be taken into account. The individual in the group does indeed act differently from the way in which he would if alone, though not without some basis for this action in his own attitudes.

Answers to these two questions indicate the answer to the final question. Some have argued that since the only *real* actions are the actions of individuals, there can be no special set of principles governing group action but merely the application of the psychology of individual behavior to action in a group context. Experience has demonstrated that regularities at the group level can be observed and generalizations formulated quite apart from the understanding of individual psychological principles underlying them. Best documented are the regularities of economic behavior. Study of the individual processes which culminate in these observed regularities of economic functioning is a useful type of investigation but does not take the place of generalizations at the collective level. Animals and plants are made of chemicals, but generalizations at the chemical level do not take the place of generalizations about the characteristics of a plant or animal as a whole. Similarly, generalizations at the group level are needed and can be made, whether the individual psychological processes underlying the group are understood or not. Each level of investigation can benefit by cues from the other, so investigators at one level keep informed of developments at the other. Each benefits from advances at the other level, but each level has its own generalizations to develop.

Irrationality and emotionality. Another recurring problem in collective behavior is the tendency to single out for study only those collective phenomena of which the observer disapproves and to depict the processes of collective behavior in value-laden terms. Alarm over the actions of destructive mobs, panics, and revolutionary or totalitarian social movements is reflected in this tendency. On this basis collective behavior is often erroneously contrasted to "rational" behavior by being designated "irrational" or "emotional." There are two important errors involved in approaching collective behavior in this way.

In the first place, the terms "irrational" and "emotional" have reference to individual behavior. In accordance with our discussion of the group mind problems, the application of these terms to the group means one of two things. Either it is a shorthand way of saying that each of the members in the collectivity is acting irrationally or it is reasoning by analogy that a group, like an individual, can be emotional or irrational. The latter procedure we recognize as fallacious, and the former assumption of homogeneity among members of collectivities is not supported by our knowledge.

In the second place, the very distinctions themselves are difficult to make. Emotion and reason are not today regarded as irreconcilables. Emotion may accompany the execution of a well-reasoned plan, and the execution of an inadequately-reasoned plan may be accompanied by no arousal of emotions. The rational-irrational dichotomy seems to have two distinct kinds of meanings. Based on external criteria, behavior can be called rational when it is an efficient way of achieving some goal. By this definition much institutional behavior is irrational and much collective behavior is rational. Who can say that the occasional lynching was not for several decades a fairly efficient way of keeping the Negro in a subordinate place? Using internal criteria, behavior is irrational when the individual does not weigh all possible alternatives of which he can be aware in deciding his course of action. By this definition most institutional behavior is irrational, since social norms narrow the range of alternatives which the individual can effectively consider. While each of the major types of collective behavior has its own characteristic ways of so restricting attention within the range of potential alternatives, collective behavior is not different from other types of behavior in this respect.

The basis for these errors lies in the fact that in folk-usage we tend to confuse rationality with behavior in conformity with the dictates of culture. When an individual follows uncritically the courses of action which are sanctioned in his society we think of him as a reasonable person, largely because he is (a) like us and (b) predictable and therefore easy to deal with. When a person challenges the established cultural dictates or is forced to act where cultural dictates are nonexistent, vague, or contradictory, his behavior becomes unpredictable to others about him, making him hard to deal with, and others may find it difficult to "understand" his behavior. Hence he is said to be acting emotionally or irrationally. The upshot of this discussion is to bring us back to our definition of collective behavior as the action of groups which operate without clear-cut direction from the culture within which they are found. To refer to this behavior as irrational or emotional is either fallacious or a tautology.

Tension theory. Another of the recurrent theoretical questions in collective behavior has to do with the application of various forms of "tension theory" as explanatory concepts. Tension theory is used to account for the motivation of individuals to engage in collective behavior—especially when the behavior is hostile and destructive or wildly expressive. Tension theory is also used to explain some of the unusual directions taken in collective behavior.

The various forms of tension theory have in common the thesis that behavior of any sort results from a state of tension within the individual. The tension in turn results from the presence of some unsatisfied need (or drive, or instinct, etc.). Satiation or satisfaction of the need resolves the tension and accordingly eliminates the impulse (or "instigation") to action or thought. Tension becomes urgent and troublesome and cumulative when it cannot be abated by need satisfaction. The experience of frustration, the blockage or lack of apparent means of need satisfaction, leads to such cumulation of tension, which then expresses itself in random or anxious or hostile behavior. In this skeletal form, though with varied terminology, tension theory is a part of nearly every approach to human behavior.

The implications of this simplest form of tension theory for collective behavior are to point toward repeated and aggravated frustrations on a wide scale as accounting for the more vigorous and unconventional forms of collective behavior. When repeated frustrations of important needs affect large numbers of people over an extended period of time, tensions accumulate. These accumulated tensions provide the motive power for behavior which deviates from the conventional. From the standpoint of the social order, the failure of the institutional structure to provide means for the satisfaction of needs generated within it leads to cumulation of tensions, making people susceptible to courses of action not normally indicated or sanctioned in the culture. To explain a wave of lynchings, of strikes, of mass confessionals, or of orgiastic behavior the investigator would accordingly search for a source of enduring and aggravated frustration within the social order.

From the foregoing simple outline, tension theory is frequently elaborated by making certain assumptions which are highly controversial. The student should be able to recognize these incompletely tested versions and avoid their uncritical use. The first of these frequent assumptions we may refer to as the "quantitative constancy" of tension. It is assumed that tension may be increased or reduced by addition or subtraction, and that the amount of behavior required to eliminate the tension is increased or reduced thereby. Tension in the human psyche is like water in an enclosed container. It is present in a measurable quantity, and the quantity remains unchanged unless added to or unless some is poured off. This point of view denies that a person can be frustrated and merely forget about it over a period of time. The tension is assumed to remain at a constant level until behavior expressing that tension takes place. If a person becomes angry, he remains angry (whether he recognizes it or not) until he has expressed a quantity of hostility sufficient to expend all of his anger.

From the simple observation that anger or other states of emotional tension can sometimes accumulate to the thesis that tension cannot be dispelled except by being expressed in sufficient quantity and that consequently unexpressed tendencies accumulate with arithmetic precision is an altogether hypothetical step. It has not been demonstrated that tensions, general or specific, cannot be dispelled without being expressed. The common belief that a person may become less angry when he sees the cause of his anger in a changed perspective has not been disproven. Nor has the common belief that an instigation may dissipate when the individual becomes preoccupied with other activities. On the other hand, it has also not been demonstrated that tension is necessarily reduced through expression. For example, proof is not at hand that a man who physically attacks another necessarily feels any less hostility toward him after the attack.

This assumed process of releasing tension (reducing instigation, etc.) by expressing it in behavior is referred to as "catharsis." The man who gets his hatred "out of his system" by bodily attacking someone is said to be experiencing catharsis. This concept appears frequently in analyses of collective behavior. Writers may contend that through crowd behavior or the participation in social movements persons express stored-up feelings and thus achieve catharsis. On the surface it appears improbable that an uninhibited one-sided race riot necessarily reduces hostility toward the group attacked, though more complex mechanisms are often introduced to reconcile the facts with the theory.

There is enough circumstantial evidence that the "quantitative constancy" assumption and the process of catharsis cannot be summarily dismissed. But there is also sufficient reason to doubt their correctness that generalizations about collective behavior had best not be made dependent upon them.

Another elaboration of tension theory asserts the transferability of tension from one object to another. Anger toward one person is dispelled by an attack on some other, more available, individual or object. Applied to collective behavior, the aggression of a race riot may be attributed to accumulated antagonism toward employers, family members, and others who cannot be attacked with impunity. All the accumulated hostility toward these various objects are then heaped upon the more available and sanctioned object. Similar explanations are offered for the "villains" as designated in the ideologies of social movements.

This idea has a background of folk observation in the everyday recognition that a mother who is angry at her husband may therefore be intolerant with her children or that an employer who has just lost badly at golf may suddenly "crack the whip" on his employees. Popularly, this redirection of feelings toward a more available or acceptable object is known as the "scapegoat" phenomenon. But scapegoating can have two meanings. On the one hand, it can mean mistaken identification of the source of one's difficulty. The message-bearer may be attacked or thanked instead of the inaccessible message-writer. The agent who is simply carrying out orders may be attacked instead of the originator of the order. Or a person may be blamed for happenings which are actually the consequence of an uncontrollable sequence of impersonal events. The individual is not satisfied by directing antagonism against just anyone or anything; he must direct it toward someone whom he can blame.

In the broader sense, scapegoating means the transfer of hostility toward any object. The term "free-floating aggression" has been used to refer to feelings of hostility which can be attached to an object apparently totally unrelated to their initial cause.

Scapegoating in the former sense is a well-established tendency which it would be difficult to deny. Free-floating aggression or other forms of the complete transferability of feelings are much more subject to question. Again, there is circumstantial evidence to support such transferability, but there is also evidence enough to suggest that other explanations are preferable. We can accept with confidence the more limited transferability of feelings as incorporated in the more limited meaning of scapegoating. But again the generalizations we formulate about collective behavior had best not be made dependent upon any generalized notion of the transferability of tension.

Chapter 2

Societal conditions and collective behavior

*D*ESPITE THE FREQUENCY with which it occurs, collective behavior stands in contrast to what we think of as "normal" or "routine" group living. Some types, such as crowd behavior, constitute brief, transitory breaks in the ordinary flow of organized group life. Other types, such as social movements, may be the processes through which, over a long period of time, widespread and lasting changes in the social order come about.

The social organization which provides the framework for traditionally patterned human behavior has certain salient features which are relevant to the emergence of collective behavior. Every group is characterized by some sort of division of labor—the relating of the tasks of individual members to each other and to group purposes. Out of this division of labor arises a structure of interdependent roles. The performance of the duties of these roles by the role occupants is necessary for the maintenance of group cohesion and the achievement of group goals.

A second, essential basis for group cohesion is a normative order, or consensus as to the behavior that is expected of the group members by each other. In a society possessing a high degree of normative integration the norms are mutually consistent and behavior closely conforms to the norms. Deviations, when they occur, are individual and exceptional. They are not cumulative in the sense of leading to further deviations and a weakening of the norms. If anything, the adverse reactions and the sanctions which occasional violations evoke tend to reinforce the norms.

Both social organization and the normative order, and hence the very existence

20

of the group as a social system, depend upon communication. If the flow of communication within the group is impeded, the coordination of the behavior of members occupying discrete but interdependent roles begins to break down. The whole system ceases to operate efficiently and fails either to achieve group goals or to provide satisfactions for the individual members. Without effective communication consensus weakens and the degree of normative integration is diminished. Different group members may come to have different understandings as to what behavior is expected of them, and all may lose confidence in their expectations of others' behavior.

Yet it is not simply the need for collective action, created by social disintegration, which leads to collective behavior. There must also be some shared image of a better state of affairs which can be attained by collective action—a hope for things to come and a belief that they can be made to come. Secondly, even though the normal processes of communication may have broken down to some extent, some basis of communication between the members of the collectivity must remain. Collective behavior does not develop in a heterogeneous aggregate of individuals. One device used by slave-holders in the early years of the United States to prevent slave uprisings was to break up tribal groups so that the slaves on any one plantation would have in common only their African ancestry and their slave status, but would lack a common culture and an established group consciousness. Unless there is a minimum of cultural homogeneity and a certain "we"-feeling in a collectivity, there will not be a sufficient basis for the communication between individuals which is necessary for the development of collective action.

Just as routine social behavior may be explained on the basis of these characteristics of social organization, collective behavior must be viewed as arising from changes in them. It has its roots in changes in these fundamental conditions for social cohesion and integrated group action.

Changes in social organization: breakdown of a system of social control. The division of labor which makes possible social organization in a group carries some provision for control of the behavior of the members. Every member of the group shares this task to some extent, but the larger and more specialized the group becomes the more the responsibility for social control is vested in certain roles. The failure of the possessor of any role to carry out its prescriptions may lead to social unrest and disorganization. The failure of persons to play properly the roles in which social control is concentrated brings into sharp relief the consequences of a breakdown in the division of labor.

The sudden and obvious breakdown of a formal system of social control as a result of the dereliction of the role occupants is illustrated in Bartlett's description of the Boston police strike. Even though there were many citizens who did not seize the opportunity to break the law, unrest and disorganization spread rapidly throughout the city. The social system began to break down. It should not be assumed that only the rioters and looters were engaging in collective behavior. Even those law-abiding citizens who began to take over the role of the police by arming themselves to protect their property were engaging in novel behavior and contributing to the emergence of a new social structure with new norms.

ANARCHY IN BOSTON

Randolph Bartlett

There had been intermittent showers throughout the day of September 9, and at 5:45 P.M. a light drizzle was falling. At Roxbury Crossing a policeman came out of the station house, his arms filled with personal belongings. There was a crowd in the street, waiting to see if the strike would actually start on schedule. A small boy decided to perform a bit of private research: gathering up a handful of muck from the gutter, he hurled it in the policeman's face, then dodged out of sight. The policeman glumly wiped away the mud and continued homeward without a word. At City Hall Avenue station, a patrolman emerged from the front entrance, carrying a pair of rubber boots, an extra uniform, a heavy overcoat, and various other articles. A burly Irish truck driver elbowed his way through the crowd at the curb. "Give me a traffic ticket the other day, would you?" he shouted, and clouted the policeman on the chin, knocking him down. The crowd jeered. The patrolman did nothing.

Such incidents as these informed the hooligans that they could do anything they liked and get away with it. The word was swiftly passed about town. In poolrooms, in speakeasies, in dingy back rooms, a sudden interest stirred. Hoodlumism began to feel its way. . . . It must be remembered that all this occurred in the year 1919, that Prohibition was still in its infancy, that organized urban crime had not yet reached the perfect blooming which was to produce the St. Valentine's massacre in Chicago ten years later. The Boston rowdies, gregarious, herd-like, followed their instincts and moved from all sections to the center of the city. Many paused on the way, diverted by the novelty of pursuing pastimes

hitherto prohibited. In front of police stations, crowds grew and crap games were started. The sergeants, lieutenants, and captains, none of whom had walked out with the patrolmen, ignored the games, realizing there soon would be more serious business at hand. On Boston Common no less than fifty games were in progress, the stakes ranging from a penny to fifty dollars. One player reaped a winning of $300, pocketed the money, and started away. He had gone hardly fifty feet when three toughs attacked him, beat him into helplessness, seized his profits, and fled.

Yet aside from promiscuous gambling and kindred activities, the first few hours of the strike produced only a highly developed spirit of mischief. Boys pulled streetcar trolleys from the overhead wires; others took possession of unlocked automobiles and drove until they discovered there was more amusement to be had on the street. Tires were removed from cars and flung about in rough hilarity. Dozens of false alarms of fire were sounded. Youths knocked off pedestrians' hats with sticks and stones. But here the urge for lawlessness ceased.

Meanwhile streams of hoodlums were pouring into Scollay, Adams, and Haymarket Squares, until these crossways of city traffic became so thronged that homeward-bound business men were compelled to make wide detours. But still there was no organization of the criminal elements; the mob, leaderless, was waiting to learn if the Law had actually decamped. As darkness fell, the crowds increased. By 11 o'clock police officers estimated that 10,000 were gathered in a tightly-packed mass near Dorchester Street, rendered harmless by their sheer inability to move. Yet the potentiality for crime soon began to produce acts of violence.

One of the first experiments was conducted in a cigar store at Friend and

Reprinted in part by permission of **The American Mercury,** from **The American Mercury,** 36 (1935), pp. 456–464.

Washington Streets. Having exhausted their cigarette supply, a dozen youths went into the shop and filled their pockets. Others observed the raid, and within fifteen minutes the store's stock had been cleaned out. Encouraged by this apparent immunity, a few bolder spirits broke the windows of a clothing establishment and looted it, many of them changing to their newly-acquired garments on the pavement. Turning down Hanover Street, the mob smashed the glass front of a shoe store and helped themselves. Swinging around Court Street toward Adams Square, they were about to seize a fruit stand when a swarm of Italians, allies of the owner, set upon them with revolvers and knives. The mob ran helter-skelter, although not a shot was fired.

Another group invaded the market section around Faneuil Hall. A wagon was stripped of its load of fruit, and the horse beaten until it ran away. Then the hoodlums began smashing the windows of wholesale stores until a lone watchman, brandishing a revolver, routed them. The raiders fled down the street, lugging bananas, pineapples, grapes, eating the fruit as they ran, strewing the pavement with debris.

The ease with which this mob was vanquished proved typical of the middle hours of the night, although the rabbit warren of streets which comprises the center of Boston was designed, however innocently, for gang operations. At Washington Street near Hanover, a crowd began smashing glass. A squad of the loyal police officers dispersed them. In a few minutes they reassembled in Haymarket Square, resuming their depredations. Another mob swung shouting down Court Street, breaking store windows and stealing articles until the officers appeared; yet even as they ran they tossed stones into shops and grabbed what they could.

These hoodlums were not professional criminals, but mostly young toughs who regarded the whole experience as a lark. More sinister individuals, however, were operating differently in smaller groups. Pedestrians were backed into doorways,

slugged, and robbed. Slot machines were demolished and their contents stolen. At the corner of State Street and Atlantic Avenue, a woman was dragged into an alley, beaten, and raped. Another woman staggered into a speakeasy, bruised and bleeding, after a similar assault. Ironically enough, she was a prostitute. Incidents of the same sort occurred in Chair Alley off Fulton Street.

After midnight passed, the individual mobs began to achieve something like organization. A gang of 400 commenced tramping up and down Washington Street from Boylston to School. In this sector were several department stores, and the outnumbered police officers concentrated here to protect these richer prizes, and the jewelry shops. A half dozen times they scattered the crowd, but each time it reassembled. A clothing store at Washington and Franklin Streets was looted while the handful of officers battled another crowd some blocks away. In the vicinity of Andrew Square, thirty stores were robbed. The pavements were littered with broken glass and articles dropped from overfilled arms. The police squad continued to patrol the area, dispersing whatever crowds it met. Yet towards dawn, the marauders began to scatter of their own accord, apparently fearing civic retaliation would commence with daylight.

There is no record of disturbances in the residential districts, although many of the burghers of Beacon Hill and Back Bay, and even sections as remote as Brookline, loaded what weapons they had and sat at darkened windows through the night, guarding their homes. Fortunately for them, the mob was not hunting prey; it was merely taking advantage of those opportunities for looting which occurred in the downtown area. Yet the night of September 9 was an alarming reminder that the lives of men, the bodies of women, the safety of property, all the decencies of ordered existence, are not worth a moment's purchase without the presence on city streets of the familiar blue-coated cop.

The breakdown of a system of social control need not be so sudden or dramatic as in this instance in order to lead to the emergence of collective behavior. In recent years, a wave of riots has swept the prisons of the United States. Floch and Hartung suggest that the critical factor leading to these riots was the disruption of the informal inmate organization, an important agency of social control. Here the key control roles were informal and, indeed, illegitimate. Apparently the functions of the inmate leaders in the informal prison community were unknown to the reform administrations, or were considered unimportant. Removal of the leaders from their positions of power and the failure of the officials to fill the gap thus created rendered the social system of a prison incapable of dealing routinely with individual and group problems, as it had in the past.

A SOCIAL-PSYCHOLOGICAL ANALYSIS OF PRISON RIOTS

Frank E. Hartung and Maurice Floch

Prison riots have frequently occurred in the past because of one or a combination of four conditions:

1. Poor, insufficient, or contaminated food.
2. Inadequate, insanitary, or dirty housing.
3. Continued sadistic brutality by prison officials.
4. Otherwise inhumane prison administration.

It seems, however, that in the riots of 1952 these four conditions were largely absent. Prison administration, it is generally agreed, has improved greatly in the past 15 years or so. And yet we have the spectacle of 1952 furnishing the largest number of riots in any one year, as well as some of the costliest, at the very time when the prisons are being administered in accordance with sounder penal principles. Why? The answer appears to lie in a combination of sociological and social-psychological circumstances that indicate the different quality of the 1952 riots:

1. The nature of the maximum custody prison.
2. The aggregation of different types of inmates within one prison.
3. The destruction of semi-official, informal inmate self-government by new administrations.

Adapted by permission of the authors and the editors from **The Journal of Criminal Law, Criminology, and Police Science**, 47 (1956), pp. 51–57.

4. The functioning of individual treatment programs.

To begin the discussion with the nature of the maximum custody prison, it is important to realize that this prison belongs to the past, even though most American prisons are still of this variety. It is generally recognized that the great majority of prisoners do not need such a high degree of security in order to keep them from escaping. Such prisons put maximum emphasis upon conformity to routine. Conformity is rewarded, initiative is punished. Each prisoner is under the scrutiny of a paid official every minute of the day and night, with the "count" and the "shakedown" being important features of the scrutiny. Each prisoner is counted about 14 times daily, and is liable to have his cell or his person searched at any time. They live in cells that range from $3\frac{1}{2}$ feet wide by 7 feet long, to about 7 feet square. At stipulated periods they can walk in the prison yard, which is, of course, limited in area, and is surrounded by a concrete wall of from 18 feet to 30 feet high. Wherever they turn, this wall is always in sight, reminding them of the outside, reminding them that they are prisoners labeled "dangerous" by society, and tending continually to stimulate ideas of escape. Their day and everything within it is ordered for them, from the time they are awakened in the morning until the lights are extinguished for them at night.

The result of continued incarceration in such a prison is some degree of breakdown in emotional stability, even in those who are fairly intact upon admission. It appears that lengthy custody under these conditions almost invariably brings emotional instability. This leads to a consideration of the second factor entering into present-day riots, namely, the mingling of different types of prisoners.

A prison encloses a conglomeration of humanity composed of men who failed to adjust to the larger community, who failed to make good under the relatively easy conditions of civilian life. Various types can be distinguished, if we simplify the complex problem of classifying the human personality. One type is composed of men who by the peculiar circumstances of their lives, and who, largely driven by powerful emotions, have become considerably deviated. These include some of the psychotic, the psychopathic, and the emotionally disturbed, whose condition the maximum custody prison always aggravates. They form a veritable witches' brew, a cauldron which is always boiling and bubbling beneath the surface. The majority of these, fortunately, are passive characters despite their various disturbances. They are passive in the sense that they dare not rebel openly against society in their criminal behavior and even in their offenses often show a form of passive resistance to society's laws. Here may be placed confidence men, forgers, embezzlers, many sexual deviates, some burglars, and most shoplifters. These people are basically unaggressive in temperament and accept the rigors of imprisonment with relative equanimity, despite their inner turmoil. Even though they are irked by the artificiality and monotony of the prison, they manage to make an acceptable life in it. By devious and stealthy ways they acquire various little refinements and privileges that put a bit of color into it. Thus, they will supplement their diet by utilizing contraband; they will smuggle in a certain amount of liquor and even sedatives. These men do not provide the active ingredients of a prison riot; they just tag along, so to speak.

The dangerous convicts are the type of offenders who have proven in their behavior previous to imprisonment that they are capable of an openly hostile and aggressive stand against society. This second category includes the various kinds of assaultive characters, including armed and unarmed robbers, forcible rapists, hoodlums, and racketeers. They are the people who have emancipated themselves from scruples against the use of force in dealing with their fellows. Many of them find it extremely difficult to become passive in the automatic, routinized life of the prison. They are consequently a continuing source of disorder, especially if the facilities provided for work, recreation, and leadership are inadequate to drain their energy and challenge their imagination. Even these divide into two distinct sub-groups. The men in the first possess qualities of leadership, as shown by their criminal careers in civilian life. They are the actual leaders in the informal prisoner community that develops in every prison. They are often two-time losers, and even more, whose role in the prisoner community enables them to continue their well-established habits of connivance. Their time in prison is therefore not so wearisome. Having become prison-wise, they attempt to observe carefully all the prison rules, and operate on the motto, "Watch that 'good' time and get out early."

The result of watching the "good" time, which is time deducted from the prison term for good behavior, is that inmate leaders use members of the second sub-group in order to gain their ends within the prison. The second sub-group includes emotionally explosive characters who lose self-control easily, the intellectually retarded who are amenable to suggestion, and a large proportion of first-termers. The latter are fairly easy prey for the inmate leaders, until they learn the dangers of being used in this fashion. The first-termers comprise a significant part of the total prison population. Thus the inmate leaders are rarely caught in violation of the rules, even though the violations may originate with them.

Why is it, then, that prisons do not continually have riots? Why is it that they are able to maintain peace for years, without even the semblance of a riot? The answer is to be found largely in the operation of the informal prisoner community. This community is a social organization which develops independently of the formal table of organization that gives the legal social structure of the prison. Many of the prisoners belonging in the second category mentioned, the prison-wise inmate-leaders, were enabled by the situation prevailing in these prisons for some years past to obtain much self-expression. This may seem paradoxical in view of what was said about the routine of the maximum custody prison. It will, however, be easily understood once details are presented.

A number of prisons were, practically speaking, administered by the informal inmate organization. This informal structure was elevated to the position of a semi-official self-government in these prisons, during the past several decades! Inmate assistants and inmate clerks of key paid officials discharged many of the major custodial duties of the prisons. These included such matters as assignments to cells and to jobs, the distribution of various privileges, such as trusty status and the sale of concessions, and even the imposition of discipline upon fellow-prisoners. When one considers that some prisons have a population the size of a small city, then it can be realized that such powers have great importance. They actually involve the major needs of a prison population. The person or group having charge of work and housing assignments, as well as privileges and discipline, controls all those elements within the institution that make prisoners' lives either bearable or difficult. The men placed in charge of these matters were logically drawn from the inmate leaders who, apart from the psychotics and psychopaths, potentially furnish the motive-power for overt prison unrest.

The question may be properly raised as to how the inmates came to occupy such important positions. The explanation is simple. Legislatures have always been loath to appropriate funds sufficient for efficient prison management. Hence inmates had to be employed in key positions to assist major officials in discharging the most important functions. Once this practice was started, primarily because of financial reasons and secondarily in order to confer trusty status upon a few prisoners, it was widely adopted. From small beginnings the usual processes of bureaucratic growth produced, in a few years, a well-knit, extra-legal prisoner self-government.

In return for being allowed to operate the prison semi-officially, the inmate leaders relieved the warden of the burden of discipline. If there was an individual prisoner who grumbled too much and too openly, he was "taken care of" by his leaders. If news of group discontent reached the warden, he suggested that the inmate leaders "knew what to do." And they did. They wanted no trouble that would endanger their positions. Thus the prison floated on an even keel for years, with no serious disturbance.

A few years ago the administration of one of the nation's largest prisons was replaced. It was then operated on sounder penal principles. The result was that conditions were at once drastically changed. The inmate clerks and assistants were shorn of their power, and replaced by paid, Civil Service personnel. Concessions were immediately and completely eliminated. All work and cell assignments were made by the custodial staff. The warden put the lid on smuggling of contraband: liquor and narcotics were reduced to a negligible minimum; and inmates were restricted to purely social visits with their female visitors. Discipline was exercised by the guards, not the inmates. The prison was thus transformed into the kind of place the public expects, namely, an institution for segregation and punishment. In short, the prison was directed from the warden's office rather than from the cell-block.

In this manner the semi-official inmate

self-government that formerly directed the prison with the benevolent consent of the warden and his assistants was totally annihilated. The reform administration filled the vacuum by establishing what was termed an individualized treatment system. It was staffed by college graduates trained in sociology and psychology. It was assumed that if inmates were given individual treatment and a chance to air their grievances to properly constituted and trained officials, many of the factors which make for prison unrest could be materially reduced. It was also hoped that a material degree of reformation could be achieved. Unfortunately, an individual treatment system composed of earnest but in many cases inexperienced young men could not substitute for what had been taken away when the inmate self-government was shattered. This kind of development occurred in a number of prisons.

One result of this development was that unrest increased by leaps and bounds in these reform prisons. Many people experienced in prison administration were of the opinion that explosions were liable to occur at almost any time. Inmates in such prisons also predicted that outbreaks were imminent. Many tried to be transferred to other prisons, complaining about the tenseness that had developed within the walls, and which increased rather than abated. Without at this point attempting a detailed analysis of any given 1952 riot it is possible to see the common ingredients of them at work.

There is, first, the very nature of the maximum custody prison, described previously, in which it is inherently difficult for almost any man to live. Secondly, there is the conglomeration of types of personalities that should never be confined together. Several types took the spotlight in the riots: the psychopathic characters, as well as those who had previously discharged the orders of the inmate leaders, namely, first-termers as yet unadjusted to prison routine (called "jitterbugs" because of their restlessness), the emotionally explosive, and the intellectually retarded. The actual inmate leaders, however, managed as always to re-main in the background. Thirdly, there is the individual treatment program. Why did these inmates continue chafing, why were they rebellious, even after this treatment program was started? At least three points must be made concerning this program. (A), there was no pretense that it was to be a substitute for the disintegrated inmate self-government. Hence the control that the inmate leaders exerted over their fellows was lifted, and nothing was put in its stead. All the convicts knew that the inmate leaders had been deprived of their semi-official power. (B), this new program, being openly no substitute for their lost power and privileges, provided no incentives for the former "big shots" to attempt to minimize and direct the growing unrest. (C), the individual treatment program was withheld from the allegedly incorrigible, explosive inmates. The benefits of the highly-praised treatment were denied these men, whose problem of adjustment was greater than that of any other groups, and who had been held in check by the semi-official inmate leadership. Officials in charge of the treatment program insisted that they preferred to work with the relatively mild first-termers, rather than with the repeaters, the incorrigible and aggressive characters. In short, the prison officials failed to fill the gap caused by their destruction of the semi-official self-government. The men who previously directed the prison to a great extent—the inmates—were shorn of their power, privileges, and leadership, and denied the chance to develop any substitutes.

It will be seen from this discussion that the prison, when viewed as a social institution, is an exceedingly complex structure. It is our contention that the chief reason for the 1952 riots is the peculiar combination of elements enumerated: the nature of the maximum custody prison, the commingling of different types of personalities, the destruction of the semi-official self-government with nothing to replace it, and the functioning of the individual treatment program.

The four elements just listed can be regarded as the mediate causes of the riots, as presenting the situation in which the direct or precipitating cause could function. The direct cause is the adoption of a technique that was quickly diffused to many prisons in which the mediate causes were present. The new element in the 1952 riots is the taking of hostages and the demand to negotiate on grievances. First used in early April, 1952, at the New Jersey State Prison, it was borrowed a few days later by the inmates of the State Prison of Southern Michigan, commonly known as Jackson Prison. Both of these institutions were being operated by what we have referred to as reform administrations. The technique was successful at Jackson Prison beyond the wildest expectations of its instigators largely, we contend, because the officials conducting the negotiations failed to make an institutional analysis of the community in which they were working.

Inadequacy of normative integration: value conflicts. Were a social system characterized by perfect normative integration there would be complete consistency between the various norms and values of the society. Such consistency does not exist in real societies, however. Every society has some degree of inconsistency between its different norms and values. In some cases different values cherished in the same society may be quite contradictory.

This inconsistency creates dilemmas for individuals and interrupts the orderly, patterned behavior of the group. Collective behavior often arises out of the efforts of the group to resolve these conflicts. Some contradictions may become acute so rarely and unexpectedly that the resulting collective behavior is ephemeral and highly localized, consisting only of crowd action. Persistent conflicts, growing in the gravity of their consequences, may lead to the development of social movements. At times conventionalized modes of dealing with a recurrent dilemma may develop.

One source of value conflict in a society is the development of subgroups with somewhat deviant norms and values. Such subgroups may arise as a consequence of the interaction of some group members with outgroups, or simply through the isolation of some members from the main body of the society. Hence value conflicts may develop in a society as a result of the infusion of alien values.

Value conflicts may also arise in the course of social change. While new ideas may be adopted, older, contradictory ones may be retained. Inconsistency develops not only in the values held by different segments of the society but also within the minds of individuals. The group as a whole may be committed to contradictory values. Gunnar Myrdal focused attention on a major value conflict in the minds of white Americans when he described the problem of Negro-white relations as "an American dilemma." * Will W. Alexander, in "Our Conflicting Racial Policies," discusses the effects of this dilemma on race relations in the South, pointing out the social unrest and tension which this persistent value conflict creates.

* Gunnar Myrdal, **An American Dilemma** (New York: Harper & Brothers, 1944).

OUR CONFLICTING RACIAL POLICIES
WILL W. ALEXANDER

While there is nowhere any official statement of the policy of this country as to its Negro citizens, an examination of our actual dealing with Negroes indicates that over the years unofficial policies have been developed. In fact, there have been two well-defined policies in race relations and only two.

The first of these is the policy that Negroes shall be educated. Negro education had its beginnings in the activities of Northern churches when, immediately following the Civil War, they established schools for Negroes in the South. These schools have had a profound influence. The increase in educational opportunity has caused the Negro illiteracy rate to drop from 95 per cent at emancipation to less than 10 per cent today. And the Southern states are showing a tendency to move toward equalization of educational funds for Negro and white schools.

Everywhere the idea of education for Negroes is accepted as part of our American way. Howard, Fisk, and Atlanta Universities have come to take their place as institutions of higher learning which are making an important contribution not only to Negro life but to national life. The superior quality of the educated American Negroes always impresses foreigners as a striking aspect of American life.

Foreigners are also puzzled by America's second policy regarding her Negro population: segregation. Segregation is not only Southern, but national—it varies not so much in degree as in method in different sections of the country. In the South segregation in schools, transportation, entertainment, and community services is maintained by law and by custom. In the North segregation is maintained by social pressure and by such quasi-legal

arrangements as restrictive covenants. In connection with many public services, such as hotels and restaurants, segregation is as rigid in the North as in the South. Thus segregation is accepted in all sections of the country to about the same degree that education is provided and accepted.

Much of the uncertainty and tension in connection with our American race relations grows out of the conflict in these policies. Education is the most hopeful aspect of American race relations. Segregation is one of the most puzzling aspects of American life, and one of the most difficult questions in American race relations. It is generally recognized by Negroes as their number-one problem and is insisted upon by many whites as the one thing in the American race scene that can never be modified or dispensed with. Here we have the greatest conflict between our professed democratic doctrines and our actual practice in day-by-day living. Segregation tends to defeat the inspiring work of Negro education. Unless the problem of segregation can be solved, there is no hope of any alleviation of the race problem in America.

Segregation in the South not only separates the races but symbolizes the idea of the inevitable inferiority of Negroes. It "keeps the Negro in his place," not only on the streetcars and busses, but in the social and economic system. It is more effective as a symbol than as a means of preventing contact between the races. In fact, racial contacts are more intimate in the South than in any other section of the country. Southerners as a rule do not object to contact with Negroes so long as the idea of Negro inferiority is maintained. Segregation does this. This fact explains why the South has never claimed that under segregation there are equal services for the races.

Under the new pressures that have come with the war to save democracy and

Reprinted in part by permission of the author from Will W. Alexander, "Our Conflicting Racial Policies," **Harper's Magazine,** 190 (1944–45), pp. 172–179.

the stronger pressures that will come when the war is won, the South will probably attempt to attain equal services within the framework of segregation. There are two reasons why this will not be possible—one psychological and the other practical. There will be resistance in the South to any modification of the symbol of the Negro's inferiority. When a person speaks of the Negro "getting out of hand," he usually means getting out of his inferior status. Therefore, equal service would destroy to some extent one of the chief functions of segregation. If Negroes in the South had equal service under segregation, they would have gone a long way toward "getting out of hand," because the symbolic function of segregation would have lost much of its meaning.

As a practical matter, separate but equal service under segregation cannot be rendered. Such service would require, for example, the duplication of the present most expensive phases of transportation, and the duplication of the state university systems, already poorly supported. Separate and equal services for the races in the South, or any other section, are a luxury which cannot be afforded.

It is generally accepted that human beings behave better in the long run when they enjoy a maximum of freedom. Human relations are certainly more satisfacfactory when they are a result of free choice. Left with the maximum amount of freedom, white and colored Americans would probably adjust amicably most of the difficulties that arose between them. Under the denial of freedom which segregation enforces, there is constant and increasing friction. An examination of incidents where tension has become acute will indicate that most of the tensions are involved in and aggravated by segregation. Rioting is less frequent in mixed residential neighborhoods than elsewhere. Segregation accentuates unduly the racial factors in our civilization and obscures the wide cultural differences that exist within the racial groups. To many white people, every Negro looks like every other Negro and any white man, no matter how unworthy, is better than any Negro, however distinguished. Segregation tends to make every row between a white man and a Negro, whatever the initial cause may have been, a race quarrel.

Most white Americans are puzzled and alarmed by the impatience and bitterness of large sections of our Negro population. They feel that Negroes are no longer pleasant to live with. Whites are inclined to charge this to some subversive influence from the outside. Many Southerners say that agitators from the North are responsible for stirring up Negroes in the South. In other sections of the country, Negro resentment and unrest are usually charged to Communists or whatever bogy happens to be current in the mind of the community.

That there is unrest and bitterness among our Negro population is a fact. This unrest is to be found not just among Negro intellectuals; it exists also in the alleys of our Negro ghettos and among the remote and inarticulate Negro sharecroppers and common laborers. It will not pass with the war. Negroes were probably never so docile as they seemed. The trouble is that they behave like other human beings. In subjecting Negroes to American education we have made them Americans. So completely American are they that they will not submit passively to being pushed around as they are under segregation. Educational opportunity for the common man is a part of the American way of life. In giving it to Negroes, we have let them in on the meaning of democracy. Their unrest under their special limitations is the result not of sinister influence from the outside, but of our education, which, with all its faults, is the best thing in our democracy.

The education of Negroes in America has not been a mistake. Here we see American faith and American idealism at their best. Segregation, on the other hand, is rooted in fear and in doubt as to whether our democratic principles will really work. It remains to be seen whether or not our faith in democracy is strong enough to overcome our fears as to what may be some of its consequences.

Social change and frustration. Social change not only leads to value conflicts; it may also give rise to widespread frustration in a society. It is a mistake to assume, as have some students of collective behavior, that culture is basically and essentially frustrating to the human individual. But while man is not just an instinct-driven animal held in tenuous check by "a thin veneer of civilization," neither is he a passive automaton, adjusting to his culture and its changes with complete facility. He is an active, striving creature with needs and motives which, even though they may be culturally defined and derived, become autonomous and persistent. In the constant interaction between individuals and their culture, both the culture and individual needs change. Hence although cultural demands and restrictions should not be regarded as foreign to the individual and thus essentially frustrating, life is both satisfying and frustrating. As R. E. L. Faris has expressed it, "All civilized societies, and perhaps most societies of any kind, are in a perpetual condition of change and partial disorganization so that persons experience conflicts and frustrations, divided loyalties, and failures of various kinds along with their good times in life." *

At times the norms and structure of a society are such that the repression and frustration of a large portion of the population are chronic. In "Mass Hysteria in Japan," the unrest and the random, often frenzied behavior which burst out periodically during a long era of dictatorial rule are described. As the author of this selection points out, there are many parallels to such outbursts in the history of other societies. It is of particular significance that these instances of "mass hysteria" do not necessarily constitute true revolutionary or reform movements, but are primarily of an expressive nature, a means of giving vent to repressed feelings. Frustration and deprivation do not always lead quickly and surely to revolt; a revolutionary goal and an organization are needed. For collective behavior of any sort to develop, there must also be a belief in better conditions which can be brought about through collective action. There are three sources from which such a belief may be derived. First, while conditions are getting worse and frustration is increasing, people may remember better conditions, a "Golden Age" which they believe can be restored. Or, as conditions are improving for a group whose plight has seemed hopeless, the members may develop an image of an even better state of affairs, as their early gains give them hope. Finally, contact with other, similar groups who do not suffer the same frustrations or, even more important, have improved their condition by collective action, may provide the sort of image which will lead to the adoption of collective behavior.

* R. E. L. Faris, **Social Psychology** (New York: The Ronald Press Co., 1952), p. 75.

MASS HYSTERIA IN JAPAN
E. HERBERT NORMAN

Stolidity, emotional restraint and stoicism are often mentioned as characteristic of

Reprinted in part by permission of the Editors, **Far Eastern Survey**, and the author, from E. Herbert Norman, "Mass Hysteria in Japan," **Far Eastern Survey**, 14 (Jan. 17, 1945), pp. 65–70.

Japanese social behavior. Like many generalizations, this description, while possibly based on observation, may in fact be misleading because it fails to explain the social reasons for this restraint, nor does it suggest that such reserve might not be so much a temperamental habit as a deliberately cultivated behavior-pattern assumed like camouflage for self-protection.

Japan is a country of social tensions. Whether in feudal or modern Japan, the social controls have been kept so tight that to succeed in a career, to protect social status, employment, or in some cases even to survive, most Japanese have been careful to conform to a rigid and often repressive standard of behavior. When the distinction between an independent and an insubordinate mind is often blurred, it is small wonder that a Japanese in the presence of his feudal lord, master, employer, or senior officer, forgets the habit of frankness and takes refuge behind the armory of equivocation, flattery, or even servility. Yet under the heaviest burden of duties and regulations, human nature, particularly when fired by the spontaneous outbreaks of more inflammable spirits, will very often express itself in the most violent and unexpected fashion.

One example of deliberate emotional restraint which often nevertheless finds an outlet is the conventional Japanese attitude towards death. Westerners who have resided in Japan may have been astonished at some instance where a Japanese would announce with a smiling face the death of a member of his family. Before the eyes of sympathetic friends and visitors the mourners preserve a wooden passivity. Yet as if to offset this restraint one notices at the theatre that during lachrymose scenes members of the audience will weep copiously, preferring to seek emotional relief vicariously in the decent obscurity of the theatre.

One need not be a Freudian to imagine what neuroses, what febrile passions are concealed behind the glacial calm of many Japanese. The emotional instability in times of stress or crises, the unbridled brutality of Japanese troops let loose upon the peaceful population of Asiatic countries, bear evidence of a diseased society where healthy outlets for self-expression, a rational ambition, or a critical intellect are effectively dammed.

The social history of Japan illustrates how the Japanese violently reacted against crushing social restrictions and inhibitions by abandoning themselves to a frenzy which periodically swept throughout the centers of population in the Tokugawa era (1603–1868). The best documented instance of this mass hysteria took place in 1867, on the eve of the Restoration.

LAST YEARS OF TOKUGAWA RULE

In the last years of Tokugawa rule the country was in turmoil. Peasant uprisings were reaching a crescendo of violence culminating in the widespread and stubbornly fought revolts of 1866 which devastated some of the richest provinces of the land. The opening of Japan in 1854, the consequent import of manufactures, chiefly cotton cloth, and the export of gold and silver precipitated a serious financial crisis marked by skyrocketing prices and inflation. Thus the machine-made goods of the Western capitalist powers contributed their part in delivering shattering blows to the foundations of feudal economy. Impoverished *samurai* and *ronin* (masterless *samurai*) were secretly plotting against the *Bakufu* (Tokugawa Government) so that the two political centers of Kyoto, the capital, and Edo (modern Tokyo) were swarming with agents of the various clans and the secret police. In order to embarrass the Tokugawa government in its relations with the Western powers, fanatical *ronin* attacked foreigners and drew down upon their clans or the Tokugawa authorities repeated protests and punitive actions. The atmosphere was charged with an aroused nationalism which bordered on hysteria as alarming rumors and handbills warned the people of the evil intentions of the foreign powers. The superstitious were shaken by such portents as a comet in 1866, following which there was a serious failure of crops threatening famine. Class feeling was at a breaking point with commoners becoming restive under the humiliations which for generations had been visited on them by a feudal bureaucracy now losing its nerve and striking back in its desperate efforts to recover an irretrievable prestige. Placards appeared in public places in Osaka, Kyoto and even Edo, the heart of Tokugawa power, ridiculing the indecision of the government, blaming it for allowing foreigners to trade and so adding to the economic distress of the people. One such placard was pasted on the approaches to the Shogun's castle with a slogan borrowed from a common sign in a pharmacist's shop: "Policy: all sold out."

Then in the autumn of 1867 on the eve of the decisive *coup d'etat* which overthrew the Tokugawa, an ominous calm spread over the country. After reaching a peak of intensity and frequency in 1866, the peasant revolts fell off in the following year for no apparent reason.[1] All political activity, superficially at least, seemed at a standstill. Then like a tropical storm a frenzy descended upon the people and it spread along the eastern seaboard highway (Tokaido) and then into the interior provinces. This phenomenon might, for lack of a better phrase, be described as mass hysteria. Fortunately we have some detailed and trustworthy eye-witness accounts; so rather than attempt to summarize them it might be more interesting to quote a contemporary observer. Perhaps the best account was given by Fukuchi Genichiro, one of the pioneer journalists of Japan who ranked with the great Fukuzawa Yukichi in versatility and literary facility. He had studied Dutch at Nagasaki and by 1859 he was employed by the authorities to translate works in Dutch, later English and French, into Japanese. Coming under the powerful patronage of Mizuno Chiun he was given some authority in matters relating to foreign affairs. After the Restoration he was the founder and editor of the government newspaper, the *Tokyo Nichi Nichi,* where he was the first Japanese to write signed editorials.

EYE-WITNESS ACCOUNT OF FRENZY

In his memoirs entitled *Kaio Jidan* which give a very interesting picture of the last years of Tokugawa rule, he writes that he was sent to accompany an impor-

[1] There are sixty-one recorded agrarian uprisings.

tant Tokugawa official, a certain Kasuya Chikushu, who was entrusted by the Edo authorities with a secret mission to Kyoto which was then the storm center of political intrigue.

Leaving Edo on November 27, 1867, they went by boat to Hyogo whence they proceeded by road to Kyoto. But at Nishinomiya, the first post station, their progress was abruptly halted. In Fukuchi's words:

When we reached Nishinomiya people were singing and dancing madly in the streets so that it was impossible to hire even one porter. Kasuya became indignant and cried out in anger at the innkeeper and he (the innkeeper) making various apologies, prostrating himself and begging his pardon, said it was quite impossible to collect the necessary porters, so we lodged that night in Nishinomiya; the next day we arrived in Osaka. This dance at that time was celebrating the appearance of placards or talismen (*fuda*) which had fallen out of the skies and were circulated from place to place.

About this time, on the road between Kyoto, Osaka, and Nishinomiya, frequently these talismen fell out of the skies and the townsmen regarded this as a happy omen of a prosperous year, and cried out in refrain, *"Eija nai ka, eija nai ka"* (isn't it good) and they inserted at random many obscene and coarse lines into the verses and the rhythm of the song was droll and amusing. They accompanied the singing with great drums and hand drums, flutes and small guitars (*samisen*). The old and young, men and women, without distinction, put on gay flower-designed clothes and wandered about the city streets making a continual uproar. Some people said that the fall of these placards had been managed by the people of Kyoto in order to excite the people's spirits. I don't know whether this was true or not but we were greatly perplexed by this wild tumult.

POLITICAL SIGNIFICANCE

This period of Japanese history is rich in diaries and journals, many of which have been collected and published. In these memoirs and diaries under the dates of October-November, 1867, considerable evidence can be found of this mass hysteria not only in the Osaka-Kyoto district but all the way along the Tokaido from Edo (Tokyo) through Yokohama and Hakone westward towards Nagoya and in such districts as Ise and Tamba.

In passing, the political significance of this mass frenzy should be noted. Thanks to the efforts of the most astute political figure of that day, Sakamoto Ryuma of Tosa, the two great "outside clans" of Satsuma and Choshu, represented respectively by Saigo Takamori and Kido Takayoshi (as he was known later) were brought together in a secret agreement committing them to attack the *Bakufu* at the opportune moment. They still lacked one essential for success, the blessing or at least tacit support of the Court of Kyoto. The Tokugawa secret police were still so alert, their net so widespread that they had foiled attempts of the anti-*Bakufu* leaders to penetrate to the capital in order to confer with the key figures among the court nobility (*kuge*), notably Iwakura Tomomi, the most intransigent anti-*Bakufu* courtier. In a letter to a friend, Iwakura acknowledged the formidable difficulties of any political activity aimed against the *Bakufu*. He wrote at the end of 1865:

> The *Bakufu* is thoroughly informed of everything and even those who are hidden away in Satsuma are known; as for *ronin*, the Tokugawa authorities insist that they know how many there are in Kyoto and Osaka. The *Bakufu* believes that it has them under control (literally, "swallowed them") but this is not so and don't put any faith in this boast.

By the summer of 1867, after two abortive *coups d'etat*, even such intrepid spirits as Saigo and Sakamoto became anxious lest their plans miscarry again through the vigilance of the Edo authorities. Then late in the year this mass hysteria swept through the heart of the country, and notably the political center of Kyoto. The Tokugawa administrative machine was paralyzed. As Fukuchi Genichiro showed in the passage quoted above, the high Tokugawa official on a confidential mission was unable to secure porterage. Iwakura comments:

> At this time people in Kyoto were crazed and danced about crying *"Eija nai ka."* When one troop departed another would come running hither and thither in the streets. Consequently, my movements were hidden, thanks to this uproar, and they escaped official attention.

LEADERS UTILIZE DISORDERS

Similarly taking advantage of the confusion and mixing freely among the milling crowds which blocked all highways leading to the capital, Okubo Toshimichi representing Satsuma met Iwakura in the village just north of Kyoto and presented him with the Satsuma plan which called for an appeal to the Throne to secure the Emperor's support in the coming campaign against the Tokugawa authorities. The plan was approved and thus the last link in the chain to bind the *Bakufu* was forged. In a letter to Iwakura, Maeda Yuzo wrote as follows, cryptically referring to this mass hysteria: "As you have heard, there is a great conflagration in the East (Kanto) and if it has been caused by our patriots it will be a good thing." These young *samurai* leaders with their keen insight into mass psychology sensed at once that this *eija nai ka* movement could be turned to good advantage by the anti-*Bakufu* forces.

It was a fitting and ironical trick which history played on the Japanese feudal authorities. Life under a heavy-handed regime had made the people credulous, superstitious, spiritually impoverished, nervously exhausted, politically frustrated. When their emotions hitherto so closely restrained sought outlet in this frenzy, like a flood it swept away the finespun, meticulous controls of the feudal authorities, thereby allowing the anti-Tokugawa coalition to execute a decisive maneuver in its grand strategy calling for the final assault upon the *Bakufu*.

FRENZY RECURRING PHENOMENON

Beyond the coincidental service which this phenomenon unwittingly rendered in breaking down the feudal controls and screening the activities of the anti-Tokugawa leaders in the critical days of late 1867, it has a wider significance. We find similar instances of mass hysteria seizing hold upon the people at intervals throughout the Tokugawa era. The *Koji Ruien* (Classified References of Ancient Things), an encyclopaedic collection of source material on a wide variety of subjects, and the *Shinto Dai-jiten* (Shinto Encyclopaedia) have preserved records of such frenzies which swept Japan in 1705, 1771, 1830, and (the one just described) 1867, that is, roughly, once a generation. The term used to describe this phenomenon is *okage-mairi* or a pilgrimage of grace, a visit to the Ise Shrine to express thanks to the Sun Goddess. But as with so many Japanese terms, there is a secondary and more specific meaning so that the pilgrimage (*mairi*) is made *thanks* (okage) *to the kindness of others.* This is a natural interpretation based on the fact that great numbers of pilgrims were given food, shelter and drink in the towns and villages through which they passed on their way to Ise. This type of pilgrimage is more popularly known as *nuke-mairi,* or secret visit to the Shrine, because so many participants, often women of good family who ordinarily would never venture out unattended, are seized with a sudden impulse to join the jostling crowd of pilgrims as it passes through the streets of their town, slipping off quietly without telling anyone of their departure. Another feature of such frenzies is that many of the pilgrims who are absent for days at a time are so nervously exhausted that after returning they appear completely stupefied and, in extreme cases, suffer from amnesia which leaves them without any recollection of their frenzy.

Motoori Norinaga (1730–1801) the famous Shinto scholar, was an eye-witness of the *okage-mairi* of 1771. He gives a detailed and colorful description but only a short example of it can be quoted here.

Every day one can see the throngs of people and each day one sees more than the preceding day so that there seems hardly to be room on the roads for them. One sees even old men of seventy and eighty. This has been known from days of yore as *okage-mairi,* and the original occasion is somewhat obscure; in recent times the phrase is used that the pilgrims are "as thick as ants going to Kumano." People go with their companions and day by day as the crowds increase it is observed that they have paper pennants, one for each group or team, telling where they are from and the province and village from which they come. This custom gradually declined and in place of it pictures were painted on these pennants so now they are mixed, some groups still using pennants with the name of the place from which the group comes and others using just pictures. These pictures are quite fantastic and depict phantasmagoric and unreal objects, others quite ridiculous and absurd, and others again are coarse and obscene. There is a nature similar to the pictures. The people go along clapping their hands, shouting, singing *"okage de sa! nuketa to sa!"* and becoming more and more excited. Both young men and old women and girls forget their natural modesty and indulge in this frenzy so that it is quite a disturbing sight to see. They seem to have abandoned themselves to utter madness, as well as ribaldry and horseplay.

HYSTERIA ACTS AS SOCIAL SAFETY VALVE

Such sudden and contagious frenzies are not confined to feudal Japan. The annual celebration of the Saturnalia in ancient Rome seems to have served as a social safety valve for the slaves and the underprivileged. There was a strange phenomenon following the end of slavery in Brazil when Antonio Conselheiro, a ragged mystic and street preacher who was acclaimed as a Messiah by thousands of primitive folk in the hinterland of Brazil, led a rebellion at Canudos, December, 1896, to October, 1897. The practice of voodoo in Haiti during the period of slavery seems to have acted as an emotional release for oppressed Negroes of that island. The most striking parallel, however, comes from the medieval history of Europe where a dancing mania seized the people after they had suffered some prolonged misery and affliction such as followed in the wake of the Black Death. Dr. J. F. C. Hecker has given us a graphic description of this mania which for the sake of comparison is quoted in part.

The effects of the *Black Death* had not yet subsided, and the graves of millions of its victims were scarcely closed, when a strange delusion arose in Germany, which took possession of the minds of men, and, in spite of the divinity of our nature, hurried away body and soul into the magic circle of hellish superstition. It was a convulsion which in the most extraordinary manner infuriated the human frame, and excited the astonishment of contemporaries for more than two centuries, since which time it has never reappeared. It was called the dance of St. John or of St. Vitus, on account of the Bacchantic leaps by which it was characterized, and which gave to those affected, whilst performing their wild dance, and screaming and foaming with fury, all the appearance of persons possessed. It did not remain confined to particular localities, but was propagated by the sight of the sufferers, like a demoniacal epidemic, over the whole of Germany and the neighboring countries to the

northwest, which were already prepared for its reception by the prevailing opinions of the times . . .
Comparison is the mother of observation, and may here elucidate one phenomenon by another—the past by that which still exists. Oppression, insecurity, and the influence of a very rude priestcraft are the powerful causes which operated on the Germans and Italians of the middle ages, as they now continue to operate on the Abyssinians of the present day.

It seems safe to generalize by saying that under any unbearably oppressive social system, whether feudalism or slave society, the emotions of the common people, curbed and repressed by the unrelenting restraints, their spirits dulled by the drab and bleak drudgery of daily life, blindly sought some outlet such as *okage-mairi*. The example of this phenomenon in 1867 seems to have been the most violent and widespread; further, it was accompanied by overtones of political discontent, with slogans and songs anticipating the advent of a new era or slyly ridiculing the malpractices of the Tokugawa Government, or rejoicing in the coming assault upon it from the west (i.e. from the anti-Tokugawa federation).

Inadequacy of communication. It has been said that both functional and normative integration depend upon the free flow of communication within a society. Human group life creates for the individual an environment far greater than he can directly apprehend. Particularly in large, complex societies, individuals and subgroups are dependent upon other members whom they may never see and with whom they may never interact directly. Yet they interact through a chain of communication which is essential to the smooth operation of the social system. One of the most dramatic instances of collective behavior arising from a false picture of the world communicated to a large number of people was the famous Orson Welles "Invasion from Mars" broadcast. Less dramatic but more common instances of inadequacy of communication channels or inaccuracy of content account for much social unrest and collective behavior. Such an instance is described in "Reflections on the Wildcat Strikes." Here inadequacy of communication led the workingmen to lose confidence in the existence of consensus in the social system. The role structure was disrupted as the authority of the union leaders was disregarded in the "quickies." The strikes themselves constituted a collective solution to what was perceived by the strikers as a breakdown of both social organization and normative integration, although it was actually the communication process that was inadequate. At the same time, well-established communication channels still existed among the workers themselves. There also existed the belief, based on past experience with the strike as an effective weapon, that conditions could be improved.

REFLECTIONS ON THE WILDCAT STRIKES
JEROME F. SCOTT AND GEORGE C. HOMANS

For a student of American industry, the wartime wildcat strikes had a malignant fascination. In the teeth of a desperate national emergency and a no-strike pledge by labor, they caused an enormous loss in man-hours of work. . . . Furthermore, they set a new pattern of industrial unrest. The responsible leaders of the unions were as weak as management in dealing with "quickies," and the government, for all its new machinery, almost as weak. The old explanations failed. Something mysterious seemed to be at work.

Last June, the authors of this paper spent some time in Detroit, not so much to make a study of the wartime wildcat strikes as to see whether such a study could be made. Detroit was chosen for obvious reasons. It was the center of the wildcat strikes, and in the closely knit automotive industry a strike in one plant can destroy effective work in many others. We had introductions to officers of some of the automobile companies, but we also talked, not systematically but as one man led to another, with officials of the United Automobile Workers (CIO) and with workingmen in the lower ranks of labor. Before going to Detroit we had read largely in the literature on the strikes, and in that city we were given access to confidential investigations of the strikes made by both management and labor. Neither from the literature nor from the men we talked with did we get enough to make a thorough study—a fact which may itself be significant. We did get some general

Reprinted in part by permission of the American Sociological Society and the authors, from Jerome F. Scott and George C. Homans, "Reflections on the Wildcat Strikes," **American Sociological Review,** 12 (June, 1947), pp. 278–287.

ideas about the strikes, the industrial scene in Detroit, and the terms in which the problem might be stated. Above all, it was brought home to us that the wildcat strike was not a matter of history. Two important quickies took place during our stay at Detroit, one of which we made some attempt to study, so far as our time, our contacts, and the feverish efforts to get the men back to work allowed.

Of one thing we felt sure: that some of the facile explanations of the quickies were almost obviously inadequate by themselves. . . . In the long run, a number of the strikes seemed to stem from faculty communication. Workingmen would call it the "run around." They use that phrase when they feel that what they consider important is not in fact being treated as such by people in authority. We tend to forget that communication is concerned with action, not with abstract understanding. Action may not be taken, but unless the man at the bottom feels that a responsible individual has given serious consideration to his concerns, communication, for him, has failed. Wartime conditions made communication, in this broad sense, much more difficult, while they made workingmen much more ready to insist, in their own way, that communication be improved. With all its good intentions, the War Labor Board may have hurt communication more than it helped. Here was an organization outside the industry. Disputes referred to it meant still longer delays before responsible action was taken. Rightly or wrongly, workers often felt that companies had used the War Labor Board to stall and to avoid dealing with matters which could perfectly well have been handled on the spot.

On management's side, the foreman may be the weak link in the chain of communication. . . . He is "the man in the middle" who is "the master and victim of double talk." Much of his old glory has been whittled away by the shop stewards, on the one hand, and by the rise of staff departments, like personnel, with its right to hire and fire, on the other. The president of the foremen's union, which comes as close to being a spontaneous development as anything which requires organization can be, observes: "The production guys have a union. The fellows at the top look out for themselves. No one looks out for the foremen. We are strictly in the middle." In a study of the foremen's problems it was found that many of the factors usually thought to bother foremen, for instance, the decreased differential between their pay and workers' wages, were not as important as the informal status problems. Thus when a grievance committee reached a decision determining policy, and the union grapevine carried the news to the floor, via the steward, before the foreman got it, the latter felt his standing lowered. Much is done in training foremen to listen to workers, but who listens to the listeners?

One must remember that during the war many of these foremen were recently promoted, unskilled, and unsure of themselves. One estimate is that half the foremen in Detroit were newly promoted. And the men the foremen had to deal with were still newer. In short, supervision's task increased at a time when its average skill and capacity had decreased. We were told by several people in management of the tendency to choose men for promotion to supervisory jobs simply on the basis of output and mechanical skill. At the same time, according to union people—and their statements must be discounted, just as management evaluations of union representatives must be discounted—carelessly selected men were being put in personnel and labor relations departments. One union committeeman illustrated with a bulletin board notice in one of the plants: "Anybody between the ages of 25 and 40 that wants to be a personnel man show up and have an interview." Certainly this is not typical of the facts, but it illustrates an impression of the facts that was rather widely held. We talked with a former worker who had represented the 7,000 or 8,000 men in building in one of the larger plants. He had been offered a job in the company's industrial relations department at an attractive salary, but refused because he felt that he would lose standing in the eyes of his friends. This is a comment on the relations between company and workers, as on the relation of this man with his group. He had also found his union job a thankless one, and took a position in municipal government.

The difficulties are not all on management's side. Although the union organization had in part arisen as a new and more rapid channel of communication, in the sense in which we have used the word, than the one offered by management, yet even this channel tended to break down during wartime. Many of the labor leaders had moved up in the union pyramid to the point where they were dealing more with War Labor Board decisions and policies relating to the union as a whole than with the feeling of the men in the lines. The problem of communication here tended to parallel management's own. Certainly no company president could have been more bewildered and irritated than a representative of the central office of the union, called in to stop a wildcat strike. We might mention here an observation by a worker and former union president that the increased dependence of the men on union officers for knowledge of "what goes on behind closed doors" was noticeable. Failures to report explicitly and more or less formally on meetings with management had irritating effects which tended to snowball. Apparently the "grapevine," which has always been so important and effective in industry, had become frayed in spots, though it is remarkable, all things considered, how well it did work at times.

In short, the feeling of the workingman that he was at last in a position to insist on being heard became strong at a time

when the actual avenues of communication, both for the company and the union,
became weaker and more indirect than
they had been in the past.

The complexity of conditions giving rise to collective behavior. It is evident that the division of labor, the normative order, and communication are interdependent and interacting features of social organization. Changes in one are likely to be accompanied by changes in the others. By the same token, collective behavior arises out of a complex of societal roots and not from a single condition. In different instances one factor may be of greater weight than others, but some degree of inadequacy of all of these basic features of a social system is likely to be present.

Human social organization, with its norms, its structure, and its web of communication, provides an indispensable framework for the social behavior of the individual. Within this framework he is able to build up his own actions in terms of what he can expect of other people and what he assumes they expect of him. Changes in the salient features of the social matrix of behavior create for him an "unstructured" or critical situation in which action becomes more problematic than usual. Hence the nature of individual reactions to such situations must be taken into account in understanding how collective behavior develops.

Chapter 3

Individual reactions to crises

$\mathcal{S}$INCE individual human behavior can be understood only as taking place within a matrix of socially-defined meanings and expectations, the development of *new* forms must be studied in the context of a changing social milieu. Social changes should not be regarded as autonomous, however, but as the products of the interaction of individuals. Culture does not "change itself" in an impersonal, automatic fashion. Individuals change culture, even though they may change it unwittingly and in minute details. Inventions usually have unplanned and unanticipated consequences for the cultures into which they are introduced. At times men deliberately, "with malice aforethought," create confusion, dissatisfaction, and insecurity, as happens when agitators spread rumors or saboteurs disrupt the productive processes of a society. Such human actions, as well as such forces of nature as earthquakes, floods, droughts, and hurricanes, may disrupt the physical and cultural milieu in which individuals must function.

But again, culture does not automatically adjust to such disruptions, and no group mind emerges to guide the individual in his adjustment to the changing situation. Social adjustment is the product of the interaction of numerous individual responses. Hence it is in the reactions of individuals to critical, unstructured situations that some of the roots of collective behavior are to be found. These individual responses must be considered as a necessary background to the analysis of the development of new group norms and structures.

Research on individual reactions to crises. The reactions of individuals to critical situations are often difficult to observe or reconstruct. Often it is easier to see the products of these individual reactions—the actions of the group. Students observing such group products have inferred individual psychological states and behavior patterns from them. Such inferences have not, however, been derived from careful study of individuals as discrete, although interacting, parts of the collectivity. In many instances conclusions have stemmed, instead, from preconceived theories of human behavior. These inferential conclusions have tended to lead to a stereotyping of the behavior of individuals in the collectivity, rather than to an awareness of the variety of individual reactions and the reciprocal effects of these different types of behavior.

Extreme and critical situations, such as those created in war or in peacetime disasters, provide opportunities for the investigation of individual reactions to the sudden and drastic disruption of the social framework of behavior. Largely as the result of World War II and the subsequent threat of atomic warfare, there has been a recent upsurge of interest in the empirical study of both individual and group response in critical situations.

Crises, particularly those involving some disturbance of the physical environment, pose a threat to the individual and his values. Fear may result from such a threat if the individual is in physical danger or believes that cherished objects are endangered. But from the standpoint of collective behavior there is an even more important aspect of the crisis, even though danger may not be great. This is the sudden, unexpected disorganization of the world with which the individual is familiar. His normal expectations as to what other objects, both human and inanimate, will do next, and as to what he himself should do, are no longer appropriate to the situation. The situation has become ambiguous and unstructured for him. The uncertain, relatively unstructured nature of the critical situation is of as much interest as is the danger that may exist in it.

TYPES OF INDIVIDUAL REACTIONS

Defense reactions. One result of a crisis, found especially in potentially traumatic situations, is the inability of the individual to act in more than a very limited fashion. Even in the absence of physical injuries sufficient to cause brain damage or a physiological state of shock, some people seem unable to comprehend what has happened or to cope with the new situation. S. H. Prince observed this reaction among survivors of the great explosion at Halifax in 1918:

> The first of these phenomena was the "stun" of the catastrophe itself. The shock reaction at Halifax has been variously described. It has been graphically likened "to being suddenly stricken with blindness and paralysis." It was a sensation of utter helplessness and disability.*

It may be that such a "dazed" or "stunned" state is a psychological defense against a terrifying world which it would be painful to comprehend. Some people in this state may act quite positively, with complete disregard for physical injuries and personal losses. Others are unable to act of their own volition except in a very limited way, but are highly amenable to suggestions from others and may obey orders readily. A doctor described such a condition, observed in a man who had suffered only minor injuries but narrowly escaped death in an explosion, in the following way:

> This man was "shocky"—just stunned. He was not in what we call "wound shock" —he had only a few small cuts and had suffered no serious loss of blood. But I

* S. H. Prince, **Catastrophe and Social Change,** Studies in History, Economics, and Public Law, 94, No. 1 (1920–21) (New York: Columbia University, 1921), p. 36.

wouldn't dismiss him from the hospital. He seemed shell-shocked, and appeared to be very apathetic. You could ask him questions and he'd answer you, but he didn't show any emotional reactions at all. Had it been necessary, I believe I could have sutured his cuts without any anesthetic.*

Restriction of attention. Another reaction frequently occurring immediately after the impact of a violent disaster is impulsive, apparently irrational, action. The individual seems to engage in action unconsciously, without making designations to himself of what he is doing. Later his actions may seem ridiculous to him; sometimes he cannot even remember doing such things or, if he can remember them, why he did them. Sometimes he finds it almost incomprehensible that he was able to do them. Such reactions are described by a man who was caught in the midst of a tornado and responded with great disregard of personal danger:

> I was sitting in a cafe while my son and daughter were at a picture show across the street. The first I knew what was coming was when the pressure started hitting my eardrums. I knew it was a tornado then because I'd been in one before—in a cellar, though. As soon as I felt it, I started for the door. As I started out, the glass in the front of the cafe was bulging in. A fellow caught me and drug me back. Then I drug a lady back and pushed her under one of the tables. By that time the glass had all blowed in, and I went out the door. *I don't hardly remember what happened after that. You don't act like a human being when something like that happens—you're just mechanical.* I knew my kids were in that theater and I was going over there. I went down twenty times between the cafe and the theater—the tornado was still over the town. When I got to the theater the cars in front of it was just moving back and forth and up and down. I had to make two runs to get to the door. The first time I started in I saw the cars coming together and I had to stop. The second time I got in between two cars and just as I did they started coming together. I just put one foot on each car and stood on them as they came together. *I thought about that later on—I couldn't have done that again if I tried.***

It appears that in such behavior there is a restriction of the individual's attention to a very narrow portion of the total situation in which he must act. It is not that he acts unconsciously, but he pays attention to relatively few features of the situation and makes only limited designations to himself about the consequences of his actions. In ordinary, noncritical situations people do not consider the full range of possible consequences of their actions; in critical situations, their attention is even more narrowly restricted.

Fear reactions. The notion of a "critical situation" suggests the existence of some threat to the individual and his values. Whether the danger is real or imaginary, fear is a frequent response to critical situations. Fear may find expression in many forms, ranging from covert changes in physiological and emotional states, to overt behavior, such as screaming or running wildly.

Fear seems to be augmented by vagueness or uncertainty about the danger. The uncertainty of the situation leads to feelings of insecurity and helplessness which arise in the individual because he does not know with what he must cope or what actions he can take to protect himself. Killian and Giffin, in studies of the reactions of firemen to their work, found that many of them did not regard a fire as dangerous or fear-provoking so long as they believed that they had the skills and equipment with which to cope with it. The type of fire which inspires

* Case material from the files of Lewis M. Killian.
** Ibid.

fear is one which contains an element of uncertainty and unpredictability, such as oil fires and "inside" fires where there is dense smoke. Such statements as the following suggest the basis for their fear of such fires:

> The worst thing about a fire is not being able to see what it is. Any time you can't see what you are working against you're in trouble.
> The worst thing about any fire is not knowing what it's going to do. That's the worst thing about an oil fire—you don't know whether it's going to blow up or just fizzle out.*

Irving Janis, in *Air War and Emotional Stress,* concludes that during World War II night air raids were more frightening to civilians than were day raids. He emphasizes the importance of general situational uncertainty in augmenting fear.

* Case material from the files of Lewis M. Killian and James R. Giffin.

NIGHT VERSUS DAY RAIDS
IRVING JANIS

The vast majority of a cross section of German civilians reported that they were more frightened by raids occurring at night than by those occurring during daylight. When bombing was light, however, there was a slight tendency to fear either day raids or night raids, depending on which kind was experienced more often. In general, the vast majority of those who experienced both day and night raids considered the latter much worse. Parallel results are reported by the United States Strategic Bombing Survey of a cross section of Japanese civilians. One of the most common reasons for fearing night raids is that it is more difficult to get away from the fires and destruction at night when orientation is more difficult. Interview comments indicate that "in the darkness the flashes and sound of bombs are psychologically exaggerated and produce more fear." Glover also mentions that among the British, night raids evoked

Reprinted by permission of McGraw-Hill Book Company, Inc., and the author, from Irving L. Janis, **Air War and Emotional Stress** (New York: McGraw-Hill Book Company, Inc., 1951), pp. 119–120.

more sensational reactions but that these were usually dispelled the next morning if there was little visible evidence of widespread destruction.

Similar observations have been reported in connection with other types of danger situations. For example, it has been noted that frontline combat troops also tend to be more fearful at night than during the day. As Sullivan points out, "terror is far more commonly experienced in darkness than in daylight and in fog than in clear weather." Thus, the observations on augmented emotional reactions among civilians exposed to night raids can be subsumed under a more general proposition: in any danger situation, anything interfering with clear visual perception tends to diminish feelings of security. Darkness reduces the opportunity for sensory discriminations and thereby interferes with the individual's ability to evaluate the dangerous and safe features of his environment. Under these conditions, the fear-evoking effects of loud noises and of other salient danger cues tend to be augmented.

Efforts to redefine the situation. Not all individuals confronted with a critical situation react in either an apathetic, highly emotional, impulsive, or reflexive manner. Many of them remain relatively calm and self-controlled, but still do not know how to assess the situation nor how to behave in response to it. Many of their initial reactions to an unstructured situation may be classified as "redefining" or "restructuring" activity—efforts to find out just what the situation is and what it means.

Much of this redefining activity is covert, consisting of attempts to interpret the new situation in terms of familiar expectations. In his narrative of the atomic bombing of Hiroshima, John Hersey tells how some survivors attempted to fit even this most drastic of critical situations into their familiar conceptions of the world.* They could think only that a conventional bomb had fallen directly upon them. But now that the atom bomb is a familiar part of the world for millions of people, any loud explosion in an American city is likely to cause some people to conclude that an A-bomb has been dropped!

Other forms of restructuring activity are overt—rushing about, looking around, asking questions. One form all too familiar to policemen, firemen, and ambulance drivers is "going to see what happened." The heedless rush of the curious to the center of a disaster area is a familiar feature of such situations. While some people may engage in the rush because of official duties or anxiety about relatives, many go simply out of curiosity.

Restructuring activity may consist of communication acts. As familiar as the rush of the curious to the scene of a disaster is the flooding of telephone switchboards with hundreds of calls. The following account by a Houston, Texas, newspaper reporter describes this reaction.

* John Hersey, **Hiroshima** (New York: Alfred A. Knopf, Inc., 1946).

AFTERMATH CAME IN FRENZIED RUSH
FRANKLIN REED

In addition to death and injuries in Friday's explosion at the Alco Fireworks and Specialty Co., there was yet another aftermath—frenzy.

Excited Houstonians by the hundreds, most of them not knowing what had happened and many of them fearing the worst, jammed the telephone lines into the massive City of Houston switchboard.

Mrs. Alma Robins, the chief operator, said the board "was lit up like a Christmas tree," and the eight switchboard operators on duty at the time "were operating at capacity."

And within minutes after the explosion, calls began flooding the *Post's* switchboard.

Callers wanted to know: "What blew up?" "Where is it?" "Anybody killed? Anybody hurt?" There were many questions. Persons several miles away from the blast were calling.

Reprinted in part by permission of the Editor and the Publishers, the Houston, Texas **Post**, from Franklin Reed, "Aftermath Came in Frenzied Rush," the Houston **Post**, June 6, 1953.

Allport and Postman, in their "Basic Law of Rumor," have suggested that ambiguity is one of the essential conditions for the spread of rumor.** Susceptibility to rumor is, in part, a function of the need of the individual to restructure an ambiguous situation. Even to know the worst seems to be better than the anxiety of an unstructured, but ominous, situation. A young man who was sep

** Gordon W. Allport and Leo Postman, "An Analysis of Rumor," **Public Opinion Quarterly,** Vol. 10 (Winter, 1946–47), pp. 501–514.

arated from his family during a tornado said, when he finally found the bodies of his mother and father, "Now all I have to do is find my brother!" A husband, after searching for his missing wife after a tornado had struck, found that she had been killed instantly. His first words were, "Thank God—at least I know now that she isn't somewhere suffering!" *

Role conflicts in critical situations. Even after the individual is able to find a clear and apparently correct perceptual structure in a critical situation, he still may find that he is confronted with a dilemma in determining what his actions should be. It is in the nature of a critical situation that the tempo of action is speeded up: choices which ordinarily can be postponed must be made immediately; conflicts which normally may be minimized and endured must suddenly be resolved. The types of conflicts and dilemmas which may arise in time of disaster, and the difficulties which individuals encounter in resolving them, are discussed in "The Significance of Multiple Group Membership in Disaster."

* Case material from the files of Lewis M. Killian.

THE SIGNIFICANCE OF MULTIPLE-GROUP MEMBERSHIP IN DISASTER

In a study of the reactions of people in four Southwestern communities to physical disasters—explosions and tornadoes— . . . it was found that conflicting group loyalties and contradictory roles resulting from multiple-group membership were significant factors affecting individual behavior in critical situations. The dilemmas created by the disasters also brought to light latent contradictions in roles not ordinarily regarded as conflicting.

In spite of the fact that multiple-group memberships do create dilemmas and inconsistencies, the majority of people in modern urban society manage to function efficiently as members of many groups, often being only vaguely aware of contradictions in their various roles. . . .

A man may play the role of a businessman, acting in terms of the work situation, during most of the day. For a few hours in the evening he may play the role of "the family man," leaving his work at the office. In a small community he may, on certain occasions, act as a functionary of the town government, as a volunteer fireman, or as a town councilman. Simultaneously, he has other group memberships which call for certain behavior—in a social class group, in a racial group, in the community of which he is a citizen, and in "society-at-large."

When catastrophe strikes a community, many individuals find that the latent conflict between ordinarily nonconflicting group loyalties suddenly becomes apparent and that they are faced with the dilemma of making an immediate choice between various roles. . . .

People who had been present in the explosion port of Texas City and in three Oklahoma tornado towns during disasters were asked, among other questions, "What was the first thing you thought of after the disaster struck?" and "What was the first thing you did?" Their answers revealed not only the conflict between loyalties to the family and to the community, . . . but also dilemmas arising from conflicting roles derived from membership in other groups. The individuals concerned were not always conscious of the dilemmas or of the existence of "cross-pressures," but even in such cases the choice of roles which the person made was significant in affecting the total pattern of group reaction to the disaster. In some

Reprinted in part by permission of The University of Chicago Press from L. M. Killian, "The Significance of Multiple-Group Membership in Disaster," **The American Journal of Sociology**, 57 (1952), pp. 309–313.

cases subjects indicated that they recognized *after* the emergency that their reaction had been of critical social importance. On the basis of the experiences of people involved in these four community disasters it is possible to suggest the types of groups between which dilemmas of loyalty may arise in modern communities. Tentative generalization as to how these dilemmas will be resolved and as to their significance for *group* reactions to disaster may also be formulated.

The choice required of the greatest number of individuals was the one between the family and other groups, principally the employment group or the community. Especially in Texas City, many men were at work away from their families when disaster struck and presented a threat to both "the plant" and "the home." In all the communities there were individuals, such as policemen, firemen, and public utilities workers, whose loved ones were threatened by the same disaster that demanded their services as "trouble-shooters." Even persons who had no such definite roles to play in time of catastrophe were confronted with the alternatives of seeing after only their own primary groups or of assisting in the rescue and relief of any of the large number of injured persons, regardless of identity. Indeed, only the unattached person in the community was likely to be free of such a conflict.

. . . The great majority of persons interviewed who were involved in such dilemmas resolved them in favor of loyalty to the family or, in some cases, to friendship groups. Much of the initial confusion, disorder, and seemingly complete disorganization reported in the disaster communities was the result of the rush of individuals to find and rejoin their families. Yet in none of the four communities studied did the disastrous consequences contemplated above seem to have materialized. In the first place, there were important exceptions to the tendency to react first in terms of the family. Most of the refinery workers in Texas City did stay on the job until their units were safely shut down, as they had been trained

to do. The significance of conflicting group loyalties in a disaster situation is underlined, however, by the importance of the actions taken by a few exceptional individuals in each town who were not confronted with such conflicts. In Texas City the chief of police remained at his post from the moment of the first explosion until seventy-two hours later, never returning to his home during the entire period and playing a vital part in the reorganization of the community. He ascribed his ability to give undivided attention to his official duties to the fact that he knew that his family was safely out of town, visiting relatives, at the time of the explosion.

. . . Devotion to the family as the primary object of loyalty did not always redound to the detriment of aid to other groups, however. Many people who served as rescue workers, assisting injured people whom they did not even know, were drawn to the areas of heavy casualties because of concern for members of their own families whom they believed to be there. Apparently they found their identification with society-at-large, and the emphasis of American culture upon the importance of human life, too great to permit them to pass an injured stranger without assisting him. Hence, many stayed to assist in the common community task of rescuing the injured, in both Texas City and in the tornado towns. In one of the latter a man sensed the approach of the tornado only minutes before it struck. In spite of great personal danger he rushed through the storm to a theater where his children were attending a movie. There he prevented the frightened audience from pouring forth into the storm by holding the doors closed. Later he was acclaimed as a hero whose quick action had saved the lives of many of his fellow-citizens. He himself denied that he had any thought of taking the great risk that he took for the sake of the anonymous audience itself; he was thinking only of his own children.

A second, but less common, type of conflict was found in the case of people who were confronted with the alternatives of playing the "heroic" role of rescue worker and of carrying out what were essentially "occupational roles." In terms of group loyalty, they were impelled, on the one hand, to act as sympathetic, loyal members of society-at-large and to give personal aid to injured human beings. On the other hand, they were called to do their duty as it was indicated by their membership in certain occupational groups.

One such person was a minister in Texas City who, upon hearing the explosion, started for the docks with the intention of helping in the rescue work. On the way he became conscious of the choice of roles which confronted him. He said:

> After I heard the first explosion my first impulse was to go down to the docks and try to help there. But on the way down I saw two or three folks I knew who had husbands down there. I saw then that my job was with the families—not doing rescue work. I had a job that I was peculiarly suited for, prepared for, and I felt that I should do that.
>
> . . . For people whose usual occupational roles bore little or no relationship to the needs created by a disaster, identification with the community as a whole and disregard of their occupational roles came still more easily. Many merchants and clerks rushed from their stores to aid in rescue work, leaving both goods and cash on the counters. The postmaster in one tornado town left the post office completely unguarded, even though the windows were shattered and mail was strewn about the floor. This was, it is true, an extreme case of abandonment of the occupational role.

A third type of conflict of loyalties was that between the loyalty of employees to "the company" as an organization and to fellow-employees as friends and human beings. It might seem that the choice, essentially one between life and property, should have been an easy one; but the fact that different choices were made by men with different degrees of identification with other workers reveals that a basic conflict was present. In Texas City

many plant officials were also residents of the community and friends of the workers. After the explosions, in which several top executives were killed, some men found themselves suddenly "promoted" to the position of being in charge of their company's damaged property. At the same time men with whom they had worked daily for several years were injured or missing. The most common, almost universal, reaction was to think of the men first and of the plant later. One plant official, active in rescue work in spite of a broken arm and numerous lacerations, described his reaction to the sudden, dramatic conflict between loyalty to the company and loyalty to the workers as follows:

> Property! Nobody gave a damn for property! All that was important was life. I've often wondered just how it would be to walk off and let a plant burn up. That was the way it was. We didn't even consider fighting the fire.

In sharp contrast to this reaction, however, was that of a man in charge of a neighboring plant. While he was in Texas City at the time of the first blast, he had never lived in the community and scarcely knew his workers. He described his first reaction in the following words:

> I got in my car and drove over to another refinery to find out what had happened. The assistant superintendent told me that their top men had been killed and asked me what I thought he should do. I told him, "You should take charge of the company's property. That's what the president of your company would tell you if he were here. You look after the property. I'm going over to Galveston to call our president, and I'll call yours at the same time."

While this reaction was exceptional, it is significant as suggesting an alternate way of resolving the conflict between loyalty to "the company" and "the men."

Finally, some individuals suddenly discovered, in the face of disaster, that there was a conflict between loyalty to the community and loyalty to certain extra-community groups. At the time of two of the disasters telephone workers in the Southwest were on strike. In both communities the striking workers were allowed to return to duty by union leaders but were ordered to walk out again a few days later. In both cases the union officials considered the emergency to be over sooner than did the townspeople of the stricken communities. In one town the workers obeyed the union's orders only to find themselves subjected to harsh criticism by their fellow-townsmen. In the other community the workers resigned from the union rather than forsake their loyalty to their other membership group. It was almost a year before union officials were able to reorganize the local in this town, and some workers never rejoined.

As was pointed out earlier, the individual may, under normal circumstances, carry out roles appropriate to membership in several groups without having to make a choice between basically conflicting group loyalties. . . . In the crisis induced by disaster, however, the individual may find that it is impossible to serve two masters, to act in two roles. An immediate choice is demanded, but it may be difficult because the demands of the competing groups may appear equally urgent. The nature of the choice made by the individual, particularly if one of his roles is associated with a key position in the community, may have important consequences for the reorganization of the community. Large-scale reorganization, co-ordination, and direction of efforts is necessary to speedy rescue work and the restoration of normalcy. Activities carried on in terms of the demands of many diverse, competing groups act as an impediment to this reorganization.

The search for security in extreme situations. In some instances the breakdown of the familiar context of meanings and values may take place over a long period of time. Instead of a brief, sudden crisis there is a long period of disorientation—what Bruno Bettelheim has called an "extreme situation." In his recollections of life in a Nazi concentration camp he describes the reactions of individuals to prolonged attack on their norms, values and self-conceptions.

Throughout this extreme situation, individuals attempted in various ways to preserve their self-esteem and their identity as the same kinds of people they were before imprisonment. A reaction to the initial shock of imprisonment and Gestapo brutality was a defense reaction akin to the "stun" of disaster victims— the development of a state of detachment in which there was a feeling "as if what happened did not really happen to them." Even after the initial shock had passed, the prisoners seemed to experience a stronger subjective response to familiar types of punishments, such as "childish punishments," than they did to unusual, even though more brutal, treatment. Finally, as the extreme situation persisted, they found themselves unable to cling to norms and values which were not appropriate to the prison situation. They became susceptible to suggestions from the strongest source of authority and meaning in their present world, and unconsciously adopted the values of the Gestapo as their own.

INDIVIDUAL AND MASS BEHAVIOR IN EXTREME SITUATIONS
Bruno Bettelheim

A prisoner had reached the final stage of

Reprinted in part by permission of the author and of the American Psychological Association, from Bruno Bettelheim, "Individual and Mass Behavior in Extreme Situations," **Journal of Abnormal and Social Psychology,** 38 (1943), pp. 417–452.

adjustment to the camp situation when he had changed his personality so as to accept as his own the values of the Gestapo. A few examples may illustrate how this acceptance expressed itself.

The Gestapo considered, or pretended

to consider, the prisoners the scum of the earth. They insisted that none of them was any better than the others. One of the reasons for this attitude was probably to impress the young guards who received their training in the camp that they were superior to even the most outstanding prisoner and to demonstrate to them that the former foes of the Nazis were now subdued and not worthy of any special attention. If a formerly prominent prisoner had been treated better, the simple guard would have thought that he is still influential; if he had been treated worse, they might have thought that he is still dangerous. This was in line with the desire to impress the guards that even a slight degree of opposition against the Nazi system led to the entire destruction of the person who dared to oppose, and that the degree of opposition made no difference in this respect. Occasional talks with these guards revealed that they really believed in a Jewish-capitalistic world conspiracy against the German people, and whoever opposed the Nazis participated in it and was therefore to be destroyed, independent of his role in the conspiracy. So it can be understood why their behavior to the prisoners was that normally reserved for dealing with one's vilest enemy.

The prisoners found themselves in an impossible situation due to the steady interference with their privacy on the part of the guards and other prisoners. So a great amount of aggression accumulated. In the new prisoners it vented itself in the way it might have done in the world outside the camp. But slowly prisoners accepted, as expression of their verbal aggression, terms which definitely did not originate in their previous vocabularies, but were taken over from the very different vocabulary of the Gestapo. From copying the verbal aggression of the Gestapo to copying their form of bodily aggressions was one more step, but it took several years to make this step. It was not unusual to find old prisoners, when in charge of others, behaving worse than the Gestapo, in some cases because they were

trying to win favor with the Gestapo in this way but more often because they considered this the best way to behave toward prisoners in the camp.

Practically all prisoners who had spent a long time in the camp took over the Gestapo's attitude toward the so-called unfit prisoners. Newcomers presented the old prisoners with difficult problems. Their complaints about the unbearable life in camp added new strain to the life in the barracks, so did their inability to adjust to it. Bad behavior in the labor gang endangered the whole group. So a newcomer who did not stand up well under the strain tended to become a liability for the other prisoners. Moreover, weaklings were those most apt eventually to turn traitors. Weaklings usually died during the first weeks in the camp anyway, so it seemed as well to get rid of them sooner. So old prisoners were sometimes instrumental in getting rid of the unfit, in this way making a feature of Gestapo ideology a feature of their own behavior. This was one of the many situations in which old prisoners demonstrated toughness and molded their way of treating other prisoners according to the example set by the Gestapo. That this was really a taking-over of Gestapo attitudes can be seen from the treatment of traitors. Self-protection asked for their elimination, but the way in which they were tortured for days and slowly killed was taken over from the Gestapo.

Old prisoners who seemed to have a tendency to identify themselves with the Gestapo did so not only in respect to aggressive behavior. They would try to arrogate to themselves old pieces of Gestapo uniforms. If that was not possible, they tried to sew and mend their uniforms so that they would resemble those of the guards. The length to which prisoners would go in these efforts seemed unbelievable, particularly since the Gestapo punished them for their efforts to copy Gestapo uniforms. When asked why they did it they admitted that they loved to look like one of the guards.

The identification with the Gestapo did not stop with the copying of their outer appearance and behavior. Old prisoners accepted their goals and values, too, even when they seemed opposed to their own interests. It was appalling to see how far formerly even politically well-educated prisoners would go in this identification. At one time American and English newspapers were full of stories about the cruelties committed in the camps. The Gestapo punished the prisoners for the appearance of these stories true to their policy of punishing the group for whatever a member or a former member did, and the stories must have originated in reports of former prisoners. In discussions of this event old prisoners would insist that it is not the business of foreign correspondents or newspapers to bother with German institutions and expressed their hatred of the journalists who tried to help them. The writer asked more than one hundred old political prisoners the following question: "If I am lucky and reach foreign soil, should I tell the story of the camp and arouse the interest of the cultured world?" He found only two who made the unqualified statement that everyone escaping Germany ought to fight the Nazis to the best of his abilities. *All others were hoping for a German revolution, but did not like the idea of interference on the part of a foreign power.*

When old prisoners accepted Nazi values as their own they usually did not admit it, but explained their behavior by rationalizations. For instance, prisoners collected scrap in the camp because Germany was low on raw materials. When it was pointed out that they were thus helping the Nazis, they rationalized that through the saving of scrap Germany's working classes, too, became richer.

The satisfaction with which some old prisoners enjoyed the fact that, during the twice daily counting of the prisoners, they really had stood well at attention can be explained only by the fact that they had entirely accepted the values of the Gestapo as their own. Prisoners prided themselves on being as tough as the Gestapo members. This identification with their torturers went so far as copying of their leisure-time activities. One of the games played by the guards was to find out who could stand to be hit longest without uttering a complaint. This game was copied by the old prisoners, as though they had not been hit often and long enough without needing to repeat this experience as a game.

Other problems in which most old prisoners made their peace with the values of the Gestapo included the race problem, although race discrimination had been alien to their scheme of values before they were brought into the camp. They accepted as true the claim that Germany needed more space ("Lebensraum"), but added "as long as there does not exist a world federation," they believed in the superiority of the German race. It should be emphasized that this was not the result of propaganda on the side of the Gestapo. The Gestapo made no such efforts and insisted in its statements that it was not interested in how the prisoners felt as long as they were full of fear of the Gestapo. Moreover, the Gestapo insisted that it would prevent them from expressing their feelings anyway. The Gestapo seemed to think it impossible to win the prisoners for its values, after having made them subject to their tortures.

Among the old prisoners one could observe other developments which indicated their desire to accept the Gestapo along lines which definitely could not originate in propaganda. It seems that, since they returned to a childlike attitude toward the Gestapo, they had a desire that at least some of those whom they accepted as all-powerful father-images should be just and kind. They divided their positive and negative feelings—strange as it may be that they should have positive feelings, they had them—toward the Gestapo in such a way that all positive emotions were concentrated on a few officers who were rather high up in the hierarchy of camp administrators, but hardly ever on the governor of the camp. They insisted that these officers hide behind their rough surfaces a feeling of justice and propriety; he, or they, were supposed to be genuinely interested in the prisoners and even trying, in a small way, to help them. Since nothing of these supposed feelings and efforts ever became apparent, it was explained that he hid them so effectively because otherwise he would not be able to help the prisoners. The eagerness of these prisoners to find reasons for their claims was pitiful. A whole legend was woven around the fact that of two officers inspecting a barrack one had cleaned his shoes from mud before entering. He probably did it automatically, but it was interpreted as a rebuff to the other officer and a clear demonstration of how he felt about the concentration camp.

After so much has been said about the old prisoners' tendency to conform and to identify with the Gestapo, it ought to be stressed that this was only part of the picture, because the author tried to concentrate on interesting psychological mechanisms in group behavior rather than on reporting types of behavior which are either well known or could reasonably be expected. These same old prisoners who identified with the Gestapo at other moments defied it, demonstrating extraordinary courage in doing so.

In conclusion, it should be emphasized again that this essay is a preliminary report and does not pretend to be exhaustive. The author feels that the concentration camp has an importance reaching far beyond its being a place where the Gestapo takes revenge on its enemies. It is the main training ground for young Gestapo soldiers who are planning to rule and police Germany and all conquered nations; it is the Gestapo's laboratory where it develops methods for changing free and up-right citizens not only into grumbling slaves, but into serfs who in many respects accept their masters' values. They still think that they are following their own life goals and values, whereas in reality they have accepted the Nazis' values as their own.

AN EXPERIMENTAL MODEL OF THE ROOTS OF COLLECTIVE BEHAVIOR

In the analysis of various life situations of a critical nature, various effects of situational uncertainty on the individual have been pointed out. Feelings of insecurity and anxiety, the need for the finding of some structure in the situation, and susceptibility to suggestions from others are important reactions. The erratic, random behavior of the individual and his increased suggestibility have been emphasized by many students as salient features of individual behavior in unstructured situations.

Sherif and Harvey have experimentally produced such reactions in an investigation, through simple judgmental reactions, of the effects of various conditions of situational uncertainty on ego-functioning. On an easily-observed perceptual level, in a laboratory situation, they have produced those individual reactions which, in life situations, constitute important roots of collective behavior—uneasiness, anxiety, random activity, and sensitivity to the suggestions of others.

As a background for their experiment, Sherif and Harvey cite evidence of the importance of the absence of stable anchorages in "life situations of little structure."

IMPLICATIONS OF OBSERVATIONS FROM LIFE SITUATIONS
Muzafer Sherif and O. J. Harvey

Experimental study must ring true to the

Reprinted in part by permission of the authors and the editor, **Sociometry**, from Muzafer Sherif and O. J. Harvey, "A Study in Ego-Functioning: Elimination of Stable Anchorages in Individual and Group Situations," **Sociometry**, 15 (1952), 272-305.

characteristics of situations and behavior in the run of things in men's lives. For our problem we are specifically concerned with life situations of little structure, that is, situations with few stable anchorages. An example is the battlefield in modern, mechanized war. In his description of the modern battlefield, Marshall [1] wrote, "The harshest thing about the field is that it is *empty*. No people stir about. There are little or no signs of action. Over all there is a great quiet which seems more ominous than the occasional tempest of fire." This is in contrast to the recruit's expectations after being trained in the presence of great numbers of men and massive mechanical power all around him. But "he finds himself suddenly almost alone in his hour of greatest danger, and he can feel the danger, but there is nothing out there, nothing to contend against." [2] "There is nothing to be seen. The fire comes out of nowhere. But that is all that he knows for certain." [3] As the men scatter under fire, they may even be out of sight of one another. And, as Vilfroy's account of the early days of the war in France (1940) puts it, he feels utterly alone, "forward and isolate." [4]

Another example is the situation of soldiers on board ship, bound for an invasion. The present situation is clear-cut enough, but the future is unknown. It was Ernie Pyle's insightful observation that "I don't believe one of us was afraid of the physical part of dying. That isn't the way it is. The emotion is rather one of *almost desperate reluctance to give up the future*. I suppose that's splitting hairs and that it really all comes under the heading of *fear. Yet somehow there is a difference* . . . When we huddled around together on the dark decks, it was these little hopes and ambitions that made up the sum total of our worry at leaving, rather than visualization of physical agony to come." [5] (Italics ours)

As Stouffer *et al.*[6] indicated, the result of such situations is anxiety and insecurity for the individual. In behavioral terms, one fruit of such unstructured situations of stress is a decrease, at least temporarily, in behavior governed by group standards for action or by possible realistic requirements of the situation and an increase in behavior aroused by the individual's anxieties. Marshall observed that as men spread apart under fire they move "individually to whatever cover is nearest or affords the best protection." Some may use their equipment, timidly at first. Others do nothing, either because lacking instructions they don't know what to do or because "they are wholly unnerved and can neither think nor move in sensible relation to the situation." [7] When the men cannot see one another under enemy fire, "all organizational unity vanishes temporarily. What has been a force becomes a scattering of individuals." [8]

Those who have spent considerable time in prisoner-of-war camps report that the uncertainty of present and future life led frequently to increased individual fantasy and increasingly difficult relations with fellow prisoners.[9]

At a simpler level, Pyle contrasted the behavior of infantry men, who were most exposed to continuing chaos and uncertainty even as to where and when they would sleep or eat, and sailors, who at least had a ship to call home. The sailors were "more like themselves. They didn't cuss as much or as foully as soldiers. They didn't bust loose as riotously when they hit town." [10]

The individual, in a situation having few or no anchorages to guide him, caught in the throes of anxiety, tries to establish some level of stability. He seeks to find some standard and is susceptible to accepting a standard from another source. Take, for example, the pilots preparing to take off from a ship before daybreak. On a completely dark deck, they must find their ships. "Old hands get used

[1] S. L. A. Marshall, **Men Against Fire.** New York: Morrow, 1947, p. 44.

[2] Ibid., p. 45.

[3] Ibid., p. 47.

[4] D. Vilfroy, **War in the West.** Harrisburg: Military Service Publishing Co., 1942, p. 105.

[5] E. Pyle, **Brave Men.** New York: Holt, 1943, p. 4.

[6] E. Stouffer, et al., **Studies in Social Psychology in World War II.** Vol. II, The American Soldier: Combat and Its Aftermath. Princeton University Press, 1949.

[7] Op. cit., p. 48.

[8] Ibid., p. 129.

[9] E.g., E. H. Vaughan, **Community Under Stress.** Princeton: Princeton University Press, 1947, pp. 133–134.

[10] Op. cit., p. 3.

to memorizing the *relative positions* of all the planes the afternoon before the next morning, which helps." [11] It is a common enough observation that some conclusion to awaiting an indefinite future, even finally entering combat, may bring intense relief and stabilization, in spite of objective dangers in the certainty.[12]

Marshall investigated the problem of why enemy fire against an advancing infantry line invariably caused a delay of from 45–60 minutes.[13] His observations (of 11 infantry companies and one reconnaissance troop) led him to conclude that the line did not proceed until *effective communication* was restored. This might be simply one bold individual standing up and shouting "Follow me! We're going on!" [14] If withdrawal becomes necessary, but is not coupled with some brief explanation (e.g. "Get the hell out of here and follow me to that tree line on the far side of the creek."), panic is likely to result.

In such stress situations, where the individual perceives only confusion, he may long for something or someone to provide standards of conduct. Thus soldiers caught in a hasty withdrawal of British forces after the breakthrough by Rommel's army in Libya, completely surrounded by confusion, "bewilderment and fear and ignorance," *wanted* to receive orders.[15] Here is the statement of a veteran wounded in the North Africa campaign: "One time we begged our lieutenants to give orders. They were afraid to act be-

cause they didn't have the rank. We took a beating while they were waiting for orders—how did they know the commander hadn't been knocked off?" [16]

In the absence of other anchors or standards for anticipating the future, men put their faith in the wisdom and experience of the captain of their vessel or the pilot of their plane.[17] In such situations, the individual becomes increasingly dependent upon his own group for feelings of security.[18]

In short, the effect of extreme stress, uncertainty, lack of stable anchorages may be to increase suggestibility—in the sense of increasing the likelihood of accepting a standard for behavior from a source other than the individual's own. When shared with others, this increasing desire for some stable anchorage leads in group process to the rise and spread of *rumors,* as the study and reports of rumor have amply shown.

Rumor may, of course, be based on some specific event or action which is not defined for those watching. Marshall who investigated the sources of panic which occurred in battle during World War II concluded that *in every case the "common denominator" was that "somebody failed to tell other men what he was doing."* [19] Thus, in one case, a sergeant wounded during battle dashed back to a first aid station without telling his squad why. They took after him, and the rumor spread through the whole line, "The order is to withdraw."

[11] M. L. Wordell and E. N. Seiler, **Wildcats Over Casablanca.** Boston: Little, Brown, 1943, p. 26.

[12] W. Simpon, **One of Our Pilots Is Safe.** New York: Harper, 1943, p. 4.

[13] Op. cit.

[14] Ibid., p. 130.

[15] A. Moorehead, **Don't Blame the Generals.** New York: Harper, 1942, pp. 69–71.

[16] Stouffer, op. cit., p. 117.

[17] E.g., Pyle, op. cit., p. 4, and R. Rehm, "Fifty Missions over Europe," in D. G. Wright (edit.), **Observations on Combat Personnel.** New York: Josiah Macy Foundation, 1945.

[18] E.g., Stouffer, op. cit., p. 144, and Marshall, op. cit., pp. 129–130.

[19] Op. cit., p. 146.

In their experiment, these two psychologists are concerned with the effects of the elimination of stable anchorages upon the individual and his self-feelings. Their general hypothesis is that in such an unstable situation the individual will experience insecurity and that his behavior will fluctuate greatly:

When, under critical circumstances, the stability of our physical and social bearings are disrupted with the subsequent experience of not being anywhere definitely, of being torn from social ties of belongingness, or when nothing but a future of uncertainty or blockages is experienced as our lot, the by-product is the experience of insecurity. The individual tossing in such a state of anxiety or insecurity flounders all over in his craze to establish for himself some stable anchorages. The fluctuations of his experience and behavior are greatly increased. In our opinion great fluctuations or variability in experience and behavior occur *first*, even in cases of persons who may *eventually* turn into themselves to build internally paranoid anchorages which are completely out of line with the facts of reality surrounding them.

The consequences of the ego-tensions, anxiety or insecurity are a state of restlessness, floundering all over to find some stable anchorages, heightened fluctuations of behavior. If these states of anxiety or insecurity are widespread among the individuals of a group, the result is an increased degree of suggestibility, the increased credulity for events that are bizarre and unexpected, a greater degree of susceptibility to the spread of wild rumors, the greater likelihood of panics.*

In this experiment Sherif and Harvey used the "autokinetic phenomenon." The autokinetic phenomenon is the apparent movement of a pinpoint of light viewed by the subject as it is exposed against an otherwise totally dark background. While the light does not actually move, it appears to move because of the absence of any stable anchorages in the background. In previous experiments Sherif had found that, in repeated judgments of the movement of the light, individuals established persistent ranges and norms for their estimates of the distance the light moved. Furthermore, it was found that when subjects made repeated judgments as members of groups, *group* norms were established reflecting the reciprocal effects of the judgments of the individuals composing the groups.

In the present experiment, Sherif and Harvey repeated the earlier experiments, using individuals as subjects both alone and in groups, but under three different conditions. Under "Condition A" the experimenter was as friendly and encouraging as he could be, the room in which the experiment took place was small, and the subjects had a brief glimpse of the interior of the room before it was darkened. Thus the subject in Condition A had some opportunity to orient himself in relation to definite anchorages, such as walls and furniture.

Condition B differed from Condition A in that a much larger room was used and the subject never saw the space relations inside the experimental hall. He was led to his chair in the dark. In group sessions under Condition B the subjects held hands and were led to their seats. Returning to the reading from Sherif and Harvey, Condition C is here described in detail.

* Sherif and Harvey, "A Study in Ego-Functioning," pp. 280–281.

PROCEDURE: CONDITION C

This was intended to be the situation in which spatial anchorages were eliminated as much as possible, hence the most difficult. *The experimenter made no attempt to establish rapport with the subjects, being matter of fact instead of warm and cordial, and engaging in only the necessary minimum of conversation throughout the sessions. More significant than the changed air of the experimenter* was the increased difficulty in the experimental conditions. The experimental room was the same one used for Condition B, but several factors were introduced which made it much more difficult.

At a distance of 12 feet from the entrance, stairs were placed containing 4 steps in the front and 3 steps down in the back. The area of the room was marked off with ropes so that the only way the subject could reach his chair was by passing over the stairs (unless he crawled through the ropes, which none did). The ropes were introduced after preliminary work showed that the subjects in search of their chairs usually ended up at the right or left wall. They tended to stick by the wall despite instructions from the experimenter on how to find their goal. Therefore, in order to eliminate vertical anchorages as much as possible, rope barriers at hip level were used. It should be pointed out, however, that when subjects lost their way and came to the ropes, the ropes did not provide any definite anchorage as to their exact location.

After finding the stairs and passing over them, it was necessary for the subject to turn exactly 45 degrees to his left and proceed straight for 39 feet before reaching his goal (chair). There was nothing between the stairs and the chair but space.

Certain landmarks in simple relation to the subject's chair were set up in order that the experimenter could direct him to his seat when he became completely lost.

Individual session. Before going to the dark room the subject was instructed:

You are to enter a dark room. (The subject had been shown the entrance he was to use previously.) After you have gone through the door, you are to pull it tight behind you and pull the curtains closed, too. (The curtains were used to insure against light leakage.) Then, place your back to the door which you have just entered and walk straight ahead. You will come to some stairs. When you have passed over the stairs, stop and turn left 45 degrees, and walk straight in the direction you are then facing. You will come to your chair and a table in front of it. After you find your chair, sit down and face directly forward. Is there anything that is not clear?

The subject was then left in an office, several doors from the experimental room, while the experimenter made his way to his chair in the experimental room. He then called the subject, who could not tell from where in the experimental room the sound had come. As soon as the subject had closed the door of the experimental room, the experimenter started recording by stop clock the time it took for him to reach his chair, as well as all pertinent remarks of the subject. The experimenter maintained complete silence despite frequent attempts of the subjects to establish contact by asking for direction and aid. The experimenter's silence was broken only after the subject had wandered for 3 minutes without finding his chair, had expressed the fact twice that he was lost and had given up, or had reached his chair. When the subject became lost the experimenter directed him to his chair by explaining the relationship of certain landmarks to the subject's table.

After the subject had reached his chair, either through his own ability or by directional aid, he was instructed:

There is a table in front of you. On this table there is a box with a button on it. You will be shown a point of light like this. (Light was shown.) It shall always appear in this place. Several seconds before it is to appear I shall tap like this. (Experimenter tapped the table with a pencil.)

The tapping was substituted for saying "ready" to reduce further the contact between experimenter and subject.

The rest of the procedure was the same as that for the individual sessions in Conditions A and B.

Group session. Here the subjects sought their seats in pairs. Before entering the dark room, the same instructions as for the individual session of Condition C were given. After the subjects had reached their chairs, the same procedure as for the other group sessions was followed except that instead of saying "ready" before the appearance of the light, the experimenter tapped his pencil.

[After the second, or group, session under each condition, each subject filled out a questionnaire. Among the items on it was an open general question concerning the subject's reactions to the individual session, and also questions about his feeling of certainty accompanying the judgments in the group session, and on the positive or negative effect of another person's presence and estimates upon his own judgments.

Responses to the questionnaire and comments made by the subjects during the experiment reveal that feelings of insecurity were actually produced in the subjects by these uncertain, though clearly not dangerous, situations.]

RESPONSES AND COMMENTS REVEALING INSECURITY

One questionnaire item concerned the subject's difficulty in making judgments. Under Condition A (relatively easy), 14 or 70% of the subjects indicated that "estimates were easy" or "no major difficulty in any estimates." In contrast, 90% of subjects in Condition C (with fewest anchorages) reported difficulty in half, the majority, or most of their estimates, only 2 subjects indicating that their "estimates were easy."

Content analysis of answers to an open general question asking for the subject's reactions to the individual session revealed increasing uncertainty and confusion from Condition A to Condition C. In Condition A, 5 (25%) subjects indicated uncertainty as contrasted to 9 (45%) in Condition B and 13 (65%) in Condition C. Typical comments of subjects in each condition reveal qualitative differences even in this experienced uncertainty, among those who spontaneously included it in their responses:

Condition A: "I felt ill at ease, but curious."

Condition B: "Bewildered. I don't ever remember even being in such complete darkness. And it was a little nerve-wracking."

"Very unsure and a little afraid, not of anything in particular, just of a strange and totally unexplained situation."

Condition C: "Felt helpless and ill at ease—was very puzzled."

"Completely confused. Lost as heck."

Further spontaneous remarks of the subjects substantiated this supposition that uncertainty and instability were not only experienced more frequently under Condition B and especially C, but that such uncertainty was more intense in the latter conditions. For example, one subject in Condition B remarked: "The first time when I was there by myself, it sometimes seemed as if the room was moving with me. Sometimes it seemed like my chair was turning over to one side. When I would move my feet away from a spot and replace them, it seemed like the floor was laying at an angle."

Statistical analysis of the fluctuations of the judgments of the subjects, in both individual and group sessions, and under the three different conditions, led to the following conclusions:

(a) The more uncertain the situation, the greater the scale within which judgmental reactions are scattered.

(b) The more uncertain the situation, the greater the magnitude of the norm or standard around which judgments are distributed.

(c) The more uncertain the situation, the larger the differences between the scales and norms of judgment of different individuals.

(d) The more uncertain the situation, the greater the tendency, on the whole, toward convergence in group situations.*

These conclusions confirm the general hypothesis that, with increasing situational uncertainty, the greater will be the fluctuations in the judgmental behavior of the individual. The last conclusion (d) suggests, furthermore, that increasing

---

* Sherif and Harvey, "A Study in Ego-Functioning," p. 303.

the uncertainty of the situation increases the susceptibility of the individual to the suggestions of others, as observation of so many life situations has also suggested.

The importance of variations in response to unstructured situations. In considering individual responses to crises and unstructured situations, it must not be supposed that all individuals in such a situation will react in the same way, or that all will react in one or another of the ways discussed above. Some individuals may remain relatively calm and arrive quickly at a course of action which seems appropriate to them. Their decisive action may, in turn, reduce the uncertainty of the situation for other individuals, and lead to the building up of group definitions and a common line of action.

An important reason for such variations in individual responses to the same external stimulus situation is the fact that whether a situation is unstructured for the individual is a function of both external and internal factors. A situation which is confusing and frightening to one person may seem well-structured and not so frightening to another with a different background of experience. Similarly, among individuals all of whom initially find a situation ambiguous, some may find meaning in it sooner than do others and thus be enabled to act.

Chapter 4

Social contagion

*I*T HAS been seen that when the social bases for integrated group action become inadequate, the group does not cease to act. Instead, in the process of collective behavior, it gropes toward new modes of action. Many observers have suggested that the greatest cohesiveness between human beings is found in collectivities which seem to be acting outside of, or in contradiction to, traditional norms and values, as the mob seems to do. One of the features of elementary collective behavior most often noted is the apparent lack of differentiation in the behavior of the individual actors. The crowd, temporary and transitory, yet dominated by a uniform mood and uniform imagery, stands in contrast to ordinary groups in its behavior.

The human crowd has been likened to the animal herd or pack; such concepts as the herd instinct, the simultaneous release of identical primordial drives, and the group mind have been advanced to account for much nontraditional social cohesion. But crowd behavior does not consist of the mere release of repressed tendencies to action; it is built up. The social cohesion of the crowd does not emerge through a sudden synthesis of common, unconscious, psychological forces; it is developed. The form of behavior which has come to be designated as "milling" is the basis of social contagion and is the fundamental process through which a uniform mood and imagery is developed in a collectivity.

A definition of milling. The term "milling" calls to mind the restless, excited circling of cattle, and the milling of human beings has often been compared to that of animals. It is true that the early stages of elementary collective behavior often involve a great deal of random, restless, physical movement, suggestive of the behavior of lower animals. But physical movement is an accident of milling, as the process is conceived here, and is not of the essence.

The solitary individual caught in the throes of uncertainty and blocked in his

58

activity may act in a restless manner. He engages in restructuring activity and finds it difficult to concentrate on anything but the source of uncertainty. He seeks repeatedly to find out what is going to happen next—looking down the track for the overdue train, listening intently for a repetition of the strange sound whose meaning he cannot fathom, sitting by the radio to catch the latest news bulletin. He also expends energy in random, nongoal-directed behavior. He may fidget, biting his fingernails, smoking, pacing, and engaging in other forms of random, nervous activity. He may be anxious, or he may be eager; it is difficult for the observer to judge, for his actions are very similar in either case.

When other people are present in the same ambiguous situation, the individual's search for meaning takes a somewhat different direction. He may now seek cues in the reactions of others to the situation. The people are an essential part of the situation; how others who are present react helps to define the situation for each individual. As individuals begin to engage in restructuring activity as part of a collectivity they may be said to mill. Milling, thus conceived, is essentially a communication process.

The restless, random movements of the uncertain individual also take on a new significance in a collective context. In addition to being a means of releasing pent-up, nervous energy, they constitute stimuli for other people. The movements themselves may become objects of attention and may serve to call the attention of members of the collectivity to each other.

Milling may thus be defined as a search for socially sanctioned meaning in a relatively unstructured situation. It is not sufficient, however, that the situation simply be unstructured for milling to begin. The situation must also have importance so that the members of the collectivity are motivated to act or, at least, to understand the situation. Under these conditions milling serves in the development of a common definition, providing a new basis for social cohesion and making possible collective action.

The nature of milling. It is evident that milling can take many forms, comprising several different behaviors. In its simplest form it may involve a minimum of physical and verbal activity. In some situations, movement and conversation are inhibited by social norms even though an ambiguous feature has been introduced, as in a religious gathering, a classroom, or a theater. In such a setting, people may respond to a distracting stimulus merely by looking about to see how other people are reacting, and perhaps by whispering to the people nearest them. This may be called "incipient milling." An example is found in the following personal experience of one of the authors:

> One day in church, in the middle of the sermon, we heard a fire engine drive into the church parking lot, next to the sanctuary. There was an uncertain feeling—were we in danger? The obvious impulse to get out of the place was countered by the obviously inappropriate character of any such behavior in the sacred setting of the church. I found myself looking to left and to right to see whether other people looked frightened, to see whether anyone was doing anything about the situation. I looked at the minister to catch any gestures which might indicate his feelings. What I saw was a lot of other people also looking about, presumably in the same way I was!

Other situations permit a greater range of activity. There may be more room to move about and fewer normative restrictions on exploratory activity. When an unusual event occurs in such a setting, very active milling may begin. Milling of this sort may be seen in a crowd waiting eagerly, but impatiently, for a parade to start. People move about from one vantage point to another, trying to see what· has happened so far. More important, milling becomes primarily a verbal process. People ask each other questions about what they've seen and heard, and answer questions with bits of information, guesses and theories. In this communication they move about, talking first to one person, then to another. Little clusters of people may form and reform, to the accompaniment of much moving about as individuals join one cluster and then another. Excited talking in one "knot" of people or the movement of a few individuals to a new point of observation may cause a sudden, brief gravitation of a large portion of the crowd to the new point of interest. All the time, communication is going on as scraps of information, guesses, and predictions are passed from one person to another.

Milling may take place over a still larger area, particularly where automobiles and telephones are part of the culture. An automobile accident, a plane crash, or an explosion occurs in some part of a city. Typically, many people who hear the sound, see smoke rising, or hear the scream of sirens will rush toward the apparent location of the event to see what has happened. Their movement attracts the attention of others, who ask questions and often join in the movement. Other people pick up their telephones to call friends, the police, or newspaper offices, to ask questions or to repeat their own versions of what has happened. In what often seems an incredibly short time, interest may be aroused and reports spread far beyond the immediate vicinity of the unexpected incident. Such "convergence behavior" constitutes a form of milling.

What has been described here can be recognized as involving rumor. Indeed, rumor is a form of milling. The receiving and passing on of rumors is milling in its essentially communicative aspect—the building up of a collectively sanctioned version of what has happened in a situation which lacks cognitive clarity. Rumor is the mechanism of social contagion which has been most frequently subjected to empirical study, and much can be learned about the principles underlying social contagion from studies of rumor.

Specific consequences of milling. The general result of milling has been said to be the development of a new basis for social cohesion where a traditional basis does not exist. This emergent cohesion may be based upon several different changes in the relationships of the members of the collectivity. The production of these specific changes may be termed the specific consequences of milling. These consequences include the sensitization of individuals to each other, the development of a common mood, and the development of a common image.

Sensitization of individuals to each other. Human beings spend a great deal of time in each other's presence without being particularly aware of one another or significantly influenced by each other's actions. Each individual may be preoccupied with his own interests and activities, being only vaguely aware of people around him except when they intrude upon his activities. Such is often the situation on a crowded street, in a busy store, or in a classroom where students are taking an examination. People gathered under such circumstances constitute hardly more than an aggregate of psychologically separate individuals.

The stir of physical movement and the murmur of conversation which accompany the beginning of milling serve to draw attention to the people in the situation and to their actions. The emerging crowd is itself an important stimulus arousing curiosity and focusing attention upon the novelty and the ambiguity of the situation. The milling of a few distracts the attention of others from their own preoccupations and focuses it upon the collectivity and the object of its attention. They, too, may then enter into the milling process.

As milling continues, with an increase of verbal activity and physical movement, it becomes a more compelling stimulus. The individual finds it increasingly difficult to disregard the distracting activity about him. Numerous individuals become acutely aware of the exciting or intriguing aspects of the situation and of each other's reactions to them. Because of this spread of interest in a common object of attention, the term "social contagion" is appropriate.

The development of a common mood. Although emotions have important roots in the psychological make-up of the individual, how a person feels in a situation is also dependent upon the emotions he perceives in others in the same situation. A person who feels and manifests amusement when others around him remain solemn experiences the pressure of their disapproval and may no longer feel amused. An individual experiencing feelings of anxiety in an apparently threatening situation may be reassured and have his fears allayed by the confident attitude of people around him. What are essentially the same phenomena can be perceived in quite different ways. An important part of the perception of an incident is the reactions of other people. How, in the milling process, a collective definition of the appropriate reaction to a novel situation arises is illustrated in the following accounts of the reactions of two college classes to a strong earth tremor which shook central Oklahoma in 1952. The two students giving the accounts were in different classes but were on the same floor in the same building.

A fear reaction emerged in the first classroom, culminating in the flight of the class from the building:

> One of the girls said loudly, "What's happening?" Immediately the room began buzzing. Everyone started talking about it. It seemed as though the room was still shaking. We heard a commotion in the halls so we all jumped up and looked out the window. People were filing out like flies, so we immediately began to talk about leaving. The poor teacher said that if it would make us feel any better we could leave. We left!

The second class, in almost the same physical setting, was exposed to the same threatening stimulus. After a brief period of milling, however, they defined the situation in a different way:

> The class went to the window and looked out. We couldn't see anything. The professor went out in the hall to see the reaction of others. The class members started joking about it and saying that the quotation the professor had just read probably caused the earth to tremble! Nobody seemed terribly interested and the class continued after a very few minutes.*

It is such mutual reinforcement of a feeling which has been called "circular reaction." It must be noted, however, that reinforcement is not all that occurs in the milling process. More than just an intensification of a feeling already experienced by everyone takes place. The circumstances which give rise to collective behavior are conducive to an initial variability of response between different

* * Case material from the files of Lewis M. Killian.

individuals and to an ambivalence in the subjective reactions of the single individual. Modification as well as reinforcement goes on as individual ambivalences are resolved and interindividual variations are reduced.

It must also be kept in mind that individual differences in response may persist in spite of social contagion. Some people "are not amused," though the crowd may roar with laughter; some go steadfastly about their business while the crowd runs after the fire engines. This immunity to social contagion may be related to rigidity of attitudes and intensity of motivation in those individuals who do not succumb. Rarely does the process of social contagion reach such intensity as to sweep all before it, but it is often powerful enough to influence many individuals in spite of their different backgrounds and preoccupations.

The development of a common image. An essential feature of the type of situation which is conducive to the development of collective behavior is a lack of cognitive clarity. There may be a lack of clarity as to what has happened. At other times, part of the cognitive picture is clear, but other parts are not, as when a crime has been committed but the identity of the criminal is unknown. Or, what has happened may be fairly evident but its significance for the individuals to whom it is important may not be apparent—this new element in their life-space cannot be immediately assimilated. This is illustrated in the reactions of a group of navy wives to the announcement of the attack on Pearl Harbor.

PEARL HARBOR DAY IN PANAMA

B. Caroline Horton

In Panama, on the morning of December 7th, my husband brought me the news that Pearl Harbor was bombed. My first reaction was one of disbelief. I didn't run for the radio; I didn't continue to cook breakfast which I had started before he brought the news. I didn't answer him; I didn't do anything except stare at him. I was dumbfounded. I must have been thinking that I heard wrong; that it wasn't possible. Perhaps I didn't want to face reality. I may have felt that the United States was too well prepared, too powerful and invincible: they wouldn't dare attack us. All these thoughts took place within a few seconds. My husband turned on the radio, and I heard it, but without details. It still hadn't "hit me." I started to rationalize. A bomb had been dropped accidentally, or maybe a few radicals, without their government's authority, had tried to take things into their own hands. I was confused.

Student Paper, Florida State University. Published by permission,

I heard the neighbors outside. They had gotten the news too. There were many voices, expressing bewilderment predominantly and, above all, the questions: What will happen? Any more news? Will they come here? What should we do? Although it was Sunday, the men started to go off to their offices and stations. They reacted more rationally than did the women. (Possibly it was because in their training provision was made for comparable situations.) Shortly after the men started to leave, word came over the radio for every man to report immediately to his station. When word came for them to report, the news took on its first serious aspect in my mind. The woman who lived in the house next door to me came out with her husband as he was leaving. She was crying and entreating him not to leave her. Naturally this caught our attention. Her husband ran down the steps and, as he passed, asked us to please take care of her. This momentary diversion was welcome, I realize now. It gave me something concrete to do. We tried to console her. At the moment I thought her childish. We were all in the same boat; we had to expect our husbands to answer the call and report in. (I still hadn't faced the reality of the bombing itself.) But as we were trying to comfort her and tell her he'd be right back, I realized there was more to it. She began to sob hysterically and, between sobs, to moan that we didn't know what we were talking about, or what it was all about. She relived her memories of France during the First World War—the bombs, the terror, the starvation, the loss of her family, everything. It was then that I saw the enormity of the news we had heard and started to feel genuine fear and, for the first time, felt the reality of possible war.

This realization must have come to the other women, too, for we kept searching each other's faces, trying to read the answer. We were trying to see what it meant to each other. What does *she* think? How should we act? What should I say? The children reacted, too. Previously they had been just questioning, but now they drew closer to their mothers and some of them started to cry. I doubt if they knew why they were crying. One of the children asked, "Will Daddy be killed?" A child had voiced what was probably unconsciously in each one's mind. He brought home to each of us the fear of death, of the death of our loved ones.

One woman had transferred her fear and the reality of what had been a distant disaster to everyone around her. A child had voiced the fear that each of us must have felt but had suppressed.

An important consequence of milling is the building up of a collective definition of the situation, of an image in which the elements of ambiguity are minimized. Foote and Hart provide an apt description of the exploratory activities of people in what we have called "milling":

> Much of their behavior under these circumstances, if it can be called intentional at all, is simply concerned with finding out what they face or what they might want. Identification of the problems proceeds by playful poking and testing, fantasy, aimless exploration, restless groping and trial definitions put forward without conviction to see if others will confirm their accuracy. Representation and misrepresentation utilize both formal analogies and verbal categories. The very lack of definition of the situation contributes to the suggestibility and imitative response which characterizes collective as against group behavior. But these trial images and unreflective impulses form the substance out of which a definition gets compounded.*

In addition to describing the essentially communicative nature of milling, this statement also designates clearly the fundamental source of suggestibility and social contagion in situations of collective behavior. In a situation which is unclear and confusing to him, the individual is responsive to cues or suggestions which promise to contribute to a sharper definition. In a collectivity other people and their groping, exploratory activities are an important source of such suggestions.

An important source of immunity to social contagion is also indicated here. To the extent that a situation is subjectively well-defined for an individual, he is not responsive to the tentative definitions advanced by other, confused persons unless they confirm his own perceptual hypotheses. Hence, even in the milling

* Reprinted in part by permission of Harper & Brothers and the authors, from Nelson N. Foote and Clyde W. Hart, "Public Opinion and Collective Behavior," in **Group Relations at the Crossroads,** eds. Muzafer Sherif and M. O. Wilson (New York: Harper & Brothers, 1953), p. 317.

process, some people may be unresponsive to the suggestions advanced by others, remaining a minority who do not accept the collective definition which emerges.

Emergent vs. precipitous crowds. Milling has been analyzed as a gradual process through which crowd action develops. It is likely to be such a slow, gradual process when certain conditions prevail, namely: (1) there is a minimum of pre-existing group feelings and channels of communication in the collectivity; (2) a strong sense of urgency is not initially present; and (3) the course of action developing in the crowd depends upon a division of labor and coordination between the actions of the crowd members. A crowd which develops through a relatively long period of milling may be called an *emergent crowd*. Sometimes, however, milling is very brief and the development of a uniform mood and imagery almost instantaneous. This is often true in cases of panic or of sudden mob action. Conditions conducive to the development of the *precipitous crowd* are: (1) there exists a high degree of presensitization and established channels of communication in the collectivity; (2) the implications of the incident seem obvious and are perceived as demanding immediate action; and (3) the course of action that seems appropriate is simple and requires little coordination. For instance, the cry, "Fire!" in a crowded theater carries clear-cut implications as to the nature of the situation and as to the type of action which seems both urgent and appropriate.

RUMOR AS A FORM OF MILLING

Milling, it has been said, is essentially a communication process. Rumor is milling in its primarily verbal aspect. From some of the many studies of rumor much can be learned about the important features of milling, as exemplified in the rumor process. These studies show particularly well the development of uniform imagery as a consequence of milling.

Rumor is the type of interaction which goes on in an ephemeral, emergent group—the people engaged in the rumor process. This group has a rudimentary structure and some norms. Since the rumor group is defined by nothing but a common concern for the subject of the rumors, however, the norms and structure are tentative and are validated in the rumor process itself. Hence, in contrast to the norms and structure of more permanent, stable groups, they shift and are reformed quickly and easily until interest in the subject subsides or some standardized, collectively sanctioned imagery has developed.

The reading "Corpus Delicti" shows in detail the process through which a crowd arrives at such a collectively sanctioned version of an event. While a generally accepted definition of what had happened developed quickly, the complexity of the rumor process and the essentially tentative character of rumors are evident in the early stages of milling. Initially a variety of tentative explanations was advanced. Some suggestions were accepted and others were rejected. Gradually the version that was finally accepted by the crowd became dominant, taking on a normative character. As this version received more general acceptance, group pressure began to be applied to individuals who advanced incompatible definitions.

Also evident in this case are the heterogeneity of the crowd and the emergence of a structure. A prestige structure developed, based not upon ordinary criteria of status, but upon the relationship of different elements of the crowd to the object of interest in this particular situation.

CORPUS DELICTI

EILEEN J. IRVIN

Shortly before 9:45 a.m. one morning a woman left the room she shared with her husband in a small hotel in a suburb of Los Angeles and went downstairs. She approached their car, which was parked in a parking lot on the property of a small venetian blind factory next door to the hotel. When she opened the door, she discovered the dead body of a man wedged tightly on the floor of the back seat. The woman, suffering from heart trouble, collapsed and was taken to her room.

Her husband told police that he had been working the previous night until two o'clock and had left the car, unlocked, in a parking lot outside a local theater. He admitted that the body might have been in the back seat when he drove home, since he had not looked in the back of the car. He denied knowing the man.

The man was a stranger. Police found on the body only a social security card, a Salvation Army meal ticket, and a crude burglar's tool. He had less than one dollar in change in his pockets.

After questioning the residents of the Salvation Army hotel in Los Angeles, where the victim had been staying, the police announced that a friend of the victim had identified the owner of the car as the man with whom he and the victim had gone on a drinking spree the night before. Police arrested both men on suspicion of murder.

The car owner then changed his story. He claimed his memories of the night before had been unclear until his identification by the other man, but he was now able to reconstruct some of the events. He admitted having met the two men the previous evening and visiting several bars with them, and with an unidentified fourth man. He said that he remembered some-

Student paper, University of California at Los Angeles. Published by permission.

one (presumably the "fourth man," since the other man left the party early) putting a "drunken buddy" in the back seat of the car. He claimed that the person then left to get some cigarettes and never returned. He forgot about the "drunk," and drove home, he said. His story aroused considerable skepticism. Both men were released the following day, however, when an autopsy revealed the cause of death to be acute alcoholism.

I was fortunate enough to be present shortly after the body was discovered. It was not yet ten o'clock when my mother phoned to tell me that a body had been discovered in the parking lot across the street from the store where she is employed.

Residents and employees of a factory, stores, and apartments facing the parking lot made up the initial crowd. Most of them were gathered in the parking lot when I arrived. Some of the residents of a hotel were standing on the steps, which afforded a clear view of the parking lot, or leaning from the windows.

The most striking thing about the crowd, from the very beginning, was the profusion of rumor. It is most interesting to note that, in the three days that the affair was a matter of public concern, I heard not one rumor which was not present in some form in the first hour after the discovery of the body. Even with the new information, no new rumors arose. I heard none about the unidentified "fourth man," probably because no one believed he existed.

It was less than twenty minutes since the discovery of the body and already rumors, misconceptions and speculations had arisen. It was, indeed, a rumor which had sent me to the scene. My mother relayed to me the information which she had received from some of the employees of the store who had crossed the street to the parking lot to see what the excitement was. Seeing that the car was parked in the factory parking lot, and hearing only fragments of the story, they assumed that the car belonged to the owner of the factory. They said that he had left it in the lot all night and that his wife had discovered the body after they arrived at the factory that morning. When I talked to them on my arrival they were still under this impression. It was corrected shortly, however, when the real story began to circulate more widely.

About this time, the other residents of the apartments and hotels in the neighborhood began to arrive. These were the people whose apartments were situated on the wrong side of the building, so that they were unable to see the lot. They had either heard the excitement or been told the story by their neighbors.

Up to this point I had not noticed much milling. The people were excited and curious, but they tended to stay in little groups of factory employees, store employees, or hotel residents. With the arrival of the other residents and some passers-by who had been attracted by the crowd, milling began, however. Movement had been restricted largely to getting up close to the car, taking a quick and cautious look at the corpse, and retreating hurriedly to one's own group to remark how horrible it all was. (Most people, of course, had no idea of how horrible the body actually looked, since only those with strong stomachs examined the body. They did what I confess to doing—took a quick look and ran, but not so far that they were out of range of the excitement.) Now, however, the newcomers, of whom I was one, began to move about from group to group. I will assume that my own explanation serves for the others, also. Those who had not been on the scene originally circulated from group to group trying to get the full account of what had happened. This movement on the part of the newcomers facilitated more general movement, and the milling process started, slowly at first, then becoming more intense.

I began to circulate among the factory employees. They had been the first on the scene, since they had answered the woman's screams for help when she discovered the body. From these people came the most factual account, and the most authoritative statements about the case— whether these statements were factual or not. They enjoyed considerable prestige in the crowd as a result of being first. In fact, before it was over, they were recognized authorities on the "murder." The rumors beginning here had considerable circulation.

Considered only slightly less important were the residents of the hotel where the couple resided. They could supply important background material on the personalities involved. Most of them seemed quite sure that the owner of the car was the murderer. It seemed that they could all remember "something queer" about him in the light of the murder. This view was shared by most of the members of the crowd. With only two exceptions, they were convinced that it was a murder, and the majority felt that the owner of the car was involved. Everyone, of course, had a solution to the murder even before the police arrived.

It is valuable here to note the types of rumors which arose. One timid voice was raised suggesting suicide, but this was scornfully overruled for the logical reason that the body had obviously been jammed into the back seat by another person, as well as because of the fact that it was contrary to the symbol of a murder which the crowd had built up.

The rest of the crowd was divided as to whether it was an accident or the result of a drunken brawl which someone had attempted to cover up by hiding the body in the car, or whether it was actually "foul play." Since those who had examined the body declared that the cuts on the face could not have been sufficient to cause death (how they knew, I cannot imagine, but it was accepted) those who believed it to be murder gave creative imagination free rein in determining the cause of death. There were probably as many causes as there were people!

Among those who believed the owner of the car to be the guilty party, reasoning was pretty much the same. They asserted that he killed the man, accidentally or otherwise, and hid the body in the car. Opinion was divided again as to the purpose of this. Some argued that he intended to find the body and act surprised, while others maintained that he intended to get rid of the body, but his wife discovered it before he could.

No rumors arose about the wife's participation in the crime. Those few suggestions which arose (usually offered by those who had not seen the woman) were vehemently rejected by the two groups with the highest prestige in the crowd—the factory employees and the hotel residents. They felt that her shock on finding the body had been too real for her to have known of its existence. Some of the hotel residents even suggested that she had collapsed not so much from the shock of finding the body, but of realizing that her husband was the murderer. There seemed to be general sympathy for the wife. She was never under police suspicion, either.

The crowd was steadily growing now. The people had spread from the parking lot to the sidewalks and the curb. They were now visible to those whose view was blocked by the front of the building, and more people stopped to inquire as to the cause of the excitement. With each repetition of the story, the excitement was heightened.

Even though the police station was a scant two blocks away, the police had not yet arrived. It was sarcastically suggested that they needed time to read up on investigating murders. This is a small town and, outside of a few robberies and waterfront brawls, the police do not have much opportunity to display their skill as investigators. A murder was an exciting event, and when the police did arrive they were as excited as the crowd.

Several cars pulled up, sirens screaming, and police piled out, all exhibiting a fine and hitherto unexpected sense of drama. They moved to the car and to the door of the hotel, clearing a path and shouting, "Get back there! Don't touch anything!" Since everyone was making way with alacrity and no one had shown any inclination to touch the car, this was rather useless, but we all decided it was part of the ritual.

By this time the crowd was really excited. This was the highest pitch of excitement and the highest phase of crowd development that the crowd attained.

Several policemen stayed outside to guard the car, while several others went inside to question the owner. Some of his story had already circulated through the crowd—spread by the hotel residents—and this was repeated for the benefit of the curious newcomers.

With the removal of the body, the first really serious opposition to the crowd image of murder was voiced. This proved later to be the correct solution! A man helping the police to move the body looked at it carefully, and then remarked scornfully and loudly, "Oh, hell! This is no murder. The guy's a lush!"

This was considered briefly, but the crowd rejected it. I rejected it myself. It was much more exciting the other way.

After the body was removed the crowd began to break up. People stayed for a while repeating the story and speculating, but the main impetus was gone. Little by little, people broke up into groups. Some went back to their work—reluctantly. Others drifted away to discuss the event over coffee or a beer. Only a few lingered on the scene, hoping for more excitement.

The most comprehensive analysis of rumor is that of Allport and Postman.* Much of their analysis of what happens to the content of a rumor is based on experiments in which a single story is passed from one subject to another in a

* Gordon W. Allport and Leo Postman, **The Psychology of Rumor** (New York: Henry Holt and Co., 1947).

chain of communication, undergoing distortion as it progresses. In these laboratory experiments the factor of "importance" was not present, participation in the experiment being the only motive the subjects had for transmitting the story of "rumor." But these writers' own formula for rumor expresses the notion that in real situations a subject must have a deeper importance than this to become the topic of rumors; moreover, this concern must be shared by all the people who enter into the rumor process. Hence rumor is a form of group interaction, but in their experimental design Allport and Postman do not treat it as such. The contrast between this sort of experiment and the situation described in "Corpus Delicti" is evident. In the latter situation rumor may be seen in its sociological aspect: as the effort of a loosely bound collectivity to arrive at a collectively sanctioned conception of a situation, a conception which will support either a particular course of action or a certain mood. The origin of the rumor in the collectively-shared concern is an essential part of the rumor process and cannot be disregarded. There is not just a single, original version which undergoes progressive distortion. Instead there are, initially, alternate conceptions of the situation which compete until one emerges as the collectively-sanctioned version and the others become unacceptable.

Gist and Peterson, in the following selection, analyze critically the formulation of the rumor process offered by Allport and Postman. They contrast the course of rumor as observed in the experimental model and in a real-life, complex, highly-motivated situation. In their case the existence of a variety of conceptions of the situation may be seen. While it is not shown in their study, it should be pointed out that some of the versions which pass as rumors may be true, but unverified. The fact that a story is true does not exclude it from the category of "rumor," nor does it guarantee that it will be accepted by the group in preference to other rumors which are not only unverified but also untrue.

RUMOR AND PUBLIC OPINION

WARREN A. PETERSON AND NOEL P. GIST

"Rumor," in general usage, refers to an unverified account or explanation of events, circulating from person to person and pertaining to an object, event, or issue of public concern. The objective analysis of rumor is contingent upon the systematic treatment of various public opinion processes.

Our present concern is with rumors which appear to arise spontaneously after

Reprinted in part by permission of the University of Chicago Press and the authors, from Warren A. Peterson and Noel P. Gist, "Rumor and Public Opinion," **American Journal of Sociology,** 57 (Sept., 1951), pp. 159–167.

a public has been formed through common interest in an issue or event. Rumors of this type can be considered the product of collective efforts to interpret a problematic situation, when the public views the situation affectively and when authoritative information is lacking.

"Public opinion," in contrast to more static concepts like "culture," designates temporary and fluctuating attitudes and beliefs resulting from collective efforts to interpret constantly emerging new situations. A group of people develops an interest in an event or issue, reciprocally communicates attitudes and beliefs pertaining to it, and interprets these in terms of the existing cultural context and their specialized frames of reference. This occurs within a social organization and is dependent upon the leadership, group affiliations, and channels of communication within the society.

Rumor "opinion" differs significantly from other forms of public opinion, in that it is not verified through customary channels. The common-sense assumption that rumor is abnormal or pathological reflects the fact that the persons involved are normally expected or accustomed to rely upon authority or a different kind of authority. A social setting conducive to rumor occurs when a public is interested and concerned about a past or anticipated event, when authoritative information and explanation are lacking, and when social controls relevant to the situation are external to most members of the public.

Under these conditions there is greater recourse to informal discussion, in the course of which the interest of individuals tends to be intensified. The public may be extended to include persons who originally were neither interested in, nor informed about, the situation. In the early stages of the process, members of a rumor public vary greatly in attitudes toward the object, issue, or event, according to the intensity and the kind of interest, concern, or anxiety. The communication of rumor tends to reduce the divergence in attitudes and to produce a common definition of the situation and a common feeling or mood. Rumor is one means by which a collectivity, albeit a temporary and unstable collectivity, emerges from an aggregate.

The work of Allport and Postman represents one of the most comprehensive attempts to examine rumor objectively. Taking methodological cues from psychological experiments on memory and recall, these investigators designed a series of carefully controlled experiments, using chains of six or seven selected subjects. A visual stimulus, in the form of a picture of a suggestive social scene, was presented to the first subject, who passed on his impressions of it to the second, who subsequently passed on his impressions of the first subject's report to the third, and so on. Conclusions about the nature of rumor were derived by comparing the "terminal report" with the initial stimulus.

Allport and Postman summarize their conclusions under the concepts *leveling, sharpening,* and *assimilation.* "Leveling" refers to the tendency of a rumor, as it travels, to "grow shorter, more concise, more easily grasped and told. In successive versions fewer words are used and fewer details are mentioned." "Sharpening" is defined as "the selective perception, retention, and reporting of a limited number of details from a larger context." And "assimilation" "has to do with the powerful attractive force exerted upon rumor by the intellectual and emotional context existing in the listener's mind."

These concepts are not offered as suggestive hypotheses but as concrete and explicit generalizations. For instance, Allport and Postman state: "What is seen or heard *must* (sic) be simplified in accordance with the economizing process of memory." "It is often assumed that rumors become embroidered in the talking or that they become enlarged like a rolling snowball. This is a misconception." "Stereotyping is a result of undue simplification in the interest of economizing mental effort."

The Allport-Postman approach is different from that which deals with rumor as a form of public opinion as a complex collective process. They assume that the social context in which rumors occur can be reduced to a single chain of subjects; that, by implication, the wide circulation of rumor is nothing more than the adding-together of such chains; and that rumor can be explained, at least in part, by reference to uniform and pervasive psychological mechanisms like "the economizing process of memory."

Moreover, and perhaps more important, Allport and Postman proceed on the assumption that rumor basically results from distortion in perception and in *unilateral* verbal communication. Thus in the course of their experiments they completely rule out changes in meaning and in motivation which occur in the give and take of informal discussion. They also overlook the possibility that the same individual, transmitting rumor to a succession of persons, may communicate a different version in each instance, not just because of faulty memory, but because of differences in his relationship with them.

It is superficially evident that persons who develop and transmit rumors are not passively reacting to a stimulus, as Allport and Postman imply, but are acting in a situation that is problematic and affectively evocative to them. Public expectations, fears, anxieties, hostilities, and aspirations are often clearly manifest in rumors. Their development and transmission involve interpretation, discussion, speculation, and creative imagination.

Similarly, simple observation discloses that communication is a complicated time-space network, relating persons who are receiving, discussing, interpreting, forgetting and transmitting attitudes and beliefs in a variety of social situations. The rapidity and complex nature of the process make rumor a difficult subject for objective examination. It is very unlikely that the methodological problems can be solved by applying the orthodox procedures of simplification and control employed in experimental psychology.

Since Allport and Postman summarize their conclusions rather precisely under the concepts of leveling, sharpening, and assimilation, it becomes possible specifically to test these concepts, to determine whether conclusions derived from their approach are meaningful and explanatory when applied to empirical cases—to "natural" rather than to experimental situations. A set of rumors investigated by the writers is presented here as an empirical test of the Allport-Postman approach and as a general case study of rumor.

Rumors were circulated in a small midwestern city during a period of public concern about an unsolved crime—the rape and murder of a fifteen-year-old girl. The rumors, or set of rumors, had many variations, but a common theme: that the householder who had employed the victim as a baby sitter for the evening had returned home without his wife and murdered the girl. Although there was no authoritative verification at the time or subsequently, the rumors circulated throughout the community, resulting in considerable excitement. Two weeks intervened between the occurrence of the crime and the circulation of these rumors. During the first two days, press and radio devoted themselves to reporting all possible details of the murder and to reviewing similar incidents in the preceding few years in the same residential neighborhood.

Later, a number of events served to stimulate interest in the case and speculation about the identity of the murderer. The police appealed, through press and radio, for any type of information that might be relevant. Citizens were requested to report to the police any male who had scratches or cuts on his face or hands. A campaign was conducted to raise a reward for information leading to the apprehension of the murderer. The National Guard was called out to screen the area for possible clues. In a neighborhood near the place of the murder the police chased and exchanged shots with a prowler, but failed to apprehend him. Police cars constantly patrolled all streets in the vicinity.

Various activities expressed the special concern of particular groups and, being noted by others, served to intensify general public interest. Large numbers of residents drove past the scene of the crime. Others devoted themselves to gathering information about the family of the girl and the family which had employed her as a baby sitter. Measures were taken to safeguard homes against intruders. Girls and young women were warned against being alone after dark. The rape-murder case became a common topic of conversation wherever persons gathered and associated.

Almost immediately after the crime, rumors began to circulate about the identity of the murderer. These rumors (or speculations) were widely varied, scattered, and of short duration. It was suggested or speculated that the murderer was a Negro; a high-school student; a cab driver, and a feebleminded boy.

There were also rumors about the inefficiency and corruptness of the police. The issue of police competence persisted as a general topic of public discussion during and after the period when the baby sitter's employer was rumored to be the murderer. The latter, whom we shall refer to as "Mr. X," was alleged to have left a party which he and his wife were attending, returned to their home, entered the house, raped and murdered the girl, and subsequently returned to the party after changing his clothes. In general, this was the common element in the rumors which circulated for three or four days.

The numerous variations which developed from this central theme indicate interpretation, speculation, and creative imagination on the part of members of the public in the direction of co-ordinating the story with previous conceptions of the murder, of attributing stereotyped sex-criminal characteristics to Mr. X, of constructing a basis for sympathizing with his wife, of supplying authentic verification, and of generally molding a sensational account.

The writers, both residents of the community, observed as carefully as possible the communication of this particular set of rumors and assembled all possible information on the preceding events. About one hundred university students, residing in various parts of the community, were asked to set down in writing any rumor or any information heard during the previous week concerning the rape-murder case. The assortment of rumors collected by this procedure presents a configuration having a basic theme but a wide variety of detailed interpretations, some of which are contradictory in ideational content.

MR. X'S ABSENCE FROM THE PARTY

"Mr. X left the party for two hours, from 9:30 to 11:30."

"When Mr. X returned to the party he had completely changed clothes, had scratches on his face."

"It is said that X left the party for about two hours. He said he was going out for more liquor . . ."

THE DETECTION AND ARREST OF MR. X

"Mr. X was picked up and questioned all day."

"Blood hounds followed the trail three times to where Mr. X was playing cards, but because of political reasons no arrests were made on this clue."

"Mr. X has confessed to the crime in Jackson City (30 miles distant)."

"I've heard that he is now being held for questioning and that the police are trying to beat it (confession) out of him."

"Mr. X is hiding out with his family in Utah."

EVIDENCE CONCERNING THE ATTACK

"He . . . entered the front door; that's why the porch light was on, because Miss B had recognized him and let him enter. He put the sawhorse by the window and broke the window to make it look as if the murderer had entered that way."

"When he and his wife arrived home that evening, he would not let his wife go into the house but insisted on going in himself and then came out and told what he had seen."

"When his little boy was asked if he had been scared that night, he had said, 'No, my daddy was here.' "

"The police have found the blood-soaked clothes he wore when he killed her."

"He undressed in the bathroom, so his wife could not see the scratches on his body."

EVIDENCE SUPPLIED BY INDIVIDUALS

"Mr. X, who hired the babysitter, was turned in by his wife because he left the party one and one-half hours at the time the murder was committed."

"Mrs. X furnished the lead which led to his arrest; she has declared her intention 'never to live with him again' as a result of previous marital disagreement."

"Mrs. X spied on him while he was undressing in the bathroom and observed scratches upon his body. This she reported to the police."

"His mother turned him in to the police, saying that he was an habitual sexual pervert, and that he had 'finally gone too far.' "

REACTIONS OF MRS. X

"His wife is covering up for him, but has gone to California to have her second child."

"Mr. X had his wife leave town until it all blows over."

"Mrs. X has gone insane."

"Mrs. X is in California, where she had a baby which was born dead, due to the effects of this case on her physiological well-being."

IMAGES OF MR. X

"I have heard that he was a known sex pervert from youth."

"He is an exceptionally intelligent man, a C.P.A. and talented in music."

"Mr. X had at one time been in an insane asylum."

"There is a connection between him and the Ferguson murder a few years ago."

It is probable that the central theme—that Mr. X had raped and murdered the girl during his absence from a party—developed in the course of speculations about the identity of the attacker. Since this theme appeared first, it is almost certain that the rumor did not emerge in full form. Among the elaborations, versions which tended to co-ordinate the story with previous conceptions of the murder seem to have followed the central theme almost immediately.

It was not, however, a simple case of one wave of elaboration spreading throughout the community, to be followed by another wave. Many persons did not hear the original version until it had been elaborated considerably. There is no reason to believe that each specialized version originated independently and ran its course in isolation from the others. There must have been additions to the rumor as it was passed from person to person, discussed in a variety of social situations, and interpreted by individuals with special interests or preconceptions.

Whether this rumor "snowballed" in the process of transmission depends upon the perspective used in interpretation. "Snowballing" suggests increasing enlargement and implies that details are retained as new ideas are superimposed.

Viewing the entire phenomenon as a *Gestalt* of interrelated rumors, probably derived from a common origin and differentiated into a profusion of details, the phenomenon does appear to have grown like a snowball. Certainly, there was an accumulation of details; whether any were completely lost in the course of transmission and elaboration is not known.

If one views each of the particular rumors as having an independent origin and a separate "career," then the case for leveling as opposed to snowballing can be supported very effectively, largely because it is logically impossible for an independent, particularistic rumor to snowball. In our opinion, such a frame of reference limits the possibility of securing information that would shed light on the nature of rumor—if rumor is fundamentally an aspect of public opinion and if communication in a public follows multilateral associational channels.

Apparently, something similar to what Allport and Postman call "assimilation" does occur. The stereotyping of Mr. X as the type of man who would commit such a crime; the portrayal of Mrs. X as reacting as a woman faced with such a situation might be expected to react; the alleged behavior of the police in apprehending and questioning Mr. X—all might be considered expressions of cultural preconceptions assimilated into the central theme, making the entire configuration more impressive and sensational but not necessarily more "coherent, plausible, and well-rounded."

The setting in which the rumors used in this report occurred was very different from an artificially constructed experimental situation. The rape and murder were real, not fictitious, events. The public was composed of girls and women concerned about their personal safety; of sympathetic friends, relatives, and neighbors; of young men who had searched for clues with the National Guard; and of a great mass of persons who took a vicarious interest in the whole range of activities. Where a public is composed of people with a variety of interests any even or situation is likely to be diversely defined and interpreted.

There is no evidence in the present study of a general "economizing process of memory." It seems more likely that persons with very little interest forget details, while those who are keenly interested remember details, at least details which they consider crucial. If persons are intensely interested and emotionally aroused, they recall certain items with clarity and accuracy; they may even take items from other experiences and, with varying degrees of accuracy, apply them to the one at hand. There was, for instance, a tendency among some persons to incorporate into the rumor information taken from the original press and radio version of the murder.

A portion of the distortion may be explained by the fact that a person, in the role of transmitter, is likely to have more personal interest in a rumor than he had in the role of perceiver. Inside information bearing on an issue of public concern places a person temporarily in a position of prestige; and the prestige-position of the transmitter is more secure if the story can be made to sound authentic.

The transmitter is sufficiently motivated to forget details that make the story dubious, to emphasize details that make it plausible and to introduce new corroborating details.

The major limitation in the experimental study of rumor and of other forms of collective behavior lies in the failure to produce, or even to simulate, affectively toned motivational states comparable to those which occur in real life. The essential characteristics of rumor are such as to require, at this stage at least, careful on-the-spot observation, preferably by a team of investigators. Although the ideational content of rumor is the easiest information to obtain and is superficially the most objective, it is not necessarily the most sociologically relevant. In the systematic investigation of rumor, attention should be given to such problems as the composition of the public, the establishment of cultural beliefs and attitudes through rumor communication, role behavior in groups where rumor is discussed, and personality characteristics of persons who specialize in rumor transmission.

This study illustrates, in addition to the initial divergence of imagery, the later convergence of different versions as they are assimilated to one theme which receives collective sanction. This is not mere distortion; it is the building up of a solution to a collective cognitive problem. Of the three processes which Allport and Postman postulate as being important in rumor transmission—levelling, sharpening, and assimilation—assimilation appears to be the most important. It is the underlying principle which determines what details are levelled and which are sharpened. In addition, assimilation to a dominant theme governs another process which Allport and Postman do not take into account. This is "completion" or "closure," the completion of the collectively-sanctioned version of filling in details, details which may be drawn from other versions or which may arise as new rumors after the process is well under way.

Festinger and his associates have conducted an important field study of rumor in which they show the assimilation of a variety of details to a central, dominant theme. It is apparent that the rumor served a very definite function for those who were most active in passing it. The reinterpretation of past events, now recalled and given a special meaning consistent with the theme of the rumor, illustrates well the operation of assimilation.

Another important aspect of the rumor process, and of milling, may be seen in this study. This is the transactional nature of the interaction which takes place.

Individuals do not merely hear a rumor and pass it on to another individual in a chain. The same people are involved over and over again in the building up of the dominant imagery. One person may hear, discuss, and shape not one but many versions. Thus the imagery which finally emerges as dominant is shaped by group interaction, not merely by a series of individual distortions.

A STUDY OF A RUMOR: ITS ORIGIN AND SPREAD

LEON FESTINGER et al.

The material presented here is a case study of the origin and spread of a rumor in a specific group—in this case a neighborhood community. In the course of conducting a research program on problems of social organization and social communication, the opportunity arose to observe the growth of a rumor.

The larger research program involved measuring the effects on the social life in a housing project of stimulating the organization of community activities. A community organizer worked with the residents of the housing project toward these ends. Resistances developed toward this process of organizing community activities from time to time and took different forms at various stages. Early in the process of community organization these resistances culminated in the creation of a rumor hostile to the continuing development of these activities.

The rumor being investigated arose in a low-rent housing project which had been built during the war for the accommodation of shipyard workers. After the war employment in the shipyards was drastically curtailed and the nature of the population of the project changed considerably. At the time of this study (the first half of 1947) more than one-third of the residents were war veterans who had moved in since the end of the war. Most of the other tenants had found new jobs so that at the time of the study only 8 per cent were still working in the shipyard. As a result of this reemployment

process, however, many of the families were unemployed for some time.

Attitudes of the tenants towards the project and toward each other were, at the beginning of the study, quite uncomplimentary. They felt ashamed of living in a low cost housing project and felt that outsiders looked down on project residents. Most of the tenants felt that the others were inferior and that they themselves were living in the project because of "unusual circumstances." A number of factors contributed to what appeared to be a high level of frustration among the project residents at the beginning of the research program. Because of their hostile attitudes towards their neighbors there was little social interaction within the project. Because of their feeling of shame about living in the project there was little interaction among project residents and outsiders. The result was that there was no social group to which they felt they really belonged. Aggravating this frustration was the employment situation where, due to the transition from war to peace, frequent job changes were taking place.

For a long time there had been sporadic efforts at organizing community activities in this project, but for the most part, these attempts had met with failure. The regulations of management required the local manager to appoint a tenants committee consisting of a group of men and women who would manage such community affairs as they wished to have. Such a tenant's committee had been appointed, but the committee had received little help from the manager largely because he had no real understanding of the

Reprinted in part by permission of the editors, **Human Relations**, and the authors, from Leon Festinger et al., "A Study of Rumor: Its Origin and Spread," **Human Relations**, 1 (1948), pp. 464–486.

functions and purposes of community activities.

With the passage of time the membership of the tenants' committee dwindled to a few women who took all the responsibility for such activities as were planned. These women maintained that they resented "doing all the work," and in turn, there was some feeling among the residents of the project of resentment against the tenants' committee because they always "ran things." At the same time, people were afraid to get involved in activities of the tenants' committee because they did not want to be subjected to the criticism and jealousies which surrounded it.

About six weeks before the research program began, a regional representative of management came in and helped the tenants' committee organize a Christmas party for the children. He succeeded in stimulating enough interest in the possibility of other activities so that the tenants' committee decided to call a meeting of the project residents to discuss further possibilities. The invitation to this meeting was added as a postscript to a routine circular and only five women, including the three officers of the tenants' committee, appeared. It was at this meeting that the community worker associated with the research program made her first appearance at the project.

EVENTS LEADING UP TO THE RUMOR

In her first contacts with the project the reasons for the community worker's participation were left unexplained except for a statement that she was "interested in community activities." She offered to obtain the assistance of consultants who would come to this meeting to discuss the plans for the community activities in which the tenants were interested.

1. *The General Meeting.*

The following two weeks were devoted to laying the groundwork for this meeting. Committees were set up to represent the different areas of interest which the women had indicated: nursery school, school-age recreation, and adult education

and recreation. These committees met separately to discuss the problems which they wished to present to the experts at the meeting, and then met again together to discuss their findings.

The night of the meeting forty women and three men came to the community hall. The meeting was organized in three parts: a panel discussion by experts whom the community worker had brought to the meeting, smaller discussion and planning groups focussing on the three types of community activities, and a movie ("The City"—a documentary about crowded city living conditions) which was included to attract people to the meeting.

2. *Progress Made Towards Community Activities.*

Within a week following the general meeting, there were meetings of the three committees. Major progress was made in the development of plans for the nursery school.

Approximately a month after the research program began, the basic committee work and planning had been completed. A widely supported program of community activities, it appeared, was about to be realized.

3. *The Rise of New Leaders.*

During this period of basic organizational work, a growing number of women became involved in the activities.

Since a much wider group of women was being included in the activity program, a shift in leadership was taking place. This change in leadership occurred because new women were becoming interested and assuming responsibilities and because the formation of various subcommittees made it impossible for all the work to be done by the same few people.

The chairman and secretary of the tenants' committee, however, continued to be active during this period of organization although neither was able to maintain her former dominant position. A number of factors combined to undermine the leadership of the chairman. She was not strongly supported by the community worker because it was felt that she would not encourage wide participation of tenants in activities.

The leadership of the secretary of the tenants' committee was also waning. She was displaced from having sole control of publicity. In other ways her own influence weakened as the influence of others grew. During this period, she saw her friend and neighbor, Mrs. C., rise to a new position of leadership in the nursery school activities and become increasingly influential.

4. The Emergence of Resistance.

During this period of preliminary work, resistances toward the action program began to make themselves known. These resistances showed themselves in three ways: first, a lasting pessimism with regard to the possibility of establishing a successful program of community activities; second, pronounced criticism of the general meeting; and third, opposition to specific features of the activities.

The chairman of the tenants' committee frequently voiced pessimism concerning the future of the activities based on her conception of the other tenants and her experience in the past. This pessimism was communicated to her associates and made them critical and defeatist.

Criticism of the general meeting also became a symptom of growing resistance. While the goal of the experts who had led the meeting had been to stimulate interest and initiative on the part of the tenants, many who attended complained that the experts had not taken enough initiative and did not seem to be of much help.

Another effect of the general meeting was to crystallize suspicion about "who all these experts were and why they were taking such an interest in the project." While it was clear to those attending the meeting that the experts were all from the same educational institution, they did not understand the reasons behind this concerted effort.

Most disruptive was the resistance shown by the secretary of the tenants' committee. Her resistance was strong enough to take the form of deliberate blocking of the activities.

5. The Groundwork for the Rumor.

At this point the people in the project were closer than they had ever been to a constructive program of community activities and at the same time overt resistance against these community activities was also at its peak. The increased number of people who were participating threatened the status position of the old leaders. If these activities were to proceed, new leaders would almost certainly become dominant. The successful progress of the various committees also contradicted the widespread conviction that such activities were impossible in this community. This unexpected progress focussed the attention of those who resisted on the outsiders whose motives for working with them they did not understand. In the absence of satisfactory information supplied by the outsiders, an explanation was found which appeared plausible to some and which justified the resistance which had arisen.

THE RUMOR

One morning late in February, 1947, when the community worker arrived at the project to attend a meeting of the school-age recreation committee, she happened to meet a member of the committee on the street. The community worker was told that this meeting and all other meetings were cancelled and that she could get more detailed information from the other women or from the local manager of the project. The woman seemed embarrassed and unwilling to talk about the reasons for this development. The community worker proceeded to talk with the local project manager to find out what had happened. The following reconstruction of events is based upon information obtained from the local project manager, from regional management, and from subsequent conversations with project tenants.

One of the three men who attended the general meeting was Mr. M., a resident of the project who was a leader of boys' activities in a local church. He was known to have close contact with a law enforcement agency and to be particularly interested in combatting communist influences.

Following the general meeting the secretary of the tenants' committee went to see Mr. M., and between them they arrived at certain conclusions which the secretary told to a number of the more active tenants as demonstrated facts. First, it was declared that Mrs. C., who had been very active in organizing the nursery school, was an "avowed communist." Secondly, it was asserted that three of the experts who spoke at the general meeting were also known to be communists.

The obvious conclusion to be reached was that the tenants should have nothing further to do with these community activities.

Armed with these "proven facts," the secretary of the tenants' committee spent considerable time talking with two other women about her discovery. Among them they decided to call a meeting of the more active leaders to decide what steps should be taken. The decision of the six women who attended this meeting was to state the case to the local project manager and to ask his advice as to what to do.

In the subsequent meeting of eight women with the local project manager (two women just happened to be in the manager's office at the time) there was some disagreement between those who wanted to drop the program altogether and those who favored a more moderate course. The secretary of the tenants' committee and a close friend of hers were most insistent on having the activities stopped immediately. The local project manager, when asked for his advice, stated that he was in a "bad position" because he himself did not fully understand who the community worker was nor why the research was being conducted. By the end of the meeting even the more moderate among the women agreed to drop the activities because the situation had become disagreeable.

The immediate effect of this series of events was the complete cessation of activities. It was almost two weeks before the community worker could do anything to dispel the rumor, since regional management, wanting to assist in counteracting the rumor, requested a delay in action. By the time the community worker resumed her activities, it had become greatly elaborated.

Once the basic premise of communism had been accepted, a cognitive reorganization took place bringing new meaning to many events which had not previously seemed at all significant. Small incidents at committee meetings, minor details of procedure at the general meeting, a chance remark in a conversation, a speaker's manner of address—all became integrated and added up to support the premise of communism. Some examples of this process may be cited.

The sudden interest that Mrs. C. (the avowed communist) had shown in nursery school activities, her repeated praise of the community worker, and the fact that the community worker had accepted an invitation to dinner at her home became the basis for the assertion that the community worker and Mrs. C. had been friends in the past.

The offer made by the community worker to provide temporarily a nursery school teacher gave rise to questions concerning the source of the money and the reason for the outsider's wanting her own teacher in the school. The communist answer seemed plausible.

The movie, shown at the general meeting, which contrasted crowded city living conditions with conditions in a planned rural community was later interpreted as being communist propaganda. This interpretation was strengthened by the belief that the music in the movie (written by Aaron Copland) "sounded Russian."

Several things happening at the general meeting were later thought to be examples of communist tactics. The suggestion made by one of the experts that the adult education group might discuss the topic of the atomic bomb and international affairs was said to have been proposed to provide an opportunity for communist propaganda.

ANALYSIS OF THE RUMOR

The functions of the rumor become clear if one relates the content and effects of the rumor to the situation from which it sprang. These functions may be analyzed in terms of the rumor's relation to areas of cognitive unclarity, personal motivations, and problems of interpersonal relations.

As indicated in discussing the events leading up to the rumor, there were many areas of cognitive unclarity for the project residents concerning the new efforts to organize community activities. The statement made by the community worker that she was employed by a research organization and was interested in community activities left many questions unanswered. The premise of communist sponsorship tied previously incomprehensible facts together into a coherent explanation. They now "understood" what was happening and why it was taking place. With communist sponsorship as an accepted reference point they proceeded to substantiate it further, as reinterpreting even events which had not been puzzling.

In describing the situation leading up to the rumor it was pointed out that the old leaders were beginning to feel their leadership position threatened. New leaders were emerging and assuming importance in the direction of new activities. The effect of the rumor was to put an end to these activities, to dissolve the new committees, and thus to preserve the old leadership structure. The communist content of the rumor served to prevent those favorable to the activities from openly supporting them out of fear that they, themselves, might become suspect.

The transmission of a rumor may be analyzed in terms of the forces acting upon people within a social structure to tell the rumor. Once having heard the rumor, a force field is set up, with the forces to relay the rumor having various magnitudes in different directions. People who were seen as working for community activities and people who were seen in the role of possible gainers from community activities were the ones who heard the rumor. A variety of factors can affect the magnitude of the restraining force against telling the rumor. The data in this study have shown that the intimacy of the relationship between two people is one of these forces. The more intimate the relationship, the less the restraining force. Thus, more of those with close friends than with only acquaintances heard the rumor. Some of the other factors which would undoubtedly affect the strength of the restraining force against communication are the ease of getting in touch with a person, the receptivity of the other person, and the like.

There remains the question of why a person tells the rumor at all. Although the answer to this question in the case of the present rumor can only be inferred from indirect evidence, several reasons for telling the rumor may be identified. The reasons which led the active instigator to conceive the rumor also led her to tell it, for only by means of its general acceptance could it become a social fact. For those who became immediately involved in the discussion of the rumor with the project manager, the tension resulting from "being in on" an exciting happening probably heightened the urge to talk about it to others. Some of these women undoubtedly also felt compelled to tell the rumor in order to account for the cessation of activity. These same factors may also have influenced further transmission of the rumor throughout the project, and one might expect them to be stronger among those people who were involved more highly in community activities. It will be recalled that those who were more highly involved in community activities were more likely to have told the rumor after hearing.

Perhaps a more basic formulation of one of the fundamental reasons for the communication of rumor is in terms of the forces arising from disparities of cognitive structure among people. If, upon hearing a rumor, a person's social behavior is to be modified by it, strong forces will be created to bring other people's cognitive structure in line with hi own. If this is not accomplished, his own behavior will not be understood or accepted by others, and joint social action will become difficult.

The extent of spread of rumor through a social structure will be governed by the factors which we have just discussed, namely, by the magnitude and direction of the driving and restraining forces. In addition, it will be governed by the structure of the group and the patterns of informal communication within the group, since duplication of communication channels and the existence of communication bottlenecks will greatly affect the extent of spread.

Types of rumor-inducing situations. Groups engaged in collective behavior may be oriented in one of two ways: externally, toward action on some object which is outside of the group; or internally, toward the production, enhancement, or validation of a subjective state which characterizes the group itself. There are corresponding types of rumors and rumor-inducing situations. The type of situation in which rumors arise accounts for the nature of the rumors and of the changes in them as much as do individual motives for rumor spreading and rumor distortion, such as guilt, hostility, or projection.

The article by Festinger shows one type of rumor-inducing situation and the type of rumors it gave rise to. Here members of the rumor group needed imagery of a sort that would support and justify a particular course of action, and the rumor which developed served this purpose. The rumors which always precede a race riot are of this type, validating a course of action which would ordinarily be inhibited by the norms of the society.

In other situations, no collective action may be possible but a commonly-shared experience may create a mood so intense that it requires validation. There may be an ambivalence of mood which can only be resolved by the development of some collectively-sanctioned imagery supporting one alternative or the other. In other cases, the mood may be stronger than the verifiable evidence seems to justify, so that the imagery developed in the rumor process validates the feeling that "things are worse (or better) than they seem." Rumors of this sort are current after a disaster. They usually include exaggerated reports of damage, rumors of disasters in other places, and forecasts of even worse catastrophes to come.

Part 2

THE CROWD

Chapter 5

The forms of crowd behavior

OF THE many forms of collective behavior, the *crowd* is the one of which most people are most aware. Crowd behavior is frequent in occurrence, often spectacular, and varies tremendously in its specific manifestations. The mob, murderous or destructive; the rioting crowd, whether angry or triumphant; crowds engaged in orgies of joy, grief, or religious fervor; audiences which "go wild"; groups in panic; clusters of gawking spectators—all these and many other types are manifestations of the crowd. The initial stages of the development of crowd behavior have been discussed in connection with social contagion. The elements common to all crowds and the features which distinguish subtypes of this form of collective behavior may now be examined.

Common characteristics of crowds. The conditions for the development of collective behavior indicate some of the features which characterize the crowd and the individuals who compose it. The situation is ambiguous or unstructured; the participants do not share pre-existing, traditional expectations as to how they should behave; the outcome is uncertain. Yet these conditions are not sufficient for the emergence of crowd behavior unless another factor is present—a sense of urgency, a feeling that something must be done *now*.

As crowd behavior develops, there is communication of mood, imagery, and a conception of what kind of action is appropriate. These are *emergent,* not traditional. While they are related to the past experiences and previously-held norms and attitudes of the participants, they constitute new products of the interaction in the particular situation.

The notion of "a conception of appropriate action" should not be understood to imply a specific plan of action. Although in some crowds a precise pattern of action may be quickly defined as appropriate, usually there exists only a sense that certain *kinds* of action are appropriate and that other kinds are not.

The mood, imagery, and conception of appropriate action are not only *com-*

municated in the cιowd; they take on a definitely *normative* character. As more and more people come to think and feel in the same way, there is a growing sense that everyone should share these feelings and definitions. There is increasing pressure on individuals to conform; a sense of constraint develops in the crowd.

Thus, on the group level, there is the emergence of a norm. On the individual level there is heightened suggestibility, but this suggestibility is not of an unfocused, indiscriminate nature. It amounts to a tendency to respond uncritically to suggestions that are consistent with the mood, imagery, and conception of appropriate action that have developed and assumed a normative character.

Finally, the crowd is permissive in that attitudes may be expressed, and actions taken, which would normally be inhibited. Ordinarily it is possible for the individual to reconcile normative conflicts by techniques of avoidance and rationalization, inhibiting certain acts inconsistent with other acts in which he is motivated to engage. He is aided in this by cultural sanctions which inhibit, modify, or limit the expression of some attitudes as against others, while still permitting the inhibited attitudes to exist.

The attitudes that are expressed in the crowd are those which, while being sanctioned in the culture of the crowd members, are ordinarily limited in their expression. But situations arise in which conflicting attitudes can no longer be reconciled, and attitudes that have previously received only limited expression are more fully expressed. Thus it may be said that the basic condition out of which crowd behavior arises is one of cultural conflict, of a breakdown of normative integration; it is not a condition of *absence of culture*. In such a situation members of the crowd may act in ways which are unusual in that they reflect attitudes ordinarily limited in expression; they may also evolve new attitudes and ways of acting in the process of resolving the dilemma of conflicting cultural demands. New forms of behavior, not previously existing in the culture of the group from which the crowd is drawn, may emerge.

These elements, then, are common to all crowds: (1) uncertainty; (2) a sense of urgency; (3) communication of mood and imagery; (4) constraint; (5) selective individual suggestibility; and (6) permissiveness. A collectivity which does not develop sufficiently to engage in a distinct, differentiating type of crowd behavior but which has these basic characteristics may be called an *elemental crowd*. As crowds develop further, they may differ markedly from each other, as is suggested by the many schemes of crowd classification that have been proposed by different writers. The dimensions in which crowds vary must also be considered to complete the analysis of the forms of crowd behavior.

The crowd objective as a basis for classification. One of the essential characteristics of a crowd is the communication of imagery, including a conception of an appropriate line of action. This crowd-defined line of action, or the *crowd objective,* is of crucial importance in determining the nature of the relations between the individuals in the crowd. On the basis of these two factors, the type of crowd objective and the type of relationship between the crowd members, the significant aspects in which crowd forms differ may be designated.

DIMENSIONS OF CROWDS

Individualistic-solidaristic. The crowd is ordinarily thought of as acting concertedly in pursuit of a group objective. Such an objective is one which the individual member of the crowd could not accomplish alone. It requires for its achievement the combined and integrated efforts of the crowd. Crowds having such a group objective may be characterized as *solidaristic*.

In some crowds the members act together, but not in an integrated way. The actions of the members are parallel and similar, but are not cooperative. The nature of the crowd objective is such that except for cultural inhibitions it could be accomplished as well by the individual in isolation as by the individual as a member of the crowd. Indeed, there is no group objective but, instead, a series of parallel individual objectives. Hence a crowd with such objectives may be called an *individualistic crowd*.

In the individualistic crowd, the action of the members is similar or even identical. It tends to become competitive, since the presence of other crowd members may interfere with the attainment of the objective by each individual. The solidaristic crowd, in contrast, tends to develop a division of labor, with the actions of the individual members supplementing rather than paralleling each other. The individualistic crowd serves primarily to provide a permissive atmosphere, one which allows people to pursue without inhibitions what are essentially private objectives. In both solidaristic and individualistic crowds there is communication of mood and the development of a common perception of the situation and of appropriate behavior.

A mixed type: the factional crowd. Solidaristic and individualistic crowds, as described here, represent polar types. Crowd behavior follows all along the continuum between these two extremes. Resembling, yet distinct from, the solidaristic crowd is a mixed type which may be called the *factional crowd*. Such a type is found in a race riot where opposing groups give each other identical treatment. The factional crowd resembles two solidaristic crowds opposing each other. It is not merely two separate crowds, however, because the communication of mood and the stimulation to action transcends the boundaries of the two factions so that the mood of each is facilitated and strengthened by the presence of the same mood on the other side. The tendency, then, is toward the development of a uniform mood and a uniform pattern of action throughout the entire crowd even though it is made up of two completely opposing factions.

Focused-volatile. The objectives of crowds may also vary in their degree of specificity. The objective may be action toward a very specific object—assaulting a particular victim or destroying a certain building. The objective may consist, on the other hand, of action on a general class of objects, such as members of a minority group in general. A crowd with the first sort of objective may be said to be *focused,* in that its attention is concentrated on one specific object. The crowd with the latter type of objective may be characterized as *volatile,* in that its objective may be accomplished by action on many specific objects of a general class. The volatile crowd may easily shift its attention from one specific object to another and, indeed, is likely to do so. Hence there is much shifting of attention and activity, as in a race riot. The volatile crowd may consist of many subcrowds, each concerned with a specific object of the general class. Yet the activities of the volatile crowd and its subcrowds are not random or uncoordinated, for they are all concerned with the same general class of objects.

Active-expressive. The type of objective which the crowd has also determines whether it may be classified as *active* or *expressive*. The objective of the *active* crowd is such that the criterion of its attainment is some action upon an external object—some physical object, or some person or persons not part of the crowd. This action need not necessarily be a direct, physical assault. It may be indirect, as when a crowd drives a speaker from his platform with boos or when a demonstrating crowd conveys its attitudes of displeasure to a public official.

The measure of achievement of the objective of the *expressive* crowd is, in contrast, the production of some sort of subjective experience or some behavior in the crowd members themselves. It may be the accentuation of a feeling state, the induction of an experience such as seeing visions, or the elicitation of a certain type of behavior such as "speaking with tongues" or vigorous cheering. Whatever the specific objective, however, the criterion of its accomplishment is subjective and internal.

EXAMPLES OF CROWD TYPES

Three dimensions of crowds have been described, each having polar types. Any crowd may be characterized in terms of these three dimensions. Logically, this should lead to the identification of eight crowd types. But the dichotomy *focused-volatile* does not apply to the expressive crowd, since its objective is production of some subjective state, not action on some *object*. There is no external object which can be either specific or one example of a general class. Hence we find six specific, composite types of crowds.

Individualistic-expressive. By being exposed to the same situation, such as a common frustration, or by perceiving an event in very much the same way, a large number of people may come to experience the same mood almost simultaneously. Even as isolated individuals away from any collectivity, they may be impelled to express their feelings in some way. On the day of Franklin D. Roosevelt's death countless Americans sat by their radios and wept silently and alone. But the presence of others who are experiencing the same mood and expressing the same feelings of joy, anger, or grief, reinforces the feelings of the individual. The expressive behavior of others stimulates him to increasingly vigorous expression of his emotion. The uninhibited acts of even a few members of the crowd may create a permissive atmosphere in which everyone feels free to "let himself go."

Such crowd behavior is *expressive* in that the crowd objective is the expression and enhancement of the mood of the members, not the effecting of any change in the external situation. At the same time, it is *individualistic* insofar as this objective is one which the participants might have had and achieved individually; the crowd has only lent a permissive atmosphere. Such an event as the "V-J Day" celebrations which took place in numerous American cities is marked by much individualistic-expressive behavior, with numerous individuals giving vent to their feelings in a variety of ways, many of which violate the usual norms of the society.

Individualistic-volatile-acting. When the members of a crowd are acting upon a variety of objects of a general class which are external to the crowd itself, the crowd is *volatile* and *acting*. If, in addition, each crowd member is acting to attain some essentially private objective, with the activities of other members merely providing cover for his own actions, the crowd is also *individualistic*.

Crowds which engage in looting or vandalism are often of this type. One of the most striking examples of such a crowd was the mob which looted the business section of Harlem on the nights of August 1st and 2nd, 1943. The mob did not act as a unified, integrated collectivity. It consisted, rather, of numerous individuals and small groups pursuing parellel individual objectives—the garnering of a variety of goods from the white-owned stores in the district. Clark and Barker, in an interview with a participant in the riot, obtained an unusually detailed, if not meticulously accurate, account of the mob's behavior. Excerpts from this interview show that the effect of the crowd situation was not to focus the activities of the participants upon any specific objective, but to provide a permissive cover for various types of aggressive behavior, including looting and vandalism. We can also see the deterioration of group relations so that members of the crowd turned on one another. The competitiveness of the individualistic crowd is evident, as is the permissiveness to act in terms of individual irritations.

A PARTICIPANT IN THE HARLEM RIOT
KENNETH B. CLARK AND JAMES BARKER

R. is a dark-brown-skinned Negro, 18 years old. He was born in New York City. For the past two years he has lived alone in a roominghouse in the center of Harlem. When the interviewer saw him for the first time on the evening of the interview he was engaged in animated conversation with two other members of his CD messenger unit.

During the course of this conversation, R., *unprompted by the interviewer began to discuss the 1943 Harlem riot and his role in it.* The riot had taken place about a month before this. After he finished his account to the group, the interviewer casually said to R., "You ought to write a book." He replied (probably because he knew that the interviewer was a college student), "Why don't you,—are you going to write a book?" This gave the interviewer an opportunity to tell him that he would like a record of his account of his experiences in the riot. He readily agreed to cooperate and the interviewer immediately made arrangements to interview him in a private office.

Adapted by permission of the American Psychological Association and the authors, from Kenneth B. Clark and James Barker, "The Zoot Effect in Personality: A Race Riot Participant," **Journal of Abnormal and Social Psychology**, 40 (1945), pp. 143–148.

[The following paragraphs are excerpts from this private interview, as recorded by Clark and Barker.]

Before the riot starts I was in the Harlem Dump theater. Some two-by-four runs in there and says that: "Harlem is on fire!" The "niggers" jump up half full of juice and running for the door, me leading of course. By this time the "niggers" have tored-off half of Harlem.

The riot started when a colored man got shot. About half hour later the riot was going full blast, and the people was going 'round stores. They messed up '25th St. badly. They hit shoe stores, beat up a cop standing there unmercifully.

The party that you're writin' about goes in a store and helps himself to the man's cash register. The store next to the A & P—goes in there. There was nothin' there. While I goes in there a lady was stealin' a man's big half-a-cow.

One boy broke into Busch, located 125th Street and 7th Avenue. A flat-foot with a sawed-off rifle watches the boy when he enters the store, wait 'til the boy comes out, draw a bead on the boy an' begins to fire. A colored lady jumps in front of the cop, turns her black ____ up the cop and tells him: "Why don't you shoot me in the back?" The cop gets excited when the rest of the crowd begins to walk over, puts the rifle down, lowered it rather, and walks away.

Walkin' a little ways, they caught a 'fay (*white*), beatin' hell outa him half ta death. The man starts throwing money into the air and runnin' like hell. The boys was fightin' left and right for a two dollar bill, tearin' it in half; one of the boys say: "You gimme your half!" the other one says: "You gimme your half!" Stubborn as they was, neither one of them gave in. As tired as I was I was scuffling, I gets myself $50.

Individualistic-focused-acting. The individualistic-focused-acting crowd differs from the type just discussed only in that the parallel, individual objective of the participants is a very specific one. The distinctive characteristics of the individualistic type of crowd are best seen in this specific crowd type.

Alexander Mintz has produced in the laboratory the type of situation which gives rise to individualistic crowd action. In this experiment the situation is defined by the participants as a highly competitive one. The factor of interaction is not important here, for the experiment is set up so that the situation is almost instantaneously perceived as demanding a hasty "every man for himself" sort of action. The definition held by the participants in this experiment is a common one and the lines of action are identical. They are not coordinated, however, and the presence of other persons does not contribute to the accomplishment of individual goals. Yet it is this very presence of others that causes the situation to be defined as it is.

NON-ADAPTIVE GROUP BEHAVIOR
ALEXANDER MINTZ

Material will be presented in this paper suggesting that violent emotional excitement is not the decisive factor in the non-adaptive behavior of people in panics and related situations. Instead, it appears to be possible to explain the non-adaptive character of such behavior in terms of their perception of the situation and their expectation of what is likely to happen. In recent times, a number of psychologists have tended to interpret features of human behavior in terms of the phenomenal properties of the situation in which it occurs. . . .

What are the reasonable expectations of people at a theater fire or in similar circumstances in which a panic is apt to develop? Situations of this type tend to

Reprinted in part by permission of the American Psychological Association and the author, from Alexander Mintz, "Non-Adaptive Group Behavior," **Journal of Abnormal and Social Psychology,** 46 (April, 1951), pp. 150–159.

have a characteristically unstable reward structure, which has been generally overlooked by social scientists as a factor in panics. Cooperative behavior is required for the common good but has very different consequences for the individual depending on the behavior of others. Thus at a theater fire, if everyone leaves in an orderly manner, everybody is safe, and an individual waiting for his turn is not sacrificing his interests. But, if the cooperative pattern of behavior is disturbed, the usual advice, "Keep your head, don't push, wait for your turn, and you will be safe," ceases to be valid. If the exits are blocked, the person following this advice is likely to be burned to death. In other words, if everybody cooperates, there is no conflict between the needs of the individual and those of the group. However, the situation changes completely as soon as a minority of people cease to cooperate. A conflict between the needs of the group and the selfish needs of the individual then arises. An individual who recognizes this state of things and who wants to benefit the group must sacrifice his own selfish needs.

It is suggested here that it is chiefly the reward structure of the situations which is responsible for non-adaptive behavior of groups at theater fires and similar situations. People are likely to recognize the threats to themselves, as they appear, and behave accordingly. These situations may be compared to states of unstable equilibrium in mechanics; a cone balanced on its tip is not likely to remain in this position a long time because a slight initial displacement of its center of gravity allows the force of gravity to make it fall all the way. Similarly, cooperative behavior at a theater fire is likely to deteriorate progressively as soon as an initial disturbance occurs. If a few individuals begin to push, the others are apt to recognize that their interests are threatened; they can expect to win through to their individual rewards only by pressing their personal advantages at the group's expense. Many of them react accordingly, a vicious circle is set up, and the disturbance spreads. Competitive behavior (pushing and fighting) may result, as e.g., at theater fires, or the group may disperse as in military panics. There is another factor which makes for further disintegration. As the behavior of the group becomes increasingly disorderly, the amount of noise is apt to increase, and communication may then become so difficult that no plan for restoring order can emerge.

This interpretation is almost the reverse of the conventional ones which ascribe non-adaptive group behavior to emotional facilitation and to the supposed alterations of personality in group situations.

The existence of mutual emotional facilitation is not denied; its operation can be readily observed, e.g., in college students during final examinations, in audiences at sports events, etc. However, it is not believed that emotional excitement as such is responsible for non-adaptive group behavior. There are many situations in which intense emotional excitement is the rule, and yet no non-adaptive group behavior appears. Thus it has been reported that intense fear is practically universally present in soldiers about to go into battle and yet no panic need develop. Similarly, participants in an athletic contest are apt to be so emotionally excited that vomiting is common; no markedly non-adaptive group behavior appears to develop as a result of this kind of intense excitement.

The assumption of personality alterations of people due to crowd membership appears to be entirely unsubstantiated in the case of panics. On the contrary, the competitive behavior or dispersal occurring in panics suggests that group cohesion disappears and that people begin to behave purely as individuals in accordance with their selfish needs. . . .

As a first step towards the verification of the proposed theory, a set of laboratory experiments was devised. It was thought that if the theory is correct it should be possible to illustrate its functioning in the laboratory. If not substantiated by laboratory findings, the theory would have to be discarded.

EXPERIMENTAL DESIGN

The experiments were conducted with groups of people, 15 to 21 subjects in each group. The subjects had the task of pulling cones out of a glass bottle; each subject was given a piece of string to which a cone was attached. Cooperation on the part of the subjects was required if the cones were to come out; the physical setup made it easy for "traffic jams" of cones to appear at the bottle neck. Only one cone could come out at a time; even a near-tie between two cones at the bottle neck prevented both from coming out because the narrow apex of the second cone, wedged into the bottle neck, blocked the path for the wide base of the cone ahead of it. The cones had to arrive at the bottle neck in order, one at a time.

Experimental Situations

1. One of the experimental setups was designed to show that it was possible to produce disorganized, uncooperative, non-adaptive group behavior resulting in

"traffic" jams by duplicating the essential features of panic-producing situations, as explained in the theoretical section of this paper. The experimental situation was represented to the subjects as a game in which each participant could win or lose money. A subject could win or lose depending on how successful he was in pulling out his cone. Success was defined in terms of arbitrary time limits in some experiments. In other experiments water was made to flow into the bottle through a spout near the bottom and the subject was successful if his cone came out of the bottle untouched by the water. Inasmuch as the rewards and fines were offered to individuals, depending on what would happen to their particular cones, it was thought that the cooperative pattern of behavior, required for group success, would be easily disrupted; a momentary "traffic jam" at the bottleneck would be perceived by some of the subjects as threatening them with loss in the game as a result of the anticipated failure of cooperative behavior. These subjects would be tempted to save themselves from the loss by pulling out of turn. Some of them would probably do so, and thus the situation could be expected rapidly to deteriorate after an initial disturbance occurred.

In order that subjects who recognized that full success was out of their reach should not stop trying, intermediate steps between full success and full failure were announced. The details and the amounts of rewards and fines are summarized in the table of results. The monetary rewards and fines were very small, the rewards for full success ranging from 10 to 25 cents, the fines for full failure from 1 to 10 cents. The very small fines were decided upon because it was intended to show that the characteristically inefficient, non-adaptive features of group behavior such as occurs in panics can be reproduced in a situation in which there was no opportunity for fear. It was not thought that the small rewards and fines were likely to constitute real financial incentives for college students. They were introduced so as to emphasize the nature of the experimental situation as a game in which individuals could win or lose.

2. In the contrasting experimental set-ups there were no individual rewards or fines, and there was no flow of water except for a few control experiments. The experiments were described as attempts to measure the ability of groups of people to behave cooperatively. Good performances of other groups were quoted. It was expected that under these conditions no "traffic jams" would develop. Subjects had no motivation to disregard any plan that might be devised by the group; the only incentive offered was membership in a group of people who were going to show their ability to cooperate effectively with each other. Thus the reward structure was the principal experimental variable studied in these two experimental situations.

3. Another variable investigated was the excitement built up by mutual facilitation. In a number of "no-reward" experiments several subjects were asked to act as accomplices. They were secretly instructed before the experiment began to scream, behave excitedly, swear, and make as much noise as possible. To limit their influence to emotional facilitation they were asked not to give specific bad advice nor to disturb the workings of any plan the group might decide upon. It was expected that the added emotional excitement, which is the major factor in Le Bon's and similar theories of panics, would not have much effect on the results.

4. In certain of the reward-and-fine experiments an attempt was made to minimize the opportunities for mutual emotional facilitation by largely preventing the subjects from seeing each other. This was accomplished by a circular screen with holes for eyes and arms and with vertical partitions on the outside, placed around the glass bottle. Each subject stood in an individual "stall" hiding him from his neighbors; he saw the bottle standing on the floor through the eye hole; only his arm and eyes could be seen by the other subjects, and the eyes were not likely to be seen because the subject

were mainly looking at the bottle tied to the floor. In order to prevent excited screams, the subjects were asked to remain silent after the experiment began, which request was largely complied with. It was expected that the results would be essentially the same as those in the other reward-and-fine experiments.

5. A third variable which was introduced in a few of the experiments was interference with the opportunity to arrive at a plan of action. In most of the experiments the subjects were not prevented from conducting preliminary discussions; in almost all instances either they started such a discussion immediately or asked for permission to do so, which was given. Only twice did a group fail to discuss and agree upon a plan when discussion was not explicitly forbidden. On the other hand, in two of the reward-and-fine experiments conducted early in the study the subjects were forbidden to talk to each other both before and during the experiment; in one reward-and-fine experiment conducted immediately after three no-reward experiments with the same group, the subjects were prevented from having a preliminary discussion so that no plan could be agreed upon beforehand, but were allowed to talk during the experiment. . . .

RESULTS

The conditions and results of all of the experiments conducted so far are indicated in a table in an appendix. Forty-two experiments with 26 groups of subjects were performed altogether, including some preliminary and control experiments conducted to investigate potential sources of error. . . .

One experiment was conducted before the procedure was fully developed; there were no fines and only one reward level was announced. No "traffic jam" resulted.

There were 16 experiments with rewards and fines. In three of them . . . discussion was interfered with before the experiment, so that the subjects had no opportunity to devise a plan of action. In all three experiments "traffic jams" developed. In only one of them did the subjects

succeed in pulling *any* cones out of the bottle—two cones out of 19 in 40 seconds; these same subjects had successfully pulled out *all* cones in 18.6 seconds and 23 seconds in two immediately preceding trials in which there had been no rewards and in which they had had the opportunity to agree upon a plan of action.

In the other 13 reward-and-fine experiments . . . discussion was not interfered with. In eight of these experiments . . . there were serious "traffic jams," the large majority of the cones failing to be pulled out of the bottle within times ranging from one to approximately two minutes. In another experiment almost half of the cones were in the bottle after 1 minute . . . In two of these experiments . . . the factor of mutual emotional facilitation was minimized by the use of the screen. The results were much the same as in most of the other reward-and-fine experiments, suggesting that this factor was not primarily responsible for the results.

In four of the reward-and-fine experiments . . . there were no serious "traffic jams"; all or almost all of the cones came out of the bottle in less than a minute. In three of these experiments the experimenter was unable to persuade the winners to take the rewards; apparently the subjects had failed to accept the situation as a game with winners and losers. In one of these experiments there was an additional factor which probably interfered with "traffic jams"; immediately before this experiment . . . these subjects had participated in another . . . in which no rewards had been offered and in which the fastest time of any group was achieved (10 seconds). The subjects knew the time of this trial; the time allowance for winning exceeded it by 5 seconds, so that the chances of losing must have been recognized as slight by the subjects.

In the remaining 25 experiments there were no rewards or fines. Twenty of these experiments were described to the subjects as measures of cooperation. These experiments fell into three groups. Experiments NR1 to NR5 were conducted with groups of subjects who had not been previously exposed to similar experiments, and under "natural" conditions, i.e., without the experimenter entering into a conspiracy with accomplices. Experiments NR6 to NR12 were similar but were conducted immediately after experiments with accomplices. Experiments ANR1 to ANR8 were the experiments with accomplices who had been instructed to make noise and to stir up excitement in the group.

No serious traffic jam developed in any of these experiments, not in those with new subjects, nor in those with accomplices, nor in those preceded by experiments with accomplices. The times for taking *all* cones out of the bottle ranged in these three groups of experiments from 10 to 22 seconds, from 10.5 to 30 seconds and from 13.4 to 59 seconds.

The experimenter's accomplices were generally able to stir up excitement but this excitement failed to disrupt the cooperative behavior of the group to an extent comparable to that of the effect of the individual rewards and fines. In most of the reward-and-fine experiments the majority of the cones were still in the bottle after a minute or longer had elapsed.

Did the accomplices have any effect? The mean times of the two groups of the no-reward, no-accomplice experiments were 16.8 seconds . . . and 19.6 seconds . . .; the mean time of the accomplice experiments was 34.4 seconds. The difference between the times of the two groups of experiments without accomplices is very small and not statistically significant. In the accomplice experiments the mean time was longer, significantly so at the .01 level of confidence, suggesting that the accomplices did have some disrupting effect. However, a closer examination of the data shows that the two longest times in the accomplice experiments were obtained when some of the accomplices had misunderstood the instructions and gave bad advice to the group. If the results of these two experiments . . . are eliminated, the mean time drops to 26.4 seconds, and the critical ratio . . . indicates that the difference between this time and that of the no-accomplice experiments is too small to reach the conventional standards of statistical significance. . . .

Thus it was not established with certainty that the accomplices who made noise and stirred up excitement without giving bad advice had a disrupting effect on group cooperation. They may have had; the evidence was inconclusive. More experiments would have been needed to establish this point. The experiments with accomplices were designed merely to discover whether an additional opportunity for mutual emotional facilitation would seriously disrupt group cooperation. They served their purpose in showing that it did not; and since the question whether it had a minor disrupting effect was not directly related to the main problem of this study in any case, the matter was not further investigated. . . .

After each experiment or group of experiments the subjects were told by the experimenter about the true nature of the experiments and about the results obtained so far. The explanations were followed by discussions. In the groups which had failed to pull out the cones from the bottle, marked tendencies towards rationalization appeared during these discussions. Subjects tended to explain the bad results of their group in terms of supposedly tangled strings, effects of the water, or insufficient time for the formulation of a plan, disregarding the fact that these factors failed to produce "traffic jams" in no-reward experiments.

DISCUSSION

The theory presented at the beginning of this paper is opposed to the common tendency to view emotion as a predominantly disruptive factor in behavior. It developed out of an attempt to reconstruct the phenomenal situation in circumstances leading to a panic. . . .

The experiments provide laboratory demonstrations for our hypothesis and partially verify the hypothesis. The behavior of the subjects did not tend towards inefficiency unless the reward structure of the situation provided them with incentives to behave uncooperatively after the cooperative pattern of group behavior was disturbed. There were no "traffic jams" in the no-reward experiments. Emotional excitement produced by the experimenter's accomplices interfered with the efficiency of group behavior only to a minor extent, if at all, compared to the effects of individual rewards and fines. On the other hand, there were inefficient behavior and "traffic jams" in more than half of the reward-and-fine experiments, in which the subjects were confronted with the probability of individual failure, as soon as the bottle neck was temporarily blocked. This result was obtained without any more serious threat to the individuals than the loss of ten cents at most and probably a mild feeling of failure in a game. Thus intense fear was not found to be an essential condition of chaotic, non-adaptive group behavior analogous to that occurring in panics.

"Traffic jams" did not occur in all of the reward-and-fine experiments and were not expected to. In an experiment with 15 to 20 subjects one cannot be certain that one or a few subjects will create a disturbance within the short time available. With larger groups the percentage of "traffic jams" should be larger; the more people there are, the more likely it becomes that one uncooperative individual will create the initial disturbance which leads to deterioration of the situation.

The theory presented here, if correct, appears to apply to many situations and to contribute to the understanding of a number of social and economic phenomena. Situations with reward structures resembling that of panics and the reward-and-fine experiments reported here seem to be numerous. Tendencies towards non-adaptive group behavior are clearly present in many such situations, regardless of the presence or absence of face-to-face contacts between people and opportunities for mutual emotional facilitation. Runs on banks resulting in bank failures, violations of price-fixing agreements among business men resulting in cut-throat competition, hoarding behavior of consumers during periods of scarcity of goods resulting in shortages are all forms of ultimately non-adaptive behavior which can be interpreted in terms of unstable reward structures of the situations. On the other hand, there are situations in which the appearance of danger does not provide incentives for anti-social behavior. In such situations no chaotic non-adaptive behavior of groups seems to occur in spite of the catastrophic nature of the danger and ample opportunity for face-to-face contacts. There seem to be no panics when people are trapped so that there can be no struggle for an exit, e.g., at submarine and mine disasters.

In "An Incident at a Train Station," the cancelling out of norms of courtesy and even honesty by the urgency of the situation is even more evident. Here, too, it may be seen clearly how the very existence of the crowd contributes to the common definition of the situation as competitive and demanding immediate action.

AN INCIDENT AT A TRAIN STATION

It was during the war that I was trying to catch the train in San Diego for Los Angeles. When I got to the station there were already throngs of people waiting for the same train. And I found myself the last in line. Naturally, I didn't expect to have a chance to get on. Numbers of

From the files of Ralph H. Turner.

people get turned away from every one of these trains. But this was one time that I outsmarted the crowd. I noticed that the last coach wasn't crowded and people were getting on without any difficulty at all. The conductor had previously told me that this last coach went only as far as Oceanside. I had nothing to lose, so I thought I would try a stunt. I ran toward the last coach, but before I left I said loudly, "Look, it isn't crowded back here and you can get on easily." Everybody else ran, too. Then I turned back to the original car and got in without any difficulty.

Mintz includes panic as one of the most significant types of competitive or nonadaptive group behavior. Fear that panic might sweep American cities in the case of enemy bombing has made the causes, the prevention, and the control of this type of behavior a matter of renewed interest to social scientists and laymen alike.

Two important facts concerning the concept "panic" have been revealed through recent research. One is that the term is vague, ill-defined, and commonly used to designate a wide variety of behaviors ranging from wild flight to paralysis, from the actions of a solitary individual to those of an entire nation. The second is that the sort of wild, terror-stricken behavior which is usually called "panic" is not as frequent as it is commonly represented as being.

Here we will restrict our analysis to the type of panic which is collective in nature and which is manifest in flight behavior. The concept "panic" remains, however, a heterogeneous term which is applied to a wide variety of terrorized behavior, both individual and collective.

The Committee on Disaster Studies of the National Research Council has defined panic as "highly emotional behavior which is excited by the presence of an immediate severe threat, and which results in increasing the danger for the self and for others rather than in reducing it." In their discussion of "The Problem of Panic" they point out that while the presence of a severe and imminent threat is necessary for the development of panic, it is not a sufficient condition. Not all excited behavior is panic, nor is all flight behavior. Panic occurs when, in the presence of severe threat, a limited number of alternative courses of action are available—including the alternatives of "taking one's chances in the situation" or striving desperately to escape through one limited route. When panic is a collective reaction the situation is essentially individualistic and competitive, in that a number of people are each trying to gain an objective whose attainment is problematic for each of them. The situation may become a competitive one not because of its objective features but because of the crowd members' perception of it, as when they overlook escape routes. In panic, as in all forms of crowd behavior, the urgency of the situation produces a restriction of attention to the alternatives available and to the consequences of various courses of action. To the extent that the individual is restricted in his perception of alternatives and in his ability to project their consequences beyond the present moment, it may be said that he is deficient in self-control.

THE PROBLEM OF PANIC

Panic is undoubtedly a dramatic term, but it is an ambiguous one. It has been used to refer to so many different kinds of behavior—ranging from a wild outburst of flight to paralysis of action—that its meaning has become vague. Often the

Reprinted in part by permission of the Federal Civil Defense Administration, from "The Problem of Panic," **Civil Defense Technical Bulletin,** TB-19-2 (June, 1955), pp. 1-2.

word is employed merely as a vivid term to refer to any kind of behavior that occurs when people feel afraid or worried. To give the word a specific meaning, it is desirable to apply it to highly emotional behavior which is excited by the presence of an immediate severe threat, and *which results in increasing the danger for the self and for others rather than in reducing it.* This concept of panic recognizes the negative connotation that the term usually carries. Thus, we avoid referring to all instances of excited behavior as panic. In these terms for example, flight is not necessarily panic, for flight may result in *reducing* the danger.

The current hunches and guesses seem to go far beyond the known facts in emphasizing the likelihood of its occurrence in this country. Many of the forecasts and discussions concerning panic which have received wide publicity assume that it will not be too difficult for an enemy nation to strike terror into the hearts of Americans—especially through the use of atomic and thermonuclear bombs. To the enormous loss of life and property—so runs the theme—panic or mass hysteria will add devastating disorganization and paralysis, a weapon more horrible in its effects than any known to man.

MASS PANIC OCCURS RARELY

An assessment of the facts shows that the existing evidence falls far short of supporting such a vivid and dramatic prediction. The authenticated instances of mass panic known to have occurred in the last 50 years have been few in number and have been very restricted in their effect. Although there has been war somewhere in the world almost continuously during this time, it is a significant and somewhat astonishing fact that there have been few instances of mass panic directly connected with enemy attack on a civilian population. Moreover, studies of terrified people who have been stunned by an overwhelming disaster indicate that panic states are usually of short duration, and that excited and irrational behavior can usually be prevented or quickly brought to a stop if effective leadership and realistic information is provided. A striking finding that emerges from observations in large scale disasters, including the A-bomb attack against Japan and the massive bombing assaults against England and Germany, is that the people who are most frightened and most upset very soon become extremely docile and can easily be induced to conform to the rules and regulations of the local authorities.

The logical conclusion from the evidence, then, is that mass panic is a rare event which arises only under highly specialized circumstances. We do know something about the conditions which give rise to panic behavior—though not as much as we would like.

There are four main factors which are characteristic of the panic-producing situation.

(1) *Partial entrapment.* There is only one, or, at best an extremely limited number of escape routes from a situation dominated by (2).

(2) *A perceived threat.* The threat may be physical, or psychological, or a combination of both, and it is usually regarded as being so imminent that there is no time to do anything except to try to escape.

(3) *Partial or complete breakdown of the escape route.* The escape route becomes blocked off, or jammed, or it is overlooked.

(4) *Front to rear communication failure.* The false assumption that the exit is still open leads the people at the rear of the mass to exert strong physical or psychological pressure to advance toward it. It is this *pressure from the rear* that causes those at the front to be smothered, crushed, or trampled. In instances where people are trampled to death, as in the Coconut Grove fire, this is usually the single, most important factor.

When a mass panic occurs, it usually happens that people do not actually see the "escape hatch," whatever its nature may be, but infer its existence from the fact that other people are moving in a specific direction. This inference made by the individual is reinforced by statements of people in the immediate vicinity. None of these communications, however, is based on realistic information about the actual conditions at the "escape hatch." The people at the rear of the mass, especially, are too far away from the exit to be able to obtain accurate information about its actual state. Thus, when the exit becomes blocked or jammed, the people at the rear behave as if it were still open.

There is some evidence to support the conclusion that when people know that the escape route is actually blocked, and that no escape is possible, they are likely to remain fatalistically hopeful or else become apathetic and depressed—but the likelihood of panic behavior is actually very slight.

In the "Cold War" period following the end of World War II the idea was frequently advanced that panic would instantly and automatically follow an atomic attack on any American city. As the Committee on Disaster Studies indicates, such a prediction is of highly questionable validity, "mass panic" being a phenomenon which occurs only under very specialized conditions. It may be, however, that the likelihood that panic will occur in American cities is increased by the prior definition of the approach of enemy planes as a panic-inducing stimulus. Paul Foreman has advanced the proposition, ". . . if a stimulus, prior to its occurrence, is linguistically defined as unmanageable, its name alone can induce immediate terror and panic." * A crowd which developed panic instantaneously in this fashion would constitute an example of a precipitous crowd, going through a very brief period of milling. Panic may also develop through a relatively long period of milling during which an *emergent* crowd arises.

One of the most tragic demonstrations of the consequences of panic was seen in the famous Iroquois Theater fire of 1903. On a December afternoon a musical extravaganza was being presented before a packed audience in this Chicago theater. Early in the second act fire broke out in draperies on the stage. The asbestos curtain caught on a wire and could not be lowered to cut off the fire from the audience. The famous comedian Eddie Foy described the individualistic-focused-active crowd behavior of the audience as he witnessed it.

* Paul B. Foreman, "Panic Theory," **Sociology and Social Research,** 37 (1953), pp. 295-304.

THE IROQUOIS THEATER FIRE
EDDIE FOY AND ALVIN F. HARLOW

As I ran around back of the rear drop, I could hear the murmur of excitement growing in the audience. Somebody had of course yelled "Fire!"—there is almost always a fool of that species in an audience; and there are always hundreds of people who go crazy the moment they hear the word. The crowd was beginning to surge toward the doors and already showing signs of a stampede. Those on the lower floor were not so badly frightened as those in the more dangerous balcony and gallery. Up there they were falling into panic.

I began shouting at the top of my voice, "Don't get excited. There's no danger. Take it easy!" And to Dillea, the orchestra leader, "Play, start an overture—anything!" But play!" Some of his musicians were fleeing, but a few, and especially a fat little violinist, stuck nobly.

Reprinted in part by permission of E. P. Dutton and Co., from Eddie Foy and Alvin F. Harlow, **Clowning Through Life** (New York: E. P. Dutton and Co., 1928), pp. 104-113.

I stood perfectly still, hoping my apparent calm would have an equally calming effect on the crowd. Those on the lower floor heard me and seemed somewhat reassured. But up above, and especially in the gallery, they had gone mad.

As I left the stage the last of the ropes holding up the drops burned through, and with them the whole loft collapsed with a terrifying crash, bringing down tons of burning material. With that, all the lights in the house went out and another great balloon of flame leaped out into the auditorium, licking even the ceiling and killing scores who had not yet succeeded in escaping from the gallery.

The horror in the auditorium was beyond all description. There were thirty exits, but few of them were marked by lights; some had heavy portieres over the doors, and some of the doors were locked or fastened with levers which no one knew how to work.

It was said that some of the exit doors leading from the upper tiers onto the fire escapes on the alley between Randolph and Lake Streets were either rusted or frozen. They were finally burst open, but precious moments had been lost—moments which meant death for many behind those doors. The fire-escape ladders could not accommodate the crowd, and many fell or jumped to death on the pavement below. Some were not killed only because they landed on the cushion of bodies of those who had gone before.

But it was inside the house that the greatest loss of life occurred, especially on the stairways leading down from the second balcony. Here most of the dead were trampled or smothered, though many jumped or fell over the balustrade to the floor of the foyer. In places on the stairways, particularly where a turn caused a jam, bodies were piled seven or eight feet deep. Firemen and police confronted a sickening task in disentangling them. An occasional living person was found in the heaps, but most of these were terribly injured. The heel prints on the dead faces mutely testified to the cruel fact that human animals stricken by terror are as mad and ruthless as stampeding cattle. Many bodies had the clothes torn from them, and some had the flesh trodden from their bones.

Never elsewhere had a great fire disaster occurred so quickly. From the start of the fire until all in the audience either escaped, died, or lay maimed in the halls and alleys, took just eight minutes. In that eight minutes more than 500 perished.

The fire department arrived quickly after the alarm and extinguished the flames in the auditorium so promptly that no more than the plush upholstery was burned off the seats. But when a fire chief thrust his head through a side exit and shouted, "Is anybody alive in here?" no one answered. The few who were not dead were insensible or dying. Within ten minutes from the beginning of the fire, bodies were being laid in rows on the sidewalks, and all the ambulances and dead-wagons in the city could not keep up with the ghastly harvest. Within twenty-four hours Chicago knew that at least 587 were dead, and many more injured. Subsequent deaths among the injured brought the list up to 602.

Solidaristic-expressive. In the other type of expressive crowd, the objective is defined in the interaction of the crowd. The mood and the appropriate expressive behavior are induced. The congregation at a highly emotional religious service constitutes this type of crowd. Liston Pope, in *Millhands and Preachers,* provides a detailed account of the development of a solidaristic expressive crowd. In this description, the essential unity or solidarity of the crowd is evident. The division of labor, not only between preacher, choir, and congregation, but within the congregation, is also apparent. Here the importance of rhythmic stimulation, stressed by Blumer, is to be seen. Anyone who has attended such a service as an "outsider" is aware, too, that the activities of the crowd create an atmosphere which is not merely permissive but is compulsive. Even lacking the "cultural conditioning" which the church members seem to have, he finds himself constrained to join in the behavior of the crowd, if only to the extent of clapping his hands.

A HOLINESS RELIGIOUS SERVICE

LISTON POPE

One traverses a grassless, rutted yard, climbs precarious 2 x 6 steps into a long, bare room filled with crude pews, and takes a seat in the Church of God. It is Sunday night, and the building is filled to overflowing, with about a thousand people present. Many stand in the doors or in the front yard of the church, including a large group of young men watching the girls go in and out. An ice cream vendor has placed his portable refrigerator near the church door, and is doing a thriving business. About 65 per cent of those present are women between the ages of fourteen and fifty-five, many of whom have sleeping babies in their laps. The atmosphere is expectant and informal; members of the congregation move about at will, and talk in any tone of voice that suits their fancy.

A crude pulpit, a piano, and a section of pews for the choir are placed at the far end of the oblong building. Back of the pulpit to the left is a homemade board on which to register weekly attendance; beneath the board, in sprawling letters, the question:

HOW WILL YOUR

REPORT IN HEAVEN BE

To the right of the pulpit is another sign:

GOD IS ABLE

A band, including three stringed instruments and a saxophone, plays occasional music.

The service begins at eight o'clock or thereabouts. Rather, the actions of the congregation become more intense and concerted in character; there is almost

Reprinted in part by permission of Yale University Press and the author, from Liston Pope, **Millhands and Preachers** (New Haven: Yale University Press, 1942), pp. 130–133.

nothing by way of formal announcement. The choir, in cooperation with the pastor, breaks into a rhythmic hymn, and the congregation follows suit. The hymn has an interminable number of stanzas, and a refrain, reminiscent of mountain ballads both in music and in narrative form. The hymn looks toward a narrative climax, and the excitement of the congregation increases as the singing proceeds. The stanzas are punctuated with loud shouts of "Hallelujah," "Thank you, Jesus," "Glory," and the rhythmic clapping of hands and tapping of feet. Almost immediately, various members of the congregation begin to "get the Holy Ghost" (as a teen-age boy awesomely remarks). One young woman leaves the front row of the choir and jerks about the pulpit, with motions so disconnected as to seem involuntary, weird. A man's head trembles violently from side to side. Another man, tieless and red-faced, laughs boomingly at odd moments, in a laugh resembling that of intoxication.

Half a dozen songs follow in succession. Then comes a prayer, with everybody kneeling on the floor and praying aloud at the same time, each in his own way. Some mutter with occasional shouts, others chant, with frequent bendings backward and forward; the volume of sound rises and falls, without unified pattern or group concentration. The pastor's voice booms out occasionally above all the others. Then, as if by a prearranged but unobservable signal, the prayer abruptly ends; the onlooker is amazed to see emerging from the confusion a concerted return to a sitting position. The cacophony of prayer is ended as suddenly as it began.

Then the pastor reads "the Scripture," after confessing that he "ain't had no time to study today," and after attempting to induce a layman in the congregation to "say something"—without avail, because the layman confesses that he "ain't had no time to study neither" and insists, "you go right ahead, brother." Reluctantly the pastor begins to read, explaining each verse with amazing exegesis and equally amazing insight. Each verse becomes the subject of a homily, and the reader works up to a climax in its exposition—a climax reflected in increase of rhythmic motions and hortatory shouts from members of the congregation. Having finished the Scripture lesson, the preacher takes up a collection, counts it, announces that he has to have "a little more," and runs around in the congregation to garner proffered contributions, acknowledging each with a receipt "God bless you, brother," and finally emptying the collection plate into his pocket.

Then the service moves toward a climax; the taking of the collection has been an emotional interlude. The preacher begins a sermon; more precisely, he enunciates verbal symbols that arouse immediate response from the congregation. Such motifs play through his shoutings as "sanctification," "the Second Coming," "the world despises and misunderstands and lies about the Church of God," "Jesus can heal your body and soul," "Believe the Word," "follow the knee-route." The Church of God is depicted as a remnant of those who have escaped from the "coldness" of the Methodist and Baptist churches. Lay preaching is urged, and personal evangelistic work. Attention is called to a number of prayer meetings to be held at various houses during the subsequent week, and to persons for whom prayer is desired—especially the family of a four-year-old girl who has just died, because "they can't hardly get over it."

Then there is a testimony meeting in which a large number of the more faithful testify to their personal experience and joy in religion, some mutteringly, some loudly, fervidly. One woman defends her right to wear long-sleeved, high-necked dresses in the summer time, because "the Spirit told me to." Nearly all say that they are proud to speak for Christ, and not ashamed to speak out for their Master in church. The man who has been indulging the intoxicated laugh defends his right to laugh in church, saying that his religion makes him feel good all over and is not like the stiff coldness of the Methodist church. Recurring phrases appear in the testimonies: "I'm glad I got over bein' too proud to be a Holiness and get all there was of the Holy Ghost"; "I'm a better wife and I've got a better husband because I joined the Church of God"; "the Baptists are all right, but I wanted more of the Lord than they had." Several testify to marvelous cures of physical illness during the past week, through prayer and the "laying on of the hands."

All the while waves of ecstatic rhythm have been sweeping over the congregation, with the actions of the preacher setting the pace. There are patterns to the rhythmic actions: running around the pulpit, holding trembling hands to the sky, very fast clogging of the feet, swinging the arms in sharp, staccato motions. One girl leaps from her seat as though struck by an electric shock, races four times around the aisles of the church, screaming "O God . . . do Jesus . . . O God . . . glory, glory, glory . . . give me more . . . more . . . glory, glory, glory"; falling over backward with hands outstretched, her whole body quivering and rhythmically jerking, she collapses at last in a dull heap on the floor, and stays there in comatose condition for several minutes. Others rise and shout at the top of their lungs for five minutes, or bang on something in staccato rhythm. The same persons respond again and again, with perhaps seventy-five individuals represented. Each responds with an individual pattern of motions, but all motions revolve around a few general types. The motions appear to have been culturally conditioned, whether immediately conditioned by the agent or not. One wonders if some form of mass hypnotism is at work.

About ten o'clock the pastor calls for sinners to come to the front and kneel around the altar (constructed of a bench quickly placed before the pulpit). About ten come, including one five-year-old boy. A hundred members of the congregation gather about, and a tremendous tumult ensues as they attempt to "pray and shout the sinners through," interspersed with wild demonstrations of joy as one is "saved."

It is nearly 11 P.M., but one stays and wonders. They cry out, and cry; they are drunken, but not with wine; they stagger, but not with strong drink. . . .

Solidaristic-volatile-acting. The chief difference between the soldaristic-volatile-acting crowd and the individualistic-volatile-acting type is found in the inter-relationships of the members. The mob in the Detroit race riot of 1943, as a solidaristic-volatile-acting crowd, contrasts with the looters and vandals of the Harlem riot described above. The crowd objective—the slaughter of members of the racial outgroup—was a group objective in Detroit. In Harlem, the mob seems to have been a congeries of individuals and small groups pursuing, often in a competitive fashion, individual but highly similar objectives. The Detroit mob was characterized by subcrowds intent on harming specific members of a general class of objects. Eyewitness accounts indicate that there was a division of labor, rather than competitiveness, within these groups, and that at times subcrowds would merge.

Solidaristic-focused-acting. The term "the mob," in popular usage, usually has as its referent the *solidaristic-focused-acting* type of crowd. Although lynchings rarely occur now, the old style lynching mob is an excellent example of this crowd subtype. Here is a crowd which is concerned with a specific object; any other objects are substitutes of lesser value. This highly preferred object is a group objective, defined in the interaction of the crowd. The sorts of action towards it which are deemed appropriate or inappropriate are group-defined, and the individual participant is strongly constrained to accept these definitions. Finally, there tends to be a division of labor among the participants in the crowd, as will be seen in the discussion of interaction in the crowd.

Other dimensions of crowds. Crowds do not readily lend themselves to classification into neat types and subtypes. Each dimension which has been proposed constitutes a continuum rather than a dichotomy of contrasting categories. There is a continuum from the *expressive* to the active crowd, so there may be behaviors which combine some of the elements of both. Elements of the *solidaristic* and the *individualistic* may be mixed and, indeed, a crowd may well be in a situation in which there is doubt as to whether it will move in the individualistic or the solidaristic direction. Finally, there are varying degrees of volatility. Some crowds accept as their objectives an extremely wide category of objects, while others accept a narrower, but still general, category of objects. Very few crowds are so narrowly focused as not to direct the same sentiments they feel regarding the principal object of attention toward objects which are symbolically connected with it in a fairly clear manner.

Crowds in which the participants are all in close and continuous physical contact, within a relatively small area, may be classified as *compact*. The discussion of crowds to this point has been concerned largely with this type. A *diffuse* crowd, in contrast, behaves in what is essentially a crowd manner although the members are disposed over a large area, with much of the interaction being indirect. An example is the widely scattered collectivity which, in a short span

of time, follows a fad such as swallowing goldfish or joining "Pyramid Clubs."
Diffuse crowd types will be discussed at greater length in a later chapter.

Crowds may also be *spontaneous, conventional,* or *manipulated.* The *spontaneous* crowd acts primarily in terms of norms emerging in a novel, unanticipated
situation. The *conventional* crowd is characterized by the communication, the
heightened suggestibility, the sense of urgency, and the permissiveness of other
crowd types. Conventional crowd behavior occurs, however, in a situation which
is anticipated or even planned, as in a religious service or a festival. There is,
moreover, a certain amount of standardization of the behavior of the individual
participants, based on past experience in similar situations. The conventional
crowd and the conventionalization of collective behavior will be subjected to
more intensive analysis in Chapter 8.

Finally, the *manipulated* crowd may have, as far as the majority of the participants are concerned, as much spontaneity as the *spontaneous* crowd. Yet certain
crowd leaders may have deliberately manipulated the situation in such a way as
to produce not only the circumstances conducive to crowd behavior but also the
mood and the imagery which the members of a crowd must share.

Chapter 6

Interaction in the crowd

ONE OF the salient characteristics of crowd behavior is the appearance of unanimity that it creates. To the casual observer, the numerous members of a crowd may appear to act in an identical fashion, dominated by a common impulse. So strong is this illusion of unanimity that it is easy to speak of the crowd in the singular, as if it were a real being—"the crowd roars," "the angry mob surges forward." Countless laymen who have never heard of Gustav LeBon and "the mental unity of crowds" speak glibly of "the mob mind" and "mob psychology." Similarly, theories of crowd behavior formulated by sociologists and psychologists have resulted in a picture of a homogeneous mass of individuals, all thinking, feeling, and acting alike.

Yet another widespread conception of the characteristics of the crowd is the notion that crowd members are almost always individuals of low social status, with little education, and personally insecure and unstable. While specific exceptions, particularly in crowd leaders, are often noted, the stereotype of the crowd as an undifferentiated "rabble" of poorly educated, low-status, highly suggestible individuals, persists.

Existing formulations of crowd behavior seem, then, to present a picture of a mass of people who are, in one way or another, identical. At the one extreme is the popular stereotype of the crowd as composed of people who are identical in social position, in motives, and in behavior. Approaching most closely the usual, empirical crowd phenomena is a conception of a collection of individuals who may be heterogeneous in many ways, particularly in initial motivation, but who go through an identical process as crowd action develops.

A theory of crowd interaction. A theory may be formulated, however, which does not focus upon the uniformity of the crowd members in motives, attitudes and behavior. It emphasizes, instead, interaction between participants who may

102

be, at various stages of the development of crowd action, feeling, thinking, and acting quite differently, yet contributing to the development of a common line of action.

Such a theory seems to be more faithful to the complexity of real crowd phenomena than are theories that require the fitting of many individuals and their behavior into one preconceived scheme of motivation. This is particularly important in view of the fact that existing characterizations of crowd members and their motives are based on knowledge secured from only a minority of the members of any one crowd. The most that can be attempted at the present stage of development of the field of collective behavior is the formulation of a typology of crowd participants, no generalizations as to the relative frequency of the various types being undertaken.

As will be seen in the descriptions of crowd behavior that follow, people may come to a crowd, even to the most violent mob, with quite different initial motives and interests. During the course of the crowd's activity different participants may behave in different ways. It appears that the unity of the crowd is often produced through the interaction of participants who are actually behaving in different fashions, and on the basis of different motivations. Hence we will examine, first, some of the types of motives that may bring people into the crowd, along with some of the other characteristics in which crowd participants may vary. Then we will consider different types of behavior that may take place within the crowd and the interaction among these various activities.

Crowd participants: some types of motives. The type of crowd participant who most readily comes to mind is the person who is motivated primarily by the sense that some sort of action is demanded. A crowd arises because of some incident which is outside the normal pattern of expectations, what Blumer has called "the exciting event." There are some people who are incensed, or frightened, or perhaps elated, over the particular incident that sets off the crowd. This type of person may not have, initially, a clear picture of what should be done. If he does visualize some line of action, he may not see how he alone can carry it out. But his feelings about the situation go beyond mere curiosity or vague concern. The incident causes him to define the situation as demanding immediate action. In some crowd situations, it is likely that the majority of the crowd participants have this feeling initially. It is evident, however, that this feeling need not be shared by all crowd members.

The motives of a second group of participants are more difficult to describe. It cannot be assumed that everyone who is concerned about an incident feels that some immediate action is necessary. Some people who share the concern of the "something should be done" type of participant may still feel that action should be left up to established functionaries of the group and that some action which is appropriate to the situation, and yet congruent with the norms of the group, should be found. Yet once crowd action has started, the orientation of these people is such that they feel that the issue must be made to go in one direction—that the side with which they identify themselves must win.

Ordinary group loyalty contributes to this sort of attitude. When an individual's group is committed to action in one direction, particularly against an outgroup, he often feels that he must support his group even if it is wrong in this particular case. Such an attitude is reflected in the traditional slogan, "My country, right or wrong." During the Los Angeles "zoot-suit" riots many sailors at the San Diego naval station had no particular anti-Mexican attitudes and didn't know what the fights were all about. They had the feeling, however, that "If a sailor and a Mexican get in a fight, what do you do? If you're a sailor, you help the other sailor!"

Some people seem to be brought into the crowd by yet a third type of motivation. These are people who derive direct satisfaction from participation in a crowd, regardless of the circumstances. It doesn't matter to them what the issue is—they get certain gratifications out of participating in the crowd itself. It is frequently observed, for instance, that adolescents make up a disproportionate element of those people who are in the active core of a crowd. Studies of "youth culture" in the United States suggest that in our society many such young people would derive gratification from any activity which represents rebellion against the ordinary controls of society.

Humphrey and Lee, in their analysis of the 1943 Detroit race riot, noted the extensive participation of adolescents in the rioting. As the following selection shows, some of these young people seem to have participated for the sheer thrill that participation gave.

AN INCIDENT FROM THE DETROIT RACE RIOT
ALFRED M. LEE AND NORMAN D. HUMPHREY

Four white youths, aged 16 to 20 years, without provocation, shot down one Moses Kiska, a 58-year-old Negro, "just for the Hell of it." Kiska was merely waiting for a streetcar at Mack Avenue and Chene Street. As John McManis wrote in the Detroit News a month later, "Sociologists may be able to give it a name, but the layman never will understand how four ordinary boys could go out and . . . shoot down innocent people." One of the boys told their story thus:

> We didn't have anything to do. We were just bumming around. Bob . . . and Blackie . . . were in the pool room. We wanted to see the fighting

From Alfred M. Lee and Norman D. Humphrey, **Race Riot** (New York: The Dryden Press, Inc., 1943), pp. 37–38. Reprinted by special permission.

but we didn't want to go where we would get hurt.

We had my gun along. It was my car. Aldo was driving. Someone—I don't know who—said: "Let's go out and kill us a nigger." We agreed that it was a good idea.

We drove around for a long time. We saw a lot of colored people, but they were in bunches. We didn't want any of that. We wanted some guy all by himself. We saw one on Mack Avenue.

Aldo drove past him and then said, "Gimme that gun." I handed it over to him and he turned around and came back. We were about 15 feet from the man when Aldo pulled up, almost stopped and shot. The man fell and we blew.

We didn't know him. He wasn't bothering us. But other people were fighting and killing and we felt like it, too.

The participation of persons of generally insecure status may also be explained under this type of motivation. Sometimes insecurity, or frustration resulting from insecurity, is treated as a basic universal motive underlying the actions of all the members of a crowd. Thus Cantril, in discussing lynching as a "solution" to the problem of defense of status, seems to combine under the same category those people who participate in the mob primarily because of this sort of gratification and those who are provoked to action primarily because of the particular incident.

A little-known but very detailed and objective study of lynchings is the pamphlet, *Lynchings and What They Mean,* published by the Southern Commission on the Study of Lynching. The authors of this report pointed out very specifically the gratification afforded insecure elements in a lynching. At the same time, they cautioned against the conclusion that it was only such types who had a part in the lynchings; saying, "It would be erroneous, however, to leave the impression that all the lynchers were of the shiftless, irresponsible, propertyless type. . . . Generally speaking, the more backward a community was, the more likely were the 'best people' to participate in the actual lynching." *

Two features of crowd behavior may be particularly appealing to the person of insecure status. In the first place, there is a terrific sense of power in the crowd. The individual in the crowd has a sense of unanimity. The crowd seems all-powerful. Hence the individual who, in his day-to-day existence, is finding things he is trying to do constantly blocked by his superiors and by other people, finds himself in a situation in which there is no obstacle. He personally partakes of this sense of power.

The other element is that of the "righteousness" of the crowd. William Graham Sumner long ago pointed out the social origin of our conventional ideas of right and wrong, of the mores. The norms of our identification groups become our own standards of right and wrong. Our idea that something is morally incontestable is essentially a conversion of our experience that nobody in the groups that mean anything to us, nobody whose opinion we consider worth listening to, contradicts this idea. The sense of absolute righteousness of an idea is derived from the unanimity with which the idea seems to be held.

In a crowd situation, however, the range of attention of the individual is narrowed. In the extreme case, the individual's orientation is determined solely in terms of the present members of the crowd. The influence of his usual identification groups and their norms is attenuated, and the individual's sense of moral rightness is determined by the compelling presence of other crowd members. The appearance of unanimity in the crowd, even though it may be illusory, gives the same kind of basis for believing that the position of the crowd is morally incontestable that the individual gets from groups with which he identifies outside the crowd situation.

A fourth category of people who have often been noted in crowds, participating in various ways, is the group of spectators. They must be regarded as part of the crowd even though they may be relatively inactive. The gathering of a crowd in the vicinity of the precipitating event, if not the incident itself, draws more crowd members who are motivated chiefly by curiosity. They may be quite unaware of the nature of the occurrence that has created the crowd situation, or they may be quite disinterested in the outcome of the crowd process. Such spectators, motivated initially by curiosity, may be absorbed into the more active core of the crowd by social contagion, however.

A personal, introspective account of the absorption of a curious spectator into

* Southern Commission on the Study of Lynching, **Lynchings and What They Mean** (Atlanta: 1931).

the activity of the crowd is found in a report written by a professor in the Sorbonne who was a spectator-participant in the Paris riots of the early 'thirties. Coming to the crowd with no inclination to engage in overt action in line with his political convictions, his initial curiosity changed to identification with the crowd as he watched the brutal actions of the police. Suddenly he found himself charging the firemen, grabbing a hose away from one of them, and becoming not only a participant but a spearhead of the crowd activity.

THE PARIS RIOTS
THE STORY OF AN EYEWITNESS

I shall try in what follows to report the point of view of the ordinary Frenchman —still more, of the ordinary Parisian— as regards the appalling massacre of quiet and ordinary citizens in the streets of our Paris on Tuesday, February 6th. The accounts of that event which I have read in the English and foreign newspapers seem to me singularly misleading, and what the foreigner should understand is that the Sixth of February saw not a revolt of the lowest elements of the Parisian population against the Chamber of Deputies, but the revolt of the Chamber of Deputies against the will of the highest elements of the people of Paris.

The demonstrators of February Sixth who marched down the boulevards were composed not merely of the Anciens Combattants, of the Croix de Feux, veterans who have received three decorations for gallantry on the field; not only of the Camelots du Roi, who are Royalists; of the Jeunesses Patriots, who are the Republican youth; or of the League des Contribuables, who represent the principal taxpayers of Paris; but one of the immense columns that massed against the parliament buildings was headed by a deputation of the Municipal Council. It is a little difficult for the foreigner to understand the particular reverence with which the Conseil Municipal is regarded by Parisians. This body has the tradition not only of having brought about and

stabilized the first French Revolution, but also of continually safeguarding the liberties and fortunes of the citizens of Paris. The real note of the Sixth of February was given in the reply of one of the Councillors to M. Frot, Minister of the Interior and responsible for the police, in the Chamber of Deputies. The column headed by the deputation of Municipal Councillors had marched from the Hotel de Ville toward the Palais Bourbon. It had been met, attacked, and broken up by M. Frot's police, three of the councillors being wounded. In spite of that, two councillors succeeded in entering the Chamber, where they were met by M. Frot and reproached for having come. M. Frot then asked the councillors, to the sound of rifle and gunfire that was going on round the Chamber, what they proposed that he should do. One of the councillors replied, "If you will authorize me to go to the Place de la Concorde and announce that you and the Daladier Ministry have resigned, I will undertake that the crowd will disperse at once, quietly and without disorder, and that within twenty minutes there will be no sign of rioting in the whole of Paris."

This attitude—and remember that it was the official attitude of the Municipal Council—is sufficient evidence of what was actually the position of M. Daladier, M. Frot, and their associates. They were the leaders of a Fascist attempt by the Radical-Socialist party of the Chamber to secure for that party a dictatorship in the face of the will of the people—to secure it with gunfire and with charges of cavalry armed with sabers, upon an orderly crowd which as I say had given no offense until, without warning, those instruments of death were launched upon them by apprentice Hitlers and Mussolinis. And I remember a friend of mine saying, "While the Government is winning votes of confidence from the Deputies in the Chamber, it is defeating itself, and being defeated by the people of Paris in the streets."

I may as well state, before recounting what I myself witnessed, that I have no political associations, that I belong to none of the parties that organized the demonstrations, and that I was present in the Place de la Concorde as a simple spectator until the brutality of the drunken Garde Mobile so aroused my indignation that I did take part with the demonstrators. This, I think, was the attitude of the great bulk of the people present in the Place de la Concorde and in the other quarters where there was trouble. Police estimated that demonstrators numbered twenty thousand in the Place de la Concorde, the Place de la Hotel de Ville and on the neighboring boulevards, and they estimated the sympathetic crowd at eight hundred thousand, many of whom, like myself, eventually took part with the demonstrators.

I should tell you too that the taxi strike which had started a few days earlier was completely effective. Without the usual speeding cabs, the streets of Paris were practically bare of wheeled traffic. The quiet of the streets struck one as unnatural and sinister.

You are to imagine, then, the wide spread of the Place de la Concorde at 6:15 of a winter's evening. The spotlights blazed up and revealed the pale obelisk of Cleopatra's Needle and the fountains spouting round it. All over the Place were black knots of police, and people going about their affairs. Though there were no taxis, occasional omnibuses and private cars still passed through the Place. Behind the railings of the Tuileries Garden that look down on the Place de la Concorde you could see the white faces of the great crowd of impartial spectators who had come to see the fun. For the Place

de la Concorde, at the end of the bridge that leads to the Chamber of Deputies, was the converging point of the various demonstrating groups. You are to remember also that while we gathered round that Place de la Concorde, we knew the Chamber was in session to meet and decide the fate of the new Daladier Cabinet, against whom public feeling had risen to the breaking point.

On the balconies of the Hotel Crillon, in the windows above the Guaranty Trust and the Admiralty, other spectators were packed, but as yet there were no signs of a demonstration. I, myself, was standing on the base of one of the statues in the southeast corner of the Place. There was a good deal of talking, but no sign of disorder, except for occasional cries of *"démission,"*—"resign"—intended for the occupants of the Palais Bourbon meeting across the bridge.

Just before 6:30 I saw the head of a crowd shouting *"démission"* debouch, black, between the buildings of the Guaranty Trust and the Admiralty. At the same time, a smaller crowd had formed in the rue de Rivoli, and from them the notes of the Marseillaise blew across the square. At once, and without warning, the Garde Mobile—the mounted police with their brass helmets and horsehair plumes—executed charges against the people in the rue Royale and the rue de Rivoli. They used their sabers without mercy on the defenseless people and they functioned to the sound of screams from spectators behind the railings in the Tuileries Garden, horrified at this wanton display of naked steel.

The demonstrators in the rue de Rivoli were driven back. I could not, of course, see how far, but I have heard that after this first charge, wounded people were picked up streaming with blood from saber cuts as far back as the statue of Joan of Arc at the other end of the Tuileries Garden. I saw several horses go down with their horsemen, and later saw them being carried away in the direction of the Palais Bourbon. These falls were caused by the horses stepping on billiard balls and bowling balls which demonstrators had rolled in great quantities across the Place. Immediately after this first cavalry charge, which had completely failed to force back the massed crowd that blocked the opening of the rue Royale, I saw an autobus topple over into the roadway and catch fire. This was done to afford the demonstrators shelter from further police charges. Until then the demonstrators had remained comparatively calm, and I had the impression that the police who surrounded the monument on which I was standing—the real police, not the Garde Mobile—were not very angry. Shortly after 6:30, the demonstrators, who had pulled up the paving stones, awaited a charge of the police; and when their batons came into play, the crowd hurled their paving blocks at the Garde Mobile behind the police.

Toward seven o'clock, however, both police and Garde Mobile withdrew to the opening of the Pont de la Concorde, which is on the other side of the Place from the Hotel Crillon and the Admiralty. The crowd—to the number of at least sixty thousand—streamed into the Place de la Concorde, opening out into a fan until the leaders were up against the police and troops stationed on the bridge itself. This withdrawal of the police was incomprehensible and one can only say criminal. They were not forced back by the demonstrators; the only action of the public had been the hurling of a few paving blocks, which seemed to wound no one. I, at least, saw no policeman or gendarmes fall out at that time, and the forces of the authorities marched back in perfectly good order.

The crowd in the Place now became enormous, fresh streams pouring in from every one of the main and side streets that enter the Place. For—and this is equally incomprehensible—the police had entirely neglected to block any of the entrances to the open Place or even to station any bodies of men along either the Champs-Elysées, the Avenue Gabriel, or the Cours la Reine. Thus the entire Place was filled with people wedged in and being constantly pressed forward by the crowds that came in behind them.

Into these wedged crowds the Garde Mobile charged, sabering, half a dozen times between 7:15 and 7:25. Before the first of these charges I heard one single bugle call, which might have been intended as the equivalent of what is called in English "reading the riot act," but which was perfectly useless if it was intended really as a warning, since no call of the sort had ever sounded in the streets of Paris for sixty years, and Parisians were utterly unacquainted with its meaning.

Interspersed with the singing of the Marseillaise and the cries of *"démission,"* there were now shouts of *"assassins";* in the open spaces where the crowds were swirling temporarily away, there were now wounded lying on the pavement. The police had made a barricade across the entry to the bridge with trolleys and police wagons. The lights playing on Cleopatra's Needle and the facades of the houses now went out, but the gas lamps were still alight and two autobuses blazed; then there shot up flames from the orifices where lamp-standards had been torn down. All these flaring lights and the shouts, screams, and clattering of horses' hooves as the Garde Mobile incessantly charged, gave the impression of a witches' sabbath. A new sound was to be added to the sinister tumult.

Suddenly—it was just 7:45—great sprays of water like white fountains began to play from the dark masses of police on to the heads of the crowd. They had brought firemen into play.

I have spared you my emotions. But I will here record that at this point I found myself running at the head of a contingent of the crowd, straight on the firemen. The fire-hose is a poor weapon. You dread it till you are wet, but once you are wet you do not mind it. A fireman surrendered his hose into my hand, phlegmatically, as if he had been giving up a hay fork or any other tool. I turned the hose upon the police; another man helped me to hold and direct it. The sound of the hose so near drowned other sounds. But one sound is unmistakable—the sound of a rifle bullet droning beside your ear. The last time we had heard it it had not been Frenchmen who had caused that familiar noise.

The man beside me fell to the ground; I directed the hose as well as I could myself. Then the water ceased and I heard the sound of the fusillade. Afraid of being wetted, the police and Garde Mobile were firing at us from the other side of the roadway that goes over the bridge, that is to say, from the Cours la Reine side; we were on the Tuileries side, in darkness. They were at a distance of about thirty meters. They had cut the firehose; my efforts were, therefore, now useless, and I understood that we were being fired on from thirty meters away by trained men using revolvers and rifles. Another man fell, throwing his arms to the sky with the familiar gesture that we had seen on the Somme. The man on the ground was dead beside me; at any rate he did not move then or so long as I was there.

I had not come there to be a hero. I sprang into one of the police wagons— long automobiles holding forty men—that had drawn up across the roadway, and there cowering down so as to have the shelter of the side, I watched from the darkness the rest of those fantastic and atrocious proceedings that were illuminated by the great jets of flame from the broken gas-standards. With that illumination the images of the cities of France sat on their high thrones, tranquil and white, round that great square. I did not know what to think when my eyes fell on the statue of Strasbourg. To the sound of what I was then hearing we had rescued Strasbourg for France: now Frenchmen were turning that sound against us. What was the moral? I don't know. Before the war that statue was always decorated with wreaths of immortelles—to show that France mourned for her lost city. They had better put some more immortelles round the base of that quiet statue, to show that France mourns some more.

Those heroes killed with a rifle bullet a chambermaid standing in the window of the Hotel Crillon!

The police fired with revolvers and rifles, with what we called *"mousquetons"* —carbines, I think. They fired steadily into the crowd. I could see them just below me. It is said that they also used machine guns. I did not see any myself. That fusillade in the night went on uninterruptedly, except at the moments when the Garde Mobile were sabering the crowd, from 7:45 till ten minutes past eight.

By that time the greater part of the Place had been emptied. I slipped down from my police car and ran along under the wall of the Tuileries Garden to the rue de Rivoli, which was also nearly empty. I helped to pick up and put into a private car a young girl—of perhaps twenty—elegantly dressed but insensible. The side of her cheek, from near the right eye to the jaw bone, had been cut away by a saber. To encourage, presumably, the future mothers of France!

I supported as far as the Café Weber an almost unconscious *ancien combattant*. He had lost a leg on the Somme. Now he had lost an ear—by saber cut from an intoxicated protector of the peace of the country.

The rue Royale was then dark except for three or four flares, and we staggered along fairly deserted sidewalks. There were no ambulances and no sort of assistance for the wounded. Several men were still lying in the gutters. There was very little sound of anything—some groans.

The Café Weber was gay—with new decorations of white and red—the white of lint and tables that had become operating tables and the carmine of blood. They had turned it into a first-aid field-dressing station—a dug-out, I think you call it. There were some dead there too.

The rest of the city was quiet; the streets rather empty as I went homewards. That was all I saw. There was more slaughter later; I preferred to see it only in imagination.

I will make the note that the police surgeons who attended to the wounded policemen and Gardes Mobiles gave evidence to the parliamentary committee which is inquiring into these incidents that none of their wounds had been caused by bullets or cutting instruments

—this proving that the crowd had come unarmed. The same witnesses gave evidence that all the wounded Gardes Mobiles—not the police—were drunk, the inference being that they had been supplied with drink by M. Frot or some other person in authority over the police. In order to give them courage to use their sabers! I find it difficult to imagine the man who will contemplate letting loose on an unarmed, singing crowd squadron after squadron of drunken cavalrymen armed with sabers. He must want to be a Hitler very badly.

In addition, the police gave evidence that not one of the hundreds of prisoners they made that night carried any weapon of any sort.

A fifth, and very important, type· of crowd participant is the person whose inhibitions are already down before crowd action develops. Crowd behavior always represents, to some extent, a deviation from the ordinary social norms. The development of crowd action is facilitated by the presence of individuals who, for one reason or another, are relatively free from inhibitions. Drunks, psychopaths, and petty criminals are frequently found in crowds and may contribute to the development of crowd behavior.

It is not suggested that such people create the crowd, or crowd behavior. They do not create the incident that gives rise to the crowd situation, and they may not even be present when the incident occurs and the crowd assembles. Nor would their irresponsible actions set off crowd behavior if the other crowd members were not present. They do serve, however, as facilitating agents, furnishing models of deviant behavior for the more inhibited members of the crowd.

In the Chicago race riots, juvenile gangs played a significant part, even being credited with the primary responsibility for prolonging the riots beyond the first clash at the waterfront. The members of these gangs or "athletic clubs" were already accustomed to public disorder and fighting, as part of their normal activities. Of even more significance is the evidence that they felt a good deal of impunity because of their political "pull."

GANGS AND "ATHLETIC CLUBS" IN THE CHICAGO RIOT

Gangs and their activities were an important factor throughout the riot. But for them it is doubtful if the riot would have gone beyond the first clash. Both organized gangs and those which sprang into existence because of the opportunity afforded seized upon the excuse of the first conflict to engage in lawless acts.

It was no new thing for youthful white and Negro groups to come to violence. For years, as the sections of this report dealing with antecedent clashes and with

Reprinted by permission of the University of Chicago Press, from The Chicago Commission on Race Relations, **The Negro in Chicago** (Chicago: University of Chicago Press, 1922), pp. 11–13.

recreation show, there had been clashes over baseball grounds, swimming-pools in the parks, the right to walk on certain streets, etc.

Gangs whose activities figured so prominently in the riot were all white gangs, or "athletic clubs." Negro hoodlums do not appear to form organized gangs so readily. Judges of the municipal court said that there are no gang organizations among Negroes to compare with those found among young whites.

The Stock Yards district, just west of the main Negro area, is the home of many of these white gangs and clubs; it is designated as District III in the discussion of the riot growth. The state's attorney, as already indicated, referred to the many young offenders who come from this particular district. A police detective sergeant who investigated the riot cases in this district said, "It is a pretty tough neighborhood to try to get any information out there; you can't do it." A policeman on the beat in the district said, "There is the Canaryville bunch in there and the Hamburg bunch. It is a pretty tough hole in there."

There was much evidence and talk of the political "pull" and even leadership of these gangs with reference to their activities in the riot. A member of "Ragen's Colts" just after the riot passed the word that the "coppers" from downtown were looking for club members, but that "there need be no fear of the coppers from the station at the Yards for they were all fixed and told to lay off on club members." During the riot he claimed they were well protected by always having a "cop" ride in one of the automobiles so everything would be "O.K." in case members of the gang were picked up. Another member of the club said he had been "tipped off by the police at the Yards to clean out and keep away from the usual hangouts because investigators were working out of Hoyne's and out of Brundage's offices, and were checking up on the activities of the 'Ragen's' during the riot."

The foreman of the August grand jury which investigated the riot cases said in testifying before the Commission:

> The lead we got to investigate the Forty-seventh Street district was from an anonymous letter stating that Ragen had such influence in the Forty-seventh Street police station that these individuals were allowed to go without due process of law.
>
> I didn't believe that was a fact in this particular instance. We did learn that Ragen was a great power in that district and at the time of our investigation we learned that some of the "Ragen's Colts" had broken into the police station and pried open a door of a closet where they had a good deal of evidence in the nature of weapons of prisoners concealed, and they got all of

this evidence out of there without the police knowing anything about it.

The station referred to is at Forty-seventh and Halstead streets. Gangs operated for hours up and down Forty-seventh, Wells, Princeton, Shields, and Wentworth avenues and Federal Street without hindrance from the police.

A judge of the municipal court said in testimony before the Commission: "They seemed to think they had a sort of protection which entitled them to go out and assault anybody. When the race riots occurred it gave them something to satiate the desire to inflict their evil propensities on others."

Besides shouting as they rode down the streets in trucks that they were out to "get the niggers," they defied the law in other ways. When the militia men came on the scene on the fourth day of the riot, they testified to trouble with these gangsters. One of the colonels testified before the Commission: "They didn't like to be controlled. They would load up heavy trucks with rowdies and try to force through the lines. They'd come tooting their horns and having back pressure explosions like gatling guns."

Some of the "athletic club" gangsters had criminal records. L- W- was accused of being one of the leaders of the gang around Forty-seventh and Wells streets. He himself said boastfully, "I have been arrested about fifteen times for 'disorderly' and never was arrested with a knife or a gun." Several witnesses said they had seen him during the riot one night leading the mob and brandishing a razor and the next night waving a gun. He was not arrested. D- H-, seventeen years old, was identified as being active in the rioting near Forty-seventh Street and Forrestville Avenue. His defense was that he was not closer to the Negro assaulted than across the street, but because he was arrested the year before for a "stick-up" people looked "funny" at him when anything happened. R- C- was accused of having been implicated in the arson cases on Shields Avenue. When his mother was interviewed, she said she knew nothing of the rioting, but said her son was at the time in the county jail, "but not for that." W- G- was identified many times as having taken part in the arson on Wentworth Avenue. He was indicted for both arson and conspiracy to riot. Two years before the riot he had been arrested for larceny.

Also to be included in this category are the deliberate instigators who sometimes play a significant role in facilitating crowd action. These are people who deliberately, in a coldly calculating manner, manipulate the crowd to accomplish their own purposes. While they may give the appearance of acting spontaneously, pretending to be "carried away" by the crowd mood, they know very well what they are doing and are acting according to some preconceived plan. Biblical prototypes of the crowd instigator are found in the chief priests and elders of Jerusalem who "persuaded the people to ask for Barabbas and destroy Jesus" (Matthew 27:20).

Differential participation in the crowd. The identification of elements in the crowd which differ in their motives, in the clarity of their attitudes towards the incident, and in degree of inhibition, suggests that there may also be differential participation in the crowd. This hypothesis stands in contrast to the notion that unified crowd action develops through circular reaction, through everyone's participating in the same way. In rare instances crowd members, initially very similar in motivation, may go through identically the same process. It seems that more frequently the crowd is initially heterogeneous in composition, and that most crowds remain quite heterogeneous during a large part of their existence. This conception of the nature of the crowd is consistent with the view that the unified character of crowd behavior is the result of interaction between elements which are participating on a different basis and in a different manner. As the crowd endures and emotions become increasingly intense, the motives of the various members become relatively homogeneous and their actions become more nearly alike. But it is proposed that this uniformity develops in the later stages of crowd behavior, as a result of the interaction of elements of the crowd which are behaving quite differently, and not as the result of a mere intensification of identical behavior.

Shifts of leadership. An oversimplification of this interactional process is to portray it as consisting of interaction between "leaders" and "followers," between those who offer suggestions for action and those who respond to the suggestions. It can be shown, however, that in the development of crowd behavior leadership may shift from one element in the crowd to another, and that those who are crowd leaders at any one time not only affect, but are affected by, other elements.

In the early stages of crowd development, those people who are incensed by the exciting event, feel that it demands action, and have some notion as to what sort of action should be taken, are most likely to be the ones who stir up the crowd, define the objective and propose a course of action. But, while the initial leaders may propose action, they cannot be sure of controlling the responses of the other elements. How the leadership of the crowd may change can be seen in the description below of a case of mob action. In this case the original crowd leaders lost control to other individuals who were ready to go far beyond the objectives originally intended, and who denounced the original leaders for opposing them.

ANTI-COMMUNIST MOB ACTION: A CASE STUDY
ROBERT C. MYERS

On Sunday evening, October 26, 1947, Gerhard Eisler, an acknowledged Communist of German nationality, was scheduled to address a public meeting under the auspices of the Communist Party of Mercer County, New Jersey, in a rented hall at Trenton. On the Sunday morning of the meeting, the residents awoke to find these page one headlines in their only Sunday newspaper:

COURT ORDERS HALL OPENED TO EISLER;
INJUNCTION ISSUED

Accompanying the two-column lead article which followed was a five by six inch photograph of the mayor being served with his copy of the restraining order by an attorney accompanied by a reporter. The photograph carried this legend:

With a look of scorn, Mayor Donald J. Connolly accepts from Solomon Golat a Chancery Court order restraining the City Commission, Police Department and the Contemporary from interfering with the Communist Party meeting at which Gerhard Eisler will speak tonight. John F. Norman, a *Daily Worker* reporter, stands at the right. Golat secured the injunction from Vice Chancellor John O. Bigelow on behalf of Manuel Cantor and the Communist Party of Mercer County.

The article explained that the Vice Chancellor in Newark had acted "after the Civil Rights Congress of New Jersey appealed to him to 'defend the civil rights of the Communist Party of Mercer County.'" It recounted the main events leading up to the securing of the injunction, and then quoted the mayor, upon receiving his copy, as saying, "It will be a pleasure to throw you and your kind

Reprinted in part by permission of the author and the editors of **Public Opinion Quarterly,** from Robert C. Myers, "Anti-Communist Mob Action: A Case Study," **Public Opinion Quarterly,** 12 (1948), pp. 57-67.

out of the City Hall any time." However, further on, the mayor was also quoted as saying, "The court has spoken and the law must be upheld. All the police facilities necessary to preserve good order will be available."

Other interesting information revealed by the article was the time (8 p.m.) and place of the scheduled Communist meeting, an announcement that veterans would group on the State House steps (across the street from the Contemporary Auditorium) at 6:15 p.m. to "plan a program against Eisler and the supporters of his Communist philosophy."

Very few people work on Sunday in Trenton, and the story about the battle between the "Commies" on one side and the mayor, the police, and the "vets" on the other was the talk of the town. There was general agreement that "something ought to be done."

AGITATION

Shortly before 6 p.m. groups of veterans, some wearing the distinctive campaign hats of their organizations, began arriving in front of the capitol buildings in response to calls from leaders of the Veterans' Alliance, representing eleven veterans' organizations in Trenton. Soon thereafter a relatively passive crowd of three or four hundred veterans had assembled, and was being addressed by several leaders of the Alliance. This original crowd, or audience, of veterans included representatives of a colored American Legion post, Catholic War Veterans, Jewish War Veterans, and Disabled War Veterans, as well as other veterans' organizations. The leaders began to shout their directions and appeals, and their lecturings quickly assumed the character of harangues.

The gist of the leaders' appeals was that the Communists were standing on the Bill of Rights, but that the veterans would see to it that the rights of patriotic Americans were upheld and not jeopardized by the Communists.

The substance of the leaders' directions and calls for action was that an endless picket line was to be formed in front of the alleyway leading to the auditorium entrance. When the doors were opened, the veterans would thus be first to gain entrance and seize most of the seats in the hall for themselves. Thereafter, they were directed to boo and hiss everything that the Communist leader Eisler, or his followers had to say. By this method, they reasoned, freedom of speech for both Communists and others would be upheld, but Communist doctrines would receive neither applause nor encouragement.

The harangues of the leaders, when referring to their own purposes, were interspersed with such symbolic references as: "The Constitution," "The Bill of Rights," "our way of life," "what we stand for," "Democracy," "what we fought for," "red-blooded Americans," and "The American Way." However, when the Communists and their purposes were being mentioned, the following symbolisms were most often heard: "Commies," "rats," "bastards," "sons of bitches," "Stalin-lovers," "dirt," and these were frequently modified by such words as "lousy" and "stinking." The only purposes ascribed to the Communists were to destroy the American way of life and turn the country over to Russia.

In effect, then, it was hammered home to the crowd over and over again that it was perfectly legal, correct, and necessary for "stinking lousy rats" to have freedom of speech, but that this right could be countered in "the American way" by giving full rein to the freedom of speech of "patriotic red-blooded Americans."

The original crowd of veterans was soon joined by 35 uniformed policemen under the direction of an acting captain of police and a deputy director of public safety. It was also augmented by the arrival of from three to four thousand residents of Trenton.

The auditorium doors were not opened until 8:30, so there was a period of two

and one-half hours for crowd growth, pushing, shoving, muttering, yelling, swirling, packing and all the other stimuli which facilitate the transmutation of a passive crowd into an active mob.

By 8 p.m. the area between the capitol buildings and the auditorium was black with gesticulating, muttering humanity. About one out of ten were females, and, except for the very young and the aged, all age groups seemed to be fairly represented. Laughter and shouts of hilarity were not infrequent, a festive spirit of revelry quite often running through the thousands of persons as their emotions began to take over from their intellects. In the vortex of the mob were the several hundred original veterans milling about the entrance to the alleyway.

ACTION

Shortly before 8 o'clock a man and his wife from Newark wormed their way through the mob and presented themselves at the alleyway demanding admission to the auditorium.

"Who the hell do you think you are?" the man was asked.

He announced that he was a representative of the Civil Rights Congress of New Jersey.

"To hell with you," he was told. "You'll get in when we let you in."

At this point the local press of October 27 states that the man "was overheard to make a remark about 'So this is American liberty.' The word spread through the crowd and (they) were 'rushed' up State Street. They were 'rescued' by State House police and finally escorted to police headquarters."

This account, however, fails to do justice to the circumstances. Actually, as soon as the stranger said, "so this is American liberty," he was struck in the face and mouth, his glasses knocked off and broken, and he was punched and kicked at. The cry went up, "Hey, fellas, here's a coupla Commies, let's get 'em!," and everyone within reach struck out at the terrified couple.

The mob had struck first blood and howled for more.

Three men arrived surrounded by police. They made up the "welcoming committee" and were to sit on the platform and introduce Eisler. They were herded by the police through the mob and into the auditorium. During this procedure the jostling and shouting reached fever pitch, and frequent cries were heard such as: "Rats like you will burn in hell," "Where's the rope, boys?," "You bastards won't get out alive," "Lousy Commies." Although two of the three Communists were of Jewish extraction, no racist appellations were shouted loud enough to be generally heard, but racist mutterings were apparent.

Tensions were built up for fifteen or twenty more minutes before the auditorium doors were finally opened. Two policemen were placed at the door where entrance tickets were sold at twenty-five cents apiece. Sixteen people are reported to have bought tickets before the shout went up, "Come on, boys, everybody in!" The mob surged forward to the accompanying sound of breaking window glass and screams of semi-hysterical females. Side doors and windows were thrown open and the hall, arranged to seat but 375 persons, was quickly filled to overflowing. Persons seated on window ledges shouted word of what was transpiring inside to those left to mill about outside.

Pandemonium was general inside the hall. The three Communist committeemen sat at a table on the stage; a colorguard of veterans surrounded a Large American flag planted in a standard nearby; twenty or more policemen ranged themselves between the stage and the riotous audience. The deputy director of public safety and the acting captain of police tried by sheer lung power alone (the hall had no public address system) to get some semblance of order, but to no avail. The principal speaker of the evening, Gerhard Eisler, did not appear, and it was later learned that the county secretary had managed to make a warning telephone call concerning the mob conditions that had arisen.

For over forty minutes various officials in the front of the auditorium, including the two police leaders and the leaders of the original veterans' groups, tried to get enough quiet so that the meeting at least could be opened officially, and thus the letter of the injunction obeyed. But each time any of the three acknowledged Communists on the stage arose to speak he was met with a crescendo of hoots, shouts, boos and stomping of feet. Some of the police-veteran pleas and shouted replies included the following:

Plea: (A leader of one of the original veterans' groups) "Listen to me, fellows, I'm one of the men that started this thing. Now we didn't intend to deny anyone free speech, but simply to boo what these rats said *after* they said it. So let's all be quiet for a minute, and let these rats talk."

Answer: "You're probably a damn Commie yourself. Why don't you get up there with them you goddamned Stalin-lover?" (At this sally the veteran leader blanched with the shock of the clear realization that a definite schism had taken place; that he and the other leaders had lost all control, and that other and perhaps more sinister leaders had taken over.)

Plea: "Men, that's certainly no way to talk to the commander of a respected (veteran's group) here in Trenton."

Answer: "Tell him to keep his mouth shut, then."

After every two or three pleas, hasty conferences took place between the police leaders and the three Communists on the stage. (There was no direct converse between the veteran leaders and the Communists.) It later was learned that the Communists were urging the police to call the whole thing off, but the police were insistent that attempts be continued to let the Communists be heard, if only for a very brief period, so that the police could report that the injunction had been obeyed.

During the forty minutes that this sort of thing had been going on there had been occasional attempts on the part of persons near the front to gain the stage. These had been gently pushed back by the police.

After the failure to gain even ten seconds of silence, the police and veteran leaders found themselves in agreement with the Communists that it would be impossible to comply with the injunction order. The press states that the reporter from the *Daily Worker* said, at this point, to the deputy director of public safety: "In the interest of their (the mob's) safety I give you permission to call off the meeting."

Plea: "The meeting's called off. Go on home."

Answer: "Come on, get the Commies to go first; we'll go after them."

The original group of veterans commenced singing "The Star Spangled Banner," and were joined in this by all in the hall, including those on the stage. Everybody stood and faced toward the flag during the singing.

Immediately upon conclusion of the national anthem cries arose: "Here they come, boys, get ready!" and the mob parted down the middle of the auditorium, making a gauntlet from stage to entrance door. Individuals along the gauntlet's sides spit upon their hands and rubbed them together. They made beckoning motions toward the stage, and shouted: "Come on you sons of bitches. We're ready for you."

Police on the stage stood in front and behind the three intended victims of the mob. It appeared as though an attempt would be made to run the mob's gauntlet. Suddenly the victims and their guardians turned on their heels and disappeared through the back exit of the stage.

For perhaps one or two seconds dead silence prevailed. Then, with a roar of rage, the mob surged up and over the stage, sweeping aside and, in one case, knocking to the floor the police left between mob and quarry. But the three Communists had escaped in a police car.

It may be postulated that such shifts of leadership at various stages of crowd development are a function of differential motivation. Those who are primarily motivated by concern over the precipitating event may be active in structuring the crowd's behavior in the early stages. Elements whose participation is based more on the satisfaction that they derive from crowd behavior, or whose inhibitions are already down for some reason, are likely to assume the leadership as crowd activity becomes more intense.

Differential expression in the crowd. The elements in the crowd may differ also as to the expression of their ideas and feelings. Hence interaction in the crowd may be said to consist, in part, of differential expression. Granted that the appearance of unanimity is a definite feature of the crowd, this impression may nevertheless be a result of differential expression rather than of a genuine homogeneity of attitudes.

It is a salient characteristic of the crowd situation that the normal give-and-take of discussion is prevented. No one in the crowd really knows what the many other members are thinking; all each member knows about is what is expressed. Hence those who speak first, most loudly, and most vigorously may create the impression that they are expressing the feelings of the majority of the crowd, especially if they are not opposed with equal vigor. In the following selection from his book *Social Psychology,* E. A. Ross comments on this feature of crowd interaction:

The man of biggest voice or wildest language, the aggressive person who first leaps upon a table, raises aloft a symbol, or utters a catching phrase, is likely to become the bell-wether.*

* E. A. Ross, **Social Psychology** (New York: The Macmillan Co., 1909), p. 47.

The mere matter of timing may put individuals who disagree with such a "bell-wether" at a disadvantage. Speaking "in second place," their proposals are likely to have a moderate, even a negative tone, in contrast to the vigorous, positive assertions which precede them. Furthermore, the acclaim of even a small portion of the crowd, accorded to the first declaration, may create the fear in those who disagree that they will be expressing an unpopular, minority viewpoint. Other features of the crowd situation may increase the reluctance of crowd members to disagree with extreme, positive declarations stated initially. One is the abuse, verbal or even physical, to which the first individual to disagree may be subjected. Other individuals who agree with him but are not sure how many other crowd members also agree are hence discouraged from expressing their doubts as to the desirability of the trend the crowd is following. They may keep silent rather than expose themselves to the same treatment. Hence only one viewpoint is expressed, and the illusion of unanimity is created.

Usually the nature of the incident itself is of such a nature as to give an intrinsic advantage to one position. When people are highly excited, perhaps indignant, over an event, the "counsel of caution" sounds weak compared with a call for vigorous, positive action. The individual who disagrees with the action proposed for the crowd may hesitate to make a more moderate proposal lest he seem insufficiently concerned, or even disloyal to an important reference group. White men who have proposed that legal procedures be followed in lieu of a lynching have been called "nigger-lovers" and thus silenced.

Keynoting. The differential effect of the first powerful, unqualified statement in quelling the expression of divergent opinions is enhanced when the feelings of many of the crowd members are ambivalent and uncertain. Many people may come to the crowd situation feeling that something should be done. They may not know, however, just what they think should be done, and they may have grave doubts as to the desirability of any action that deviates sharply from the usual social norms. The person who feels no such uncertainty but is, instead, capable of proposing extreme action, without reservations, is able to express his proposals much more tersely and forcibly. The first positive, unqualified statement may have additional power because most of the members of the crowd are tentatively, and part of the time, thinking along the same line, considering this as a possible line of action without being yet committed to it. The presentation of a positive suggestion in an ambivalent frame of reference such as this may be called "keynoting." For some people the uncertainty and ambivalence in the internal portion of their frame of reference is resolved by the keynote statement. One position is reinforced for them and they now find it easier to express themselves, agreeing with a proposal that someone else has already enunciated. As more people resolve or suppress their ambivalent feelings and vocally assent to the keynote proposal, the stronger grows the impression that this is the feeling of the majority of the crowd. Others then find it more difficult to weigh various alternatives, particularly those which run counter to the line of action that is developing.

The performer-audience relation. Another important aspect of the interaction of various elements in the crowd may be designated as the "performer-audience" relationship. Not all members of a crowd are equally active, even at the height of crowd activity. It has often been observed that only a minority of mob members perform overt acts of violence. The majority of the crowd members often play a relatively passive role and are somewhat in the relationship of an audience to the active nucleus. Their relative passivity does not mean, however, that the audience portion is unimportant in the development of the action of the crowd as a whole.

First, to the extent that individuals in the audience category engage in vocal activity they contribute to the process which builds up the impression in unanimity. This encourages the members who are disposed to be physically more active. Furthermore, as has been seen before, some members of the audience or spectator element may become identified with the active nucleus and enter into the performer group.

But crowd members who only look, even those who may covertly disapprove of what the active performers are doing, are important in crowd interaction. They make the crowd larger numerically, increasing the impression of strength and of support for what is being done. The Southern Commission on the Study of Lynchings noted that sometimes spectators constituted a source of protection for the very elements of which they might disapprove.

The onlookers play an important part in another process which we will call the process of *commitment*. In this process, the active element of the crowd becomes committed to a line of action once begun, because of the presence of a large group of observers. It is a general characteristic of human relations that an opinion formed or a resolution made in private can be changed more easily than can one to which the person has publicly committed himself. To embark upon a line of action and then to fail to pursue it is to "back down" and, if done in the presence of observers, is to "lose face." That this process of commitment operates in crowd situations may be seen in the following episode in the Chicago riot.

THE INFLUENCE OF THE AUDIENCE IN THE CHICAGO RIOT

Among the spectators of mob violence were men, women, and children of all ages; they included tradesmen, craftsmen, salesmen, laborers. Though the spectators did not commit the crimes, they must share the moral responsibility. Without the spectators mob violence would probably have stopped short of murder in many cases. An example of the behavior of the active nucleus when out of sight of the spectators bears this out. George Carr, Negro, was chased from a street car. He outstripped all but the van-

guard of the mob by climbing fences and hiding in a back yard. This concealed him from the rest of the crowd, who by that time were chasing other Negroes. The young men who followed Carr left him without striking a blow, upon his mere request for clemency. In regard to the large non-active elements in the crowds, the coroner said during the inquest, "It is just the swelling of crowds of that kind that urges them on, because they naturally feel that they are backed up by the balance of the crowd, which may not be true, but they feel that way."

Reprinted by permission of the University of Chicago Press, from The Chicago Commission on Race Relations, **The Negro in Chicago** (Chicago: University of Chicago Press, 1922), pp. 22–23.

Juror Ware said, "If sightseers were lending their aid and assistance—" Juror Dillon interrupted and finished, "they ought to be punished."

Instigators and participants. Yet another relationship that prevails between different elements in the crowd is the one between active, highly excited participants and those whom we have called instigators. There is evidence from many crowd situations that there have been people who, while they themselves may or may not have been participating in the physical activities of the crowd, were encouraging others to do so. This suggests that, contrary to the widely held view of the reactions of crowd members, some members remain sufficiently aware of what they are doing not to lose the sense of physical danger to themselves. The caution displayed by some mob members, and their activities in instigating others to action, was witnessed in the Detroit riot, as Lee and Humphrey point out in the following passage:

> A Negro woman described what she saw of Woodward rioting from a third-story window as follows: "My top view, so to speak, showed clearly men in the back of the lot pushing youngsters in their teens out into the street to do the fighting, while they themselves kept back." A Detroit *News* reporter, according to the *News* columnist Philip A. Adler, saw the same sort of thing elsewhere: "Men who led the mobs into the brawls would retreat after they had reached the fighting line, so to speak, and let others, usually boys in their teens, do the fighting." *

The recognition of the presence of such cautious, deliberative instigators in mobs necessitates a revision of the picture of the crowd as consisting of people so completely involved in the circular reaction and collective excitement that they lose all sense of personal danger, and all self-control. There is evidence that some instigators who appear, on the surface, to be highly excited members of the crowd, are deliberately assessing the effects of their own actions, particularly on other members of the crowd. The history of the anti-Semitic pogroms in Russia provides many striking examples of this. In spite of the violence, the passion, and the disorder of the mobs, it appears that the great majority of pogroms were deliberately planned and instigated. During the first great wave of pogroms the appearance of the "Bare-Footed Brigade," a band of Great Russian tramps and ruffians, usually presaged the beginning of a pogrom. The pogrom always started, of course, on some seemingly accidental pretext. Further evidence of the deliberate nature of these riots was found in the fact that the police, when they desired, could stop them almost at will, the rage of the rioters suddenly subsiding at the first show of force. As soon as the riot was over, the "Bare-Footed Brigade" would vanish as suddenly as they had arrived. In a pogrom at Warsaw in the early part of the 19th century the role of the instigators was quite evident:

> The hordes were under the command of thieves, well known to the police, and of some unknown strangers who from time to time gave signals by whistling, and directed the mob into this or that street.**

Implications for the study of crowds. It has been seen that in first-hand, detailed descriptions of crowds a variety of participants can be identified. These participants differ in their motivation and in the nature of their participation. Yet the crowd behavior that is the product of their interaction may give the impression of homogeneity of motives and uniformity of action. Research that starts with the assumption that homogeneity may be taken for granted is unlikely to lead to identification of the essential features of the process of crowd development. Research findings which will contribute to the understanding of the dynamics of crowd behavior will result from observations that focus upon differences in the crowd participants and on the interaction between them.

* From Alfred McClung Lee and Norman D. Humphrey, **Race Riot,** p. 81. Copyright 1943 by the Dryden Press, Inc. Reprinted by special permission.
** S. M. Dubnow, **History of the Jews in Russia and Poland,** tr. by I. Friedlander (Philadelphia: The Jewish Publication Society of America, 1918), Vol. II, p. 281.

Chapter 7

Crowd process: symbolization
and change

*T*HE CROWD has always had about it an aura of irrationality and unpre
dictability that has aroused awe in observers. Sudden shifts in behavior have len
to it an air of capriciousness, enhancing the appearance of irrationality. Henc
writers have been tempted to explain the crowd and its behavior in terms of a
inferior crowd mind, or of a collective psychosis.

Much of the incomprehensible, seemingly irrational behavior of crowds ma
be explained in terms of two important crowd processes. One of these is *crowd
symbolization*. The objects toward which crowds act are not simply stimuli tha
have the same meaning for observers as they do for members of the crowd. The
are *symbols,* whose development and significance must be analyzed for a fulle
understanding of the nature of crowd behavior. The second important process i
that of *crowd change*. It has been seen that the emergent crowd may culminat
in any of several forms. Similarly, even after it has developed into one type, i
may change its object or its mood.

Symbolization in the crowd. An essential part of the preparation of a crowd fo
action is the development of a shared image of the object. In crowds, no les
than at other times, man lives in a symbolic environment. Common symbols fur
nish the basis for unified action. To understand crowd behavior it is necessary t
view crowd objects in terms of their symbolic meanings to the crowd member
themselves. A classic illustration of the symbolic nature of the object of an actin
crowd is found in the storming of the Bastille.

120

THE FALL OF THE BASTILLE
CHARLES MORRIS

"To the Bastille! to the Bastille!" was the cry. Paris surged with an ungovernable mob. Month by month, week by week, day by day, since the meeting of the States-General,—called into being to provide money for the king, and kept in being to provide government for the people, —the revolutionary feeling had grown, alike among the delegates and among the citizens. Now the population of Paris was aroused, the unruly element of the city was in the streets, their wrath directed against the prison-fortress, the bulwark of feudalism, the stronghold of oppression, the infamous keeper of the dark secrets of the kings of France. The people had always feared, always hated it, and now against its sullen walls was directed the torrent of their wrath.

The Bastille was the visible emblem of that oppression. It was an armed fortress threatening Paris. The cannon on its walls frowned defiance to the people. Momentarily the wrath of the multitude grew stronger. The electors of the Third Estate sent a message to Delaunay, governor of the Bastille, asking him to withdraw the cannons, the sight of which infuriated the people, and promising, if he would do this, to restrain the mob.

The advice was wise; the governor was not. The messengers were long absent; the electors grew uneasy; the tumult in the street increased. At length the deputation returned, bringing word that the governor pledged himself not to fire on the people, unless forced to do so in self-defence. Even while the electors were reporting the governor's evasive message to the crowd around the Hotel de Ville the cannon of the Bastille were roaring defiance to the people of Paris!

That shot was fatal to Delaunay. The citizens heard it with rage. "Treason!" was the cry. "To the Bastille! to the Bastille!"

again rose the shout. Surging onward in an irresistible mass, the furious crowd poured through the streets, and soon surrounded the towering walls of the detested prison-fortress. A few bold men had already cut the chains of the first drawbridge, and let it fall. Across it rushed the multitude to attack the second bridge.

The fortress was feebly garrisoned, having but thirty Swiss soldiers and eighty invalids for its defence.

A chance shot was fired from the crowd; the soldiers answered with a volley; several men were wounded; other shots came from the people; the governor gave orders to fire the cannon; the struggle had begun.

It proved a short one. Companies of the National Guard were brought up to restrain the mob,—the soldiers broke from their ranks and joined it. Two of their sub-officers, Elie and Hullin by name, put themselves at the head of the furious crowd and led the people to the assault on the fortress.

Delaunay proposed to capitulate, saying that he would yield if he and his men were allowed to march out with arms and honor. The proposition was received with shouts of sarcastic laughter.

"Life and safety are all we can promise you," answered Elie. "This I engage on the word of an officer."

Delaunay at this ordered the second drawbridge to be lowered and the gates to be opened. In poured the mass, precipitating themselves in fury upon that hated fortress, rushing madly through all its halls and passages, breaking its cell-doors with hammer blows, releasing captives some of whom had been held there in hopeless misery for half a lifetime, unearthing secrets which added to their revengeful rage.

Elie and Hullin had promised the governor his life. They miscalculated their power over their savage followers. Before

From Charles Morris, **Historical Tales** **(French)** (Atlanta: The Martin and Hoyt Co., 1893), pp. 269-274.

they had gone far they were fighting hand to hand with the multitude for the safety of their prisoner. At the Place de Greve, Hullin seized the governor in his strong arms and covered his bare head with a hat, with the hope of concealing his features from the people. In a moment more he was hurled down and trodden under foot, and on struggling to his feet saw the head of Delaunay carried on a pike.

Meanwhile, the king was at Versailles, in ignorance of what was taking place at Paris. Louis XVI went to bed and to sleep, in blissful ignorance of what had taken place. The Duke of Lioncourt entered and had him awakened, and informed him of the momentous event.

"But that is a revolt!" exclaimed the king, with startled face, sitting up on his couch.

"No sire," replied the duke; "it is a revolution!"

That was the true word. It was a revolution. With the taking of the Bastille the Revolution of France was fairly inaugurated. As for that detested fortress, its demolition began on the next day, amid the thunder of cannon and the singing of the *Te Deum*. It had dominated Paris, and served as a state-prison for four hundred years. Its site was henceforward to be a monument to liberty.

The example of the Bastille shows that the object is not simply a stimulus which, because of its intrinsic or "objective" character, evokes a particular response from the crowd. It is, rather, an object which symbolizes the cause of the situation that the crowd members feel demands action. It has the additional characteristic of being accessible. It enables the crowd to act quickly and forcefully, permitting the expression of aroused feelings. Logical analysis may show that the action does not accomplish what the crowd thinks it will. It may change the situation little or not at all. Yet a symbol is necessary for the crowd to act, and the crowd therefore evolves some symbol or symbols that will permit action.

This reading also suggests that, in the heat of crowd action, symbols may acquire a vital significance that is carried over into the life of the society. Thus the Bastille did not cease to be a symbol after its destruction; instead its significance was enhanced and it has persisted in Western European society as a symbol of tyranny. Bastille Day has become an institutionalized celebration of French independence from oppression.

Not only does the symbol provide a basis for uniformity of crowd action. The development of an unambiguous symbol also serves to neutralize norms that might inhibit the crowd from acting in an unrestrainedly hostile manner towards its object. Turner and Surace analyze this function of the crowd symbol in the following study.

ZOOT-SUITERS AND MEXICANS: SYMBOLS IN CROWD BEHAVIOR

RALPH H. TURNER AND SAMUEL J. SURACE

In this paper we shall report the test of

Reprinted in part by permission of the University of Chicago Press, from Ralph H. Turner and Samuel J. Surace, "Zoot-Suiters and Mexicans: Symbols in Crowd Behavior," The American Journal of Sociology, 62 (1956), pp. 14–20.

an hypothesis concerning the symbols with which a hostile crowd designates the object of its action. Our hypothesis is that hostile crowd behavior requires an unambiguously unfavorable symbol, which serves to divert crowd attention from any of the usual favorable or mitigating connotations surrounding the object being attacked. The hypothesis has been tested by a content analysis of references to the symbol, "Mexican," during the ten and one half year period leading up to the 1943 "Zoot-Suit" riots in Los Angeles and vicinity. We shall begin by discussing the theory from which the hypothesis is derived, followed by a statement of findings and their interpretation in light of the hypothesis.

Theory and Hypothesis. The hypothesis under examination is related to two important characteristics of crowd behavior. Based on these two characteristics, certain conditions are indicated as necessary to the development of hostile acting crowd behavior. These necessary conditions can, in turn, be related to the connotations surrounding the symbols by which the crowd designates the object of its hostile attack.

First, crowd behavior is *uniform* behavior in a broad sense. By contrast, much noncrowd behavior exposes the infinitely varied attitudes of diverse individuals. Many attitudes and gradations of feeling can be evidenced in a group's actions toward any particular object. However, the crowd is a group expressing *one* attitude, with individual variations largely concealed. Many people are acting in accordance with a single dominant definition of the situation.

In noncrowd situations uniform behavior may be achieved in a group by a process of majority decision, acceptance of authority, or compromise of some sort. But the uniformity of crowd behavior is not mediated by such slow and deliberate procedures for reaching agreement. Within the crowd there is a readiness to act uniformly in response to varied suggestions. Until such readiness to act *uniformly* has spread throughout the crowd's recruitment group, fully developed and widespread acting crowd behavior is not possible.

The response in the community to shared symbols is crucial to this uniformity of action. Ordinarily any particular symbol has varied connotations for different individuals and groups in the community. These varied connotations prevent uniform community-wide action, or at least delay such action until extended processes of group decision-making have been carried out. But when a given symbol has relatively uniform connotations in all parts of the community, uniform group action can be taken rather readily if the occasion seems to demand it. *To the degree, then, to which any symbol evokes only one consistent set of connotations throughout the community, only one general course of action with respect to that object will be indicated, and the union of diverse members of the community into an acting crowd will be facilitated.*

Second, the crowd follows a course of action which is at least partially sanctioned in the culture, but which is normally inhibited by other aspects of that culture. Mob action is frequently nothing more than culturally sanctioned punishment carried out by unauthorized persons without "due process." The fact that such behavior has support in everyday life is attested to in many ways. Organizations such as the Ku Klux Klan and other vigilante groups act as self-appointed "custodians of patriotism," and are fairly widely accepted as such. The lynching of two "confessed" kidnappers in California in 1933 was given public sanction by the then governor of the state on the grounds of its therapeutic effect on other would-be criminals. The legal system in America implicitly recognizes these supports by including laws in the statute books designed to counteract such actions.

Hostile acting crowd behavior can take place only when these inhibiting aspects of the culture cease to operate. In a sense there is cultural conflict between the norms sanctioning the crowd's action and the norms inhibiting it. For the crowd to blossom into full-scale action the conflict must be resolved by neutralization of the inhibiting norms.

The connotations surrounding the symbol which designates the object of a crowd's hostile actions are crucial in this connection also. There is normally some ambiguity in the connotations of any symbol, so that both favorable and unfavorable sentiments are aroused. For example, even the most prejudiced person is likely to respond to the symbol, "Negro," with images of both the feared invader of white prerogatives and the lovable, loyal Negro lackey and "mammy." The symbol, "bank robber," is likely to evoke a picture of admirable daring along with its generally unfavorable image. It is our contention that these ambiguities of connotation, which evoke ambivalent feelings in persons using the symbols, play an important part in inhibiting consummatory or extreme hostile behavior against the object represented by the symbol.

The diverse connotations of any symbol normally inhibit extreme behavior in two interrelated ways. First, the symbol evokes feelings which resist any extreme course of action. A parent, for example, is normally inhibited from punishing his child to excess no matter what the child's offense may be because feelings of affection are also aroused which limit the development of anger. Sentiments of pity and admiration for courage or resolute action, or sympathy for a course of action which many of us might like to engage in ourselves, or charity toward human weakness, usually moderate feelings of hostility toward violators of the mores. So long as the individual's feelings are mixed his actions are likely to be moderate.

Second, the mixed connotations of the symbol place the object *within the normative order,* so that the mores of fair play, due process, giving a fair hearing, etc., apply. Any indication that the individual under attack respects any of the social norms or has any of the characteristics of the in-group invokes these mores which block extreme action.

On the other hand, symbols which are unambiguous in their connotations permit immoderate behavior toward the object in question. In the absence of ambivalence toward an object there is no internal conflict to restrict action. Furthermore, a symbol which evokes a pure image of a person outside the normative order provides no justification for applying the in-group norms of fair play and due process. The principle that "we must fight fire with fire," or that a person devoid of human decency is not himself entitled to be treated with decency and respect, rules out these inhibiting norms.

In summary, then, we have observed that crowd behavior consists of (a) action reflecting a uniform sentiment throughout the group involved in crowd behavior and (b) behavior which is not moderated by the usually inhibiting social norms and sentiments. *A necessary condition for both uniform group action and unrestricted hostile behavior is the presence of a symbol which arouses uniformly and exclusively unfavorable feelings in the group toward the object under attack.*

Two qualifications must be added before we discuss the empirical test of the hypothesis. First, our discussion of the connotations of the symbol refers to the manner in which the symbol is presented to the mass or partially developed crowd. Changes in the connotations of a symbol *to the mass or crowd* do not necessarily imply a generality of closely corresponding changes *within individuals.* The symbol as presented in the group context mediates the *overt expression* of attitudes in terms of *sanction* and the focus of *attention.* (a) The individual in whom a particular symbol evokes exclusively unfavorable feelings may nevertheless be inhibited from acting according to his feelings by the awareness that other connotations are *sanctioned* in the group. Or the individual in whom ambivalent feelings are evoked may conceal his favorable sentiments because he sees that only the unfavorable sentiments are sanctioned. He thereby facilitates crowd use of the symbol. (b) Furthermore, of all the possible connotations attached to a symbol, the individual at any given moment acts principally in terms of those on which his *attention* is focussed. By shielding individuals from attending to some of the possible connotations of a symbol, the unambiguous public symbol prevents the evocation of attitudes which are normally present. Thus, without necessarily undergoing change, favorable individual attitudes toward the object of crowd attack may simply remain latent because of the uniform connotations of the symbol before the crowd. This process is one of the aspects of the so-called "restriction of attention" which characterizes the crowd.

Second, while the emergence of unambiguous symbols is a necessary condition to full-fledged crowd behavior, it may also be a *product* of the earlier stages of crowd development. In some cases a rather sudden crowd development is probably facilitated by the pre-existing linkage of an already unambiguous symbol to the object upon which events focus collective attention. But more commonly we suspect that the emergence of such a symbol or the stripping away of alternative connotations from an established symbol takes place cumulatively through interaction centered on that object. Over a period of time, community-wide interaction about an object takes on increasingly crowd-like characteristics, as there is a gradual preparation for the final consummatory crowd action.

With this latter qualification in mind we shall hypothesize that *a period of overt hostile crowd behavior is usually preceded by a period in which the key symbol is stripped of its favorable connotations until it comes to evoke unambiguously unfavorable feelings.*

The "Zoot-Suit Riots." Beginning on June 3, 1943, Los Angeles, California was the scene of sporadic acts of violence involving principally United States Naval personnel with the support of a sympathetic anglo community and members of the Mexican community. This period of crowd violence has come to be known as the "zoot-suit riots." The designation "zooter" referred mainly to two characteristics. First, the zoot suit was a style of clothing featuring long suit-coats and trousers which were extremely pegged at the cuff, draping fully around the knees and terminating in deep pleats at the waist. Second, the zooters wore their hair long, full, and well greased.

We shall not describe the action in detail. It is sufficient to state that many attacks and injuries were sustained by both sides. Groups of sailors were frequently reported to be assisted or accompanied by civilian mobs who "egged" them on as they roamed through downtown streets in search of victims. "Zooters" discovered on city streets were assaulted and forced to disrobe amidst the jibes and molestations of the crowd. Streetcars and buses were stopped and searched. "Zooters" found therein were carried off into the streets and subjected to beatings. Cavalcades of hired taxicabs filled with sailors ranged the east-side districts of Los Angeles seeking, finding and attacking "zooters." Civilian gangs of east-side adolescents organized similar attacks against unwary naval personnel, inflicting injury and swelling the cries of "outrage."

It is, of course, impossible to isolate a single incident or event and hold it responsible for the riots. Local, State, and Federal authorities, and numerous civic and national groups were ultimately involved in the attempt to assess blame and prevent further violence. The most prominently reported *claim* of both antagonists referred to the other as molesting "our girls." For example, it was reported that sailors became enraged over learning that zoot-suiters were responsible for "assaults on female relatives of servicemen." Similarly, the claim against sailors was that they persisted in molesting and insulting girls belonging to the Mexican community. While many other charges were reported in the newspapers, including unsubstantiated suggestions of sabotage with respect to the war effort, the *precipitating* context was dominated by implications of acute and improper sexual competition.

Method. In the absence of any direct sampling of community sentiment in the period preceding the riots we have assumed that the use of the symbol, "Mexican," by the media of mass communication can be taken as an indication of the connotations prevalent in the community. In making this assumption we beg all questions of moral responsibility for the riot and of direction of influence between community sentiment and the mass media. Whether the mass media passively reflect community sentiment or whether they actively mold it, or whether, as we suppose, some combination of the two processes occurs, we should still be justified in using the content of mass media to indicate community feeling. Ideally we should have sampled a variety of mass media to correct for biases in each. However, with the limited human resources at our disposal we chose one newspaper, the *Los Angeles Times*. The *Times* has the largest circulation of the four major newspapers in the Los Angeles area. It is conservative in emphasis, and tends away from the sensational treatment of minority issues. In the past a foremost romanticizer of old Mexico had been a prominent member of the *Times* editorial staff and Board of Directors.

In order to uncover trends in the connotations of the symbol under study, one newspaper per month was read for the ten and one half year period from January, 1933, until June 20, 1943. These monthly newspapers were selected by assigning consecutive days of the week to each month. For example, for January, 1933, the paper printed on the first Monday was read; for February, the paper printed on the first Tuesday was read. After the seven day cycle was completed the following months were assigned, respectively, the *second* Monday, the *second* Tuesday, etc. To avoid loading the sample with days that fell early in the first half of the month, the procedure was reversed for the last half of the period under consideration.

In order to secure an intensive picture of the critical period, consecutive daily editions were read for one month starting with May 20, 1943, through June 20, 1943. This covered approximately ten days before and after the period of violence. Data gathered from this group of newspapers will receive separate analysis.

Any editorial, story, report, or letter which had reference to the Mexican community or population was summarized, recorded, and classified. The articles were placed in five basic categories: favorable themes, unfavorable themes, neutral mention, negative-favorable mention, and "zooter" theme.

If the hypothesis of this paper is to be supported, we should expect a decline in the favorable contexts of the symbol "Mexican," as it manifests itself in the newspaper content throughout the indicated time span. The change should serve to produce the type of symbol suggested by the hypothesis, a symbol dominated by unambiguously unfavorable elements.

Findings. The favorable and unfavorable themes are reported alone in Table 1 for the ten and one half year period. The table by itself appears to negate our hypothesis, since there is no appreciable decline in the percent of favorable themes during the period. Indeed, even during the last period the mentions appear predominantly favorable, featuring the romanticized Mexican. However, there is a striking decline in the total number of articles mentioning the Mexican between the second and third periods. Treating the articles listed as a fraction of all articles in the newspapers sampled and using a sub-minimal estimate of the total number of all articles, the "t" test reveals that such a drop in the total number of articles mentioning Mexicans could have occurred by chance less than twice in one hundred times. We conclude, then, that the decline in total favorable and unfavorable mentions of Mexican is statistically significant.

While the hypothesis in its simplest form is unsubstantiated, the drop in both favorable and unfavorable themes suggests a shift away from *all* of the traditional references to Mexicans during the period prior to the riots. If it can be shown that an actual *substitution* of symbols was taking place, our hypothesis may still be substantiated, but in a somewhat different light than anticipated.

From the distribution of all five themes reported in Table 2 it is immediately evident that there has been no decline of interest in the "Mexican," but rather a clear-cut shift of attention away from traditional references. The straightforward favorable and unfavorable themes account for eighty-nine percent, seventy-four percent, and thirty percent of all references respectively during the three periods. This drop and the drop from sixty-one to twenty-five percent favorable mentions are significant below the one percent level. To determine whether this evidence confirms our hypothesis, we must make care-

Table 1

FAVORABLE AND UNFAVORABLE MENTION OF "MEXICAN" DURING THREE PERIODS

Period	Favorable Themes	Unfavorable Themes	Percent Favorable
Jan., 1933–June, 1936	27	3	90
July, 1936–Dec., 1939	23	5	82
Jan., 1940–June, 1943	10	2	83
Total	60	10	86

ful examination of the three emerging themes.

The *neutral* theme shows a steady increase throughout the three periods. While we have cautiously designated this "neutral," it actually consists chiefly of unfavorable presentations of the object, "Mexican," without overt use of the symbol, "Mexican." Thus it incorporates the unfavorable representation of Mexican, which we assume was quite generally recognized throughout the community, without explicit use of the symbol.

The *negative-favorable* theme, though small in total numbers, also shows an increase throughout the period examined. At first we were inclined to treat these as favorable themes. However, in contrast to the other favorable themes, this one gives recognition to the extent of negative connotation which is accumulating about the symbol, "Mexican." By arguing openly against the negative connotations these articles acknowledge to the reader that there is widespread community sanction for such negative connotations. When the implicitly favorable themes of romantic Mexico and California's historic past give way to defensive assertions that all Mexicans are not bad, such a shift can only reasonably be interpreted as a rise in unfavorable connotations.

The most interesting shift, however, is the rise of the *Zoot-suit* theme, which did not appear at all until the third period when it accounts for thirty percent of the references. Here we have the emergence of a new symbol which has no past favorable connotations to lose. Unlike the symbol, "Mexican," the "Zoot-suiter" symbol evokes no ambivalent sentiments but appears in exclusively unfavorable contexts. While in fact Mexicans were attacked indiscriminately in spite of apparel, the symbol *Zoot-suiter* could become a basis for unambivalent community sentiment supporting hostile crowd behavior more easily than could "Mexican."

It is interesting to note that when we consider only the fifteen mentions which appear in the first six months of 1943, ten are to *zooters*, three are *negative-favorable*, two are *neutral*, and none are the traditional favorable or unfavorable themes.

In Table 3 we report the results of the day-by-day analysis of the period immediately prior, during, and after the riots. Here we see the culmination of a trend faintly suggested as long as seven years

Table 2

DISTRIBUTION OF ALL THEMES BY THREE PERIODS

	Percent Favorable	Percent Unfavorable	Percent Neutral	Percent Negative-Favorable	Percent Zooter	Total Percent	Total Number
Jan., 1933–June, 1936	80	9	11	0	0	100	34
July, 1936–Dec., 1939	61	13	23	3	0	100	38
Jan., 1940–June, 1943	25	5	32	8	30	100	40

before the riots and clearly indicated two or three years in advance. The traditional favorable and unfavorable themes have vanished completely and three-quarters of the references center about the *zooter* theme.

Discussion. From the foregoing evidence we conclude that our basic hypothesis and theory receive confirmation, but not in exactly the manner envisaged in advance. The simple expectation that there would be a shift in the relative preponderance of favorable and unfavorable contexts for the symbol "Mexican" was not borne out. But the basic hypothesis that an unambiguously unfavorable symbol is required as the rallying point for hostile crowd behavior is supported through evidence that the symbol "Mexican" tended to be displaced by the symbol *Zoot-suiter* as the period of actual crowd behavior was approached.

It should be recalled that the conception of the romantic Mexican and the Mexican heritage are deeply ingrained in Southern California tradition. The Plaza and Olvera Street in downtown Los Angeles, the Ramona tradition, the popular-

Table 3

DISTRIBUTION OF ALL THEMES FROM
MAY 20 TO JUNE 20, 1943

Theme	Percent of All Mentions
Favorable	0
Unfavorable	0
Neutral	3
Negative-favorable	23
Zooter	74
Total	100
Total (number)	(61)

ity of Mexican food, and many other features serve to perpetuate this tradition. It seems quite probable that the force of this tradition was too strong to be eradicated entirely from community awareness, even though it ceased to be an acceptable matter of public presentation. In spite, then, of a progressive decline in public presentation of the symbol in its traditional favorable contexts, a certain ambivalence remained which prevented a simple replacement with predominantly unfavorable connotations.

Rather, two techniques emerged for circumventing the ambivalence. One was the technique of presenting the object in an obvious manner without explicit use of the symbol. Thus an obviously Mexican name, a picture, or reference to "East side hoodlums" was presented in an unfavorable context. But a far more effective device was uncovered with the emergence of a new symbol whose connotations at the time were exclusively unfavorable. This symbol provided the public sanction and restriction of attention essential to the development of overt hostile crowd behavior. The symbol, *Zoot-suiter,* evoked none of the imagery of the romantic past. It evoked only the picture of a breed of persons outside of the normative order, devoid of morals themselves and consequently not entitled to fair play and due process. Indeed, the zoot-suiter came to be regarded as such an exclusively fearful threat to the community that at the height of rioting the Los Angeles City Council seriously debated an ordinance making the wearing of zoot-suits a prison offence.

The *zooter* symbol had a crisis character which simply unfavorable reference to the familiar *Mexican* symbol could never approach in effectiveness. And the zooter was an omnibus symbol drawing together the most reprehensible elements in the old unfavorable themes, namely, sex crimes, delinquency, gang attacks, draft dodgers, etc. Any one of these elements by itself lacked the wide applicability possessed by the *zooter* symbol.

The *zooter* symbol also supplies an objective tag with which to identify the object of attack. It could be used, when the old attitudes toward Mexicans were evoked, to differentiate Mexicans along both moral and tangible physical lines. While the active minority were attacking Mexicans indiscriminately, and frequently including Negroes, the great sanctioning majority heard only of attacks on *zoot-suiters.*

Once established the zooter theme assured its own magnification. What previously would have been reported as an adolescent gang attack would now be presented as a zoot-suit attack. Weapons found on apprehended youths were now interpreted as the building up of arms collections in preparation for zoot-suit violence. In short, the *zooter* symbol had absorbed many of the elements formerly present and sometimes associated with Mexicans along with the objective accoutrements of the zoot-suiter into a new unity. This new unity relieved the community of ambivalence and moral obligations toward the objects who could then become the sanctioned victims of widespread hostile crowd behavior.

APPENDIX

The following themes and sub-themes were found to recur in the data. The sub-themes were not used separately in the report.

(1) *Favorable*
  (a) Old California Theme
     This is devoted to extolling the traditions and history of the old rancheros as the earliest California settlers.
  (b) Mexican Temperament Theme
     This describes the Mexican character in terms of dashing romance, bravery, gaiety, etc.
  (c) Religious Theme
     This has reference to the devout religious values of the Mexican community.
  (d) Mexican Culture Theme
     This pays homage to Mexican art, dance, crafts, music, fifth of May festivities, etc.

(2) *Unfavorable*
  (a) Delinquency and Crime Theme
     This theme includes the specific mention of a law violator as "Mexican," associating him with marihuana, sex crimes, knife wielding, gang violence, etc.
  (b) Public Burden Theme
     This attempts to show that Mexicans constitute a drain on relief funds and on the budgets of correctional institutions.

(3) *Neutral*
  This is a category of miscellaneous items including reports of crimes committed by individuals possessing obvious Mexican names but without designation of ethnic affiliation.

(4) *Negative-Favorable*
  This category consists of appeals which counter or deny the validity of accusations against Mexicans as a group. For example, ". . . not all zoot-suiters are delinquents; their adoption by many was a bid for social recognition . . ."; or ". . . at the outset zoot-suiters were limited to no specific race . . . The fact that later on their numbers seemed to be predominantly Latin was in itself no indication of that race . . ."

(5) *Zooter Theme*
  This theme identifies the zooter costume as "a badge of delinquency." Typical references were, "reat pleat boys," "long coated gentry," coupled with mention of "unprovoked attacks by zoot-suited youths," "zoot-suit orgy," etc. Crime, sex-violence, and gang attacks were the dominant elements in this theme. Almost invariably, the "zooter" was identified as a Mexican by such clues as "Eastside hoodlum," a Mexican name, or specific ethnic designation.

Symbols justifying crowd action. The crowd may also develop symbols which refer to what the crowd is doing and serve to justify its actions. Symbols arise to characterize the crowd itself, legitimatizing its actions in the eyes of its members. Lynch mobs or rioting crowds may be designated by their members as "all self-respecting white men" or as "patriotic, red-blooded Americans." Members of religious crowds may refer to themselves as being "saved," in contrast to all the other people who are "lost" or "living in the world."

Symbolic acts in the expressive crowd. In the expressive crowd, yet another form of crowd symbolization may be seen. Here the crowd behavior itself consists of symbolic actions. Just as the active crowd acts on objects which symbolize intangible, inaccessible conditions, the expressive crowd engages in behavior which symbolizes states or experiences which cannot be otherwise made evident. In the following selection Clark shows the importance of the concept of the state of "sanctification" in Negro holiness religion. Yet "sanctification" is a mystic, thoroughly subjective experience. Its attainment is symbolized, both for the individual who experiences it and for onlookers, by certain expressive acts, the induction of which is the crowd objective.

SANCTIFICATION IN NEGRO RELIGION
WILLIAM A. CLARK

Sanctification in religious doctrines is not new. It is mentioned in several instances in the ancient Hebrew scriptures. Originally, it was a designation of the activities by which individuals consecrated themselves to the services of their Supreme Beings. The place and objects of consecration were parts of the total concept. Sanctification thus meant a separation of the sacred and mundane, the holy and profane. To be consecrated to the sacred meant that one had to taboo many of the customary actions and thoughts of the ordinary mortal. Normal passions, appetites, and material ambitions had to be suppressed. Those who could learn so to deny themselves looked upon their activity as a process of purification. Hence, sanctification came to mean freedom from sin, freedom from earthly bonds, and becoming heavenly or holy in being. Imagination is exercised on the concept until a phantasm is produced of direct communion with the Trinity—the Father, Son, and Holy Ghost. In both thought and deed, those who profess sanctification attempt to live as they believe these Supreme Beings live. To the convert, such a life is not only possible but also very real. The true believer actually thinks he is living above earthly things, away from reality.

Among Negroes there is only one organized body that advocates sanctification as its major element of doctrine. That is the "Church of God in Christ," started by

Elder Charles H. Mason in 1895, at Memphis, Tennessee. The church doctrine is Trinitarian. God is the Father; Christ was, and is, the Son of God, equal in wisdom and power. The communicants believe in the personality of the Holy Spirit; ". . . that He proceedeth from the Father and the Son; that He is equal in power with the Father and Son; and that the Holy Spirit is the chief executive of the Trinity through which the plan of salvation is carried on in this earth."

The members believe in the possibility of entire sanctification, in evidence of which they are given power of speaking with new tongues and gifts of divine healing. These beliefs are loudly and actively expressed as the predominant part of their frequent religious services.

The services in the Holiness church are divided into three parts. They begin on a very simple level. All communicants, or those who want to participate, bow on their knees in prayer. Each one prays in his own way. A general humming, groaning, and moaning begins, with occasional comprehensible utterances of prayers made by some. This goes on sometimes for more than an hour. The praying gradually grows louder until the interior of the building is filled with a confusion of sounds, and individual utterances are lost in the din.

As this part of the services proceeds the more sensitive and susceptible communicants can be observed to become more physically active. Muscular twitchings become observable, and automatic motions of limbs become more frequent in some. Others demonstrate changes in

Reprinted in part by permission of the editors of **Social Forces,** from William A. Clark, "Sanctification in Negro Religion," **Social Forces,** 15 (1937), pp. 544–551.

the form of facial tics and distortions. Still others get worked up to a state in which they seem to writhe in pain and go through several forms of bodily contortions, even doubling up with the head drawn between the knees so as to form a ball of the body. Fixed in this position by muscular catalepsy, they easily fall from their position and roll aimlessly about. Another type of cataleptic manifestation is the communicant whose body, on being permeated with the Holy Ghost, slowly straightens up and becomes rigid. This type of worshiper also easily gets out of equilibrium with gravity, falls, and rolls about on the floor. It was these types that brought the Holiness groups into disrepute in the early days and earned for them the name "Holy Rollers."

The purpose of this first part of the services is to "get the spirit," "to get a new baptism of fire from the Holy Ghost," or "to get in tune with the Infinite," to put it the way a more sophisticated young evangelist expressed the purpose of this part of their worship. "It is through prayer," he said, "that we unlock the gates of heaven, walk into the sanctum sanctorum and commune with the Holy Ghost." This evangelist further explained, in answer to some questions, that the various forms of muscular reactions were manifestations of the degree of closeness the individual got to the Holy Spirit. Said he, "When you get very close to the Holy Ghost you get a lot of this essence; a lot of His power just knocks you out, a little of His force just moves you slightly."

This expression of the evangelist represents the general belief underlying most of the practices in the worship of this sect. Many individuals and sects have from time to time proclaimed their powers to get personal contact with Supreme Beings. Witness the early prophets, the ascetics, the mystic cults of the Dark Ages, the Shaking Quakers, and the Holiness groups. However, it appears that the Negro Holiness group lays more stress on the idea of nearness to the Holy Spirit than any of the other Holiness organizations.

The belief in the possibility of getting near the Holy Spirit through prayer encourages the communicants to work themselves into a hypnotic frenzy, and the cataleptic or epileptic states which seize some of them. The ideal of the more devout members is to get into the state manifested in the extreme seizures, because it is believed that when one is in this state he has succeeded in getting extremely close to the Holy Ghost. Actually, on coming out of the seizures, some loudly and joyously exclaim that they have "touched the hem of His garments."

The second part of the services of this sect consists of three types of activities, singing, handclapping and dancing, and recitation of experiences.

When the praying is over, and everyone is "in tune with the Infinite," a song is started. Anybody who happens to feel the Spirit starts the song. When the song is started the musicians, usually a pianist and drummer, pick it up, always in good jazz rhythm, usually to the tune of one of the classical blues songs. Instantly all participants stand, start clapping hands and marking time to the rhythm of the music. Ardor increases, action of hands and feet grows more vigorous until a stage of ecstasy is reached that requires a more thorough release of the spiritual forces acting within. One begins to speak in tongues, "Me, me, me . . ." Then another, "Tut tut tut . . ." So it goes. Speaking in tongues is contagious. The worshipers seem to feel that they are closely approaching the sacred realm of the Holy Spirit. Some appear to be trying to carry their mortal parts with them in their ecstatic flights, for they seem actually to try to fly.

The worshiper who first began to speak in tongues is seized with an urge to dance. She dances with great vigor, a dance which she executes with a degree of gracefulness that indicates she has put in a great deal of time practicing it. Others join in the dancing until a large number are participating, and the building is creaking from rhythmic vibrations. Each one has enough individuality to enable an observer to distinguish her dance as her own pattern.

Dancing, singing, and handclapping go on at high pitch until exhaustion slows the action to a pace of weakly raising the feet from the floor. The song ends. Exhausted and perspiring, the participants seat themselves.

A member rises and fervently tells the group how good God has been, how firm in the faith she has been, how holy, sanctified and free from sin she is. Someone bursts into song again and the process is repeated until the spirit has worn off.

The third and concluding part of the services is a sermon which reminds one very much of the old-fashioned, fundamentalist sermons of evangelistic days. The minister shows a degree of action during his exhortations comparable to that of the worshipers during the first and second phases of the services. His bounding action, his high voice and tonal effects arouse his communicants to exert their remaining energy to raise a chorus of statements of approval and shouts of joy. Great emphasis is given to heaven and all that it is alleged to offer for so little effort. Hell is practically forgotten by the ministers. The whole group seems to be pulled by anticipation of heaven, never pushed by fear of hell. All ideas of pain and unpleasantness, defeat and failure are lost in the temporary projection of self beyond reality to a changeless, deathless world of perpetual happiness, that exacts not thought or work from the individual, and where others cannot block satisfaction of desires.

Crowd change. A salient characteristic of crowd mood and imagery is their emergent, nontraditional nature. It is not surprising, therefore, that they should be typically tenuous and easily changed. Change, in the form of shifts in object or mood, is a normal crowd process.

Shifts in object. Crowds have been classified on the basis of the nature of the crowd object. Yet this object is not necessarily fixed and unchanging, once defined. By virtue of the symbolic character of the object a variety of objects can serve to make crowd action possible and to permit it to continue when it is interrupted.

A shift from one specific object to another may occur in any type of crowd. The most common instances of shifts from object to object are found in volatile crowds. Here the collective imagery of the crowd may remain vague or incomplete. A general class of objects may be sufficient to permit action consistent with the mood of the crowd. In the Chicago, Detroit, and Harlem riots there was no collectively defined, specific crowd object. In none of these riots were the real or alleged assailants in the precipitating incidents the objects of the crowd action. Many mob members had no idea what had started the riots. Yet a mood of hostility towards a general class of objects was created, and the crowd shifted easily from one specific object of this class to another.

Another cause of shift of object is the relative inaccessibility of the original object. After imagery develops, the object which is perceived as suitable may not prove accessible. It may be an intangible condition, such as injustice. Another object, related symbolically, but more tangible even though more limited, may serve as a substitute. The Bastille was such a limited, symbolic, but tangible object.

Even after a specific object has been defined and action toward it initiated, a shift may occur. One type of shift may come when something interferes with the action of the crowd toward the original object. Such an obstacle may become a new, substitute object of the crowd's action. In the crowd situation, ambiguities are resolved, doubts dispelled, and feelings of tolerance suppressed. As the feeling of universal approval, and hence of absolute rightness, reaches a maximum, dissent from the intended course of action of the crowd takes on a new aspect. First, it constitutes a source of frustration of an on-going course of action to which the crowd is now committed. The source of this frustration easily becomes an object of attack. Furthermore, the crowd becomes a powerful, even though temporary, reference group and in-group for its members. Interference is perceived as disloyalty and opposition to its righteous purposes. The person who interferes, whatever his motives, is identified in the participants' minds with the original object of their aggression. Hence he may easily become an acceptable substitute object, symbolically linked with the original object. This happened, it has been seen, to the erstwhile leaders of the anti-Communist mob in Trenton. Another illustration of such a shift is found in the near-lynching of the mayor of Omaha, described below.

OMAHA

The feature of the Omaha riot that somewhat differentiates it from previous crimes of the same nature, while emphasizing the sinister spirit of anarchy that inspires them all, is the murderous assault upon Mayor E. P. Smith when he attempted to address the mob. Omaha dispatches report a recent epidemic of crimes committed by Negroes in that city. On Sunday night, September 28, the correspondents tell us, a mob of five thousand stormed the court-house where the Negro charged with this crime was imprisoned, and demanded that the authorities hand him over to them. When this demand was refused they set fire to the court-house with incendiary bombs, imperiling the lives of more than a hundred prisoners and officials, and turned upon the building a fusillade of shots. When the Mayor appeared on the court-house steps and began to address the mob as "fellow citizens"

the leaders interrupted him with shouts of "give us that nigger." When he replied, "I can't do that, boys," he was seized by the men nearest him and dragged to a point several blocks away. "Lynch him," shouted some one in the crowd, and in a moment a rope was strung up to a trolley-wire. Somebody cut him down, but the mob readjusted the rope and pulled him up again. When a group of policemen rescued him he was bleeding at the nose and mouth, but still conscious. At the hospital where he was taken his condition was found to be critical, but he ultimately rallied. In the meanwhile, the mob wreaked its fury on the Negro, Brown, who had been handed over to it by his fellow prisoners when they faced the alternative of being burned alive. His body was riddled with bullets, partially burned, and dragged through the streets behind an automobile. Afterward rioting continued, with threats against the Negro population, until Federal troops under Gen. Leonard Wood took charge of the situation.

"Omaha," **The Literary Digest,** 63 (Oct. 11, 1919), 16.

Sometimes a crowd shifts to another object and even to another objective after it seems to have vented its aggression on the original victim. The Leeville, Texas, lynching of 1930 illustrates the latter type of shift, as well as a shift to a frustrating object. When the mob discovered that their would-be victim was confined in the vault of the courthouse and was not readily accessible, they turned their fury on the courthouse itself, burning it recklessly and gleefully. Then, having killed their now accessible victim, they took his body to the Negro section of town, mutilated and burned it, and wreaked havoc on the property of many innocent Negroes.

Cantril points out that almost everyone in the community participated in the lynching in one way or another.* This offers one clue as to the reason for the shift in crowd objective, from killing the Negro to torturing his lifeless body and vandalizing Negro property. This prolongation of the crowd activity provided an opportunity for direct participation on the part of many who had been restricted to a more passive role in the assault on the courthouse. A more significant reason for the shift seems to be that the success of the crowd in attaining their first objective served to pave the way for the subsequent actions. The aggressive crowd mood had been intensified as the activity progressed. Sanctions for aggressive action had emerged. The troops and Rangers had indicated that they would not offer firm resistance. A large part of the population of the town, including many respectable citizens, had cheered the active portion of the mob as they burned the courthouse. A permissive atmosphere for further aggression had been developed, not only for the initially bold active participants but for the more cautious spectators. It appears from Cantril's description that both elements participated in the burning and looting.

Finally, a shift of object may occur because the original object is, in a sense, a superficial or substitute one. The antagonism of the crowd participants may be directed at some object which, nevertheless, is not initially attacked. The norms of the society and the attitudes of the individual participant may inhibit them from focussing initially on this "real" object of their hostility. It is in this sense inaccessible and they may act on a substitute object. Action against the more available object may, however, intensify the crowd mood, relax the inhibitions of members, and create a sense of power and unanimity. Then the crowd may shift to the more hated objective.

In Lofton's description of the Civil War Draft riots in New York City it may be seen that the draft proclamation served as a precipitating incident to arouse the long-standing, deep-seated hostility of the Irish laborers against their alleged Negro competitors. These so-called "Draft Riots" were ostensibly protests against conscription. They began with walkouts and attacks upon the military as well as upon Negroes. Soon, however, the Negro residents became the primary object of attacks and the riot became a full fledged anti-Negro riot. Apparently by this time it mattered little to the rioters that such action led them to be branded "Rebel sympathizers," although the implications of disloyalty acted as a deterrent at first.

* Hadley Cantril, **The Psychology of Social Movements** (New York: John Wiley & Sons, Inc., 1941), pp. 97–110.

NORTHERN LABOR AND THE NEGRO DURING THE CIVIL WAR

WILLIS H. LOFTON

The hostile attitude of a large segment of Northern labor to the Negro and toward plans for emancipation was a major prob-

Reprinted in part by permission of the editors, **The Journal of Negro History**, from Willis H. Lofton, "Northern Labor and the Negro During the Civil War," **The Journal of Negro History**, 34 (1949), pp. 251–273.

lem which President Lincoln and his administration had to consider during the Civil War. It influenced the policies of the administration for the conduct of the war and the emancipation of the blacks. There had long been a not so latent fear among many northern workers that if the slaves were freed they might move northward seeking work and thus offer competition in the labor market. The anti-slavery leaders had been forced to meet this issue in appealing to the workers for their support. This same fear was to lessen the whole-hearted support which many workers would otherwise have given the Union cause.

Though generally giving support to the war, the Northern workers were often suspicious of the supposed sympathy for the blacks and sometimes showed little interest in proposals to emancipate them. Indeed, too often this coolness toward emancipation of the slaves crystallized into open hostility toward the colored workers in Northern communities. For many white workers these Negro laborers in Northern cities represented the sort of labor competition which they would be forced to meet if the masses of slaves were emancipated. The extent which the free colored people of the North actually offered labor competition is difficult to determine. Professor Fite has given the opinion that, "the competition offered by negroes was small, but in many places it called forth opposition which frequently passed beyond mere protest into bloodshed and murder." This is probably an accurate summation of the matter of labor competition. However, it must be kept in mind that it was not actual competition from colored workers which fixed the pattern of the attitude of the white workers. It was, rather, the idea and fear of probable competition which would result if the masses of slaves were emancipated. This was the spectre before many urban workers of the North.

It seems that the Irish workers exhibited a greater enmity toward colored workers than did any other group of white workers. This hostility had been noted before the Civil War and it seemed to increase as the war progressed. Hostility of the Irish workers toward the Negroes living among them at the North and toward projects to liberate the slaves was encountered in nearly all sections of the Union. Opposition to the presence of Negro workers expressed itself in strikes against employers using colored help, in agitation in the public press, and often in violence against the Negroes. This use of force was one of the most unfortunate features of the labor difficulties of this period.

The hostility of the white workers toward Negroes reached its climax at the time of the so-called "New York Draft Riots" of July, 1863. Though called "Draft Riots," the rioters more often than not made the colored people of the city the object of their fury. On March 3, 1863, Congress passed the first comprehensive conscription law in order to fill the ranks of the Union armies. The $300 exemption clause of the act made it appear to many white workers that the true purpose of the law was to conscript the poor, and not to bother the wealthy. Then, too, for many northern workers the draft seemed only "another name for forced military service in behalf of the hated negro rivals."

The opposition to the enforcement of the draft law was on two points: 1. it seemed that the act bore especially heavily upon the poor; 2. it would force white workers to fight to free the slaves who would soon become rivals for employment. It was because of this twofold character of the opposition to the Draft Act in New York that the rioters turned against the military forces, against persons of wealth and their property, and against the Negroes of the city.

Opposition to the $300 exemption clause of the law drew the fire of workers' organizations as being unfair to the laboring people and "advantage was taken of this feeling to create disloyalty to the Union and bitterness against the negro." That the Negro should have been the object of the opponents of the draft was illogical, for as one daily paper pointed out in reference to the colored people, ". . . are they not almost uniformly poor men, themselves exposed to the draft, and unable to pay the $300?" However, from the time of the passage of the law the draft was connected in the public mind with the Negro and the emancipation of the slaves. Why should the workingman allow himself to be drafted in order to fight in a war, the successful conclusion of which would release a horde of potential labor competitors?

When the registration of men for the draft began in the city on July 12, there was little evidence of opposition, but on the following morning "organized parties of men went from yard to yard, from shop to shop, to compel the workmen to leave their labor, and join the several processions which were wending their way toward the corner of Third Avenue and Forty-sixth Street." Another report warned that the laborers of the city were preparing to resist the draft.

On the next day rioting began with attacks upon the military and upon the colored residents of the city. One observer felt that "the fact that nearly all the men drafted were laborers and mechanics added fuel to the flame." It seemed that the outbreak had some organization and planning and was not chance attacks by inflamed workers. It was reported that on the morning of July 14, a large number of "respectable workmen and others, were seen to assemble at certain specified spots, and between eight and nine o'clock began moving along various avenues west of Fifth Avenue towards their appointed place of general meeting." From the beginning the rioters were chiefly workingmen. As the mobs formed those composing them forced employers to release their workers under threat of destroying the shop if the demands were resisted.

The rioters turned with great intensity against the colored people, even more than against the military officers and soldiers of the city, who were aiding the metropolitan police in enforcing the Draft Law. As soon as the disturbance began mobs threatened to burn factories and foundries, giving as the reason that "negroes were employed in them." Some employers sought to forestall the rioters by discharging their colored workers.

By the second day of the rioting the anger of the mob seemed to be turned more and more against the Negro population of the city. The draft seemed to be forgotten. The police and the few soldiers aiding them were attacked as a rule only when they went to the aid of the helpless people of color. The charge was made that the outbreak could not be attributed to "anything else than sympathy with the Rebels." The cry of the rioters was raised against "nigger, Abolition, Black Republican," along with denunciations of prominent members of the Republican party.

The Negroes of the city were hunted down, beaten, and killed with unbelievable ferocity. One of the city's newspapers reported that,

A perfect reign of terror exists in the quarters of this helpless people, and if the troubles which now agitate our city continue during the week it is believed that not a single negro will remain within the metropolitan limits.

Other evidence indicated that when Negroes were caught by the rioters "they were hung up to lampposts, or beaten, jumped on, kicked and struck with iron bars and heavy wooden clubs." Not only were men attacked but women and children felt the hands of the rioters. Homes were sacked and the inmates driven to the streets.

The sacking of the homes of Negroes was not only evidence of the anti-Negro spirit of the mobs, but was also a display of the desire for loot. As it happened, the riot once under way took curious turns. Grogshops, stores, and the homes of the wealthy were looted.

The vicious attacks upon the Negroes drove them from the city by the thousands. By the time that thousands of soldiers had been brought into the city to restore order over 3,000 colored people had been made homeless, and hundreds of others were lurking about the suburbs on Long Island and in the woods along the Harlem River. It seemed that they sought especially to escape their Irish persecutors. It was reported that many Negroes had fled to Hoboken because that place "has been a pretty safe refuge for them, as there are but few Irish living in that city." If the desire of the Irish was to intimidate the Negro workers of New York, they succeeded. By the third day of the riot one observer stated that "the negroes have entirely disappeared from the docks. Many of them, it is said, have been killed and thrown into the river."

Though the New York City riots attracted the attention of the nation, outbreaks of a similar type occurred in other places. These were on a lesser scale and did not draw the eyes of the country as did the New York catastrophe, but they revealed the same pattern of anti-Negro and anti-emancipation feeling. This indicates the extensiveness of the opposition to the Negro, especially if there were likelihood that he would become a competitor in the labor market.

The open hostility of northern white workers toward the Negro workers and their fear of the results of emancipation were logical sequences in view of labor attitudes before the Civil War. The workers were, by and large, loyal to the government and the Union, but their status as wage-earners made them view efforts to free the slaves with skepticism. For them it was a practical matter. If the slaves were liberated it might endanger their own chances of finding employment.

Emancipation of the slaves was not objected to very seriously by the workers if they could be assured that the freedmen would remain in the South. But the ideas of many of the radical Republicans did not seem to encompass a fixed geographical location for the former slaves. The hostility toward the free Negro workers in the North and the attacks upon them during the Civil War are to be interpreted in the light of the labor situation. Only then do these attacks become clear. The Negro worker was a symbol of what the Civil War and emancipation would bring. The fear of the black worker as a weapon in the hands of the employer, which has been characteristic of the labor movement, became a fixed pattern during the Civil War. Subsequent reaction to the competition from Negro workers has been only an accentuation of this earlier reaction to this competition, whether real or imaginary.

Shifts in mood. Even more perplexing are instances in which the mood of a crowd shifts without a change in object. Some changes in crowd mood are simply an intensification of the existing mood, but other shifts constitute an actual transformation change of mood.

One factor which is related to mood shifts of both types is interference with the developing crowd action. A mildly aggressive crowd may be enraged, and their mood raised to a high pitch of hostility, when resistance to the accomplishment of their objective arises. In Trenton, for example, the mob initially was relatively restrained in mood and object, but was determined to prevent the communist speaker from being heard. Then the police and the veteran leaders attempted to insure that the letter of the law guaranteeing free speech was observed. This attempted interference with the attainment of the objective only helped to heighten the mood of aggressiveness. Toward the end of the demonstration, actual physical violence to the communists became the goal of the crowd. When the police enabled the would-be speakers to escape unharmed they themselves became the object of aggression.

Interference with its activities may also cause a major transformation of mood. The police often find themselves objects of aggressive mob action when they interfere, or even seem to interfere, with the revelrous behavior of an expressive crowd. At the height of the 1955 Mardi Gras festivities in New Orleans, the attempted arrest of one of the merrymakers changed the gay mood of the crowd to one of aggressiveness. Officers who came to the assistance of their fellows were beaten and pummeled. Even after the original disturbance was quelled, the aggressive, destructive mood continued to prevail, and repeated riot calls were put in as the crowd expressed its aggressive mood by hurling rocks at cars and busses.

A second cause of mood shift is a change in composition of a crowd. This may result in an intensification of mood, as happens when certain types of participants join a crowd. As has been indicated in Chapter 6, aggressive crowd action, regardless of objectives, may attract participants who derive gratification from such behavior. Their relatively uninhibited, sometimes pathological behavior may serve to heighten the aggressive mood of the crowd and provide models for extreme behavior.

A change in composition of the crowd may, however, cause a transformation of both mood and imagery. Here again it must be remembered that the crowd is not a collectivity without culture, but that the participants bring to the situation part of their culture. Hence the pre-existing attitudes and identifications of the members are one variable affecting the responses of the crowd. How the mood may shift as a result of the addition of members with different attitudes is well illustrated in the following account. The increasing number of young people in the crowd, which was characterized initially by an "anti-youth" mood, contributed strongly to the subsequent shift in both mood and imagery.

A CROWD OBSERVATION
LELAND LAYNE NICHOLS

At four-twenty on Sunday a grey Studebaker swung down Malibu canyon road to the highway. The young driver and his date had been swimming at Malibu Lake and both were still wearing only their swim clothes and both were wet and tired, chilled now by the breeze that blew in from the sea. The boy put his foot on the brake pedal as they approached the intersection. A nearly solid thread of traffic wound down the coast. The north-bound lanes were clear, everyone was returning to the city.

The boy plunged the pedal downward, the force of his thrust and the resistance of the pedal set his cold, wet foot slipping wildly to the right. He hit the accelerator and in an unmeasurable instant of time the car shot out into the highway, crashing into the left front fender of a new Pontiac which was hurrying to keep up with the pack which was now four car lengths ahead. They joined in a weird *pas de deux* and slipped to the shoulder. The Studebaker was freed by the twisting and it stopped on the road, but the Pontiac tipped on its right wheels, hesitated, and slipped down the embankment, tipped

Student paper, University of California at Los Angeles. Published by permission.

over on its side and came to rest. Traffic stopped and within a minute a crowd had gathered. Over the rhythmic crash of the sea and the irregular swish of the north-bound traffic the wail of a girl could be heard.

The boy got out of his car and stood looking dully at the sea. Of the crowd, one went up to see if he was hurt. Neither he nor the girl was and now the girl had stopped her fitful wailing. The crowd stood looking down the slope at the Pontiac—not a sound nor movement came from it.

The crowd quickly grew to twenty, three couples in their twenties and the rest middle aged. One woman, the oldest in the group and the most vocal, was informing the newcomers about the accident. As she saw it youth was careless and full of blame. She told her story with the authority and enthusiasm of a revival minister, "He never tried to stop—he was going to sneak in ahead of them others, poor folks. These youngsters should not be allowed to drive."

One of the older men and two younger ones went down the slope to the other car. A few others followed behind. There were two people in the car—both unconscious, both wearing swim suits and both young, a fellow and a girl.

The crowd still standing on the highway gathered around the old woman. She was repeating her story. No one questioned her, or doubted her. Others took up some of the newcomers and repeated much the same story in answer to the inevitable, "What's happened?"

The group down at the Pontiac was younger, by and large, than that on the road. As new people arrived the younger ones clambered down the slope, the older stayed on the level ground. Someone suggested that they ought to get the car back on its wheels, "Better get them out first," another thought. "Maybe we ought to wait for the cops," a timid third said. One of the younger ones crawled up on the car to open the driver's door. The boy was conscious now and struggled to get out. He had a cut on his hand where he had hit some of the dash instruments. He was helped to the ground, he looked around for a minute, then, "Turn my car over," he said weakly. He repeated this again and again; whether in shocked description or imperative it was impossible to tell. He kept avowing that he was not hurt. They talked him into lying down and the boy who had opened the door climbed back up to look at the girl. She was conscious now too, but in pain and she whimpered as they laid her down on a blanket which had appeared in the crowd.

With both of the people out of it the men set to the job of righting the car. They had it on its feet when the police arrived. The next few minutes are familiar to anyone who has ever been at a wreck. Talking, taking names, looking at identification, getting opinions, measuring, talking, and being official.

The boy in the Studebaker said he had tried to stop. Others agreed that he had hesitated. The old woman was then questioned, "What happened?" "Where were you when the accident took place?" Her answer was delivered in the same voice, full of authority, that she used before. "The boy was coming down the canyon," she said, "he started to stop then he

whizzed into the street. Guess he must have had something go wrong with his car—engine stuck, or something. If he hadn't hit them he would have shot right into the ocean, poor boy."

The ambulance arrived and the two girls and the boy from the Pontiac were loaded aboard. With a shrill scream it took off for Santa Monica. The other boy stayed with his car, the police were still talking to him. A tow-truck was on its way to pull the other car up from the sand.

The crowd scattered and now passers-by only slowed down, then drove on.

ANALYSIS

The most important thing to be noted is the shift in crowd mood. Initially the crowd was apparently convinced that the boy in the Studebaker was at fault; heedless and careless. By the time the police arrived this view had changed to one of such a different mood that people were reporting things favorable to the lad which they were in no position to have witnessed.

Two factors account for this shift, in the main. The first is the constitution of the crowd—or its heterogeneity. The second is the function and character of the rumors which were circulated. These points will be discussed separately.

Composition of Crowd. Until the time when the police appeared on the scene the crowd had continued to add new members. The original group of seven persons grew quickly to twenty or twenty-five and never changed from this figure by more than five. At the time of the key note by the old woman the crowd was still predominantly middle aged. Her remarks about the general irresponsibility of youth were not ill-received by the group. As the crowd grew it became more evenly balanced with regard to the age distribution. Four motorcyclists stopped as did several groups of younger people going home from a day at the beach. At this time also the occupants of the Pontiac were discovered to be at least as young as the other couple. It would have been very difficult to continue to support an anti-youth bias since this would mean placing the blame for the accident on both parties, a singularly unsatisfactory way to solve the problem of who's to blame for an accident. With the announcement that the Pontiac couple was also young the old woman ceased her recounting of the story. She engaged her traveling companion in conversation and talked to nobody else until the officer asked her his questions.

As the police arrived several cars left—none containing any of the young people. When the questioning started there were only a few people left over thirty or thirty-five, among them the old woman and her friend.

Rumor. Rumor served to provide a collective image around which the attitudes and possibilities of action could be organized. The rumors all seemed to contain the same essential parts with material and emphasis changing as the mood changed. The rumors of the first stage might be combined as follows: "This young kid in the Studebaker came barreling out of the canyon without stopping and tried to sneak in ahead of the Pontiac. He must have been drunk to try to make it. After the crash he got out of the car and started to cry—sort of crazy, ya know what I mean?"

By the time the police arrived the rumors were of a very different sort, or of two sorts, rather. Collecting several direct quotations we may combine these into one full rumor showing each type: "The fellow in the grey car tried to stop but his brakes didn't work and he shot into the traffic and hit the Pontiac. If he had been a minute sooner he would have shot into the brink—lucky thing they hit, nobody was hurt this way." The other version would be: "The Studebaker was just trying to get into the traffic and the Pontiac speeded up. They're lucky they didn't get killed."

From these examples the change in mood is clear. Rumor functioned to inform the crowd about what had happened, as those who saw it interpreted it. These rumors were modified or re-emphasized to fit the changing feeling of the crowd as it, in turn, changed its composition to one which was more sympathetic with the young drivers. Then new versions, and new "slants" were given to the stories to buttress and reinforce the new mood, or to justify it.

Changes in Leadership. Of great importance was the fact that the crowd did not have a fixed membership. There were new faces every few minutes and these had to be informed and integrated into the group. As the mood changed these new ones became recruits for the now stronger faction. These took over the leadership of the crowd and gave it direction and orientation.

An even more dramatic shift in the mood of a crowd from hostile to friendly and sympathetic is portrayed in "Sendoff for Devil's Island."

Several reasons for the shift in mood of this and other crowds are suggested by this account. First, it is evident that ambivalence within a crowd and within its individual members may persist even after it seems to have been resolved in the initial interaction. Differential expression may conceal differences of attitude on the part of the silent participants, creating the illusion of unanimity. Ambivalence may also continue to exist in the feelings of some individual members of the crowd, even as they act in terms of one set of attitudes. Yet even a slight change in the situation may lead to overt expression by members who previously dissented, but silently. A new keynote may be struck, suppressed feelings may be aroused again, and a new and different crowd mood may develop.

One such change in the situation may be some development which renders incongruous the crowd image of the object. The gentlemanly gesture of the convict who bowed his thanks for a carton of cigarettes seems to have caused such a shift in objective. The crowd now perceived the thinly masked misery of the prisoners and the mood changed to one of compassion. Perhaps the weeping boy and the old man came to dominate the crowds' conception of the object, rather than the tough, recalcitrant murderers.

Another change may be a redefinition of the situation in which the crowd action occurs, here exemplified by a change in locale. It was at the quayside that the shift in crowd mood and the first friendly gesture towards the prisoners came. Now the convicts no longer marched through the streets under guard, but sat jammed together hugging their pitiful belongings. As the launches pulled away from the shores of France, the finality of the prisoners' departure and the horror of their destiny became figure rather than ground in the crowd's perceptual field. Sentiments of compassion, of fair play, of "not kicking a man when he is down," seem to have asserted themselves and been reflected in a transformation of the crowd's mood and actions.

SENDOFF FOR DEVIL'S ISLAND
W. A. S. Douglas

For 28 years now—ever since the end of the first World War—France has been talking about cleaning up its private hellhole to the south of us, the convict settlement of French Guiana. Matter of fact, the movement began after it was learned that Maj. Alfred Dreyfus was not a traitor to his country—as were those who had sent him there. All that was done at that time was to clean up the place a little—a very little.

We once watched the loading of the prison ship which, before the German occupation of France, used to make a twice-a-year journey to the penal colony. The march of the doomed over the cobblestones of Marseilles was the most disgusting sight we have ever witnessed—and we have had our full share of disgusting sights. The prisoners tramped along between long lines of guards, old men, middle-aged men and boys; their crimes ranged from murder through treason to petty thievery; some were in the lineup through the machinations of political enemies.

A THROWBACK

Here was a throwback to France at her 18th-century worst. While weeping men

and women walked outside the line of guards seeking a last glimpse of someone who, no matter how hated by others, was loved by them, other men and women— yes, and children, too—howled and cursed at the convicts. Outside the thin line of family mourners, outside the packed mass of men without hope, the people were on cruel holiday.

In the front row of the sentenced were two notorious murderers who had managed to cheat the guillotine—if it was cheating to trade an easy if gory death for a lifetime in the nearest place on earth to the popular conception of purgatory. The pair was singled out for special attention—but they gave back as good as they got, at any rate in filthy vituperation, though they were hampered by a lack of rotten vegetables. The audience had plenty, however.

As well as we can remember there were between 200 and 300 convicts in that shipment. The general attitude on their part was one of bravado. The really tough ones cursed, spat, howled and laughed at their tormenters; and those who were not so tough but pretended to be followed suit. In the lost column that tramped past us we saw only two in tears —a very old man and a boy who appeared to be no more than sixteen.

THE CROWD RELENTS

But at the quayside an extraordinary

Reprinted by permission of the editor and publisher, Chicago **Sun-Times,** from W. A. S. Douglas, "The Sun Beam," Chicago **Sun,** May 3, 1946.

change came over the watching, hitherto howling populace—one of those mass switches of the mind which make the people of France so ununderstandable to the rest of us. The first of the launches had been loaded with the unfortunates, what was left of the column was moving to another launch. The convicts sat jammed together, hugging their pitiful belongings, still cursing, their misery masked by the forced grins of the toughs as well as the would-be toughs.

A woman, seemingly as hard-boiled in appearance as any of the men in the launch, threw a carton of cigarettes at random into the boat. It was caught by a shackled convict who rose as well as he was able and bowed his thanks in the approved fashion of French upper-crust society. The tossing of the carton seemed a signal to others on the quayside. More cigarettes followed, flowers followed, boxes of food went through the air, some to break in transit, others to land more or less whole in the laps of the prisoners. Before the launch pulled out for the convict ship, about every man aboard, including the guards, had a flower or food or cigarettes or all three.

A public denunciation had changed in a twinkling to a public ovation. Curses had changed to almost affectionate farewells. You would have thought—if you had not viewed the preliminaries—that these were soldiers of France off to do battle for their motherland.

Now we are assured that the tropical prison colony is to be liquidated. Twenty eight hundred "libérés"—men who have completed their sentence but who were doomed to live out their miserable lives in the jungle—are to be brought home. Twenty three hundred others—the balance of the convict population—are to be either pardoned or sent to serve the balance of their terms in more healthful places. Marseilles will miss its twice a year parade.

Chapter 8

Crowd conventionalization
and control

$\mathcal{C}$ROWD behavior consists, in essence, of deviations from the traditional norms of society. Hence it is often regarded as undesirable and pathological. Societies tend to attempt to prevent, control or terminate it, especially when it threatens to go against the more important norms. Consideration of methods by which its behavior is controlled is, therefore, essential in the study of the crowd.

But there is an ambivalence in the reactions of groups and individuals to crowds. Giving free play to his feelings, without designating to himself all of the consequences of his acts, and escaping for a time from the bonds of convention can be an enjoyable experience for the individual. Furthermore, the sense of unity and power produced when a group becomes a crowd is a potent force in reinforcing the solidarity of the group, as Durkheim pointed out. Kingsley Davis has said of this force: "It would be amazing if such a potent force were not socially utilized in some way . . . The crowd situation is constantly being planned for and utilized by every type of social system." *

Hence, while societies attempt to control and terminate crowds, they also harness and utilize the force of the crowd. It may be said, then, that *conventionalization* of crowd behavior occurs, as Blumer suggests in his concept of "the conventionalized crowd." At times, also, the force of the crowd is deliberately utilized by individual leaders or by small power-groups, although the crowd members are unaware of this and feel that their activities are spontaneous. The phenomenon of crowd manipulation must therefore be considered in connection with the process of conventionalization and control.

* Kingsley Davis, **Human Society** (New York: The Macmillan Co., 1949), p. 351.

Crowd control and termination. In complex societies, with laws and law-enforcement agencies, it is the law-enforcement agents who most often have the job of controlling crowd situations. Their duties may range from maintaining order in an amiable crowd at a ball game to breaking up a rioting mob.

If sufficient force of men and arms can be mustered, a police force can overwhelm even the most violent mob. The use of force as the means of crowd control is likely to entail great costs, however. As was shown in Chapter 7, frustration of a crowd in the pursuit of its objective is likely to intensify the angry mood and make the frustrating individuals themselves objects of aggression. History is replete with tragic incidents in which police or soldiers have engaged in pitched battles with mobs. Often the victims prove to be ordinarily peaceful, law abiding citizens, members of the in-group. Hence law-enforcement agencies are inhibited from the unrestricted use of force as a means of crowd control.

In recent years the practical experience of police officers and the studies of social scientists have together served as the basis for the formulation of principles of crowd control. One such formulation is found in the manual "The Police and Minority Groups," prepared for the Chicago Park District Police by a sociologist in collaboration with supervisory police officers. In the selection below, five methods of controlling and terminating a potentially riotous crowd are suggested:

(1) Removal or isolation of the individuals involved in the precipitating incident before the crowd has begun to achieve substantial unity.

(2) Interruption of communication during the milling process by dividing the crowd into small units.

(3) Removal of the crowd leaders, if it can be done without use of force.

(4) Distracting the attention of the crowd from its focal point by creating diversions at other points.

(5) Preventing the spread and reinforcement of the crowd by isolating it.

THE ROLE OF THE POLICE OFFICER IN CROWD CONTROL
Joseph D. Lohman

The steps in the development of an aggressive and destructive crowd can be identified. The first stage in the transformation of a collection of separate individuals into a mob is the occurrence of some exciting incident. Whatever the nature of the incident, if it is sufficiently exciting and commanding of attention, it will attract a group of onlookers who will mill about the scene of the incident and who may have occasion to take sides. In the early stages of the gathering of crowds, it is often possible for the police

officer to isolate an incident by making a quick, yet adequate, determination of the facts. Then, by taking immediate action— e.g., the taking of the parties into custody —he may avoid the involvement of many onlookers. The speed with which the police officer operates in these situations is the measure of the extent to which onlookers can accumulate. By cutting short such an accumulation, he can prevent an incident from becoming an affair which it will be impossible for him to handle. The following incident, related by one of the supervisory officers, illustrates the way in which incidents can be expeditiously handled in such a manner that more serious developments are avoided:

A cab load of white sailors were

Reprinted in part by permission of the Chicago Park District and the author, from Joseph D. Lohman, **The Police and Minority Group** (Chicago: Chicago Park District, 1947), pp. 80–86.

having an argument with a cab driver over the payment of their fares. This argument took place in a Negro area at 47th and Michigan, and a crowd of curious onlookers began to gather. The sailors, who were under the influence of liquor, began to hurl insults at the Negro bystanders. An ugly situation was in the making when a police officer appeared on the scene. He immediately ordered the cab driver to take his cab with the load of sailors to a point several blocks distant. The removal of these sailors from the crowd which had collected made it possible for the officer to deal with the dispute between the cab driver and the sailors and prevent what otherwise might have been a dangerous race incident.

Many times an officer does not arrive upon the scene of an incident until after a crowd has assembled and achieved a degree of aggressive unity. As an incident proceeds to attract numbers of individuals, they are pressed together. They quite naturally begin to brush and contact one another, even to initiate conversation with utter strangers. This activity is somewhat akin to the behavior of sheep crowded together in a corral. They move around and about in rather aimless fashion, all the while communicating to each other the collective excitement of the situation. This is known as the milling process.

This process creates among the members of the crowd an internal rapport, a kind of collective hypnosis in which the individual loses his self-control and responds only to the dictates of the crowd as a whole. Here is an important fundamental fact which every police officer who has dealt with a crowd has had occasion to experience. In the mob the individual loses his ability to act in terms of cool and rational considerations. He is swayed by the moods and sentiments of the mob. He begins to act in quite different terms than if he were alone or out from under the influence of the mob. In this fact exists the immense potentiality for evil behavior which crowds often exhibit. Quite often individuals find it difficult to understand how they could possibly have acted as they did while part of a crowd or mob.

Notwithstanding the increasing difficulties which confront a police officer in coping with a milling crowd, there are control measures which can be employed at that stage. One effective handling of a milling crowd is indicated in the following incident related by one of the supervisory officers.

A relief agency had sent out notices that it would employ men at a certain hour at Humboldt Park field house. When an officer arrived on the scene, a crowd of several thousand had gathered in front of the field house. The officer was confronted by a sea of heads milling about the doors. Excitement was rising, men pushed against one another, and there was danger that a protecting rail would collapse from the weight of the pressure against it. If left to its own devices, the crowd would soon have broken the railing, with resultant injuries, and might have stormed the building. The officer took a position where he could command the attention of the crowd and told them that if they would form an orderly line, they would all be registered in due course. He selected four men as the first elements in a column and began to march them in zig-zag fashion around and away from the field house. Soon he had the whole crowd arranged in a column of fours stretched around and away from the field house.

In this incident the officer acted in terms of a practical understanding of the potentialities of the milling crowd. He realized that the milling must be broken up before the crowd became hysterical and aggressive. He introduced the regular formation in order to isolate individuals from each other in groups of fours. Thus, he transformed the crowd and potential mob into an orderly assembly.

In many cases, however, the crowd or mob has already achieved a degree of unity and purpose that makes it unresponsive to this kind of suggestion. When this is the case, it becomes necessary for police officers to remove the most excited individuals from the crowd. The most excited individuals are always a focus of attention in the organization of an aggressive mob. Their removal will contribute to, and make possible, the dissolution of the remaining less excited individuals. In the removal of these individuals, the police officers must make a *show of force*. However, it does not necessarily mean that they should *use* force. The difference is an important one, and a failure to make the distinction may result in unnecessary bloodshed. The mere presence of sufficient numbers of men in uniform is what is meant by a *show of force*. This awes the crowd so that it becomes unnecessary to *use* force in removing key persons. The idea of individual heroic police action is not only unnecessary, it may be positively damaging and foolhardy. A police officer who attempts single-handed to subdue a mob or grapple with individuals puts his own safety in jeopardy. In the violence that then is bound to ensue, he merely stimulates the ugly tendencies of the crowd. It is of prime importance that such situations be avoided. It can be done if supervisory officers so arrange and instruct their personnel that reinforcements can be mobilized at any point in the shortest possible time and in numbers appropriate to the situation.

In the following incident related by one of the supervisory officers unpleasant results followed an *inadequate* show of force:

> A mob had gathered who were being harangued by an inflammatory soap-box orator. The officers drove up in a squad car and decided to place the speaker under arrest. Drawing their clubs, they made their way to the center of the crowd, where the speaker stood. The speaker, however, was surrounded by sympathizers. So were the two police officers. The members of the crowd set upon the officers, wrested their clubs from their hands, knocked them down, and kicked them. They were unable to arrest the speaker. Only with the arrival of reinforcements and a considerable *use of force* were arrests made and the mob dispersed.

In this instance the law was represented in too little strength. There was an *inadequate* show of force, with the result that the crowd was not overawed. The mere presence of a larger group of uniformed men would have made unnecessary the later resort to the *use of force*.

Tension in a crowd is usually highest at a point-front and center. Here the excited individuals who exercise such unusual influence on all the others are located. These are the points upon which police attention should be centered and the approach made if the exciting influence of strategic individuals needs to be checked. A tactic used in the Harlem riots by the New York police and also by the Milwaukee police in the dispersal of dangerous crowds met with considerable success. It is that of directing the crowd from its outer edges to "break up and go home." This was done by means of a public-address system mounted on a sound truck. The blare of the speaker and the authoritative tone of the commands attract the attention of the individuals in the crowd. In so doing, it turns them away from the excited individuals and breaks up their influence. This technique is unquestionably helpful in breaking up crowds in their early stages and can be useful in penetrating the consciousness of a group which is already well organized.

The final stage in the development of a mob has been called the phase of social contagion. In this period, the small original crowd is swelled by numbers of bystanders. They usually have little, if any, knowledge of the precipitating incident. They are impelled by curiosity and are merely attracted by the sight of gathering people. Innocent as they are of the incident, they are, nevertheless, quickly captured by the mood of the crowd and begin to share its collective excitement. A supervisory officer furnishes the following incident to indicate that innocent bystanders are drawn to and become a part of the mob:

> A crowd had collected in Douglas Park and were being incited by questionable leadership. It began to collect people passing by and before long it became necessary to break it up by positive police intervention. Considerable force was used, and later it was found that the greater proportion of those who received injuries were innocent bystanders who had drifted into the crowd from 12th Street.

In the early stages of the formation of the crowd, a cordon of police would have been effective in minimizing such injuries. By means of the police cordon, individuals could be permitted to escape from the crowd, but not to enter it. In the handling of mob situations, the police cordon prevents the riotous infection of great masses of individuals by preventing social contagion. In the Harlem riots, the cordon was used with great success. By throwing police cordons around danger areas, thousands of curiosity seekers were prevented from being exposed to the mob situation and in that way becoming infected with its spirit. Letting people out means freeing them from the excitement of the mob; keeping them out of the area means that the mob spirit will not be able to possess them.

A significant characteristic of the participant in the crowd is that his attention is narrowly focused on the immediate situation. The seemingly unanimous support and approval of his immediate group encourage the immediate, uncritical translation of his impulses into action. Therefore any technique which reduces the feelings of anonymity and invincibility of the individual, forcing him to focus his attention upon himself and the consequences of his own actions, is likely to be effective in controlling a crowd.

The use of such a technique by the police, in preference to a resort to force, is illustrated in the following incident witnessed by the authors.

WHO'S NEXT?
Lewis M. Killian

Shortly before 7 A.M. one November morning in 1949 a crowd of 750 union members marched *en masse* before the doors of a strike-bound factory on Chicago's West Side, in defiance of a court order limiting the number of pickets to four. The illegal pickets came from the struck plant and from a score of other plants whose workers belonged to the same amalgamated union local. Their purpose was to demonstrate union solidarity to their various employers and to strikebreakers who were being employed at this plant.

The demonstration had been carefully planned during the preceding weeks by union officials, and the crowd was skillfully manipulated by these leaders. Many of the union members had gathered near the plant under the impression that they would merely stage a peaceful, legal demonstration in a public park opposite the plant, proceeding afterwards to their own home plants. Instead they found their officers leading them in a line of pickets packed solidly, six abreast, across the sidewalk. Actually, the illegal picketing had been planned by the union leaders as a test of the injunction provisions of the then new Taft-Hartley Act.

The Chicago police had learned in advance of the plans, and the Labor Squad was out in force in the early morning hours. The mass of pickets marched steadily to a position blocking the doors of the plant, despite the immediate arrest of their leaders, and mild resistance offered by the police. As some fifty strikebreakers arrived for work their entrance to the plant was barred, and those who attempted to break through the picket line were shoved back. Excitement was high in the crowd as it milled around in a tight circle, defying the orders of the police to disperse. The police were greatly outnumbered and the crowd was defiant. For a few tense moments it seemed likely that if the demonstration were to be broken up a pitched battle between police and strikers would occur.

Based upon materials in the files of Lewis M. Killian.

Then the police went into action, but not with any assault on the crowd as a unit. Rather, they began to pick off individuals from the edges of the milling mob, calmly, firmly, and indiscriminately. There seemed to be no particular logic in their selections, but whatever individual came within reach of the heavy hand of the law was pulled away from his fellows and marched off to a waiting patrol wagon. One wagon after another was loaded with strikers, and driven away. Before the demonstration was over 180 persons were arrested.

Although this was only a minority of the mass of picketers, the demonstration was over soon after the police began making their indiscriminate arrests. Each time a picket was led off to a patrol wagon, several others dropped out of the crowd. The strength that lay in the size and unity of the crowd was lost, for the police made no effort to deal with the crowd as a whole nor to make the pickets disperse simultaneously and precipitously. Instead, they made it plain that they would deal with the pickets individually but indiscriminately, and that while the majority might escape, some would be jailed. Since no one knew who would be arrested next, the safety of each was threatened, and only the heartiest remained long to try their luck. Within 25 minutes from the time the demonstration started four lone pickets remained to march in front of the plant, under the watchful eyes of a pair of policemen, while a few of their erstwhile comrades watched from a safe distance. No blood had been shed, no clubs wielded, but the crowd had been effectively dispersed.

Crowds can be terminated or controlled by means other than the show of force and by individuals other than police officers. Sometimes a solidaristic crowd may be transformed into an individualistic crowd and thus controlled. Presented with opportunities for looting, a hostile solidaristic crowd may be diverted from its common object, with concerted pursuit of a common objective being abandoned for individual competition to attain parallel goals. A quick-thinking individual may deliberately terminate solidaristic-focused crowd action in this manner, but such a transformation may also occur without deliberate effort by anyone.

Another means of controlling a crowd relies upon the creation of some incident that changes the mood of the crowd. Such an incident may be an appeal to in-group mores that have not yet been completely suppressed from the attention of the crowd members. As the following incident shows, a suggestion that the crowd's action is violating important norms is likely to be accepted if it comes from a person who appears to be "with" the crowd. Such a technique is not as likely to work, however, in the later stages of crowd development, when the dominant mood and imagery have become more strongly established.

INGROUP NORMS AND CROWD CONTROL

RALPH H. TURNER

On Thursday evening, February 11, 1954, Senator Joseph McCarthy was guest speaker at a regular meeting of the Freedom Club held in a fashionable Congregational church in Los Angeles. The

Based upon materials in the files of Ralph H. Turner.

meeting came at a time when the controversy surrounding McCarthy was at its height. Wilbur Jerger, a Democrat, parked a station wagon equipped with loudspeaking equipment in a private driveway immediately adjacent to the church parking lot. From this vantage point he harangued the group as they left the meeting on the evils of McCarthyism. The result was the quick development of a hostile crowd, separated from Jerger by a chain-link fence and police cordon, but managing to break one of the loud speakers and to do other damage to his car. Unlike most reported crowds, this one was observed to consist chiefly of middle-aged, middle-class men and women. At a point when more serious action appeared likely, Jerger was safely escorted from the scene under police protection and the crowd gradually dispersed.

One incident which occurred before Jerger left is instructive regarding the manner in which crowd behavior may be controlled. The episode centered about a man who had not attended the McCarthy meeting, but had come with a female companion simply to watch the group leave the church. He was an outspoken opponent of McCarthy. The following slightly adapted account is taken from a tape-recorded interview with him a few days after the event.

I was there with a young lady, and we'd resolved that it would be the height of unwisdom to make any comment, because the atmosphere at the conclusion of the meeting would undoubtedly be charged with tension. And frankly, I debated the wisdom of being there at all, since I am somewhat well known locally. Even my presence there might give cause for some sort of demonstration. We stood by and watched this particular performance.

Then a man next to me said, "Oh, I know that Wilbur Jerger. He's a teacher in the Valley and a yid." To this the young lady with me said, "Well, he's got a right to speak." And then all my resolutions just flew out the window. I said, "Yes, he's got a right to speak." And he said, "He's a yid; he doesn't have a right to speak." And I said, "Everyone has a right to speak." And he said, "If you think everyone has a right to speak, you must be a Red." And I said, "Well, if believing that everyone has a right to speak makes me a Red; then I'm a Red!"

That was probably a very silly thing to have said, but I was defiant and this led to a call on his part, "Here's a Red, here's a Red, here's a Red." Well, from every direction they came. I was pretty terrified and looked about frantically for a wall or fence—something to which I could put my back and at least fight in one direction. I was rendered completely inarticulate and frightened by the horde converging upon me. I felt that I was surrounded in every direction. There must have been a hundred people in the group that came around me. They were throwing punches. And I was trying to protect the young lady, whose arms were catching the blows, and holding her with one arm and swinging with the other as well as I could. I was swinging in a wide arc to keep people away. Then somebody jumped me from the back, got me by neck and applied pressure, but it didn't hurt too much. I tried to make a hasty decision as whether to bend over and throw him. But then I felt that that would merely have exposed me to being jumped from the front. In a way he was paradoxically protecting my back. So I just let it go at that, let him stay there and punched in a wide arc.

The battle went on, it may have been a minute, it may have been two minutes—it would be absolutely impossible for me to estimate its duration. It seemed like hours while looking up at the fear-crazed faces of these people—elderly people for the most part. By their very numbers they constituted a threat. The strange part of it is that I never felt those punches, though I may have received a hundred of them. And even later I bore no scars or bruises. They certainly weren't in fine Marciano athletic trim . . . no Bobo Olson or Kid Gavilan.

As they went on for, as I say, a minute or two, a young fellow came up. He must have been 18 or 19, tall, I think almost 7 feet tall. This may sound strange—as though I was not in possesion of my faculties. But I'm 6 feet 3 myself and he was very, very considerably taller than I, with long, long arms. He approached the group and said, "We don't want any violence on this church property. Violence on church property won't help our cause. We don't want violence on church property." This had an almost magical effect upon the group. The whole group dissolved just as rapidly as it had gathered together. And quite shaken, I proceeded then to walk away from the scene. No one followed me, no one made any attempt to, no one threatened, no one threw a blow.

Then this young fellow came up to me and said, "Man, you're a fool. I'm not with these people. I'm here for the same purpose that you are, but I have better sense than to make any remark at all before these people. They're a bunch of animals. They're crazy. You could have been killed." And without even stopping to take his name or thank him, because I certainly wasn't in possession of my faculties, I just let him go.

Almost certainly the stature and poise of the man who dispersed this segment of the crowd were crucial in accounting for his success. But it should be stressed that his action consisted of *manipulating ingroup mores*. The Freedom Club was firmly grounded in the church and centered about its minister. The minister and members believed their political convictions to be a practical expression of their Christian faith. Consequently, the mores of Protestant Christianity were present as a common bond among the crowd participants. The disavowal of violence, while recognized as a Christian tenet, has not been accorded a sufficiently high place in the hierarchy of norms in most of the standard Protestant denominations to be effective in extreme situations. However, in this instance the disavowal of violence was specifically linked to preserving the sanctity of the church property. The fundamental protection of sacred property from contamination by the profane world which Durkheim stresses as a key element in every religion was the effective appeal. While violence may be accepted as a necessary compromise in an unchristian world, its use within the sacred bounds of church property becomes serious profanation. By defining the crowd's action as

profanation of sacred values which they self-consciously shared, the anonymous individual was able to disperse them.

But a further fact about the case points to a second condition which had to be met for this action to be effective. According to Wilbur Jerger's account, while the crowd was attacking his car he shouted, "How can you do this? You've just come out of church!" His remarks merely infuriated the crowd further. His attempt to cite the sacred context and suggest the ingroup mores was utterly ineffectual.

An important difference appears to lie in the image which each principal established. The first referred to "our cause." The effect he created upon the crowd was that of being one of them. Jerger was clearly an outsider. As such he had no right to cite ingroup mores. His attempt to assert them fell in the same category of blasphemy as the Devil quoting scripture. Ingroup mores can only be legitimately cited by an ingroup member.

From the foregoing analysis it appears that a person of impressive stature and bearing was able to stop crowd violence by (a) citing ingroup mores which were self-consciously shared by crowd members and (b) effectively creating the image of himself as an ingroup member. Certain characteristics of the crowd undoubtedly facilitated this action. The membership were probably not accustomed to the use of violence and did not employ it particularly effectively, because of both their socio-economic position and their religious activity. The crowd development had never reached the more advanced stages, and lacked any but sporadic leadership. And the object of attack in this episode was quite secondary and incidental to the major recipient of crowd hostility. Under different circumstances the technique might not have been effective.

Part of the effectiveness of force as a means of dispersing a crowd lies in the threat that it poses to the safety of the individual. Yet not all forms of attack are equally effective, for some, such as the blows of clubs, can be directed at only a small part of the crowd. The effectiveness of "mass weapons" such as tear gas, machine guń fire, or Napoleon's famous "whiff of grapeshot," seems to lie in the fact that their incidence falls indiscriminately on the major portion of the crowd, "atomizing" it in a sense.

Crowd manipulation. Crowd control is not always exerted for the purpose of limiting or terminating crowd action. Crowds may also be manipulated to serve the purposes of individuals or groups who, so to speak, exploit the crowd participants. The majority of the participants in a manipulated crowd may feel that their behavior is entirely spontaneous. Yet this behavior may actually have been induced by the skillful operations of agitators within the crowd. In Chapter 6 it was shown how the "Bare-footed Brigade" aroused and fostered anti-Semitic sentiments in local population in Russia. The agents of revolutionary political parties have stirred up and manipulated crowds in order to embarrass established authorities, provoking them to violence and sometimes creating martyrs.

Many expressive crowds are skillfully and patently manipulated, although the participants are likely to ascribe their expressive behavior to some metaphysical source rather than to the skill of the manipulators. The religious crowd in which an evangelist, with skillful use of music, rhythmic preaching, and careful staging, induces a high state of emotional expression, is an example.

Perhaps the ultimate in deliberate manipulation of crowds, as well as of the utilization of crowd behavior to reinforce group solidarity, is found in the carefully staged political and patriotic rally of the modern state. Thornton Sinclair describes how the Nazi leaders used the annual Party Rallies at Nuremburg to strengthen the "bond of faith, love, and loyalty" between them and their followers. The similarity between the expressive behavior of this patriotic crowd and that of a religious crowd is evident.

THE NAZI PARTY RALLY AT NUREMBERG
Thornton Sinclair

The Nuremberg party rally (Reichsparteitag), which is now held in September of each year, is one of the most remarkable of the Nazi creations. Although in theory only a party affair, it broadens into a "review of the German nation," to give expression to the Nazi theory of the *Volksfuhrerstaat* (people's leader state) which, we are told, is a new and ennobled type of democracy.

According to this theory, the leaders, as a natural elite, make decisions for which they bear complete responsibility, while followers follow faithfully. Over all

Reprinted in part by permission of the editor, **Public Opinion Quarterly,** from Thornton Sinclair, "The Nazi Party Rally at Nuremberg," **Public Opinion Quarterly,** 2 (Oct., 1938), pp. 570–578.

is Hitler whose single will ultimately guides the Reich. He is finally responsible. Between leader and follower there is said to be a strong bond of faith, love, and loyalty.

Designed as the most striking demonstration of this theory, the Party Rally is not only the most important link between leader and follower and a place of accounting for leaders, but it is also intended to be a center of propaganda and political regeneration, a sounding board for announcements to Germany and to the world.

In order that the rally may serve these purposes, lavish and skilful propaganda and pageantry are brought into play.

The buildings and grounds of the Party

Rally reflect its grandiose character. What has already been done on them is impressive, but what has been planned is truly staggering. The fields—the Luitpold Arena and the Zeppelin Field—are equipped with extensive stone stands and striking decorations. A vast area has also been set aside for the projected congress building, the main hall of which will seat 60,000 people. The German Stadium, which will accommodate 450,000 spectators, is the latest undertaking to be announced.

Just as the buildings are designed to create confidence in the future, so close adherence to tradition in the congress is an example of Nazi effort to create a sense of security among the German people. The self-styled Nazi revolution developed in a country plagued with doubts about tomorrow and hungry for security. Since the Nazis asserted that they were breaking with traditions of the past, and since revolutions are notoriously uncertain things, the Nazi aim was to build up Third Reich traditions as quickly as possible. The strong drive toward this objective is reflected in the Party Rally, in which even details of procedure, persons, and place remain nearly always the same.

Long after the expectant audience has assembled, blasts of trumpets herald the arrival of the *Fuhrer*, who, with his retinue, makes his triumphal entry, marching down the long center aisle to the stage to the strains of the "Badenweiler March" and shouts and cries of "Heil!" After the *Fuhrer* has reached the stage, the blood flag is borne in, followed at a distance by the standards of the movement. Guarded by three SS men (*Schutzstaffeln*—Special Guard), all of whom wear the medal of the blood order evidencing their long membership in and special services to the party, the blood flag is carried to a position in the middle aisle between those sitting on the stage and directly behind the speakers' platform, where it is held in turn throughout the proceedings by its guardians standing at attention. The standards follow the blood flag, finding their positions further to the rear of the stage and furnishing a wall of color for background at one end of the gaily decorated hall. Men stand holding them there during every session.

The demonstrations manifest the frankest emotional appeal. Somewhat diverse in character, they involve expert staging, elaborate use of flags, manuals of arms, a sham battle, marching, rousing short speeches, singing, and impressive ritual.

The demonstrations of particular units vary little from year to year. The following descriptions of those which the writer witnessed in 1936 may be taken as typical, even to the language employed.

In 1936, forty-five thousand Labor Service men, using the newly improved Zeppelin Field, passed in review before the *Fuhrer*, marched around behind the crowded stands, and then entered the opposite end of the field in mass formation, filling a large part of it. The picture of discipline and precision, they shouldered spades as one man. Well spaced, using numerous flags, they presented a striking picture. *Arbeitsdienst* leader Hierl reported to the *Fuhrer*, who shouted, *"Heil Arbeitsleute,"* and they, as with one voice, replied, the whole 45,000 at times singing, they went through lines to the following effect:

> The hour has come when once a year we lay aside our work and appear before the *Fuhrer*. We stand in common work and uniform. No one is too good to work for the fatherland, and thus this service has become the duty of all. The *Fuhrer* wants to give peace to the world and we are ready to follow him where he leads. We are troops of peace, making new land to protect our homes. Firm in our belief and true to the command of the *Fuhrer*, we march proudly into the future. When our work is hard we think of those brothers who died for Germany in the trenches or in the streets. We may live for Germany. We now lay four wreaths at the labor column—one for the heroes of the war, one for the martyrs of the movement, one of the victims of labor, and one for the comrades who die in our camps. We carry the fatherland in our hearts, we praise the *Fuhrer*, and our whole

lives will be one great labor service for the German people.[1]

Then they sang their song, "God Bless the Work," after which Hitler spoke shortly. Hitler answered that he was so filled with emotion it was difficult to reply. The Labor Service men had won the love of the whole German people and had become a part of German national life in this short time. The Labor Service had become a new higher school of German youth, a step in German education, an education to a common society without class, something much more beautiful than the class struggles in the lands of Germany's critics.

Speaking, singing, and precision were the fields in which the Labor Service excelled. For pure pageantry and grandeur there was no comparison with the assembly of the Political Leaders the following evening on the same field. For spectators arriving with the last of the afterglow, the 90,000 Political Leaders in their brown uniforms were already in place. The large

[1] **Der Parteitag der Ehre,** vom 8, bis 14 (Munich, 1936), pp. 71–85.

middle way running from the front to the back of the field and a few parallel lanes were the only breaks in the dimly visible sea of brown. At the rear entrance to the field and opposite the speakers' tribune, high steps had been built overnight. Blue light thrown suddenly from one hundred and fifty giant search-lights surrounding the outside of the field appeared to converge on one point in the sky, giving the onlooker the impression of sitting under a blue dome reaching high into the heavens. Over the steps and down the center way marched the *Fuhrer,* followed by district and Reich leaders. At an order, twenty-five thousand flags began streaming from the rear stands into the long gaps in the brown ranks. As other search-lights played upon them they seemed streams of fire on which floated glistening silver. After the banners had come to rest, from their special positions in front, the students of the school for future Political Leaders, the Ordensburg Vogelsang, sang their oath song; and bands played "I Had a Comrade" in honor of the dead. Then Hitler spoke. . . .

Crowd conventionalization. The crowd which gathered annually at Nuremberg for the Nazi Party Rally was not only a manipulated crowd, but was also a conventional crowd. It could be termed conventional because of two salient aspects. First, the participants gathered with the anticipation of taking part in highly emotional, yet socially sanctioned, crowd behavior. Secondly, as the experience was repeated year after year, the forms of the behavior became standardized, although the crowd situation continued to be necessary for their emergence. These are the marks of the conventional crowd, and they may be analyzed separately.

Kingsley Davis characterizes conventional crowds as being "articulated with the social structure." From the time of the Roman Saturnalia, and no doubt before then, societies have provided traditional, conventional situations in which people could to some degree "let themselves go," abandoning themselves to relatively unrestricted following of impulses that are ordinarily inhibited and limited in expression. Yet the behavior is not traditional, nor does it follow the ordinary, day-to-day pattern of behavior of the group. Although the situation may be anticipated and even planned, it is still an unusual situation in which unusual norms prevail. The behavior may still properly be termed crowd behavior because the stimulating influence of crowd interaction is necessary in order that the ordinary inhibitions against such behavior may be overcome. There is, furthermore, a permissiveness about the conventionalized crowd which allows and sometimes encourages the emergence of novel and extreme forms of behavior so long as they are consistent with the dominant mood.

Such occasions provide a satisfying, yet legitimate, escape from the restrictions of the usual social norms. Particularly in modern society, the maintenance of reserve and dignity is inculcated in the person as an important value from childhood. It is not easy for the individual to drop this decorous posture and, most of the time, the norms do not permit him to do so. At times, the norms of propriety may seem confining and frustrating. The conventionalized crowd, such as is found at sports events, in holiday crowds, and at parties, provides a socially sanctioned setting in which, with the aid of crowd facilitation, members of the society may enjoy the excitement, the loss of self-consciousness, and the relaxation that crowd participation affords.

In "The Importance of the Audience," dramatic illustration of the relaxing of inhibitions in a crowd is found. Kjerbuhl-Petersen describes the extent to which spontaneous, expressive, uncontrolled behavior may develop in a formal audience. The conventionalized nature of this crowd situation is suggested by the author's comment that this is a "large group of people whose emotions and thoughts are consciously directed towards an expected artistic pleasure."

THE IMPORTANCE OF THE AUDIENCE
LORENZ KJERBUHL-PETERSEN

Not every large group of people forms a mob, but every mob implies a large group, the strength of which may vary. The throngs of people, thousands in number, for example, who enliven the Potsdamer Platz in Berlin shortly after six o'clock in the evening, do not comprise a mob, in our sense of the word, while the few hundred people who fill up a small intimate theater do make one.

What welds a large group of people into a psychological mob is the "orientation of emotions and thought in a certain determined direction." This orientation may be accidental, that is the unforeseen result of unexpected external events, or may be intentional. We are concerned with the latter case alone. According to this a public, as we use the term, is a large group of people whose *emotions and thoughts are consciously directed towards an expected artistic pleasure.*

When a psychological mob has been formed it acquires a train of provisional but determinable features to which are joined special variable characteristics, ac-

cording to the elements of which the mob is composed, and through which its mental texture may be modified. . . .

It is not otherwise with the theater public. At the moment that they become part of the psychological mob, all of them, uneducated and savant, become incapable of observation or criticism. John F. Schinck confesses of himself: "During the performance, I felt myself to be merely a participator in it and the art critic in me ceased to be." Friedrich Ludwig Schroder "could not cease to be amazed that every audience can, in the same quarter of an hour, admire truth and falsehood." In general every one can verify this fact from his own observations. Who has not been a little ashamed subsequently, in the privacy of his own chamber, when he realized what stale jokes those were at which he had laughed so heartily, and by what false sentimentality he had been so deeply moved.

The fact that extravagance of emotion may under some circumstances, take actually pathological forms and destroy all artistic pleasure, is shown by many examples which the history of the theater has preserved for us—note as *curiosities!* A few will suffice here. Apropos of the

Reprinted in part by permission of the Expression Co., from Lorenz Kjerbuhl-Petersen, **Psychology of Acting** (Boston: 1935), pp. 29–32.

irst performance of "Othello" under the direction of Schroder it is reported: "One fainting fit followed another during the narrowing scenes of the first performance. The doors of the boxes banged open and shut as people went out, or were carried out in case of necessity, and (according to accredited reports) miscarriages, resulting from premature confinements of this or that prominent Hamburg matron were the consequences of this too torturing tragedy. In London the audience contented themselves at least with accompa-nying Garrick's playing of "Lear" by loud wails of grief. During the performance of "Die Rauber" in the National theater in Mannheim "the theater was like a madhouse, rolling eyes, clenched fists, stamping feet; hoarse shrieks in the auditorium! Men, strangers to each other, fell sobbing into each other's arms, women staggered, almost fainting, to the door. There was a general disintegration, as in chaos, from the midst of which a new creation emerges."

Conventionalized crowd behavior serves another important function in facilitating the resolution of cultural conflict. Men are capable of adhering to inconsistent and conflicting cultural values, even though they ordinarily act in terms of one rather than of the other. This is most likely to be true when the formal order and the explicit, official ideology support certain values in preference to others. In critical situations, when the value conflict becomes acute, crowd interaction facilitates the translation into action of the ordinarily neglected, suppressed values. Over a period of years, a conventionalized pattern of crowd behavior may arise to support the neglected values.

The pattern of lynching and vigilante action that persisted for many years in the South and West exemplified the support of implicit values by conventionalized crowd behavior. As Myrdal has pointed out, respect for law and belief in its efficacy have long been an important tenet of the American Creed. This value is formally supported by the "due process" clause of the 14th Amendment to the Constitution. At times, however, adherence to other important values may conflict with this value. Such values as "keeping the Negro in his place" or "showing a horse thief no mercy" cannot always be attained through due process. The following account from a period when racial mob violence was a frequent occurrence shows clearly the conventionalization of a pattern of crowd behavior to support such an "unofficial" value.

THE RACE WAR IN THE NORTH
William E. Walling

"Lincoln freed you, we'll show you where you belong," was one of the cries with which the Springfield mob set about to drive the Negroes from town. The mob was composed of several thousand of Springfield's white citizens, while other thousands, including many women and children, and even prosperous business men in automobiles, calmly looked on, and the rioters proceeded hour after hour and on two days in succession to make deadly assaults on every Negro they could lay their hands on, to sack and plunder their houses and stores, and to burn and murder on favorable occasion.

The American people have been fairly well informed by their newspapers of the action of that mob; they have also been told of certain alleged political and crim-

From William E. Walling, "The Race War in the North," **The Independent,** 65 (1908), pp. 529-531.

inal conditions in Springfield and of the two crimes in particular which are offered by the mob itself as sufficient explanation why six thousand peaceful and innocent Negroes should be driven by the fear of their lives from a town where some of them have lived honorably for half a hundred years. We have been assured by more cautious and indirect defenders of Springfield's populace that there was an exceptionally criminal element among the Negroes encouraged by the bosses of both political parties. And now, after a few days of discussion, we are satisfied with these explanations, and demand only the punishment of those who took the most active part in the destruction of life and property. Assuming that there were exceptionally provocative causes for complaint against the Negroes, we have closed our eyes to the whole awful and menacing truth—that a large part of the white population of Lincoln's home, supported largely by the farmers and miners of the neighboring towns, have initiated a permanent warfare with the Negro race.

We do not need to be informed at great length of the character of this warfare. It is in all respects like that of the South, on which it is modeled. Its significance is threefold. First, that it has occurred in an important and historical Northern town; then, that the Negroes, constituting scarcely more than a tenth of the population, in this case could not possibly endanger the "supremacy" of the whites, and, finally, that the public opinion of the North, notwithstanding the fanatical, blind and almost insane hatred of the Negro so clearly shown by the mob, is satisfied that there were "mitigating circumstances," not for the mob violence, which, it is agreed, should be punished to the full extent of the law, but for the race hatred, which is really the cause of it all.

For the underlying motive of the mob and of that large portion of Springfield's population that has long said that "something was bound to happen," and now approves of the riot and proposes to complete its purpose by using other means to drive as many as possible of the remaining two-thirds of the Negroes out of town,

was confessedly to teach the Negroes their place and to warn them that too many could not obtain shelter under the favorable traditions of Lincoln's home town. I talked to many of them the day after the massacre and found no difference of opinion on the question.

"Why, the niggers came to think they were as good as we are!" was the final justification offered, not once, but a dozen times.

On the morning after the first riot I was in Chicago and took the night train for Springfield, where I have often visited and am almost at home. On arriving in the town I found that the rioting had been continued thruout the night, and was even feared for the coming evening, in spite of the presence of nearly the whole militia of the State. Altho we visited the Mayor, military headquarters, the leading newspaper, and some prominent citizens, my wife and I gave most of our attention to the hospital, the Negro quarters and the jail.

We at once discovered, to our amazement, that Springfield had no shame. She stood for the action of the mob. She hoped the rest of the Negroes might flee. She threatened that the movement to drive them out would continue. I do not speak of the leading citizens, but of the masses of the people, of workingmen in the shops, the storekeepers in the stores, the drivers, the men on the street, the wounded in the hospitals and even the notorious "Joan of Arc" of the mob, Kate Howard, who had just been released from arrest on $4,000 bail. (She has since committed suicide.—Editor) *The Illinois State Journal* of Springfield exprest the prevailing feeling even on its editorial page:

> While all good citizens deplore the consequences of this outburst of the mob spirit, many even of these consider the outburst was *inevitable,* at some time, from existing conditions, needing only an overt act, such as that of Thursday night, to bring it from latent existence into active operation. The implication is clear that conditions, not the populace, were to blame and that many good citizens could find no other

remedy than that applied by the mob. It was not the fact of the whites' hatred toward the Negroes, but of the Negroes' own misconduct, general inferiority or unfitness for free institutions that were at fault.

Having participated in a satisfying, thrilling crowd experience people tend to try to recapture the excitement of the moment again and again. Having found that, through the fury of the mob, neglected values can be supported despite their conflict with other values, people may be predisposed to utilize such means again when these values are threatened. Yet the crowd experience cannot be consciously and deliberately reproduced; there must be an element of spontaneity and release from inhibition. The type of situation in which such an experience is likely to occur can be reproduced, however, and people can enter into such situations with an expectant, relaxed attitude. Hence one aspect of crowd conventionalization is the conventionalization of situations favorable to crowd development.

As such crowd experiences are repeated, another aspect of crowd conventionalization occurs. Although the spontaneity and relaxation of self-control remains, the modes of behavior become patterned without becoming merely formal. Certain sorts of expressive or even aggressive behavior come to be defined as appropriate to this type of situation. These definitions persist from one specific type-situation to another, emerging as the crowd mood develops to a sufficiently high pitch of excitement. Such conventional crowd patterns reflect, in part, the unique features of the type of situation in which they occur. Thus, at the peak of excitement during a hard-fought football game, part of the crowd may, quite spontaneously, begin to chant "Hold that line" and, after a victory, they may rush to tear down the goal posts. Such behavior would be obviously inappropriate at a baseball game, merely because of the nature of the game. These patterns also reflect the cultural milieu within which the crowd behavior takes place. In "The Paris Riots," the writer notes the traditional pattern followed by Paris mobs of tearing up the paving stones and using them as missiles.

In his analysis of Negro religious expression, E. T. Krueger emphasizes many of the salient aspects of conventional crowd behavior. While stressing the elements of spontaneity, expressiveness, excitement, drama, and mysticism as essential, he shows that the forms of expression have become nevertheless "fixed and traditional." The roots of these forms in historical religious revivals, both white and Negro, are indicated. Finally, he discusses briefly the relationship of the Negro subcultural milieu to the survival of these highly expressive forms in rural, lower-class Negro churches.

NEGRO RELIGIOUS EXPRESSION
E. T. KRUEGER

Negro religious practices vary widely. It would be a serious mistake to assume otherwise. There are Negro churches with distinctly formal and intellectualized expression and there are those which are highly expressive and informal. The latter are, of course, in the vast majority. In spite of this diversity of practice, common elements and forms of religious expression are discernible. We shall mean, by

Reprinted in part by permission of the University of Chicago Press, from E. T. Krueger, "Negro Religious Expression," **American Journal of Sociology,** 38 (1932–33), pp. 22–31.

elements, the psychic qualities of response, and by forms, the objective modes of response.

A chief element in Negro religious expression is spontaneity. Many Negro religious services are so informal and spontaneous as to appear, to the casual observer, without order or without pattern. It is not uncommon to see several persons participating at the same time, and neither the audience nor the participants are concerned over the fact. Songs may break out at any time, and the preacher readily pauses to permit outbursts of religious melody. The religious service of the Negro seems to have developed its general pattern upon the basis of informality and spontaneous participation.

Closely allied with the element of spontaneity is that of expressiveness. The Negro in his religious expression is not bothered with inhibitions; he gives vent to his feeling whenever so moved. He is profoundly explicit. Inner ecstasy gives way immediately in shouts, musical responses, and songs, the latter often accompanied with rhythmical patting of hands and feet.

A third element is excitement. A Negro religious service moves by concerted participation, at first slowly, but finally with rapid tempo, to a profound state of rapport and mutual responsiveness, which assumes the character of the so-called psychological crowd. It is the crowd which is expressive but does not act, to distinguish it from the crowd which becomes destructive. In the anticipation and formation of this crowd aspect a feeling of expectance develops, culminating in intense excitement whenever the preacher succeeds in reaching a dramatic climax in his sermon. At this point the responsiveness of the audience is at its height, and individuals begin to exhibit ecstatic manifestations.

Queer as it may seem to those unfamiliar with the phenomenon, the excitement is pleasurable, joyous, and intermittently mirthful. In the long pre-sermon stage of the religious service, mirth breaks out frequently in spite of the occasional exhibitions of agony on the part of those who wrestle with the spirit in long and soul-wracking prayers and in spite of the mournful character of many of the songs. During the sermon the preacher may dwell upon the sins of his people, but his people are more interested in the drama of his presentation than in their sins. If conversion takes place they do not mean moral reconstruction but divine visitation and recognition. For the evidences of divine acceptance are an exultant mood, a flooding of the soul with pleasant feeling, a desire to shout and to sing. The effect of the service is, hence, one of exaltation, of ecstasy and joyous religious expressiveness.

The fourth element of Negro religious expression is rhythm. Rhythm gets its chief expression in singing and in the physical accompaniments of singing. When a service is well under way and the audience becomes expectant, song breaks out spontaneously, hands and feet move with the musical measures, and often bodies begin to sway in unison with the melody. The shouts and the responses become musical. At vivid points in the sermon the audience will break out with "Well," "Help us, Lord," and similar expressions, sung with a sustained note. Here and there in the audience the responses of individuals sometimes assume a lilting form almost birdlike in cadence. Even the preacher falls into musical expression, intoning or chanting his phrases.

Rhythm undoubtedly lends itself to expressiveness of feeling; it creates, in part, excitement and intensity of mood. It stimulates participation. It is highly contagious and aids greatly in creating the crowd effect of rapport and mutual responsiveness.

The fifth element in Negro religious expression is interest in the dramatic. The Negro is intensely theatrical, if one may use the term in other than an artificial sense. Meditative and reflective religious practices are foreign to his mode. He prefers the outward manifestation, hence his love of musical expression, his shouts and calls, his often violent prayers, his rituals and ceremonies, and his tendency toward ecstatic manifestation. All of these have the dramatic qualities of expressive action, suspense, and excitement. Moreover, the content of his songs is pictorial and seldom abstract. Inanimate objects are personalized and thus dramatized. His religious imagery is concrete. God, the angels, and the devil are realistic anthropomorphic creatures who play definite and purposive roles in human affairs. It is in the sermon, however, that the dramatic element finds its most perfect expression. For Negro sermons are narrative in form, they tell a story and are often replete with character dialogues and soliloquies.

The sixth element of Negro religious expression is love of magic. The Negro is vastly interested in phenomena which are mysterious and unusual. His everyday life may be drab, but magic makes it colorful, as it has in all ages for all peoples. But the Negro is still largely unacquainted with modern techniques of control, hence needs a magical element to meet his conflicts and to gain his wishes. Religion furnishes him with a superb repertoire of magical beings and magical formulas . . .

In the above classification of elements —spontaneity, expressiveness, excitement, rhythm, interest in the dramatic, and love of magic—no mention is made of emotion. The omission needs explanation. We are suggesting that Negro religious expression is based upon feeling rather than emotion, if we assume that feeling is orgiastic and expressive, and emotion moralistic and introspective. The Negro is not greatly concerned with his own moral life nor in intellectual aspects of dogma and tenets of faith. He prefers in religious expression to submerge himself in the engulfing waves of ecstatic feeling produced in the religious crowd. When he attains this he transcends reality, and his spiritual catharsis is complete. For religion is to the Negro what music and poetry are to the white man. In religious expression he finds rhythm and harmony, color and aesthetic feeling.

No lengthy description of the forms of Negro religious expression is necessary. They vary considerably as cultural forms usually vary through local cultural fixations. The most common forms may be classified as: antiphonal singing, approving responses often musically expressed, prayers, rhythmical patting of hands and

feet as an accompaniment to singing, shouting, testifying, hand-shaking and collection ceremonies, and in certain churches physical manifestations, such as seizures, paroxysms, jerks, and dancing. In the sermon the pictorial narrative and the dramatic dialogue are prevailing forms.

The Negro church today seems to be dropping many of these forms, and making some of them less expressive and more formal. It is in the churches which are isolated or which include the lower and submerged classes that the traditional forms are chiefly retained. The majority of the Negro churches in our cities, both South and North, have dropped the more physical forms of expression and even much of the shouting. Indeed, morning services in modern Negro churches are much like white services; the evening service, however, remains very informal and truer to type . . .

Our interest here, however, is not in the separate forms of religious expression but their description as a whole. Close observation reveals that the forms are true forms in the sense that they are patterns which by long usage have become fixed and traditionalized. It is a mistake to assume that Negro religious expression is wild and uncontrolled. Such commonly used terms as emotional instability, hypnotic suggestion, emotional fury, and religious frenzy indicate that observers have failed to see that Negro religious expression follows well-defined patterns and is heavily ritualized. Odum has rather accurately described and analyzed the traditional Negro prayer and the preacher's sermon. He calls the Negro prayer "natural" and says that when "reduced to particulars it is very formal." [1] By natural he means that the prayer flows directly from inner feeling, and by formal he means that it possesses a well-defined pattern. It begins with invocational and petitioning phrases, uttered in a low tone, delivered very slowly and with precision; moves then to shorter phrases, more rapidly spoken and rhythmically punctuated, fervently expressed, often tremulous with

[1] Howard W. Odum, **Social and Mental Traits of the Negro,** p. 68 ff.

feeling, rising in pitch and volume, eloquent with vivid imagery; and ends in a brief recurrence to slowly and softly spoken phrases or in abrupt subsidence when physical exhaustion is reached.

The sermon also follows a set pattern and one much like the prayer. It begins in a low-pitched conversational tone. As telling phrases are caught by the audience and answered by responses of "Well," "Yes, Lord," "Lift him up," and so on, the preacher begins to stride the platform, raises his voice, and becomes more fervent. The audience increases its response. Songs break out, shouts and calls multiply. It often takes an hour before the sermon reaches the point of full fervor. The speaker's voice is soon shattered; his words become interspersed with a peculiar exhalation sound resembling "huh" or by gasping inhalation sounds which pass description. Physical exhaustion is finally reached, or simulated, the sermon reaches its climax, and the preacher is through . . .

A study of the cultural history of the Negro in America, especially of his contact with the white religious revivals which swept over America from the Great Awakening of 1734 to the Kentucky-Tennessee revival of 1875, affords a wealth of materials to account for the cultural transmission of the elements and forms of Negro religious expression. We know that the Negro population was in close contact with these revivals, participating at first on the fringes of the crowds which gathered, but gradually being drawn into the movement by its excitement and its fervor. Separate Negro gatherings were organized, in the beginning under white leaders and finally under Negro preachers and evangelists produced in the revivals . . .

In the years which have intervened between the last of the great revivals and the present, white religion has for the most part become formalized and stereotyped. The frontier life of early America has passed away, and with its disappearance have come education, cultural expansion, science, and art. These have transformed white religious expression. But the Negro has remained on a cultural frontier. Only in recent years has the Negro group begun to feel the impact of the educational process and of cultural expansion, but the effect is already discernible in the changes now taking place in religious expression . . .

The church is the center of Negro social organization. It is in his church that the Negro is least open to criticism and most free to express himself. His religion is a form of escape, a way of securing relief and catharsis. His outmoded theology with its emphasis upon a magical divine manipulation and intervention and upon a glamorous future world still provides opportunity to drench his spirit in rapturous feeling as an antidote for a realistic world . . .

Limitations in the conventional crowd. The conventional crowd permits the lowering of normal inhibitions but, at the same time, it sets strict limits to behavior and expression. This seeming paradox is very important to the explanation of the uninhibited quality of conventional crowd behavior. Observation of such behavior at parties, celebrations, or sports events will show that if the behavior of some crowd members goes beyond certain tacitly accepted bounds the mood of spontaneity and relaxation is destroyed; "the fun is spoiled." Waller and Hill, in their analysis of "party behavior" among groups of married couples, observe that at parties a certain relaxation of the sexual norms takes place but that tacit understandings still exist as to "how far" the participants may go.* Violation of these crowd norms puts an end to spontaneity of the party. It may be postulated that one of the factors which permits normal inhibitions to be lowered in the

* Willard Waller and Reuben Hill, **The Family** (New York: The Dryden Press, 1951), pp. 584–587.

conventional crowd is the shared confidence that relaxation of inhibitions will not go beyond an understood point. This may even apply to conventionalized forms of violence, such as lynching. Even when lynchings were relatively frequent in the South it was observed by the Southern Commission for the Study of Lynchings that a lynching often seemed to give a community a period of immunity from the repetition of such behavior. The explanation of this and the almost complete disappearance of lynching in the South may lie in the fact that so many lynch mobs went to such excesses in their torture of victims, and extended their activities to generalized attacks on Negroes, thus going beyond the limits understood by most of the crowd members to exist.

Part 3

THE DIFFUSE COLLECTIVITY

Chapter 9

Mass society and mass communications

*T*HE TERM "crowd" usually brings to mind a group of people in close physical contact and within earshot of one another. But already in our discussions of the crowd we have dealt with instances in which not all persons are in immediate contact with all others. For example, rumor can travel among persons all of whom are not in direct or simultaneous contact with one another. And yet this rumor process among individuals dispersed throughout the community is quite like that which takes place among milling individuals in close contact. Furthermore, terms such as "crowd-mindedness" are often used to accent the resemblances between the behavior of a whole nation in war hysteria or adopting some fad and that of the crowd of persons in immediate contact with one another.

Two conditions must necessarily be met if we are to speak of collective behavior among dispersed individuals. First, there must be *uniformity of response* to a common object of attention. And second, this uniformity of response must be that of a group of individuals *acting in awareness of group membership*. Uniformities based merely on learned cultural prescriptions do not constitute collective behavior. The role played in the individual's behavior by the sense that he is a member of a collectivity is the crucial determinant. If a person feels that he is a member of a nationwide audience, for example, and if he has some image of how the rest of this audience are acting and lets this sense influence his attitudes and behavior, we may justifiably speak of collective behavior, even though the individuals are not in direct contact.

Apart from the individual psychopath who may acquire a sense of membership in a unanimous collectivity through sheer hallucination, some sort of communication is essential to create collective behavior. There are two types of communication through which this is achieved. First, there is the *interaction chain*. Communication may be from individual to individual and from small

165

group to small group. The sense of a universe of persons much larger than those immediately present at the time of communication is created when each rapporteur tells his story as something which everyone is talking about or will soon be discussing. This sense is reinforced since each listener will in all probability hear the same item from several unrelated persons within a short space of time. Such an experience very quickly creates an impression of overwhelming preoccupation with the matter at hand.

The process of *mass communication* is the second means through which the sense of membership in a collectivity is created. Unlike the communication chain, mass communication refers to the relatively simultaneous exposure of a large number of people to identical communication emanating from a limited number of sources. We think of the printed word, radio, motion pictures, and television as the major agencies of mass communication. The recipient of mass communication may, of course, define his experience as a solitary one and, hence, in no sense become part of a collectivity. But often he finds himself defining his experience as one that is extensively shared and he in some sense interacts with his image of the large body of fellow-viewers and listeners. Various conditions facilitate this type of experience. Past experience tells the listener that many share his experience. Advertising and cross-referencing in mass communication media foster the impression. The media themselves are skillfully used to create this impression by the mode of addressing people; by the development of symbols which are meaningful only to the regular audience of a particular program, column, etc.; by the creation of audience effects through studio audiences, publishing letters to the editors, and the like. These are merely a few of the conditions contributing to such an effect. Perhaps the most important such condition is the supplementation of mass communication by the direct interpersonal interaction chains. The sense of being one of millions who read a given comic strip or listen to a given program is made vital by the fact that if one mentions the item among a group of associates there is immediate recognition. Mass media content provide common subjects of casual conversation.

To the degree, then, to which large numbers of individuals act as if they were part of a large group of like-minded persons, or to the degree to which interpersonal communication chains are geared into mass communication media, we may justifiably speak of a type of collective behavior that takes place among dispersed individuals. Since it will most certainly appear that there are some consistent differences between the collective behavior of dispersed individuals and that of persons in immediate contact, it will be useful to designate two types of collectivities. We shall call those groups whose members are in one another's immediate presence *compact collectivities* and those whose members are dispersed *diffuse collectivities*. The nationwide public concerned with a current foreign policy issue, the followers of a popular recreational fad, and a community aroused over some crime or public scandal are all examples of diffuse collectivities. The compact collectivity can exist in a pure form, but the diffuse collectivity probably cannot exist in any genuinely functioning sense without the presence of a large number of small compact collectivities. However, when the participant interprets these small groups as primarily indicative of a larger grouping, and when the small groups are linked through a communication network, the essential characteristics of the diffuse collectivity will be present.

The mass and mass society. The prevalence of mass communication suggests the need for another distinction. Responses to the media of mass communication fall along a continuum according to the degree to which they may be adequately designated as collective behavior. At one end of the continuum is the fully "collective" behavior in which extensive interaction chains are established in response to mass communication, and various types of concerted action occur. For example, the readers of a sensationalized newspaper account of a crime may be aroused to the extent of discussing the matter and organizing to demand stricter law enforcement. At the other end of the continuum is the uniform response of a large number of disparate individuals to the same content, but without interaction and without any sense of being part of a large body of co-reactors. As an ideal construct, we refer to the latter as the *mass*. The men who individually respond to an advertised sale of suits at half price form such a mass provided they do not anticipate and try to beat the crowd to the sale. *In its simplest form the mass is a number of separate individuals each responding independently to the same stimulus in the same way.* The mass is more than an aggregate, since it involves a common focus of attention and a common response. But it is less than a collectivity since it lacks interaction tying the entire group together.

The mass in its theoretically pure form would not be appropriate subject matter for the study of groups, since the behavior is entirely individual. But in several ways the mass is so interrelated with forms of collective behavior that its characteristics must be explored.

In the first place, neither the mass nor the diffuse collectivity is often found in pure form. Empirical instances generally fall at intermediate points along a continuum, with elements of the mass and of the diffuse collectivity intermixed. Hence considerable understanding of the mass is necessary to the interpretation of most actual instances of diffuse collective behavior. The audience of a popular television program, for example, acts partly like a diffuse collectivity and partly like the mass.

Second, the mass represents the *source* and the *residue* of much diffuse collective behavior. The uniformization that takes place in the mass is a constant preparation for collective behavior. The uniformity of response means a constant readiness to interact because of a common universe of discourse, because of common preoccupations, because of common symbols and meanings. Followers of such comic strips as "Little Orphan Annie" may acquire uniform and ready-made notions about how to deal effectively with spies and saboteurs. Furthermore, the directions taken in collective behavior are probably largely predetermined by the preoccupations and the common definitions of technique formed within the mass.

Even though diffuse collective behavior may be of short duration or sporadic, the mass becomes the repository of the end products of collective behavior and the agent of continuity among succeeding instances of such behavior. There is, indeed, a dynamic interaction between mass behavior and collective behavior. The agencies of mass communication respond quickly to collective behavior, oftentimes serving to perpetuate or strengthen the preoccupations and significations of collective behavior, to extend their application beyond the locale of collective behavior, or to contradict and modify them.

Third, the media of mass communication are important as agents through which collective behavior is initiated and fed. Reports of American race riots, for example, indicate with great frequency that newspapers communicate the basic rumors which seem important in starting the riot. News reports, merely through conveying the fact that crowd action is under way, are regarded as so important a factor in enlarging and extending crowd behavior that maintaining voluntary newspaper silence is a major technique of crowd control.

The nature of the mass and the problems of communication in that type of society in which the mass is a predominant form are discussed by Louis Wirth. His discourse is of interest in several respects. First, he elaborates upon the definition of the mass, and in particular describes it as a realistic rather than as an ideal concept. Second, he presents the idea of *consensus* as a basis for uniform response within the mass. And third, he discusses the lines of communication and the problem of converting mass behavior into collective behavior.

CONSENSUS AND MASS COMMUNICATION
Louis Wirth

I have chosen to discuss the topic of consensus because I believe it provides both an approach to the central problem of sociology and to the problems of the contemporary world. I regard the study of consensus as the central task of sociology, which is to understand the behavior of men in so far as that behavior is influenced by group life. Because the mark of any society is the capacity of its members to understand one another and to act in concert toward common objectives and under common norms, the analysis of consensus rightly constitutes the focus of sociological investigation. But to discuss the nature of consensus in all kinds of human groups in different cultural settings would be a formidable task. Similarly, an analysis of the conditions conducive to consensus under varying circumstances would be a vast undertaking. My observations will therefore be directed to the conditions under which consensus functions in mass societies as distinguished from more compact, intimate groups, such as the family and other primary associations.

Before exploring the nature and conditions of consensus, it seems appropriate to indicate the salient characteristics of mass societies. As we look back upon previous social aggregations, such as those of the ancient kingdoms, or at their great-

est extent the Roman Empire, we wonder how, given the primitive communications that obtained, such impressive numbers and territories could be held together under a common regime over any considerable span of time. If we discover, however, that these aggregations were not truly societies but were little more than administrative areas, creatures of military domination along the main arteries of communication from some center of power, and that the economic base of their cohesion rested on exploitation of the outlying territories and peoples by the power holders at a center through their representatives who were scattered thinly over the territory, the magnitude of these aggregations does not seem too impressive. Mass societies as we find them today, however, show greater marks of integration. They are aggregations of people who participate to a much greater degree in the common life and, at least in democratic parts of the world, comprise people whose attitudes, sentiments and opinions have some bearing upon the policies pursued by their governments. In this sense mass societies are a creation of the modern age and are the product of the division of labor, of mass communication and a more or less democratically achieved consensus.

Since we shall speak of our society as a mass society and of the communication that it involves as mass communication, it behooves us to depict the characteristics

Reprinted in part by permission of The American Sociological Society, from **American Sociological Review**, 13 (Feb., 1948), pp. 1-15.

of the mass. Its most obvious trait is that it involves great numbers, in contradistinction to the smaller aggregates with which we have become familiar through the study of primitive life and earlier historical forms of human association. Second, and again, almost by definition, it consists of aggregates of men widely dispersed over the face of the earth, as distinguished from the compact local groups of former periods. Third, the mass is composed of heterogeneous members, in that it includes people living under widely different conditions, under widely varying cultures, coming from diverse strata of society, occupying different positions, engaging in different occupations, and hence having different interests, standards of life and degrees of prestige, power and influence. Fourth, the mass is an aggregate of anonymous individuals, as may be indicated by the fact that though millions of individuals listening to a radio program, reading a newspaper, or seeing a movie, are exposed to the same images, they are not aware of who the fellow members of the audience are, nor are those who transmit these images certain of the composition of their audience. These anonymous persons who constitute the mass may be, and usually are, of course, aware that they are part of a mass and they make some assumptions as to who their fellow members are and how many of them there are. They are likewise capable of identifying themselves with their anonymous fellows who are exposed to the same images and may even gain some support from the knowledge of their existence. They may even act as if they had their unanimous support as is illustrated by the slogan "Fifty million Frenchmen can't be wrong," or by the much disputed band-wagon effect resulting from the publication of the results of public opinion polls. Fifth, the mass does not constitute an organized group. It is without recognized leadership and a well-defined program of action. If it acts collectively at all it does so only as a crowd or as a mob, but since it is dispersed in space it cannot even move as these elementary social bodies are capable of action, al-

though it may be far from constituting, as Carlyle thought, "an inert lump." Sixth, the mass has no common customs or traditions, no institutions and no rules governing the action of the individuals. Hence, it is open to suggestions, and its behavior, to a greater degree than that of organized bodies, is capricious and unpredictable. And, finally, the mass consists of unattached individuals, or, at best, individuals who, for the time being, behave not as members of a group, playing specific roles representative of their position in that group, but rather as discrete entities. In modern urban industrial society, our membership in each of the multiple organizations to which we belong represents our interests only in some limited aspect of our total personal life. There is no group which even remotely professes to speak for us in our total capacity as men or in all of the roles that we play. Although through our membership in these organized groups we become articulate, contribute to the moulding of public opinion, and participate more or less actively in the determination of social policies, there remains for all of us a quite considerable range of ideas and ideals which are subject to manipulation from the outside and in reference to which there is no appreciable reciprocal interaction between ourselves and others similarly situated. It is this area of life which furnishes the opportunity for others to entrap us or to lead us toward goals with the formulation of which we have had little or nothing whatever to do. Hence, all of us are in some respects characterized in our conduct by mass behavior.

The fragmentation of human interests in heterogeneous, complex modern societies is so far advanced that as Robert E. Park put it, "What a man belongs to constitutes most of his life career and all of his obituary." The trend in group organization is not merely toward the multiplication and diversification of organizations, but also toward bodies of enormously increased size.

Many of these organizations have become so colossal that they themselves come to approximate masses. The sense of belonging and of participation which smaller and more compactly organized groups are able to generate is hence largely frustrated by the very size of the typical organizations of our time.

The problem is complicated by the fact that not only is mass democratic society enormous in scope and intricate in structure, but it presents a dynamic equilibrium in which one of the principal condiitons of effective collective action is the accuracy and speed with which the shifting interests and attitudes of great masses of men, whether organized or unorganized, can be ascertained and brought to bear upon the determination of policy.

Another significant feature of modern mass society, and especially of mass democracies, is the instability of the interests and the motives of the members, and the correspondingly frequent changes in leadership and the consequent uncertainty as to the locus of decisive power at any one juncture of events. If the spokesmen in any group are to know whom they are speaking for they must be able to assess how strong or enduring the interests are that they profess to represent, and whether, indeed, the groups for which they speak are at all interested in the issue.

Mass societies, furthermore, involve vast concentrations of power and authority and complicated machinery of administration. Perhaps the most urgent need that goes unmet in such a society is the capacity for prompt decisions in the face of recurrent crises. The fact that concerted action in such societies, if they are to remain democratic, must take into consideration the shifting constellation of public opinion imposes upon those who guide its destinies a responsibility which can only be met by the utilization of all the relevant sources of knowledge and the perfection of very much more advanced techniques than we now seem to possess.

A thoughtful student has described society as "a highly intricate network of partial or complete understandings between the members of organizational units." Consensus is the sign that such

1 Edward Sapir: **Encyclopedia of the Social Sciences,** "Communication."

partial or complete understanding has been reached on a number of issues confronting the members of a group sufficient to entitle it to be called a society. It implies that a measure of agreement has been reached. The agreement, however, is neither imposed by coercion nor fixed by custom so as no longer to be subject to discussion. It is always partial and developing and has constantly to be won. It results from the interpenetration of views based upon mutual consent and upon feeling as well as thinking together.

If men of diverse experiences and interests are to have ideas and ideals in common they must have the ability to communicate. It is precisely here, however, that we encounter a paradox. In order to communicate effectively with one another, we must have common knowledge, but in a mass society it is through communication that we must obtain this common body of knowledge. The resolution of this paradox seems to lie in the possibility that though men of diverse backgrounds, experiences and interests, when they first come in contact, are incapable of communicating with and understanding one another, much less arriving at agreement, they must initially be content to grope haltingly for such elementary understandings as can be supplied on the basis of the scanty and superficial common experiences that even the most casual and superficial contact supplies.

There are many ways that society has developed of inducing consent. We may first point to the kind of acquiescence induced by superior force. Power is not equally distributed among the members of most societies and there probably is no society where it is so equally distributed that all the members are equally capable of exerting their will upon the others. In its extreme form, this inequality of power and influence is exemplified by dictatorship. But even in a dictatorship, while the ultimate monopoly of violence rests with the dictator, the members of the society count for something, and the dictator does not enjoy unlimited opportunity to coerce his subjects. Although, for instance, in the case of the present Soviet regime we are convinced of the actuality of its dictatorial character, we recognize nevertheless that there are certain limits beyond which the dictators cannot go, and that if the conditions of life which they can provide for their people and the hopes that they can hold out to them fall below a certain minimum, there will be rebellion and counter-revolution. Similarly, we act, at least with reference to the Voice of America broadcasts to the Soviet people, as if even their public opinion were of some importance.

Though social cohesion in a dictatorship rests ultimately upon force and violence, it need not at all times exercise this force and violence brutally and arbitrarily. It can be held in reserve for occasions when it is absolutely necessary, and indeed the wise dictator knows this principle of prudence in the exercise of his unquestioned power. Suppression may be the first or last stage in the life cycle. It can, for instance, be translated into law, however authoritarian and arbitrary its character, and into a religious control which may rest upon fear. This attenuated form of the exercise of force has been the practice at least of modern dictators ever since Machiavelli offered his counsel to the dictators of his day. It should be noted, of course, that people may never know that they are exploited and oppressed until they see their own humble status juxtaposed to an actual condition of relative freedom and opportunity that exists in some other society with which they are in contact, or unless they can recall some previous condition of existence in which these forms of oppression did not prevail, or unless, finally, there is held out to them some ideal condition which is possible of achievement and to which they consider themselves entitled. The idea of natural rights is an example of injecting into the minds of men an ideology which serves as an ideal against which they can measure their actual condition, and the experience with this ideology in recent times shows that it has made dictatorship of any kind untenable in the long run. The notion of the inalienable rights of man and of the dignity of the human personality is at work in increasing measure over all the world to challenge autocratic rule in every realm of human life.

Closely related to the type of basis of consensus provided by force and authority is the consensus that rests upon a common identification with great heroes or leaders, of which the charismatic leader depicted by Max Weber is perhaps the fittest example. There are many roads that lead to leadership, although they are not the same roads in all societies. Force and ruthlessness, law and authority, the sacred sanctions of religion or of tradition, or the wisdom or personality of the leader himself, or even the belief in his wisdom or personal qualities, separately or in combination, may establish a man or a group in a position of leadership which can evoke consensus on the part of the followers. Whatever these original sources are, they may be reinforced by propaganda and education and thus come to have a symbolic significance far out of proportion to the original sources.

Just as leaders can serve as instruments for building consensus, so ideas and ideals and the symbols with which they become identified can create cohesion in the group. The Cross and the Crescent, the Stars and Stripes, and the Hammer and Sickle, the Magna Charta, the Declaration of Independence, and the Four Freedoms, not to speak of the popular stereotypes and the slogans which are the stock-in-trade of so much of our present-day propaganda and public relations, are and will continue to be potential forces for creating and maintaining consensus. The instrumentalities of mass communication lend themselves particularly well to the dissemination of these symbols on a scale hitherto thought impossible. We happen to live in a world in which, despite barriers of technology and of politics, the whole human race becomes potentially exposed to the same symbols. They are weapons of offense and of defense, and they are bonds of union or of discord, depending upon the purposes which those who use them have in mind. Sociologists have long been accustomed to analyze in particular one of the bases of consensus, namely, the consensus that derives from the social heritage of a people, from a common culture, a common history and set of traditions, from the mores, which can make anything seem right, true, good, beautiful and possible. It is this basis of common social life as patterned by these traditions that makes it possible in the last analysis for any group to think of itself and to act as a society, to regard itself as a "we" group and to counterpose this "we" experience to all that is alien. The extent to which force and authority, law, religious sanction and leadership, propaganda and education, and the apparatus of symbols can be used effectively depends in large part upon this substratum of a common basis of knowledge, belief and standards molded by tradition and reinforced by the ongoing social life which embodies that tradition.

The fact that the instrumentalities of mass communication operate in situations already prepared for them may lead to the mistaken impression that they or the content and symbols which they disseminate do the trick. It is rather the consensual basis that already exists in society which lends to mass communication its effectiveness. A number of changes have, however, occurred since the days of the primitive local and isolated group life of our ancestors which have profoundly affected the force of tradition. The movements of population and the contact between people from the ends of the earth, the opening of world markets, and the spread of modern technology, the growth of cities, the operation of mass media of communication, the increasing literacy of the masses of people over all the world, have combined to disintegrate local cohesion and to bring hitherto disparate and parochial cultures into contact with each other. Out of this ferment has come the disenchantment of absolute faiths which expresses itself in the secular outlook of modern man.

One characteristic of this secularism is the increasing skepticism toward all dogmas and ideologies. With this goes the reluctance to accept things on faith or on authority, and the substitution of more or less rational grounds for believing, and where reason fails, to seek legitimation for a belief in personal tastes, preferences and the right to choose.

Another feature of this secularism is the change from naïveté to sophistication. One of the prime virtues on which the modern man prides himself is that he will not be taken in by anybody; that he offers sales resistance to those who offer him a pig-in-a-poke; that he suspects the motives of the salesman of goods or of ideas; that he wishes to see the evidence upon which the appeal rests; and that he claims the right to exercise independent judgment on the validity of that evidence. This has in turn led to a perfection of the means of persuasion through the invention of ways of making the irrational appear rational and of subtle means for making people interested in things that may not be to their interest. It has led to an enormous interest in discovering through scientific means what the interests, prejudices and predilections of men are and how they can be manipulated by appropriate appeals.

This secularism carries with it the disintegration of unitary faiths and doctrines, on the one hand, and their blending into new syncretisms which seek to combine a variety of hitherto incongruous elements in such a way as to attract the greatest number of followers. The symbols and slogans that formerly were characteristic of one party become mingled with those of others in order to woo more effectively the greatest number of adherents. Ideas and ideals that formerly stood for one set of objectives come to be perverted and diluted until they can comprise objectives which formerly seemed incongruous and until it seems that the unambiguous labels under which men formerly united not only no longer differentiate parties but actually can come to have the most contradictory content in order to appeal to all parties.

In addition to force and authority, leadership and personal prestige, ideas, ideals and the symbols into which they are incorporated, and social traditions we must consider an aspect of the basi of consensus which, though it overlaps with others, is nevertheless so distinctive of our society as to require separate treatment. I refer to public opinion. This, of course, is not an independent force but is an aspect of every ongoing society.

Public opinion is formed in the course of living, acting and making decisions on issues. It is precipitated through the clash of representative ideas reflecting more or less faithfully the positions confronting the respective groups that compose the society. Our society, and others comparable to it, are composed of varieties of constituent groups, occupational and economic, racial and ethnic and religious. Each of these groups articulates its own interests, has its own powers, leadership, creed, political and corporate organization.

Not all members of each group have an equal share of influence nor is the strength of each group determined solely by the size of its membership. These groups are not loose aggregations of men, and it is not necessary for all members of each group to share the official view of the group to which they give their adherence. There will be some who are indifferent or even hostile to what the group stands for without rebelling, as can clearly be seen by looking at our present day political parties or major economic or religious organizations. The role which the individuals play is not determined alone by their age, sex, race, occupation, economic or educational status, although these may significantly influence the character and policies of the groups to which the individuals belong. What counts, rather, is their power, prestige, strategic position, their resources, their articulateness, the effectiveness of their organization and leadership. Within the group those who make the decisions and who exercise the dominant influence are subjected to pressures from all sides and radiate influence upon their group. The old saying: "I am your leader, therefore I must follow you," suggests the extent to which independent judgment is limited even among the leadership. The decisive part of public opinion, then, is the organization of views on issues that exercise an impact upon those who are in a position to make decisions. The characteristic feature of public opinion in our society lies both in the fact that so many human beings are affiliated with a variety of organized groups, each of which represents only a segment of their interest, and that another large proportion of our fellowmen are unattached to any stable group and in that sense constitute unorganized masses and thereby leave the decision-making to those who are organized and can exercise their corporate power.

In modern democracies, and to some extent in all inclusive societies on the scale of modern states, men exercise their influence and voice their aspirations through delegated powers operating through functionaries and leaders, through lobbies, party organizations, religious denominations and a variety of other organized groups having a complex internal organization of their own. This seems to be the characteristic way of representative democratic government. In the course of the flow of communication the interests and grievances, the sentiments, attitudes and opinions of the people at the bottom may become grossly distorted, and the people at the top may find themselves so remote from their constituents that they may either be ignorant of their actual feelings or may seriously misinterpret the fragmentary knowledge that they do have. It is at this point that public opinion studies may prove significant. We have already witnessed in the United States the rise of what might be called government by Western Union, which is instanced by the story of the lady who went to the telegraph office and said, "I should like to send a telegram to my Congressman to use his own judgment."

Consensus in mass democracies, therefore, is not so much agreement on all issues, or even on the most essential substantive issues, among all the members of society, as it is the established habit of intercommunication, of discussion, debate, negotiation and compromise, and the toleration of heresies, or even of indifference, up to the point of "clear and present danger" which threatens the life of the society itself. Rather than resting upon unanimity, it rests upon a sense of group identification and participation in the life of a society, upon the willingness to allow our representatives to speak for us even though they do not always faithfully represent our views, if indeed we have any views at all on many of the issues under discussion, and upon our disposition to fit ourselves into a program that our group has adopted and to acquiesce in group decisions unless the matter is fundamentally incompatible with our interests and integrity.

Consensus is supported and maintained not merely by the ties of interdependence and by a common cultural base, by a set of institutions embodying the settled traditions of the people, and the norms and standards that they imply and impose, not merely by the living together and dealing with one another, but also, and not least important, by the continuing currents of mass communication, which in turn rest for their meaningfulness and effectiveness upon the pre-existence of some sort of a society, which hold that society together and mobilize it for continuous concerted action.

To the traditional ways of communication rumor, gossip and personal contact, to the pulpit, the school and the forum, we have added in our generation the mass media of communication, consisting of the radio, the motion picture and the press. These new media represent giant enterprises, dependent upon and designed to reach a mass audience. By virtue of the fact that they are dependent upon mass patronage, these media transcend both in their content and in their mode of presentation the peculiar interests and preoccupations of the special and segmental organized groups and direct their appeal to the mass. To reach their mass audiences they are constantly tempted to reduce their content, whether it be that of entertainment, enlightenment or appeal

to action, to the lowest common denominator, to what is believed will interest the greatest number, if not everybody. Since these mass media are so often tied to a mass market for their sustenance, they tend furthermore to be as near everything to everybody and hence nothing to anybody as it is possible to be.

It is upon these mass media, however, that to an ever increasing degree the human race depends to hold it together. Mass communication is rapidly becoming, if it is not already, the main framework of the web of social life. In retrospect we can see how shrewd Hitler and his cohorts were in recognizing that in these instrumentalities they controlled the principal means for moving great masses of men into at least temporary adherence to their objectives and in using them for their own purpose.

There has been much discussion recently, more with reference to the radio and motion picture than the older medium of the press, concerning the concentration of control over these mass media of communication. The fact that the media of communication tend toward monopolistic control, as is evidenced by the building up of industrial empires in this field of enterprise has serious implications for mass democracy. The concentration of such power in a few hands—whether through press associations, newspaper columns syndicates, radio networks or motion picture combines may create great imbalance in the presentation of divergent, especially minority views. It may result in the danger of censorship no less real for being unofficial, and may threaten the free and universal access to the factual knowledge and balanced interpretation which underlie intelligent decision.

In a society dominated by centers of unquestioned power and authority, reinforced by sacred traditions and rituals and capable of eliciting unquestioning loyalty to its norms and purposes, such mass communication devices would not constitute a serious problem. They would reinforce, but would not greatly alter the social structure. But in a society where all men irrespective of race, creed, origin and status claim and are to be granted an increasing share of participation in the common life and in the making of common decisions, the control of these media of mass communication constitutes a central problem. If it is consensus that makes an aggregate of men into a society, and if consensus is increasingly at the mercy of the functioning of the mass communication agencies as it is in a democratic world, then the control over these instrumentalities becomes one of the principal sources of political, economic and social power.

Mass media: cause or effect? In oversimplified form one fundamental question underlies any discussion of the relation of the mass to collective behavior. Assuming that some correlation exists between the content of the mass media and the preoccupations and imagery of the mass we may ask whether the mass media chiefly *shape* the mass imagery or whether the mass media principally *reflect* the mass imagery. For example, do adolescents accept romantic love because it is depicted in most of the motion pictures, or is it depicted in motion pictures because it is what adolescents want to see? Undoubtedly the most general answer is that the relationship operates in both directions. But a more specific answer would enumerate ways in which each relationship operates and circumstances determining the degree to which each operates.

There is abundant evidence that the media of mass communication are not neutral in their handling of content. Some types of slanting stem from the editorial convictions, the special interests, the private imagery, and the techniques which are believed to have mass appeal by those responsible for production of a particular newspaper, radio series, etc. However, this type of bias may merely reinforce the imagery of segments of the mass rather than modifying it. When members of the mass are free to select from among the available media those which are most congenial with their points of view, the media may provide *validation* for preconceptions and focalize existing inclinations through giving them specific direction and ideology.

Other types of bias characterize an entire medium, so that members of the mass have no opportunity to make comparison or selection. Such a generalized bias may be due to the content of imagery that is communicated. The predominance of the romantic image of courtship found in the movies, the tendency for most media to depict events in terms of the actions of great men, and the prevalence of stereotypes of occupations, nationalities, and the like, illustrate this type of bias.

A bias which applies to an entire medium may also be a product of technical characteristics of the medium, generalized views concerning the appropriate uses of the medium, or the development of uniform techniques for exploiting the mass appeal of the medium. The way in which television imparted a very special impression to a public spectacle with definite political implications is described in the following selection.

THE UNIQUE PERSPECTIVE OF TELEVISION AND ITS EFFECT: A PILOT STUDY

KURT LANG AND GLADYS ENGEL LANG

This paper aims to investigate a public event as viewed over television or, to put it differently, to study in the context of public life, an event transmitted over video. The concern is not with the effects of television on individual persons, irrespective of the spread of this effect. Our assumption is, on the contrary, that the effect of exposure to TV broadcasting of public events cannot be measured most successfully in isolation. For the influence on one person is communicated to others, until the significance attached to the video event overshadows the "true" picture of the event, namely the impression obtained by someone physically present at the scene of the event. The experience of spectators may not be disseminated at all or may be discounted as the biased version of a specially interested participant. Or, again, the spectator's interpretation of his own experience may be reinterpreted when he finds the event in which he participated discussed by friends, newspapermen, and radio commentators. If the significance of the event is magnified, even casual spectatorship assumes importance. The fact of having "been there" is to be remembered—not so much because the event, in itself, has left an impression, but because the event has been recorded by others. At the opposite extreme, privately significant experiences, unless revived in subsequent interpersonal relations, soon recede into the deeper layers of memory.

By taking MacArthur Day in Chicago, as it was experienced by millions of spectators and video viewers, we have attempted to study an event transmitted over video. The basis of this report is the contrast between the actually recorded experience of participant observers on the scene, on the one hand, and the picture which a video viewer received by way of

Reprinted by permission of The American Sociological Society, from **American Sociological Review**, 18 (Feb., 1953), pp. 3–12.

the television screen, and the way in which the event was interpreted, magnified, and took on added significance, or the other. The contrast between these two perspectives from which the larger social environment can be viewed and "known," forms the starting point for the assessment of a particular effect of television in structuring public events.

THE RESEARCH DESIGN

The present research was undertaken as an exploration in collective behavior. The design of the communications analysis differs significantly from most studies of content analysis. The usual process of inferring effect from content and validating the effect by means of interviews with an audience and control group is reversed. A generally apparent effect, i.e. the "landslide effect" of national indignation at MacArthur's abrupt dismissal and the impression of enthusiastic support bordering on "mass hysteria," given to him, was used to make inferences on given aspects of the television content. The concern was with the picture disseminated, especially as it bore on the political atmosphere. To explain how people could have a false imagery (the implication of participant observational data), was necessary to show how their perspective of the larger political environment was limited and how the occasion of Chicago's welcome to MacArthur, an event mediately known already, was given particular structure. The concern is how the picture of the events was shaped by selection, emphasis, and suggested inferences which fitted into the already existing pattern of expectations.

The content analysis was therefore focused on two aspects—the selections made by the camera and their structuring of the event in terms of foreground and background, and the explanation and interpretation tations of televised events given by commentators and persons interviewed by them. Moreover, each monitor was instructed to give his impression of what was happening, on the basis of the picture and information received by way of television. The monitors' interpretations and subjective impressions were separately recorded. They served as a check that the structure inferred from the two operations of "objective" analysis of content were, in fact, legitimate inferences. At the same time, utilizing the categories of the objective analysis, the devices by which the event was structured could be isolated, and the specific ways in which television reportage differed from the combined observations could be determined.

Thirty-one participant observers took part in the study. They were spatially distributed to allow for the maximum coverage of all the important phases of the day's activities, i.e., no important vantage point of spectatorship was neglected. Since the events were temporally distributed, many observers took more than one station, so that coverage was actually based on more than 31 perspectives. Thus the sampling error inherent in individual participant observation or unplanned mass-observation was greatly reduced. Observers could witness the arrival at Midway Airport and still arrive in the Loop area long before the scheduled time for the parade. Reports were received from 43 points of observation.

Volunteers received instruction sheets which drew their attention to principles of observation and details to be carefully recorded. Among these was the directive to take careful note of any activity indicating possible influences of the televising of the event upon the behavior of spectators, e.g., actions specifically addressed to the cameras, indications that events were staged with an eye towards transmission over television, and the like.

SUMMARY OF FINDINGS

The Pattern of Expectations. The mass-observation concentrated on discerning the psychological structure of the unfolding event in terms of present and subsequent anticipations. Certainly the crowd which turned out for the MacArthur Day celebration was far from a casual collection of individuals: the members *intended* to be witnesses to this "unusual event." One may call these intentions specific attitudes, emergent acts, expectations, or predispositions. Whatever the label, materials on these patterns of expectations were taken from two sources: (1) all statements of spectators recorded in the observer reports which could be interpreted as indicative of such expectations (coded in terms of the inferences therein); (2) personal expectations of the 31 study observers (as stated in the personal questionnaire).

Though not strictly comparable—since the observations on the scene contained purely personal, very short-range and factually limited expectations—both series of data provide confirmation of a basic pattern of observer expectations. The persons on the scene *anticipated* "mobs" and "wild crowds." They expected some disruption of transportation. Their journey downtown was in search of adventure and excitement. Leaving out such purely personal expectations as "seeing" and "greeting," the second most frequent preconception emphasizes the extraordinary nature of the preparations and the entertaining showmanship connected with the spectacle.

As a result of an unfortunate collapsing of several questions regarding personal data into one, the response did not always focus properly on what the observers "expected to see." In some cases no evidence or only an incomplete description of this aspect was obtained. Of those answering, 68 per cent expected excited and wildly enthusiastic crowds. But it is a safe inference from the discussion during the briefing session that this figure tends to underestimate the number who held this type of imagery. The main incentive to volunteer resided, after all, in the opportunity to study crowd behavior at first hand.

To sum up: most people expected a wild spectacle, in which the large masses of onlookers would take an active part, and which contained an element of threat in view of the absence of ordinary restraints on behavior and the power of large numbers.

The Role of Mass Media in the Pattern of Expectation. A more detailed examination of the data supports the original assumption that the pattern of expectations was shaped by way of the mass media. For it is in that way that the picture of the larger world comes to sophisticated as well as unsophisticated people. The observers of the study were no exception to this dependence on what newspapers, newsreels, and television cameras mediated. They were, perhaps, better able than others to describe the origin of these impressions. Thus Observer 14 wrote in evaluating his report and his subjective feelings:

> I had listened to the accounts of MacArthur's arrival in San Francisco, heard radio reports of his progress through the United States, and had heard the Washington speech as well as the radio accounts of his New York reception. . . . I had therefore expected the crowds to be much more vehement, contagious, and identified with MacArthur. I had expected to hear much political talk, especially anti-Communist and against the Truman administration.
>
> These expectations were completely unfulfilled. I was amazed that not once did I hear Truman criticized, Acheson mentioned, or as much as an allusion to the Communists. . . . I had expected roaring, excited mobs; instead there were quiet, well ordered, dignified people. . . . The air of curiosity and casualness surprised me. Most people seemed to look on the event as simply something that might be interesting to watch.

Other observers made statements of a very similar content.

Conversation in the crowd pointed to a similar awareness. Talk repeatedly turned to television, especially to the comparative merit of "being there" and "seeing it over TV." An effort was consequently made to assess systematically the evidence bearing on the motives for being there in terms of the patterns of expectations previously built up. The procedures of con-

tent analysis served as a useful tool, allowing the weighing of all evidence *directly* relevant to this question in terms of confirmatory and contrary evidence. The coding operation involved the selection of two types of indicators: (1) general evaluations and summaries of data; and (2) actual incidents of behavior which could support or nullify our hypothesis.

Insofar as the observers had been instructed to report concrete behavior rather than general interpretations, relatively few such generalizations are available for tabulation. Those given were used to formulate the basic headings under which the concrete evidence could be tabulated. The generalizations fall into two types: namely, the crowds had turned out to see a great military figure and a public hero "in the flesh"; and—its logical supplement—they had turned out not so much "to see *him,* as I noticed, but to see the spectacle (Observer 5)." Six out of eleven concretely stated propositions were of the second type.

An examination of the media content required the introduction of a third heading, which subdivided the interest in MacArthur into two distinct interpretations: that people had come to find vantage points from which to see the man and his family; or, as the official (media and "Chicago official") version held, that they had come to welcome, cheer, and honor him. Not one single observer, in any generalized proposition, confirmed the official generalization, but there was infrequent mention of isolated incidents which would justify such an interpretation.

TABLE 1

Types of Spectator Interest

Form of Motivation	Per Cent
Active hero worship	9.2
Interest in seeing MacArthur	48.1
Passive interest in spectacle	42.7
Total	100.0

The analysis of actual incidents, behavior, and statements recorded is mor revealing. A gross classification of the anticipations which led people to participate is given (according to categories outlined above) in Table 1.

A classification of these observations by area in which they were secured gives a clear indication that the Loop throngs thought of the occasion *primarily* as a spectacle. There, the percentage of observations supporting the "spectacle hypothesis" was 59.7. The percentage in other areas was: Negro district, 40.0; Soldiers Field, 22.9; Airport, 17.6; University district, 0.0. Moreover, of the six generalizations advanced on crowd expectations in the Loop, five interpreted the prevalent motivation as the hope of a wild spectacle.

Thus, a probe into motivation gives a confirmatory clue regarding the pattern of expectations observed. To this body of data, there should be added the constantly overheard expressions—as the time of waiting increased and excitement failed to materialize—of disillusionment with the particular advantage point. "We should have stayed home and watched it on TV," was the almost universal form that the dissatisfaction took. In relation to the spectatorship experience of extended boredom and sore feet, alleviated only by a brief glimpse of the hero of the day, previous and similar experiences over television had been truly exciting ones which promised even greater "sharing of excitement" *if only one were present.* These expectations were disappointed and favorable allusions to television in this respect were frequent. To present the entire body of evidence bearing on the inadequate release of tension and the widely felt frustration would be to go beyond the scope of this report, in which the primary concern is the study of the television event. But the materials collected present unequivocal proof of the foregoing statements, and this—with one qualified exception—is also the interpretation of each one of the observers.

Moreover, the comparison of the television perspective with that of the participant observers indicates that the video aspects of MacArthur Day in Chicago served to *preserve* rather than disappoint the same pattern of expectations among the viewers. The main difference was that television remained true to form until the very end, interpreting the entire proceedings according to expectations. No hint about the disappointment in the crowd was provided. To cite only one example, taken from what was the high point in the video presentation, the moment when the crowds broke into the parade by surging out into State Street:

> The scene at 2:50 p.m. at State and Jackson was described by the announcer as the "most enthusiastic crowd *ever* in our city. . . . You can feel the tenseness in the air. . . . You can hear that crowd roar." The crowd was described as pushing out into the curb with the police trying to keep it in order, while the camera was still focusing on MacArthur and his party. The final picture was of a bobbing mass of heads as the camera took in the entire view of State Street northward. To the monitor, this mass of people appeared to be pushing and going nowhere. And then, with the remark, "The whole city appears to be marching down State Street behind General MacArthur," holding the picture just long enough for the impression to sink in, the picture was suddenly blanked out.

Observer 26, who was monitoring this phase of the television transmission, reported her impression:

> . . . the last buildup on TV concerning the "crowd" (cut off as it was, abruptly at 3:00 p.m.) gave me the impression that the crowd was pressing and straining so hard that it was going to be hard to control. My first thought, "I'm glad I'm not in that" and "I hope nobody gets crushed."

But observers near State and Jackson did not mention the event in an extraordinary context. For example, Observer 24 explained that as MacArthur passed:

> Everybody strained but few could get a really good glimpse of him. A few seconds after he had passed most people merely turned around to shrug and to address their neighbors with such phrases: "That's all," "That was it," "Gee, he looks just as he does in

the movies," "What'll we do now?" Mostly teenagers and others with no specific plans flocked into the street after MacArthur, but very soon got tired of following as there was no place to go and nothing to do. Some cars were caught in the crowd, a matter which, to the crowd, seemed amusing.

The Structure of the TV Presentation. The television perspective was different from that of any spectator in the crowd. Relatively unlimited in its mobility, it could order events in its own way by using close-ups for what was deemed important and leaving the apparently unimportant for the background. There was almost complete freedom to aim cameras in accordance with such judgments. The view, moreover, could be shifted to any significant happening, so that the technical possibilities of the medium itself tended to play up the dramatic. While the spectator, if fortunate, caught a brief glimpse of the General and his family, the television viewer found him the continuous center of attraction from his first appearance during the parade at 2:21 p.m. until the sudden blackout at 3:00 p.m. For almost 40 minutes, not counting his seven minute appearance earlier in the day at the airport and his longer appearance at Soldiers Field that evening, the video viewer could fasten his eyes on the General and on what could be interpreted as the interplay between a heroic figure and the enthusiastic crowd. The cheering of the crowd seemed not to die down at all, and even as the telecast was concluded, it only seemed to have reached its crest. Moreover, as the camera focused principally on the parade itself, the crowd's applause seemed all the more ominous a tribute from the background.

The shots of the waiting crowd, the interviews with persons within it, and the commentaries, had previously prepared the viewer for this dramatic development. Its resolution was left to the inference of the individual. But a sufficient number of clues had already come over television to leave little doubt about the structure. Out of the three-hour daytime telecast, in addition to the time that MacArthur and party were the visual focus of attention,

there were over two hours which had to be filled with visual material and vocal commentary. By far the largest amount of time was spent on anticipatory shots of the crowd. MacArthur himself held the picture for the second longest period; thus the ratio of time spent viewing MacArthur to time spent anticipating his arrival is much greater for the TV observer than for the spectator on the scene.

The descriptive accounts of the commentators (also reflected in the interviews), determined the structure of the TV presentation of the day's events. The idea of the magnitude of the event, in line with preparations announced in the newspapers, was emphasized by constant reference. The most frequently employed theme was that "no effort has been spared to make this day memorable" (eight references). There were seven direct references to the effect that the announcer had "never seen the equal to this moment" or that it was the "greatest ovation this city had ever turned out." The unique cooperative effort of TV received five mentions and was tied in with the "dramatic" proportions of the event. It was impossible to categorize and tabulate all references, but they ranged from a description of crowded transportation and numerical estimates of the crowd to the length of the city's lunch hour and the state of "suspended animation" into which business had fallen. There was repeated mention that nothing was being allowed to interfere with the success of the celebration; even the ball game had been cancelled. In addition to these purely formal aspects of the event, two—and only two —aspects of the spectacle were *stressed* (1) the unusual nature of the event; (2) the tension which was said to pervade the entire scene. Even the references to the friendly and congenial mood of the waiting crowd portended something about the change that was expected to occur.

Moreover, in view of the selectivity of the coverage with its emphasis on close ups, it was possible for each viewer to see himself in a *personal* relationship to the General. As the announcer shouted out "Look at that chin! Look at those eyes! —each viewer, regardless of what might have been meant by it, could seek a personal interpretation which best expressed, for him, the real feeling underlying the exterior which appeared on the television screen.

It is against the background of this personal inspection that the significance of the telecast must be interpreted. The cheering crowd, the "seething mass of humanity," was fictionally endowed by the commentators with the same capacity for a direct and personal relationship to MacArthur as the one which television momentarily established for the TV viewer through its close-up shots. The net effect of television thus stems from a convergence of these two phenomena; namely, the seemingly extraordinary scope of the event together with the apparent enthusiasm accompanying it and personalizing influence just referred to. In this way the public event was interpreted in a very personal nexus. The total effect of so many people, all shouting, straining, cheering, waving in personal welcome to the General, disseminated the impression of a universal, enthusiastic, overwhelming ovation for the General. The selectivity of the camera and the commentary gave the event a personal dimension, non-existent for the participants in the crowds, thereby presenting a very specific perspective which contrasted with that of direct observation.

Other Indices of the Discrepancy. In order to provide a further objective check on the discrepancies between observer impressions and the event as it was interpreted by those who witnessed it over television, a number of spot checks on the reported amount of participation were undertaken. Transportation statistics, counts in offices, and the volume of sales reported by vendors provided such indices.

The results substantiate the above finding. The city and suburban lines showed very slight increase over their normal loads. To some extent the paltry 50,000 increase in inbound traffic on the street cars and elevated trains might even have been due to rerouting. The suburban lines had their evening rush hour moved up

into the early afternoon—before the parade had begun.

Checks at luncheonettes, restaurants, and parking areas indicated no unusual crowding. Samplings in offices disclosed only a minor interest in the parade. Hawkers, perhaps the most sensitive judges of enthusiasms, called the parade a "puzzler" and displayed unsold wares.

Detailed Illustration of Contrast. The Bridge ceremony provides an illustration of the contrast between the two perspectives. Seven observers witnessed this ceremony from the crowd.

TV perspective: In the words of the announcer, the Bridge ceremony marked "one of the high spots, if not the high spot of the occasion this afternoon. . . . The parade is now reaching its climax at this point."

The announcer, still focusing on MacArthur and the other participating persons, took the opportunity to review the ceremony about to take place. . . . The camera followed and the announcer described the ceremony in detail. . . . The camera focused directly on the General, showing a close-up. . . . There were no shots of the crowd during this period. But the announcer filled in. "A great cheer goes up at the Bataan Bridge, where the General has just placed a wreath in honor of the American boys who died at Bataan and Corregidor. You have heard the speech . . . the General is now walking back . . . The General now enters his car. This is the focal point where all the newsreels . . . frankly, in 25 years of covering the news, we have never seen as many newsreels gathered at one spot. One, two, three, four, five, six. At least eight cars with newsreels rigged on top of them, taking a picture that will be carried over the entire world, over the Chicagoland area by the combined network of these TV stations of Chicago, which have combined for this great occasion and for the solemn occasion which you have just witnessed."

During this scene there were sufficient close-ups for the viewer to gain a definite reaction, positive or negative, to the proceedings. He could see the General's facial expressions and what appeared to be momentary confusion. He could watch the activities of the Gold Star mothers in relation to MacArthur and define this as he wished—as inappropriate for the bereaved moment or as understandable in the light of the occasion. Taking the cue from the announcer, the entire scene could be viewed as rushed. Whether or not, in line with the official interpretation, the TV viewer saw the occasion as *solemn,* it can be assumed that he expected that the participant on the scene was, in fact, experiencing the occasion in the same way as he.

Actually, this is the way what was meant to be a solemn occasion was experienced by those attending, and which constitutes the crowd perspective. The dedication ceremony aroused little of the sentiment it might have elicited under other conditions. According to Observer 31, "People on our corner could not see the dedication ceremony very well, and consequently after he had passed immediately in front of us, there was uncertainty as to what was going on. As soon as word had come down that he had gone down to his car, the crowd dispersed." Observer 8 could not quite see the ceremony from where he was located on Wacker Drive, slightly east of the bridge. Condensed descriptions of two witnesses illustrate the confusion which surrounded the actual wreath-laying ceremony (three other similar descriptions are omitted here).

It was difficult to see any of them. MacArthur moved swiftly up the steps and immediately shook hands with people on the platform waiting to greet him. There was some cheering when he mounted the platform. He walked north on the platform and did not reappear until some minutes later. In the meantime the crowd was so noisy that it was impossible to understand what was being broadcast from the loudspeakers. Cheering was spotty and intermittent, and there was much talk about Mrs. MacArthur and Arthur . . . (Observer 2).

Those who were not on boxes did not see MacArthur. They did not see Mrs. MacArthur, but only her back. MacArthur went up on the platform, as we were informed by those on boxes, and soon we heard some sound over the loudspeakers. Several cars were standing in the street with their motors running. . . . Some shouted to the cars to shut their motors off, but the people in the cars did not care or did not hear. . . . The people in our area continued to push forward trying to hear. When people from other areas began to come and walk past us to go toward the train, the people in our area shrugged their shoulders. "Well, I guess it's all over. That noise must have been the speech." One of the three men who had stood there for an hour or more, because it was such a good spot, complained, "This turned out to be a lousy spot. I should have gone home. I bet my wife saw it much better over television" (Observer 30).

Regardless of good intentions on the part of planners and despite any recognition of the solemn purpose of the occasion by individuals in the crowd, the solemnity of the occasion was destroyed, if for no other reason, because officials in the parade were so intent upon the time-schedule and cameramen so intent upon recording the solemn dedication for the TV audience and for posterity that the witnesses could not see or hear the ceremony, or feel "solemn" or communicate a mood of solemnity. A crowd of confused spectators, cheated in their hopes of seeing a legendary hero in the flesh was left unsatisfied.

Reciprocal Effects. There is some direct evidence regarding the way in which television imposed its own peculiar perspective on the event. In one case an observer on the scene could watch both what was going on and what was being televised.

It was possible for me to view the scene (at Soldiers Field) both naturally and through the lens of the television camera. It was obvious that the camera presented quite a different picture from the one received otherwise. The camera followed the General's car and caught that part of the crowd immediately opposite the car and about 1 rows above it. Thus it caught that part of the crowd that was cheering, giving the impression of a solid mass of wildly cheering people. It did not show the large sections of empty stands, nor d it show that people stopped cheering as soon as the car passed them (Observer 13).

In much the same way, the television viewer received the impression of wildly cheering and enthusiastic crowds before the parade. The camera selected shots of the noisy and waving audience, but in this case, the television camera itself created the incident. The cheering, waving, and shouting was often largely a response to the aiming of the camera. The crowd was thrilled to be on television, and many attempted to make themselves apparent to acquaintances who might be watching. But even beyond that, an event important enough to warrant the most widespread pooling of television facilities in Chicago video history, acquired in its own right some magnitude and significance. Casual conversation continually showed that being on television was among the greatest thrills of the day.

CONCLUSION

It has been claimed for television that it brings the truth directly into the home: the "camera does not lie." Analysis of the above data shows that this assumed reportorial accuracy is far from automatic. Every camera selects, and thereby leaves the unseen part of the subject open to suggestion and inference. The gaps are usually filled in by a commentator. In addition the process directs action and attention to itself.

Examination of a public event by mass-observation and by television revealed considerable discrepancy between these two experiences. The contrast in perspectives points to three items whose relevance in structuring a televised event can be inferred from an analysis of the television content:

(1) technological bias, i.e., the necessarily arbitrary sequence of telecasting events and their structure in terms of foreground and background, which at the same time contains the choices on the part of the television personnel as to what is important;

(2) structuring of an event by an announcer, whose commentary is needed to tie together the shifts from camera to camera, from vista to close-up, helping the spectator to gain the stable orientation from one particular perspective;

(3) reciprocal effects, which modify the event itself by staging it in a way to make it more suitable for telecasting and creating among the actors the consciousness of acting for a larger audience.

General attitudes regarding television and viewing habits must also be taken into account. Since the industry is accustomed to thinking in terms of audience ratings—though not to the exclusion of all other considerations—efforts are made to assure steady interest. The telecast was made to conform to what was interpreted as the pattern of viewers' expectations. The drama of MacArthur Day, in line with that pattern, was nonetheless built around unifying symbols, personalities, and general appeals (rather than issues). But a drama it had to be, even if at the expense of reality.

Unlike other television programs, news and special events features constitute part of that basic information about "reality" which we require in order to act in concert with anonymous but like-minded persons in the political process. Action is guided by the possibilities for success, and, as part of this constant assessment, inferences about public opinion as a whole are constantly made. Even though the average citizen does, in fact, see only a small segment of public opinion, few persons refrain from making estimates of the true reading of the public temper. Actions and campaigns are supported by a sense of support from other persons. If not, these others at least constitute an action potential that can be mobilized. The correct evaluation of the public temper is therefore of utmost importance; it enters the total political situation as perhaps one of the weightiest factors.

Where no overt expression of public opinion exists, politicians and citizens find it useful to fabricate it. Against such demonstrations as the MacArthur Day, poll data lack persuasiveness and, of necessity, must always lag, in their publication, behind the development of popular attitudes. For the politician who is retroactively able to counter the errors resulting from an undue regard for what at a given time is considered overwhelming public opinion, there may be little significance in this delay. The imagery of momentary opinion may, however, goad him into action which, though justified in the name of public opinion, may objectively be detrimental. It may prevent critics from speaking out when reasoned criticism is desirable, so that action may be deferred until scientific estimates of public opinion can catch up with the prior emergence of new or submerged opinion.

Above all, a more careful formulation of the relations among public opinion, the mass media, and the political process, is vital for the understanding of many problems in the field of politics. The reports and telecasts of what purports to be spontaneous homage paid to a political figure assume added meaning within this context. The most important single media effect coming within the scope of the material relevant to the study of MacArthur Day was the dissemination of an image of overwhelming public sentiment in favor of the General. This effect gathered force as it was incorporated into political strategy, picked up by other media, entered into gossip, and thus came to overshadow immediate reality as it might have been recorded by an observer on the scene. We have labelled this the "landslide effect" because, in view of the widespread dissemination of a particular public welcoming ceremony the imputed unanimity gathered tremendous force. This "landslide effect" can, in large measure, be attributed to television.

Two characteristics of the video event enhanced this effect (misevaluation of public sentiment). (1) The depiction of the ceremonies in unifying rather than in particularistic symbols (between which a balance was maintained) failed to leave any room for dissent. Because no lines were drawn between the conventional and the partisan aspects of the reception, the traditional welcome assumed political significance in the eyes of the public. (2) A general characteristic of the television presentation was that the field of vision of the viewer was enlarged while, at the same time, the context in which these events could be interpreted was less clear. Whereas a participant was able to make direct inferences about the crowd as a whole, being in constant touch with those around him, the television viewer was in the center of the entire crowd. Yet, unlike the participant, he was completely at the mercy of the instrument of his perceptions. He could not test his impressions— could not shove back the shover, inspect bystanders' views, or attempt in any way to affect the ongoing activity. To the participant, on the other hand, the direction of the crowd activity as a whole, regardless of its final goal, still appeared as the inter-play of certain peculiarly personal and human forces. Political sentiment, wherever encountered, could thus be evaluated and discounted. Antagonistic views could be attributed to insufficient personal powers of persuasion rather than seen as subjugation to the impersonal dynamics of mass hysteria. The television viewer had little opportunity to recognize this personal dimension in the crowd. What was mediated over the screen was, above all, the general trend and the direction of the event, which consequently assumed the proportion of an impersonal force, no longer subject to influence.

This view of the "overwhelming" effect of public moods and the impersonal logic of public events is hypothesized as a characteristic of the perspective resulting from the general structure of the picture and the context of television viewing.

Certain characteristics of the mass media place them in a potentially powerful position for modifying mass preoccupations. The absence of other sources of information, combined with the corroborative nature of the communications from different agencies, makes considerable influence probable. Communications stemming from the mass media are often assigned a special quality of authenticity because of respect for the printed word or the large-scale production. The prestige of numbers may be assigned such communications, so that the listener or reader assumes that the degree of attention devoted to particular items reflects the degree of attention, or conviction, of the mass. The mass media may provide a shared system of symbols that become the accepted vehicles of interpersonal communication. Such symbols may exercise important influence because of the values they imply and because they impose upon the user, without his awareness, a frame of reference for perceiving, thinking and acting. Herbert Blumer and Philip Hauser, in an early study, showed the influence of the movies in providing imagery for the child viewer.* As has further been suggested by Martin Millspaugh, the mass media may become the effective arbiters in a criminal court case by presenting so unbalanced an image to its audience that an unbiased jury is unlikely to be found.**

The following experimental study presents rather carefully the evidence for the shaping of mass tastes by the media. Certain alternative interpretations of these particular findings cannot altogether be ruled out. And the dynamics of the relationship between the mass media and mass tastes are not clarified in the study. However, the fact of a relationship is clearly documented. A plausible interpretation might emphasize the prestige aspect in preferring the "right" popular songs, which creates a particular mass susceptibility to the shaping of tastes by the indications of popularity inferred from the frequency with which musical numbers are played on the radio. Whether the same type of influence characterizes matters in which the prestige of being in agreement with the majority is less, we do not know.

* **Movies, Delinquency, and Crime** (New York: The Macmillan Co., 1933).
** "Trial by Mass Media," **Public Opinion Quarterly,** 13 (1949), pp. 328–329.

THE EFFECT OF RADIO PLUGGING ON STUDENTS' OPINIONS OF POPULAR SONGS

Gerhart Wiebe

The question investigated here is: Does extensive broadcasting (called plugging) of a song influence students' opinions about the song?

Twenty-four songs were chosen at random from the inexhaustible supply of advance copies which publishers distribute to the broadcasting networks. Six songs were used with each of the four cooperating groups of subjects.

The subjects were members of two high school and two college classes. The high school students were slightly above

average high school IQ, of ages 15 to 17, from fairly representative urban homes. The college students were from two classes, one in Psychology and one in Sociology. In all, there were 136 subjects.

The four groups of students were assembled and each heard six new popular songs, each played twice. A few subjects had heard a few of the songs previously. They were asked to rate each of the songs on a ten-point scale and also to answer seven questions concerning the song. Each group was reconvened about four weeks after its first sitting and again about four weeks later for a third sitting. Since it was known from another study that

Reprinted in part by permission of The American Psychological Association, Inc., from **Journal of Applied Psychology,** 24 (Dec., 1940), pp. 721–727.

style of performance, and especially of vocal performance, strongly influences attitudes towards popular songs, a good consistent commercial pianist was used at all sittings and only choruses were played.

The magazine *Variety* lists each week those songs which have been most broadcast. Playing of new popular songs over the air is called plugging and those songs which appeared *once* or more in *Variety's* lists of most broadcast songs during the first month of this study were classified as Much-Plugged (P). All other songs are called Little-Plugged or Un-Plugged (U). Although several of these songs had been plugged for two or three weeks before the first sitting (the number of plugs before was 282, or 14 per cent of the total number of plugs) the subjects, except for a few individuals, reported that the songs were new to them at the time of the first sitting. A fortunate though fortuitous fact is the comparative constancy of plugging of the songs throughout the experimental period. This constancy entitles us to investigate the significance of differences between sittings 1 and 2 as well as overall differences, between sittings 1 and 3. A Chi-square calculation shows that the number of plugs is essentially constant throughout the period of the experiment.

Table 3 shows the mean rating at each sitting for the ten plugged and the twelve unplugged songs.

TABLE 3

Ratings for Plugged and Unplugged Songs, by Sittings

	Sitting		
	1	2	3
Plugged	6.5	6.6	6.4
Unplugged	6.4	5.9	5.9

Statistical test shows that the only significant difference (at the "0.05 level") is that between the first and second sittings for unplugged songs. This state of affairs may be interpreted as follows.

Plugging maintains students' ratings of songs at a constant level. Songs which are *not plugged are rated lower when they are heard again.*

It appears, then, that extensive plugging does not increase the liking of students for popular songs. But if songs are not plugged, they fall off in rating, and the plugging can be expected to hold the rating up to a level of roughly 6.5 on a ten point scale. Due to the small number of songs used in this study the constancy of rating of the plugged songs can only be asserted with an accuracy of about 0.5 of scale unit. The expected drop in rating of unplugged songs is only just over this critical limit.

The effect of plugging might be expected to be different for songs originally better liked and for those originally less liked. To test this hypothesis, the plugged songs were divided into two groups, those (5) above their median score (6.67) and those (5) below this score. Similarly the unplugged songs were divided into two sub-groups, above (7) and below (6) their median (6.28). The above-median sub-groups are called better liked and are labelled B in column 7 of Table 1. The below-median sub-groups are called less liked and labelled L.

Table 4 shows the mean ratings for the four sub-groups.

TABLE 4

Ratings of Liked and Plugged Songs, by Sittings

	Sitting		
	1	2	3
Better Liked Songs			
Plugged	7.7	7.4	7.1
Unplugged	7.4	7.1	6.8
Less Liked Songs			
Plugged	4.9	5.7	5.6
Unplugged	5.6	4.9	5.0

The only statistically significant difference between sittings in this table is that between the first and second sittings for less liked unplugged songs. But the general trend of the four groups must also be viewed as significant. It is seen that those songs that were initially better liked fall off slightly in rating whether or not they are plugged. It is in the less liked groups that the importance of plugging appears, for here the trend is upward for plugged and downward for unplugged songs. It should be possible to study the effects of desire-to-be-fashionable, of musical competence, and of ability to play the piano.

Table 4 justifies the following contention:

Plugging does not affect students' ratings of better liked songs. Plugged and unplugged songs fall off together at the rate of about 0.3 of a scale unit for each sitting.

Plugging does affect the rating of songs originally less well liked. Such songs are rated about 0.3 of a scale unit higher for each successive sitting.

We have made, then, one differentiation with respect to a property of the *songs,* namely better liked and less liked; and one distinction with respect to an outside *influence,* namely much plugging and little plugging. It remains to investigate differences between the *subjects.* The important difference here is taken to be between those who are more and those who are less interested in popular music. As an index of interest the subjects were divided into those who listened to the radio more than two hours a day, and those who listened less than two hours a day. Table 5 shows the difference in ratings for these two groups.

In the first place, those who listen more to the radio rate the songs consistently higher for every sitting and whether or not the songs are plugged. This measures the greater enthusiasm of the habitual listeners. The difference in rating is about 0.6 of a scale division for each sub-group. Secondly, the plugging of songs is no more effective with those who listen more

TABLE 5

Ratings of Songs by Those Who Listen More, by Sittings

	Sitting		
	1	2	3
More daily listening			
Plugged	7.2	7.6	7.2
Unplugged	6.6	6.1	5.9
Less daily listening			
Plugged	6.5	6.9	6.7
Unplugged	6.1	5.3	5.5

than with those who listen less. The differences in rating as between plugged and unplugged songs are almost exactly the same for those who listen more (0.6, 1.5, and 1.3) and for those who listen less (0.4, 1.6, and 1.2).

SUMMARY

One hundred thirty-four high school and college students liked ten popular songs that were later widely broadcast, no better than thirteen songs that were seldom or never broadcast. After a month, however, the plugged songs were liked as well as before, while the unplugged songs were rated somewhat lower. After a second month, there was no change in rating of plugged or unplugged songs. Dividing the songs into those that are initially well-liked and less well-liked, it is found that plugging does not affect the ratings of the more-liked songs. Plugged and unplugged songs fall off in rating together. Plugging does affect the rating of songs originally less well-liked. These songs, if plugged, increase slightly in rating at each sitting.

There was no observable difference in effectiveness of plugging for radio-enthusiasts as against casual listeners.

At times, however, there develops some sort of collective or highly organized resistance to the content of mass communication, and effective pressure may force change. The organized campaign against indecency in the movies, spearheaded by the Catholic Church during the 1930's, led to the establishment of a system of self-regulation and self-censorship within the movie industry. The following account tells of a more recent protest action which forced the withdrawal of a series of advertisements by the television industry. But even as this incident shows that organized activity may force a change in communications content, it leaves open the question of whether the advertisement that first appeared was rendered any less effective by virtue of the action. A plausible interpretation might be that the vigorous collective response was a reflection of the *effectiveness* of the appeal which presented in exaggerated form a sentiment which many parents had already felt. The resentment was that of people who had indeed been hit in a vulnerable spot.

THE BRUISE INSIDE

The millions of U.S. parents who don't own TV sets were whipsawed last week by full-page ads in 1,100 newspapers and sudsy commercials pouring from 250 radio stations. The American Television Dealers and Manufacturers Association was spending $2,000,000 to feature the sad plight of a winsome, pigtailed little girl blubbering on the shoulder of her pouting, sad-eyed brother. Warned the A. T. D. M.: "There are some things a son or daughter won't tell you . . . Do you expect him to blurt out the truth— that he's really ashamed to be with the gang—because he doesn't see the television shows they see? . . . How can a little girl describe the bruise deep inside? . . . Can you deny television to your family any longer?"

To this heartbreak harangue, Columnist Angelo Patri, child guidance expert, added his voice of authority: "Youngsters today need television for their morale as much as they need fresh air and sunshine for their health . . ."

Protests crackled from coast to coast. A Washington *Post* reader denounced the "vicious" attempt to "blackmail parents into buying a product." The Washington *Star* editorially conceded that the ad "was in bad taste" and regretted its publication. Cried the Los Angeles *Mirror's* Columnist Hal Humphrey: "How neurotic can you get?"

Reprinted by permission of Time, Inc., from **Time,** 56 (Nov. 27, 1950), pp. 74–75. Copyright Time, Inc.

In Nashville, a convention of 90 Methodist church leaders took time out to denounce the campaign as "a new low" in advertising. Asked one embattled parent in the Nashville *Banner:* "Should I go into debt . . . in order that my children can see highlights of football, an ancient fourth-rate movie followed by a full program of wrestling?"

Angelo Patri's syndicated column was promptly dropped by the Providence, R. I. *Journal-Bulletin,* even though Patri himself had withdrawn his endorsement and returned the check he had received for it.

By the time the first returns were in and counted, several papers had announced that they would run no more ads in the campaign. Editor Frank A. Clarvoe of Scripps-Howard's San Francisco *News* said shortly: "It was a damned stupid campaign and whoever thought it up ought to have his head examined."

In Manhattan, ad agency Ruthrauff & Ryan, which is handling the campaign, was only mildly repentant, admitted that the "negative approach" may have been a mistake. Announcing the withdrawal of the second ad in the series (a freckle-faced, tearful boy described as "the loneliest kid on the block"), Ruthrauff & Ryan decided to accentuate the "positive, happy approach." The first "happy" ad: a picture of two smallfry embracing their father over the caption: "You'd give them the world if you could—this Christmas you can."

Alongside of these emphases on the power of the mass media we must consider the manner in which the media *express* mass sentiments and preoccupations. In an interesting investigation, W. Lloyd Warner and William Henry answer criticisms of daytime radio "soap operas" by saying that these serials are a response to the unmet needs of a certain segment of the female population rather than creators of attitudes. In their study 62 Chicago and Detroit women belonging to the "common man" class level, most of whom were married, were studied with a variety of techniques. All were regular listeners to "Big Sister," one of the most popular of such programs. A partial thematic apperception test was administered to each listener to secure personality information. A verbal projective test, consisting of five incomplete stories involving the major characters of the radio serial which the respondents were instructed to complete, helped to establish the manner in which listeners understood the program. Interviews were further employed to uncover linkages between personality characteristics and the appeal of the program. For contrast, a small number of women from the "upper-middle class" who did not follow the serial were given the same set of tests. While techniques are not yet available which can establish connections between personal needs and receptivity to particular ideological content unequivocally, the authors have made a series of reasonable interpretations from their data. We present only the summary statement, which is a brief portion of the entire monograph.

THE RADIO DAY-TIME SERIAL: SUMMARY OF FINDINGS

W. LLOYD WARNER AND WILLIAM E. HENRY

This pilot research on the responses of the audience and the effect of this serial on its listeners yielded a number of important conclusions which are stated here in the form of a series of interconnected propositions:

A. THE PROGRAM FUNCTIONS TO IDENTIFY THE AUDIENCE WITH THE CHARACTERS IN THE PLOT

1. The Big Sister serial is a drama which functions to express the hopes and fears of its audience.

a. Its basic themes portray these anxieties and hopes.

b. The themes are symbolically expressed in the plot and action through the personalities of the characters.

c. The audience, identifying with the plot and characters of Big Sister, relate their own personal problems to those of the play.

2. The program is a drama of the middle-class family.

a. "Everything in the world" is centered within the focus of an upper-middle class family (Big Sister's). Consequently, social realities outside the family are secondary and enter only as reflected in the structure and action of the family.

3. As conceived by the listeners, the program expresses the psychological realities of their place in life, for it states the traditional symbolic themes of family life they have learned from our culture. This statement means that for most listeners:

a. The present characters motivate the plot and their motives are usually plausible.

b. New themes can only be added (to this serial and others like it) if they conform to the basic one of the drama.

c. Social and economic situations (the realism of social science) can only be developed in a very secondary way, never as basic to the story.

B. THE SYMBOLIC CONTENT OF THE PROGRAM IS DEFINITE AND CLEARLY DEFINED

1. The characters in the Big Sister program are men and women of the upper-middle class and, for the great majority

"Summary of Findings" reprinted by permission of The Journal Press, from W. Lloyd Warner and William E. Henry, "The Radio Day-Time Serial: A Symbolic Analysis," **Genetic Psychology Monographs,** 37 (Feb., 1948), pp. 61–64.

of the audience (those from the Common Man level of America), 65 per cent of our population, this is essentially an emulatory device where the behavior and morals of the heroine are copied by the listeners because she is of higher status and because she expresses the moral ideals of the listeners.

2. The basic and primary theme is that good and noble women who are wives and mothers are invincible within their own arena of life, the American family. Men, who are superordinate elsewhere, are subordinate and dependent on the wisdom of the wife. This primary theme always triumphs over the secondary theme which runs counter to it, that family ties can be broken and a woman's security threatened chiefly by the loss of the husband to other women and, quite secondarily and obliquely, by death. From the point of view of middle-class culture to which most of the listeners to Big Sister belong, these two themes are expressions of social reality.

3. The basic themes of the Big Sister program express the spartan, restrictive virtues of American middle-class morality; the good, well-disciplined woman who is the mother (sexless) of all living is praised and rewarded.

C. THE MAJORITY OF THE WOMEN WHO LISTEN HAVE THE SOCIAL CHARACTERISTICS OF THE COMMON MAN LEVEL OF AMERICAN SOCIETY

1. The women who listen, being normally distributed through the several socio-economic levels of our society (27), belong in most cases to the Common Man social level. At this social level ordinarily:

a. The woman is economically dependent upon the moderate salary or wage of her husband.

b. The world beyond the family is largely outside her sphere of action, but it threatens her security.

c. Her security, as well as that of her dependent children, depends upon her husband.

d. The moral code is more rigid and strict, particularly for women, than at the top and bottom social levels.

e. Adaptation and real anxiety about it are morally phrased, for the behavior of the woman must be highly prescribed and closely regulated or she will lose her position as wife and mother and, thereby, her security.

f. Because her economic position and her larger social situation are dependent upon others (particularly a male) and beyond her control, anxiety develops. Also, with the decreasing role of the housewife in this society, she often questions her utility and, consequently, worries about being a good wife and mother.

(The above, *a* through *f,* were first learned from previous community and personality researches on American women but were further strengthened and confirmed by this research.)

D. THE BIG SISTER PROGRAM HAS SPECIFIED PSYCHOLOGICAL FUNCTIONS THAT WERE EXPRESSED IN THE RESPONSES OF THE WOMEN STUDIED

1. The Big Sister program arouses normal and adaptive anxiety in the women who listen.

2. The Big Sister program directly and indirectly condemns neurotic and nonadaptive anxiety.

3. This program provides moral beliefs, values, and techniques for solving emotional and interpersonal problems for its audience and makes them feel they are learning while they listen (thus: "I find the program is educational").

4. It directs the private reveries and fantasies of the listeners into socially approved channels of action.

5. The Big Sister program increases the women's sense of security in a world they feel is often threatening by:

a. Reaffirming the basic security of the marriage ties (John's and Ruth's).

b. Accentuating the basic security of the position of the husband (John Wayne is a successful physician).

c. "Demonstrating" that those who behave properly and stay away from wrong-doing exercise moral control over those who do not.

d. Showing that wrong behavior is punished.

6. The Big Sister program, in dramatizing the significance of the wife's role in basic human affairs, increases the woman's feeling of importance by showing that the family is of the highest importance and that she has control over the vicissitudes of family life.

7. It thereby decreases their feeling of futility and makes them feel essential and wanted.

8. The women aspire to, and measure themselves by, identification with Ruth, the heroine; however, the identification is not with Ruth alone, but with the whole program and the other characters in the plot. This permits sublimated impulse satisfaction by the listeners', first, unconsciously identifying with the bad woman and, later, consciously punishing her through the action of the plot.

9. Unregulated impulse life is condemned since it is always connected with characters who are condemned and never related to those who are approved.

E. THE PROGRAM HAS SPECIFIC SOCIAL FUNCTIONS (AS EXPRESSED IN THE RESPONSES OF THE WOMEN STUDIED)

1. The primary social function of the program (how it works) is to strengthen and stabilize the basic social structure of our society, the family. It so functions by dramatizing family crises and the ideals and values involved, as they are understood and felt by the women who listen, and by making the good wife (Ruth) the center of action and power.

2. Our society, by offering a choice to women between being housewives or career women (usually professional), frequently creates a dilemma for them: The career woman's role is attractive because it is usually of higher status than the occupation of the Common Man level and offers more moral and emotional freedom. On the other hand, such a role is often frightening, demands hard work, ability to buck the system, and the capacity for self-initiated action. Most of the life of such women is outside the family. The Big Sister program plays up the importance of the role of the wife and therefore obliquely depreciates the role (career women) the ordinary listener has avoided, or not been able to take. It helps resolve any conflict she may have within her for not choosing the other role (that once might have been open to her) and reinforces her present position.

F. EVALUATION OF THE PSYCHOLOGICAL AND SOCIAL EFFECTS OF THE PROGRAM CAN BE MADE

1. Essentially the Big Sister drama is a contemporary minor morality play which expresses, as did the morality plays of ancient times, the feelings and beliefs of its audience by use of idealized symbols of good and evil and of things feared and hoped for (the characters and their actions). It differs from the morality play of earlier times primarily because modern culture is secularized, whereas our earlier society was dominated by sacred beliefs and values.

Mass media as a reflection of mass preoccupations. Certain conditions must be present if the mass media are to function in a neutral manner as the "daydreams of the mass." In the absence of these conditions the media will diverge from mere image-reflection and wish-fulfillment to become a potential influence on mass and collective preoccupations.

The first limitation on the degree to which mass media can become the mere reflection of mass preconceptions is imposed by the heterogeneity of the mass. When there is mass consensus the mass media *can* provide faithful reflections. But in the areas of heterogeneity which are so crucial a part of modern society, such reflection is limited. To some degree the specialized audiences to which different communications appeal permit correspondence. But the fact of multiple-group membership makes it unlikely that content can be pitched to a specific enough group to fit preconceptions fully. One of the consequences of this is that the same content will involve multiple appeals. In the same "western" movie the small boy responds to the shooting that his fifteen-year-old sister dislikes while refusing to look at the romantic scenes that appeal to her. In modern society an undue impress is frequently made upon the content of communication by very inconsiderable but articulate minorities who presume to speak for the total mass.

Even when the mass is sufficiently homogeneous, the content of mass media can only be brought into correspondence with mass preoccupation in two general ways. Either (a) the producers of the content must be themselves representative of the mass, sharing its imagery *and* reflecting these characteristics naively in the material they produce, or (b) there must be selective mechanisms operating whereby inappropriate content is being constantly eliminated and appropriate content brought into prominence.

(a) While the producers of content may reflect mass views in a fairly naive manner, it is unlikely that they will do so fully. First, every occupation draws upon a special kind of person because of the special skills it requires, its general recruitment methods, the appeal of the general style of life which goes with it, and the many rewards and risks involved in the occupation itself. The work of Leo C. Rosten, Hortense Powdermaker, and others demonstrates such selection in the motion picture colony. Second, the in-grouping of an industry means establishing patterns of behavior and belief which are requisite if one is to gain entry into the industry. And third, the development of self-conscious efforts to take account of assumed audience characteristics and of "what the public wants" may lead to distorted reflections. A systematic study of stereotypes which the mass media functionaries hold regarding the mass would be quite informative.

(b) The operation of selective mechanisms likewise rests upon the existence of a number of facilitating conditions. In the first place there must be alternatives among which to choose. Without an awareness of alternatives dissatisfaction is not likely to be strongly enough focalized for the producers of mass media to be able to modify their product to a better fit. Without alternatives people may continue to turn on television or go to movies in the absence of something better to do and register an unenthusiastic acceptance of the existing pattern. Not only can people not formulate dissatisfaction in the absence of alternatives, but there is often no means of *registering* preferences apart from choosing within what is available. When monopoly control characteristics, predominance of stereotyped thinking, and band wagon practices within the industry limit the alternatives from which the mass may choose, there can be little effective pressure brought to bear on the producers to align their product with public preoccupation.

Besides the awareness and availability of alternatives there must be a focusing of the issues of choice. If primary choice is through box office or "Hooper rating" or volume of sales, there must be effective ways of making correct interpretations of the issues which determined preferences. The practice of putting something in each newspaper or motion picture to appeal to everybody leads to purchase by persons who find no appeal in much or most of the content, but respond favorably only to a minor aspect of the total.

Finally, there must be a pattern and means of two-way communication between the industry and mass if preferences are to be recognized and issues defined.

The degree to which these several conditions are met will vary with time, place and medium. But there are sufficient limitations in modern society that we may expect considerable divergence between the content of the mass media and mass preoccupations. This divergence in turn opens the way for the media to operate importantly in shaping mass and collective behavior.

Chapter 10

The diffuse crowd

*T*HE INTENSITY of activity and rapidity of communication decline as one moves outward from the center of a crowd. But even on the outskirts where the activity is least the essential crowd processes are still likely to be found among small knots of people. The interaction within these peripheral groups gives support to the more dynamic center and feeds new members to it.

Similarly, any crowd of considerable intensity and duration is likely to be supplemented in the community by the constant formation and interchange of small knots of people who are intensely concerned about the same situation as is the compact crowd and are duplicating many of the processes which occur within that crowd. These knots are connected through a community-wide network of rumors about the compact crowd itself and of rumors that duplicate those being passed within the compact crowd. This community-wide arousal and milling-rumor process that accompanies a compact crowd is the most obvious instance of what we shall call the *diffuse crowd*.

The mere presence of community-wide interest in the compact crowd is not sufficient justification for speaking of a *diffuse crowd*, however. The characteristics of the *elemental crowd* as we have discussed it earlier must be present. These include uncertainty, urgency, communication of mood and imagery, constraint, individual suggestibility, and permissiveness.

The diffuse crowds typically show the same sort of restriction of attention as the compact crowd. The collectivity sanctions only one type of sentiment and sanctions the exploration of only a few out of many possible interpretations and courses of action. It will not tolerate a challenge to the basic truth of the imagery on the basis of which the crowd is acting. It tolerates only sentiments which duplicate those of the compact crowd. The diffuse crowd exists as a network of communication chains, and as the same individual encounters the same sentiments being expressed in a succession of small knots of people, he quickly acquires the sense that he is part of a collectivity sharing uniform sentiments and encompassing the entire community. With this sense, he is able to act in many respects like the member of a compact crowd, to speak with minimum reflection and without qualification, to express feelings that would place him in a bad light under more typical circumstances, and to disregard many of the more routine demands of everyday living.

Diffuse and compact crowd. The diffuse crowd is not merely similar to the compact crowd. The two are dynamically interrelated in such a way that the course of a compact crowd of any considerable duration is not fully comprehensible without attention to the processes in the environing diffuse crowd. At least five such interrelations are deserving of attention.

First and most obvious, the diffuse crowd is the major *mechanism through which new members are recruited into the compact crowd*. The diffuse crowd instills the essential imagery, sentiments, and conviction of group unanimity in advance of contact with the compact crowd. When persons thus prepared join the compact crowd they are likely to intensify its tempo, since they do not need to pass through a gradual period of induction into the crowd mood.

It is a plausible hypothesis that a considerable portion of the most extreme crowd participants are recruited in this way. Just as a child talking about what he is going to do to "that bully" next time he sees him can more easily build up a misconception of his own prowess and the bully's weakness than he can in the bully's presence, so the members of diffuse crowds may develop a less ambivalent image of their object and be less restrained by the dangers involved because of the fact that they are removed from the scene of action. Thus, newcomers recruited from the diffuse crowd may enter with less inhibitions than those who have been members of the compact crowd from the start.

Second, the diffuse crowd *precipitates new compact crowds* in other locations, crowds which are concerned with the same objects as the original crowd. Thus, in the Southern California "Zoot-Suit" riots of 1943, the initial major crowd action in downtown Los Angeles was reflected in a widespread diffuse crowd. Newspaper headlines and person-to-person communication reiterated the phobia and hatred toward the Mexican-American youth and the determination that things had now reached the point where something had to be done. Newspaper reports of the next few days reported a whole series of attacks on Mexican-Americans similar to the original attack, though smaller in scope, throughout Los Angeles county and as far away as San Bernardino (50 miles) and San Diego (100 miles). People who discovered a unanimity of sentiment through reading newspaper accounts, listening to radio reports, and engaging in informal communication were either provoked to action by the sight of a Mexican-American or assembled and hunted out a suitable object. The widespread sentiment also provoked counterattack by Mexican-Americans against Anglos in several dispersed locations.

In this connection, one of the important features in preventing the spread of anti-Negro rioting at certain public housing projects in Chicago during 1946 and 1947 to city-wide race riots was undoubtedly the cooperation of major newspapers in not reporting the events and thus helping to confine the crowd behavior.

The diffuse crowd operates in a third way *to maintain the continuity of the interrupted compact crowd*. The famous Chicago race riots of 1919 consisted actually of a series of daily riots, beginning seriously each day sometime after noon and continuing into the early hours of the morning. The crowd spirit was maintained in the interim through the diffuse crowd which dominated discussion at work, in the neighborhoods, and throughout the community.

Fourth, the diffuse crowd often *maintains an effective crowd situation for a considerable period after the compact crowd has dispersed.* The long-range effects of crowd behavior depend upon the character of this diffuse crowd. In many instances, especially in those involving an acting crowd that has been controlled by force, the original crowd atmosphere persists long enough to create enduring attitudes which leave their impress on the mass. In other instances the diffuse post-crowd may convey attitudes that are a reaction against the excesses of the compact crowd. If we may judge from contemporary news reports, a diffuse crowd must have developed in the case of the 1921 anti-Negro riot in Tulsa. The riot was followed by a marshalling of community energies to rebuild the Negro neighborhood and demonstrate that "the real citizenship of Tulsa weeps at the unspeakable crime and will make good the damage, as far as it can be done, to the last penny."

Finally, a diffuse crowd may develop prior to the compact crowd and *constitute the situation out of which the latter develops.* Typically those crowds which revolve about a long-standing aggravation and are community-wide in scope develop first as diffuse crowds, often referred to as a state of community tension or unrest.

In pointing out that the diffuse crowd may precede the compact crowd, we have also indicated that a diffuse crowd may develop in other ways than as an extension of a compact crowd. A diffuse crowd may develop like other crowds, as a sudden response to an unanticipated crisis or through an abruptly accelerating process of intercommunication. The national response to the Japanese attack on Pearl Harbor on December 7, 1941, is an instance of precipitous crowd behavior. Radio reports were conveying completely unfounded rumors about fleet engagements thousands of miles away from Pearl Harbor and the populace demanded more such accounts. Public officials rushed to outdo one another in declaring that they stood unqualifiedly for immediate retaliation. Even many who had previously doubted that our interests would be served by defending the Philippines and other Asiatic locations gave their support to the new sentiment.

The media of mass communication transmit not only a point of view but also a sense that the voice of thousands of persons is being expressed. The result is frequently a merging of mass behavior and crowd behavior to the extent that they are indistinguishable. Such merging is exemplified in a famous instance of mass panic. On October 30, 1938, Orson Welles produced a radio program based upon H. G. Wells' story, "The War of the Worlds." It was handled as a series of special news bulletins, including on-the-scenes reports, concerning a successful invasion by mechanical monsters from outer space. Landing at various places in northeastern United States, the monsters crushed all resistance before them. Some thousands of people are estimated to have fled from the area in panic upon hearing the radio reports. While most of these people were acting as individuals responding to a common stimulus, they were acting in the belief that there was already a great crowd of fleeing persons whom they were but joining. The sense of being part of the crowd, effectively conveyed through the radio presentation, undoubtedly was a part of the cause of the resulting mass panic.*

Incidents that outrage the mores, such as certain sex crimes, create diffuse crowds, which are fed in large part through the media of mass communication. The power of some diffuse crowds is such that a judge will fear to give any sex offender probation while one is active. Efforts to extend treatment rather than punishment programs for such offenses will be suspended or kept behind the scenes.

Helene Veltfort and George Lee have prepared an informative description of a diffuse crowd which followed a panic and catastrophe with several hundred people killed in a night club fire. Two among the many interesting features of this account should be noted. First, the diffuse crowd mood was structured from the standpoint of those who were in the night club disaster. In the search for an explanation and an object of antagonism, only those suggestions consistent with this orientation were acceptable. Second, the paper shows well the function of the mass media as *tentative keynoters*. The newspapers offered a succession of objects to the diffuse crowd. But reflecting and responding to the crowd pattern themselves, the writers continued to offer new keynotes until those most acceptable to the diffuse crowd were found. Thus the tentative process through which the crowd defined the object of its pre-existing mood consisted of keynote, response, and modified keynote between the mass media and the bulk of the crowd.

* Hadley Cantril, Hazel Gaudet, and Herta Herzog, **Invasion from Mars** (Princeton: Princeton University Press, 1940).

THE COCOANUT GROVE FIRE: A STUDY IN SCAPEGOATING

HELENE RANK VELTFORT AND GEORGE E. LEE

The word "scapegoat" is part of our everyday language, yet the term is not easily defined. The following definition of the process whereby individuals become scapegoats will serve our present purposes:

> Scapegoating is a phenomenon wherein some of the aggressive energies of a person or group are focused upon another individual, group, or object; the amount of aggression released is greater than that usually released by similar provocation; the fixing of blame and the release of aggression are either partially or wholly unwarranted.

Reprinted by permission of The American Psychological Association, Inc., from Helene Rank Veltfort and George E. Lee, "The Cocoanut Grove Fire: A Study in Scapegoating," **The Journal of Abnormal and Social Psychology**, 38, Clinical Supplement (April, 1943), pp. 138–154.

Scapegoating as a means of fixing blame and relieving guilt is age old; its practice was ritualized in Biblical times. In those days, however, so long as the scapegoat was only a *goat* no harm came of this convenient practice. But in our society today scapegoating is harmful. Particularly is this true in wartime. Scapegoating of our allies, of government officials, of minority groups not only misdirects our aggression away from the common enemy; it also impedes the war effort by causing internal dissension and thus prevents us from attaining maximum production and cooperation within the nation and with our allies.

The Cocoanut Grove fire provides an object lesson in scapegoating, perhaps not typical of all cases of scapegoating, but undoubtedly revealing some of its basic mechanisms. The writers were residing in

Boston when the disaster took place and were able to follow the day-to-day attempts of the newspapers and of the public to fix the responsibility for the catastrophe. The complexity of the case, as evidenced by the many scapegoats that emerged in the aftermath of the tragedy, held the promise of a fertile ground for testing certain hypotheses concerning the dynamics of scapegoating. Further, although the background of Boston's political life cannot be completely overlooked in this analysis, the scapegoating in the Cocoanut Grove fire was relatively free from the entanglements of the complex social, political, and economic forces of the past and present which make it so difficult to analyze completely the scapegoating of the Jews, of the British, or of our government officials. Had the Cocoanut Grove tragedy occurred in any other metropolitan city of the United States, the scapegoating might well have taken a similar form.

THE FACTS OF THE FIRE

Before proceeding with the study of the scapegoating which took place in connection with the disaster, we shall give a summary of the facts pertaining to the tragedy up to and including the return of indictments by the Grand Jury on December 31, 1942.

On Saturday night, November 28, 1942, a violent fire swept the Cocoanut Grove, a popular Boston night club, causing the death of nearly 500 people. The fire started when Stanley Tomaszewski, a 16-year-old busboy, lit a match in order to replace a light bulb which a patron of the club had removed. An artificial palm tree, one of the many used for decorative purposes, immediately caught fire and from there the flames spread swiftly through the several rooms of the club. The cause of the rapid spread of the fire has not been exactly determined, but it is assumed to have spread so rapidly because the ceilings and walls of the club were covered with various highly inflammable materials. Firemen arrived within a few minutes and the flames were quickly brought under control. Yet

the death toll that first evening was about 450 victims. Subsequent deaths at the hospitals brought the total to 488. This tremendous loss of life for a fire which lasted only twenty minutes was attributed in great part to the insufficient number of exits and to the panic which the sight of the flames created. Although the Grove had at least five exits (a number later admitted to be legally sufficient), one of these was locked, the "panic lock" on another was not functioning, and a third was a revolving door. The latter was the main entrance, and it is when this door jammed because of the pressure of the panicky crowd that many people became trapped inside the night club and died not only of burns but also of suffocation.

The investigation also brought out the following facts:

Although in its application for a license the Grove management specified it had 460 seats, it was the general consensus of all witnesses that there were about 1,000 people in the club that night.

The physicians attending the victims, many of whom died subsequently, felt that in most cases these deaths were caused by the inhalation of noxious fumes. Testimony of witnesses who survived, coupled with that of experts, suggested that these fumes were probably nitrous oxide. It is generally accepted that these fumes were given off by the materials used in the club decorations.

Fire Inspector Frank Linney had inspected the Grove a week earlier and recorded the condition of the club as "good."

The inflammability of the materials used in the club was never clearly agreed on. The decorators declared that they bought the material as fire- or flame-proof. There is also a record of the delivery to the club of several cans of a well-known flame-proofing compound. Further, Fire Inspector Linney testified that he put a match to one of the palm trees when he inspected the club and found that the tree did not burn. On the other hand all the tests made on the materials after the fire showed that they burned like tinder.

The Cocoanut Grove had recently been enlarged and the wiring in the new section was done by a nonlicensed electrician. The owner of the club received several notices from the city threatening the cutting-off of electricity unless the club employed a licensed electrician.

After more than a month of investigation by Attorney General Bushnell, ten men were indicted by the Suffolk County Grand Jury. The list of the defendants and the charges against them follow:

MOONEY, JAMES H., Boston Building Commissioner. Failure to enforce law prohibiting use of place of public assembly until a certificate had been issued by a Building Department inspector.

WELANSKY, BARNETT, principal owner of the Grove. Manslaughter and conspiracy to violate the building laws.

WELANSKY, JAMES, brother of Barnett and in charge of the club the night of the fire. Manslaughter and conspiracy to violate the building laws.

GOLDFINE, JACOB, manager of the night club. Manslaughter.

LINNEY, LIEUT. FRANK J., Fire Department Inspector. Accessory after the fact of manslaughter and willful neglect of duty.

BUCCIGROSS, CAPT. JOSEPH, Night Captain of Division 4. Wilfully and corruptly failed, neglected, and omitted to enforce the fire laws.

BODENHORN, REUBEN, designer of the night club; RUDNICK, SAMUEL, contractor; GILBERT, DAVID, foreman for Rudnick. Conspiracy to violate the building laws.

ELDRACHER, THEODORE, Boston City Building Inspector. Failure to report violations of the building laws and to report insufficient exits at the Grove.

All the defendants pleaded "not guilty." They are expecting trial in February.

The above facts as well as the evidence presented subsequently in this study were taken from several Boston newspapers, especially the *Boston Traveler* (an evening paper) and the *Boston Globe* (morning edition). The *Boston American,* the *Boston Post* and the *Boston Herald* were also consulted. These papers have of course quite divergent political tendencies, but the similarity of their approach to the Grove fire by far outweighs their differences.

In addition to the analysis of the news stories and editorials, our study relies heavily on the *letters to the editor,* especially those published in the *Traveler,* which seemed to feature more than any other paper the public's reaction to the fire.

FIXING THE BLAME

The immediate reaction to the fire was one of horror. The early edition of the *Herald* the morning after the fire spent pages describing the tragedy and the mutilation of the victims, with photographs as supporting evidence. The horror thus aroused gave rise to an outcry for avenging the victims; those responsible must be found and punished. This intense desire for "fixing the blame" is the predominant feature of the Cocoanut Grove case and is the subject of the present study. Many of the accusations made by the papers and the public were no doubt well founded; some of the persons involved in the case seem to be actually guilty of violation of safety ordinances. Yet whether these violations were the cause of the fire and of the terrific death toll is far from established. From the beginning, however, the papers and the public assumed that such violations, if not actually deliberate, were certainly among the *causes* of the catastrophe. The people felt some person or persons must be held responsible; attaching responsibility to mere laws or to the *panic* provided neither sufficient outlet for their emotions nor opportunity for punishment. Whenever Boston's lax and insufficient laws were blamed, the matter was personalized by blaming the *City Council* or *public officials* for failure to pass or to enforce laws; or more rarely by the public's blaming the *people* for failure to demand better laws. This personalization is the rule in scapegoating.

Significantly, newspapers and public alike overlooked the fact that the panic created by the fire must have been largely responsible for the great loss of life. In spite of statements by officials immediately after the fire, the people were not ready to accept the fact that "the Boston tragedy was due in part to a psychological collapse." To the extent that they ignored this fact, the blame that the newspapers and public placed on various persons involved in the fire was disproportionate to their responsibility.

An important contributing factor in the campaign to fix the blame was the recall in editorials and news stories of two similar catastrophes some years earlier: the Iroquois fire, Chicago, 1903, and the Pickwick Club disaster, Boston, 1925. In both these cases indictments were returned against several persons but none was found legally guilty and thus all escaped punishment. Editorials and letters alike demanded that such should not happen again.

In the course of this analysis of scapegoating, we shall examine several aspects of the case. The most prominent feature was the number of diverse persons who were chosen as scapegoats by the newspapers and public alike. We shall try to show why these particular scapegoats were chosen, how they were scapegoated and how they responded to the accusations leveled against them. Another important contribution this study can make to an understanding of scapegoating is the exposition of the motivations involved.

THE SCAPEGOATS

The Busboy: As soon as a city dumbfounded with horror and shock had regained itself sufficiently to speak, Boston echoed the universal question: "Who started it?" The Boston press answered a few hours later: on their front pages for November 30 the newspapers featured prominently the story of "The Busboy," and his full confession; of how in striking a match to replace a light bulb removed by some prankster he had accidentally set fire to one of the decorative palm trees. The ordinarily conservative *Globe* declared in two-and-a-half-inch headlines: "BUSBOY BLAMED" and ran a three-column picture of the 16-year-old "offender" on its front page. The busboy was

Stanley Tomaszewski, Dorchester high-school student, who was employed by the Grove during week-end rushes. Thus emerged the first "scapegoat" of the Cocoanut Grove case.

To exactly what extent Stanley was acceptable to the public as the *immediate* scapegoat is difficult to ascertain. To some people at least he may have been a satisfactory object of blame during the first period of emotional upheaval, when little else was known factually about the disaster besides his admission. This admission was the determining factor in the selection of Stanley as the first scapegoat.

Just as quickly and decisively as had the press pointed the accusing finger at the youth, just as quickly did the majority of the public force the press to withdraw it. By Wednesday, December 2, the *letter to the editor* sections were flooded with letters protesting vehemently against this "persecution." On December 3, every letter printed in the *Globe* contained some agitation for the boy's exoneration. Most of these letters seemed to be from persons who had never blamed Stanley; others may have been from persons who had been inclined to scapegoat him originally but had since changed their views. At any rate the "Busboy Movement" passed the stage of full exoneration and soon reached one approaching near adulation. Proposals were forthcoming that he be appointed to West Point, and he received a substantial number of "fan letters," in one of which was included a check for $25.

What accounted for this sudden rise to the defense of Stanley? Quite a number of facts were in his favor. First of all, the admiration of the public was aroused by his straightforward, voluntary admission of having started the fire, and by his teachers' and friends' testimony that he was a model young man. Secondly, discovery that his family was impoverished and that his mother was seriously ill aroused general public sympathy. Thirdly, his youthfulness seemed to convince that he could not be held as responsible as could an adult. Finally, and perhaps most significantly, further acquaintance with the facts of the case revealed to the public he possibility of more satisfying scape-goats.

It was acknowledged that Stanley started the fire; but the public set out to discover who was *responsible* for it and or the staggering loss of life.

The Prankster. Sharing the spotlight of press blame in the early returns following the fire, though to a lesser degree, was the prankster who had removed the light bulb which Stanley had sought to replace. The *Globe* on November 30, the same day that the "Busboy Blamed" headline appeared, ran an article on page one headlined "Prankishness Real Cause of Club Tragedy."

Immediate acceptance of the prankster as the scapegoat instead of Stanley no doubt occurred among some people. The majority who pointed to the former seemed to do so as a protest against the publicizing of the busboy as the "cause of the disaster." There was not, however, any wholesale or continued blaming of the prankster. His exact identity was never discovered, whether it be because he perished in the fire or because he never came forward to admit his part in the disaster. Also, in itself, his action in removing the bulb was not sufficient to make him legally culpable; indeed the connection between his act and the starting of the fire was not sufficiently direct for even logical condemnation. As in the case of the busboy, psychologically more satisfying scapegoats soon emerged as the investigation proceeded.

The Public Officials. The public had not long to wait for detailed reports on the circumstances of the disaster and the emergence of eagerly awaited successors to the exonerated busboy and the soon-forgotten prankster. The *Globe* sounded the keynote blast typical of the entire press on Tuesday morning, December 1, with its terse headline: "O.K.'D GROVE— FIRE DEPARTMENT APPROVED CLUB WEEK AGO." Thus an entire scapegoat group, the public officials, took over the unwelcome spotlight, and, unlike their two predecessors, held it.

Although it was the Fire Department that bore the brunt of the initial attack, it was followed by others, department by department, official by official. Press indictments were strongly phrased and in some instances inflammatory against Lieutenant Frank Linney, Fire Inspector. The text of his latest inspection report on the Grove, made just eight days previous to the fire, was printed in each of the papers with special emphasis placed upon sections of the report which labeled the exits and extinguishers "sufficient" in number and the general condition of the club as "good." His testimony at the inquest that he had tested the inflammability of the decorative palm trees and found them "treated (with flame-proofing liquid) to my satisfaction" was also relentlessly and unfavorably publicized. The *Boston American* seized upon an ill-chosen statement by Linney to the effect that he had taken fire-proofing of certain of the club's furnishings "for granted" and ran the following headline on December 1: "INSPECTOR TOOK GROVE'S SAFETY FOR GRANTED!" The Fire Commissioner, William A. Reilly, took his share of journalistic flailing, although the accusations leveled against him were not as specific as were those against Linney. The accusation seemed to be that, as commissioner, he was responsible for his subordinate's performance of duty.

Shifting momentarily to the Police Department, the press lashed Captain Joseph Buccigross, who, the papers pointed out, was inside the club at the time of the fire, allegedly engaged in routine inspection duties. Much was made of the fact that he had been dressed in plain-clothes, the general implication being that perhaps his presence was more social than professional in nature. Furthermore, the papers revealed that while there he had made no effort to enforce the laws against overcrowding or the employment of under-age workers. No mention was made of any effort on his part to quell the panic that broke out at the first sign of fire. Police Commissioner Frank J. Timilty was portrayed either directly or by implication as being lax, negligent, and incompetent in not checking to see that his subordinate rigidly enforced the laws. The inference to be drawn was that his entire department was similarly ill-managed and undisciplined.

Surging onward and upward, the wave of journalistic censure inundated even the ultimate governing agencies of the city, namely the City Council and Mayor Tobin. On December 1, the *Globe* revealed that a building code, similar to those effective in some other cities, had been in the hands of the City Council for the past four years. The paper scored this body for having taken no action upon it.

The press had also opened fire indirectly upon the mayor. At first, though his name was not actually mentioned in this connection, the constant references to the negligence and laxness of certain heads of departments, along with their subordinates, brought to mind the fact that the mayor had appointed these same heads of departments; such associative thought could hardly reflect credit upon the mayor's administration, his exercise of discretion, or even his personal integrity. Secondly, in regard to the building code, it appeared that the mayor had exercised neither pressure nor influence upon the City Council to speed the code's adoption. Finally, and most significantly, the press gave reams of publicity to a statement allegedly made, some time before the fire, by Barnett Welansky, owner of the Cocoanut Grove, to the effect that "The mayor and I fit"; the immediate response of many readers was undoubtedly to picture the mayor as something other than the upright, honest servant of the people.

Through its news reports and featured articles, the press had directed its wrath against the public officials individually. The latter had been selected one by one for headlined denunciations; but throughout each had been scored as an individual official separately and uniquely culpable. It was almost as if the press had lined them up and said to the public: "Here you are; take your choice." Under these circumstances it would appear likely that different readers would either select different individual scapegoats or that there would occur a focusing of condemnation upon one or two individuals. Significantly,

however, such was not the case; the reaction of the public was essentially against the public officials *as a group or class*. Since the time of the fire, of the letters to the editor printed by the *Traveler*, over 90 per cent which blamed any of the public officials refer to their *collective* negligence, laxness, and incompetence.

Just why this "blanket scapegoating" occurred is not immediately evident; perhaps desire for a simplification of the issues involved may partially account for it. Certainly the picture would be clearer if blame were focused on a minimum of persons; yet for some reason a blanket condemnation of officials was more satisfying. Why? The acknowledged complexity of the building laws with the consequent confusion as to the function of various city officials made blaming them collectively much simpler than blaming them as individuals. So complex was the issue and so equally was responsibility distributed among officials accused that it was simpler to select all than logically and rationally to select one.

Furthermore, the public officials were not normally separate in the public eye; they were a symbol of interacting function, a symbol of the city government; and often a symbol is as simple a mental concept as is an individual. Collectively they were "the rascals," for among certain elements of the public there is a deep-rooted, perhaps unrecognized latent hostility toward all political authority, toward those "higher up." Expression of this latent hostility is usually suppressed because such expression is not ordinarily in keeping with social convention. But, whenever the situation changes so that self-expression formerly frowned upon becomes socially approved and even encouraged, the latent hostility will become active and find immediate aggressive outlets. These circumstances probably help to account for the collective rather than individual nature of the scapegoating. People *preferred* to attack the entire administrative set-up rather than certain specific individuals.

The Owners. While engaged in wholesale denunciation of the city officials, the press was at the same time heaping abuse upon the owners and operators of the ill-fated Grove—an abuse calculated not only to emphasize their responsibility but also to disparage their personal characters. Thus in its editorial columns on December 10, the *Traveler* referred openly to the "greed and cupidity of the owners"; similar attacks by this and other papers, though usually more subtle, were nevertheless as damaging.

Significantly, indictment was almost invariably against "the owners" and seldom by name against Barnett Welansky, the acknowledged owner of the establishment. A number of factors may have accounted for this. First, at the time of the fire and during the investigation that followed, Welansky was confined to the hospital with a serious illness. Thus the press may have forsaken any direct charges against his name since he was unable to answer them personally. Another consideration was the attempt of the press to imply that actual control of the Grove was in the hands of some secret and probably subversive syndicate for which Welansky was a mere "front." This last explanation is partially substantiated by the editorial, appearing on December 7 in the *Traveler,* asking: "Who really owns the Cocoanut Grove?"

The means employed by the press to fix the responsibility of the owners and at the same time to disparage them personally were quite ingenious. One of these techniques was to give the impression that the owners were cheap, money-hoarding profiteers and that their so-called avarice had contributed to the huge death toll. Subtly colored words and phrases were frequently resorted to. Upon testimony of an expert that the lethal fumes might have come from the imitation leather covering the chairs, the *Globe,* among other papers, announced: "CHEAP LEATHER CAUSE OF FUMES." In like manner much was made of the "flimsy, tinsel-like" decorations.

Disproportionate space was alloted to the revelation that the reserve supply of liquor, stored in a fire-proof vault, remained intact: implication—the Grove protected its liquor but not its patrons.

The testimony of an amateur electrician that he had been employed for a nominal wage to do the wiring in the club, despite the fact that he had no license, was prominently featured. Similarly, emphasis upon the employment of the "under-age busboy" implied that the owners were not willing to pay a "man's wage."

The press also tried to create the impression that the owners operated the club in direct, wilful disregard of the law. The emphasis upon the unlicensed electrician and the under-age busboy are also applicable here. The fact that a revolving door was used at one of the exits and that the decorations were not adequately fire-proofed received enormous attention despite the fact that the existence of laws covering the use of either was never proved.

Further, the public was given the impression that the owners were "shady" in their dealings, that their pasts were somewhat soiled. The *Boston American* ran a serial feature entitled "The Rise and Fall of the Cocoanut Grove," in which the club was described as having been historically a base for racketeers and bootleggers. All the papers mentioned Welansky's association, as his lawyer, with the late Charles "King" Solomon, notorious lord of the underworld. James Welansky, brother of Barnett and in charge of the club the night of the fire, was "casually" mentioned by the *American* as a witness in a murder case some years before.

A consideration which must not be overlooked in accounting for "the owners" phraseology is the latent hostility that certain elements of the public maintain against those highly successful financially. They regard the latter as a class of profiteers with their hands in the pockets of the poor. As in the case of hostility against public officials, this latent hostility is usually suppressed but may become socially approved under certain circumstances. For the public Welansky as an individual object of wrath was not as satisfying as was the class he symbolized; and in this case the class could be most nearly represented by the term "the owners."

There is no doubt that the public was

solidly behind the press in its scapegoating of the owners. The *Traveler's* editorial on "greed and cupidity" was taken up as a battle-cry by its readers, several of whom congratulated the paper for its "crusading spirit." Likewise the character disparagement of the owners which the paper often only implied was accepted as fact by irate readers.

Tie-up between Public Officials and Owners. While simultaneously flailing public officials and owners, the press was constantly seeking and playing up the slightest thread that might link the two in political intrigue. Mention has already been made of the "Mayor and I fit" statement attributed to Welansky. The papers immediately implied the existence of a Tobin-Welansky coalition involving the exchange of legal indulgence for political patronage. The mayor vigorously denied having made the statement; but such damage had already been done. Subsequently there were discovered in the ruins of the club a collection of unpaid checks; the *Traveler* headlined: "Grove Took Good Care of 'Right People.'" The *American* asserted that on these checks were "names you won't have to ask how to spell." Perusal of the tax-assessment records indicated that in 1942 the Grove had paid less taxes than in 1941; the implication was that city officials had secretly "taken care of" the Grove. When the Grove's account books were found the papers promised "startling developments" upon revelation of their contents.

In all these instances nothing even nearly conclusive was ever proved by the papers. But the public nevertheless went all-out for reform. "Corruption," "vice," "rotten mess," "crooked politics" were standard terms to be found in the correspondence. The press had failed to establish the link between officials and owners; the public readily supplied the connection.

MOTIVATIONS

The frustrations and fears aroused by the tragedy underlay much of the scapegoating that followed. During the initial period of shock and confusion there was a need for the release of emotional tensions created by the *frustrating* situation.

Nearly five hundred lives had been lost and nothing could be done to restore them, no constructive action was possible; some outlet was required for the feelings of aggression aroused; the busboy and the prankster were the first scapegoats available. However, as the facts in the case developed more clearly, the actual selection of the scapegoat became gradually a more rational process. The frustrations still existed but other motivations played an increasingly important part.

Another important factor in the early stages was *fear*. Fear arose because people imagined themselves as being trapped in the flaming night club and they also feared the occurrence of similar tragedies, this time involving themselves or their loved ones. This fear might be alleviated by attacking some immediately responsible person—at first either the busboy or the prankster. By the time the public officials and the owners became objects of blame, these fears had been greatly diminished through the passage of time and the increase in rational control.

"Tabloid Thinking," expressing the desire for simplification of the issue, was from the outset conducive to scapegoating. The very confusion engendered by conflicting reports and lack of knowledge created within the people a desire for clarification, for establishment of some cause-and-effect relationship. By choosing definite scapegoats some simplification was achieved.

How *latent hostilities* led to the choice of public officials and owners as scapegoats has already been discussed. This aggression was most strongly expressed when owners and officials were linked in joint accusations, for then all the hostilities the people had accumulated against "political bigwigs" and "money czars" could be focused on this relationship. There is also evidence in some letters to the editor that peoples' prohibitionist sentiments and their grievances against both low wages for public employes and high taxes were responsible in part for the scapegoating of owners and officials.

It also seems probable that through debasing of officials and owners certain elements of the public may have found opportunity to *enhance* their own self-conceived prestige; they could, by scapegoating, feel, at least momentarily, superior to these so-called "higher ups."

Finally, it cannot be overlooked that the people themselves felt in some way responsible for the tragedy. For most this feeling of *guilt* was unconscious, and was eased by pointing out the culpability of some more directly involved. However a small minority did realize their responsibility for having elected the city administration. In their letters they said that "the public is responsible," and in these letters there was no evidence of scapegoating.

The above discussion does not attempt to trace the intricate patterning of motivations for individual scapegoats and for individual scapegoaters. We have merely indicated some general motivational trends which seem to be basic to the scapegoating.

THE INDICTMENTS

The immediate and desired objective of the scapegoaters was to relieve their feelings of frustration, of fear, of hostility, of guilt, by legally fixing the responsibility on the guilty so that they might be punished. Ten indictments were returned on December 31, and according to Attorney General Bushnell more were to come. But even in the drawing-up of the indictments there are indications of scapegoating. On January 13, the *Globe* reported a violent exchange of words between Bushnell and defense lawyer John C. Johnston. The latter was asking for a quashing of the indictments on the allegation that they were improperly drawn, for they do not specify the acts of the accused. In fairness to the allegation advanced, the generalized nature of the official charges does smack of scapegoating tactics, an impression strengthened by what followed. After Johnston presented argument for his petition, Bushnell is reported to have shouted: "Hair-splitting technicalities have no place here. . . . The voiceless public is not interested in a lot of words. We're dealing with a case where the death toll amounted to nearly five hundred—half a hundred of them our men in uniform. . . ." To

which Johnston replied: ". . . The defendants should be tried by law and not by public clamor. The defendants should be tried by law and not by lynch law, which is the apparent tendency from the argument I have just listened to." No, scapegoating has not yet ceased in the Cocoanut Grove case.

CONSEQUENCES

The Government. During the past year, the *Traveler* has conducted several vigorous campaigns against state and federal officials; at the time of the fire, Oil Coordinator Ickes and Price Administrator Henderson were the targets of its attacks. In this atmosphere of resentment against federal officials, antagonism against city officials involved in the Cocoanut Grove case was easily aroused. In turn, the expose of alleged corruptibility and inefficiency of the latter can hardly fail to undermine even more the already shaken confidence in government officials generally.

Anti-Semitism. Another possible consequence of the scapegoating in the Cocoanut Grove case is the fanning of the anti-Semitism which Father Coughlin's followers have spread in Boston. To people who have learned to make the words "jews" and "cupidity" or "greed" synonymous, the editorial of the *Traveler* of December 10, declaring that "Human greed and human negligence cost human lives," strengthens the implication: "The Jews were responsible for the loss of lives." There is evidence that this implication was caught by many, in reported conversations blaming the "Jew Welansky" and "those dirty Jews." Some admit that their prejudices against the Jews have increased because of the Grove fire. We are not claiming that anti-Semitism was deliberately raised as an issue, but are simply pointing out that the scapegoating of the Grove owners furnishes ammunition to the "merchants of hate."

PRESS COVERAGE

Figure 1 shows the number of column-inches of news-space which the *Boston Traveler,* an evening paper, devoted to the fire over a period of approximately a month. News stories, editorials, letters to the editor, and photographs were all considered in the day-by-day accountings. However, the number of column-inches devoted to the photographs, lists of victims, obituaries, and accounts of funerals is reduced by half in the graphical repre-

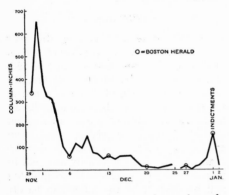

FIG. 1. *Amount of space devoted to the fire in the* Boston Traveler, *Nov. 29, 1942 to Jan. 2, 1943* [1]

sentation. If we consider that over a period of a week the average daily amount of space devoted to news is 1350 column-inches (exclusive of 14 pages of sports, financial, social, women's, and entertainment features), we see that the ratio of Grove news to other news was rather staggering, especially during the first few days following the tragedy. At the peak of interest, stories and features about the Grove case constituted almost 50 per cent of the total news. Also significant is the length of time that the case was continually publicized, even late in January hardly a day passed without some reference to it. Although some of these articles were brief, they assumed front-page importance from November 29 to December 19, and took the limelight again from December 29 to January 1, the period of indictment. Banner headlines about the fire and the investigation that followed

overshadowed war news throughout the first week and part of the second.

The importance of the entire case was further indicated by the number of editorials and letters to the editor devoted to the subject. Altogether, during this period thirteen editorials touched upon at least one aspect of the case, during the first week and part of the second week, this was the *lead editorial*. Most of these editorials were intent upon fixing the blame on one scapegoat or another.

Figure 2 shows the number of column-inches devoted to the letters alone. It is especially significant that the letters about the Grove took up almost all the space of the *People's Forum* (two full columns devoted to letters to the Editor), at least for the first three weeks. The great majority of these letters demanded the punishment of the guilty and named one or more scapegoats. These letters were particularly useful in ascertaining the motivations for scapegoating.

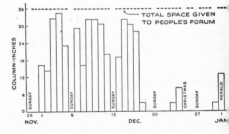

FIG. 2. *Proportion of all letters devoted to the fire in the* Boston Traveler, *Nov 29, 1942 to Jan. 2, 1943* [2]

SUMMARY

Frustrations and fears aroused by the Cocoanut Grove holocaust created a desperate desire on the part of the people of Boston to fix the blame and punish those responsible for the catastrophe. There resulted violent accusations, if not unwarranted, at least out of proportion to the possible guilt of the accused. The scapegoating was most intense against the owners of the Grove and against the public officials responsible for the safety of Boston's citizens. Officials and owners were

---

[1] The **Traveler** does not publish on Sundays or holidays, hence figures for Nov. 29, Dec. 6, 13, 20, 27, and Jan. 1 were taken from the **Boston Herald,** the **Traveler's** morning edition.

[2] See footnote 1.

especially satisfying scapegoats since the tragedy permitted the releasing of much latent aggression. It is when such latent hostility is present that scapegoating is most dangerous. Because in Boston hos-tility against the Jews and hostility against our federal officials has been smoldering for months, the Cocoanut Grove fire may well have serious consequences beyond the loss of five hundred lives.

Fads and crazes. The type of diffuse crowd that is exemplified in the post-Cocoanut Grove case and throughout the preceding discussion bears considerable resemblance to fads and crazes. These terms refer to an exceptional preoccupa-tion with a single viewpoint, a single object of interest, or a single line of behav-ior, which is of limited duration. The preoccupation is exceptional in its intensity, in the uniformity with which it is exhibited, and in the number of people it includes.

Whereas the type of diffuse crowd we have been discussing is commonly a response to a provocative situation or to a series of such events, the fad is thought of as arising rather unpredictably. The sudden popularity of miniature golf during the 1930's, with courses being built on widespread sections of vacant land, only for the majority to go bankrupt within a few months as interest de-clined, was not in any direct sense a collective response to a group crisis. Careful quantitative studies of fads over a long period might reveal that they are espe-cially numerous in periods of group crisis, suggesting that recreational fads divert attention from the problems at hand. However, the fads are not created by the participants as a recognized effort to cope with any particular crisis.

Popular depictions of fads and crazes tend to overdramatize them and equate them more closely with compact crowd behavior than is justified. In the true compact crowd the mood and attention are sustained without interruption, and the excesses of crowd behavior are often attributable to the fact that participants have no chance to relax and survey their behavior. The fad or craze, however, is sustained with constant interruptions. In spite of the interruptions, the atten-tion of the faddist is severely restricted to the point that alternatives pass unno-ticed. Consequently, money may be invested in highly improbable schemes or exaggerated fears maintained, when the evidence against both is clear to the non-faddist. Or people may undergo privation by paying inflated prices and wait-ing in long lines in order to participate in the current fad when other recreational opportunities lie neglected close at hand.

Phenomena of this sort cover a wide range, from the recreational to quite serious types of activities. Fads in amusements, fads in adolescent language, fads in music, goldfish swallowing and the like may have little significance for the participant beyond identifying him with an in-group and giving him a type of prestige. Fad participants develop strong in-group feelings, with special terms for the outgroup, such as "squares." More serious activities involving financial spec-ulation sometimes show similar characteristics. In the famous Holland Tulip Mania during which the value of tulip bulbs came to exceed their weight in gold, in the South Sea Island Bubble, the Florida Land Boom, and many other such episodes, the worth of some object became inflated because of the confidence in its speculative value. Tulip bulbs were not used, but bought and sold among spec-ulators. Florida lands were sold and resold at ever higher prices without even being seen. As soon as the speculative market declined and the objects had to be valued in terms of use, the entire structure crumbled quickly.

Fears, belief in special formulae, and moods of all sorts may also have this faddish character. The image of the "terrible Turk," the "red scare" of the 1920's, the confidence in learning a few simple techniques to "win friends and influence people," or the repetition of the formula, "Every day in every way I'm growing better and better," are instances of this sort. The fad may also exist as a *permission* to act contrary to the folkways and mores, as in the example of college "panty-raids." Finally, the fad may exist simply as a direction or content given to activity which it does not create. At various times motion picture heroes or comic strip figures, such as "the little tough guy," have been emulated by juvenile delinquents on a wide scale. There is no clear evidence that delinquency was increased by these activities, but the *pattern* of the activity was adopted and spread widely.

There is a frequent tendency to emphasize the spread of fads among adolescents and among persons somewhat detached from the stable aspects of society. On the basis of such emphasis, theories are spun which attribute fad-susceptibility to value-conflict, social detachment, personal insecurity, etc. Undoubtedly some kinds of social isolation foster susceptibility in some persons and heighten fad-resistance in others. But by examining a fad in an area not usually included in such discussions, we may demonstrate that no abnormal degree of isolation or insecurity is necessary to faddish behavior.

It has often been proposed that cultural change proceeds by spurts of creativeness. These spurts are attributed to the discovery of "key" inventions, or the discovery of a new theme or approach in art. The key invention opens up heretofore unrecognized possibilities, so there is a rush to apply it in as many ways as possible. The creative spurt subsides when the full range of possibilities has been exhausted. The resulting curve of activity and interest resembles that of a fad.

Such a focus of attention on newly-uncovered possibilities is not a fad, however, unless it includes diversion of attention away from what the participants might otherwise regard as unpleasant features of their behavior. L. S. Penrose has shown how restriction of attention sometimes characterizes the rising period of such a preoccupation, while the declining period shows an increased awareness of limitations. As his example he cites a scientific fad.

ANALYSIS OF CRAZES
L. S. Penrose

A new idea which suddenly becomes important in the life of a community and which nevertheless does not appreciably disturb the pre-existing order can be called a craze. Examples are easy to find.

Reprinted in part by permission of H. K. Lewis and Co., Ltd., and the author, from L. S. Penrose, **On the Objective Study of Crowd Behavior** (London: H. K. Lewis and Co., Ltd., 1952), pp. 18–22.

A new game or pastime becomes popular almost overnight. The cult of a toy Yo-yo, Bifbat, the crossword puzzle or comic strip character, arises in an apparently unpredictable manner and vanishes again. Fashions in food and novelties in male and, especially, in female attire often show the same type of capricious adventure. There can also be periodicity dependent upon the seasons of the year. Some crazes are merely magnifications of activities which are part of the normal life of members of the community, that is, endemic. Quite frequently, after the disappearance of a craze, the activity remains as part of the stock of possible pastimes without commanding any special attention when it occurs. When they hear an old-fashioned popular tune, people only remember vaguely that at one time everybody was expected to react to it with considerable emotion. The characteristic features of the craze, though they may seem trivial at first glance, are of great importance in the study of crowd psychology because, in the craze, we are able to examine in its purest form the behavior of a crowd under the influence of an infectious idea.

Judged from the psychopathological point of view, a craze is a crowd disorder so mild that it can be compared with an outburst of enthusiasm, excitement or anger which occurs in the ordinary daily life of an individual whose mind ranks as entirely normal. An idea which can infect the community, moreover, is not necessarily harmful or unreasonable because it is infectious. The only justification for including such activities under the heading of crowd mental illness would be that, during a craze, an abnormal amount of energy is discharged in one direction, and that, as a result, matters more vital to the welfare of the group may be neglected.

The course of any craze is marked by certain phases, which sometimes can be very clearly distinguished and which follow closely the pattern shown in an epidemic physical disease. First there is a latent period, during which the idea, though present in the minds of a few, shows little sign of spreading. Next comes the phase during which time the idea spreads rapidly. The number of people who accept the new idea mounts with an increasing velocity which may develop an almost explosive character. As the market of susceptible minds becomes saturated, the velocity of the wave—as shown by the number of articles bought in a given time, for instance—begins to slacken. This is the third phase. The fourth phase is marked by the development of mental resistance against the idea which resembles immunity to infection in the sphere of physical disease. During this period, the mental infection wanes; in those already infected, the enthusiasm becomes weaker and there are few new cases. In the fifth or final phase, if the idea still persists, it remains stagnant; either it is incorporated into the occasional habits of many or kept alive in the minds of a few enthusiasts. In favourable circumstances, it may remain latent to blossom again at some future time, when the immunity has disappeared.

If any person should doubt the reality of mental resistance to an idea which has recently been the virus of a craze he should enquire into the experience of commercial firms which manufacture or sell material involved in these mental epidemics. The immunity has two important characteristics. In the first place, once started, it develops rapidly—probably the degree of rapidity depends directly upon the degree of explosiveness of the outbreak, though this needs to be fully investigated. Secondly, the immunity is highly specific. There is resistance to exactly that form of the idea which caused the craze, but another idea, in many respects similar, may produce another craze soon after the first.

In spite of the great prevalence of crazes in human communities, precise data for the numerical analysis of their development are difficult to obtain. The type of data which would be valuable from this point of view could be obtained from a study of the actual sales of craze pastimes during the critical periods. The demand rather than the supply would perhaps furnish the best index of the crowd's state of mind but there are complicating factors which make the investigator pause before embarking upon the arduous task of collecting the data. Commercial reticence is also a serious obstacle. The example chosen here for analysis is imperfect in many respects, as an instance of a craze, but it has the advantage that the data were easy to obtain. It concerns the development of a fashion in medical therapy. Crazes of this kind are common among physicians and they are, to some extent, the inevitable result of natural enthusiasm over fresh discoveries in medical science. As will be seen, however, there can be more than one side to the picture.

The use of thallium in the treatment of skin diseases, as a preliminary measure to remove the hair, was first advocated in 1914 both in Germany and in Mexico. The pioneers who drew attention to the possible therapeutic use of the metal were careful to issue the warning that poisonous effects of a most dangerous character might arise if an overdose were given. A survey of medical literature between the years 1914 and 1925, charted in Figure 1, reveals the fact that the drug

ever, was masked by the rapid growth of the realization of the dangers attached to the treatment. Several fatalities resulted from overdoses. Some medical authorities proclaimed that the treatment was far more hazardous than the diseases which it was intended to cure. The fourth phase, which coincided with increasing immunity to the idea of this treatment, was reflected in the medical literature by a preponderance of writings which described experiments on laboratory animals and emphasized the poisonous nature of thallium compounds. At the same time, the total number of writings on the subject declined. From 1928 until 1940, this

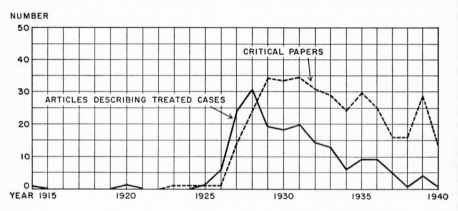

FIG. 1. *Literature on thallium therapy (from* Index Medicus)
——————— *Articles describing treated cases*
– – – – – – *Critical papers*

was, in fact, very little used during this period, which corresponded to the first phase or latent stage of the mental epidemic under discussion. In the next two years, however, use of the drug became rapidly fashionable. Thousands of children were treated in centres widely distributed over the globe. During this second period of the infection of the medical profession with the new idea, a large body of literature sprang into existence in which the results of treatment were described and commented upon, for the most part very favourably. The saturation of all possible clinics for skin diseases with the new idea would inevitably have slowed down the craze and produced the third phase about 1927. This effect, how-

decline in interest was fairly continuous and recent scientific publications on the use of thallium have, for the most part, been confined to experimental studies, to warnings against proprietary preparations, which might poison unsuspecting lay people, and to descriptions of instances where thallium had been used for attempted murder or suicide. Notwithstanding, medical textbooks now accept that the treatment has value in selected cases under very carefully controlled conditions. The fifth phase has been reached and the craze is over.

Meteorologists have more knowledge of the origins of cyclones than of local storms. Similarly, it is more difficult to identify the predisposing causes of crazes than those of more disruptive mental epidemics. In the example which has just been analysed, there were elements which are commonly found in all types of crowd infection. The new idea gave a pleasurable feeling of superior power, and was probably welcomed by physicians as a visible proof of omnipotence which they might wish to possess. Furthermore, the factor of relative isolation from the general public, which the medical profession enjoys, possibly favours the development of crowd mental aberration among its numbers. Such epidemics as that described in the example might be even more frequent or significant among medical workers than is actually the case were it not for the lengthy and humiliating training in scientific caution which physicians undergo before qualification. A comparison of mental epidemiology between members of the medical profession with members of other groups, whose training is much less intensive from this point of view, such as osteopaths and chiropractors, might be instructive.

Indifference or opposition to a fad is not treated with toleration. In spite of the fact that some of these phenomena are distinctly competitive in nature (e.g., real estate booms), they are still universally accompanied by both active proselyting and penalties for those who resist.

This proselyting attitude is more than a by-product. It is actually an essential part of maintaining the fad and justifying the behavior of the faddist. In cases where the prestige of participating in the latest fad is important in motivating the faddist, prestige will only be accorded if enough people follow the fad. In speculation booms the amount of money each person makes will be determined by how many others join the speculation. In cases in which the mores or conventional inhibitions are challenged, as in contagious mass religious confessions, membership in a large group similarly preoccupied is effective protection against self-criticism in light of these conventional codes. The rewards which the individual receives from participation in the fad require that other persons be constantly adopting the fad, and these rewards cease when adherence to the fad starts to decline.

Intolerance toward the nonfaddist serves both to bring more people into the fad and to protect the member from seeing his behavior through the eyes of nonfaddists. By placing the outsider in the category of a person who simply doesn't know what is going on, the faddist is shielded from the need to respond to his judgments. An essential mechanism of the fad, then, as of the crowd in general, is the formation of a sharp ingroup-outgroup dichotomy which insulates the participant against the impact of any reference groups except the faddists themselves.

Diffuse crowd as an organizational adjunct. We have noted already that fads and crazes may appear as aspects of such organizational behavior as economic pursuits (land booms, for example) and scientific investigation. A margin of diffuse crowd behavior may also be an enduring aspect of organizational behavior. This margin appears when the rules and traditions governing organized behavior are in some respect incomplete. Phases of group behavior not fully governed by established rules and traditions may be governed by crowd mechanisms.

Whenever a group is involved in some unusual venture or in a conflict situation, the outcome is not wholly predictable. This indeterminacy provides room for the establishment of a group sense of confidence or hopelessness in the venture.

A shared conviction concerning the worth of the group goal and a confidence in the eventual success of the group constitute *morale*. Morale may be simply a common reasonable response to the facts of the situation. Thus, troops that are winning battles have higher morale than those who are losing. The crowd element cannot be said to enter until the group sense becomes vital enough to maintain a degree of high morale or low morale in the face of apparently inappropriate circumstances. A college with a losing football team may sustain high morale in spite of continued defeat. Or a school with a winning team may still share a communicated sense of dread of each new game. The diffuse crowd processes fill the gap of uncertainty by establishing a collective mood.

Morale combines a collective attachment to a group goal with a spirit of fellowship and attachment to the group, with each aspect reinforcing the other.

> If the members of a group develop a collective goal which is highly valued, they become much more disposed to camaraderie and fellowship. Conversely, if the members have a strong feeling of common identification, and sense in one another congeniality and a readiness to mutual aid, there are imparted extra significance and value to the goal.*

A classification of morale has been proposed by Herbert Blumer on the basis of the way in which the collective goal is viewed. *Practical* morale develops about a goal of expediency. Morale in the United States during World War II was of this type, without positive enthusiasm for the goal at hand, but with a determined conviction that there was no alternative to winning the war and getting it over with. *Romantic* morale develops about a goal depicted in glorious terms, bringing prestige, adventure, wealth, or power. The goal is overvalued and surrounded with myth, and attention is drawn away from practical consequences and immediate necessities and turned toward the romantic future. *Sacred* morale centers about a goal that is pursued from duty and divine injunction. A sense of mission, a conviction of unquestionable rightness, and a sense that ultimate attainment of the goal is inevitable mark this type of morale.**

These three types of morale in different ways give a group the necessary determination to carry through an enterprise that is bound to encounter serious obstacles. The reinforced conception of the worth of the goal and the sense of group cooperation prevent each setback from seriously weakening group determination. Practical morale tends to be negative, holding the group together only so long as there is present danger, while romantic and sacred morale tend to build a group enthusiasm which carries beyond attainment of immediate goals.

The inclusion of land booms and other economic crazes in the discussion of diffuse crowds has already shown that economic enthusiasm and confidence may contain a crowd element. Many writers, observing the excesses and contagiousness of confidence during prosperity and of fears during depression, have suggested that crowd mechanisms contribute to the business cycle. While the principal explanations for prosperity and depression are undoubtedly to be found elsewhere, it is possible to identify the element of indeterminacy through which crowd mechanisms can operate. Following the lead of the economist, Keynes, and others, Gottfried Haberler shows how the necessity for participants in eco-

---

* Herbert Blumer, "Morale," in William F. Ogburn (ed.), **American Society in Wartime** (Chicago: University of Chicago Press, 1944), p. 210.
** Ibid., pp. 207-231.

nomic activity to anticipate the behavior of others permits the entry of crowd mechanisms.

PSYCHOLOGICAL THEORIES OF THE BUSINESS CYCLE
GOTTFRIED HABERLER

1. INTRODUCTION

There is really no fundamental difference between the "economic" theories and the so-called "psychological" theories. Both make assumptions as to economic behavior in certain situations. The real difference is sometimes this. The "psychological" theories introduce certain assumptions about typical reactions, mainly on the part of the interpreneur and the saver, in certain situations; and these reactions are conventionally called psychological, because of their (in a sense) indeterminate character. But the distinction between the writers who give prominence to these "psychological" factors and the writers so far reviewed is, taken as a whole, a distinction of emphasis rather than of kind. The "psychological" factors are put forward as supplemental to the monetary and other economic factors and not as alternative elements of causation, while on the other hand, though they may be assigned a less prominent place in the chain of causation, they are in no sense overlooked by the majority of writers of the other group.

2. ANALYSIS OF THE PSYCHOLOGICAL FACTOR IN THE EXPLANATION OF THE BUSINESS CYCLE

The writers who have laid the greatest stress on "psychological" reactions in the explanation of the various phases of the cycle are Keynes, Lavington, Pigou and Taussig.

Of the writers whose theories have been analysed earlier in this report, Mitchell, Robertson, Ropke, Spiethoff all attach a certain importance in their system to "psychological" elements.

It remains to define more precisely the

actions and reactions in connection with which the operation of "psychological" factors is postulated by these writers in their explanation of the cycle. "Psychological" factors come into consideration in economic theory in connection with anticipations and expectations.

With the introduction of the element of expectation, uncertainty enters the field. Future events cannot be forecast with absolute precision; and the farther they are distant in the future, the greater the uncertainty, and the greater the possibility of unforeseen and unforeseeable disturbances. Every economic decision is part of an economic plan which extends into the more or less distant future. In principle, there is therefore always an element of uncertainty in every activity. There are, however, certain cases where the element of uncertainty is especially great and conspicuous, such as the case of investment of resources in long processes and durable plant and the provision of funds for these purposes. The longer the processes in which capital is to be sunk, and the more durable the instruments and equipment to be constructed, the greater the element of uncertainty and risk of loss.

Naturally, economic actions and reactions in such cases are less rigidly determined by observable facts than in other cases. It is therefore mainly here that the "psychological" theories make their essential contribution. Optimism and pessimism are introduced as additional determinants. An attitude of optimism is an attribute to the prosperity phase of the cycle, and an attitude of pessimism an attribute of the depression; and the turning-points are marked by a change from optimism to pessimism and vice versa.

What do these new elements add to the picture of the expansion and contraction process which has emerged from the

From Gottfried Haberler, **Prosperity and Depression** (Geneva: League of Nations, 1941), pp. 142–149.

analysis of the "non-psychological" theories reviewed so far? If the psychological argument that during the upswing people take a more optimistic, and during the downswing a more pessimistic, view meant no more than that people invest more freely during the upswing and are reluctant to invest during the downswing, it would add nothing at all to the picture of the upswing and downswing as drawn by the monetary over-investment theory. But the psychological theories mean, of course, more than that. Optimism and pessimism are regarded as causal factors which tend to induce or intensify the rise and fall of investment which are characteristic of the upswing and downswing respectively. But are optimism and pessimism really separate factors definitely distinguishable from those analysed in the non-psychological theories of the cycle? The factors and forces making for cumulative expansion may be defined, broadly speaking—as they are defined in these theories—as low interest rates and/or the appearance of new investment opportunities as a result of inventions, changes in demand, etc., which are themselves the consequences of growth of population, the need for replacement of outworn equipment and so on. An increase in investment, however brought about, leads to an inflow of new money into the circulation and so to a rise in the money demand for goods in general which in turn stimulates investment: the process is cumulative. An indispensable condition is of course an elastic money supply. What now is changed, if to this list of factors optimism and pessimism are added as intensifying elements? If all that is meant is that a fall in the rate of interest, or the appearance of an invention requiring for its application a heavy investment of capital, or a rise in demand makes people anticipate better returns from particular investments, there is no new element in the mechanism as pictured by, say, the monetary over-investment theory, since to the latter too profits can only mean expected profits.

But the introduction of optimism and pessimism as additional factors signifies more than this. It implies that the connection between a fall in the interest rate and a change in the other objective factors, on the one hand, and the decision of the entrepreneur to invest more, on the other hand, is not so rigid as the "economic" theories sometimes maintain. If in a given situation the rate of interest falls, or demand increases, or there is a change in the technological situation (exploitation of an invention or introduction of an innovation), it is not possible on the basis of these data alone to predict the strength of the entrepreneurs' reactions or the extent to which they will increase investment. It is true, such phrases as "the degree of optimism" or "a change in optimism" are omnibus formulae which conveniently cover a number of other factors such as the general political situation and other elements likely to influence the outcome, though to an unknown extent. It should be clearly recognized that, while it is true that developments are not determined wholly by the objective factors with which the non-psychological theories are concerned, the introduction of the determinants "optimism" and "pessimism" makes no positive contribution to the explanation of the cycle so long as the optimism and pessimism remain purely psychological phenomena—i.e., states of mind of the entrepreneurs (or other members of the economic community with whose behaviour the theory is concerned). We cannot observe states of mind; but it is possible to make certain observations from which states of mind or changes of mind can be inferred. It is at this point that the "psychological" theories have a positive contribution to make.

What observable factors are there (other than those which have already been taken into account by the "non-psychological" theories) that go to make people optimistic or pessimistic—i.e., that stimulate or discourage investment? There is in the first place the fact that, in a period when demand and production are rising in many branches of industry, producers in branches which have not yet felt an increase in demand are inclined to expect one. The connection between the objective factors (interest rate, etc.) with which the non-psychological theories are concerned and the volume of investment is, as it were, loosened. The response of total investment to changes in the objective factors becomes stronger than "rational" economic considerations would suggest. Professor Pigou, in this connection, speaks of "errors of optimism." Lavington likens businessmen who infect each other with confidence and optimism to skaters on a pond. "Indeed, the confidence of each skater in his own safety is likely to be reinforced rather than diminished by the presence of numbers of his fellows. . . . The rational judgment that the greater their numbers the greater will be the risk is likely to be submerged by the mere contagion of confidence which persuades him that the greater the numbers the more safely he himself may venture."

Another point to which the psychological theories direct attention is the fact that, when demand and prices have continued for a while to rise, people get into a habit of expecting more and more confidently a further rise of equal or approximately equal extent—that is to say, they project current experience too confidently into the future. All this leads them to an excessive valuation of capital assets. As Mr. Keynes says: "It is an essential characteristic of the boom that investments which will in fact yield, say, 2% in conditions of full employment are made in the expectation of a yield of, say, 6%, and are valued accordingly."

The theorists who stress the psychological factor, especially Professor Pigou and Mr. Keynes, point out, furthermore, that the discovery of errors of optimism gives birth to the opposite error of pessimism. Professor Pigou speaks of "the mutual generation of errors of optimism and pessimism." The above passage from Mr. Keynes continues: "When disillusion comes, this (optimistic) expectation is replaced by a contrary 'error of pessimism,' with the result that the investments which would in fact yield 2% in conditions of full employment are expected to yield less than nothing; and the resulting collapse of new investment then leads to a state of unemployment in which the investment, which would have yielded 2% in conditions of full employment, in fact yields less than nothing."

Fashion. Fashion is a process centered about the diffusion of changes in taste. A style of clothing which was admired at one time looks ridiculous or passé later. An automobile or a coiffure which swept the country in one year looks strangely inept in another year. It is important to note that behavior is not all that changes. No matter what initial opposition to a fashion change may develop, even the tastes of its opponents usually change once the style has become established.

Unlike fads, which also have to do with taste, fashion is a continuous process. Each style follows the preceding and replaces it with a continuity in the style changes themselves. Automobiles may become lower and squarer each year and the length of dresses may increase a little each year.

Characteristically the spread of fashion supports the established status structure in the society, while fads often do not. New styles are available to those at the upper status levels first, and persons at the lower levels emulate them. The reward for adopting a new style early is the prestige of possessing a symbol of a high status. The penalty for adopting the style too early is the judgment that one is trying to act above his station in life. Rapidly changing fashion, therefore, depends upon a society in which upward mobility and prestige striving are favorably valued. The rapid succession of styles becomes necessary when the higher social strata are not able to maintain a monopoly of the symbols of high status.

While fashion tends to reinforce established status distinctions, fads may establish prestige at variance with the conventional scale. The pace-setters of a fad may come from any stratum, and the fad may be adopted more quickly within the lower levels of the society. Based upon priority of adoption of the fad and intensity of activity in its behalf, the prestige accorded may be a substitute for established prestige. Thus fashion is conservatizing with regard to the social structure, while fads may promote change.

The cyclical character of style changes in fashion is often stressed, but with a false impression of fixed repetition of styles. Of necessity the variation of some specific elements of style—such as dress length and width—will be cyclical within the limits of practicality and mores. However, style consists of the total effect rather than single elements. A. L. Kroeber's studies of fashion have shown that the periodicity of cycles in dress styles during recent centuries is different for different dimensions of the dress. Furthermore, specific embellishments are added or eliminated in no necessarily regular sequence. While there is a tendency to put together items which are regarded as harmonious, there is seldom a total repetition of style. The cycles of recurrence which have been noted are fairly irregular, showing constant minor variation within the larger cycle.* Thus, in the sense that a particular culture makes possible only variations of style within certain limits (e.g., restrictions imposed by canons of decency), there must necessarily be some alternation and recapitulation of styles. But the conception of any precise, total, predictable recurrence of identical styles is not justified by evidence at hand.

The important question in deciding whether collective behavior concepts can be applied to fashion concerns the relative determinacy and spontaneity of fashion behavior. Vigorous adherents to the cyclical theory of fashion have argued that individual choice does not enter into the selection of styles. It is possible to overlook the evidence against such complete predetermination and still grant the intervention of crowd mechanisms. So long as the ordinary participant in fashion behavior cannot predict the direction of style changes, the diffuse crowd can serve as the *means* through which consensus regarding new styles is established, even though that consensus reflects a principle of regularity.

It is sometimes contended that fashion is entirely "rigged" by the leaders of the industry involved. Industries have geared their production to an artificially high demand which can be maintained only by the regular obsolescence of goods on account of style before their intrinsic useful life has been exhausted. Consequently, there is much fashion planning and deliberate acceleration of normal rates of style change. But a large part of fashion planning is not the creation of fashion so much as the careful study of fashion trends in order to anticipate changes which will take place regardless of who assumes the style leadership.

Neither the cultural determinacy nor the organizational control of fashion change seems to be complete. Typically, the mass has presented to it not a single style but several, by competing *style planners.* Selection of the dominant style is made with the help of *style leaders,* persons of prestige who have personal followings and whose selections among available styles are watched by bodies of *style followers.* The style planners often present styles to select groups of known fashion leaders for trial reactions, and after a style is fully launched they watch

---

* A. L. Kroeber, "On the Principle of Order in Civilization as Exemplified by Changes of Fashion," **American Anthropologist,** n.s. 21 (1919), pp. 235–263.

carefully the general reactions. Thus there is abundant opportunity for popular selection and for establishment of a partially spontaneous consensus through crowd mechanisms operating within the channels of the established status system.

At times of more radical style change, or of reversal in direction of style change, there is often an aroused collective opposition. Such aroused opposition developed at the close of World War II when the "new look" was abruptly introduced following wartime interruptions of normal style fluctuation. The resulting process is less like a public discussing an issue than it is like the rumor process in which a variety of possible definitions of the situation are heard and screened for consistency with the emerging collective image. The little-understood transformations whereby the reluctant and the violently opposed imperceptibly come to acquire the very tastes which they initially resisted offer one of the most potentially fruitful subjects for research on the operation of the diffuse crowd within the institutional structure of fashion.

Nature of the public
and public opinion

*T*HE PUBLIC is less often thought of as a type of collectivity having structure and dynamics than as the adjective in the concept, *public opinion*. In definitions of the latter concept, the stress tends to be placed on the term "opinion," leaving the word "public" as a rather unimportant modifier. Those who use public opinion in this sense agree that it refers to opinion (a) as verbalization rather than action, (b) regarding a matter of concern to a plurality of persons, and (c) about a matter which is regarded as controversial rather than consensual. Most students would further restrict the term to opinions (d) to which the individual is willing to give overt expression, whether he has actually done so or not. Under this general approach the fundamental datum of public opinion, the unit of observation and measurement, is the individual expression. The group enters only implicitly with the assumption that interaction is an element in the formation of public opinion.

Usages vary in the degree to which public opinion is conceived in individual terms. First, there are some writers who speak of opinion toward a "public object" and can discuss the formation of public opinion entirely as a process within a single individual. Second, public opinion more often refers to some sort of summation of individual opinions. Thus public opinion becomes *majority* or *preponderant* opinion, or a statement of the relative numerical support for the alternative positions regarding the issue at hand. A third group of writers distinguish public opinion as statements that are actually made overtly in the presence of others from *private opinion* which remains unspoken except to one's most intimate associates.

None of these conceptions introduces a collectivity as a necessary component. Only the existence of a mass is required in the first of these definitions. A bounded aggregate, i.e., a definite universe of persons not necessarily in interaction, is required in the second case, but no collectivity need be assumed. In the third instance some person-to-audience relation is assumed, but still there need be no collectivity.

Such definitions place the field of public opinion quite legitimately within the study of the formation and expression of individual attitudes. For those primarily interested in group characteristics and processes, however, a different conception is necessary. From this standpoint public opinion may be defined as *the effective expression of a public.* So defined, it need not be either majority opinion nor any sum of individual opinions, unless the mode of expression available to the particular public at the moment is the ballot box. *Public opinion becomes that which is communicated to the effective decision-makers as a consequence of the functioning of a public.* From this standpoint a precise definition of the public becomes essential.

The public, as a diffuse collectivity, must consist of persons in interaction, and consequently must be something more than a mere audience. *The public, then, is a dispersed group of people interested in and divided about an issue, engaged in discussion of the issue, with a view to registering a collective opinion which is expected to affect the course of action of some group or individual.*

In order to sharpen the distinction between the public and the diffuse crowd some further refinement is necessary. While registering opinion as its ultimate performance differentiates the public from many diffuse crowds, some crowds do not go beyond the "referee" function, which is essentially that of registering an opinion. Furthermore, some crowds, such as a race riot or labor strife, are involved in controversy. Of these latter it is clear in some cases that there is no single over-all collectivity, but rather two sharply divided crowds with strong outgroup relations between. These are not difficult to distinguish from the public, but other cases offer a greater problem.

As a basis for distinguishing the crowd from the public, Dawson and Gettys divide collective behavior into two types, "collective-emotional" and "collective-rational." * Such a distinction is difficult to apply, however, for at least three reasons. First, the rational can hardly be differentiated from irrational behavior without some judgment from the investigator concerning that which is logically correct, a definition which is prone to reflect cultural orientation. Second, rational and emotional are not polar concepts, since a person may become emotionally aroused in the course of pursuing a rational course of action, either because of enthusiasm such as accompanies the sight of success or because of an obstacle to his course of action. Finally, rational *forms of expression* are used so extensively as part of the crowd, and emotional appeals are so much a part of the public, that the distinction does not seem to be the critical one.

The key to a useful distinction can be found in further examination of the idea that the public is built about an issue. An issue is not merely a matter on which people disagree. It is a matter regarding which people are thought to have a *right* to disagree. The public, then, is crucially distinguished from the crowd by

* C. A. Dawson and W. E. Gettys, **An Introduction to Sociology** (New York: The Ronald Press Co., 1948), p. 605.

the fact that interaction within it is governed by the assumption that disagreement, argument, and counterargument are *legitimate*. This does not mean that the other side is necessarily thought to have any worth-while points, nor that members of the public listen to the other side with any intention of subjecting their own position to test, nor that the appeals need even follow principally rational form. But conceding the other man's "right to be wrong if he wants to" keeps discussion open, restricts the public to registering an opinion rather than taking consummatory action, and makes the ascertainment of the "opinion of the public" important to those effectively concerned about the issue.

In keeping with the general point of view developed above, Carroll D. Clark extends further our discussion of the nature of the public, describes the circumstances under which the public arises, and makes a much-used distinction between general and specific publics.

THE CONCEPT OF THE PUBLIC
CARROLL D. CLARK

Social research and social theory are increasingly obliged to take account of that vague and amorphous entity, the public. At one stage or another every social problem has a way of involving the problem of public opinion. It is perhaps not too much to say that one reason we have social problems, or at least recognize them as such, is due to this same phenomenon of public opinion.

In spite of their growing importance in affairs, the public and public opinion as concepts for group analysis remain wrapped in a haze of confusion and doubt. Their definitions and interpretations seem likely to rival in variety the views of political theorists as to the nature of the state. (1) This situation became acutely apparent in 1924 when a Round Table on Political Statistics of the National Conference on the Science of Politics found it impossible to agree on a standardized meaning, and concluded it best "to avoid use of the term public opinion, if possible." In spite of this recommended abstinence, the question of what the public is has continued to dog the steps of the political scientist, and there has been no perceptible diminution in the employment of the concept. (2)

The public may be, as Walter Lippmann has concluded, only a phantom, but it is one that continually haunts discussions of social and political problems.

However, some progress has recently been made in the clarification of the public. One of the noteworthy trends of current work in sociology has been a reexamination of basic concepts in an effort to develop a more coherent frame of reference, and it was natural that public opinion should receive some critical attention. The chief recent contribution is a behavioristic view of the process of public opinion set forth by George A. Lundberg. He finds the principal sources for existing confusion in the meaning of the term "public opinion" to lie in the subjective vagueness lent to the term "opinion" by the old individualistic psychology and the recrudescence of the realist nominalist controversy with respect to the reality of group concepts, such as "social mind," the "crowd," and the "public." He defends, most ably, the reality of these social organisms as functional units and puts forward a behavioristic definition of public opinion.

"It is therefore just as permissible," he concludes, "to speak of public opinion as of individual opinion, and as permissible to speak of the thinking, feeling, and acting of a group as it is to attribute these

Reprinted by permission of **Southwestern Social Science Quarterly**, 13 (Mar., 1933), pp. 311–320.

phenomena to individuals. In both cases, those words merely indicate a deliberative technique through which the unit referred to achieves a tentative adjustment." [1]

With the "group fallacy" bogey at least temporarily out of the way and a rough but objective definition of public opinion at hand, we are in a better position to describe the phenomena falling in this field of collective behavior in generic and mutually comprehensible terms. The profile of the public, however, is not yet clear. How are we to distinguish this unit whose "tentative deliberative adjustments" constitute public opinion? What, fundamentally, are its characteristics, and how does it come into existence?

The position to be here maintained is that public opinion is most fruitfully conceived from the standpoint of collective action. From this standpoint not just the formal contest of views and registering of ballot-box decisions constitute public opinion, but the whole series of reactions involved in collective deliberation. Public opinion then becomes a form of group thinking, and the process bears more than an analogous relation to the individual's "complete act of thought."

At the inception of the public-opinion process, as in the case of the individual thought process, we have interruption of routine action and the disturbance of the preexisting equilibrium. Tension grows as responses are held up and an effort made to define the situation. Group attention is more or less sharply focalized on the issue. All of these phases have their counterpart in the individual act of thought. The group discussion which now ensues corresponds to the "inner forum" by means of which the individual rehearses tentatively alternative lines of action, weighing them with a view to probable consequences. The rational or deliberative aspect of public opinion as distinguished from crowd behavior, and of individual thought as distinguished from impulse, lies in both cases in the controlled quality

of the action—the checking or delaying of overt responses until incipient tendencies or programs of action compete, modify each other, and eventually take shape in a judgment or line of conduct that has, to some degree, been measured with respect to projected ends.

If the foregoing statement be in the main acceptable, what indications does it afford concerning the social situation in which the public can arise? Evidently it implies a situation where differences can be talked out instead of fought out, and where a common interest transcends, or at least permeates, conflicting interests in such manner as to make possible their mediation in a common motive or judgment. For a group with unified attitudes and a definitely organized action-structure to function in this manner would present no problem, but a public is characterized by its spontaneity, diversity of attitude, and lack of a formal action-pattern. How are the individuals composing it to find a common motive and to function as an organized whole?

Park and Burgess have already given an indication as to how this is accomplished. "A public is, in fact, organized on the basis of a universe of discourse, and within the limits of this universe of discourse, language, statements of fact, news, will have, for all practical purposes, the same meanings. It is this circle of mutual influence within which there is a universe of discourse that defines the limits of the public." [2] A universe of discourse arises spontaneously in a primary society as a result of directly shared experiences and a traditional system of collective representations. In a secondary society, however, it depends upon more complex factors—upon organization of interests and complicated indirect methods of communication. It is the latter type of universe of discourse that underlies the public.

But there must be more than a shared interest and common understanding before the public appears on the social horizon. The simple, static society which has

[1] "Public Opinion from a Behavioristic Viewpoint," **American Journal of Sociology,** XXXVI (November, 1930), p. 396.

[2] Robert E. Park and Ernest W. Burgess, **Introduction to the Science of Sociology,** p. 254.

both these attributes, does not, typically, function as a public. Nor is it because conflicts in purpose do not arise, nor because there are no opinions. In this connection the distinction drawn by Professor Park between the mores and public opinion has marked significance. Opinion does not become public opinion, in the sense we have given that term, so long as it merely expresses a judgment rooted in the mores. Public opinion involves "live" issues; the mores are residues of long since threshed out and, for the time being, settled issues. Where standards are absolute and values are personal, as in the static primary society, there may be controversy but not deliberation; gossip, but not, in the fullest sense, discussion. For while views may clash in interpreting and applying the existing rules of behavior to specific cases, the rules themselves remain unchallenged. Before a group can become a public there must be a confrontation of divergent attitudes involving the tacit or expressed rules that set the pattern of behavior and fix judgment of consequences.

If this distinction between public opinion and the mores be allowed we need to employ a separate term to denote the processes of group opinion where judgments are based on the mores alone. The term "social opinion," as applied by Thomas and Znaniecki to the primary-group controls of gossip, social appreciation, and community-wide feeling, seems satisfactory for this purpose. Social opinion is "the common factor which holds the community together, besides and above all the particularities which unify various parts of the community, individuals, or smaller groups with each other, and it is the only indispensable factor." [3] In the mechanisms of its operation, three original elements, according to the authors, are to be noted: an extraordinary occurrence that focuses attention, the development of an identical attitude toward this phenomenon, and the awareness of this identity.

In the description of its workings in Polish primary-group society, the characteristics that mark off social opinion from

[3] **The Polish Peasant in Europe and America** (1st ed.), I, 144–45.

public opinion are quite clearly distinguishable. The attitudes toward the attention-compelling occurrence are spontaneously assumed in accordance with tradition as preserved in the mores and customary behavior-patterns, and while gossip and persuasion are necessary to reconcile divergent interpretations based on personal diversities of experience or interest, nevertheless the generalized traditional attitude and its correlative behavior-pattern are already present to be applied to the given class of occurrences, and remain essentially unmodified throughout the process. The estimates and decisions made in social opinion are personal and absolute; the valuations that serve as criteria for defining the occurrence have their origin in the circumscribed, though ancient, heritage of the group. Social control based on the mores assumes unanimity. Civil law and legislation cannot develop until divergent interests, attitudes, and points of view are tolerated. Hence, as Professor Park has pointed out, in a primitive, stable society all law is sacred and civil law does not exist. Even in so complex a society as China, as long as custom holds its fixed and sacred character, civil law does not make a beginning. Public opinion operates as an indispensable factor in civil law; in criminal law, it is social opinion that operates.

In the clash of primary-group attitudes —as in the conflict of groups of kin or opposition of family interests—no elements of fact or interpretation that possess other than a traditional connotation enter into the formation of social opinion concerning the controversy. That is why we may say that discussion does not enter as a creative factor into the opinion arrived at. Social opinion is essentially the process of bringing predetermined attitudes to fit novel but classifiable cases.

When the social organization is widened and complicated by economic and cultural differentiation that entail incompatible schemes of group behavior, issues cannot always be met by the application of uniform traditional controls. It is at this juncture that publics come into existence and public opinion commences to function.

The market place may be taken as the type of situation conducive to the rise of the public. As the center for the exchange of economic goods and services, that is, of values that can be treated impersonally, it demanded adjustments based not on the irrational control of the mores but upon fact and news. Commodity values, credit, and enterprise are determined by the current situation rather than by tradition, and for this reason the market place became more than a mere trading institution. It served as a news center, a focal point for intelligence, and a station for the mobilization of novel ideas.

In short, when current events rather than arbitrary standards became the controlling factor in directing activities, and when interests began to be organized functionally rather than traditionally, the public was born. Modern industrial civilization may, for present purposes, be regarded as a vast extension of the market place—a scheme of economic order that pushes its frontiers ever further into regions where the social organization is and for ages has been static and traditional. Wherever it has penetrated, it has profoundly modified the systems of social and political organization. To carry out the division of labor and organization of functional activities that are its inevitable accompaniments, special agencies of communication have developed as coordinating mechanisms. All indirect means of communication, but especially the newspaper, serve to facilitate the collective acts of special-interest groups. Informational news having a relatively objective factual content, as distinct from human-interest news of emotional appeal, has developed in most fields of organized special interest, and helps to create in each a universe of discourse.

Thus the market place in its broader phase tends to take on a "soviet" character by virtue of the functional organization of interests and special universes of discourse. Each of these "soviet" organizations—banking, the bar association, welfare work, the real estate board, etc., —carries with it a wider following than the "members" or active participants, a following that is indirectly, if not directly, concerned with the activities and programs falling in the special field, and possessing more than a lay knowledge of these operations. The whole body of active participants and "interested" supporters or followers share in an on-going collective act and become a public with reference to the special undertakings in the given field. When the indirect consequences of these undertakings affect other groups or society at large and these consequences are perceived and reacted to by the latter, a still wider public comes into being.

In other words, there are special as well as general publics, and failure to recognize this fact prevents a full appreciation of the functions of public opinion. Walter Lippmann's lucid analysis of the functions of the public clears away the misconception of a single public omnicompetent to deal with the manifold problems of democracy, but when he limits the actual publics to the bystanders, as distinct from the "insiders," or active participants in a controversial affair, he restricts unduly the public's scope and reduces to a shadow its functions. The "insiders," in most cases, are the special publics or their representatives. When interests ordinarily left in their hands come into collision with other interests or produce undesired consequences affecting a wider social body, the general public, of which they remain an active part, begins to function.

Special publics, with "soviet" organizations at their core, have developed as a phase of the secularization of society that has gone *pari passu* with the extension of the market place, or, as most would put it, with the growth of modern civilization. To the extent that group behavior is secularized, it comes under the control of objectively determined fact and rationally predicted consequences instead of tradition, magic, or irrational sentiment. The interests defining a special public are to some degree technical and participation in its activities requires a certain amount of special knowledge. The universe of discourse of such a public, as a natural consequence, takes on a somewhat esoteric character. The activities, as well as the vocabularies of the publics of *belles lettres,* of banking and finance, of racing or organized baseball, of welfare movements and reform, and so on, are likely to be rather mysterious to the uninitiated, while the operations and discourse of science appear not infrequently to be downright magical.

Special periodicals, technical journals, the departmentalized sections of the daily press, and other communicational mediums cater to the interests of "soviet" groups and their publics, centering attention on common objects and coordinating activities to common ends. News in such fields tends to be stripped of sensational and symbolic qualities, and to approach the accuracy of scientific fact. The degree of secularization of a public may be measured more or less reliably by the objectivity of its news.

The competence of a public to deal with its problems is a variable depending upon such other variables as its equipment of special knowledge, the efficiency of the communicative devices that supply it with news and facts, and the effectiveness of its organization. The special public, within its own field, has special competence. All publics, it is true, think largely in terms of stereotypes, but the latter are indispensable factors in thought of whatever sort. Whether they falsify the environment or effectively simplify it for practical action depends upon how they are built up, checked, and utilized. It is not the purpose here to minimize the significance of irrational factors in public opinion, but to insist that the range and influence of such factors rest not upon their inherent nature or the inherent limitations of the public so much as upon the variables of the public's organization and functioning.

There is, no doubt, a sharp contrast between the competence of the special public dealing with issues in its domain and the general public as it functions through the feudal set-up of party politics. The news and the data affecting the deliberative adjustments of the latter, unlike the former, are largely selected for their power as emotional stimuli or their congruity with prevailing stereotypes with little regard for their accuracy or relevance as facts. Mr. Lippmann is not far wrong in restricting the competence of such a public to a few crude discernments which enable it to throw its force behind one or the other of the contestants.[4] But it should be remarked that the general public in its political capacity is functioning in a region that is still largely magical, traditional, and unsecularized. Encompassing the most divergent experiences that our highly mobile and heterogeneous social life has evolved, this public possesses scant means of translating such experiences into generally intelligible purposes and meanings. As a consequence its universe of discourse (if indeed it may be said to have one) is fragile and tenuous, its common motives are transitory and ephemeral, and its focus of attention is as wayward and evanescent as the front-page content of the newspapers it reads. At the same time, the problems with which it has to cope are notoriously complicated and profound. This is the state of affairs that has brought many protagonists of democracy to the verge of despair.

The performance of the general public, after all, partakes more nearly of the nature of social opinion, as heretofore described, than of public opinion. Its fugitive attention is largely preoccupied with scandals, trivia, and sensational occurrences. One may say without serious exaggeration that its only universe of discourse is in the news of mass appeal. But if such news is considered not from the standpoint of taste or esthetics but from that of social interaction, it takes on a new significance. For it becomes unmistakable that the human-interest and sensational material on which is centered so largely the public's attention presents exactly those "extraordinary occurrences" that set in motion the processes of social opinion and provide data for the formation of moral judgments. The communications of the general public, then, turn out to be largely concerned with getting

4 **The Phantom Public,** pp. 77ff.

a basis for a larger common understanding, with funding diverse experiences into intelligible wholes—in short, with establishing a wider consensus and a moral order.

The growth of social competence on the part of this wider public will proceed only as fast as interests are rationalized. This implies more than the free flow of facts which, according to some theories, is all that is necessary to set in motion an enlightened public opinion. Facts get their meaning from their relationships within a universe of discourse and their effective utilization depends upon the adequacy of this basis for interpretation as well as upon their being given free play in reorganizing stereotypes and the ongoing course of action. The wider public not only is deficient in a background of common meanings that might enable it to employ facts in defining and interpreting situations, but it lacks a technique for organizing the experiences of its diverse elements, or for integrating the productive but dispersive activities of interest-groups launched on separate and often conflicting careers.

The rationalization and organization of specific interest, however, have the effect of relieving the wider public of all but the most general responsibilities in the fields involved. As affairs long private,

like the state of one's health or the treatment of one's children, are made matters of public concern, they present at first issues with which the general public is poorly prepared to deal. In time, however, special organizations and "soviet" groups spring up and assume the major responsibilities in each field. These "voluntary associations" are the core of special publics, but at critical junctures they appeal to the general public, often in the capacity of propaganda agencies.

In conclusion, it would appear that the basic functions of the general public will, as time goes on and the functional organization of activities proceeds, be restricted increasingly to settlement of broad matters of policy, such as those dealt with by the board of directors of a very large and far-flung business or philanthropic institution. The simile has its disadvantages but it at least suggests that the "meddling" of the general public in matters requiring technical knowledge is likely to have consequences similar to those produced by over-zealous boards. With special publics assuming the chief responsibility in their own fields, the general public will be left the problem of integrating more or less unrelated specialisms and of defining the common objectives of the Great Society. This appears to be its unescapable burden.

The issue. A fundamental aspect of the public is the issue about which it forms, and one of the fundamental processes within the public is the definition and change of issues. Occasionally an issue may be fixed in advance, but usually the public defines and redefines the issue in the course of its deliberations. Not all issues that can be posed and that are logically relevant are necessarily the subject of public opinion. The public rejects or ignores certain statements of issues. In so doing an atmosphere is created in which those who define the issue in a manner acceptable to the public can communicate intelligibly and those who define issues in other ways are thought to be confused, dealing with irrelevancies, and the like. The issue, then, consists of those points of dispute about which people agree to do their disagreeing.

From this point of view a major task in studying public opinion is to ascertain how the public defines the issue. When people are polled on a synthetic issue, i.e., an issue created in the public opinion laboratory, they may provide answers whose interpretation will be misleading, or answers that seem to shift rapidly and fortuitously. For example, individuals have been polled at various times concerning their willingness to enter service in the event of war. Such a question is unlikely to become an issue in public opinion for at least two reasons. First of all, people sense that in the face of organized authority there will be no organized resistance in large numbers, and comments along this line are understood as merely "letting off steam." Second, the issue is an unpleasant one since no conceivable alternative course of action will be a gratifying one. Hence, people avoid facing this issue until the choice is forced upon them, while concentrating their attention and discussion on issues that can be phrased in more hopeful terms.

When the public must register its opinion through such measures as electing a public official, the issues about which the public made its decisions may not be indicated. Errors may also arise in predicting the outcome of elections by misdefining the issue. The accurate prediction by Louis Bean of the unexpected outcome of the 1948 presidential election in which Harry S. Truman was returned to office led some persons to predict mistakenly a similar outcome in 1952. The error in prediction probably lay not so much in erroneous procedure or in any general shift in people's attitudes toward the economic and social issues involved, but in a shift in the predominance of particular issues. Thus people who had not changed in their judgment of the economic issues involved may have felt that in 1952 the war and international issue was more important than the economic issues and hence shifted their vote to the Republican candidate.

Evidence of the constant shift in definition of issues is provided in a study of public opinion during the period leading up to American entry into World War II. Hadley Cantril has effectively pointed out that public opinion shifted in the direction of war not so much by the conversion of individuals from the anti-war to the pro-war position as by a succession of issues, each of which aligned people progressively closer to war participation. This approach has at least two important implications. First, we may hypothesize that many, and perhaps most, changes in public opinion consist of redefinitions of issues which group people differently. And second, public opinion may change without any necessary change in the attitudes and opinions of individuals.

PUBLIC OPINION IN FLUX

HADLEY CANTRIL

John Adams once wrote that "public information cannot keep pace with facts." What was true in the early nineteenth century is not so true today. Our country is for the first time in a war during a period when the development of reporting and communicational facilities makes it possible for nearly everyone to keep pace with the facts. At least 90 per cent of us either have radios or read daily newspapers.

Reprinted in part by permission of The American Academy of Political and Social Science, from **The Annals of the American Academy of Political and Social Science,** 220 (March, 1942), pp. 136–150.

This familiar situation is more revolutionary than we may realize. Among other things, it means that public opinion in our democracy has become sensitized to events. We take it for granted that we shall be widely and instantaneously informed. And we take it for granted that the opinions we hold or evolve are important—for us and for the country of which we are a part. We, the people, feel and know that we have become more significant than ever before, with the narrowing of the barrier that separates "us" and our range of experiences from our elected representatives and their range of experiences.

This is also the first critical period in our Nation's history when it has been possible to determine rapidly what opinion is —a possibility Lincoln craved when he said just before the Civil War, "What I want is to get done what the people desire to have done, and the question for me is how to find that out exactly." The social scientist is, therefore, at last able to examine systematically the effect of events on a sensitive public. At the present time, data are being gathered more rapidly than they can be exhaustively analyzed. But the flux of American opinion since the outbreak of the war in Europe can at least be outlined.

THE ISSUES CHANGE

Under present conditions it is even more difficult than usual for us to look at the recent past with any perspective. Issues have changed with the march of events. We can recapture some impression of the war issues we faced at different stages of the conflict if we sample the answers to questions asked at six scattered intervals.

1. *Just before the outbreak of hostilities in Europe.* In the fall of 1938 most of us thought England and France had made a mistake when they gave in to Germany's Sudeten demands. We also thought at that time that the Munich agreement had increased the likelihood of a general European war. But in the bright summer of 1939 we refused to believe that the squabble over the Polish Corridor would cause a war, almost two-thirds of us saying there would be no major war in Europe during the next year. At the same time, however, the overwhelming majority of us who had opinions thought Hitler's claims to the Corridor were not justified.

The chief issue at that time was *whether or not we should sell war materials to England and France.* When we were asked what we *should* do if war broke out between England and France on one side and Germany and Italy on the other, we were about evenly divided on the question of selling food and war supplies to the democracies. Two-thirds of us believed that if we did sell war materials to England and France there would be little

or no chance of our staying out of the war. When asked what we probably *would* do if a war broke out, about one-third of us thought we would remain neutral, one-fourth of us believed we would send troops to Europe, and almost half of us thought we would send war materials but no troops. When asked what side we wanted to see win if war should break out, 14 per cent of us had no opinion, 84 per cent of us voted for England and France, 2 per cent for Germany.

2. *The first two weeks after the outbreak of the European war.* During this period we harbored a complacent optimism. We wanted to watch and wait. The issue was still whether or not to help England and France by selling supplies. The great majority of us expected England and France to win the war; half of us believed the war would last one year or less. Slightly over half of us thought this country should sell supplies to the democracies, but if we did sell supplies, over 90 per cent of us thought we should be paid in cash. Almost half of us with opinions said at that time that if it looked as though England and France would be defeated in the next few months, we should declare war on Germany and send our troops abroad. But as further events showed, this opinion seemed based more on a remote sense of duty than on any sense of probable urgency.

3. *Month following French armistice.* We were aroused from our complacency with a horrified shock by the lightning successes of the German Army in the spring of 1940. Whereas fewer than half of us had thought we would be personally affected by a German victory before the conquest of France, by now two-thirds of us thought we would be affected. Our reaction was to turn our attention to our own defense. Approximately three-fourths of us were now saying that all able-bodied men should serve one year in the Army and that the National Guard should be called up for training. Most of us thought our defense production was inadequate.

Things looked dark on the Continent. We were not so sure of a British victory. The majority of us said it was more important for us to stay out of war than to help Britain. A majority of us were not in favor of sending food to Britain in our own ships. A majority of us felt we should try to have friendly trade and diplomatic relations with Germany if she won the war. The issue *now was whether or not we should give up our neutrality to help the British.*

4. *Mid-fall 1940.* By late October, after the British demonstrated their capacity for resistance and after it became clear that the foreign policy of the Roosevelt Administration remained firmly set against appeasement and withdrawal, the question facing most people was *whether or not we should resist Hitler by aid to Britain short of war.* The emphasis shifted from a program of passive aid to Britain to a program of more active resistance to Nazi Germany. About half of us were now willing to let England borrow money to buy food and war supplies from this country. Over half of us were willing to send more planes to England, even though this might delay our own national defense program. Forty per cent of us with opinions were in favor of changing the Neutrality Law to permit American ships to carry war supplies to England.

5. *Late spring 1941.* After the Balkan invasion the issue was *whether or not to resist Hitler at any cost.* . . . Over half of us with opinions favored convoying ships to Britain. Over two-thirds of us approved the recent passage of the Lend-Lease Act.

. . . opinion varies when questions are stated under different contingencies, interventionist opinion vacillating from 78 to 8 per cent. . . . insofar as general objectives were concerned, two-thirds of us seemed definitely agreed that we should follow through with our aim of defeating Nazi Germany, even though this program seemed likely to involve us in war.

6. *Just before declaration of war.* By late November 1941 the question seemed to be *when will we fight?* Over 80 per cent of us thought we would get into the war in Europe; over two-thirds of us with opinions thought we would soon be at war with Japan. Seventy per cent of us said that if our present leaders and military advisers believed the only way to defeat Germany was for this country to go into the war, then we would go in. Approximately the same number thought it was more important to defeat Germany than to stay out of war. Almost a third of us

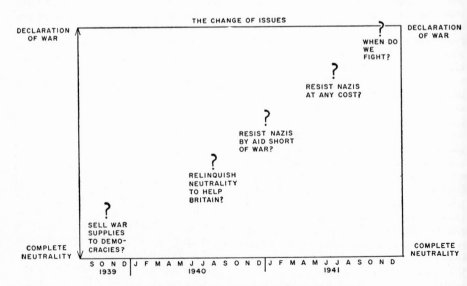

FIG. 1. *How public opinion stepped to war*

now said we would vote to go to war against Germany if we had a chance to vote. Furthermore, we had a growing confidence in the armed forces of our side. Over four-fifths of us said Germany would lose the war. Only 5 per cent thought Germany would win. Of the great majority of us who thought Germany would lose the war, over two-thirds believed Germany would be brought to her knees only after our own Army, Navy, and air force had joined the fight. We were practically unanimous in saying that we could beat Japan. Eighty per cent of us were sure our Navy could beat the Japanese Navy.

This change of issues through time, leading step by step from complete neutrality to a declaration of war, is diagrammed roughly in Figure 1.

TRENDS OF OPINION

Since the social context changes so rapidly with events, questions that make sense one week may be meaningless the next. It is therefore difficult to frame many questions which can be repeated over a considerable period of time for trend purposes. But some questions have been appropriate since the beginning of the war in Europe, and others have been repeated for shorter intervals. Some of these trends of opinion are shown in Figures 2, 3, and 4.

In general, these diagrams tell their own dramatic story. However, a few observations are noteworthy.

1. The ups and downs in the diagrams, especially Figure 2, show beyond any shadow of doubt that public opinion is sensitive to events.

2. The curve most sensitive to the course of events is that indicating which side people think will win the war. Here wishes are most closely related to opinion. Also, the average man has little solid and long-time strategic information on which to base his judgments. When separate trend curves of expectation are made by economic class, there is clear indication that persons of the upper income groups are more vacillating in their opinions than persons in the low income group. The relationship between the curve representing

those who think England will win and the unadjusted Dow-Jones Stock Index is close but not surprising. Again, if upper income people are separated out, their expectations are found to approximate more closely the trends in the Dow-Jones Index.

3. During the early period of the "phony" war, most Americans felt that we would not become involved. When hostilities began, however, more people thought we would be drawn in, but this expectation suddenly dropped when it seemed too late to help. Since late summer 1940, the number predicting our entrance has steadily risen.

4. A close relationship between our desire to help Britain and our expectation of a British victory is seen by comparing Figures 2 and 3. We do not like to bet on a loser, even if he is a friend.

5. The American people easily decided to resist Japanese aggressions. There have been no signs of appeasement on the part of public opinion.

6. The higher number of people (shown in Figure 3) who would "vote to go to war against Germany" than who thought we "should enter the war" was due chiefly to the fact that people were more willing to go to war if they felt they could personally play some part in making the decision.

7. The American people did not change their opinion concerning Britain's war aims. Approximately a third of them believed at the beginning of the war that Britain was fighting to preserve democracy. This figure remained constant.

8. The diagrams show the effect of certain events. For example:

a) The signing of the German-Italian-Japanese Pact of late September 1940 did not scare Americans away from their policy of aid to Britain at the risk of war.

b) During October 1940, when both major Presidential candidates were minimizing the probability of actual intervention, there was over a 10 per cent drop of those who favored aid to Britain at the risk of war and also of those who thought we would become involved in the war.

c) The President's fireside talk of December 29, 1940 increased by about 8 per cent the number who thought it was more

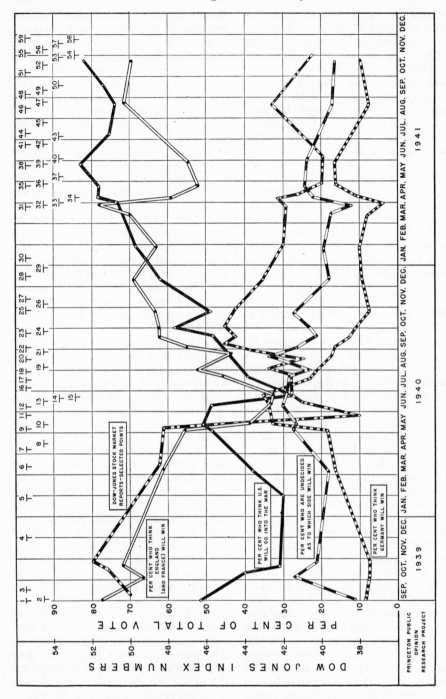

FIG. 2

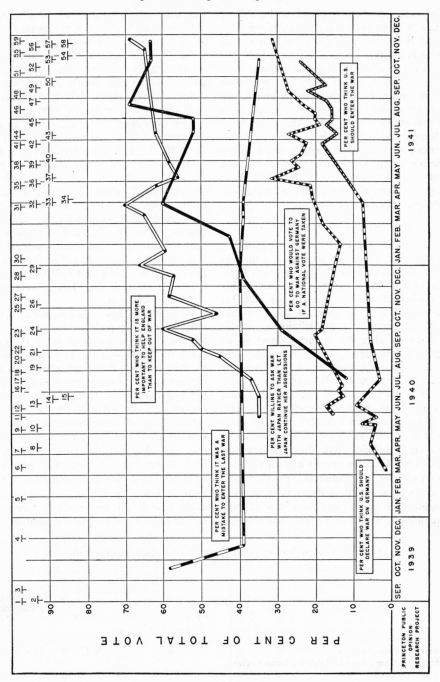

FIG. 3

important to help England at the risk of war than to keep out of war. If this talk had been sustained by some action, the rise in opinion might easily have held.

d) The effect of Russia's entrance into the war was to lift American optimism concerning the war's outcome and to decrease slightly the number of people who thought we would enter the war. After Russia was invaded, there was a slight increase of those who thought it was more important to aid Britain than to stay out of war. Hitler's talk of his Holy War against Communism made no impression on the American people.

OPINION AND POLICY

Early in May 1941 the Gallup poll first asked the question "So far as you personally are concerned, do you think President Roosevelt has gone too far in his policies of helping Britain, or not far enough?" . . . In spite of the fact that United States aid to Britain constantly increased after May, the proportion of people who thought the President had gone too far, about right, and not far enough remained fairly constant.

This does not mean, however, that even a President with Roosevelt's popularity could have carried the 50 per cent middle-of-roaders as he did with any radically different policies than those he actually pursued. It seems almost certain that the majority of the American people, with access to news telling them of totalitarian aggressions and of our own state of preparedness, would never have followed ei-

ther an appeasing Roosevelt or a Roosevelt obviously trying to hurry us into war. A close examination of poll results does show, however, that since the late spring of 1941 the public has been considerably ahead of the President's official stated policy. For example, if instead of using the President's name in the question above, the question is changed to "So far as you personally are concerned, do you think the United States has gone too far in its policies of helping Britain, or not far enough," the "not far enough" alternative generally draws about 32 per cent of the vote, instead of the usual 20 per cent when the President's name is mentioned. If the President had chosen to "get us into war" somewhat faster, there is every evidence that he could easily have done so. The public was half waiting for a push from its leader. The reverse may also have been true.

Anyone who has followed public opinion through the polls or any other systematic device knows that since the outbreak of World War II, the common man in this country has been ahead of his Congressman in urging more aid to Britain and her Allies. The complete record cannot be given here; but in Table 1 are listed at random some of the more important issues that have come before Congress, together with the dates on which at least 50 per cent of the people who had opinions voted for implementation of the interventionist program indicated. In every case it will be seen that Congress lagged behind the people—sometimes ten

TABLE 1. *Comparison of public opinion and congressional legislation*

	Public Opinion		When Passed by Congress
	Per Cent of Those with Opinions Who Voted "Yes"	Date	
Repeal arms embargo	50	8–17–39	11– 3–39
Make war supplies available to democracies on noncash basis	52	5–14–40	3–11–41
Conscript man power	50	5–14–40	8–28–40
Use U.S. Navy to convoy supplies	53	4–25–41	11–13–41
Use American ships and crews to carry supplies	55	10– 1–41	11–13–41

months, sometimes only one month, an average of about four months on our small sample. The figures err, of course, on the conservative side, since the polls did not tap opinion each week during the period when people were making up their minds.

With respect to Japan, the record shows that by late March 1941, 60 per cent of the total population wanted to stop Japanese aggressions at the risk of war, and as early as June 1938, over three-fourths of the total population favored an embargo on all war supplies to Japan—an embargo finally put into effect by the President more than three years later.

SOME CHARACTERISTICS OF OPINION

The trend charts and the national averages reported refer only to the *direction* of opinion. As we have already noted, the general orientation of opinion was set before the war began—only 2 per cent of us said we wanted Germany to win. To learn how we got more specific directives and to appreciate the dramatic climax of opinion with our entrance into World War II, it is therefore necessary to see what other dimensions of opinion were operative.

Intensity. Changes of opinion depend in part upon how strongly people hold their opinions—how convinced they are of their beliefs. For a number of reasons, this dimension of intensity is difficult to measure in large population. What measures we have made are at least consistent with one another, and show that by and large, the ratio of "strongly" held to "mildly" held opinion was greater among interventionists than among noninterventionists (Figure 4). They also show a progressive increase in the intensity of interventionist opinion. With the possible exception of the brief critical period in midsummer 1940, it would have been consistently more difficult for interventionists than for noninterventionists to reverse their opinions.

Stability. The stability of opinion is essentially a measure of both the direction and the intensity of opinion at different times and under different circumstances. It is readily tested with polling devices by the use of split but comparable samples of the population, each of which receives questions biased in various directions. The results of many such tests indicate that opinion concerning war aims and objectives has been stable since the spring of 1941—the majority of us were convinced that the Nazis had to be defeated; however, opinion concerning the instrumenta-

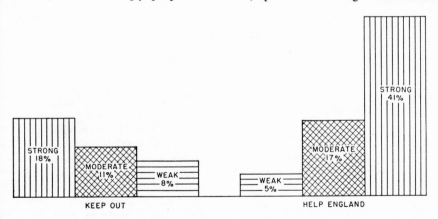

FIG. 4. *Intensity of opinion*

Question: "Which of these two things do you think is the more important for the United States to try to do—to keep out of the war ourselves, or to help England win, even at the risk of getting into the war?"

April 25, 1941:	Keep out	37%
	Help England	63%

tion of these aims, or opinion on topics which the common man knew little about or had little interest in, has been relatively unstable. Two examples of the stability of opinion concerning war aims may be cited. In both these instances, biased wordings produced no differences in results.

In April 1941 the Fortune poll reported results on a number of questions deliberately biased in opposite directions when asked of two populations (A and B below) but asked in a straightforward way of a third comparable population (C below).

Population A:
Hitler will never be satisfied unless he dominates the U.S. because it is the richest country in the world.

Agree	68.3 per cent
Disagree	22.8 per cent
Don't know	8.9 per cent

Population B:
Hitler is only interested in making Germany a powerful nation in Europe, and talk about his wanting to dominate this country is just British propaganda.

Disagree	68.0 per cent
Agree	21.3 per cent
Don't know	10.7 per cent

Population C:
Do you think that Hitler wants to dominate the U.S.?

Yes	69.3 per cent
No	23.0 per cent
Don't know	7.7 per cent

July 1941 the Office of Public Opinion Research asked the following questions of comparable sample populations:

Population A:
Some people say that since Germany is now fighting Russia, as well as Britain, it is not as necessary for this country to help Britain.

Agree	20.2 per cent
Disagree	72.4 per cent
No Opinion	7.4 per cent

Population B:
Some people say that since Germany will probably defeat Russia within a few weeks and then turn her full strength against Britain, it is more important than ever that we help Britain.

Agree	71.0 per cent
Disagree	18.9 per cent
No Opinion	10.1 per cent

Breadth. A third dimension of opinion is its inclusiveness, or generality. We want to know if a person's attitude toward one problem has any bearing on his attitude toward another problem. Is one opinion merely something to which a person has become conditioned, or is it something related to a larger mental context? By and large, as we should expect, opinions concerning the war form consistent patterns, indicating that the various opinions in a common pattern trace back to the same roots or standards of judgment.

The way opinions hang together is illustrated in Table 2. If the opinion pattern of the "Keep Out" group is compared to the pattern of the "Help England" group, the significance of each becomes more apparent. Particularly noteworthy in this table is the fact that interventionist or noninterventionist opinion appears entirely unrelated to the presence or absence in the family of men of military age.

Depth. For the psychologist concerned with motivation, the most fascinating chapters in the story of public opinion during the war are those which trace different opinions of different people back to their basic determinants. From what comprehensive frames of reference are opinions derived? What are the bases of these frames of reference? How are opinions related to the ego? Each psychologist will explore the dimensions of depth according to his own conceptual framework.

We cannot describe this search for determinants here, but it is vital for us to record in the story of opinion flux the rationale behind opinions before this country became a partner in the shooting war. . . . Three conclusions stand out especially from [a classification of] the chief reasons people gave in June 1941 for thinking it was more important to try to keep out of war or to help England at the risk of war. . . . First, the great majority of people who favored an aid-to-Britain policy did so for hard-headed, realistic, selfish reasons. Second, nonintervention-

TABLE 2. *Relationship of opinions*

Other Opinions		"Which of these two things do you think is more important for the United States to try to do: To keep out of war ourselves, or To help England win, even at the risk of getting into the war?" (3–12–41)	
		Keep Out (Per Cent)	*Help England* (Per Cent)
National Total		32	68
Any men in family between 16 and 36?	Yes	66	66
	No	34	34
Willing to fight or have family member fight?	Yes	33	75
	No	62	20
	No Opinion	5	5
If Germany defeats England will she attack U. S. in next ten years?	Yes	33	75
	No	54	19
	No Opinion	13	6
If England falls, will Germany control trade?	Yes	32	73
	No	53	21
	No Opinion	15	6
Was it a mistake for U. S. to enter last war?	Yes	66	26
	No	17	58
	No Opinion	17	16
Which side will win?	England	44	75
	Germany	20	12
	Neither	11	3
	Undecided	25	10
If Germany wins, will you be as free to do what you want as you are now?	Yes	52	24
	No	38	72
	No Opinion	10	4
If Germany wins, will we have to pay for strong defense and be poorer than we are now?	Yes	54	78
	No	35	16
	No Opinion	11	6

ist attitudes were based primarily on traditional pacifist appeals, applicable to any war at any time. Third, the character of Britain's war aims was quite incidental in determining opinion.

In view of the nature of opinion as revealed by these dimensions, the increasingly belligerent interventionist answer of the American people to the course of world events is easily understood. Most of us were simply convinced that it was to our own self-interest to defeat the Nazis; this determination was so deeply rooted that it could not be sidetracked; our extensive news services and mass media of communication won our confidence and kept us so well informed that we became increasingly alert to the implications events and courses of action had for our self-interest. . . .

Often it is an oversimplification to speak of a public as a group divided about an issue. Rather, the public may be organized about a matrix of issues that are conceived by the members of the public as belonging together. In some instances there may be a clearly-defined hierarchy of issues, in some instances the public may evidence uncertainty as to just what it is supposed to be deciding, and in other cases there may be definitely factional definitions of issues.

The presence of competing definitions of the issue may create a public opinion consisting of sharply opposed groups made up of individuals who are only slightly divergent in their individual opinions and attitudes. The public which was concerned about the activities of Senator Joseph McCarthy and his investigations of "un-American activities" represented such a polarity more in terms of issue-definition than in terms of individual opinions. The anti-McCarthy group tended to define the issue as that of preserving free speech and thought against totalitarian inroads, and consequently defined the opposition as fascistically inclined. The pro-McCarthy group defined the issue as the protection of America from the fifth-column activities of an enemy power, and hence regarded the opposition as "soft" toward communism or unwilling to protect their nation from danger. Among those who see the opposing argument more clearly, there is likely to be a partial admission of the charges accompanied by an insistence that they do not refer to the most important issue. Thus, on one side a defender of freedom from "thought control" speaks of the necessary "calculated risk" of subversives in certain types of organizations. On the opposing side a pro-McCarthy speaker declared:

> I was six months in the State Department, and I know how dirty they can play. It takes a dirty fighter to fight a dirty fighter. The junior Senator from Wisconsin has made a lot of mistakes but he has been pointing at the right thing.*

A further aspect of the public is the nature of the divisions of opinion which develop about the issue. Out of an initial variety of responses there evolves through discussion a consolidation of points of view into a limited number of alternatives. Once such a consolidation takes place it is difficult for any individual to communicate within the public any view other than one of those predefined. Each participant is assigned to one of the accepted divisions, and those who resist such classification are said to be confused and inconsistent. By such an attitude the public resists modification of its pre-established divisions.

The number of different positions that are recognized may be intrinsic to the issue or, more often, a function of the intensity of interest, the sense of urgency, and the type of action indicated. Within a public not marked by a sense of urgency there are likely to be a large number of recognized positions which can be taken, but as a greater sense of urgency prevails there is a tendency toward the consolidation of positions ultimately into only two opposing views. The public then treats all expressions as indicative of adherence to one of these two positions. A person who refuses to adopt completely either point of view is told to stop hedging, to come out in the open and reveal his true colors. This principle may be illustrated by contrasting the diversity of viewpoints regarding the toleration and recognition of communist activity in the United States during the early 1930's to the polarization during the "cold war" period of the early 1950's.

Mode of expression of public opinion. A public is necessarily shaped by the manner of registering public opinion toward which it is oriented. If public opin-

---

* From the files of Ralph H. Turner.

ion is to be registered through the secret ballot, the efforts of partisans within the public will be directed toward getting the maximum number of individuals committed to going to the poll and voting. If public opinion is to be registered through testimony before a congressional committee, the emphasis is more likely to be concentrated on securing a wide range of organizational representation buttressed by convincing evidence of public support. If public opinion is to be registered through informal influence upon official decision-makers, the incorporation into the public of persons respected by decision-makers may be crucial.

The very existence of a public may be dependent upon some sense that there are effective ways in which public opinion may be registered and that some noticeable effect upon the course of action will result. In a book entitled *The Phantom Public,* Walter Lippmann suggests that "The private citizen today has come to feel rather like a deaf spectator in the back row, who ought to keep his mind on the mystery off there, but cannot quite manage to keep awake. . . . He lives in a world which he cannot see, does not understand and is unable to direct." Problems of communication in modern society have already been underlined in the selection by Louis Wirth. As the conviction becomes general that nothing can come of public discussion, interest drops, activity subsides, and publics as we have defined them disappear. There may be unfocused discussion and random complaining, but there will be few genuine publics entering into discussion with a purpose.

One feature in the mode of expression of public opinion is the overlapping of publics and the intertwining of issues. When certain issues are thought to be closely related, a fairly definitive registration of public opinion on one issue may effectively structure the less definitive public opinion on a related issue. Such was the case in the unseating of the Pasadena Superintendent of Schools following the rejection by the voters of a proposed tax increase for the schools. The latter seemed to be accepted by the community and the public itself as indicating public opinion regarding the superintendent and his policies in general, though a subsequent poll of individual voters produced different evidence.

THE ENEMY IN PASADENA
Carey McWilliams

Last summer the delegates to the National Education Association's convention were told that a general attack is being organized on public education in the United States. "The enemy," warned Harold Benjamin, dean of the University of Maryland's school of education, "is trying our lines with a number of local, probing raids, attempting to find out where we are weak or strong, testing his methods of attack, recruiting and training his forces,

building up his stockpiles." Even then it was clear, as Dr. Benjamin pointed out, that the issue shaping up in Pasadena was likely to be the test engagement.

In selecting Pasadena as the testing ground, the Enemy demonstrated real insight. Pasadena is not only a well known community but it has been rated the model small city of the nation. If the control of its schools could be captured, the school systems of even larger communities might be captured and by the same methods. In Pasadena, also, the opposition was commanded by Willard E. Goslin, one of the outstanding public school

Reprinted in part by permission of the editors, **The Christian Century,** from **The Christian Century,** 68 (Jan. 3, 1951), pp. 10–15.

administrators in the country. If Goslin could be routed—so the Enemy reasoned —lesser administrators would be easy victims. The victory which the Enemy has just won in Pasadena, therefore, demands careful study as a model in miniature of the big battle for control of public education which is now shaping up in the United States.

I

Like almost everything else in Pasadena, the schools had always been run by the "better elements." School board elections were a mere formality, educational controversies were unknown, and general school policies were accepted as fixed and ordained, like the Ten Commandments. Then in 1947 the unheard-of happened: rebel candidates defeated two incumbents, both prominent Pasadenans who had served for more than a decade. To run for the school board without being "invited" to do so was audacious, but to unseat two incumbents endorsed by the "better elements" was dangerously "subversive." Today this election has been forgotten; it is noted here merely to indicate that the crisis in the schools had begun a full year before Willard E. Goslin came to Pasadena.

The two rebel candidates had campaigned on the single issue that, after twenty years, the Pasadena schools needed a new superintendent. The incumbent resigned with their election and the board then asked 75 civic organizations what kind of superintendent they wanted. The answer was unanimous: "The best that money can buy." The board's choice was Dr. Goslin, then in charge of the public schools in Minneapolis. Named as one of the five outstanding public school administrators in America, Dr. Goslin had just missed, by one vote, being selected to direct the New York school system. For a city of 112,000 population to walk off with an educator of this prominence was quite a feat. The bait that attracted Goslin was the promise of a free hand, including permission to select a small nuclear staff. The board knew, and all Pasadena knew, that some changes might

be needed in the schools after twenty years under one administration.

To Dr. Goslin the public school is the central institution in American life. It is not an adjunct to the community; it *is* the community, organized to achieve its highest purpose. One of his first acts therefore was to appoint a series of advisory committees made up of teachers and parents, of administrators and laymen. The committees were not only to work out solutions to particular problems but to create a new awareness of the schools as a community concern. The committee on conservation and outdoor education came up with a recommendation for a year-round camp, where youngsters might study animal life, soil erosion and conservation problems generally and, at the same time, live together for short periods as a miniature community. The committee on child guidance and counseling, finding that the Pasadena schools fell below desirable norms, recommended the appointment of a full-time psychiatric case worker and suggested greater emphasis on child guidance and mental health. The committee on human relations stressed the need for greater emphasis on racial understanding and social democracy. And so it went.

While the committees were at work, Dr. Goslin brought in a number of "outside" experts as part of an in-service training program, it being his theory that the teaching staff and the administrative staff should keep abreast of what was happening in some fields outside their own specialties. He was anxious also that the staff should be a team, sharing the same values, goals and understandings. Among these visitors was William Heard Kilpatrick of Columbia University, who conducted a workshop in the summer of 1949 on the subject, "We Learn What We Live." At this point there were a few raised eyebrows but no audible protests or demurrers.

II

Dr. Goslin soon discovered that his predecessor had retired at a most opportune time. From 1940 to 1948, enrollment had steadily climbed but the school plant had not expanded nor had the tax levy been increased. A building program could not, of course, be carried out during the war, and in the postwar period everyone was of the opinion that costs would eventually decline. Faced with an emergency that had been building up for eight years, and sensing a still greater emergency, Goslin proposed, and the school board approved, an increase in the tax levy from 90 cents to $1.34 per $100 assessed property valuation. An increase of this size, proposed by a *new* administration, doubtless seemed excessive. Older residents in California never appreciate the consequences of migration, nor are the newcomers always aware that they create special problems. By 1948 old-timers were complaining that there were "whole streets in Pasadena on which the people have not lived for more than five years." It was against this background, then, that an election to approve the new tax levy was scheduled for June 2, 1950.

Feeling confident that an expansion program would be approved, Goslin then proceeded to draw up a proposed rezoning of school districts—a routine procedure, since population increases and the construction of new schools usually call for some revamping of districts. But there was an additional reason in this case, for Dr. Goslin had unearthed the paradoxical fact that in Pasadena racial and ethnic minorities were concentrated in the newer and more modern schools. This refreshing reversal of custom had come about by reason of long adherence to a zoning system under which the "better elements" could have their children transferred to certain preferred schools—preferred, that is, in terms of social prestige. These schools were the older schools, located in the elite neighborhoods; but, in these same neighborhoods, small pockets of Mexican and Negro settlements were to be found in which servants and domestics lived in close proximity to their employers. Ordinarily their children would have attended the schools in the neighborhood, but Pasadena's elite, with characteristic politeness, had sorted out the minority children and routed them to new schools,

outside the district, in which enrollment was often 60 per cent of capacity by comparison with 120 per cent capacity enrollment in the so-called "better" schools. Goslin wanted the new districts to be based on standard norms and to ignore social and racial preferences.

With tempers rising over the proposed tax increase, a huge crowd surged into the regular board meeting at which the rezoning proposal was to be discussed. In fact the crowd was so large that the hearing had to be adjourned to the auditorium of near-by Junior high school—an occurrence without precedent. The session lasted for five hectic hours; the discussion was loud and vehement; and the press reported the meeting as "a lively and free-swinging affair." In a new and strangely tense atmosphere, divisions which had long been latent suddenly yawned like chasms across which neighbors hurled epithets at each other. Frustration accounted in part for this intensity of feeling: the opposition hesitated to discuss the racial issue and felt compelled to rest its case on other grounds. Everyone sensed, moreover, that rezoning in itself did not warrant all this excitement; the growth of the city alone made some rezoning imperative. Although no one said so, everyone sensed that rezoning, like the approaching election, had suddenly become a gambit in a larger struggle for power.

III

As June 2 approached, Pasadena found itself divided from top to bottom over an issue which had suddenly become invested with unspoken implications. The issue was clearly not economy *vs.* extravagance, retrenchment *vs.* expansion. The Pasadena chamber of commerce had endorsed the proposed increase in the tax levy and the opposition frankly conceded that its objections were ideological as well as fiscal. The immediate issue was simply whether more funds should be raised to finance the construction of new schools; yet, in some mysterious way, this issue had become charged with an entirely different meaning; namely, Who is to control the schools and for what purpose?

The verbal violence which now echoed

in the staid precincts of Pasadena was quite unheard-of. The school board election of 1947 had been lively, to be sure, but this was a real brannigan. Supporting the increased tax levy were such groups as the P.T.A., the League of Women Voters, the American Association of University Women, the B'nai B'rith, the local chapter of the National Association for the Advancement of Colored People and the Pasadena chamber of commerce. Nominally the opposition was led by a group known as the Pasadena School Development Council, directed by one Frank Wells, of whom little was known. Indeed little was known about the council except that it had come into being a year or so earlier but had been inactive until the increase in the tax levy had been proposed. In the opposition, also, was Pro America, under the spirited direction of Mrs. Morgan G. Padelford, one of Pasadena's more formidable society matrons and the daughter of Albert W. Hawkes, former senator from New Jersey. But just as the real issue was not openly voiced, so the real opposition was silent or remained undefined. This opposition was "the Enemy"; that is, no one in particular but rather a tendency, a situation. Before discussing the campaign, therefore, this impersonal Enemy must be brought into a little sharper focus.

IV

Curiously enough, the Enemy had tried to schedule the first test engagement in Los Angeles. On January 16, 1950—some months before the Pasadena school situation became a focus of interest from coast to coast—the *Los Angeles Herald-Express* launched a series of articles on the subject, "What's Wrong with the Schools?" Repeating stock charges against public education, the articles were agitational rather than critical; familiar complaints were repeated as "signals," for clearly agitational purposes. Based on interviews with "rank-and-file" citizens, the articles indicated that everything was wrong and nothing right with the schools.

The reporter who prepared the articles kept insisting that he was being bombarded with letters from complaining parents; that many parents feared the schools were being taken over by dictators masquerading as progressive educators; and that the three R's had been supplanted by "calcimine, clay and confusion." Many of the articles were made up of quotations from letters written by irate parents, uniformly critical in tone, and published with such terse captions as "Deplorable," "Wants Results," "Boiling Mad," "Untaught," "Who Is to Blame?" "Long Overdue," "Powder Keg," "Foreign Born," "Progressive Rot." The articles had no theme, reported no facts, reached no conclusions. Clearly the purpose was to use a loaded question—"What's wrong with the schools?"—to encourage the articulation of all sorts of discontents as a means by which Alexander J. Stoddard, superintendent of the Los Angeles schools, might be publicly "persuaded" to softpedal an expansion program. Dr. Stoddard got the point and the agitation promptly subsided.

Up to this time, the Pasadena newspapers had indicated little awareness that there was or might be anything wrong with the city's schools. But extras carrying the first of the *Herald-Express* articles were hardly on the streets before the *Independent,* recently converted from a shopping guide to a newspaper and anxious to take circulation from the conservative *Pasadena Star-News,* began to sneer and snarl: "Kindergarten to college in twelve easy lessons," "Too much paint daubing," "Parents raising Hail Columbia in L. A.," and so forth. And now, for the first time, a new note was struck: "more and more parents" were sending their children to parochial schools, where discipline was stressed. This plug for the parochial schools was coupled, rather significantly, with the charge that the public schools were costing "more and more" every year.

A clue to the appearance of the articles in the *Herald-Express* may be found in the fact that on January 26, 1950, the Los Angeles chamber of commerce had devoted the occasion of its fifty-ninth annual banquet to the thesis that federal aid to education would be "subversive." The ay before the banquet, the *Los Angeles Times* carried an editorial captioned, "If he Schools Would Only Educate." The aption, related to the following day's headlines, suggested that federal aid to education should be opposed because the public schools weren't doing a good job.

As the election approached, the Pasadena situation became of ever increasing interest to the *Los Angeles Times.* Under he heading, "Pasadena Becomes Schools' Test Tube," the *Times* ran six articles on he Pasadena school situation during the week preceding the election. Curiously enough, these articles were all devoted to issues of educational policy. Readers might well have concluded that the voters of Pasadena were about to pass judgment not on a proposed increase in the tax levy, but on matters of educational policy which were being debated by American educators twenty years back. But perhaps a discerning reader might have concluded that the *Times,* in the guise of stalking John Dewey, who had just celebrated his ninetieth birthday, was inciting voters to rebel against an increased tax levy.

The articles in the *Times* did reveal, however, a good deal about the nature of he Enemy's propaganda. Goslin's emphasis on race relations, human rights and the United Nations became, in this lurid reading, a plot to indoctrinate children with dangerous thoughts. The proposal to add a full-time psychiatric case worker was interpreted as a scheme to alienate kiddies from their mommies and daddies. Similarly, the mountain camp proposal was described as a technique by which "the child" was to be turned against his family. Large attendance at recent board meetings was presented not as a healthy manifestation of public interest, but as an attempt to "load" meetings with individuals interested in "political sociology" rather than education. Only one of the six articles even touched upon the merits of the proposed tax increase. But to understand just how John Dewey, pragmatism and progressive education got involved in the June 2 election, one must cut back to the campaign.

V

There is a fable that in Pasadena's precincts the rich and retired dwell in a seclusion so complete and silent that nothing can be heard there save the ticking of the clocks and the hardening of the arteries. This seclusion, however, was rudely violated in the weeks which preceded the June 2 election. Both sides took to the airways; telephone campaigns were organized; leaflets fluttered from the skies and pamphlets were tucked under doorways. The little known Pasadena School Development Council was suddenly well financed and extraordinarily active. On the morning of the election, ten thousand telegrams went to voters from selected mailing lists. Noting the excitement, all sorts of organizations began to dabble in the election for strictly private purposes. For example, the P.T.A. had earned the enmity of Pasadena's "senior citizens" by opposing a pension scheme at a prior statewide election; now the "senior citizens" saw a chance to settle scores with the P.T.A. On election day, the School Development Council carted the aged off to the polls, not a few in wheelchairs and ambulances. Prior school elections had seldom brought out a vote of even 7,000, but on June 2 a record 32,000 votes were cast and the increased tax levy was snowed under by some 22,000 votes.

During the campaign Max Merritt Morrison, of the Westminster Presbyterian Church, disturbed over the tenor of a meeting sponsored by the School Development Council, preached a sermon about it. He said:

It was one of the most disturbing experiences we have had since we came to Pasadena eight years ago. If anyone had told us that "it can happen here," we would not have believed them. At this meeting we heard good American citizens—men and women of Pasadena whom we have learned to admire for their unselfish service to our community—ridiculed, accused of giving sympathy to un-American activities, and our free public school education referred to as "rubbish." All the speeches made were against the tax measure and our school authorities, and anyone who attempted to speak on the opposite side or to ask a simple question was shouted down and told to go home. . . . I went home from the meeting heartsick.

One of the things that most disturbed Dr. Morrison was the distribution, at this meeting, of large quantities of vicious anti-public-school propaganda. Among the items were pamphlets with such titles as *Progressive Education is Subverting America, Must American Youth Be Taught that Communism and Socialism are Superior to Americanism? They WANT Your Child! Progressive Education Breeds Delinquency* and *How Red are the Schools?* All these pamphlets were written by a Mr. Zoll and carried the imprint of the National Council for American Education.

Thanks to Dr. Morrison, Pasadenans learned that A. Alderson Zoll, "Ph.D.," had been an ardent Coughlinite in 1942; that he had worked with Gerald L. K. Smith, Joe Kamp, Upton Close and Merwin K. Hart; that the National Council for American Education is merely Zoll's alter ego; that such sponsors of the council as General Jonathan M. Wainright, Senator Arthur Vandenberg, Senator Karl Mundt, and Stanley High of *Reader's Digest* had resigned when Zoll's well known anti-Semitic background was publicized in the New York World-Telegram on August 25, 1948.

The Pasadena School Development Council promptly published a statement repudiating any connection with Zoll but echoing his favorite themes. The theories of John Dewey and William H. Kilpatrick, the council added, were "as great a threat to the American system of government . . . as any subversive threats by parties of the right or the left . . . Regardless of what Zoll or his group may be, the material . . . is about as subversive as the American Constitution and the Bill of Rights" (that is, the material attacking the public schools).

The defeat of the proposed tax increase did not, of course, appease the School Development Council. Almost before the votes were counted, the council leveled its first direct attack on the teachers: all teachers must take a loyalty oath. The Pasadena education association, composed of a majority of the city's 1,200 public school teachers, promptly agreed and asked the council members to join with them in making the affirmation. The council agreed but countered with the charge that the teachers' oath was nothing more than "a fancy flag salute"; something stronger was required. Too long to quote here, the oath which the council proposed is, without doubt, the most complicated and detailed "ism" disavowal yet concocted. Among other renunciations is this: "I do further swear that I have not attempted to influence anyone—child or adult—by innuendo or by direct or indirect statements tending to create doubt or to weaken anyone's faith in American institutions and the superiority of the American system over all others." At the same time the council insisted that its real concern was with curriculum and educational ideologies, and it has since demanded a general textbook inquiry. Also, hardly was the election over before Frank Wells, director of the council, left for San Diego to launch a similar campaign there, the San Diego schools having been "redefined and reanalyzed" as late as 1948 by the heretic, William H. Kilpatrick.

VI

That the election settled nothing is conclusively shown by a public opinion survey prepared by the John B. Knight Company for the Pasadena teachers, who were anxious to find out why the proposed tax increase failed. Was discipline satisfactory? "Yes," replied 63.6 per cent of the parents with children in the schools, 46.6 per cent of the nonparents and 83 per cent of the teachers. Was enough emphasis being placed on the three R's? "Yes," said 46.5 per cent of the parents, 30.9 per cent of the nonparents and 74.4 per cent of the teachers. Were classes too large? "Yes," said 52.5 per cent of the parents, 47.2 per cent of the nonparents and 85.1 per cent of the teachers. Were students getting enough personal attention? "No," said 55.15 per cent of the parents, 56.8

per cent of the nonparents and 79.8 per cent of the teachers. Should pupils be graded on how they compared with other pupils or on their own effort? "On their own effort," said 70.6 per cent of the parents, 68.4 per cent of the nonparents and 66.7 per cent of the teachers. Of the entire sample, 77.5 per cent thought the schools should provide guidance, 89.2 per cent favored vocational guidance, and 90.5 per cent approved educational guidance. By and large these replies indicate a surprisingly large measure of agreement on most issues, but this agreement was concealed and negated by the election.

Even more revealing were the answers to the key question: "If you voted against the tax levy, why?" "Too many taxes already," said 39.1 per cent; "Don't need money, system not being run well now," said 20.9 per cent; "Money would be misspent," said 20 per cent, with other objections shading off in minor percentages. Only 4.6 per cent of the sample voted against the levy because of any lack of confidence in the superintendent, and only 10 per cent voted against the levy because they were opposed to "progressive education"!

Who, then, were those who voted at the election? Only 52 per cent of those having children in the schools bothered to vote, by comparison with 60.9 per cent of the nonparents. Of the property owners, 58 per cent voted, by comparison with 25.7 per cent of those who did not own property. In a narrow sense, therefore, the election simply determined that property owners without children in the schools do not like to pay higher school taxes. But the election unfortunately had many larger meanings. . . .

VII

All summer long the issue of Goslin's retention was debated in Pasadena. Would the board stand firm or, yielding to pressure, would it demand his resignation? The school term opened with no overt indication that any change was contemplated. But the Pasadena School Development Council was determined to exploit the victory which it had won in June. A call was sent out for the state senate committee on education to hurry to Pasadena to aid in the movement to oust Dr. Goslin. The day the committee arrived in Los Angeles, the board of education in Pasadena demanded Dr. Goslin's resignation in order, so it was said, "to restore harmony" in the schools (November 10, 1950). A few days later the *Los Angeles Times* carried the triumphant headline: "Progressive Education Tossed Out—Pasadena Schools to Abandon Policy After Years of Trial."

Before Goslin acted on the board's request, however, the state senate committee convened in a crowded hearing room in Pasadena's city hall. Here the full fury and incredible wildness of the attack against Goslin were unleashed. Witnesses for the Pasadena School Development Council implied that Goslin was a "Red" on the basis of his membership in the National Conference of Christians and Jews and the fact that he served on an advisory committee for UNESCO! The showing of such films as "The Brotherhood of Man" was denounced, with the hearty approval of the committee, as "subversive." In fact the entire intercultural educational program was denounced as subversive.

Thus, while hundreds of Pasadenans sat back, stunned and amazed, the public school system was attacked with a fury and violence shocking to witness. The attack was so violent, and was so clearly based on elements of pure delusion, that public opinion began to rally rapidly to Goslin's side. When Dr. Goslin was finally heard, he was given a standing ovation by the crowd as he left the stand. The *Los Angeles Mirror* (November 17) carried a story with the headline, "Pasadena Board May Rescind Act to Fire Goslin," and for a time it seemed that the opposition's attack had backfired.

But the sane and sensible "middle-of-the-road" opinion in Pasadena had learned too late the real nature of the attack; namely, that it was not against Goslin or "progressive education" so much as it was a carefully laid plot to capture control of the public schools. The finale came on November 21 when Dr. Goslin resigned. Even before he resigned, however, the papers announced that a "civic association" in Denver had renewed the campaign to force the resignation of Kenneth E. Oberholtzer, another outstanding public school administrator. There again the familiar demand was voiced that Oberholtzer resign "unless the 'progressive education' system was abandoned" (*Denver Post*, November 16, 1950). . . .

In the analysis of public opinion, avenues of expression other than the ballot have seldom been explored. Herbert Blumer calls our attention to the great importance of other modes of expression. Even when issues are supposed to be settled by public election, much of the total impact of public opinion occurs during the period when decision-makers are trying to assess the issues upon which public decision hinged. At this point the representatives of various organized groups play a major role and the individual within the public is able to express himself only through organizational membership. Blumer also discusses certain aspects of the composition of the public which are relevant to the following section.

PUBLIC OPINION AND SOCIAL ORGANIZATION
Herbert Blumer

1.) Public opinion must obviously be recognized as having its setting in a society and as being a function of that society in operation. This means, patently, that public opinion gets its form from the social framework in which it moves, and from the social processes in play in that framework; also that the function and role of public opinion is determined by the part it plays in the operation of the society. If public opinion is to be studied in any realistic sense its depiction must be faithful to its empirical character. . . .

2.) A society has an organization. It is not a mere aggregation of disparate individuals. A human society is composed of diverse kinds of functional groups. In our American society illustrative instances of functional groups are a corporation, a trade association, a labor union, an ethnic group, a farmers' organization. To a major extent our total collective life is made up of the actions and acts of such groups. These groups are oriented in different directions because of special interests. These groups differ in terms of their strategic

position in the society and in terms of opportunities to act. Accordingly, they differ in terms of prestige and power. As functional groups, that is to say as groups acting individually in some corporate or unitary sense, such groups necessarily have to have some organization—some leadership, some policy makers, some individuals who speak on behalf of the group, and some individuals who take the initiative in acting on behalf of the group.

3.) Such functional groups, when they act, have to act through the channels which are available in the society. If the fate of the proposed acts depends on the decisions of individuals or groups who are located at strategic points in the channels of action, then influence and pressure is brought to bear directly or indirectly on such individuals or groups who make the decisions. I take it that this realistic feature of the operation of our American society requires little explication. If an action embodying the interests of a functional group such as a farmers' organization depends for its realization on decisions of Congressmen or a bureau or a set of administrators, then efforts on behalf of that action will seek to influence such Congressmen, bureau, or administrators. Since in every society to some de-

Reprinted in part by permission of The American Sociological Society, from Herbert Blumer, "Public Opinion and Public Opinion Polling," **American Sociological Review**, 13 (Oct., 1948), pp. 543–46.

gree, and in our American society to a large degree, there are individuals, committees, boards, legislators, administrators, and executives who have to make the decisions affecting the outcome of the actions of functional groups, such key people become the object of direct and indirect influence or pressure.

4.) The key individuals referred to who have to make the crucial decisions are almost inevitably confronted with the necessity of *assessing* the various influences, claims, demands, urgings, and pressures that are brought to bear on them. Insofar as they are responsive and responsible they are bound to make such an assessment in the process of arriving at their decisions. Here I want to make the trite remark that in making their assessments these key individuals take into account what they judge to be worthy of being taken into account.

5.) The above points give a crude but essentially realistic picture of certain important ways in which our society operates. The fifth feature I wish to note is that public opinion is formed and expressed in large measure through these ways of societal operation. This point requires a little elaboration. The formation of public opinion occurs as a function of a society in operation. I state the matter in that way to stress that the formation of public opinion does not occur through an interaction of disparate individuals who share equally in the process. Instead the formation of public opinion reflects the functional composition and organization of society. The formation of public opinion occurs in large measure through the interaction of groups. I mean nothing esoteric by this last remark. I merely refer to the common occurrence of the leaders or officials of a functional group taking a stand on behalf of the group with reference to an issue and voicing explicitly or implicitly this stand on behalf of the group. Much of the interaction through which public opinion is formed is through the clash of these group views and positions. In no sense does such a group view imply that it is held in equal manner and in equal degree by all of the members of the group. Many of the members of the group may subscribe to the view without understanding it, many may be indifferent about it, many may share the view only in part, and many may actually not share the view but still not rebel against the representatives of the group who express the view. Nevertheless the view, as indicated, may be introduced into the forum of discussion as the view of the group and may be reacted to as such. To bring out this point in another way, one need merely note that in the more outstanding expressions of view on an issue, the individuals almost always speak either explicitly or implicitly as representatives of groups. I would repeat that in any realistic sense the diversified interaction which gives rise to public opinion is in large measure between functional groups and not merely between disparate individuals.

I think that it is also very clear that in the process of forming public opinion, individuals are not alike in influence nor are groups that are equal numerically in membership alike in influence. This is so evident as not to require elaboration. It is enough merely to point out that differences in prestige, position, and influence that characterize groups and individuals in the functional organizations of a society are brought into play in the formation of public opinion.

The picture of a series of groups and individuals of significantly different influence interacting in the formation of public opinion holds true equally well with reference to the expression of public opinion. By expression of public opinion I mean bringing the public opinion to bear on those who have to act in response to public opinion. This expression is not in the form of a parade or array of the views of disparate individuals, in an open forum. Where the views are voiced in open forum they are likely, as has been indicated, to be in one way or another the expression of group views. But in addition to the voicing of views in the open forum, the expression of public opinion is in the form of direct influence on those who are to act in response to public opinion. Through such means as letters, telegrams, petitions, resolutions, lobbies, delegations, and personal meetings interested groups and individuals bring their views and positions to bear on the key persons who have to make the decisions. I am not concerned with whether such forms of expressing public opinion should occur; I merely wish to emphasize that in any realistic consideration of public opinion it must be recognized that such means of expressing public opinion do occur. A society which has to act will use the channels of action that it has in its structure.

6.) The last feature of public opinion that I wish to note is that in *any realistic sense* public opinion consists of the pattern of the diverse views and positions on the issue *that come to the individuals who have to act in response to the public opinion*. Public opinion which was a mere display, or which was terminal in its very expression, or which never came to the attention of those who have to act on public opinion would be impotent and meaningless as far as affecting the action or operation of society is concerned. Insofar as public opinion is *effective* on societal action it becomes so only by entering into the purview of whoever, like legislators, executives, administrators, and policy makers, have to act on public opinion. To me this proposition is self-evident. If it be granted, the character of public opinion in terms of meaningful operation must be sought in the array of views and positions which enter into the consideration of those who have to take action on public opinion.

It is important to note that the individual who has to act on public opinion has to *assess* the public opinion as it comes to his attention, because of the very fact that this public opinion comes to him in the form of diverse views and usually opposed views. Insofar as he is responsive to public opinion he has to weigh the respective views. How this assessment is made is an obscure matter. But one generalization even though trite, can be made safely, to wit, that the individual takes into account different views only to the extent to which such views count. And views count pretty much on the basis of how the individual judges the "backing" of the views and the implication of the backing. It is in this sense, again, that the organization of the society with its differentiation of prestige and power, enters into the character of public opinion. As was explained above, the key person who has to act on public opinion is usually subject to a variety of presentations, importunities, demands, criticisms, and suggestions that come to him through the various channels in the communicative structure of society. Unless one wishes to conjure in his imagination a very fanciful society he must admit that the servant of public opinion is forced to make an assessment of the expressions of public opinion that come to his attention and that in this assessment consideration is given to expressions only to the extent to which they are judged to "count." . . .

Chapter 12

Dynamics of the public

*I*N A SENSE the issue and the mode of registration of opinion are the pivots about which interaction within the public must develop. The issue provides reason for the existence of a public, and the registration of opinion is the accomplishment of the public. Within this framework, the intrapublic processes take place.

Aspects of the public. Nelson N. Foote and Clyde W. Hart have proposed that the processes within the public be viewed according to an idealized series of *phases*.* In the first or *problem phase* a group of people come to recognize their common situation as problematical and to experience discontent. In the second or *proposal phase* a dominating sense that something has to be done leads to the advancement of many plans of action, some of which are rejected and others of which are accepted. During these first two phases the communication is only partially verbalized. Much of it consists of vague feelings and gestures hardly recognized consciously by the participants themselves. During the third or *policy phase* there is explicit discussion revolving about the plans for action that have been selected in the preceding phase and culminating in group decision and responsible commitment. This phase prepares the way for the final or *program phase* in which the decision is converted into action. In a sense, with this phase the public as a collectivity is supplanted by an organized group—"a self-conscious organization of functionally differentiated persons cooperatively pursuing common objectives." The authors suggest that there may also be a sort of transitional phase that links the completed cycle to the beginning of a new cycle. This they call the *appraisal phase,* in which new problems are defined because of the discrepancy between what was sought and what was attained.

* "Public Opinion and Collective Behavior," in **Group Relations at the Crossroads,** eds. Muzafer Sherif and M. O. Wilson (New York: Harper & Brothers, 1953).

In some situations these phases follow one another, but many publics exist about enduring problems that are in a continuous state of redefinition, with group decision of a sort being registered and affecting programs continuously. Thus the phases are often better labelled *aspects,* all of which occur simultaneously and continuously rather than cyclically in the usual public opinion situation.

Even when there is a defined procedure and moment for the registration of opinion, preceded by an extended preparatory period, the *effective* registration of opinion is continuous. We may illustrate this in the case of the 1954 gubernatorial election in California. Prior to election day, the formally designated time for registering opinion, considerable sentiment was expressed that the incumbent state administration had neglected the Southern California "smog" problem. Just a few weeks before election the governor took several dramatic steps to guarantee state assistance to Los Angeles County and to obtain federal assistance. On election day the governor's wide margin of victory left little doubt that he would have been re-elected even without taking these steps. However, the administration was already committed to a new program which the election results could not alter. Thus the informal registration of opinion during the period when the public had not yet reached a firm decision actually determined program on this matter as much as the subsequent formal registration of opinion.

As we discuss the internal dynamics of the public, therefore, we shall speak of the intercommunication processes among members and groups constituting the public as being simultaneously concerned with all of these aspects—the definition and redefinition of issues, the effort at decision and selection of an effective program, and the effective registration of opinion.

Individual attitudes within the public. Underlying the entire public opinion process are the attitudes, beliefs, images, and sentiments of individuals. The formation and change of these individual attitudes are an important subject matter of social psychology. Much of this area, however, lies outside the field of collective behavior. Only as attitudes get *expressed* and *modified* within the public and, in so doing, make an impact on the opinion of the public, can we be concerned with individual attitudes.

If we think of opinion as an alignment on more immediate issues and of attitude as the more durable inclination toward general values, then the problem for collective behavior becomes how individuals with given attitudes come to express certain opinions. In the formation and change of public opinion the crucial problem is not how *attitudes* change. The problem is how people come to regard certain attitudes rather than others as relevant to the situation at hand, and how they alter opinions by applying different attitudes to the situation. The opinions of individuals may change radically or only slightly while the public is in existence, but we do not look principally to changes in attitudes to account for these shifts.

Addressing himself to the more dramatic switches of opinion that occasionally take place, Edwin H. Paget suggests six general conditions any one of which makes an apparently stable public opinion likely to change. In each instance the condition is one which permits opinion to shift without waiting upon the slower process of fundamental attitude change.

SUDDEN CHANGES IN GROUP OPINION

EDWIN H. PAGET

. . . "Why should there ever be a sudden reversal of group opinion?" Some students of social psychology might deny that these sudden reversals do occur, pointing to customs which go on from generation to generation with little change. But unfortunately, as we have already seen, we cannot accept this conclusion. Although a change may, at times, take many years, at other times the transition is very brief indeed. The results of years of effort may be destroyed in even a few weeks, a warning which cannot be too often repeated. Admitting the danger, then, we must explain its sources. Why are there so many contradictions to the axiom that all things change slowly? And the first major reason for these sudden reversals is that most people act with little reason for acting. During the last war, to take a well-known example, millions of Americans were persuaded by effective propaganda that Germany intended to "conquer the world," that the Kaiser was a lieutenant of Satan. They had very little evidence to support this conclusion. Indeed, historians are still studying the origins of the World War, and although their conclusions are far from final, the verdict of history will probably fail to substantiate the conquest of the world accusation. But in 1917 even unusually intelligent men refused to concern themselves about the historical evidence of war guilt. Instead, their minds were dominated by somewhat unreal but very vivid pictures of Belgium invasions and the resulting cruelty to the population, secret councils of haughty Prussian militarists, and the vision of democracy ultimately triumphant in nearly every country of the world. The foundations of belief, therefore, were very shaky. Then the peace

treaty was signed. A year or two passed. We came to see "glorious" France as an unwilling debtor, trying to "cheat" us of our billions. The news reels showed the ex-Kaiser, a harmless and even kind looking man, chopping wood in his Dutch retreat, certainly no imperial demon. Also, our interest in internationalism and world-wide democracy became confused when confronted by the tangled plans for the League of Nations. We came to think "America first," and our enmity towards Germany was no longer vivid enough to prevent our enjoying plays glorifying the student life of old Heidelberg or cheering the German flyers who had crossed the Atlantic.

An understanding of this change will give us our first conclusion—a group opinion which is neither founded in a thorough comprehension of the points at issue nor supported by strong associations with some enduring prejudice, may easily disintegrate. A man may cheer for a program, but his convictions may be shallow. He may be stirred emotionally, but there may be no permanent basis for his emotions. Yet uncritically, all things seem alike.

But this sudden-reversal problem has a second aspect, one of even greater seriousness to those who guide our social institutions. In forming our conclusions concerning the drift of public opinion, we are all too easily satisfied by a purely formal response. Since millions attend church regularly on Sunday, many conclude that the nation is safely Christian. This complacency may go on for years and even decades. Suddenly we find that in many communities, at least, there is widespread skepticism not only among those who do not attend church but among those who do. Even while they contribute to the church fund and play base ball on the church picnics, many of the members no longer "take religion seriously." It is "all

Reprinted in part by permission of The University of North Carolina Press, from Edwin H. Paget, "Sudden Changes in Group Opinion," **Social Forces**, 7 (Mar., 1929), pp. 440-44.

right for Sunday, but don't preach to me now; I get enough of that from the minister." And although millions openly profess a belief in life immortal, they secretly come to regard death as the end of all things. Yet the *formal response* to religion continues. And those who still examine only the surface fail to see the spread of a skepticism or, worse, of an indifference which should frighten the thoughtful student of religious influence.

The lulling effect of the formal (but semi-meaningless) response which we all make in assenting to beliefs we no longer hold, has a further danger. Those who attempt to direct group opinion tend to neglect the vehement and aggressive persuasive campaign which alone can protect their plans from the callousness of "all too human nature." It is easy to underestimate the need for this conditioning. Of late years many "liberals" have objected to the extremely patriotic history books assigned for study in the elementary grades. They ridicule the picture of the heroic American patriots opposing the heartless British villains. And although we may grant that many of our histories are too nationalistic and too militaristic, we must not forget that these same texts have aided in producing a national consciousness invaluable to this country in hours of crisis. If our educators are to revise the history texts, the nation must find other means of teaching a reasonable patriotism. Merely singing the *Star Spangled Banner* and taking a holiday on Independence Day do not insure us that future generations will understand love of country as it was once understood. And as with patriotism, so with other matters. The response sought should never be a meaningless formality. It should come from a thoughtful understanding of that to which we assent, and from a legitimate but vehement emotional reaction to its many connotations. Only constant alertness assures effective social control.

The third major reason for sudden changes in group opinion results usually from the unwise and over-aggressive actions of those who attempt to direct that opinion. Here is the old story of carrying an acceptable plan to an illogical extreme. Encouraged by group support, men advance rapidly beyond the sympathy of the group. Thus, with little warning, a seemingly safe majority will shrink to an impotent minority. This is a constant danger. A recent illustration is the so-called "reform" movement. It gained considerable public support by advocating the abolishment of the saloon, the closing of all gambling houses, the barring of horse racing, the censorship of obscene books. But their widespread success increased the ambitions of the reformers. They determined to make prohibition "bone-dry" in the dryest possible sense of the word, even though its enforcement necessitated a spy-system repugnant to the public. At the height of their victory, some of the reformers rejoiced that certain alcohol had been poisoned. "They who violate the constitution deserve death." Nor did the reformers stop here. They suppressed books which in other times would have been considered harmless enough. They announced their intention of abolishing ultimately all use of tobacco. Blue laws were to be extended in all directions. Most of this, of course, was mere talk, but there seemed to be enough reality to their plans to alarm the public. As a result, we are now witnessing a reaction which threatens to destroy even the legitimate accomplishments of the reform group. Success is often the prelude to defeat. This should never be forgotten by those who would direct any movement making for social improvement. When we are at the height of victory, we are often but a step from the edge of the cliff.

The fourth reason for the sudden reversals is somewhat related to the one just considered. Here the reversal is made possible by the normal person's willingness to say "yes" to a plan of action, even though that person hold certain less powerful (at the time) objections to that proposal. Thus a man may say, "I like Taylor; he is a good friend of mine." And yet at the same time he may be thinking, "Somehow I don't completely trust Taylor. If it were to his own gain, he might e willing to injure me." Shrewd students of human behavior have long since noted that a man will often defend a belief more warmly when he is not completely certain of its validity than when he is calmly confident that it cannot be disproved. When we are very vehement, we are often endeavoring to convince ourselves as well as our listeners. This conflicting state of mind increases the danger of the reversal in group opinion, for we have as yet very crude means of measuring the degree of popular assent. If we question an individual closely, he may qualify his admiration for his friend, Taylor; but the members of a large group are rarely given an opportunity to state their beliefs exactly. Thus year after year in a certain city hundreds of thousands may vote for extensive bond issues. The politicians may assert loudly that the money expended is greatly improving the city. Those who consistently vote for the bond issues may outnumber those who vote against them by five to three. And yet the political leaders who are planning extensive and necessary improvements (let us assume that they will be improvements) may have either a safe majority or a very shaky one. That is to say, five eighths of the voters may be enthusiastically in favor of the issues. Or this same majority may, for the most part, be very doubtful of their real value and yet, at the same time, be afraid to risk stopping "the growth of the city" by voting against the bonds. This example, you may think, is not entirely a fortunate one, since most politicians are careful to measure the actual strength of the voters' enthusiasm. And probably the more successful do. The all-important fact for us to remember is that the "amateur" politician often neglects to make his study. And yet it is to the unselfish and intelligent interest of these amateur politicians that we must look for a large part of our political and social improvement. Perhaps this explains why the professional politician is usually victorious in his struggle with the so-called better elements. The novice is notoriously content with one or two victories. He fails to realize that the public must be watched

constantly; that even while they vote for a project, a deadly doubt or indifference may be growing in their minds.

The fifth major cause for sudden reversals in group opinion is akin to the one just discussed in that it arises from hidden factors which the untrained observer may easily overlook. In the final analysis, any group is often opposed not to an evil or an undesirable *force* but rather to an evil or undesirable *situation*. If, therefore, this threatening situation comes later to assume a pleasing aspect, the opposition may quickly collapse. The real evil may continue as before, but few look below the surface of things. Thus a corrupt mayor will order the police department to enforce very strictly all laws against vice for the six months preceding the majority election. And when election day comes, thousands of otherwise intelligent people will vote for the incumbent mayor, the friend of law and order. True, the return to the old situation may cause them to turn against their favorite again, but with election necessary only once every four years, the latitude is great. And as with politics, so with all other social functions. A corrupt or incompetent man may long remain in control.

Those who would check the possibilities of such reversals of well-founded group indignation, must stress the fundamental evils *inherent* in the forces they oppose. They must resist the alluring temptation to give undue emphasis to temporary embarrassments of their opponents. This temporary embarrassment will surely pass. It may even be succeeded by a very favorable outlook. At the least, the gloom of the present may make even a brief rift in the clouds seem the coming of perpetual sunshine. But the fundamental causes for the evils will probably remain. And although it is more difficult to educate the group to understand the underlying and less obvious forces making for maladjustment or corruption, such an education once accomplished is reasonable surety for permanent support. And here again we see the need for a complete study of this sudden reversal phenomenon in all its phases. Those who would advance their own selfish and often anti-social interests have little to lose by playing the game of expediency. But those who direct any extensive plan for progressive action are in grave danger at every turn. They must constantly guard against any sudden reversal which would destroy years of work. And yet these same workers are, for the most part, astonishingly ignorant of the real cause for these disasterous reversals. Time after time they exaggerate and magnify the unpleasant situations which their opponents have created, not realizing that by doing so they give the opposition an opportunity to win widespread public favor by even a comparatively slight amelioration of that situation.

There is, in addition, a sixth cause for any sudden change. Here the danger arises from the possibility that a leader of an opposing and reactionary movement may be given an opportunity to capture the imagination of the public. "Imagination" is a vague word, of course, but there is as yet no better word to describe the object of the appeal. In Italy, for example, the socialistic groups, who were endeavoring to work out an extensive social program, were rather suddenly overcome by Mussolini and his Facisti. Because of the peculiar conditions existing before the rise of the Facisti, conditions conducive to the advancement of radical

experimentation, the student of history might have concluded that the liberal and socialistic forces would retain control for some years before being overthrown by the inevitable reaction. Instead, their downfall was sudden, complete, and final. Mussolini appealed to the "imaginations" of the Italian people. He became the new Caesar, the strong, fearless man destined to restore order and prosperity to a weary nation. He promised to place Italy in her proper place, a leader in European affairs. Rome was to be born again. Glory and a New Order! For the first time in decades, Italy turned her eyes toward the future.

Mussolini is, I grant, an extreme example, but fairly similar changes occur everywhere. "Facts," "reasons," and "evidence" have rarely gained a secure hold on the minds of most men. On the contrary, the logical elements very often create a "heavy and dry" atmosphere, an admirable time for a reactionary movement to win a sweeping victory by some bold appeal to the imagination. Those who are directing social improvements forget at their peril to advance some symbol which will catch the fancy of the group whose support must be maintained. They who pride themselves upon their logic and reasonableness are only too prone, at times, to overlook the far different forces motivating most human action.

Some of Paget's discussion deals with the frequent difference between what people may be thinking, or perhaps only vaguely feeling, and what they are saying. What they are saying or not saying and the way they are saying it are crucial to the momentary state of public opinion. But the discrepancies between these expressions and the unstated thoughts and feelings may become a dynamism leading to opinion changes. This thesis has been elaborated by Tom Harrison on the basis of a distinction between public and private opinion.* What a person says only to his wife, to himself, or in his sleep constitutes his private opinion. What he will say to a stranger is public opinion. (It should be noted that public opinion is being used here as the opinions people will express as members of a public rather than as the effective opinion of a collectivity.)

Harrison argues that the private opinion is unlikely to become public opinion unless it has social sanction. Such sanction may be provided by the support of a single prestigeful person or by the prestige of large numbers of lesser individuals.

* "What is Public Opinion?" **Political Quarterly**, 11 (1940), pp. 368–83.

In the absence of such sanction private opinion may gradually veer away from the prevalent public opinion. At the moment when sanction is forthcoming public opinion may change drastically, almost overnight. Those who have listened only to public opinion will be shocked at the seeming fickleness of the public. Those who have been paying attention to more indirect and subtle indicators of private opinion will have been able to anticipate the change.

In presenting the idea of *social sanction,* Harrison is pointing out that the individual's *group identifications* determine the opinions he will express. Not only the superficial expression of opinion but the genuine convictions of an individual at any given time are extensively affected by his group identifications. To the extent to which a person identifies himself strongly with any group, he feels ill at ease when his opinions are not those of the group. To the degree to which he feels that the members of a group are "his kind of people," he will be inclined to bring to the fore those attitudes within himself which will permit him to hold the group opinion as his own.

The foregoing idea has been expressed under various labels. The term "reference group" is sometimes used in the sense of an *identification group* with the implication that the process takes place as described above. Leon Festinger has restated the same principle in distinguishing the circumstances under which a person's external compliance with the norms of any group will be accompanied by a private acceptance of those norms or will take place without such private acceptance. "Public compliance *with* private acceptance will occur if there is a desire on the part of the person to remain in the existing relationship with those attempting to influence him." *

Under some circumstances it is useful to think of the units composing the public as groups rather than individuals. To the extent to which the members of a family feel constrained to present a common front on issues of public dispute, the family rather than the individual becomes the unit of participation. The same principle applies to larger groups. Members of a group may take a strong and uniform stand on an issue concerning which they neither know nor care anything except that they have been informed of the group position.

Communication and decision patterns within the public. Both the course of communication and the content of communication within the public depend first of all upon the pre-established channels of communication within the society. The pre-existing conceptions of what it is proper to say to a minister, to a politician, to a neighbor, to an employer, to a competitor, etc. will affect the opinions that get communicated to persons in any of these roles. The pre-existing *directions* of communication, as between persons of high and low prestige, are likely to be maintained within the public, and the unequal influence of different individuals will extend to the public.

Among the consequences of the pre-existing status system may be the existence of a sort of *elite public* which maintains a continuity of membership from issue to issue. Such a group constitutes the forum to which the official decision-makers refer questions of policy and program, and upon whose decision they depend, so long as the larger publics retain them in power. An *elite public* may

* Leon Festinger, "An Analysis of Compliant Behavior," in **Group Relations at the Crossroads,** eds. Muzafer Sherif and M. O. Wilson (New York: Harper & Brothers, 1953), pp. 232–55,

be entirely unofficial, and its function is not only to decide issues as an independent public, but to interpret and take account of the broader public opinion so that in a crucial test its decisions will be backed by those of the larger publics Floyd Hunter has contended that such an elite public, to which the Republican national administration referred issues of policy and program, was an important force in the United States in 1954. The elite public consisted of a core of about twenty individuals, located throughout the nation, some of whom held public office and some of whom did not, but all of whom knew each other on a somewhat informal basis. Through the informal discussions of this elite public in primary group situations many of the important policies of the national administration were shaped.

Superimposed upon the established community prestige structure is a structure peculiar to each public. Participants divide into *instigators* and *receivers* according to the direction of persuasive efforts, and into *opinion leaders* who mediate and interpret the communication for most of the receivers. The difference between instigators and receivers is one of degree, since anyone who expresses an opinion or asks a question is exercising some influence. Furthermore, the roles of particular individuals and groups may shift in the course of the public, so that a receiver becomes actively identified with a position and attempts vigorously to shape the definition of issues and the alignments of others within the public. The instigators are often representatives of formal organizations, such as political party organizations, industries, labor unions, and churches. Since members of the public are likely to discount communications from organizations which have too obvious a stake in the outcome of public deliberations, such organizations frequently attempt to remain hidden while cultivating other conspicuous instigator groups. The organizational instigators then operate through some "citizens' committee," which is represented as being spontaneously aroused about the issue under consideration. Public opinion often revolves as much about the question of who are the true instigators as it does about the merits of the issue itself.

Opinion leaders are those upon whose judgment other members of the public depend. Most of them are not the instigators, but merely those among the receivers to whom others turn because of their generalized prestige or because they are thought to have special competence in the matters under discussion.

While there are communication chains linking all sections of the public, most of the discussion takes place within separate *discussion universes*. Discussion universes tend to be separated from one another in at least three important ways. First of all, the amount of discussion that takes place among people within any such universe is greater than that which takes place between people from different universes. Second, the frankness and completeness of discussion are greater within a discussion universe than between universes. And finally, each discussion universe is characterized by a somewhat distinctive framework of values and thought within which the issues are defined and interpreted and the arguments evaluated. Fundamentally, it is this third characteristic that creates the discussion universe and leads to the first two characteristics.

The discussion universes are, in a sense, subsidiary publics within the larger public. The members of a discussion universe do not necessarily agree on the issue, but they do argue on the basis of a common frame of reference. Occupational groups, people from common educational backgrounds, people with similar religious orientations, people with common economic interests, are among the kinds of groups which may become discussion universes. People with a common religious frame of reference may disagree on the issue of participation in war, but they will agree in relating the concrete issue before the larger public to their shared religious values and conceptions. The same individual may be a member of several different discussion universes, but the manner in which he defines and argues the issues will be different in each discussion universe.

Discussion universes with sharply defined frames of reference and with commitments which preclude members' participation in other discussion universes become *interest groups*. In the broadest sense interest groups are bodies to whom a standing issue is of such general and sustained importance that they assimilate current issues to this standing issue, rather than treating each current question in its unique aspects. Thus a group may be committed to the cause of labor to the extent that they will subordinate the consideration of any specific issue to the general question of whether their vote is pro-labor or anti-labor. Since many individual members of these interest groups might otherwise be inclined to examine issues on their individual merits, or may not see the strategic relation of any particular issue to the interests of the group, spokesmen play an important role in translating particular issues into interest-group terms.

In popular usage, "interest group" is a term of invective rather than a term of analysis. To label a group an interest group is to condemn its members as having ulterior motives. But everyone has "ulterior motives" in the sense of pre-existing conceptions in terms of which they view current issues. It is only from the vantage point of one interest group which regards its own frame of reference as the only justifiable one that the motives of other interest groups are labelled "ulterior."

To some degree all people belong to interest groups, but certain interest groups may be more conspicuous in their operation than others. Such is the case of minority groups, among whom each issue is frequently translated into its significance for minority-majority relations before a judgment is made. With the tenuousness of the relation between many current issues and minority interests, there is abundant opportunity for minority leaders to manipulate "blocs," either in terms of their honest assessment of the issues or considerations of personal gain. Henry Moon offers a generalized judgment regarding the role which Negroes as such an interest group have played in American politics.

VOTES FOR SALE
HENRY LEE MOON

That the Negro vote is singularly ignorant, venal, and corrupt is a widely held generalization in American politics. Indeed no other segment of the American electorate has been so consistently maligned with the charge of vote selling.

Professed liberals and confirmed conservatives alike share this appraisal of the Negro's political morality and frequently express it in such a manner as to convey the impression that venality is a uniquely racial trait practically unknown among voters of other races. The supporters of the party or candidate *against* whom the bulk of the Negro vote may be cast can be depended upon to raise this cry. It has

Selections from Chapter II, "Votes For Sale," in Henry Lee Moon, **Balance of Power: The Negro Vote** (Garden City: Doubleday & Co., 1949), pp. 39–53.

proved to be a much easier way of accounting for the preferences of the Negro voters than an honest examination of the failings of the repudiated faction, party, or candidate. A common complaint of a defeated candidate in any community where there is a sizable Negro vote is his lack of funds to "buy" that vote.

Certainly some Negroes have sold their vote for cash or other considerations. There is, however, no evidence that this practice has been more common among Negroes than among other voters. . . .

The average reformer's cavalier unconcern for the welfare of the race, his remoteness from the day-to-day problems which confront Negroes, and his post-election forgetfulness all present hazards to the Negro voter who may desire to support certain reforms. Half a century ago Du Bois discerned this dilemma in his study of the Philadelphia Negro. Then a young man of high ideals, he was shocked and disturbed by the common-place political bargaining through which the machine controlled the city. Even so, "the paradox of reform" was clear to him. "Suppose," he ventured, "the Municipal League or the Woman's School-board movement, or some other reform is brought before the better class of Negroes today; they will nearly all agree that city politics are notoriously corrupt, that honest women should replace ward heelers on school-boards, and the like. But can they vote for such movements? Most of them will say No; for to do so will throw many worthy Negroes out of employment: these very reformers who want votes for specific reforms will not themselves work beside Negroes, or admit them to positions in their stores or offices, or lend them friendly aid in trouble. Moreover Negroes are proud of their councilmen and policemen. What if some of these positions of honor and respectability have been gained by shady 'politics' —shall they be nicer in these matters than the mass of the whites? Shall they surrender these tangible evidences of the rise of their race to forward the goodhearted but hardly imperative demands of a crowd of women? Especially, too, of women who

did not apparently know there were any Negroes on earth until they wanted their votes? Such logic may be faulty, but it is convincing to the mass of Negro voters." [1]

Most Negroes would agree with Gunnar Myrdal that they "are grossly discriminated against in what they get from politics just as they are in their exercise of the right to vote." From the reformers, at least until the advent of Franklin D. Roosevelt in the White House, they got practically nothing—or, too often, a post-election kick in the face. What little they have obtained in the way of benefits has come most generally from machine politicians—often the heads of corrupt machines—all the way from Republican President U. S. Grant to Democratic Mayor Ed Kelly of Chicago. To a people such as the American Negro, socially circumscribed and economically depressed, the most important spoils of politics are job opportunities in both public and private employment and on varying levels, protection of civil rights, equality of access to public facilities, and adequate provisions for housing, health, schools, and recreation. For a small but often politically influential group there is the added demand for protection of illicit practices, most frequently policy and other forms of gambling, and soft penalties for infractions of the law.

In terms of these objectives, the Negro probably attained his greatest recognition under the lush administrations of Big Bill Thompson of Chicago, 1915–23 and 1927–31. It was generally acknowledged that Mayor Thompson leaned heavily upon the Negro vote for his repeated victories at the polls. He discharged his obligation to this electorate to such a conspicuous extent that his political enemies —and they were many and powerful— dubbed the City Hall "Uncle Tom's Cabin." Unabashed, the mayor "did not hide his colored appointees in the back rooms but he gave them the regular places to which their positions entitled them. As the size of his majorities in the Black Belt increased at each election, so the amount

---

[1] W. E. B. Du Bois, **The Philadelphia Negro** (Philadelphia: University of Pennsylvania publication, 1899), pp. 383–84.

of recognition he gave this section in the form of patronage also increased." [2]

Under Mayor Thompson's administration the Negro forged ahead politically as he had not done anywhere since Reconstruction. This was not alone a measure of the mayor's attitude or his political sagacity. It was primarily the result of an exceptionally astute Negro leadership which knew what it wanted and how to go about getting it. In Edward H. Wright the Negro community had a skilled and seasoned politician. Associated with him were others who, under his guidance, quickly learned the art and science of ward politics at a time when they could turn this knowledge to effective use. Thompson came to power during the period of accelerated expansion of the black belt. Attracted by the high industrial wages of World War I and driven from their homes by discrimination and lynch terror, tens of thousands of southern Negroes flocked to Chicago during the decade 1910–20. This influx more than doubled the black belt population, which rose from 44,103 to 109,458. In the next decade the Negro population continued to grow, expanding by 114 per cent—to 233,903. It was these new voters, Republican by tradition, who, crowded into the black ghetto, supplied the base of operations for the Negro politicians and gave to the latter power in the city's politics through solid support of the Thompson faction in the Republican party.

The eagerness with which these migrants turned to political action gave ample refutation to the charge that their acceptance of disfranchisement in the South was an expression of apathy. Organized on a ward and precinct basis, they responded to the exhortations of their new leaders, who developed an enviably effective political machine. As a result, 77 per cent of the potential Negro vote was registered in 1920 as compared with 68 per cent for the city as a whole. This heavy registration gave to the Negro leaders the necessary bargaining power. In four primaries Thompson received more than 80 per cent of the Republican vote in the Second Ward, in which most of the Negroes were concentrated. In the 1927 primary he received 94 per cent of the party vote in that ward. This support was essential to his nominations and elections. Negro support of Thompson, Gosnell reports, survived "political landslides, economic depressions, graft revelations and other ground swells that affected voters in other parts of the city." [3]

It was not mere loyalty to the party of Lincoln and Thompson which consolidated the Negro vote behind the mayor. It was the conviction that Negroes were getting something out of this political solidarity. The ambitious young men were finding a new outlet for their talents. Thompson appointed Bishop Archibald E. Carey to the Civil Service Commission and Wright as assistant corporation counsel. These were just the opening appointments. In the various legal departments of the city, county, and state, Negroes were represented, not by one, but, in many instances, by several appointees. The number of Negro police, teachers, and other public servants was greatly increased and opportunities for promotion facilitated. Young Negro women who previously had but little opportunity to use their training as stenographers and clerks found openings in the civil service. Negro candidates, running on the Thompson ticket, were elected to the Board of Alderman and to both houses of the state legislature. One became the first Negro judge in the North elected on a city-wide basis. And finally it was in this period that with Thompson's aid, Oscar De Priest was elected to Congress in 1928 as the first Negro representative since 1901.

What else did Negroes get out of their support of Thompson, whose regime has been widely publicized as the acme in corrupt machine politics? It was Thompson's boast that he started the playground movement in America when he established the first public playground in a predominantly Negro neighborhood. Yet recreational facilities for Negroes re-

[2] Harold F. Gosnell, **Negro Politicians** (Chicago: University of Chicago Press, 1935), p. 55.

[3] Ibid., p. 43.

mained woefully inadequate. It was during one of Mayor Thompson's administrations that the disastrous race riot of 1919 occurred. Contributing to this outbreak were the insufficiency of recreational outlets, the lack of adequate housing to meet the needs of the swelling Negro population, as well as the economic fears and tensions which were the aftermath of the war. Thompson's regime further offered the protection which the Negro underworld demanded, but the activities of these black parasites were neither as vicious nor as remunerative as those of white gangsterdom which flourished in the Chicago post-war era. While the Negro made gains under Thompson, his regime was not an unmixed blessing.

The temptation to irregularity was certainly present, but it was not always a matter of pecuniary gain. The Negro voter certainly has been no less hesitant than other citizens to align himself with corrupt political machines in his group interest. Thus in the Democratic primaries in 1946, Negro voters supported the Pendergast machine of Kansas City, Missouri, in a successful effort to retire Representative Roger C. Slaughter. The Missouri representative, as a key member of the important House Rules Committee, had been, perhaps, the one person most responsible for the refusal of that committee to submit to the House the bill for a permanent FEPC. He had boasted: "I sure as hell opposed the bill for a Fair Employment Practices Commission, and I'm proud of the fact that my vote [in the Rules Committee] was what killed it." The labor movement, through the CIO-PAC, joined in the fight against Slaughter. President Harry S. Truman personally intervened to assure the defeat of the man who had held up legislation which the President had expressed a desire to have enacted.

In the Fifth Congressional District which Slaughter represented there were 21,000 potential Negro voters, constituting approximately 15 per cent of the total vote. In the 1944 general election, Slaughter had been re-elected, with the support of the Pendergast machine, by a margin of 5193 votes. In view of the strength of the Negro vote in his district, his open hostility to FEPC seemed to indicate that Congressman Slaughter did not care for this vote or that he did not believe colored citizens were intelligent enough to vote in their own interest. In the next election he was defeated by a margin of 2783, with 7000 Negro votes cast against him. His vote in the thirty predominantly Negro precincts was negligible. In two of these precincts he received not a single vote, and the highest was 35. This solid Negro vote was the decisive factor in the defeat of Slaughter. In the subsequent general election, the Democratic nominee was defeated by the Republican candidate. Later, charges of fraud in the primary election were made. To the Negro voter, however, the important thing was the retirement from public life of a man who sought to deny them equality of job opportunity, their paramount demand today.

Except for Chattanooga and Memphis, Tennessee, and San Antonio, Texas, Negroes have not been an important factor in recent years in the political machines of any southern city. What they have been able to get out of these political organizations is far less than what their brothers have been able to get out of political machines in Chicago, New York, Philadelphia, or Cleveland. While in San Antonio the Negro vote has been for years vital and, indeed, at one time the virtual political boss of the city was a Negro, little recognition has been given to the race in the form of patronage. The chief reward has been in the form of protection for the illicit practices of the Negro boss and his fellow gamesters. In Memphis, Negro supporters of Boss Crump point with pride to the overcrowded colored schools (better equipped and more numerous than elsewhere in the South), the recreation center, the shabby Negro park, the paved streets in the ghetto, the flourishing Negro businesses as evidences of Crump's beneficence and the opportunities for racial development afforded by his control of that city. In none of these cities have reform movements been able to make any appreciable headway, in part at least, because they have been unable or unwilling to offer Negro voters even as little as they now get from the machine. In Memphis, reformers commonly begin their attack upon Crump by focusing attention upon and discrediting his Negro supporters. This does not make for votes in the Negro community, even though many of its citizens may be dissatisfied with the present regime. Maury Maverick made this mistake in San Antonio in 1938 and alienated potential Negro support.

What is the price of the Negro's vote? What does he demand for it and what has he been able to buy with it? The price he can command depends upon a number of factors: the number and strategic location of qualified colored voters; the type of leadership and the degree of organization; the possibilities for favorable alliances, as with a labor or progressive group, or a political machine; the extent of division prevailing in the community at large and the competition for his ballot; the local political climate; the presence or absence of race as an issue in the campaign, and the degree of integration into the existing party structures. These are the factors which determine the value of the Negro's vote. How much can he buy with it? In general, he has not been able to get as much for his vote as have members of other groups. However, in some instances, as Bunche points out, the Negro population "has been given an opportunity to exert a political influence often far in excess of its numerical strength in the particular locality." Nowhere, however, has he been able to use the ballot to solve his basic social and economic problems. Amelioration—yes. Solution—no.

Expansion and contraction of the public. Public opinion and deliberations within the public may change without alteration of existing alignments through the addition of new members or the withdrawal of old members. The public expands as more people become interested enough to enter into discussion of the issue. The public contracts as persons lose interest and cease to participate in the interaction processes contributing to the registration of public opinion.

The boundary of a public may exist more as a theoretical construct than as an empirical reality. Mere interest and attention to communication do not necessarily constitute membership in a public. Studies indicate that many persons listened to enemy radio propaganda during the war for amusement and because it provided interesting material for conversation, but without ever thinking of taking the material seriously. On the other hand, the listener group included proportionately somewhat more people from these groups who were inclined to be discontented with policies of their own government, suggesting that in some vague sense they may have been exploring issues which they did not verbalize to themselves.

For an election public, the extent of nonvoting may be sometimes taken as an indication of the numbers outside of the public. However, nonvoting may itself be an important way of registering opinion, or it may reflect an inability to resolve conflicting opinions of a vital sort.

Nonmembership in a public may reflect mere lack of interest, or it may reflect withdrawal and suppression of interest because of unwillingness to suffer the psychological turmoil which the issue creates in the individual. Martin Kriesberg shows how such loss of interest may be one of the consequences of conflicting pressures on the individual.

CROSS-PRESSURES AND ATTITUDES
MARTIN KRIESBERG

In recent years, organized pressure groups have increasingly concerned themselves with activities designed to influence public opinion. Public relations budgets of many organizations have been increased; groups hitherto confining their activities to informing their membership have taken to mass media; "institutional" and "ideological" advertising appear more and more frequently in newspapers and magazines. America is characterized by considerable freedom for the political propagandist and by consummate skill in promotional campaigns.

These attributes of our society raise problems in public opinion analysis which merit serious study. One such problem is the effect which conflicting propaganda has upon people's attitudes. In the face of conflicting propaganda will people's opinions be more or less moderate? Will the individual become more interested and better informed on the issue, or less so?

The following study, designed to investigate these questions in connection with attitudes on American foreign policy, suggests these conclusions:

First, in an environment where people are exposed to contending propaganda regarding issues of foreign policy, relatively few individuals are aware of the conflicting interpretations to which they are exposed. Most of the people do not know that they are subjected to conflicting propaganda, and many, consciously or unconsciously, avoid continued exposure to the contradictory influences.

Second, those who remain exposed to conflicting propaganda on a foreign policy issue are more moderate in their opinions, but moderation is manifested in various ways, according to the individual's

Reprinted by permission of the Princeton University Press, from Martin Kriesberg, "Cross-Pressures and Attitudes: A Study of the Influence of Conflicting Propaganda on Opinions Regarding American-Soviet Relations," **Public Opinion Quarterly,** 13 (Spring, 1949), pp. 5–16.

interest and information on the subject. The unconcerned and the uninformed tend to be unaware that they are exposed to conflicting influences; their attitudes tend toward uncertainty and inconsistency. The interested and the informed tend to be aware of conflicting influences and to consciously select one point of view, while rationalizing their rejection of the others. However, although these individuals give greater credence to one body of propaganda than the other, their resultant opinions are more moderate than those of people not in a conflict situation.

Third, those who remain exposed to strong cross-pressures appear to be less interested in the controversial foreign policy issue than those primarily subject to one or the other influence. The effect of conflicting propaganda upon levels of information could not be ascertained.

THE RESEARCH DESIGN

Creating a research design which would reveal the effect of conflicting influences upon attitudes is complicated by the multiplicity of variables affecting opinions. The problem is somewhat simplified by constructing a study around those determinate influences which, in a given situation, are likely to have a decided effect upon attitudes, as for instance the factor of race on opinions about anti-lynching legislation. This suggests that one might begin with a particular issue and work back to specific factors or forces which are likely to affect opinions on that issue. Then, by selecting those forces which are in conflict regarding the issue and by locating an environment in which these forces are operative, the effect of cross-pressures may more readily be ascertained.

With this approach in mind, the subject of American-Soviet relations was selected for study as one of intrinsic interest and importance and one upon which determinate forces were likely to have a decided influence. Two polar opinion groups which exercise conflicting influences on opinions about American-Soviet relations immediately came to mind: the Catholic Church and the Communist Party. Having arrived at this juncture, the problem was to locate people who were subject simultaneously to the influence of the Church and the Party.

Investigation of various geographic and social groupings led to the search for a trade union population in which Catholic and Communist influences might be evidenced. Both organizations were known to participate actively in certain trade unions and, taking unequivocal stands on the subject of American-Soviet relations, both were likely to urge their views upon union members.

A trade union was located which seemed to meet the research prerequisites. The probability of conflicting influences was high, since more than 65 per cent of the group were Catholics and a number of the union's local officers and rank and file admitted to Communist Party membership. Moreover, the trade union was reputed, in union circles, to be Communist led at the national level. The survey took place in an eastern city with a large Catholic population. During the period of the study, 1946, the secular press in the area tended to reenforce the Church viewpoint on American-Soviet relations. At the same time, rank and file members of the union were not only exposed to union members purveying the Party viewpoint but also to the union newspaper. This newspaper, mailed weekly to every member of the union, closely followed the line of the *Daily Worker* on the subject of American-Soviet relations.

After a population which was apparently exposed to conflicting influences had been selected, the cooperation of union officials and rank and file was solicited. In every local, cordial relations were established.

Pretest interviews were first made among members of two other trade unions and one local of the union population studied. The pilot survey was designed to test the questionnaire and the manner of interviewing to be employed. As a result of the pretest, it was decided to conduct interviews at union meetings, since interviewing the workers at home or in the shop proved to have several shortcomings. Of these, the most important for purposes of this study was that only a small proportion of those interviewed at home or at the shop came to union meetings or read their union newspaper. It appeared that people who did not come to meetings and did not read the union paper were less likely to be exposed to the Party point of view—one of the two conflicting influences.

Before each meeting, the author was introduced to the membership by the local business agent or presiding officer. The author would then indicate the nature of the study and solicit cooperation. The introduction pointed out the nature of the study: a public opinion poll among working people to learn their views on foreign affairs. At the conclusion of these brief remarks, the author introduced an assistant interviewer and informed the membership that he and his assistant would pass among them soliciting interviews.

Respondents were asked to accompany the interviewer to a convenient place in the rear of the meeting hall or to an adjoining room; almost none were reticent in responding. While a standard questionnaire was used, interviewers were instructed to use probes extensively. Each local was visited several times until approximately 10 per cent of the number usually present had been interviewed. In all, 103 interviews were made from the six locals included in the analysis.

FEW RESPONDENTS AWARE OF CROSS-PRESSURES

Perhaps the most important finding in this study of cross-pressures is the small number of individuals who evidenced awareness of conflicting influences. While all those interviewed were subject to some degree of conflicting propaganda and one-fourth could be classified as subject to "strong" cross-influences only a handful indicated that they were conscious of the contending influences.

Three probable reasons for widespread unawareness may be advanced: (1) Opinions are functional and the process of individual adjustment to conflict situations operates against acceptance of both Catholic and Communist viewpoints; (2) a large proportion of those interviewed lacked interest in issues of foreign policy and therefore both sets of propaganda were ineffectual; (3) the Communist propaganda was operative in an "inhibitive" context and even in the selective population studied was relatively weak compared to the Catholic.

Opinions, like group membership, are functional; they are part of the individual's social and psychological adjustment. From his earliest years the individual learns that certain opinions bring social approbation; others bring disapproval. He learns that certain opinions are approved by some people and disapproved by others. Opinions serve to rationalize social and physical environments. One individual believes that success accrues to hard work and frugality, another that it depends on luck and "drag." Both views help give meaning to a given situation, such as the individual's position in society. The body of beliefs which make up Catholicism and Communism, the cross-influences involved in this study, tend to be mutually exclusive means to comparable end satisfactions. In terms of psychological satisfaction, the two systems may be viewed as similarly authoritarian, similarly offering an integrated explanation of the individual's world, and offering similar satisfactions as a faith larger than the individual.

The functional nature of opinion suggests that cross-pressures are likely to be avoided. Among the respondents there was a tendency to change either their beliefs or their allegiance and thereby to resolve the conflict. Catholics who most nearly reflected the opinions of the Left tended to draw away from the religious fold. Several of the men in this category remarked that while their wives or their families went to church, they did not; others reported that the Church was biased or should stay out of politics. It is also likely that a number of those interviewed, having been perturbed by the conflicting influences, had achieved a resolution of the difficulty by rejecting the subject of American-Soviet relations, as well as, or together with, the contestants.

Another means of avoiding conflicting influences, and a second factor making for relatively few cases in which cross-pressures were felt, is lack of interest in the issue involved. Apathy about foreign affairs was manifested by many respondents, and suggests that arguments presented by the Left frequently fell on non-absorbent minds; Church pronouncements on the subject probably met with similar disinterest. Therefore neither contradictions nor conflicts were perceived. Closely related to lack of interest, and perhaps causally related, is lack of information by which to evaluate arguments of either Church or Party. Inability to see the relationship between conflicting arguments or their relevance for the individual further militates against their having a serious effect upon him. This was particularly the case among women in the population studied. On the one hand, the Church had a greater influence upon their opinions than it did on the views of their menfolk. On the other hand, the women interviewed were generally members of locals where the Left influence was strongest. Despite this environment of cross-pressures, few women interviewed were conscious of conflicting influences.

A third factor making for a paucity of cross-pressure consciousness was the "inhibitive" context in which the Party line was conveyed and perceived. Despite the selective nature of the population studied, Communist propaganda was less pervasive than that of the Church. The Left influence was retarded by the status of its purveyors in relation to other sources of information. Opinions presented by most fellow workers tended to be discounted when opposed by the more widely accepted authority of Church or of secular commentators and columnists. Time and again respondents reported that none of the men in the shop or union were better informed on Russia than they. Nor did the rank and file ascribe superior knowl-

edge to the union leadership; to most respondents, they were merely fellow workers. Moreover, ideas presented by the
Church, the secular city press, and the
national mass media tended to reinforce
one another, thereby increasing the disparity in weight between the views of the
Left and of the prevailing environmental
ideology.

The Left was further handicapped because its protagonists were occasionally
tagged "Communist." Opinions advanced
by men so labelled were discredited or derided by many of the workers interviewed.
Moreover, formal discussion of Russia
was usually avoided at union meetings.
Where pro-Party men were in power,
Communists were content to remain in-
cognito and preferred not to raise "disruptive" issues. Where anti-Party men
were in office, issues related to Russia
were generally considered outside the pale
of union activities.

EFFECT OF INTEREST AND INFORMATION
ON OPINIONS UNDER CROSS-PRESSURES

What were the reactions of those people who, despite the inhibitive context of
Communist propaganda and the individual tendency to avoid cross-pressure situations, were subject to strong conflicting
influence of Party and Church? As might
be expected, strong cross-pressures made
for moderation of opinions but, significantly, moderateness was manifested differently according to the respondent's
interest and information on American-
Soviet relations. Among respondents who
were unconcerned and uninformed, there
was unawareness of conflict and moderateness was manifested by uncertainty and
inconsistency. In the long run, these people might be expected to withdraw from
both influences and to move toward general apathy on the issue.

None of the respondents subject to
strong cross-pressures were vehemently
anti-Soviet or doctrinaire pro-Soviets.
This moderation was probably the result
of several contributing factors. First, such
cross-pressures occurred among individuals who were open to influence by both
sides. When the individual dogmatically
adhered to one viewpoint, he was not
likely to listen to propaganda for the
other. Second, the individual was cate-
gorized as subject to strong cross-pressures only if he had been exposed to
considerable influence from both sides.
Finally, many respondents subject to
cross-pressures were worried about American-Soviet tension. For some of these,
anxiety was related to a desire to see Russia in a more friendly light.

While cross-pressures tended to induce
moderation, this absence of polar opinions was manifested differently according
to the respondent's interest in and information on American-Soviet relations.
Among the more interested and informed
respondents there was a recognition of the
conflicting views to which they were exposed; they were aware of both Catholic
and Communist ideologies. While recognizing the opposite view they consciously
accepted one in preference to the other.
The positions of these respondents were
frequently well structured; their views
were consistent and often cogently expressed.

Among the respondents who were interested in American-Soviet relations,
cross-pressures also tended to induce
skepticism of information sources. For
example, among informed respondents
who were subject to strong cross-pressures
there was a tendency to believe that both
Church and union reports were slanted.
For them either the secular press was a
poor best choice or they trusted none of
the three sources.

Among the less interested and the less
well informed, moderateness was manifested by uncertainty and inconsistency.
The number of "don't know" and "no
opinion" responses increased in inverse
proportion to the level of interest and information. Frequently respondents who
were little interested and poorly informed
indicated that they were uncertain of the
position they took or the "correctness" of
their opinion. However, they were less
skeptical of the honesty of their information sources. Unfamiliar with world affairs generally, these respondents were
uncritical of the information they received. They were often inconsistent in

their views, reporting undigested phrases of both Party and Church ideologies. For example, they would favor international control of the atomic bomb and yet want the United States to have a preponderant voice in the UN; they would state that the Communist Party was controlled by Russia but was not a threat, or vice versa.

This lack of structured opinions on foreign policy issues may be contrasted to attitudes on election issues. For a great many people the social mores of their community or their group affiliation makes voting more or less mandatory. The individual is pressed to decide between alternative views in order to offer some rationalization for his vote decision. However, for most people there is no equivalent social compulsion impelling decisions on foreign policy issues. It is socially acceptable to throw up one's hands at the complexities of America's international relations. While people frequently apologize for not voting, they readily admit their ignorance and indecision on foreign policy issues.

EXPOSURE OF CROSS-PRESSURES ASSOCIATED WITH REDUCED INTEREST

What is the relationship between cross-pressures and information and interest? Are cross-pressures associated with increased interest owing to the suggestion of conflict which makes the issue exciting—or with reduced interest and an expedient adjustment to a difficult decision situation? While the findings are not conclusive, the evidence does suggest that continued exposure to cross-pressures and reduced interest in the issue are correlated.

The assertion that cross-pressures are associated with reduced interest is supported by responses to a question on the importance of American-Soviet policies in influencing voting behavior. Among respondents who were subject to strong cross-pressures, America's Soviet policy was a less important vote determinant than among people primarily subject to only one propaganda. This suggests that respondents subject to strong cross-pressures of Party and Church were less con-

cerned and less interested in the issue of Soviet relations. These people also tended to be less certain of the relative importance of policy toward Russia versus domestic policy as a factor affecting their vote; a larger proportion of them answered the question with "don't know." The evidence apparently confirms Paul Lazarsfeld's finding that cross-pressures tend to reduce interest in election issues.

Although people who remained exposed to cross-pressures were less concerned over U.S. policy toward Soviet Russia, they appeared to be better informed and more prone to discuss the subject than those primarily influenced by the Church. People who were primarily subject to Church influence scored lower on the information and articulation scales than those who were at the same time subject to Communist influence. Indeed, levels of information and articulation were both positively correlated with exposure to Left propaganda.

The fact that respondents who were subject to both influences made higher information scores than those who were primarily influenced by one contestant may, however, be explained as an artifact of the criteria used in categorizing the individual as subject to strong conflicting influences. One of the criteria of strong influence by Church or Party was that the individuals regularly read their respective publications, and readership of the partisan periodicals was highly correlated with wide press and periodical readership generally. Furthermore, respondents under cross-pressures tended to be more concerned with foreign affairs generally than those subject to a single preponderant influence. These factors, suggesting greater familiarity with the subject, may also explain the higher articulation scores made by respondents under strong cross-pressures over those primarily under Church influence. Since the higher information score made by cross-pressure respondents may be an artifact, the relationship between cross-pressures and information is not illuminated by the data.

POSSIBLE POLITICAL IMPLICATIONS

If the findings of this study may b

generalized, the political implications are noteworthy. It has been said that a prerequisite of an informed public opinion on foreign relations is "competing analyses" of the world situation and of America's role in world affairs. It has also been asserted that the answer to certain evils of pressure group propaganda is more propaganda. These arguments are well taken; a multiplicity of viewpoints is essential for an enlightened public opinion. This study suggests, however, that an informed public opinion cannot be left entirely in the hands of interests competing for public acceptance of their particular views. Unless the people have a framework of information in which the arguments may be set, conflicting propaganda may lead to confusion rather than clarification, and may not be conducive to a more enlightened public opinion.

In the first place, the bulk of the people are likely to be unaware of, and unable to differentiate between, conflicting propagandas on foreign policy issues. They may assimilate views of contending interests without being aware of the source or significance of the ideas suggested. Such absorption of information would seem to contribute little toward an enlightened public opinion.

Secondly, people are prone to avoid the conflict of contending propagandas by rejecting one of the contestants or by withdrawing their attention from the contest. The study produced no conclusive evidence that exposure to conflicting opinions makes people better informed, though it presents some evidence that they become less interested in the contested issue. Moreover, if, as seems likely, the uninformed and uninterested tend to avoid the conflict situation by withdrawing attention from the issue, this point takes on special importance because so many Americans lack information and interest in the nation's foreign policies.

Third, although continued exposure to conflicting propaganda apparently makes for moderation of opinion, such moderation is more likely to be a manifestation of confusion and contradiction than the result of a careful weighing of the different viewpoints. Exposure to conflicting influences may not lead to further polarization of opinions, but without an underpinning of interest and basic information it may not mean a more considered opinion at any particular point on an attitude scale.

SUGGESTIONS FOR FURTHER RESEARCH

The effect of cross-pressures upon political attitudes may be studied apart from omnibus national surveys on political behavior. Representative samples of national or community populations are not essential when the hypotheses to be tested are not related to such populations. Instead, small, relatively inexpensive studies may be designed around those groupings which are included in the hypotheses. However, special care is necessary to integrate the small study with related experiments and research programs in order to maximize its contribution.

A study of cross-pressures may be concerned with different levels or kinds of conflicting forces. The study reported here dealt with rather obvious influences, namely, propaganda by specific organizations. The analysis might well be carried on at other levels, e.g., cross-pressures of family group vs. friendship group, work affiliations vs. religious affiliations, personal influences vs. nonpersonal influences. Such an analysis could probably be accomplished by more intensive interviewing and by relating the respondents' opinions to those expressed by the groups with which they are associated. This information would help to establish a rough hierarchy of group influence and to throw light on the broader question of how different group affiliations affect opinion formation.

In designing research to study the influence of cross-pressures it would be profitable to use a longitudinal approach, i.e., to interview the same people over a period of time. This would facilitate an appraisal of the impact made by each body of propaganda or other source of pressure. A study over time would also aid in analyzing the metamorphosis of attitudes when subject to cross-pressures; factors which influence the direction as well as incidence of change could be explored.

To maximize the value of the research, the attitudes assayed should be related to actions such as voting, attending political rallies, or writing members of Congress. A study on action-oriented attitudes is not only more significant politically but facilitates measuring the activating or inhibiting effect of cross-pressures. Where attitudes may be channelized into socially prescribed courses of action, people are more likely to react to their cross-pressure environment in a way permitting measurement.

Political thinking and action are group phenomena, and the importance of group activities in the political life of the nation has not declined but has increased since Pendleton Herring's study stimulated research in the field of pressure groups and politics. There is need for additional research in this area, particularly of pressure group influence upon the political opinions of its members and the public generally. Such studies, drawing upon the instruments and insights of psychologists and sociologists as well as political scientists, would redound to the benefit of the several disciplines.

Except as issues undergo steady revision and events keep alive a vital interest, the large public tends to dwindle rapidly or to become transformed into some other type of group. If interest is kept alive about a somewhat stable issue, the members of the public tend to become *converts,* and the public is transformed into a number of organized groups with embryonic traditions and patterns of group behavior. At this point little is to be gained by trying to change people's affiliations since these are too well stabilized, and what remains is chiefly a power struggle between organized bodies.

Also, as alignments become fixed, there is a tendency for conventions against discussion of the issues to arise. Thus it is regarded as poor manners to discuss religion or politics because the resulting controversy might interrupt the serenity of the trivial. It is thought better that each person should make up his mind in private and register his vote in secret than that tempers should flare in public discussion. The result is the transformation of a public into the mass.

While *enduring* issues tend to destroy the public by turning it into organized groups or into mass behavior, *intense* issues tend to convert the public into crowd behavior. On the one hand, intense convictions giving rise to intolerance may transform the public into separate crowds corresponding with each pre-existing faction. When one faction refuses to let the other be heard, employs physical violence, or in any way refuses to tolerate other positions, the public has ceased to exist. On the other hand, an event may eliminate the issue as a point of controversy and unite the entire public in a single intolerant group. Such was the consequence of the December 7, 1941, Japanese attack on Pearl Harbor. What had been a public concerned with the issue of America's involvement in the war became a single crowd intolerant of any who questioned the necessity of active retaliation and defense.

Conventionalization of the public. The theoretically "ideal" public reflects a spontaneous arousal of interest about an issue that develops out of mass preoccupations with the events of the day. Most of our knowledge concerning the public however, is based on that kind of public which is perhaps furthest from this ideal namely, the election public. Just as we must qualify the application of the principles of crowd behavior when we examine the conventional crowd, so we must note that many of the principles of the public become distorted when the public is conventionalized. The election public is a highly conventionalized type. Alignments of members are largely predetermined by party loyalties. The rules of interaction are largely prescribed and the manner of registering opinion is formally designated. The occasion for the public is a predetermined calendar interval rather than heightened mass preoccupation with particular problems. The margins of indeterminacy are small, though the consequences of small shifts may be proportionately larger for this very reason.

In stressing the extent to which actual voting could be predicted in advance of an actual election, Paul Lazarsfeld points to some of the aspects of conventionalization. Within the context of such a public, he gives us a general overview of the processes of opinion determination and influence in a single American community.

THE ELECTION IS OVER

Paul F. Lazarsfeld

In an important sense, modern Presidential campaigns are over before they begin.

This is the conclusion that emerges from an intensive study of Erie County, Ohio, during the campaign of 1940. Erie County has a population of about 46,000 people, half of whom live in the industrial town of Sandusky and half in the surrounding rural area. The county was chosen for analysis because for decades it has rested nearest the national average in the quadrennial national elections.

The technique employed was not the usual one of polling different representative groups at different times. The same representative sample of 600 people was interviewed seven times, every month beginning with May and ending the week after election day. Four other comparable samples of 600 people each were interviewed at different times during this period, partly for control purposes and partly to get a broader statistical base on the more crucial issues.[1]

In the course of the study the members of the main panel were asked approximately 250 questions. A number of these questions were repeated at each interview: whom they intended to vote for, whom they expected to win, etc. If the vote intention of a respondent had changed between two interviews, he was subjected to a more detailed inquiry centering on why he had changed his mind.

Three types of information resulted from this polling: (1) the kind of material which comes from any regular public opinion poll, with the distinction that more detailed questions than usual were asked; (2) information on the same respondents obtained at different time periods (this made possible a new kind of analysis: studying what happens to a declared political opinion with the passage of time and under different propaganda conditions); (3) the detailed reasons of those people who changed their vote intention.

SOCIAL GROUPING AND THE VOTE

Throughout Erie County there was the usual increase in Democratic votes as the income scale went down. On the same socio-economic level rural people voted more Republican than the residents of Sandusky. Religion played a very large role. On each socio-economic level the

Reprinted by permission of the Publishers, Public Opinion Quarterly, Inc., from Paul F. Lazarsfeld, "The Election is Over," **Public Opinion Quarterly,** 8 (Fall, 1944), pp. 317–30.

[1] Special tabulation showed that the repeated interviews, in themselves, had no influence on opinions. In regard to vote intention, for example, the repeated interviews induced people to make up their minds more quickly but do not change the proportion of Democrats and Republicans as compared with the control groups that were not interviewed repeatedly.

proportion of Republican voters among the Protestants was two to three times as large as among Catholics. The age divisions were striking. Among Protestants, the older the group, the more Republi-

portions of men and women who said they intended to vote. In October, just prior to the election, about 6 per cent of the men and 20 per cent of the women said they did not expect to vote. (It is

POLITICAL PREDISPOSITION

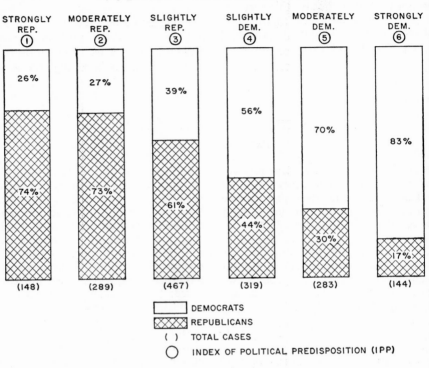

CHART I

This chart illustrates the high correlation of the index of political predisposition to vote intention. High SES level, affiliation with the Protestant religion, and rural residence predispose a voter for the Republican party; the opposites of these factors make for Democratic predisposition.

cans; among Catholics, the older the group, the more Democrats. The younger generation seemed to have a tendency to vote against the trend prevailing in its own socio-religious circle. If socio-economic level was held constant, occupations did not make much difference, although white-collar workers on each level tended to vote slightly less Democratic than other workers.[2]

There was no marked sex difference among the Roosevelt and Willkie voters, but there was great variation in the pro-

usually overlooked that the vast majority of "Don't Know's," just prior to an election, are women who end up by not voting or by going to the polls under the influence of their husbands.) Especially striking was the large number of female

[2] The marked correlation between social groups and votes raised the question whether the voters themselves saw the election in class terms. Here again the more detailed interviews proved valuable. The explanations of the voters made plain that a considerable proportion saw the difference between Republicans and Democrats as one of conflicting class interests.

citizens who bluntly stated that they did not see why women should vote at all.

It became plain, then, that three social factors—religious affiliation, economic status, and residence (urban or rural)—could be combined into a crude *index of political predisposition* (IPP). Thus people could be classified according to whether their social characteristics made it likely that they would vote Democratic or Republican. Chart I, for example, shows that wealthy Protestant farmers, who would have the lowest (i.e., Republican) IPP, had 74 per cent Republicans among their voters, whereas poor Sandusky Catholics, whose IPP was highest, had only 17 per cent Republican voters.

The results of Chart I are based on the interviews made in May with 3,000 people and, of course, pertain only to those respondents who had a definite vote intention at the time. Presumably people with more permanent political allegiances are influenced by their social situation, whereas those who form their decisions in the course of the campaign are freer in their choice. This, however, did not prove to be the case. One group, who might be called the crystallizers, entered the study as "Don't Know's" and made up their minds only during the campaign. These crystallizers were classified by their IPP scores according to whether their social characteristics indicated a Republican or a Democratic predisposition. Seventy-six per cent of those whose IPP suggested Republicanism finally voted for that party; only 26 per cent of those with Democratic IPP voted Republican. The same is true for the people who underwent actual party shifts. The majority changed so that their final vote was more in accordance with their political predisposition than was their vote intention at the beginning of the campaign. There is a mass of additional evidence that as the campaign goes on people are more and more inclined to vote for the party which prevails in their social group. What the campaign seems to do is to activate the political predispositions of people.

One way in which this activation comes about can be traced by studying the common media of communication to which people are exposed. In the course of the repeated interviews we were able to build up a fairly extensive inventory of the items our respondents had read or listened to at different times during the campaign. Chart II pertains to those panel members who did not have a vote intention in August; they are classified according to their political predispositions as indicated by their social characteristics. Clearly their propaganda exposure was closely related to their IPP score. The campaign propaganda does not reach the citizen in the

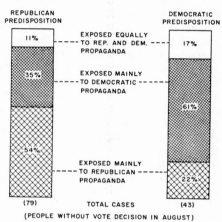

REPUBLICAN PREDISPOSITION — DEMOCRATIC PREDISPOSITION

11% | EXPOSED EQUALLY TO REP. AND DEM. PROPAGANDA | 17%

35% | EXPOSED MAINLY TO DEMOCRATIC PROPAGANDA | 61%

54% | EXPOSED MAINLY TO REPUBLICAN PROPAGANDA | 22%

(79) TOTAL CASES (43)

(PEOPLE WITHOUT VOTE DECISION IN AUGUST)

CHART II

People who have not yet decided about their vote expose themselves more to propaganda of that party to which they are predisposed by background.

proportion in which it is offered. Social environment sifts propaganda; the undecided ones are not easily reached by the propaganda of the party to which their group is generally hostile.

Only about 4 per cent of the Erie County families contained members who had different vote intentions; and when this was the case, the vote intention of each single member was unstable and easily susceptible to influence. The sample was not large enough to permit a study of special social organizations, such as fraternities, Rotary groups, etc. But an interesting result is obtained if people who did and those who did not belong to such organizations are compared.[3] The general finding is that belonging to an organization accentuates political predisposition. Members of the higher socio-economic levels were more likely to vote Republican if they belonged to a social organization. Those on lower socio-economic levels were more likely to vote Democratic if they were members of such formal groups. Superimposed on this result, however, is another trend. If a person of low income happened to belong to an organization the majority of which belonged to higher social strata, then he was more likely to vote Republican.

One other observation furnishes evidence for what might be called the social character of political behavior. One always found people who had a contradictory opinion pattern. They intended to vote for one party but held opinions on one or two specific issues which were more characteristic of the other party. At the time of the next interview many of these respondents had become consistent, inasmuch as their vote intention and their opinion on a specific issue followed the prevailing pattern. In the large majority of cases the people who started out with an inconsistent opinion pattern kept their vote intention but shifted on the specific issue to the opinion prevailing in the political group with which they had associated themselves. Material of this kind bolsters the conclusion that people vote with the social group to which they belong and that these groups in turn are strongly determined by a few basic social characteristics.

RADIO AND PRINT IN THE CAMPAIGN

If the vote of the people who make up their minds during the campaign is so strongly determined by predispositions, then we cannot expect formal media of communication to have a very great effect. What do we know on this subject?

[3] Such a comparison has to be carried through separately on different socio-economic levels because otherwise we would be misled by the fact that the more well-to-do people are, the more likely they are to belong to formal associations.

Detailed analyses were made of the radio, newspapers, and magazines in the early, middle, and late part of the campaign. The content of the local newspapers was about 2-1 favorable toward the Republican Party and, surprisingly enough, the radio had about the same ratio. This is partly due to the fact that the Republicans bought more time on the air for speeches. It also came about because the opposition candidate had more news value. The magazines were the most partisan medium in favor of the Republicans (3-1). In the early part of the campaign they published a considerable number of articles on Willkie, who was a comparatively new figure and whose career lent itself especially well to magazine treatment.

A considerable part of the population was scarcely touched by the political content of the media. In October, when the campaign was nearing its peak, people were shown the front page of the newspaper they regularly read, a list of political articles appearing in the mass magazines with the highest circulation in the

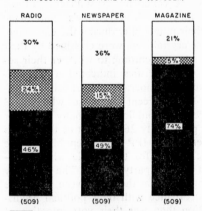

EXPOSURE TO POLITICAL ITEMS (OCTOBER)

RADIO	NEWSPAPER	MAGAZINE
30%	36%	21%
		5%
24%	15%	
		74%
46%	49%	
(509)	(509)	(509)

☐ EXPOSED TO TWO OR MORE POLITICAL ITEMS IN THAT MEDIUM

▨ EXPOSED TO ONE POLITICAL ITEM IN THAT MEDIUM

■ EXPOSED TO NO POLITICAL ITEMS IN THAT MEDIUM

CHART III

A considerable proportion of voters untouched by the political content of radio speeches or newspaper and magazine articles.

area, and a list of the five main radio speeches which had been on the air the day preceding the interview. Chart III shows the striking results. Similar inquiries at earlier stages of the campaign showed even less exposure. Except for an extraordinary occasion, it is safe to say that during an average day of the campaign more than half the sample were not exposed to any political topics in the mass media of communication. Characteristically enough, the people who read political items in the newspapers were also those who listened to political speeches. Those who had not been reached by propaganda at the time of one interview usually proved to be still unexposed at the time of the second interview.

The importance of this lack of reading and listening on the part of about half of the population is further accentuated by two facts. The people who read and listened were usually those who had well-established political opinions and affiliations. Those less set in their ways and, therefore, theoretically more susceptible to influences, were also less likely to be reached through the formal media of communication. In addition, a very marked exposure bias was found. For those who had already formed a vote intention, it was found that the political color of their exposure had a correlation of about .6 with their vote intention. The more interest people had in the election, incidentally, the higher was this exposure bias.

A number of comparative remarks can be made about the role of radio and newspapers. The radio is probably more effective than newspapers. The measure of effectiveness here is the number of people who can give concrete instances of how at some point in their deliberation

a newspaper or a radio item entered as a conscious factor. Content analysis showed that local newspapers cut reports of speeches short and so gave little room to direct or indirect argumentation. They had to lay stress on news, and the news of the campaign comes from actual campaign events, predictions as to outcome, and reports on people who have taken a definite stand. About two-thirds of the political content of newspapers was concerned with such campaign matters. On the other hand, over the radio candidates spoke for themselves, and much time was given to actual argumentation. No wonder, then, that this kind of material lent itself to closer integration with the thinking people did for themselves.

In the 1940 campaign, there was an interesting relationship between supporters of the two parties and the two main media of communication. We have seen that the content of press and radio was equally strongly favorable toward the Republican side, but in the mind of the audience, the situation was different. The [table at the bottom of this page] lists a number of questions and percentage answers by which people's attitudes to media were gauged.

Note that in answer to both questions the Democrats considered the radio more their medium, while the Republicans leaned toward the newspapers. And these differences repeated themselves at other points of the study. Republicans read more political items in the newspapers, Democrats listened to more radio speeches. And when it came to explaining changes in votes, again people who during the campaign decided to vote for Willkie mentioned newspapers more frequently as influences, while respondents who finally cast their vote for Roosevelt

Questions	*Republicans* Newspaper	Radio	*Democrats* Newspaper	Radio
1. "Which do you think is closer to the truth (more impartial)—the news you get in the newspapers or on the radio?"	41%	32%	30%	39%
2. "Where do you find ideas on the coming election which agree most closely with your own ideas?"	35	37	26	39

reported more incidents where the radio played a role. All these differences, moreover, hold true for all educational levels, thus eliminating any effect of the lower educational status of the average Democratic voter.[4] Obviously a considerable selection bias exists because people tend to expose themselves to the side with which they agree anyhow. The stereotype of the impartial voter weighing all the evidence offered by both political parties is just another political myth.

THE ROLE OF PERSONAL CONTACTS

The strongest influence discovered was face-to-face contact. Whenever the responders were asked to report on their recent exposure to campaign communications of all kinds, political discussions were mentioned more frequently than exposure to radio or print. On any average day at least 10 per cent more people participated in discussions about the election —either actively or passively—than listened to a major speech or read about campaign items in a newspaper. And this coverage "bonus" came from just those people who had not yet made a final decision as to how they would vote—those who were still open to influence. Three-fourths of the respondents who at one time had not expected to vote but who were finally "dragged in" mentioned per-

[4] The fact that more than 80 per cent of the newspapers all over the country were in favor of the Republican candidate cannot be a complete explanation for the above finding, for the three local papers in Sandusky were evenly divided, one for each major party and one neutral. It is more likely that the regular and skillful use which Roosevelt makes of the radio has built up the idea of radio as more friendly to the Democratic side.

sonal influences. After the election, the voters were given a check list of "sources from which they got most of the information or impressions that caused them to form their judgment." Those who had made some change during the campaign mentioned friends or members of their family relatively more frequently than did the respondents who kept a constant vote intention all through the campaign.

It is worthwhile at this point to introduce a table [below] cross-tabulating people's vote intention on the eve of election day as against the actual vote decision they reported right after November 5th.[5]

Even at this late date there occurred a considerable turnover, although from a general political point of view most of the changes cancelled each other. The main point here is that many of the changers did not hesitate to report personal influence. We can take as an example the sixteen people who had no definite vote intention in October but who went to the polls on election day. Half of them report incidents such as the following: "I was taken to the polls by worker who insisted

[5] The translation of vote intentions into voting action as discussed here and as traced in the table has implications of interest for those who want to understand the workings of the regular public opinion polls. It is the task of an election forecas to infer from the intended vote prior to the election the actual vote after the election Some of the major hazards of making election predictions are nicely exemplified here (1) the difficulty of predicting what the "Don't Know's" will do on Election Day (2) the fact that those people who had intended to vote Democratic were more likely not to vote in the end than those who had intended to vote Republican; and (3) the fact that all of the people who voted despite an original intention not to vote, voted for Willkie.

Vote Intention in October

Actual Vote	Rep.	Dem.	Don't know	Don't expect to vote	Total
Republican	215	7	4	6	232
Democrat	4	144	12	0	160
Didn't vote	10	16	6	59	91
Total persons	229	167	22	65	483

that I go. . . . My husband persuaded me to vote for Willkie. He was opposed to the third term. . . . The lady where I worked wanted me to vote—took me to the polls and they all voted Republican so I did, too. . . . My parents are Republican but I didn't have any interest in the election at all. . . ."

A more detailed study of all of the cases interviewed in the course of the campaign permits us to list the factors which make personal contacts so influential:

a. Personal contacts are more flexible. The clever campaign worker, professional or amateur, can fit the argument to the person. He can shift his tactics as he analyzes the reactions of the other person.

b. Face-to-face contacts make the consequences of yielding to or resisting an argument immediate and personal. The mass media can only intimate or describe future rewards or punishments; the living person can create them at once in the form of smiles or sneers.

c. More people rely upon personal contacts to help them pick out arguments which are relevant for their own good in political affairs than rely upon the more remote and impersonal newspaper and radio. They are used to relying upon the judgment and evaluation of the respected people among their associates.

d. Personal contacts are more casual. If we read or tune in to a speech, we usually do so purposefully and in doing so have a definite mental attitude which tinges our receptiveness. On the other hand, people we meet for reasons other than political discussions are more likely to catch us unprepared and so cut through our barriers more easily.

e. Finally, personal contacts can get a voter to the polls without relying to any extent upon comprehension of the issues of the election—something the formal media can do less easily.

It is possible to characterize the people

from whom much of the personal talk about the election came. By appropriate questions and by getting advice from people who knew the community well, about 20 per cent of the sample were spotted as opinion leaders. These were not necessarily prominent community figures; they were simply people who were likely to be asked their opinion and were eager to give their advice. The following table indicates how these opinion leaders were found in all walks of life.

Occupational group	Number in sample	Percentage of opinion leaders
Professional	17	35
Proprietary, managerial	28	25
Clerical	21	33
Commercial, sales	16	44
Skilled workers	37	35
Semi-skilled workers	31	32
Unskilled workers	47	23
Farmers	46	15
Housewives	230	13
Unemployed	13	15
Retired	23	35

In answer to all relevant questions these opinion leaders showed themselves more involved in the campaign than the rest of the population—the largest difference being in the extent to which they read political matter in magazines. It therefore makes sense to talk of a two-step movement of propaganda. In a somewhat crude generalization, one can say that the formal media reach mainly the opinion leaders, who in turn pass it on to the rest of the people by word of mouth.

THE AVAILABLE VOTE

All this raises the practical question: who are the people who make their decision during the campaign and thus are available for propaganda? Restricting this analysis to the respondents who actually went to the polls, we find that Erie County split as follows: about one-half the voting sample made up its mind before May and did not change its vote intention; another 30 per cent made up their minds as soon as the candidates were nominated by the conventions; the other 20 per cent hesitated long enough to be considered at least theoretically susceptible to propaganda influences. (This count excludes the 20 per cent of the total sample who were psychologically so outside of the campaign that they did not vote at all.)

Two facts are closely related to the time of decision. The first is interest in the election. The less interested people were, the later they made up their minds. In the course of the study we used a considerable number of indices by which interest in the election could be reasonably measured. It turned out that people's own statement as to whether they had a great, a moderate, or no interest in the election was about as good an index as could be found. In Chart IV, therefore, the panel members are divided into those who exhibited great interest and those whose interest was less strong. For both groups, the chart indicates at what time they formed the vote intention with which they went to the polls. (This chart, therefore, contains only the panel members who actually voted.) By comparing the two bars we see that about two-thirds of the greatly interested people knew in May for whom they would vote, but among those with less interest less than half were that constant in their vote intention. Twice as many with less interest made their final decision between September and November. In the later phases of the campaign, then, the propagandists have to address themselves more and more to the least interested sector of the population.

People susceptible to campaign influences can be characterized in still another way. It is possible to set up a number of criteria of what can be called "cross-pressures." We saw, for instance, that well-to-do people and Protestants were much more likely to vote Republican than poor people and Catholics. A well-to-do Catholic, therefore, was under cross-pressures. Another index of cross-pressure can be developed by dividing the respondents into those whose family members are all in agreement and those with a political deviate or, at least, someone who had not yet made up his mind. Another type of cross-pressure exists around a citizen who intends to vote for a party but does not agree with all its tenets. By such considerations we were able to develop a cross-pressure index which consisted of six elements. Only 15 per cent had no cross-pressures at all. From Chart V it can be seen that the people who waited for the campaign before making a final vote decision were quite clearly those who live under the greatest variety of such pressures. The table is set up so that it is possible to compare the effect of cross-pressures independently of the role of interest. By comparing, for instance, the first and

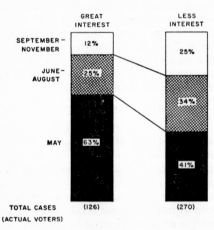

CHART IV

People greatly interested in the election make their final vote decision earlier than less interested people.

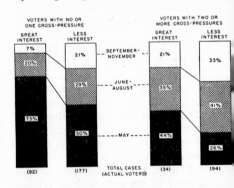

CHART V

Both cross-pressures and lack of interest delay the final vote decision. Separately they show about equal strength. Their joint effect is especially strong.

third bar in Chart V we see that if people had great interest in the election, they still decided their vote later if they were subject to many cross-pressures.

The joint effect of interest and cross-pressure can be seen by comparing bars 1 and 4—an effect which is very great indeed. People who had great interest and few cross-pressures were three times more likely to make up their mind before the campaign. But only a quarter of those who did not care much about the political situation or found themselves under a number of cross-pressures decided that early. Inversely, in the last weeks of the campaign, the propagandists dealt almost exclusively either with people who had no interest or with people who found themselves in a contradictory social and psychological situation.[6]

THE TOTAL EFFECT OF THE CAMPAIGN

Erie County had voted 58 per cent Democratic in 1936 and voted 46 per cent Democratic in 1940. When we entered the county in May, 1940, it had already a solid Republican majority, which increased only slightly in the course of the

[6] As can be seen from the base figures in Chart V, there exists a noteworthy relationship between cross-pressures and interest. One might have expected that people whose social situation contained conflicting elements became very alert to campaign events. This, however, is not the case. If a person belonged to a constellation where neither of the two candidates was a "natural" solution to his problems, the whole campaign seemed to be of less importance to him and he lost interest.

campaign. Here is the best indication that elections are decided by the events occurring in the entire period between two Presidential elections and not by the campaign. The evidence presented in this paper makes such a conclusion even more plausible.

The study of Erie County does not, to be sure, suggest that a party could give up campaigning and win. Propaganda has to reinforce and keep in line the vote intentions of the approximately 50 per cent of the voters who have made up their minds before the campaign starts. The campaign has, moreover, to activate the latent predispositions of most of those who are undecided. The campaign is like the chemical bath which develops a photograph. The chemical influence is necessary to bring out the picture, but only the picture pre-structured on the plate can come out.

Only a very small percentage of people can be considered so truly undecided that propaganda can still convert them, and those are likely to be of a special kind: not much interested and living in a social constellation which makes neither of the two candidates a very convincing solution. As a result, these people are especially sensitive to the social pressures around them; and if they finally make up their minds, their vote is likely to be proportional to the group influences exerted upon them. This means that in the end their decision will not considerably alter the ratio of Republican and Democratic vote intentions which existed prior to the beginning of the campaign.

Chapter 13

Manipulating the diffuse collectivity

*W*HILE deliberate attempts to control the thoughts and actions of large numbers of people are by no means recent, widespread concern about the techniques of manipulation is a phenomenon of modern times. As the mass and the public have emerged to self-consciousness, jealously protecting their right to challenge the sacrosanct, there has been accompanying preoccupation with identifying and resisting propaganda. At a time when the ultimate test of truth was the word of legitimate authority, propaganda was a term with favorable connotations referring to the approved education of the masses in those matters in which it was proper that they should be informed. When the conception of the public as the legitimate agency of ultimate decision became dominant, the effort to indoctrinate with predetermined truths by the careful selection and slanting of facts and accompanying censorship came to be feared. Thus the term propaganda became a bad word.

Since the term propaganda is part of the folk-language, its evaluative connotations are more prominent in determining usage than any precise denotations. In popular use propaganda is likely to mean simply any arguments in behalf of a position with which we disagree heartily. More sophisticated usage makes propaganda the promotion of an idea or position through means of which we disapprove. Groups with vested interests in persuasion attempt to spread definitions which protect their activities from the invidious label, propaganda. Education, for example, is differentiated from propaganda in accordance with the current philosophies of education. Training to think, to keep an open mind, to see all sides, is called education, while propaganda tries to insure a closed mind. Unfortunately, the question of whether a man who argues his own convictions is thereby educating or propagandizing depends upon an exploration of his most obscure motivation and a delving into matters of which he is not himself necessarily

276

ware. Businessmen also fear that their culturally sanctioned efforts to depict merchandise in the best possible light may be challenged, and consequently they try to differentiate advertising from propaganda. As the conceptions of legitimate advertising undergo change and as philosophies of education evolve, so will the boundaries of the concept propaganda be altered.

For purposes of practical social control and applied philosophy it may be useful to make the foregoing distinctions. However, except in recognizing that people label what they see and hear and then react accordingly, it is probably not useful to differentiate propaganda as a special kind of influence. To the degree to which communications identified by the recipients as propaganda are discounted and responded to differently from other communications, we must consider this labelling procedure a part of the total communication process.

There are important differences, however, in the type of collectivity toward which the communication is directed and the kind of reaction sought. (1) Efforts may be directed simply toward the mass, seeking only the separate responses of a large number of individuals. Most advertising is of this sort, aimed only at maximizing the number of individuals who will buy a given product. (2) Efforts may be directed toward a public, intended to influence public opinion in a context of open controversy. (3) Efforts may be directed toward a group with the objective either of promoting solidaristic crowd behavior such as morale or of breaking down solidarity. (4) And finally, the objective may be the more complex one of breaking down existing solidarity and promoting collective action contrary to the initial group orientation.

We shall discuss manipulative efforts in the foregoing order. While all of these types of activities are taking place constantly, the first two are likely to attract greatest attention within a society functioning under normal peacetime conditions. The latter types gain characteristically more attention as aspects of psychological warfare. The effort to strengthen the morale of the in-group, to break down the morale of the outgroup, and to promote organized dissension within the outgroup has come to be known as an important branch of military strategy. Basically the same strategies are constantly in use, however, whenever groups are in competition, although they are less likely to be openly admitted than in the relations between warring nations.

Mass appeals. Certain fundamental conditions will determine the effectiveness of attempts to manipulate any type of collectivity. These conditions may be viewed in their simplest form in appeals to the mass.

(1) All effective influence obviously depends first of all on gaining *access* to the group to be influenced. Many of the problems in this connection are entirely technical matters, having to do with the coverage of any particular medium of mass communication. Recurrent questions deal with the relative merits of a few major appeals as contrasted to a large number of brief appeals. Will the political candidate, for example, gain a better hearing by having one or two spectacular television rallies or by a large number of brief "spot" announcements? The problem of reaching specialized audiences and the merits of mass appeal as opposed to selective appeal confront the advertiser or propagandist. In promoting a school bond election, for example, in which only a minority can be expected to take the trouble to vote, the problem of access is not the number of persons reached but rather the number of parents—the persons who are directly affected—who

can be reached. Or in promoting a measure to benefit the underprivileged, the key problem may be how to get to those who neither read a newspaper nor listen to political discussions on the radio, but who constitute the potentially strongest body of supporters. The problem of access also includes the question of whether to make a mass appeal or to reach key persons who can then be expected to influence others. In advertising it may sometimes be more important to sell to a recognized fashion leader than to try to sell directly to the masses.

(2) The second condition determining the effectiveness of manipulative effort is the *receptiveness* of the mass toward the proposed course of action or thought. In the mass, the receptiveness is that of the individuals, since individuals must decide and act. While the statement sometimes made that "a propagandist can convince people only of what they already believe" is too extreme, manipulator activities must take advantage of at least partial readiness to act in the indicated direction.

Receptiveness is compounded of *interest, motivation,* and *understanding.* Without interest there is no attention to the communications. Without motivation verbal assent will not be followed by action. Fund drives for various "worthy causes" are particularly likely to encounter verbal acceptance without being able to dislodge people from a state of normal passivity.

Robert Merton, on the basis of interviews with a sample of persons, some of whom did and some of whom did not contribute in response to a war bond drive has shown the importance of guilt feelings in motivating people to buy bonds. Those persons who already felt some guilt over the paltriness of their own contributions to the war effort were led by the appeal to contrast themselves even more sharply with others who were making very great sacrifices. The intensification of pre-existing guilt feelings provided the motive power to make them buy bonds.*

Receptiveness toward any proposed course of action or thought also includes the ability to "get the point" of the communication, to see the implications of the facts or arguments presented. The recipients must possess the frame of reference necessary for understanding the message. Eunice Cooper and Marie Jahoda have demonstrated clearly how the entire theme of a communication can be completely distorted when the recipient does not share the frame of reference of the communicator. Their study reports the ineffectiveness of certain efforts to alter the attitudes of individuals toward minority groups.

* Robert K. Merton et al., **Mass Persuasion** (New York: Harper & Brothers, 1946).

THE EVASION OF PROPAGANDA: HOW PREJUDICED PEOPLE RESPOND TO ANTI-PREJUDICE PROPAGANDA

EUNICE COOPER AND MARIE JAHODA

A. PROPAGANDA EVASION AS A PROBLEM
Communication research points up the fact that it is difficult in general for a

Reprinted by permission of The Journal Press, from **The Journal of Psychology**, 23 (January, 1947), pp. 15–24.

communication to reach people who are not already in favor of the views it presents. It is well-known that many people evade points of view which are at odds with their own by the simple expedient of not exposing themselves to such views

Those who most need to be influenced by certain communications are least likely to be reached by them.

Thus, the bulk of the listeners to educational radio programs are among the better educated segment of the listening audience. A study of a radio program designed to promote friendship, cooperation, and mutual respect among various immigrant groups showed that a program about Italians was listened to chiefly by Italians, a program about Poles was listened to chiefly by Poles, and so on. In the same way, anti-prejudice propaganda is likely to reach or affect a considerably smaller proportion of the prejudiced group in the population than of the non-prejudiced.

This is, of course, not a denial of the value of pro-democratic propaganda. The audience of such propaganda is composed of sympathizers, neutrals, and opponents. Although the opponents may be largely unaffected, the other two groups may still be influenced. Here, however, we are chiefly concerned with the reaction of the prejudiced person to anti-prejudice propaganda. What happens when in an experimental situation they are involuntarily confronted with it?

There are, theoretically, two possibilities: they may fight it or they may give in to it. But our research in this field has shown us that many people are unwilling to do either: they prefer not to face the implications of ideas opposed to their own so that they do not have to be forced either to defend themselves or to admit error. What they do is to evade the issue psychologically by *simply not understanding the message.*

It is true that understanding of communications is related to the amount of education of the audience. However, even among people on the same educational level, those who are prejudiced are more apt to misunderstand a message than the unprejudiced.

This article deals with two aspects of the problem of propaganda evasion: its mechanisms and its cultural basis. The first part is drawn from evidence collected in about a dozen studies of the public's

response to anti-prejudice propaganda; the second part is speculative and hypothetical. Considerably more research would be needed to verify our tentative ideas on the motivation of propaganda evasion.

B. THE MECHANISMS OF PROPAGANDA EVASION

The evidence for the techniques employed by a prejudiced respondent in order to avoid understanding is, of necessity, inferential. The process of evasion occurs in the respondent's mind some time between the presentation of a propaganda item and the respondent's "final" statement in answer to the interviewer's questions. The mechanisms involved in evasion, although they may be rather complicated and may appear to be deliberate, are in most cases probably unconscious. It is impossible to determine from even depth interview data at what level of consciousness the process occurs, that is, to what extent the respondent is aware of his evasion.

Evidence of the evasion process is often revealed in the course of the interview, if the interview is considered as an integrated whole and individual statements are not accepted in a disjointed, static fashion as isolated answers to isolated questions.

1. Identification Avoided—Understanding "Derailed"

An example of how a dynamic interpretation of the whole course of the interview reveals evidence of the process of evasion is provided by a recent study of a cartoon series. The cartoons lampoon a character dubbed Mr. Biggott. To bring home the satire of the cartoon, he is shown as a rather ridiculous prudish figure, with exaggerated anti-minority feelings.

What the producers of the cartoon intended was roughly this: The prejudiced reader would perceive that Mr. Biggott's ideas about minorities were similar to his own; that Mr. Biggott was an absurd character; that it was absurd to have such ideas—that to have such ideas made one as ridiculous as Mr. Biggott. He would, then, as the final stage in this process, presumably reject his own prejudice, in order to avoid identification with Mr. Biggott. The study showed a very different result. Prejudiced respondents who understood the cartoon initially—that is, they went through the first three stages mentioned above—went to such lengths to extricate themselves from their identification with Mr. Biggott that in the end they *misunderstood the point of the cartoon.* To use the phrase of the writers of this report, there was a "derailment of understanding."

Here is an example of one of the ways in which the cartoons were misunderstood:[1] The respondent at first identified with Mr. Biggott, saying, among other things which indicated this identification, "I imagine he's a sour old bachelor— (laughing)—I'm an old bachelor myself." He also seemed to be aware of Mr. Biggott's prejudices. As the interview progressed, in order to differentiate himself from Mr. Biggott, he concentrated on proving that Mr. Biggott's social status was inferior, that he was a *parvenu.* This led to a loss of focus on the real problems presented by the cartoons.

"Sixth generation American blood. He don't want anything but sixth generation American blood! Ha! That's pretty good."

At this point the man begins to focus on Mr. Biggott's social inferiority and his attention is deflected from the issue of prejudice more and more as the process continues:

"Well, you know, *I'm eighth generation myself,* of English descent on both sides. My family settled up on Connecticut, C_____, Connecticut, in 1631. A sixth generation American —he's a man of six generations himself. *Maybe less than that.* . . . (What is the doctor thinking?) He's astonished, I guess. He thinks this man has an awful nerve. He looks like a crabby old man. *He may not be the best blood either."*

[1] In the particular cartoon discussed, Mr. Biggott is shown lying in a hospital bed with a doctor in attendance, and saying that for his blood transfusion he wants only "sixth generation American blood."

Mr. Biggott's prejudices have become snobbish pretensions and as the interview continues, the respondent regards him more and more as a "lower class" symbol:

"(Do you know anyone like him?) *No, I have no interest in knowing anyone like that. I've known some like him* up in C_____. This particular man was in the Congregational Church— of course that's the church to which my family belongs. . . . He made plenty of money as an undertaker too. You know, my father died a few years ago. The burial cost $180. He knew that at the time I didn't have any money. He trusted me, let me pay it gradually. But, you know, he charged me 6 per cent interest. Yes, *that's what he charged me. Even though he knew my family and all that.* . . ."

By this time the issue of prejudice has been completely side-tracked. Biggott reminds the respondent only of an old acquaintance whom he considers rather crude. At the end the cartoons become for him only a kind of test for judging personality characteristics:

"(What do you think is the purpose of these cartoons?) To get the viewpoint of anyone. From the viewpoint you can form some opinion of that person. You can get different answers—some agree and some say something else. You can compare them and draw some conclusions. . . . (What is the artist trying to do?) To get the *viewpoint of people to see if they coincide with the artist'* idea of character and all. Some would some would differ."

In the same study there were other variations in what might be called the path of the misunderstanding. Some people caricatured Mr. Biggott, made him a target of ridicule; others made him appear intellectually inferior; still other transformed him into a foreigner or a Jew. Regardless of the particular line developed, the process is essentially the same. Whether or not a respondent follows one of these lines rather than another is probably a matter of temperament and character.

Such complicated forms of arriving at

cuitously at misunderstanding when there is good evidence that spontaneous understanding was present at first are, of course, not the only form of evasion that the prejudiced person takes to escape facing the criticism implied in the message of a propaganda item; but they are the most revealing forms as to the influence of prejudice on comprehension. The conflict about having prejudices must be strong, and at the same time the prejudice must be deeply rooted in the character structure. Under the pressure of this psychological predisposition the respondent takes the roundabout way of first understanding the content of the propaganda item; then identifying with the prejudiced figure, perceiving the criticism of his own position involved in the item; inventing means of disidentification from the special instance of prejudice depicted by the propaganda item; and in the process losing the original understanding of the message. Apparently this process occurs frequently; the unconscious ingenuity of the respondent sets in mainly during the last two steps.

2. The Message Made Invalid

In other cases the process of disidentification leads to more rationalized argumentation. Understanding has been admitted too openly to permit distortion of the message. The respondent accepts the message on the surface but makes it invalid for himself in one of two ways. He may admit the general principle, but claim that in exceptions one is entitled to one's prejudices; or he may admit that the individual item is convincing in itself, but that it is not a correct picture of usual life situations involving the minority group discussed. There is evidence in our studies of both types.

The first type of distortion occurred as a common reaction to a pro-tolerance propaganda booklet. This was presented in the form of a series of well-drawn comic cartoons exposing the absurdity of generalizations about various groups. It concluded with the Golden Rule, "Live and let live." Prejudiced persons frequently followed the whole story with interest and amusement to the end, accepting the Golden Rule, but added: "But it's the Jews that don't let you live; they put themselves outside the rule."

Perhaps even more frequent is the tendency to accept the isolated story presented in propaganda as "just a story." The need to maintain the attention value of a propaganda item through a human-interest appeal has led many propagandists to exemplify by one outstanding dramatic story the general principle for which they wish to enlist support. This technique was used in a broadcast dramatization, "The Belgian Village," presented on the CBS series, "We, the People." In the story, a Jewish couple in an occupied Belgian village are saved by the loyal support of the villagers who hide them from the Gestapo. The dramatization was followed by a direct appeal, spoken by Kate Smith, for sympathy and tolerance toward the Jews. Considerably more of the apparently prejudiced respondents than of the others in the test audience refused to admit the applicability of this dramatic story to other situations. They called it an "adventure story," a "war story," they discussed the dramatic highlights with great interest, but treated the explicit appeal attached to the incident either as if it had not occurred or as an unjustified artificial addition.

3. Changing the Frame of Reference

There remain to be discussed two other forms of misunderstanding by prejudiced persons. One of them is of greater interest than the other; in these cases the prejudiced person's perception is so colored by his prejudice that issues presented in a frame of reference different from his own are transformed so as to become compatible with his own views. Quite unaware of the violation of facts he commits, he imposes on a propaganda item his own frame of reference. This type of response was found in a study of a cartoon depicting a Congressman who has native fascist, anti-minority views. The cartoon series seeks to expose and ridicule him so as to focus the readers' attention upon such native anti-democratic movements and to cause them to disapprove of these tendencies. For example, in one cartoon, the Congressman is shown interviewing an applicant in his office. The man has brought a letter of recommendation saying that he has been in jail, has started race riots, has smashed windows. The Congressman is pleased and says, "Of course, I can use you in my new party."

One respondent commented: "It might be anything crooked. . . . might be a new labor party. That shady character makes me think so, the one applying for a job."

Another, in response to the second picture in the series, said: ". . . . a bunch of men down in Congress that are more interested in keeping their jobs, interested in the votes rather than anything else. . . . I never liked Senator Wagner. . . ."

Another: "It's about a strike. . . . about trouble like strikes. . . . He is starting a Communist party."

The type becomes clearest in the following reply: "It's a Jewish party that would help Jews get more power."

The only clue that these respondents took from the cartoon was the fact that it tried to show up a bad politician. The rest they supplied themselves by identifying the Congressman with whatever appeared to them to be "bad politics." Thus they imposed their own ideology on the cartoon and arrived at an interpretation satisfactory to them—an interpretation which, however, represented a complete misunderstanding of the cartoon's message.

4. The Message is Too Difficult

The remaining type of misunderstanding can be dismissed quickly. This takes the same form as misunderstanding by unprejudiced people. Some respondents frankly admit that "they don't get the point." This is most frequently due to intellectual and educational limitations of these respondents or to defects in the propaganda.

These evasion processes have obvious implications for the producers of cartoons (and probably of propaganda in general). Given the tendency to evade opposition propaganda, evasion is facilitated by making the message subtle or satirical. How-

ever, simplifying the message may lessen its emotional impact. What seems to be indicated is that the more subtle—and therefore the more easily distorted and misunderstood—forms may be appropriate for neutrals and for inactive sympathizers of the anti-prejudice message: these people do not show evidence of thi tendency to *evade* the message although they may misunderstand for other reasons; and the impact of the item may make stronger supporters of them. For the prejudiced person the research suggests that this approach is ineffective.

For a better understanding of the evasion mechanism we must turn to an examination of the motivation underlying it and its role in our culture.

C. EVASION—A CULTURAL PATTERN

A thorough examination of the motivation underlying evasion would require a much more extensive treatment than we can provide here. However, certain cultural features may be mentioned which seem to bear out in other areas the kind of evasion mechanism discussed above.

1. Fear of Isolation and the Threat to the Ego

The fear of isolation is a major force in our society, where the majority of people are dependent upon group membership not only for their physical well-being but also for psychological support. They rely upon group codes and group values as guides for their behavior and their ideals. Nearly everyone wants to "belong." At the same time this is complicated by the fact that assembly-line production and the general complexity of modern life tend to drive people into more and more atomistic contacts with their fellow men, thereby increasing the fear of losing identity with the group.

From a psychological point of view the evasion of a propaganda message with which one disagrees functions as a defense mechanism. Such defense mechanisms come into play whenever an individual senses a danger to his ego structure—that is, whenever his self-confience hangs in the balance. As we have seen, the steps involved in the evasion process are fairly complicated. However, these complications are obviously negligible compared to the discomfort that would be created by facing the message.

The printed propaganda items that attack prejudice are an attack on the ego of the prejudiced person. Moreover, they constitute an attack made with the authority of the printed word, thus presumably speaking for a large part of the world that disapproves of the respondent. He is confronted with a two-fold threat to his security: On the one hand he is an outsider in the world represented by the propaganda item; on the other hand, giving careful consideration to the validity of the propaganda and possibly accepting it threatens the individual's security in the group to which he feels he belongs and which supports his present ideas. The interviewing situation increases the threat to the security of the individual who feels attacked by anti-discrimination propaganda. Interviewers are trained to use an engaging, polite, and friendly manner when approaching a respondent; they are selected, not only for the skill they have acquired, but also for neatness and pleasantness of appearance in order to facilitate their contact with strangers. The respondent, who is on the defensive, probably links the person of the interviewer with that outside world which may disapprove of him. The interviewer's reluctance to voice his own opinion creates the suspicion that he, too, might disapprove of the respondent's attitude.

The emotional nature of prejudice has been well enough established to explain why the prejudiced respondent often does not trust his own capacity for logical argument on the subject. He feels himself attacked in spheres that actually transcend logic. So where possible, he evades the issue. Although there is insufficient evidence on this point, we venture the guess that the less a person has rationalized his prejudices, the greater will be his tendency to evade an attack on them. Those who are most advanced in the rationalization of prejudice will not feel

the need for evasion to the same degree as their less ideologically developed supporters. Witness the pseudo-science on race questions developed by the Nazis and their followers in this country. Those however, who are infected without having made the decisive step over to the "lunatic fringe," and who are only dimly aware of the irrational basis of their particular attitude, will try to weasel out of their difficulty when confronted with the disconcerting anti-discrimination message.

2. The Multiplicity of Value Systems

Another dimension must be added to the phenomenon of propaganda evasion before it can be understood. This dimension is closely related to that part of our life experience which involves inconsistencies or contradictions. There exists in our society a culturally conditioned habit of evasion, a product of the fact that each individual is compelled to participate in many different groups, each of which has its own more or less well defined value systems. Often, these value systems are somewhat inconsistent with each other; sometimes they imply a different hierarchy of values.

Examples of simultaneous acceptance of inconsistent value systems abound. The obsequious bookkeeper who assumes a dominant role in political discussions with his barbershop cronies is a familiar figure in the modern literature of the western world. We are not surprised when a store owner who privately champions progressive causes, refuses to hire a Negro salesclerk on the grounds that his customers will object. The example of the bookkeeper illustrates the necessity for flexibly shifting from one social role to another. The storekeeper, too, is involved in a conflict between his public and private attitudes. He keeps the solution of this conflict in abeyance by setting up a special hierarchy of values for his business role: he knows that he is supported by the generally accepted view that taking care of one's profits takes precedence over other considerations.

Thus, two possible alternatives are available. These contradictions may either be recognized and resolved; or they may be evaded. Instead of looking squarely at the inconsistencies, one may divide one's life into so many little pockets in which behavior is determined by independent and even contradictory values; or one may realistically examine and compare the values involved in his various day-to-day roles and then weigh their relative merits as behavior guides.

Evidence of this was found in a study of the impact of factory life on children who had just left school. The moral values they had been taught in school were confronted in the factory with an inflation of the importance of efficiency to the exclusion of morality. Nevertheless, the absorption of this new value system was achieved with incredible speed. But the two systems were not reconciled, nor was one abandoned for the other. They coexisted in strictly separate compartments of the personality; the issue of conflict was evaded by the departmentalizing of the personality.

3. Other Cultural Factors in Evasion

In this context the lack of spontaneity so characteristic of people living in our culture must be considered. The public which comprises the audience for the mass media of communications is entertainment hungry. Many of them are lulled into boredom and fatigue by their jobs; outside their jobs they want to have fun. They want to be entertained without having to think. And they are encouraged to persist in this mental laziness by the stereotypy of these communications. Not only are they continually confronted with entertainment cast in the same mold; they are even told how to react to it. Everything is, as it were, pre-digested for them. They are informed by advertisements that a comedy will make them "laugh 'til their sides ache," that a sentimental love story will "wring their hearts," to mention only the most superficial appeals. As one writer has put it, "they march to their destiny by catch-words." Ideas are adopted, not as ideas, but as slogans. Where ideas infiltrate in the guise of entertainment the habitual shying away

from effort comes to the rescue of the person who is the propaganda target and helps him to miss the point of the message. The only alternative would be to face the implications of the message and think about them, and this they neither want nor are habituated to do.

Also involved but probably less important in the complex of propaganda evasion is the factor of recognition-value. Audiences tend to prefer the things which are familiar to them. The best-liked music is the music one knows. What is new is a little suspect, requires more effort in listening, and has no pre-established associations which prescribe a pattern of response. Hence it is rejected. It is quite likely that a similar tendency makes itself felt in the consideration of new (and oppositional) ideas.

4. Why Evasion?

Why has evasion become so general? The answer lies partly in the difficulties the individual must face to achieve uniformity in the various areas of his everyday experience. To face the contradictions and try to resolve them would undoubtedly set up disturbing tensions which would in turn involve serious difficulties for most individuals. For example, consider the fact that most people agree with the ideas of their own social group; they are conditioned by the people with whom they live and, in turn, they choose to be with people whose attitudes are compatible with their own. Adopting a conflicting attitude would create antagonisms in inter-personal relationships, requiring considerable adjustment on the part of the individual. Even *considering* an opposing point of view may create great discomfort.

Thus evasion appears as a well-practiced form of behavior, which receives encouragement from the social structure in which we live. In connection with response to anti-prejudice propaganda it serves as a defense against group attack. This may partly explain why persons with a poorly developed ego structure tend most frequently to take this easy way out.

(3) A third general condition governing the effectiveness of manipulative efforts is the possibility of carrying out the proposed action. Much advertising, for example, is premised on the assumption that listeners already want new cars, but that they have to be convinced that it is easier for them to buy a car than they think. To elicit a workman's support for a labor union it may be chiefly necessary to assure him protection against possible retaliation from an anti-labor union employer. To make a man actively advocate a point of view it may be essential to provide him with arguments and techniques of debate with which he can feel confident of holding his own in a controversial discussion. Widespread defection within enemy forces cannot be secured until the means for deserting safely are assured.

(4) With the inclination and opportunity to act, the recipient still makes some evaluation of the appeal itself and of the assumed source of the appeal. When the perceived source is an individual or group of high prestige and respected competence who is judged as having nothing to gain personally, the communication is likely to be well received.

While the identification of any communication source as biased will frequently work to its disadvantage, recognized bias does not negate the communication's effectiveness in all situations. This is especially true in the realm of advertising, where the bias is recognized in all materials.

The appeal itself may be such as to make it easy or difficult to respond. The recipient may feel insulted by too childish, too demanding, too intimate appeals, or he may feel indignant over unfair or intemperate appeals. The very appeal may impede action by making the recipient feel that he is gullible if he complies.

Appeal to the Public. In our earlier discussion of processes within the public we have pointed out some of the circumstances under which public opinion changes. Effective influence will be directed toward creating or utilizing such conditions favorable to change.

The conditions for effective influence which we have discussed under the mass apply equally to the public, but in somewhat different form. To the extent to which the strategy is that of a "grass roots" appeal, individuals will be the recipients, and most of what has been said about the mass is applicable. However, the "possibility for action" will refer to the opportunity for each individual to engage in discussion in such a manner as to affect the decision being registered by the public.

For many issues serious efforts must be devoted not only to propagandizing persons to a particular point of view, but to preparing them—making them *receptive*—before the propaganda can be attempted. Efforts may also be necessary to stir people up about the positions which they accept so that they will contribute to an effective public. Frequently these efforts to ready people to listen to persuasive attempts and to stir them into becoming ardent advocates are referred to under the term *agitation*.

Among the varied usages of the concept *agitation* two important elements are generally found. First, agitation is concerned with motivation, the arousal of feelings, more than with the promotion of a particular belief. Propaganda, persuasion, and similar terms connote persuasion to a particular point of view or plan of action, while agitation connotes excitement and arousal, with or without a very specific program. Indeed, agitation may serve to arouse people to a danger, alert their suspicions, or convince them of the necessity for drastic action, while strengthening, however, quite antithetical programs.

Second, agitation tends to be negative in emphasis, creating, reinforcing, or redirecting discontent. To say that agitation is negative does not mean that it is only negative or destructive in its *consequences*. It is the sense of discontent that makes the individual receptive to a program of change, that makes him listen to reform programs as more than an intellectual game or a self-righteous broadmindedness. The well ingrained sentiments in support of the established order override the intellectual understanding of arguments for reform unless these sentiments are already weakened through a personal dissatisfaction.

Attempts to win support for any program are likely to fall short of creating the sense of issue which is necessary if a public is to appear. Such attempts may fail because of a pleasant agreement with the speaker—a sort of "Isn't that a fascinating idea!" kind of reaction. There is a considerable market for amusement over our foibles, the inconsistencies in our formal associations, and for strictly in-group self-criticism. It is the sense of satisfaction and security with present conditions that allows this broadminded acceptance of our own shortcomings to be present without the least thought of taking self-criticism seriously. Or within a group which has become narcotized to suffering, committed to the view that life is hard and that one can learn to accept anything, programs of change only threaten to disturb the nice balance whereby the impact of suffering is subjectively lessened.

On the other hand, attempts to promote programs of change may fail because they outrage the sense of loyalty to prevailing institutions. Patriotism and the "free-enterprise system" are sacred values which must be preserved even at the cost of some suffering to individuals. As long as confidence in the general outlines of the established order is unshaken, a serious proposal for reform will provoke a sense of outrage which completely obscures any potential response to the arguments of the propagandist.

Agitation is a process whereby the mass is prepared for the establishment of a public by creating a sufficiently aroused sense of discontent that there will be other reactions than the aforementioned unmotivated acquiescence or indignant repudiation. Agitation is a crucial step in the creation of a public about a new issue. Agitation may be an important auxiliary technique when the propagandist appeals to an established public. But it must be the major activity until a public has actually been developed and the issue has been accepted as a real one having important consequences for the members of the public.

Herbert Blumer has called attention to an important difference in the manner in which an agitator must function if he is to be effective, depending upon the extent of prior development of a public.* Where no public or sense of issue exists, any frontal attack on alleged "problems" will be dismissed or resisted violently depending upon the forcefulness of the agitator. However, the agitator, by concealing his purpose and working through indirection, may call people's attention to sources of discontent that they had but faintly sensed. He must maintain the

* Herbert Blumer, "Collective Behavior," in **Principles of Sociology,** ed. A. M. Lee (New York: Barnes & Noble, Inc., 1953), pp. 203–205,

safe appearance of a member of the in-group, a person whose loyalty to the system is not seriously questioned. He must also be a poised, quiet individual, not given to violent expression or unpredictable outbursts. Thus safely defined as a solid and respectable citizen, he may ask the kinds of questions that start people wondering why conditions are not as they should be. He may point out discrepancies that lead them to fairly obvious conclusions about the motives of their present leadership, about the justice of the present system, or about the inevitability of current inequities, without himself directly suggesting the conclusions. As the impact of this agitation develops, the amount of undercover protest talk grows, until beneath the cover of overt conformity there has developed widespread covert ill will. Until such covert discontent has been widely expressed and discussed so that many people have become personally convinced that all is not right and strongly assured that their feeling is widely shared and supported, any frontal attack will still evoke the conventional responses. Indeed, as the discrepancy between overt conformity and covert discontent becomes greater, the agitator or propagandist who attacks conditions frontally is more and more likely to be dealt with by indignation and violent repression, as the very responsive chord he has struck makes people more fearful of the consequences of unleashing such discontent.

However, once the fear of bringing discontent to the surface has been overcome, the problem of the agitator is then to push people to the point of acting upon their discontent. No longer is the quiet, poised individual effective, but rather a person with the enthusiasm that infects others, with assurance that makes others forget their doubts, and with extremity of conviction and feeling to make others forget their moderation. The agitator at this stage fits more closely the popular image of the agitator—the daring, contentious individual, the human dynamo.

Selective appeal to the public. The locus of agitation and attempts to influence public opinion may not be the mass or the undifferentiated membership of a public. The "grass roots" appeal may be displaced by efforts to reach the effective decision-makers more parsimoniously. Access to key persons may be all that is required in some publics.

A few spokesmen may be won over and create public opinion that does not depend upon large numbers of unpredictable individuals. Strategy may concentrate upon interest groups. Or appeals may be directed toward the elite publics, so that only a small number of persons need be won over. In all these instances the bulk of individual members of the public are by-passed and their receptiveness, opportunities for action, and evaluation of the appeal itself are of little consequence.

Under the auspices of the American Council on Race Relations, a survey was made of the strategies employed in various campaigns to enact state "Fair Employment Practices" legislation. The findings were summarized in a manual intended to guide those who would participate in subsequent campaigns. In the following excerpt a strategy of working through established groups rather than through mass appeal is stressed.

STATE CAMPAIGNS FOR
FAIR EMPLOYMENT PRACTICES LEGISLATION

Political and Social Factors. Between 1944 and 1949 inclusive, FEPC bills have been introduced 59 times in 27 states, and have passed in 10 states. In two of these, Indiana and Wisconsin, "voluntary" commissions were established; that is, commissions without the power of enforcement.

Republican controlled legislatures passed FEPC 7 times, while Democratic legislatures passed it once. One bill passed in a divided legislature, and one other passed as a result of Democratic action in a legislature with a Democratic House and an evenly divided Senate. Republican controlled legislatures defeated FEPC 30 times, Democratic legislatures, 6. In legislatures where each party controlled one of the houses, Republicans were responsible for 9 defeats, the Democrats, for 2. Both Republican and Democratic legislators from rural areas were usually opposed to FEPC; Democrats from urban areas were usually for it, and Republicans from urban areas were split on the issue.

The governor appears to play a decisive role only when he controls the majority party. His influence is almost directly proportionate to the power he holds in that party. Thus, in New York for example, the legislature easily disposed of FEPC in 1944 when Dewey showed no interest in the issue, and just as easily passed it in 1945, when he said that he wanted such legislation. In California and Minnesota, on the other hand, the majority has consistently opposed the governors, from the same party, and defeated FEPC despite their expressed desire to see it passed.

Legislative committees are a significant stumbling block in the way of the passage of FEPC. Of the 40 out of 47 defeats for which we have complete information, FEPC bills died in committee 20 times, and were defeated 8 times.

American Council on Race Relations (Chicago: 1949).

Another significant fact is that FEPC bills died as a result of inaction, or incomplete action on the part of committees and the legislature proper, in 26 cases, and were defeated by vote in only 14. Thus it may be concluded that legislators prefer to avoid action if possible, and usually send the measure to committee as a technique for getting rid of it.

Of a series of six socio-economic and demographic factors examined, only two appear to be related to the passage or nonpassage of FEPC. States that passed FEPC had, on the average, a higher percentage of foreign-born whites in the population. In addition, they had a higher average urban population. However, there were important variations in this pattern.

In summary, FEPC cannot be characterized as "Democratic" legislation.

Rural legislators are almost always opposed to FEPC, and proponents have failed to deal effectively with this problem.

Legislative committees so often are the end of the line for FEPC bills, that proponents would do well to give them more attention, with the following objectives in mind:

1. The selection of the committee to which the bill will be sent.
2. The selection of the members of that committee.
3. Influencing action by, and the vote of, the members of the committee.

Organizational Support for FEPC. FEPC campaigns have usually been led by organizations concerned with the rights of ethnic and other minorities. These include Negro and Jewish agencies, as well as interracial and interdenominational groups, and civic unity councils.

Various church groups have been active on the local and state levels, endorsing FEPC, appearing at hearings, and working in the campaigns. Because of heir different structures, the Protestant and Catholic church groups must be approached in a different manner. The role of organized labor has been particularly disappointing in view of the professed stand it has taken. On the national level, both the AFL and the CIO have expressed support for FEPC. On the state level, the unions have testified at hearings, and endorsed FEPC generally. However, the AFL has, in some states, worked behind the scenes against FEPC. On the local level, various AFL unions have actively opposed FEPC, though not always openly. The support of the unions nominally in favor of FEPC, except for several instances, has been substantially less than was possible. Unions have passed resolutions and endorsements, and occasionally put educational material in their publications, but there has been no concerted effort to make FEPC a vital issue to union members. The responsibility for this lies both with the proponents of FEPC and the unions. The proponents for the most part have not worked out an effective approach to the unions, and as a result, the unions have remained concerned with other problems. The unions at the same time, have often found it expedient, for purposes of union politics, to ignore discrimination, and thus are not always too anxious to become involved in more than a token way, with campaigns for FEPC.

Veterans' organizations have usually stayed clear of the issue of FEPC: Catholic and Jewish veterans' organizations have occasionally endorsed FEPC, but essentially have shown little awareness of its significance for them. The American Veterans' Committee has been somewhat more active, but here again, proponents have not brought this organization into the mainstream of the campaigns. The American Legion, despite its formal policy on the national level, has rarely supported FEPC, and has opposed it in several states, though not openly.

The League of Women Voters, while primarily an educational organization, is potentially a great asset to proponents of FEPC. Wherever the League has discussed the issue, it has approved it, and often endorsed it. In some cases, local Leagues have assisted in the campaigns for passage of FEPC. The state Leagues are an excellent educational medium, and an important political factor when they support an issue.

In summary. Despite the important role played by the minority group agencies, there remains a great deal of room for the expansion of these activities, and especially for their extension beyond the large metropolitan areas.

Churches today are moving towards a greater awareness of the need to do away with discrimination against minorities, and proponents of FEPC would do well to enlist their support. It is especially important to keep the local clergy well-informed and supplied with material. The prestige value of endorsement by the churches is an important asset in the FEPC campaigns, but in addition, bodies such as social action committees are potential sources of active workers.

Proponents of FEPC have, on the whole, failed to enlist the effective support of organized labor.

Similarly, they have failed to organize effective support among the veterans' groups, such as the Catholic War Veterans, the Jewish War Veterans, and the American Veterans Committee, which has shown some interest in FEPC.

The above remarks are premised on the demonstrated need for "grass-roots" support, no matter what type of campaign strategy is employed. The functional groups mentioned above, minority groups agencies, civil rights organizations, church, labor and veterans' groups, etc., have potentialities not merely for educational purposes, but also for political pressure.

Organizational Opposition to FEPC. Overwhelmingly, opposition to FEPC has come from those associations and other organizations representing the business and industrial interests in the states under consideration. In addition, there has been some opposition from farm organizations. The opposition has used a wide variety of arguments, but essentially they revolve around the following points: tolerance cannot be legislated; such legislation will not work; business does not want to be bothered with government interference. Proponents must examine both the content of the arguments and their intent, in order to counter them effectively.

It would be incorrect to work on the assumption that opposition is based upon misunderstanding. The opposition is capable of understanding the FEPC bills, but interprets them in the light of its own interests and aims. Proponents should not fall into the error of thinking that the facts alone will convert the opposition.

Strategy of FEPC Campaigns. The use of a state committee to integrate the work of the proponents and lend direction to the campaign has been found to be the most efficient method of coordinating such a campaign. Some state committees established local committees throughout the state, and this permitted wider and more intensive coverage. Such an arrangement also enables the proponents to exert political pressure in the home constituencies of those representatives who express opposition to FEPC, and this is the type of pressure that is most effective.

Generally, two types of strategy have been employed—"grass-roots" and "top-level." The former relies upon the development of mass public support as a base for political pressure; the latter upon dealings with key legislators and party leaders. Both strategies have succeeded, and both have failed. It is important that proponents realize that neither is the one and only answer. Proponents should decide upon their strategy after careful analysis of the situation rather than on the basis of vague personal preferences.

When a legislature is in the substantial control of one party, proponents will have to work through the majority party if they hope to succeed. When power is more evenly divided, proponents may choose to work with one of the parties, or rely upon a bipartisan approach. In such a situation, the bipartisan approach has one advantage, in that the majority party is usually not solidly in support of FEPC, and therefore the proponents will have to rely upon the support of some members of the minority party.

Proponents of FEPC have dealt with the problem of "left-wing" support in many ways. Opponents will make use of every opportunity to describe FEPC as "communist-inspired," and the proponents as "communist-tools." Realistically, there is little that can be done about this, except to repudiate such support, and this will not in itself assure that the opponents will view the issue differently. The use of top-level strategy avoids the need to rely upon the "left-wing" groups. In some states, their support has been repudiated, though occasionally far more violently than one would expect from civil rights' advocates. A positive solution, but one more difficult than the above, is so to organize the elements in the community that the "left-wing" groups become an unimportant minority.

Defeat of FEPC by the legislature does not permanently ruin the chances for subsequent success. Defeat by referendum is far more serious, since here, for one reason or another, the public itself may be said to have repudiated the measure.

Proponents have found it a distinct advantage to have an FEPC committee in existence continuously, rather than merely during the year when the legislature is in session, even though that committee consists only of a few people. If this is not possible, proponents should begin to plan before the legislative elections, so that FEPC may be made an election issue. Party conventions can be asked to endorse FEPC, as can candidates for election.

Tactics of FEPC Campaigns. The facts alone are not sufficient to pass FEPC, but such legislation will not be passed without them. The two most important sets of facts are those dealing with 1) employment discrimination in the states; and 2) the experience of FEP Commissions and employers in other states. These are necessary to counter the arguments that FEPC is not needed "here," and that "it won't work."

Public meetings of a general nature have been found to be of little value. They involve too much time and money and reach too few people not already convinced of the need for FEPC. They may, however, be instrumental for purposes of organization and to build morale among those who are disposed to support the measure but need the confidence that they are not alone.

For the most part, formal meetings with business associations and similar organizations have not been fruitful. Possibly an informal approach would prove more successful. Similarly, few successful attempts have been made to organize special meetings for union members. It is felt that the best tactic is to have the discussion of FEPC as a part of the regular agenda of a meeting. This was found to be true with most organizations that were willing to listen to speakers explain FEPC.

Little use has been made of newspaper advertising because of the expense, and there is no gauge of its effectiveness. Because of the tendency of the press to be opposed to FEPC, proponents can facilitate matters by making special efforts to have concise and accurate press releases prepared when the occasion warrants.

Radio stations do not editorialize, and often will give free time to both sides of a public issue. Proponents can also present their views through "forums" and other similar programs. In some states, proponents have used "canned" programs, prepared by national agencies.

Extensive use has been made of printed materials of all kinds. Little attempt has been made to determine the relative effectiveness of this literature, but proponents are of the opinion that such material should be prepared with special audiences, for example, labor, church groups, etc., in mind. This literature should concentrate on bringing out the following points: the need for FEPC in the state; description and explanation of the bill; the results and effects of FEPC in other states.

The main tactic of the opposition, and this should be differentiated from the arguments used, has been to stall on the FEPC bill, so that the legislative session will end without action having been completed. This also permits legislators to express support for the bill, without having to vote for it. Proponents must anticipate such maneuvers, and their intent.

Organizational Problems. Proponents of FEPC have failed to give adequate attention to the opposition from suburban and rural areas. The least effort has been expended in these areas where we find widespread public opposition.

An effort such as that to pass FEPC will generally arouse personal and organizational jealousies and antagonisms with reference to publicity and the desire to run the campaign. To reduce this to a minimum, the state committee should attempt to have publicity divided among the supporting agencies, as well as reflect emphasis upon itself. Control should be decentralized to the extent that cooperating agencies are given a feeling of responsible cooperation.

It is important that the FEPC bill be correctly drawn and include all that is considered essential. There are numerous sources of legal advice with regard to the mechanics of drawing up such a bill. As a minimum, an FEPC bill should create a paid commission with the power to conduct investigations, to render judgment, and to have sanctions enforced.

Proponents of FEPC must agree before the campaign begins, or at least before the legislative session begins, on the type of bill that will be supported. Further, it is necessary to agree beforehand as to the minimum that will be accepted as a compromise. Finally, it is essential to have legislators agree, not merely to the principle of FEPC, but to a specific type of bill—one with "teeth." Only in this way can a united front be maintained, and legislators be prevented from supporting FEPC in principle, while finding fault with one and all bills.

Creation and destruction of morale. The manipulation of morale and other diffuse crowd behavior must deal seriously with the relations among individuals as well as with the promotion of a particular course of action. The adherence sought is to a course of action which is felt to be shared. A sense that the goal is a matter of enthusiastic consensus becomes as vital an element as adherence to the goal itself. Along with this conviction goes greater suggestibility toward other members of the same collectivity and a sense of both the rightness and the power of the group.

The attempt to destroy morale may often be an effort to convert a solidaristic type of crowd into an individualistic crowd. In the extreme instance a group with high morale may be caused to panic. In the more typical instance efforts are made to heighten awareness of disparate individual objectives at the expense of the shared objectives. Confidence in the group and its leaders is attacked, with suggestions that many are actually putting individual gain above the group welfare. If the strategy is sufficiently effective the mood of mutual suspicion may be as effectively diffused as the original mood of confidence. During World War II Nazi propaganda in the United States appeared to be directed toward this end. There was probably never any illusion that the United States might be brought into the war on the side of the Axis, but the effort was made to render American assistance to the Allies either unlikely or ineffectual because of internal dissension.

The recognized source of communication is always an obstacle to its effectiveness in psychological warfare, and frequently the opportunities for those within enemy territory to carry out the urgings of the propagandist are meager. Receptiveness to enemy appeals depends on the extent of enthusiasm for the war and the degree of internal unity. When the fortunes of war are favorable, internal divisions tend to be overlooked and it is unlikely that psychological warfare can be effective. Psychological warfare serves chiefly to hasten defeat that is already in the making. Dealing with these problems—the enemy as the source of propaganda, the limited opportunity for defection, and the actual course of war—Martin F. Herz outlines some of the practical lessons that were learned from the psychological warfare activities of the United States government during World War II.

SOME PSYCHOLOGICAL LESSONS FROM LEAFLET PROPAGANDA IN WORLD WAR II

Martin F. Herz

The effectiveness of leaflets which were used in combat propaganda during the past war could be gauged to a much larger extent than was possible in the case of most other forms of propaganda. Continuous prisoner interrogation about the impact of combat leaflets, for instance, permitted the elaboration of certain principles, and their confirmation and subsequent refinement, whereas with respect to the effectiveness of strategic propaganda it has been possible to make only broad and very general observations. Our mistakes in combat propaganda were often readily apparent, while correct psychological judgments could be confirmed by observing the behavior of enemy troops. It is the purpose of this article to set forth some conclusions about leaflet writing and propaganda in general which resulted from this experience.

Reprinted in part by permission of the Princeton University Press, from **Public Opinion Quarterly,** 13 (Fall, 1949), pp. 471-86.

THE INSUFFICIENCY OF TRUTH

During the early days of combat leafleting, the psychological warfare field team with the Fifth Army in Italy was partially dependent on shipments of propaganda material from governmental agencies in Britain and the United States. One leaflet sent to Italy seemed a first-rate job. It described, with many pictures and a brief text, the life in "British, American and Canadian Prisoner-of-War Camps." It showed, for instance, a Canadian base camp that had formerly been a hotel, a camp orchestra, a well-groomed prisoner (an officer) sitting in an overstuffed chair, and other prisoners playing billiards or sitting on a porch listening to the radio. Everything this leaflet said or depicted was true. It was thought best, however, to test it first on some of the prisoners in the Aversa P/W enclosure.

As a result of those tests, the entire shipment had to be discarded. The prisoners were by no means uncooperative—in fact, many of them stated that if only they had known that treatment would be as good as it was in Aversa, they would have surrendered earlier. Nevertheless, they simply refused to believe that conditions in P/W camps in America could be as shown on the leaflet.

Although it was true that prisoners in American P/W camps received eggs for breakfast, further testing showed us that this notion was so preposterous to the Germans on the other side of the firing line that they simply laughed at the idea. Since this discredited the balance of our message, it became another favorable truth which we learned to suppress. The same, incidentally, applied to an important strategic propaganda theme, that of war production. We had to refrain from telling the Germans that Henry Kaiser put ships together in five days. Although this spectacular fact was true, we had to stress the less spectacular and more general fact that we were building several times the tonnage sunk by the U-boats. Intelligence on what the Germans believed, and what they could be expected to believe, forced us to do this.

Eventually, as the result of extensive prisoner interrogations, a basic theme on P/W treatment was worked out, which found its widest application on the Western Front. Instead of picturing captivity in the U.S. as the outrageous idyll which it really was, we used the slogan: *"It's no fun being a prisoner-of-war!"* and went on to show that it was a grim but tolerable fate for anyone who had fought hard but who nevertheless had been unable to evade capture. We did point out, however, that being a prisoner had certain redeeming features. The punch line to this type of appeal was: *"Better Free Than a Prisoner-of-War, Better a Prisoner-of-War Than Dead."* That line proved highly effective. Understatement, in this instance, was probably the only viable means of communicating with the enemy.

HOW CAN EFFECTIVENESS BE JUDGED?

At this point, the question may legitimately be asked just how it was known, during the last war, whether a combat leaflet was more, or less, successful. After all, the psychological warfare intelligence officer could only in the rarest instances observe the behavior in battle of those enemy units which had been subjected to a specific leaflet message. Since this question is important to consideration of the following case material, we will dwell on it briefly.

Evidence of effectiveness, or of lack of effectiveness, was obtained chiefly from the following sources: (a) quantity of leaflets found on the persons of prisoners; (b) recollection of leaflets by prisoners, and comments about them; (c) favorable mention, and detailed discussion by soldiers behind the German lines, as reported by cooperative prisoners; (d) detailed description of their surrender by prisoners; (e) preoccupation of German counter-propaganda with specific Allied leaflets, including plagiarism by German combat propagandists; (f) comments by the enemy command, as learned from captured documents on troop morale.

In some cases, where continued dissemination of one special leaflet was deemed desirable, prisoner reactions could even be used to sharpen its effectiveness, as in the case of the well-known SHAEF Safe-Conduct leaflet. The first edition of that leaflet, produced in the early days of the Normandy invasion, showed merely the seal of the U.S. and the British royal crest, together with a standard text in English and German which called upon the Allied front-line soldier to accord his prisoner good treatment. By the time the Safe-Conduct leaflet went into its sixth printing, the following changes had been made as the result of P/W interviews; (a) the German text had been placed above the English; (b) a note had been inserted, stating specifically that the English text was a translation of the German; (c) General Eisenhower's signature had been added; (d) his name had been spelled out, because it was learned that Germans did not recognize the written signature as Eisenhower's; (e) the leaflet was printed in red rather than in green, which made it more conspicuous on the ground; and (f) a note had been added under the word "Safe Conduct," pointing out that the document was valid for "one or several bearers." These improvements resulted from continuous testing of the leaflet's effectiveness.

In planning for propaganda exploitation of our landing at Anzio and Nettuno in January 1944, we provided for dissemination of a leaflet on the main (Cassino) front as soon as we knew that our troops were ashore. In this leaflet we committed the mistake of making specific predictions, speaking of the German retreat being blocked and of a "battle of encirclement" that would commence with the landing operation. When the beachhead was subsequently contained, the Germans were so elated about the falsity of our prediction that they disseminated replicas of our (German-language) leaflet to the American soldiers at the front, jeering at us and delighting in proving us wrong. It need hardly be pointed out that this was rather foolish on their part: our soldiers had never seen our German-language leaflet and did not care what it said. What the Germans might have done, but failed to do, was to disseminate the leaflet *to their own troops,* thus demonstrating the falsity of our propaganda.

THE HANDLING OF PROPAGANDA DEFEATS

The lesson to be learned from this experience would seem to be that it is highly risky to make predictions about a forthcoming operation, and also quite unnecessary. The argument was advanced during the planning stage before Anzio that we "owed it to our boys to assume that they would be successful," since "if they fail, the incidental propaganda defeat won't matter." In other words, it was contended that the propaganda risk was part of the major military risk. Experience proved this attitude to be wrong. While it is necessary to take military (and political) risks, it does not appear to be necessary to take propaganda risks. If facts go against us, we can still salvage some propaganda honor from them by admitting that the facts are against us. If we make false predictions, however, subsequent admissions have much less value because our whole credit has been undermined. Victories, after defeats in battle, may restore the enemy's fear of our weapons; but truth, after falsity, does not necessarily restore the belief in our truthfulness.

The second instance of an Allied propaganda defeat also contains food for thought. We had achieved considerable success with a leaflet which factually and in pictures described the first day in the life of German P/W's captured on the Cotentin peninsula. The leaflet was widely disseminated all over the Western front. When we broke out of the beachhead and captured Paris, the last picture on the leaflet (which showed P/W's being embarked on an LST) was overprinted in red to show that henceforth prisoners would not longer be shipped to America but would remain in enclosures in Western France. This was a correct decision based on interrogations which showed that many Germans, feeling that the war was about to end, were fearful of being shipped to America, from where it would presumably take longer to get home after the armistice.

German counter-propaganda selected this widely disseminated leaflet to "prove" that since "prisoners are no longer sent to America"—they were being shipped to

Siberia instead. The accusation was substantiated in no other way. It was very widely made, however, and eventually expanded into the general slogan *Sieg oder Sibirien!* (victory or Siberia) which tied in with Goebbels' brilliant "strength through fear" propaganda on the home front. This confronted us with the problem of how to meet a preposterous falsehood that apparently was having some success in bolstering German troop morale.

After careful discussion, it was decided not to respond directly, because (a) any reply could be picked up by the Germans as similarly spurious "proof" of the correctness of their contention; and (b) we did not wish to give additional currency to the idea of Siberia. It was assumed that every denial of a flagrant lie lends it a certain dignity that it did not possess before. The word "Siberia" was consequently never mentioned in our output, and the German campaign eventually died a natural death. During the entire period, we continued our regular output on P/W treatment, ignoring the question of shipment but playing up somewhat more heavily the guarantee, under the Geneva Convention, that prisoners would be returned home "as soon as possible after the war."

In general, to deny a lie disseminated by the enemy is in most cases merely to give it additional circulation. (The Soviets are experts at picking up a denial and using it to revitalize the original falsehood.) Disputing a specific point with an opponent usually means descending to his level. When the enemy has scored, it is usually best to chalk up the score in his column and then to hit him somewhere else. If we dispute a point with him, we meet him on ground which he has chosen and engage in defensive propaganda. Later it will be demonstrated that defensive propaganda is—at least in combat propaganda—a virtual impossibility. Propaganda is essentially an offensive weapon.

TARGET: THE MARGINAL MAN

The marginal man in propaganda is the man who does not believe everything we say, but who is interested in our message because he does not believe everything our opponents say either. In war, he is the man who distrusts us and has reasons for fighting, but who also has good reasons for not fighting. He is the *potential waverer*. (Real waverers are presumably already convinced, and thus are not strictly marginal targets.) In our combat propaganda we always tried to address ourselves to potential waverers, to the men who despaired of victory but were reluctant to draw the consequences, the men who were still willing to fight but who fought without determination, who would "never surrender" but who might submit to capture "if the situation were hopeless." To address the out-and-out fanatics would have been a waste of time, and would have harmed us with our other listeners and friends. On the other hand, to address directly the defeatists and those waiting to desert harmed us with the potential waverers.

The concept of the marginal propaganda man may be a useful one for peacetime propaganda also. Too much output may be addressed to persons who already agree with us. With battle lines fairly clearly drawn, communications which meet the approval of completely pro-American elements are less important than those which appeal to potential waverers on both sides of the ideological front (i.e., we must not forget potential waverers in our own democratic ranks). That is why public opinion polling on the effectiveness of our peacetime propaganda, if it does not weight its samples in favor of the critical strata of the population, may be misleading. If, for instance, a theme of ours elicits exceptional enthusiasm on the part of extreme rightist elements abroad, while intensifying doubts about us on the part of potential waverers among the democratic left, then such a theme has done us more harm than good.

The reasoning behind this conclusion is similar to that which made us forego outright appeals to the German soldier to desert, on the assumption that the desertion-minded would in any event receive our message warmly, whereas a blunt appeal for desertion would have harmed us with the potential waverers. For the potential waverer needs more than "just one little push" to make him topple. To address him with overly partisan, overly direct, overly anti-enemy propaganda might sour him on us completely. Similarly, if propaganda favoring American "rugged individualism" is directed to potential waverers abroad who are convinced that they want economic security most, but who are not yet convinced that it is worthwhile to surrender freedom for it, equally adverse results might be expected.

NECESSITY OF CONCENTRATING
PROPAGANDA FIRE

During the war, demands were continuously made upon our propagandists to "tell the enemy" a large number of things, to attack him on a variety of fronts and to undermine his credit in numerous ways. These demands tended to lead to output which devoted a small amount of attention to a large number of subjects.

The dispersion of themes in some of our combat propaganda may also have been caused in part by the advertising and journalism background of many of our propagandists. Yet combat propaganda and other propaganda addressed to enemy populations in wartime posed quite different problems than domestic advertising. The advertising man need only imagine that he is charged with publicizing Fleetfoot automobiles in publications which contain anti-Fleetfoot material, both editorial and advertising, in about twenty-five times the lineage that he has at his disposal. Let him imagine that the publications on which he must rely to communicate with his public will contain material such as the following:

A news item describing how a certain individual sat down at the wheel of his Fleetfoot, switched on the ignition, stepped on the starter, and was blown to smithereens by gasoline fumes which had accumulated under the hood, due to imperfections of the carburetor . . . Pictures of the man's funeral . . . Resolutions of the bereaved of other families similarly stricken to

boycott Fleetfoots . . . A news item about another Fleetfoot driver who dizzily careened down a steep incline when his brakes failed to function, and a picture of the resulting smashup and carnage . . . Reports of protest meetings against the slipshod manufacturing methods and repressive labor policies of Fleetfoot . . . Pictures of disorders at the Fleetfoot plant, and articles describing the disorganization of the production line, which resulted in rejected parts being inadvertently built into cars on the assembly line . . . Stories about the cost-cutting policies of the Fleetfoot management which brought the elimination of many safety features ordinarily present in other cars . . . Statistics proving the falling-off of Fleetfoot sales and production, and the increase in complaints and fatalities . . .

To appreciate the situation of the wartime propagandist one need only imagine such items appearing in all newspapers and other media of a country, in a volume many times that of any message that the Fleetfoot advertiser can bring to bear. For in a totalitarian country, the mass and insistence of domestic propaganda is altogether out of proportion to what the enemy can offer. Only an occasional leaflet and snatches of radio programs, and often only messages passed on at second hand, can be brought to the attention of the average enemy target. Under such circumstances, it would be idle to speak of the beauty, low price, popularity, engineering advances, etc. of the latest model—as one would do in domestic advertising. There is only one thing, under such circumstances, that can and should be pounded home: namely, that Fleetfoots *work*.

In peacetime, preparatory to possible hostilities, the basic desideratum of propaganda addressed to potential enemy populations is that it should contain proof of our veracity. Praising the excellence of our product is not only secondary but rather beside the point. As we have seen it would be difficult to sell the beauty and stylishness and engineering advances of Fleetfoots to potential customers who are day in, day out, told that Fleetfoots are a danger and a menace.

During the last war, many well-meaning critics of our propaganda effort thought that we should have re-educated the Germans while trying to make them surrender. To this day there are some who do not understand why our propaganda to German soldiers did not characterize Hitler as the villain he indubitably was. To convince German soldiers of the iniquity of the Nazi system, however, would have been a task infinitely more difficult and time-consuming than merely to convince them *that they were being defeated and that it was sensible to give up*. Re-education is not a task of psychological warfare, but of postwar reconstruction. Many men surrendered during the last war who had been convinced by our combat propaganda that to fight on was hopeless and that they would be well treated if they gave up. To convince them of the falsity of Nazism and of Hitler's iniquity might have taken many months and perhaps years longer.

The correctness of this finding is well demonstrated by the failures of Soviet Russia's initial combat propaganda effort against Germany during the last war.

MAKING EXCESSIVE DEMANDS UPON
THE ENEMY

All through the bitter winter of 1941 in front of Moscow, when the Soviets might have had an excellent opportunity to appeal to the frustrated attacking troops, German morale was perceptibly stiffened by injudicious, doctrinaire Soviet propaganda. Conversations with Austrian Communists who participated in that propaganda effort reveal that a bitter fight raged between Soviet propagandists and political officers, with the latter insisting that Soviet combat propaganda be "revolutionary." Soviet leaflets thus initially called upon German soldiers in the front-line to "overthrow Hitler in order to save Germany."

It is a well-established principle of psychology that if pressure is put on a person to perform an act of which he is incapable, serious internal strains and disturbances are set up which may even culminate in hostility toward the person who is making the demands. To call on people who are completely incapable of "overthrowing Hitler" to do so in order to attain their salvation, only means that such people will either despair of their salvation or will turn their backs altogether on the message and its source.

The Soviets eventually learned their lesson and strictly divorced their ideological propaganda from their combat propaganda, but only after caricatures of Hitler, messages exalting the bravery of the Soviet Army and denouncing fascism, etc., had done them immeasurable harm. Even after the break had been made, however, the spilling-over of Communist concepts and nomenclature (including occasional domestic propaganda caricatures and words such as "bankruptcy," "lackeys," "cliques") continued to give their propaganda an outlandish flavor, in spite of their brilliant use of captured German generals for combat psychological warfare purposes. It is an axiom of all propaganda of the written word, of course, that the language must be truly that of the recipient—and that any queerness of idiom severely detracts from the effectiveness of the message. This is so obvious that we may forego the pleasure of offering Japanese exhibits which convincingly demonstrate the point.

"EXPORTING" DOMESTIC PROPAGANDA

Generally speaking, it can be said that domestic propaganda and propaganda addressed to the enemy simply do not mix. It follows that exceptional loathing and hatred of the enemy, perhaps derived from personal humiliation, persecution, and other on-the-spot experiences, do not by any means constitute good qualifications for combat propagandists. Thus persons who returned from Germany and Japan shortly before the war, and considered their primary mission to be spreading knowledge in America about the iniquity and menace of the systems there, found it extremely difficult to achieve the necessary adjustments that would make them useful for propaganda directed toward the enemy civilian populations. Similarly, in combat propaganda, the propagandist's exultation over the enemy's discomfitures should not be too apparent in his output. Leaflets gleefully pointing at weaknesses and absurdities of the enemy, jibing and jeering at his travails, (the "We hear you have a one-legged man in your company" type) generally proved unsuccessful during the last war. It was difficult to prevent the production and dissemination of such material, however, since intelligence officers, for whom propaganda inevitably means capitalizing on all weaknesses and mistakes of the enemy, frequently pressed very strongly for leaflets of this type.

The above point is by no means as obvious as it seems, for while in theory many might agree, in practice it seemed unreasonable to some that we did not fight "ideologically" in our combat propaganda. To clinch this point, therefore, it is well to observe the effect on ourselves of enemy propaganda which incorporated domestic propaganda elements.

One example may be found in German anti-Semitic propaganda. The Nazis, to whom it seemed obvious that the Jews were behind America's entry into the war, found it impossible to contain themselves on that score. As a result, leaflets and radio programs which otherwise might have had a measure of success became even queerer and stranger to the American soldiers—for instance, the Axis-Sally programs with their reference to the "Jewnited States," or leaflets about wartime profiteers which pictured a character named Sam Levy who had been helped up the ladder to fame and fortune by Mr. Mordecai Ezekiel. To the Nazis, the name of a real-life figure such as Mr. Ezekiel seemed a God-given propaganda asset which the propagandist simply could not pass up. After all, did not that name clearly convey the idea of an untrustworthy, scheming and grasping individual? To Germans who had been steeped in Nazi anti-Semitic propaganda it undoubtedly had such a connotation. To American GI's, however, such leaflets looked more like "propaganda" than they would have otherwise, and the entire venture acquired a fatally alien and unreasonable quality.

A second example is afforded by German and Japanese anti-Roosevelt propaganda. Let it not be said that the average American was more loyal to his President or more convinced of Roosevelt's essential honesty than the average German wa of Hitler's. Many a German who consid ered the war a mistake, and perhaps ever a crime, nevertheless resented slurs on Hitler, especially when made by the en emy. The same, *mutatis mutandis,* wa true of many American soldiers. An anti Roosevelt leaflet had a decidedly adverse (i.e., anti-enemy and morale-strengthen ing) effect on our troops.

The third, and most recent, example may be taken from the propaganda now being directed to Europe. In this the So viets, whose propagandists appear to have their hands tied by directives, have with out question sinned and failed the most in Austria, for instance, the Soviet news paper *Oesterreichische Zeitung,* with it alien make-up, its queer wording ("over fulfilled the norm," "miasmas of capital ism," etc.) and its preponderance of out landish news items, has lost nearly al reader interest—although the Austria Communist paper, which is written by Austrians, is quite another story. Wa films of all nations, in which enemy sol diers are shown, have met with unfavor able receptions in ex-enemy territory Plays, such as the eminently successfu "Watch on the Rhine," which packe them in on Broadway, elicited genera astonishment and dismay over what Ger man and Austrian theatergoers (includin; violent anti-Nazis) considered to be in accuracies and "patent propaganda."

DOCTRINE OF LIMITED AGREEMENT

Thus it can be said that in comba propaganda it would be fatal to expec the enemy to identify himself with ou side. Totalitarian enemies do not revo because they cannot, and they do no change sides because they rarely under stand the truth until it is too late. Conse quently, we cannot expect an individua enemy to agree with us on more than on point at a time.

In order to find any common groun

at all, to find a point of departure for the psychological manipulation of the enemy, it may even be necessary to select a point of his own creed on which to register agreement. During the last war, the elements of the German propaganda position which we used as such "points of departure" were (a) the belief in the excellence of the soldierly qualities of the German infantryman; and (b) the belief that he was being crushed by Allied superiority of materiel, rather than outfought man for man. No propaganda to enemy targets can be successful unless some such common ground which can be used as a point of departure for the message is found.

As an example of the validity of this doctrine, there is featured what was probably the most successful combat leaflet of the last war. This leaflet is usually passed over by chroniclers of our combat propaganda record because of its seeming lack of originality or insidiousness. Yet it was again and again adjudged the most successful venture of this type (next to the SHAEF Safe-Conduct leaflet). It was found in large numbers on the persons of prisoners, was republished in many variants at various stages of the campaign in the West, and was also reprinted and used with good success by combat propagandists in the Mediterranean Theater. It salved the feelings of the enemy by crediting him, by implication, with great soldierly virtue; it accommodated his alibi of material inferiority; it described him in soldierly (non-political) terms, avoiding any political arguments; it did not overly praise captivity; and it "left the decision to the reader," seemingly not urging him to desert. Also, on its reverse side, along with a dry, curt summary of the essential facts about captivity, it spelled out the behavior necessary to effect surrender.

Propaganda to non-enemy targets is governed by the opposite considerations. In addressing ourselves to an enemy-occupied country, for instance, the audience's identification with our side must obviously be *taken for granted*—even if it does not completely obtain. It must always be assumed that citizens of occupied countries will greet us as liberators when we redeem them. (This assumption also immeasurably lightens the task of consolidation and post-war reorientation propaganda in occupied territories.) To make concessions to the Quisling point-of-view in any particular would be quite out of place.

WEDGE-DRIVING AND APPEALS TO THE UNCONSCIOUS

To "widen the gulf" between two enemy nations, to "drive a wedge" between officers and enlisted men, or to "exploit the cleavage" between elite troops and combat infantry, or "between the party and the people," are ever-cherished objectives of the propaganda directive writer. As objectives they are of course entirely sound. Implementation may, however, involve so many psychological difficulties that more harm than good is done. For sometimes it will suffice for a latent dissatisfaction to be brought out into the open by the enemy, for it to disappear.

Witness the German propaganda at the Anzio beachhead in February 1944, which reasoned quite correctly that British troops, who had borne the heaviest brunt of the German offensive at Aprilia (Carroceto), were apt to grumble about the seemingly less dangerous role played by the Americans. Several wedge-driving leaflets along such lines were disseminated, including some titillating ones showing British girls being undressed and fondled by Americans. The German approach, however, was so lacking in subtlety that according to British officers on the beachhead the comradeship-in-arms between British and Americans there was enhanced rather than diminished by the Nazi propaganda effort. Also—possibly through the projection of a theme that was vexing and frustrating to the reader without his being able to do anything about it—anti-German sentiment among British troops may even have increased.

The Japanese combat leaflet writers also attempted to capitalize on the known sex-frustration of American soldiers in the jungles of the South Pacific, but again the result was so crass and clumsy that if it lowered the morale of any American soldier reading such a leaflet, at the same time it quite likely made him want to vent his pent-up feelings upon the enemy. Although there were some abler attempts in the same direction, all suffered from the directness of the appeal: it simply is not for the enemy to remind us of our desire for women, or, for that matter, of our desire to get out of the battle alive. What goes for sex goes even more for cowardice. Enemy media can hardly appeal plainly and directly to the individual's unsoldierly, unheroic desire for self-preservation. Perhaps it could if he were alone, but since powerful group pressures work upon him, and feelings of duty, comradeship, fear and patriotism intervene, the overt appeal cannot run directly counter to them. German appeals to our GI's, slogans such as "Take it easy, you'll last longer," fall into this category.

DANGERS OF BLACK PROPAGANDA

It may be said, in view of the above—and there are many other examples—that to bring out and nourish any subconscious feelings of resentment on the part of the enemy soldier may be beyond the capabilities of "white" propaganda (the source of which is admitted) and instead is a fitting subject for "black" or "gray" propaganda (ostensibly produced by dissident elements within the enemy population, or mentioning no source at all). The difficulty there, however, is that detection of the origin of such propaganda will not only result in heightened hatred against the actual originator for having thus invaded the most private recesses of the enemy's mind, but it will also redound emphatically to the detriment of all "white" propaganda from the same source.

As a good example of this danger, mention might be made of an Allied "black" or "gray" leaflet of the last war that was designed to fan the sex-starved German soldier's resentment against the alleged increased latitude given foreign laborers in Germany. The leaflet in question showed a swarthy foreign worker shamelessly disporting himself with a naked Teutonic maiden, and was decidedly apt to arouse the passions of a front-line soldier. Had it been possible to conceal the source completely, beyond the shadow of a doubt, this leaflet might well have been a smashing success in undermining German troop morale. As it was, however—and this is a criticism of most of our naive "black" and "gray" activity of the last war—the enemy could easily see from the elaborateness of the leaflet (which in this case was printed in four colors) that this was Allied propaganda. Even though he might agree with the message, he would resent it since it was painful to him. Moreover, since at the same time all our "white" media were laboring hard and patiently to establish the essential honesty and forthrightness of our propaganda, some harm was probably done to the credit of our white media.

No nation can talk out of two sides of its mouth at the same time: we cannot on the one hand speak nothing but the truth and then, with a changed voice and pretending to be someone else—but quite obviously still ourselves—say things which we don't dare to say straight out. Black propaganda must be like the voice of a master ventriloquist which really appears to come out of the mouth of an entirely different individual. In the case of the "gray" leaflet under discussion, the general make-up of the message and especially the elaborateness of its presentation, made it quite obvious that it was not the product of a clandestine printing press in Germany. Had it been possible to create such an impression, however, or had it been possible to make it seem an inadvertent German disclosure, it might have been the important adjunct to our overt program which it was originally intended to be.

ON THREATS AND "TOUGHNESS" IN PROPAGANDA

There does not appear to be a single case on record in the last war when an ultimatum resulted in surrender of a surrounded enemy unit. On the other hand we know of many cases when, in the face f a hopeless situation, commanders sent or received emissaries to discuss surrender. Because, in a sense, a totalitarian country at bay resembles a beleaguered fortress, the question of collective surrenders in the face of collective threats is ll-important. First of all, it must be said that the threat of force is only effective if immediately followed by force—nothing s more damning than an empty propaganda threat. Second, a message written rom the strength of one's position cannot be hedged or qualified, or couched in defensive tone, and should not attempt o answer imaginary counter-arguments. 'he German appeal to the American orces in Bastogne, in fact, might have een written by an American fifth columnist in the ranks of a German combat propaganda company, or by American lack operators attempting to raise the morale of the defenders. Instead of emphasizing all factors of German strength, he writer attempted to answer all imaginable counter-arguments and thus practically created the impression that the jermans at Bastogne were the beleaguered ones and that the Americans really had no reason to be as self-confident" as he imagined them to be. This is n excellent example of the general proposition that defensiveness has no place in combat propaganda and little place in any propaganda.

Threats, however, do occasionally have place in propaganda. In order to describe the conditions under which they may have a salutary effect, it is necessary o differentiate among four basic situations: (a) the situation of the enemy soldier—if he can do something about getting out of the fight, and (b) if he can o nothing about getting out of the fight; milarly (c) the situation of the civilian who is in a position to act, and (d) that f the civilian who can do nothing about le war. If these differentiations are not orne in mind, the effects of propaganda may be diametrically opposed to those hich have been intended.

As to the enemy soldier, if he is in ny position to surrender, a threat followed up with a display of strength (e.g., overwhelming artillery superiority) may make him ripe at least for capture. If he is in no position to surrender, however— and most members of beleaguered garrisons belong in this category—he is quite likely to be galvanized into especially fanatical resistance by the threat, because of the psychological mechanism of frustration which has been mentioned above.

As to civilians, those who are in no position to do anything about the war— and these constitute the overwhelming majority of the population of all totalitarian countries—will quite likely be embittered by threatening propaganda. Occasionally, however, such bitterness can be exploited for tactical purposes. The Germans are said to have used terror propaganda during their Blitzkrieg in 1940 specifically in order to create panic and encourage civilians to take flight and thus clog the roads. They also attempted to use scare tactics during their Ardennes offensive, when they cynically advised unfortunate French civilians in the Strasbourg-Mulhouse area (where they had temporarily recrossed the Rhine) to "save yourselves—for we will treat you just as well as we have treated your comrades during the last four years!" The Western Allies also used such tactics when, at the behest of Prime Minister Churchill, they unfolded a propaganda effort early in 1945 which was designed to start large numbers of Germans trekking from certain specified "danger areas." These are the only known instances in the last war when threatening propaganda to civilians had the intended effect.

THE "HELPLESS CIVILIAN" TARGET

By far the most important category of targets, however—in point of numbers, at least—is the civilian population (category "d") that can do nothing to end the war, consisting as it does of persons who cannot even remove themselves from the impact of bombing attacks. To threaten them—however gratifying it may be to the enemy-hating propagandist—is psychologically unsound. Rather, the propagandist must seek, by continuous analysis of the patterns of life in the enemy country, to discover those actions which the enemy civilian can reasonably take in his own interest, and where his own interest coincides with ours. To find such actions may afford the key to propaganda to enemy civilians. In the absence of that key, most propaganda directed to enemy civilians will have little concrete effect on the course of a war. In fact, when it is considered that military defeats in any event constitute psychological blows of the first magnitude against the enemy civilian, it would seem that, prior to the time when mutual-interest situations begin to obtain, little can be gained from propaganda directed toward enemy civilians in wartime, except by way of building up credibility. Thus our enormous leaflet output which was dropped on Germany during the war, on which so little evidence of effectiveness has been obtained, can really be judged only in terms of whether it built up belief in our essential honesty. This confidence was needed in the final months of the war when we were in a position to exploit mutual-interest situations.

This—the seeking of mutual-interest situations—constituted by far the most difficult and delicate psychological warfare research project of the last war. Whereas at the beginning of the war, "tough" propaganda from the West was received with derisiveness; whereas during the invasion period it produced sullenness and frustration; at the end of the war our propaganda was all too often greeted by German civilians with the remark: "*I agree with everything you say, but what am I to do?*" In a war against a different country, entirely different mutual-interest situations may obtain. The important lesson is that the earlier such instructions can be formulated and the better they can be presented as being of mutual interest and as being *feasible,* the more successful will propaganda against enemy civilians be.

To a considerable degree morale in a group involved in a collective enterprise will develop apart from deliberate efforts at its cultivation. Indeed, too constant attention to morale may serve to reinforce any suspicions that all is not really well, that there may be more to fear than is generally known. The existence of an essential objective shared by all will lead to spontaneous group pressure upon the individual who openly pursues his disparate individual ends. The sense that the objective is worthy and the conviction that success is inevitable will bear considerable relation to values and events which preceded the current enterprise. But to the degree to which deliberate efforts can strengthen morale, they may require a carefully balanced role for the propagandist. Talcott Parsons has proposed that morale-building propaganda, to be effective, requires such a special role. He suggests that certain distinctive characteristics of the physician's role vis-à-vis his patient have important features in common with those of the effective propagandist for national morale.*

The physician-patient relation allows the patient to make intimate self-revelations in the presence of the physician without expecting comparable revelations from the physician. The institutionalized trust in the physician and the prestige of his professional competence help to make possible such intimacies. The physician stands unquestionably for approved behavior, but passes no moral judgments on the patient's behavior and does not take the latter's rationalizations at face value by arguing with them. Self-examination in such a relationship permits the patient to see his rationalizations for what they are and apply a more realistic perspective to his own behavior. Similarly, in morale-supporting propaganda the

---

* Talcott Parsons, "Propaganda and Social Control," in **Essays in Sociological Theory Pure and Applied** (Glencoe, Ill.: The Free Press, 1949), pp. 275–309.

objective is to control deviant tendencies and to reinforce a realistic perspective. The agencies of propaganda, like the physician, must be identified with those aspects of the government which symbolize the unity of the society, avoiding involvement in partisan struggles. They must establish a reputation of scrupulous honesty in reporting events about which the individual cannot learn from other sources. They must cultivate the unquestioned assumption that they are identified with the national welfare. And they must operate not through answering particular arguments against national unity but by constantly keeping before the people the fundamental definitions of the situation that are conducive to national unity.

Eliciting active support from the enemy. Strategies may call for more than the promotion of morale in the in-group and the destruction of morale in the out-group. They may call for eliciting active support from among the enemy. The task is thereby made more complicated. For example, such tactics as the creation of widespread fear may destroy enemy morale but also prevent effective collective action to assist the group. Again, the propaganda efforts must be supplemented by concrete means to act collectively. Hans Speier has examined this question of how propaganda directed toward enemy civilians in wartime can effectively promote collective action.*

A nation attempting to create organized opposition within the enemy ranks must make the most effective use of those areas in which it has greatest power over the receivers' responses, and attempt to work in areas in which the enemy exercises little effective control over its own citizens' behavior. This general principle has many applications. Because of the power of the enemy to block mass communications the most effective procedure may be to send information to organized resistance groups which then relay the material through their own channels. By using persons of international prestige to deliver propaganda the communicating nation can maximize listener interest. Coordination of propaganda with military initiative heightens the impact of propaganda. Realistic account must be taken of the extent of freedom permitted its citizenry by the enemy. Incitement to types of resistance which the enemy can easily block is futile. General efforts to destroy civilian enemy morale are not likely to promote effective resistance or revolutionary movements. Effective strategy is to facilitate the efforts and reinforce the morale of already dissident organizations within enemy territory, looking toward ultimate defection among the police or armed forces.

These points underline a more general principle that solidaristic collective behavior can operate effectively only by taking advantage of weaknesses in the established power structure. The task of the propagandist is to keep alive the morale of those groups within the enemy nation that already show promise of gaining some control over the police power, and to provide them with the means for making rebellion an effective rather than a futile gesture.

* Hans Speier, "The Future of Psychological Warfare," **Public Opinion Quarterly,** 12 (1948), pp. 5–18.

Part 4

THE SOCIAL MOVEMENT

Chapter 14

Social movements:
character and processes

$\mathcal{C}$OLLECTIVE behavior is the study of those phenomena which fall between on the one hand group behavior, which is organized on the basis of rules and tradition, and on the other mere disparate individual behavior. The boundaries of the field of study tend to be vague, shading both into the study of organized group behavior and into the dynamics of individual behavior. Perhaps the most ephemeral type of collectivity and that which merges most closely with disparate individual behavior is the momentary panic. The social movement falls toward the other extreme of the area of study, with a considerable degree of organization, the emergence of rules and tradition, and stability and continuity in time. Indeed, the longer the life of a social movement and the larger and more powerful it is, the more it takes on the characteristics of an association rather than a collectivity.

We have observed that the crowd tends to develop and enforce on its members a uniform course of action. The public determines a course of action that takes account of acknowledged differences of position. If the crowd develops a more enduring sense of group-identity and pursues a plan of action requiring more sustained activity than can be maintained through crowd conditions, a social movement is emerging. Or if members of a public who share a common position concerning the issue at hand supplement their informal person-to-person discussion with some organization to promote their convictions more effectively and insure more sustained activity, a social movement is incipient.

In spite of the relation of social movements to other forms of collective behavior, social movements are different in important respects. Popular writers often

307

treat a social movement as a sort of extended crowd made up of people acting under a delusion fostered by the mechanisms of crowd behavior. Because the members of a movement are in constant contact with persons who do not adhere to the movement, because sustained activity and enthusiasm over an extended period of time is required, and because some sustained division of labor is required within the movement, the members' activities on behalf of the movement must be disciplined rather than chiefly impulsive. At times the provocation and manipulation of crowd behavior is an effective tactic, either in making the opposition afraid of the movement, in arousing the enthusiasm of outsiders for the movement, or in strengthening the *esprit de corps* of the members through crowd experience. At other times the spontaneous resurgence of crowd behavior may lead members of a movement to excesses of behavior that discredit the movement within the public to which it is appealing. In either case, however, the crowd behavior is a phase of the movement rather than the whole of it.

Definition of a social movement. A social movement is a collectivity acting with some continuity to promote a change or resist a change in the society or group of which it is a part.

As a collectivity, a movement is a group with indefinite and shifting membership, with leadership whose position is determined more by the informal response of the members than by formal procedures for legitimizing authority.

The movement is marked by continuity in several respects. First, the movement's objective must be of a type that requires sustained activity. A movement could hardly be said to develop over so short-range an objective as lynching a single kidnapper, though the determination to control kidnapping in general could give rise to a movement. Likewise, there will be some continuity in movement strategy. There will also be some continuity in the division of function, with some stability of leadership and other roles. There will be continuity in the sense of group identity, so that even with rapid turnover of large portions of the membership the sense of group continuity prevails.

In saying that a social movement promotes or resists change we are differentiating it from an informal group whose activities are entirely self-contained in their implications. A group of people who assemble strictly for their own enjoyment or their own betterment without making any demands on the community would not be a social movement.

There are three types of groupings which we may call *quasi-movements* because they possess some but not all of the characteristics of a movement.

First, the term *mass movement* is applied to phenomena that fall somewhere between the mass and a true social movement. In a mass migration or a gold rush, for example, there is a certain amount of social contagion and we-feeling though in the final analysis the behavior remains individual. There may be considerable activity in the common interest, such as combined activity to protect migrants from hostile natives or to promote favorable political measures. But the governing objectives and plans of action remain individual. The numbers involved are likely to be great, and the implications for change in the society considerable. We may learn a good deal about the grass roots, mass support aspects of social movements from the study of this type.

Second, the term *following* is applied to a collectivity that is united in its attention to and admiration of a public individual. The attachment to a hero is the basis for continuity, and the subject of interaction among "fans." The attachment is to the hero himself rather than to any cause that he represents. Hence, while there may be some organization and a vitally developed we-feeling, the following is short of being a collectivity concerned with promoting some program. However, the following is seldom an altogether neutral force in the larger society since the members seek to imitate the hero in numerous ways. Hence the difference between a following and a true movement built about an admired leader tends to be one of the degree to which admiration for the leader causes the followers to promote a program of social change.

Third, a *cult* is a collectivity that has the continuity of a social movement, but that makes demands only on the behavior of its members. A religious cult may demand of its members behavior that is quite different from the established social conventions while making no effort to promote acceptance of such a program in the society. The cult membership is content to remain withdrawn from the society in general. In many collectivities the members believe that the world can be changed by winning large numbers of people to their way of behaving. Hence they attempt to modify the social order by extensive proselyting—by incorporating more people within their movement and enforcing their behavioral demands upon them. Although this procedure is different from that of the typical movement which attempts to modify society through legislation or influence on policy, it also distinguishes these movements from simple cults. To the degree to which collectivities proselytize as a means toward changing society, they become true social movements.

Life-cycle of a social movement. One of the approaches frequently used to study social movements has been to describe the typical life-cycle of social movements in general or of certain types of social movements in particular. The life-cycle consists of an idealized series of stages from the origin to the success or other final form of the movement.

This approach is one of value in several ways. It places emphasis on process, which is particularly important in the study of phenomena whose most important characteristic is change. Furthermore, the life-cycle is a way of organizing our knowledge about movements so as to permit prediction of forthcoming events. The life-cycle also offers a framework within which the many aspects of a movement may be seen working together—leadership, ideology, tactics, membership, etc., rather than each studied separately. Finally, it provides a framework within which the determination of "success" of a movement may be approached.

On the basis of an historical study of political revolutions in South America, Rex Hopper has sketched a typical life-cycle. While the cycle is only supposed to apply to revolutions, it incorporates generalized life-cycles proposed earlier by Park and Burgess, by Blumer, and by Dawson and Gettys as applying to most types of social movement. It should be read as a generalized cycle, applicable to most kinds of social movements in its broad outlines. At the same time the reader should constantly consider the degree to which such an idealized scheme can correspond to the actual events of any movement.

THE REVOLUTIONARY PROCESS: A FRAME OF REFERENCE FOR THE STUDY OF REVOLUTIONARY MOVEMENTS

REX D. HOPPER

. . . The hypothesis to be discussed is an example of what is known as the *natural history* approach to the study of human behavior. . . . "The natural history method is nothing more nor less than an account of an evolutionary process— a process by which not the individual but the type evolves."

This approach when applied to the study of revolutionary movements has yielded the postulate that such movements pass through four stages in their development: the Preliminary Stage of Mass (Individual) Excitement, the Popular Stage of Crowd (Collective) Excitement and Unrest, the Formal Stage of Formulation of Issues and Formation of Publics, and the Institutional Stage of Legalization and Societal Organization.

To prevent what we are here doing from being judged as merely another in a series of clever surmises, it is important to realize that the hypothesis just formulated has a history. By collating the work of such pioneer students as Sorokin, Edwards, Gettys, Blumer, and Brinton, it is possible to draw a general picture of revolutionary behavior in which the nature and interrelationships of the different aspects of a revolutionary movement are rather clearly indicated. . . .

Before undertaking to outline the revolutionary process, it is necessary to undergird such a description of revolutionary behavior with a brief statement of the way *human* behavior looks to contemporary students of the "science of human relationships." In answer to the question, "What is human behavior?" there is an increasing tendency to reply that *human* behavior is a function of the development of socially-acquired attitudes toward culturally-held values.

What does this point of view mean when applied to the analysis of the rev-

olutionary process? Expressed otherwise, what happens when one social order collapses and another emerges? It means first, that any social order or society may be viewed as a sort of moving equilibrium of culturally-held values and socially-acquired attitudes. In relation to the social order, then, it consists of a system of relatively orderly values. From the point of view of the people living in the culture and responding to its values, a social order consists of a system of commonly held tendencies to act toward a given system of values. Thus men call the times orderly, speak of social order and organization, and believe that they live in a *cosmos* when the values deposited in their culture satisfy the attitudes in terms of which they tend to act. On the other hand, men deem the times to be out of joint, speak of social disorder and disorganization, and fear that they live in a *chaos* when the values deposited in their culture no longer satisfy their attitudes.

It means, second, that social order is disturbed and the process of social disorganization sets in when for any reasons all attitudes and values begin to diverge.

It means, third, that social change has taken place if and when social disorganization eventuates in the reorganization of attitudes and/or values.

It means, fourth, that significant social change always has to do with change on the institutional level—that is, with changes in the attitudes-values that are deemed to be basically important. Changes on this level are very disturbing and result in great disorganization and unrest until the changed attitudes and their corresponding values have been worked into the institutional structure of the culture and a new social order has been built. Therefore, an understanding of the process of social change on this level is imperative to those interested in doing something about social change.

Reprinted in part by permission of the editors, from **Social Forces,** 28 (March, 1950), pp. 270–79.

It means, finally, that *revolutionary change* is precisely that kind of social change which occurs when the basic institutional (i.e., legally enforced) values of a social order are rejected and new values accepted.

We may now ask what a revolutionary movement looks like when historical events are re-examined in terms of the hypothesis which the events themselves have suggested to trained observers. Arranged in terms of the postulated four stages and in a fashion designed to indicate the interdependence of the various features of the movement during each stage, the answer runs as follows.

THE PRELIMINARY STAGE
OF MASS (INDIVIDUAL) EXCITEMENT
AND UNREST

Characteristic Conditions

In this stage socio-psychological conditions (meaning simply the traits which people tend to manifest in a society where a revolutionary movement may be getting under way) may be grouped under six headings, so arranged as to reveal a socio-psychological sequence or orderliness.
1. General restlessness which manifests itself in:
   A. Wish repression
   B. Development of a balked disposition mind-set
   C. Restless behavior of individuals
   D. Increase in crime, vice, insanity, suicide, agitation, and travel (wandering individuals of all classes, and emigration)
2. The development of class antagonisms as shown by:
   A. The increase in wealth, intelligence, and power of "repressed groups"
   B. The separation of economic power from political power and social distinction
   C. The development of a condition wherein men of ability are shut out from careers of any consequence
3. Marked governmental inefficiency
4. Reform efforts on the part of the government

5. Cultural drift in the direction of revolutionary change
6. Spread and socialization of restlessness as evidenced by:
   A. Increased tension, cramp, and irritation
   B. Increased talk of revolution
   C. Wandering of attention from one individual, object, or line of action to another

It is suggested that this arrangement of the dominant characteristics of the preliminary stage portrays what happens as a society breaks up into a mass, a process that is necessarily preliminary to the initiation of a revolutionary movement.

Typical Process

How may people like this be expected to behave? Or, what process is *typical* of the Preliminary Stage? They will be susceptible to the *milling* process or "circular interaction" as it is sometimes called. . . . When translated into the terms used in our earlier description of the nature of human behavior, this means that milling occurs in the early stages of the process by which disparity is produced between the attitudes of a group and their social values. This disparity is initially expressed by a sort of unorganized and unformulated restlessness, the causes of which are unknown, hence unrecognized. The diffused nature of the discontent makes impossible the projection of any plan of action and accounts for the random character of behavior at this stage as well as the uncertainty with references to the ends toward which action should be directed.

Effective Mechanisms

How may people so behaving be influenced? What mechanisms or devices must be employed by those presuming to positions of leadership in the Preliminary Stage? In general terms, of course, the mechanisms employed to control people must be suited to their dominant mood. When applied to the present problem this means that people who exhibit the socio-psychological characteristics already outlined can be influenced by such devices as agitation, suggestion, imitation, propaganda, et cetera. It also means that those men will emerge as leaders who are most able and skilled in the use of such control devices. Thus it may be said that the dominant socio-psychological conditions determine both the nature of the leadership and the choice of mechanisms of social control.

Types of Leaders

What kind of leader will potential revolutionists follow? This stage belongs to the agitator and, as Blumer has shown, there are two types of agitators who correspond to the two types of situations in which they function.

Dominant Social Form

In what sort of groupings do such people as we have been describing act? In other words, what is the *form* of elementary collective behavior, or the sort of behavior characteristic of the Preliminary Stage of a revolutionary movement?

It is suggested that possible participants in such a movement constitute a "psychological mass," a form of human collective behavior with the following features: first, the people composing it come from all walks and levels of life; second, the mass is made up of anonymous persons, responding to common influences but unknown to each other; third, because they are unknown to each other, there is little interaction or exchange of experience between the members of the mass; fourth, there is little or no organization on the level of mass behavior.

In short, the nature of the mass is determined by what the people composing it are like. And the people behave as they do because of the characteristics they share. Thus persons who participate in mass behavior do so because the objects of interest which gain their attention lie outside of the local culture and groups and are something for which the mores of the local groups offer inadequate explanations. In consequence, the members of the mass are detached and alienated individuals, both with reference to the

mores of their old culture and the new objects of attention. They are in a marginal position. A disparity of attitude and values has developed and the process of social disorganization has set in.

THE POPULAR STAGE
OF CROWD (COLLECTIVE) EXCITEMENT AND UNREST

Whether a movement passes from the preliminary stage of mass (individual excitement and unrest into this stage depends on the nature of developments in the first stage. The hypothesis under examination does not postulate an inevitable sequence of events. Quite to the contrary, it recognizes that in a variety of ways a possible movement may be indefinitely postponed or completely redirected. For example, governments sometimes use war with another nation as device for keeping down threatened internal disturbances. Or, the unrest may be drained off in non-political directions This seems to have happened in England when the development of Methodism redirected a movement that might have had catastrophic revolutionary effects.

However, failure to deal with the underlying causes of unrest and discontent will mean that the evolution of the movement will continue. If it does, the basic socio-psychological conditions typical of the second stage will emerge and their general nature is suggested by the name given to the period. It is a time of the *popularization* of unrest and discontent; time when the dissatisfaction of the people results in the development of *collective excitement*. It is not implied that unrest and discontent become popular in the sense that they spread to every last man in the population. Rather, popularization takes place among those psychologically prepared to share in the movement. On the part of the opposition, the very popularization of unrest and discontent serves to intensify their resistance to the spread of the movement. Thus popularization one section of the population is paralleled by resistance in another.

This is the stage when individuals participating in the mass behavior of the preceding stage become aware of each other. Their negative reactions to the basic factors in their situation are shared and begin to spread. Unrest is no longer covert, endemic, and esoteric; it becomes overt, epidemic, and exoteric. Discontent is no longer uncoordinated and individual; it tends to become focalized and collective.

Characteristic Conditions

In consequence of all this, the socio-psychological conditions typically present in this stage can be classified under six headings.

1. The spread of discontent and the contagious extension of the several signs of unrest and discontent as manifested in:

  A. Increased activity

  B. Growing focus of attention

  C. Heightened state of expectancy

2. The transfer of allegiance of the intellectuals, including:

  A. Wish reformulation

  B. Loss of faith in their leadership on the part of the repressed classes and the loss of faith in themselves on the part of the leaders

  C. Spread of rumor and scandal and the development of a literature of exposure

  D. Emergence of the "good man fallacy"

  E. Identification of a guilty group, focusing of attention on it, and the development of an "advertising offensive" against it

  F. Development of an "oppression psychosis"

3. The fabrication of a social myth with these allied characteristics:

  A. Creation of collective illusions, myths, and doctrines

  B. Emergence of the economic incentive to revolutionary action

  C. Development of a tentative object of loyalty

4. The emergence of conflict with the out-group and the resultant increase in in-group consciousness

5. The organization of the discontented for the purpose of remedying the threatened or actual breakdown of government

6. The presentation of revolutionary demands which if granted would amount to the abdication of those in power.

Typical Processes

With reference to the processes functioning at this level, there is a marked intensification of milling. But, it is not quite so random and aimless. People develop more definite notions of the causes of their difficulties and of what should be done to resolve them. This intensification and speeding up of the milling process results in so changing it that *social contagion* and *collective excitement* are better terms for describing what is going on. The attention is being caught and riveted and the people are becoming emotionally aroused and more likely to be carried away by impulses and feelings. Hence collective excitement serves to integrate unrest and discontent, break down old behavior patterns, and prepare the way for new patterns of behavior. Where collective excitement is intense and widespread there is also the possibility of social contagion: that is, there occurs the relatively rapid, unwitting, and non-rational dissemination of a mood, impulse, or form of conduct.

Social contagion, then, is simply an intense form of milling and collective excitement in which rapport is established. These processes serve to unite the individuals of the mass into the crowd and so lay the foundations for further development.

Effective Mechanisms

It is necessary again to remind ourselves that the four stages of a revolutionary movement are not clear-cut and mutually exclusive. No such claim has ever been made for them. The concept "stage" is simply a means of describing dominant tendencies and makes no pretense of dealing with absolutely delimited periods.

This reminder is particularly desirable when considering the processes and mechanisms of the Popular Stage. Milling continues, though there is a basic, if subtle change. There is a focusing of attention on a tentative objective to be realized that was absent in the previous age. Agitation, suggestion, imitation and propaganda continue in use. But the change in the nature of the processes gives new direction to the mechanisms already in operation and calls into play certain additional devices.

Of these the effort to develop *esprit de corps* is especially important. Leaders who desire to intensify rapport as a means of transforming a mass of individuals into a psychological and/or acting crowd will employ esprit de corps as a means of social control. That is, they will foster it as a way of organizing and integrating loyalty to the movement—as a way of making people feel that they belong together and are identified with and engaged in a common undertaking. It is at once evident that esprit de corps is very necessary as a means of developing unity and solidarity in a movement. Its use prevents disintegration and permits the organization of unrest and discontent in such fashion as to forward the evolution of the movement. It is achieved through promoting the in-group relationship, the formation of informal fellowship associations, and participation in informal ceremonial behavior.

Another important mechanism that is brought into use at this stage has been called the "social" or "revolutionary" myth. In order to mobilize unrest and discontent and prepare for action, the people must be led to believe that they are on the march toward a New Order—a potential Utopia which it is their duty to help actualize.

In addition to these two major devices and as aids to their realization rumor, scandal, a literature of exposure, pamphlets, plays, protests, and many other mechanisms are also employed.

Types of Leader

The conditions of the period and the skills requisite to the use of the necessary mechanisms determine the requirements for successful leadership. Thus the Popular Stage provides opportunity for the talents of the *prophet* and the *reformer*.

The prophet feels set apart or called to leadership; that he has a special and separate knowledge of the causes of unrest and discontent which the agitator has already brought to the attention of the people. He speaks with an air of authority, revealing a new message and a new philosophy of life, though always in general terms. He formulates and promulgates the social myth. He uses his belief in himself and his confidence in his message as a means of articulating the hope and wishes of the people.

The reformer is a somewhat different type. He is produced by and is reacting to the same basic conditions, but the nature of the reaction is different and it is likely, too, that he appears somewhat later than the prophet, whose aims are general and vague. The reformer attacks specific evils and develops a clearly defined program; he attempts to change conditions in conformity with his own conceptions of what is good and desirable.

Dominant Social Form

The above brings us to the consideration of the social form typical of the Popular Stage. For the fact that the mass of the first stage evolves into the crowd of the second is the most obvious difference between the two. . . .

It remains only to remark that the evolution of the mass into the crowd is the result of the changing socio-psychological situation and the work of the leadership. Given the characteristics present, the processes operative, and effective leadership, the crowd emerges as the form within which collective behavior goes on.

THE FORMAL STAGE
OF THE FORMULATION OF ISSUES AND FORMATION OF PUBLICS

Transition from the Popular to the Formal Stage marks a crucial point in the development of a revolutionary movement. Esprit de corps must be buttressed by devices designed to develop group morale and ideology if disintegration is to be avoided. Furthermore, collective excitement and social contagion are not ad quate to serve as the processual foundation for enduring social change. For this he formulation of issues and the formalization of procedures are demanded. In ther words, the roots of the movement nust strike deeper than sensationalism, ashion, and fad. It must come to appeal o the essential desires of the people.

Characteristic Conditions

The typical characteristics found at nis stage may be classified in terms of ne two major developments which occur.

1. The fixation of motives (attitudes) and the definite formulation of aims (values). This major characteristic is paralleled by these developments:

A. A struggle between the conservative, moderate, and radical factions of the revolutionary group; the continuation of the in-group–out-group conflict, and the intensification of class antagonisms

B. The moderate faction gains control to the accompaniment of these typical events:

1) Release of prisoners
2) Apparent co-operation of reformers and revolutionists
3) Abortive attempts of the radicals to seize power
4) Radical-conservative coalition attacks on the reformers
5) Evidence of manifest incompetence on the part of the reformers

C. The reformers are confronted with three typical handicaps:

1) Fear of armed invasion
2) Fear of internal rebellion
3) Political inexperience

D. The desertion of lukewarm supporters

E. The elimination of the conservatives by the reformers

F. A movement toward the "left," or an "uncontrollable swing of the masses toward radicalism"

G. The emergence of the typical "perversions"

H. The development of a set of norms formally stated in dogma and formally expressed in ritual, together with a marked increase in the use of shibboleths

I. The fusion of patriotism and the social myth elevates the radical to power

J. The radicals are also confronted with three typical dangers:

1) The danger of conservative opposition and foreign invasion or intervention
2) Domestic insurrection
3) Political inexperience

2. The development of an organizational structure with leaders, a program, doctrines, and traditions. This is accompanied by:

A. The increasing recognition of organizational breakdown and Governmental inefficiency

B. The development of a condition of dual sovereignty

C. The occurrence of an immediate precipitating factor and the seizure of power by the radicals

D. The presence of conflict within the ranks of the radicals

E. The formation of a provisional government

F. A "lull" between the seizure of power by the radicals and the initiation of the Reign of Terror

G. The use of the Reign of Terror as a control technique

Typical Processes

Because of the character of the events of this stage the behavior of the participants in the movement may be described under three headings: (1) discussion and deliberation, (2) formulation, and (3) formalization.

Since the terms discussion and deliberation are self-defining they are introduced here only to show the inter-relation of the different phases of a revolutionary movement. Given the typical events, interaction *must* take the form of discussion and deliberation, and the public is the social form within which such interaction must take place. In other words, this is the stage when issues emerge with reference to which there are differences of opinion. Publics form to discuss these issues. Discussion as a process is marked by the effort to interpret the issues under debate, by dispute, and by the dominance of conflict relations. This results in the participants becoming more self-conscious and critical. This, in turn, makes for opposition and disagreement and places a premium on the careful consideration of pertinent facts, and produces arguments and counter-arguments.

The process of formulation may be thought of as both a continuation and a result of discussion. In the give and take of argument over and critical analysis of possible lines of action with reference to the issues under examination, policies begin to take shape and programs are formulated.

As the movement proceeds through the third stage a development occurs that may be called formalization. That is, wishes (attitudes) that have been reformulated, goals (values) that have emerged, and policies that have been developed get worked into the mores of the participants and become a formal part of their behavior in preparation for subsequent institutionalization.

Effective Mechanisms

In general, the mechanisms characteristic of this stage are those devices that are effective in developing group morale and ideology.

Morale is the device by which a developing movement is given cohesion, solidarity, and unity—just the qualities needed for its on-going. It roots in three convictions: (1) that the purposes and objectives of the movement are right and just and that victory will initiate a sort of Golden Age; (2) that these purposes will actually and ultimately be realized, with all the intense motivation deriving from this faith; and (3) that these purposes represent a sacred responsibility which must be fulfilled.

The ideology of a movement consists in a body of doctrines, beliefs, and myths which provide direction and ability to withstand the opposition of out-groups. The following elements are usually present: (1) a statement of the objectives, purposes, and premises of the movement; (2) a body of criticism and condemnation of the existing social order which the movement is attacking and seeking to change; (3) a body of defense doctrine serving to justify the movement; (4) a body of belief dealing with policies, tactics, and practical operations; and (5) the myths of the movement. From all this it is evident that it is the *function* of an ideology to give an answer to the unrest and discontent of the people. Unless such an answer is provided the movement cannot move forward.

On a slightly different level propaganda —"The deliberately evoked and guided campaign to induce people to accept a given view"—is also of major importance at this stage.

There is no thought of presenting here a complete list of possible mechanisms. Rather, the important point to be established is that whatever mechanisms are employed, they serve to facilitate the process of formalization. Various types of leaders and various types of mechanisms combine to realize this end. Historians, apologists, poets, hymnologists, and propagandists use the radio, the press, pamphlets, books, the stage, the movie, the platform, the pulpit, cartoons, posters, slogans, banners, insignia, and so forth to carry the movement along its way.

Types of Leaders

As might be expected in view of the nature of the period, leadership is in the hands of statesmen. That is, the leaders are those who are able to formulate policies and will attempt to carry social policy into practice. They are those who are skilled in estimating and evaluating the nature and direction of the prevailing social forces. They are those who will try to understand and champion the beliefs and convictions that have become established in the thinking of the people. They are those who will propose the program which promises to resolve the issues and realize the objectives of which the people have become aware.

Dominant Social Form

As already intimated, all this goes on in a *public*. Because of the interdependent character of the different features of a revolutionary movement, discussion and

liberation, formulation and formaliza-
n can only occur in a public; these
ocesses cannot function in a mass or a
owd. . . .

THE INSTITUTIONAL STAGE
OF LEGALIZATION AND SOCIETAL
ORGANIZATION

We come now to the final stage in the
velopment of a revolutionary move-
ent: The period in which institutional-
tion takes place. If the revolutionaries
e to avoid the stigma of permanent
ssification as "rebels" this must occur.
at is, the out-group must finally be
le to *legalize* or *organize* their power;
ey must become the in-group of the
ucture of political power. When the at-
udes and values of the revolutionary
adership have thus become the legal
d political foundation of social organ-
tion, a new *society* has been formed
d the revolution has been consum-
ated.

haracteristic Conditions

The socio-psychological conditions
ich indicate that a revolution is mov-
g from the Formal into the Institu-
nal Stage may be classified as *causal*
transitional and *resultant* or accom-
dative.
1. Causal characteristics:
   A. Psychological exhaustion which
   undermines the emotional foundations of the revolution
   B. Moral let-down and return to old
   habits (attitudes), including "escape
   recreation" and the re-emergence of
   graft, speculation, and corruption,
   become deterrents to continued revolutionary behavior
   C. Great economic distress, mount-
   ing almost to chaos, demands a settling down
2. Resultant characteristics:
   A. End of the Reign of Terror;
   granting of amnesty; return of ex-
   iles; repression of extremists; and
   search for scapegoats
   B. Increase in powers of central government, frequently resulting in dictatorship

C. Social reconstruction along lines
of the old social structure but with
the new principles (values) essentially intact
D. Dilution of the revolutionary
ideal; transformation of evangelist
fervor for social change into the desire for conquest; transformation of
the "revolutionary sect" into a "political denomination"
E. Re-accommodation of church
and state
F. "Reaction to the reaction" represented by escape recreation
G. The revolution becomes attitudinally established and develops a permanent organization that is acceptable to the current mores; that is, it
is institutionalized

Typical Processes

From a processual point of view, the
movement increasingly relies on discussion and deliberation as the means for
fixing policies and determining action.
That is to say, the unrest and discontent,
and collective excitement out of which
the movement came, together with the
correlative behavior, slip into the background and mechanisms and processes
emerge that are appropriate to the prevailing mood of the participants. The
process of institutionalization results: the
process by which collective behavior
which begins outside formal offices and
without formal rules, engaged in by unconventional groups of people, in unexpected situations, or in ways contrary to
use and wont, develop formal offices, organized groups, defined situations, and
a new body of sanctioned use and wont.
It is obvious that this description covers the entire process by which any area
of behavior becomes institutionalized. It
also describes the entire revolutionary
process by which mass behavior, originating in unrest and discontent generated by
the institutional inadequacies and inef-
ficiencies of a society, becomes popular-
ized and finds expression in the *crowd;*
begins to acquire form in the *public;* and
finally legalizes a new body of sanctioned

use and wont. That is, a new *society* emerges, its core being a new constellation of institutions. Our present concern is with the final stage of this process.

It is also helpful to relate the revolutionary process to such basic sociological concepts as conflict, accommodation, and assimilation. In the Preliminary Stage, conflict remains covert and endemic because the causes of unrest and discontent have not yet been identified. In the Popular Stage it becomes overt and endemic, increasing in intensity as issues emerge and are recognized. However, it is in the Formal Stage that conflict becomes violent, organized and directed toward the realization of definite objectives.

Evidence that the movement is moving through the Formal into the Institutional Stage is found in the subsidence of conflict and the emergence of accommodative and/or assimilative processes. That is, the people involved in the movement are becoming reconciled to changed conditions of life through the formation of attitudes adequate to the changes that have occurred; and they are beginning to recognize and accept a new set of values —a new set of defined relationships which fix a new status system.

The success of the entire revolutionary movement hinges on what happens at this point in its evolution. If the objectives (values) that were formulated in doctrine, written into the constitution, and expressed in ritual and ceremony, are really attitudinally accepted and become the bases for behavior, the goals of the movement have been assimilated and victory has been relatively complete.

What more frequently occurs makes for a condition in which the new values are *legally* but not *attitudinally* accepted. The legally-defined values are then held as ideals; the behavior of the people falls far short of them. A compromise is effected between the values of the decadent old order and the emergent new society. In short, what might be called incomplete or imperfect institutionalization results, and the movement comes to rest at a point that is short of its expressed purposes.

Effective Mechanisms

With reference to the mechanisms employed at this stage two observations a in order: (1) they are well-nigh innume able, for, conceivably, any device which the behavior of people can be i fluenced may be used at some time another; therefore, (2) a general stat ment regarding such mechanisms must concerned with the ends sought rath than with the specific devices employed

From this point of view, it may be o served that the movement now inten fies the development of its ideology a perfects the tactics previously employ to carry people along in the desired rection. The use of established mech nisms and procedures takes preceden over "personalities"—"personal ascen ancy is less essential to this stable a established order than the impersonal i struments it has forged for itself: t laws, descriptions, faiths, dogmas, a ideals."

Type of Leader

Given what is going on at this stage, follows that the movement now requir the services of the administrator-exec tive. This does not mean that a socie does not and cannot always use agitato prophets and reformers, as well as state men and administrators. On the contrar it could be argued that sound admin tration would deliberately employ these various types of leadership. T only point here being urged is that are dealing with another aspect of t division of labor in leadership and th this function must be fulfilled if the mov ment is to reach full institutionalizatio The policies formulated by the statesm —in order to satisfy the demands for a tion voiced by the prophets and refor ers in consequence of the unrest and d content generated by the agitator—m be administered. Herein lies the fun tional justification for the rise of the a ministrative type of leadership.

Dominant Social Form

This brings us to the consideration the prevailing social form in which t havior is channeled in the Institutional Stage. We have seen that the mass, the crowd, and the public are the dominant social forms of the first, second, and third stages. These have been called "Forms of Elementary Collective Behavior" because they "arise spontaneously and their action s not set or determined by existing cultural patterns. Each has a distinctive character and each arises under a special set of conditions." Thus, from the point of view of the social forms within which collective behavior goes on, a revolutionary movement may be thought of as a development in the course of which a mass is transformed into a crowd, a crowd becomes a public, and a public evolves into a society. That is, the movement 'acquires organization and form, a body of customs and traditions, established leadership, and enduring division of labor, social rules and social values; in short, a culture, a social organization, and a new scheme of life."

The resultant society or social order may be said to possess the following characteristics:

1. A body of common expectations upon the basis of which people are able to co-operate and regulate their activities to one another. This procedure yields them customs, traditions, rules and norms. (It was this aspect of society that Park had in mind when he defined it as a "network of accommodative arrangements.")
2. A set of values which are attached to these expectations and which determine how important they are, and how readily people will adhere to them.
3. The conceptions which people have of themselves in relation to each other and to their groups.
4. A common subjective orientation in the form of dispositions and moods.

In terms of what was said earlier about the nature of human nature and social change, this means that a destroyed equilibrium between the attitudes of the people and the values of the culture has been re-established; attitudes have been reformulated, values have been redefined, and a new social order has been built. . . .

Interpretation and use of the idealized life-cycle in the examination of particular movements and the formulation of generalizations is not a simple matter. Statements of "typical life-cycles" are frequently hedged about with qualifications. Thus we are often told that a movement may change either backward or forward in the cycle and that a movement does not necessarily have to pass through the entire series of stages. But with such qualifications, what is left of the cycle?

The life-cycle approach became popular in the early period of sociology when organismic analogies were in favor. Social forms were thought to have invariant stages of development from birth to maturity to death in the same manner as living organisms. With this approach discredited, the life-cycle is sometimes regarded as merely an empirical sequence of events that has been noted in the examination of several cases.

However, the life-cycle acquires significance in causal analysis when each stage is regarded as containing some of the causal preconditions for the development of the following stage. Without the preceding stage, any particular stage cannot come about. However, since each stage includes only a portion of the preconditions to the following stage, the progression to succeeding stages is not inevitable. Frequently there will be not merely one stage but alternative stages that may follow any given stage.

The special value of the life-cycle, then, is to permit us to discover the *additional conditions* that have to be present if a movement is to proceed from any given stage to the next. The causes that push a movement from the first stage to the second may not be the same as those pushing it from the second to the third stage. Thus we can refine any general discussion of the factors contributing to success of a movement by observing that these factors may not be the same in the early and late periods. Through such analysis we can find explanations for movements that make impressive beginnings and then fail of further achievement and for movements that have weak beginnings and suddenly burst into rapid development. We should also be able to discover the crucial conditions that cause a movement to take one rather than another direction when alternatives are present.

Success and crucial aspects of a movement. In speaking of a cycle from beginning to success of a social movement, we have been taking for granted the idea of success. In actual practice, however, the term *success* is likely to have several meanings. Often a movement is regarded as successful so long as the number of its adherents is increasing. However, not all movements depend upon support by large numbers to accomplish their objectives. The labor movement in America for example, was more successful in collective bargaining and in securing desired legislation when it reduced the base from which its members were drawn for the sake of homogeneity of interest. Success of a movement is sometimes viewed as the perpetuation of the movement itself and its organization. However, a movement may cease to exist because its objectives have been largely achieved, or a movement may persist at the cost of extensive departure from its original goals.

Even measuring success by the degree to which the values that the movement promotes are achieved introduces difficulties. Seldom is there a simple, clear-cut value being promoted. A movement to remove a corrupt political administration may "succeed" in the sense of winning a recall election, but the entrenched power of the old machine may be such that the new officials are never able to gain complete control of the governmental machinery. Or a movement may be unsuccessful in winning its specific goal, such as the adoption of a particular statute, but the strength of the movement may lead to the adoption of other measures that give substantially the same benefits. Or, finally, the very strength of a movement may result in its objectives being "stolen" by some established party or stronger movement. Thus, the Socialist party in the United States lost a great deal of support during the 1930's because the Democratic party adopted some of its proposals.

In each of these instances the decision to describe a movement as successful or unsuccessful depends upon the perspective of the observer. The various criteria of success are all found to some degree in every movement and represent essential pursuits. Thus we may conclude that among the essential aspects of a social movement are, first, a program for the reform of society; second, the promotion of membership gratifications; and third, the establishment of power relations favorable to the movement. But so long as the importance of these various activities is evaluated differently in different movements, we shall have to examine particular kinds of success rather than success in general. It appears, then, that some effort to classify significant types of social movements should precede discussion of the conditions making for success.

Classification of social movements. The commonest basis for classifying social movements has been the type of activity and objective with which they are concerned. Movements are frequently grouped as political, religious, social reform etc. Another frequent type of classification concerns the movement's relation to the direction and rate of social change. Thus movements may be labelled progressive, conservative, reactionary, etc., according to whether they are in accord with the prevailing direction of change or contrary to it. And movements may be labelled as reform and revolutionary according to whether the change they foster is gradual or sudden.

None of these bases is adequate as a framework for the sociological and social-psychological analysis of movements. The first is deficient because we cannot take for granted that merely different types of purpose give rise to movements that are structurally or dynamically different. Thus, we cannot assume just because a movement has religious rather than political aims that the leader-follower relation will be different, the tactics will be different, or that the internal organization or the appeal of the movement to mass membership will be fundamentally different. Classification should be based on differences in the function and structure of the movement, irrespective of whether the resulting divisions between types correspond to the "content" or purpose differentiations or not.

The other types of classification have more justification because they relate the change promoted by the movement to the general pattern of change in the society. However, in practice such criteria are difficult to use and tend to become seriously confused with the evaluations of the investigator. The rapidity of change advocated by a movement becomes a point of debate between the advocates and opponents of the movement, and the term "revolutionary" tends to become a term of condemnation rather than of analysis. Likewise, each movement urges that its program expresses the trend of the future. We do not have at hand techniques that would enable us to identify the direction and rate of social change in values with sufficient confidence to make this the key criterion for examining movements. It may be essential that such judgments be made when the interest in social movements is subordinated to the study of social change, but it seems preferable not to do so when the movements themselves are the principal focus of interest.

As a guide to some major principles that should be incorporated into a sociological classification of movements we may examine Louis Wirth's definition of the types of minority and nationalist movements. In attempting to find a basis for generalizing about minority movements anywhere in the world, Wirth devises a set of ideal types. He then indicates the interrelations among these types of movements and the circumstances governing which type will be found in any given situation. While the movements discussed are exclusively minority movements, the general approach to the establishment of types has much wider applicability.

TYPES OF MINORITY MOVEMENTS
Louis Wirth

[We can come closest to the actual minor-

Reprinted in part by permission of Columbia University Press, from Louis Wirth, "The Problem of Minority Groups," in Ralph Linton, editor, **The Science of Man in the World Crisis** (New York: Columbia University Press, 1945), pp. 354–58, 360–64.

ity problems that plague the modern world] by analyzing the major goals toward which the ideas, the sentiments, and the actions of minority groups are directed. Viewed in this way minorities may conveniently be typed into: (1) pluralistic; (2) assimilationist; (3) secessionist; and (4) militant.

A pluralistic minority is one which seeks toleration for its differences on the part of the dominant group. Implicit in the quest for toleration of one's group differences is the conception that variant cultures can flourish peacefully side by side in the same society. Indeed, cultural pluralism has been held out as one of the necessary preconditions of a rich and dynamic civilization under conditions of freedom. It has been said in jest that "tolerance is the suspicion that the other fellow might be right."

Toleration requires that the dominant group shall feel sufficiently secure in its position to allow dissenters a certain leeway. Those in control must be convinced either that the issues at stake are not too vital, or else they must be so thoroughly imbued with the ideal of freedom that they do not wish to deny to others some of the liberties which they themselves enjoy. If there is a great gulf between their own status and that of the minority group, if there is a wide difference between the two groups in race or origin, the toleration of minorities may go as far as virtually to perpetuate several subsocieties within the larger society. . . .

The range of toleration which a pluralistic minority seeks may at first be quite narrow. As in the case of the Jews in medieval Europe, or the Protestants in dominantly Catholic countries, it may be confined to freedom to practice a dissenting religion. Or, as in the case of the ethnic minorities of Czarist Russia and the Austro-Hungarian empire of the Hapsburgs, it may take the form of the demand for the recognition of a language as the official medium of expression for the minority and the right to have it taught in their schools. While on the one hand the pluralistic minority craves the toleration of one or more of its cultural idiosyncrasies, on the other hand it resents and seeks protection against coerced absorption by the dominant group. Above all it wishes to maintain its cultural identity.

The nationalities of Europe, which in the nineteenth and early twentieth centuries embarked upon a course of achieving national independence, began their careers as pluralistic minorities bent merely upon attaining cultural autonomy. Some of these minorities had enjoyed national independence at an earlier period and merely wished to recover and preserve their cultural heritage. This was the case in Poland, for instance, which sought to recover from Czarist Russia a measure of religious and linguistic autonomy. Czech and Irish nationalism was initiated under similar historic circumstances.

It would be an error, however, to infer that the claims for cultural autonomy are generally pursued independently of other interests. Coupled with the demand, and often precedent to it there proceeds the struggle for economic and political equality or at least equalization of opportunity. Although the pluralistic minority does not wish to merge its total life with the larger society, it does demand for its members a greater measure of economic and political freedom if not outright civic equality. Ever since the revolutionary epoch of the late eighteenth century the economic and political enfranchisement of minorities has been regarded not merely as inherent in the "rights of man" but as the necessary instrument in the struggle for cultural emancipation. Freedom of choice in occupations, rights of landownership, entry into the civil service, access to the universities and the professions, freedom of speech, assembly, and publication, access to the ballot with a view to representation of minority voices in parliament and government—these and other full privileges of citizenship are the foundation upon which cultural freedom rests and the instruments through which it must be achieved and secured.

Throughout the period of awakening of dominant ethnic minorities in Europe in the nineteenth century and subsequently in all parts of the world the first stages of minority movements have been characterized by cultural renaissances. The primary emphasis in this stage of development has been upon accentuating the religious, linguistic, and cultural heritage of the group and driving to obtain recognition and toleration for these dif ferences. This movement goes hand in hand with the clamor for economic and political equality. In the course of such movements what at first are marks of inferiority—a homely folk tongue, an alien religion, an obscure lore, and eccentric costume—are transformed into objects of pride and positive group values in which the intellectuals among the minority take an especially avid interest and the promotion of which becomes the road to their leadership and power. The aim of the pluralistic minority is achieved when it has succeeded in wresting from the dominant group the fullest measure of equality in all things economic and political and the right to be left alone in all things cultural. . . .

It should be recognized however that pluralistic minorities, like all structures expressive of dynamic social movements, are merely waystations on the road to further developments. They move on inexorably to other stages where correspondingly new types of social structures emerge. Unlike the pluralistic minority, which is content with toleration and the upper limit of whose aspiration is cultural autonomy, the assimilationist minority craves the fullest opportunity for participation in the life of the larger society with a view to uncoerced incorporation in that society. It seeks to lose itself in the larger whole by opening up to its members the greatest possibilities for their individual self-development. Rather than toleration and autonomy, which is the goal of the pluralistic minority, the assimilationist minority works toward complete acceptance by the dominant group and a merger with the larger society.

Whereas a pluralistic minority, in order to maintain its group integrity, will generally discourage intermarriage and intimate social intercourse with the dominant group, the assimilationist minority puts no such obstacles in the path of its members but looks upon the crossing of stocks as well as the blending of cultures as wholesome end products. Since assimilation is a two-way process, however, in which there is give and take, the mergence of an assimilationist minority rests upon a willingness of the dominant group to absorb and of the minority group to be absorbed. The ethnic differences that exist between the minority and the dominant group are not necessarily an obstacle to assimilation as long as the cultural traits of each group are not regarded as incompatible with those of the other and as long as their blending is desired by both. The "melting pot" philosophy in the United States which applied to the ethnic minorities but excluded the racial minorities, notably the Negro, in so far as it was actually followed, tended to develop both among immigrants and natives an atmosphere conducive to the emergence of a crescive American culture to which both the dominant and minority groups contributed their share. This new culture, which is still in the process of formation, comprises cultural elements derived from all the ethnic groups constituting the American people, but integrates them into a new blend.

The success with which such an experiment proceeds depends in part upon the relative numbers involved and the period of time over which the process extends. . . .

No ethnic group is ever unanimous in all of its attitudes and actions, and minority groups are no exception. They, too, have their internal differentiations, their factions and ideological currents and movements. It should be understood, therefore, that the difference between a pluralistic and an assimilationist minority must be sought in the characteristic orientation and directing social movement of these groups. The Jews furnish an excellent illustration of a minority which especially in modern times has vacillated between these two types. When the "out" group was favorably disposed toward the Jews, assimilation proceeded apace, even in the face of occasional rebuffs and persistent discrimination. When the dominant group made entry of the Jews difficult, when intolerance movements became powerful and widespread, and when persecution came to be the order of the day, the Jews as a minority group generally withdrew into themselves and by virtue of being excluded became clannish. The most conspicuous example of this transformation is to be found in the shift in the attitude of the German Jews who—before the anti-Semitic wave climaxed by the Hitler epic—could have been correctly characterized as an assimilationist minority and whose optimum longing upon the advent of Hitler was for even a modicum of toleration. Among Jews in this country a similar differentiation is contemporaneously found. The older settlers and those who have climbed the economic and social scale seek on the whole full incorporation into the larger society and may truly be regarded as an assimilationist minority; but the later comers and those whose hopes have been frustrated by prejudice, those who through generations of persecution in the Old World retain a more orthodox ritual and a more isolated and self-sufficient community life, generally do not seek full cultural identification with American society at large. To be sure they aspire to full social and economic equality with the rest of the population but they seek to retain a degree of cultural autonomy. . . .

The secessionist minority represents a third distinct type. It repudiates assimilation on the one hand, and is not content with mere toleration or cultural autonomy on the other. The principal and ultimate objective of such a minority is to achieve political as well as cultural independence from the dominant group. If such a group has had statehood at an earlier period in its career, the demand for recognition of its national sovereignty may be based upon the cultivation among its members of the romantic sentiments associated—even if only in the imagination—with its former freedom, power, and glory. In such a case the minority's cultural monuments and survivals, its language, lore, literature, and ceremonial institutions, no matter how archaic or reminiscent of the epoch of the group's independence, are revivified and built up into moving symbols of national grandeur.

In this task the intellectuals among the minority group play a crucial role. They can find expression for their talents by recovering, disseminating, and inspiring pride in the group's history and civilization and by pleading its case before world public opinion. Having been rejected by the dominant group for higher positions of leadership, and after having been denied equal opportunity and full participation in the intellectual, social, economic and political life of the larger society, the intellectuals of such minorities tend to be particularly susceptible to a psychic malady bordering on an oppression psychosis. They find their compensation by plunging into the life of the smaller but more hospitable world of their minority.

The Irish, Czech, Polish, Lithuanian, Esthonian, Latvian and Finnish nationalistic movements culminating in the achievement of independent statehood at the end of the first World War were examples of secessionist minority groups. The case of the Jews may also be used to illustrate this type of minority. Zionism in its political, as distinguished from its cultural variety, has acquired considerable support as a result of the resurgence of organized anti-Semitic movements. The forced wholesale migration out of the countries practicing violent persecution and extermination has changed the conception of Palestine from a haven of refuge in which Jews are tolerated to a homeland to which Jews lay official claim.

The protest against the dominant group, however, does not always take the form of separatism and secessionism. It may, under certain circumstances express itself in movements to get out from under the yoke of a dominant group in order to join a group with whom there exists a closer historical and cultural affinity. This is particularly true of minorities located near national frontiers. Wars, and the accompanying repeated redefinitions of international boundaries, rarely fail to do violence to the traditions and wishes of some of the populations of border territories. It is generally true that these marginal ethnic groups exhibit more fervid nationalistic feelings than those who have not been buffeted about by treaty-makers.

Secessionist minorities occupying border positions, moreover, generally can count upon the country with which they seek reunion for stimulation of minority consciousness. When France lost Alsace and Lorraine at the end of the Franco-Prussian war in 1871, the French culture of these "lost provinces" became the object of special interest on the part of Frenchmen in and out of these territories. And when these same provinces were lost to Germany at the end of the first World War, a similar propaganda wave on the German side was set in motion. When the Nazis came to power and embarked upon their imperialistic adventures they made the "reunion with the Fatherland" of such territories as the Saar, Alsace, Lorraine, Eupen-et-Malmedy, Sudetenland and the Danzig Corridor an object of frenzied agitation. By every means at their command they revived the flagging or dormant secessionist spirit among these ethnic groups. They created incidents wherever the slightest pretext existed to provoke violent outbreaks so as to elicit from the neighboring governments countermeasures that could be exploited for the purpose of creating a world opinion that the German minorities in these territories were suffering from extreme persecution and were anxiously waiting to be rescued by the armed might of the fatherland.

The solidarity of modern states is always subject to the danger of the undermining influence of secessionist minorities, but it becomes particularly vulnerable if the minorities are allied with neighboring states which claim them as their own. Out of such situations have arisen many of the tensions which have provoked numerous wars in recent times.

There is a fourth type of minority which may be designated as militant. Its goal reaches far beyond toleration, assimilation, and even cultural and political autonomy. The militant minority has set domination over others as its goal. Far from suffering from feelings of inferiority, it is convinced of its own superiority and inspired by the lust for conquest. While the initial claims of minority movements are generally modest, like all accessions of power, they feed upon their own success and often culminate in delusions of grandeur.

Thus, for instance, the Sudeten Germans, aided and abetted by the Nazi propaganda, diplomatic, and military machine, made claims on the Czecho-Slovak republic which, if granted, would have reduced the Czechs to a minority in their own country. The story, let us hope it is legendary, of the slave who upon his emancipation immediately proceeded to buy himself a slave, suggests a perverse human tendency which applies to minorities as well. No imperialism is as ruthless as that of a relatively small upstart nation. Scarcely had Italy escaped the humiliation of utter defeat in the first World War when she embarked upon the acquisition of *Italia Irredenta* far beyond her own borders across the Adriatic. In recent times, the rise of the relatively obscure Prussian state to a position of dominance in Central Europe is illustrative of the dynamics of a militant minority in quest not merely of a secure basis of national existence but of empire. The none too generous treatment accorded by the newly emancipated Poles between the two World Wars to the Ukranian, White Russian, Lithuanian, Jewish, and other minorities allotted to the Polish state offers another case of the lack of moderation characteristic of militant minorities once they arrive at a position of power.

The problem of finding a suitable formula for self-government in India would probably have been solved long ago if the Hindu "majority," which considers itself a minority in relation to British imperial rule, could have been satisfied with an arrangement which stopped short of Hindu domination over Moslems. Similarly the problem of Palestine could be brought much nearer a sensible solution if certain elements among Jewish and Arab groups were less militant and did not threaten, in case either were given the opportunity, to reduce the other to the status of a minority.

The justification for singling out the four types of minorities described above for special delineation lies in the fact that each of them exhibits a characteristic set of collective goals among historical and contemporary minority groups and a corresponding set of motives activating the conduct of its members. These four types point to significant differences between actual minority movements. They may also be regarded as marking crucial successive stages in the life cycle of minorities generally.

The initial goal of an emerging minority group, as it becomes aware of its ethnic identity, is to seek toleration for its cultural differences. By virtue of this striving it constitutes a pluralistic minority. If sufficient toleration and autonomy is attained the pluralistic minority advances to the assimilationist stage, characterized by the desire for acceptance by and incorporation into the dominant group. Frustration of this desire for full participation is likely to produce (1) secessionist tendencies which may take the form either of the complete separation from the dominant group and the establishment of sovereign nationhood, or (2) the drive to become incorporated into another state with which there exists close cultural or historical identification. Progress in either of these directions may in turn lead to the goal of domination over others and the resort to militant methods of achieving that objective. If this goal is actually reached the group sheds the distinctive characteristics of a minority.

It should be emphasized, of course, that this typology of minorities is a theoretical construct, rather than a description of actually existing groups. We should not expect to find any one of these types to occur in pure form either in history or in the present. All minorities contain within themselves tendencies and movements in which we can discern the characteristic features of one or more of these types. Using such a typology as a tool we are in a better position to analyze the empirical problems of minority situations and to evaluate the proposed programs for their solution.

The first principle that emerges from Louis Wirth's statement is that the same movement—or at least a movement recruited from the same group—may fall into different types at different times. The type refers to the current characteristics of the movement rather than to any immutable characteristics. Such a basis for classification acknowledges that the entire dynamics of a movement may change from time to time. With each type, the kind of accomplishment that constitutes "success" for the movement is different. Achievements which would be regarded as substantial success for one type may be regarded as failure for another.

The second principle in Wirth's system is the construction of types from the way in which the movement seeks to relate itself to groups outside the movement. Thus the minority movement may be directed toward gaining certain concessions from the majority, disengaging itself from the majority, or securing domination over the majority.

Third, these categories refer to ideal types, since any movement is likely to combine elements of each. In order to gain concessions (as the *pluralistic* type does) or even effective separation from the majority (as the *secessionist* type does) it may be necessary to obtain control over some of the machinery of the majority group. Consequently both of these types are to some degree *militant* movements. A movement may be examined according to the degree to which each of these elements prevails and determines in part its course of action, its recruitment of members, the response of outsiders to the movement, etc. Only in those instances in which one of the tendencies becomes so clearly dominant as to shape the whole internal and external dynamics of the movement can the movement be placed in just one of the categories.

With these principles in mind we may return to the three fundamental aspects of social movements indicated earlier. While a program of social change, gratifications of membership, and external power relationships are all present to some degree in every movement, the degree to which success is measured by any one of the three and the degree to which the dynamics of the movement are shaped by each aspect will vary. In the Nazi movement the power relationship seemed to be the major element, so that ideology and the gratifications of membership fell into place as subordinate to the quest for power. Franz Neumann in his analysis of the ideology of the Nazi movement has concluded that there was no stable ideology, but that the ideology was changed from time to time to fit the strategy of power.*

Movements of this sort will differ in important respects from movements that are closely bound to a particular program for change in the society. Any effort by movements of the latter type to gain power through methods that compromise their program will damage the movement. The achievement of effective power will not be regarded as success unless the program remains intact, and the movement may be judged successful if its program is adopted and carried out by another group. The crucial, decision-making core of members will be recruited and guided more by the needs of promoting the ideology and by the need to be consistent with the general scheme of values contained in the ideology than by the sheer effort to establish favorable power relations.

Both of the foregoing types of movements will differ from that in which the provision of personal satisfactions to members becomes the orienting feature. In some movements the ideology of societal change and the movement's power situation may have little to do with the continuity of membership, the sense of the members regarding the movement's success, and the character of decisions rendered within the movement. Thus a cultish group may depict itself as the ultimate inheritors of society and adhere to an ideology of widespread change. But the hold of the movement on its members may be quite unaffected by the failure to gain any power or to take any effective steps in the direction of modifying society, and the crucial interaction within the movement may be little related to ideology.

Thus we have identified three fundamental ideal-types of movements, based upon the degree to which the internal interaction, the maintenance of membership, and the conception of what constitutes success are oriented about the predominance of one aspect of the movement. In general we may speak of *value-oriented, power-oriented,* and *participation-oriented* movements. No movement will be a "pure" instance of any type. Many, if not most, movements will have to be described as mixed. But to the degree to which they are mixed in different combinations, the types will be useful in their analysis.

Additional classifications. These three types do not exhaust the useful classifications of social movements. There are other important criteria which crosscut them. From the many, we shall select two of the most important for special exposition.

The distinction commonly made between the reform and revolutionary types of movement suggests a dimension of classification not yet touched. Besides the rate of change, to which we have already referred, this distinction often refers to the movement's relationship to the fundamental values of society. The revolu-

* Franz Neumann, **Behemoth: The Structure and Practice of National Socialism** (New York: Oxford University Press, 1942).

tionary movement is said to challenge the fundamental values while the reform movement seeks modifications within the existing value scheme. The reform movement advocates a change that will *implement* the existing value scheme more adequately than present conditions, while the revolutionary movement urges *replacement* of the existing value scheme.

Taken literally, such a distinction puts the investigator in the position of having to judge the ultimate relation between the movement's program and society's values. No movement advocates total overthrow of existing values. Indeed, the ideologists of the most revolutionary movement argue that it seeks to re-establish the most fundamental aspects of the current value scheme by doing away with other aspects which adulterate them. Furthermore, it is commonplace that apparently innocuous changes may sometimes have altogether revolutionary consequences and that our advance predictions concerning the ultimate consequences of any movement are highly fallible.

But this distinction, when considered from a different standpoint, is quite useful. The fact is that every movement is *viewed in the society* either as generally consistent with or as fundamentally antagonistic to the established value scheme. How it is viewed will determine crucially the type and tactics of opposition with which it is confronted, the circumstances under which it may recruit members, the degree to which it may operate openly through legitimate means, and many other conditions.

Every movement, through defining and promoting consideration of an *issue,* thereby creates or fosters a public concerned both with the issue and with the movement itself. Part of the function of the public will be to define the movement's relations to society's value scheme. The effective definition that emerges from the public will determine the access that the movement has to legitimate means for promoting its program in society. Whether a dispassionate or retrospective evaluation would determine that the movement's objectives were or were not *in fact* consistent with the basic value structure of society is not the important question. The manner in which the movement will be required to operate within the society is determined by the effective definition that emerges from the public. Consequently, movements may be classified usefully as *respectable* or *revolutionary* on the basis of the prevailing public definition. In addition to this dichotomy there is a sort of intermediate category. Some movements are regarded as odd, peculiar, or queer. While they are inconsistent with the basic value structure of society, they are thought to be harmless and consequently can be tolerated and permitted considerable access to legitimate means of promoting their objectives. They are opposed largely through ridicule, isolation, and ostracism of their members rather than by condemnation and deprivation of access to legitimate channels of promotion. Oftentimes the difference between a revolutionary and a *peculiar* movement is simply one of apparent strength, so that change of a given movement from one to the other type is frequent.

Classifying types in terms of public definition, character of the opposition evoked, and access to legitimate means of action suggests a further subdivision of the respectable movement into the *factional* and *nonfactional*. Certain movements must cope primarily with competing schemes claiming to promote similar ends by superior means. Hence they are likely to be concerned not so much with gaining adherence to their general objective as to promoting their own particular scheme for attaining it. Other movements must overcome primarily lack of inter-est or enthusiasm rather than factional opposition. Thus a movement like Moral Rearmament has been respectable and largely nonfactional. That is to say, it has received widespread lip-service from respectable community leaders and no real organized opposition. Its problem has consisted of marshalling effective support in lieu of mere token support, rather than of combatting active opposition or competition.

In sum, we have suggested four types of movement, based upon the public definition of the movement's relation to the basic value scheme of the society, and accordingly involving the general type of opposition that will be evoked and the access to legitimate channels of action. The four types are schematized below:

Public Definition	Type of Opposition	Means of Action
(1) Respectable-nonfactional	Disinterest and token support	Legitimate means
(2) Respectable-factional	Competing movements advocating same general objective	Legitimate means
(3) Peculiar	Ridicule and ostracism	Limited access to legitimate means
(4) Revolutionary	Violent suppression	Chiefly illegitimate means

Movements may finally be differentiated according to the manner in which they "act." Some movements promote their particular program chiefly through the creation of a public concerned with the movement. Most limited social reform movements depend heavily upon securing a large favorable public, assuming that in the last analysis public definition will determine whether the desired reforms are achieved or not. Other movements depend largely upon creating a public that fears the movement and consequently will not risk opposing it.

Movements of a contrasting type, however, place less dependence on creating any particular type of public. These movements depend upon the actions of their members to accomplish their objectives. When such movements are concerned with more than personal reform, they act by incorporating into their membership those persons who are in a position to take the crucial actions themselves. For example, the progressive education movement in the United States has operated chiefly through enlisting teachers and professors of education into their membership. The movement has been effective in modifying educational practices throughout the country in spite of apathetic reactions outside of the teaching profession and in the face of powerful counter-movements that have created quite hostile publics in some locations. While a movement of this sort is impeded to some degree by a hostile public, it is much less vulnerable than one exclusively dependent upon a public.

Outline of discussion. In the remainder of this section we shall take up first the three major aspects of a social movement as we have defined them, and the characteristics of the corresponding broad ideal-types of movements. We shall examine the sources and characteristics of the values and ideology that movements seek to promote, and point out some features of those movements that are primarily value-oriented. Next we shall view the power orientations of movements and examine in some detail a subtype, the separatist movement. Then we shall consider the nature of the participation-oriented types of movements and explore the different types of participation orientations that are found in movements generally.

Supplementing the discussion by types we shall first look at leadership phenomena and the characteristics of the following, and secondly at the various ways in which movements terminate or reach a more or less permanent form.

Chapter 15

Value-orientations of social movements

$\mathcal{T}$HE FIRST question we normally ask about any social movement concerns its program. We ask just what kind of changes it seeks to promote in the society. While few investigators today would fall into the error of limiting their study to the content of a movement's program, as did many writers of an earlier generation, neither can we overlook the pivotal character of the program in any movement. The program must be acceptable to the bulk of the movement's adherents. The program will be interpreted by outsiders as part of the basis for determining what reaction there shall be in the larger society. And there is an enforced commitment within every movement to its original program that predetermines the movement's course and limits its adaptability to changed circumstances.

Movements will vary, however, in the degree to which the support of their members is derived from a conviction of the worth of the movement's manifest program and in the degree to which the key decisions which govern the movement's course from within are directed toward promoting the manifest program. We refer to *manifest* program to eliminate from consideration private understandings at variance with the publicly-understood program of the movement. Those movements whose publicly-understood program is more crucial in the sense indicated above will be referred to as *value-oriented* movements, in contrast to other types of movements. Those respects in which any movement whatever is directed or limited in its activities and recruitment of adherents by its publicly understood program will be called *value-orientations*.

At the outset we may distinguish the particular program of change that a movement advocates from the conception of society through which it justifies that program. The latter we shall call the *ideology* of the movement, while bear-

331

ing in mind that other usages of the term are prevalent in the literature on movements.

Ideology includes many elements. Normally there is an interpretation of the historical processes that have led to the present state of affairs. An ideology of impersonal historical processes, such as the Marxian dialectic, will necessarily be associated with a program aimed at altering the social structure directly, while an ideology attributing present conditions to a moral decline among the people will follow a program of individual regeneration like that of Moral Rearmament. The ideology also usually extends the historical interpretation into a prediction for the future, either by depicting the ultimate consequences of adoption or non-adoption of the program in utopian and catastrophic terms respectively, or through preaching the inevitable success of the movement. The ideology also usually includes a re-evaluation of the worth of population segments, such as social classes, minorities, and the like. It is possible that the most influential consequence of the various movements for old-age pensions since World War I has been the diffusion of that portion of their ideology which holds that elderly people deserve more than it is possible for many of them to have in modern society. And running through each of these elements is the designation of a villain—some entrenched group whose selfishness or limited vision prevents immediate acceptance of the movement's program.

The ideology and program usually evolve interdependently. "Men of action" may be attracted to the movement because its program appeals to them, while more contemplative persons may be won to the movement by its ideology. But there is a constant interplay, for the ideology must justify the program and the program must be sound in light of the ideology. At certain stages the ideology may be more salient than the specific program, while the ideology may take a back seat at other times. Such movements as those in the fields of art, literature, and thought may have little in the way of program to supplement the ideology which they promote.

As a consequence of the foregoing considerations we have sought a broader term than either ideology or program to encompass the two in combination. The ideology and program are linked together in their espousal of certain changes in the *values* of the society. These values, though often vaguely felt rather than explicitly stated, are the criteria by which the ideology and program are both judged, and which both are designed to express.

A value is any category of objects that are felt to have worth, that ought to be protected and promoted rather than treated with indifference. Objects of value can range from tangible things to broad ideas and their related activities. People "feel good" when an object of value is being honored; they feel distressed or outraged when it is being disregarded or profaned. An object of value is felt to merit some sacrifice of less highly valued objects for the sake of its attainment or preservation. A program to change the values of a society is a proposal that some gratifications that are currently being enjoyed should be given up for the sake of attaining or preserving the newly emphasized value.

The program of a movement is the more-or-less definite set of procedures for getting the value reflected in the social organization, while the ideology is a way of viewing reality that supports the value. In its fullest sense, however, the value includes both ideology and program. The abolitionist movement, for example, was directed toward eliminating slavery. Various proposals were followed at different times for achieving this value. To justify the high value placed on abolition of slavery, an ideology developed which pictured slave owners as insensitive to the human needs of their slaves and often sadistic. The ideology also helped to divert attention from the problems of readjustment for both slave-owners and slaves that were certain to follow abolition. In the operation of the movement the ideology and the specific programs were seldom distinguished from the general objective of eliminating slavery. The movement promoted a value-complex consisting of ways of viewing slaves and slave-owners, interpretations of history, a series of proposals for action, and a general objective of abolition.

"Ideology and Utopia." A distinction has been made between *ideology* and *utopia* by Karl Mannheim. Although his usage differs from our own, the distinction rests on an approach which has been extensively incorporated into the analysis of social movements. Mannheim subdivides our conception of ideology into two kinds according to a relation to the historical process of change. Ideas that depict the world in such a manner as to render the inequities of the existing order acceptable and right are called *ideology*. Thus ideology is conservative in its implications. Ideas that stir people to break away from the existing order to bring about new conditions that seemed unrealizable and fantastic at the time are *utopian*. Mannheim recognizes the difficulty in telling which ideas are utopian and which ideological in the present, but argues that the criterion of realization enables us to separate the two in past history:

> Ideas which later turned out to have been only distorted representations of a past or potential social order were ideological, while those which were adequately realized in the succeeding social order were relative utopias. The actualized realities of the past put an end to the conflict of mere opinions about what in earlier situationally transcendent ideas was relatively utopian bursting asunder the bonds of the existing order, and what was an ideology which merely served to conceal reality.*

Societal manipulation vs. personal transformation. As we have suggested, there are two broad directions in which the program and ideology may point. They may point toward changing individuals directly or toward changing social institutions. The circumstances under which a movement sets about converting masses of people to a faith that requires a moral or intellectual transformation on their part but does not seek to manipulate social institutions directly are not well understood. Movements of limited scope whose special way of life serves principally to advance the special interests of a small segment of society are properly treated only as participation-oriented movements. But those more ambitious movements which seek to establish the Kingdom of Heaven on earth or to promote international peace by conversion on a mass scale are genuinely value-oriented. The major religions of the world, such as Christianity and Buddhism, have sought to promote a new set of values on a society-wide basis through attention to the "hearts" and motives of men.

We may suggest tentatively three conditions that are essential if movements are to take this direction rather than the direction of reforming society's institutions. First, there must be a world-view prevalent in the society that incorporates a basis for believing that widespread self-improvement is possible. The Judaic

* Karl Mannheim, **Ideology and Utopia** (New York: Harcourt, Brace and Co., 1946), p. 184.

conception that man was made in the image of God and Greek and Roman versions of the belief in human perfectibility set the stage for the Christian doctrine resting upon the divinity of man. Second, the conception of the universe must be such as to lead people to assume that the state of the social order will reflect the integrity and character of individual men. The belief in a punishing and rewarding supernatural is one such belief; a view that society is what the sum-total of its individual members make it is another such belief. Third, the circumstances giving rise to the movement must be such that the people can take some responsibility upon themselves for their present unsatisfactory condition.

For this third reason such movements as the woman suffrage crusade, the abolitionist movement, and the labor movement could only take the direction of societal manipulation. The women could feel no personal responsibility for their position and had necessarily to force suffrage upon the men. Abolition was a movement among nonslaveholders self-righteously forcing the abandonment of slavery upon slaveholders. And the labor movement explicitly rejected the employers' view that the laboring man deserves his fate for not having initiative enough to get out of the ranks of labor.

Some of these movements begin as quite limited messianic movements or as movements of resignation within subjugated classes. But because of the foregoing conditions they do not take on their full value-oriented character until they become dominated by a better established membership and subordinate their messianic emphasis. Thus the Christian movement, beginning as a nationalistic messianic movement, only became the movement we know when it centered among the gentile populations of the Roman empire.

Movements of this sort are also not likely to have their main strength in completely depressed classes of people. Such groups are unlikely to have a basis for believing that man's will can transform the world. Consequently these movements are not so much associated with serious deprivation as with loss of a sense of personal purpose and worth in life. In the presence of a certain amount of material comfort, combining a sense of individual capability with an absence of meaningful direction, people are prepared to assume personal responsibility and feel guilt for the current state of affairs. A movement for social reform through convincing men at large to adopt a particular set of values as their guide in everyday life is the natural outcome of this widespread feeling of directionlessness coupled with experiences that suggest that man can better himself when he will.

Movements for personal transformation characteristically exhibit tendencies to shift toward a societal manipulation emphasis when they have achieved some success and added to their membership persons of influence in society. Most Christian codes, for example, have been translated into laws imposed upon the general populace at one time or another. The upsurge of the "social gospel" in Christendom during the depression period of the 1930's suggests that the personal transformation emphasis may also lose ground to societal manipulation during periods when there is pressure for a more immediate solution of social problems than the gradual process of winning men's souls can promise.

Keeping in mind that no social movements are simple examples of pure types, these two forms of the value-oriented movement represent tendencies corresponding to the other two major types of movements. The value-oriented movement stressing societal manipulation necessarily combines some of the features of the power-oriented types. The strategy will have to include some preoccupation with gaining power over the legitimate institutions in society. The value-oriented movement working through the conversion of personal attitudes and behavior moves in the direction of the participation-oriented movement, gaining much of its strength from the sense of personal satisfaction which follows the conversion. These participation gratifications may explain why a few such movements appear to have outlasted in time all movements that have sought to modify society directly.

Value-oriented movements. For the value-oriented movement success is measured by the degree to which desired changes are promoted in the larger society. It is appropriate, therefore, to formulate hypotheses about these movements in terms of their ability to marshal effective support for such changes.

(1) The ability of a value-oriented movement to marshal effective support for change in society depends upon combining within the program and ideology both a promise of societal betterment and a promise of immediate and tangible benefits to the members of an important segment of society. Research has not yet been focussed in a manner that would tell us how these two themes must be combined, but each serves an essential function in promoting the movement.

The appeal to self-interest of an established segment of society not only insures a vigorous rather than lip-service support from a group of people, but it also gives the movement access to the pre-established organization and communication networks of a group with some pre-existing homogeneity. By appealing to farmers, laborers, or elderly people, a movement taps the informal communication nets which already link people within these categories, and it may make use of the prestige of already recognized leaders.

A movement that has had powerful support may lose it when the tangible benefits it can offer to its major *carrier group* come to an end. Seymour M. Lipset points out this difficulty as it has applied to the Canadian Commonwealth Federation, a farmer's movement with a socialistic program and ideology:

> Most C. C. F. leaders assume that if farmers are given enough economic security and increased social services they will continue to support the movement in its efforts to socialize the rest of the economy. Experiences in other countries do not lend weight to this assumption. In fact, the contrary seems to be true—farmers tend to become conservative when they achieve their economic goals. The farmer is radical vis-à-vis the larger society when his economic security and land tenure are threatened. He may join other exploited groups, such as the workers, to win his own economic demands. However, once the farmer achieves these immediate goals and becomes a member of the secure property holders of society, he resents government controls and labor or tax legislation that interferes with the expansion of his business.*

A movement that presents as its value only the self-interest of a segment of society can hardly be effective except through sheer power-subjugation of the larger society by a group who are willing to repudiate their identification with that society. Members of the self-interest group themselves will be hesitant openly to pursue so unidealistic an objective. And all but actively revolutionary movements depend upon a permissive atmosphere in which to work in the larger society. The *passive sympathy* from the great mass of people which contributes

*Seymour M. Lipset, **Agrarian Socialism** (Berkeley: University of California Press, 1950), p. 229. Quoted by permission of the publisher.

to such a permissive atmosphere will be replaced by fear and intolerance when the group's self-interest is not felt to be subordinated to the general welfare. When passive sympathy prevails, overly aggressive opposition to the movement enlarges the sympathetic public. When such sympathy is replaced by fear, aggressive opposition encourages more widespread active opposition.

The self-interest group need not be large if it is crucially related to the legitimate means for realizing the movement's values. W. F. Ogburn has pointed out the rapid success of the movement for safety in industry *after* laws had been enacted making employers liable in case of injury to their employees. The employers, though a relatively small group, possessed the legitimate means to establish and enforce safety procedures and to install safety devices.

(2) To achieve sustained effectiveness a movement must present a hierarchy of goals, ranging from some that are fairly immediately attainable to others that are practically unattainable. Movements for the reform of civil government are notably ineffective in the long run because they marshal their forces for a single accomplishment, such as recall of a corrupt official or the sensational clean-up of a single vice condition. After this accomplishment the movement quickly dissipates and the old conditions are quietly reinstated. Unless the members are convinced before the first accomplishment that it is merely an important step toward the ultimate goal, the movement will be difficult to revive. Efforts to revive support will lead to disillusionment rather than renewed enthusiasm.

On the other hand, movements that can claim no proximate successes but only preparation over a long period for an ultimate triumph are unlikely to maintain popular support. Movements like Technocracy and Upton Sinclair's "End Poverty in California" (EPIC) movement offered no halfway accomplishments but only finished programs to be established *in toto*. Each movement had a period of great popular support followed by a fairly rapid falling-away of membership and public interest.

Ultimate objectives conceived in fairly general terms permit flexibility in the more specific short-range objectives. Movements that do not subordinate their specific goals to more general goals cannot substitute one scheme for another when conditions demand. The pressure for old-age pensions in the United States, for example, has come from a series of competing and relatively short-lived movements rather than from a single sustained movement. Each movement has been attached to the promotion of a particular plan—the Townsend Plan, "Thirty Dollars Every Thursday," etc. As each plan reached its apex and its program came under attack, the movement declined in spite of its effect in forcing liberalization of existing pension schemes and other improvements.

(3) In order to retain access to legitimate means of creating a favorable public a movement must justify its values by the sacred values of the society and must avoid infringing the sacred values. The Townsend Plan, the New Deal, the American Federation of Labor all sought changes in our economic system which were carefully justified as means of preserving the free enterprise system. The Constitution, certain religious symbols, historical personages such as Washington and Lincoln, all constitute such sacred values in American society.

Many of these sacred values are only sacred for purposes of public representation, but their defamation is nevertheless dangerous for a movement. Though many people were privately thinking and saying the same. Charles Lindbergh's famous remark in a public address in 1941 that Jews were unduly seeking American involvement in the war against Nazi Germany made the "America First" movement vulnerable to attack. Opponents of the movement made use of the statement to discredit the entire basis for opposing America's entry into World War II, and many leaders of the movement felt compelled to disavow Lindbergh's remarks. Tolerance as a public value, particularly in consequence of Hitler's attacks on Jews, was sacred.

(4) To the degree to which a movement incorporates only major sacred values its power will be diffused by a large body of conspicuous lip-service adherents who cannot be depended upon for the work of the movement. Too widespread support is a danger to any movement. A movement needs enemies who threaten its success so as to marshal the determination of its members to overcome the obstacles.

(5) To maintain its effectiveness a value-oriented movement must reveal publicly only tactics that are in keeping with its values. Practical tactics of compromise are often gainsaid for a movement whose ideology is presented in absolute terms. Tactics that can be interpreted as a group's taking the law into its own hands are dangerous. The labor movement has been through a series of struggles as it tried out new tactics of force, ranging from the strike to the sit-down strike and open violence, each new tactic evoking public fear and frequently damaging the position of the movement.

There is, however, an ill-defined line separating tactics consonant with the sacred values of the society and those which outrage these values. The most respectable movements are able to argue that the ends justify the means in some instances and are able to win support by taking direct action to "cut through red tape," or to argue that "you have to fight fire with fire." Arousal of an attitude of righteous indignation seems to be the general condition that permits such violations of customarily sacred values. Indignation is a sentiment that is directed against persons and conditions whose behavior deprives individuals of the rights of due consideration and due process that normally apply. Indignation calls for decisive action and the movement that can take advantage of such opportunities will increase its popular strength. An important and neglected area of research concerns the circumstances under which an indignant public can be created and successfully manipulated.

Tactics must also be consonant with those aspects of the movement ideology which concern the dignity, rectitude, and power of the movement and its figureheads. When subpoenaed before a Congressional investigating committee, Dr. Francis E. Townsend, the originator of the Townsend Plan, had little choice but to accept the martyr role and go to jail for contempt. In thus defying review of his activities by an unfriendly body he was maintaining his own sanctity as figurehead of the movement.

With respect to these last three propositions, a movement that openly accepts revolutionary definition will adopt a different pattern of tactics and necessarily challenge some of the society's sacred values, though still retaining some. The usual course for a revolutionary movement is to retain several identities, the effort being to create or capture respectable movements while retaining a separate revolutionary identity. The success with which this may be done is indicated by the appearance of an article in a political science journal in 1943 reporting that the American communist party had changed from a revolutionary movement to a pressure group.

Sources of value-orientation. We may look for the sources of ideology and program of movements either in the current situation and mentality of the major group from which the movement is recruited (the *carrier* group), or historically in changes that have prepared the way for an ideology of this sort. The two approaches are complementary.

In following the first approach the commonest oversimplification is to regard the values of any particular movement as a simple expression of the self-interest of the carrier group. Our traditional moral attitudes lead us to think in terms of an unjustifiably simple dichotomy of self-interestedness versus altruism. Three points must be understood in viewing the relation of a movement's values to the interests of any group.

First, very few groups conceive their own interests as antithetical to the interests of the rest of society. Most groups think of a community of interest shared by most legitimate segments of the society. Their definition of this community of interest is shaped largely by their own situation, but their definition of their own interests is also restricted by their unwillingness to find themselves in sharp antagonism to the entire society. The billboard advertisement of a nationwide business organization depicting a baby, with the slogan "What's good for business is good for me," is typical of the sincere belief of any interest group.

Second, there are many ways in which any group may conceive its self-interest. As Talcott Parsons has pointed out, an elaborate body of ideas which are not subject to immediate empirical verification have a part in shaping a group's interests. Max Weber has shown that not only the search for religious salvation but the entire conception of the manner in which salvation is to be achieved shaped the activities of early Protestants.

Finally, an objectively identifiable group does not automatically conceive of itself as an interest group. As Rudolph Heberle points out, *economic classes* are not necessarily *social classes*. Persons in similar economic position do not develop a class consciousness or sense of likeness and identification, except from "repeated experiences of class differentiation, discrimination, and antagonism." *

In a classic statement, Selig Perlman has attempted to explain the type of ideology and program that dominate successful labor movements. The contrast between the intellectuals' program for labor and the "grass roots" program is a contrast in conceptions of what *is* labor's self-interest. Only brief selections could be abstracted from this important book, and the interested student will wish to read more extensively in the original.

* Rudolph Heberle, "The Sociology of Social Movements," **American Sociological Review,** 14 (1949), pp. 346–57.

ECONOMIC OPPORTUNITY AND LABOR UNION PHILOSOPHY
SELIG PERLMAN

A theory of the labor movement should include a theory of the psychology of the laboring man. The writings of socialists, syndicalists, anarchists, communists, and "welfare" capitalists abound in embroideries on the theme of "what labor wants" or "what labor aspires to." But the safest method is to go to the organizations of labor's own making, shaped and managed by leaders arisen from labor's own ranks, and to attempt to discover "what's really on labor's mind" by using as material the "working rules," customs and practices of these organizations. A study of such "rules" and customs, the products of long drawn out, evolutionary developments, will aid in distinguishing fundamental from accidental purposes. No such certainty can attach, of course, to the formulations by the "ideologists" of labor, just because these latter, being intellectuals and without the workingman's shop experience, are unable, for all their devotion, to avoid substituting their own typical attitudes and wishes for the genuine philosophy of the laboring man.

There are, by and large, three basic economic philosophies: the manual laborers', the business men's, and the intellectuals'. Werner Sombart, in his definitions of "handicraft" and of capitalism, offers the best clue to an explanation of the essential psychologies of the "manualist" and of the business man. He points out in these definitions the wide gulf between economic motives in the mediaeval economy and in modern business. A secure livelihood for everyone was the aim of the gilds, but the business man has from the first been inspired by a boundless desire to amass wealth. This thought, which is one of Sombart's many illuminating

contributions to economic history, can be made the starting point of a more comprehensive theory of economic group psychology. It can be done by showing, first, how the psychological contrast between the two historical epochs, the gild and the capitalistic, continues in our own day, in the contrast between the psychology of trade unionism and the psychology of business, and second, how each and every type of such group psychology, past and present, can be explained through a common theory.

In an economic community, there is a separation between those who prefer a secure, though modest return,—that is to say, a mere livelihood,—and those who play for big stakes and are willing to assume risk in proportion. The first compose the great bulk of manual workers of every description, including mechanics, laborers, farmers, small manufacturers, and shopkeepers (since petty trade, as Sombart correctly points out, is also a manual occupation); while the latter are, of course, the entrepreneurs and the big business men. The limited or unlimited purpose is, in either case, the product of a simple survey of accessible economic opportunity and of a psychic self-appraisal. The manual worker is convinced by experience that he is living in a world of limited opportunity. He sees, to be sure, how others, for instance business men, are finding the same world a storehouse of apparently unlimited opportunity. Yet he decisively discounts that, so far as he is himself concerned. The business man, on the contrary, is an eternal optimist. To him the world is brimful of opportunities that are only waiting to be made his own.

The scarcity consciousness of the manualist is a product of two main causes, one lying in himself and the other outside. The typical manualist is aware of his lack of native capacity for availing himself of economic opportunities as they lie amidst

Reprinted in part by permission of the author, from Selig Perlman, **A Theory of the Labor Movement** (New York: Augustus M. Kelley, 1949), pp. 237–43, 246–47, 249–53, 273–78.

the complex and ever shifting situations of modern business. He knows himself neither for a born taker of risks nor for the possessor of a sufficiently agile mind ever to feel at home in the midst of the uncertain game of competitive business. Added to this is his conviction that for him the world has been rendered one of scarcity by an institutional order of things, which purposely reserved the best opportunities for landlords, capitalists and other privileged groups. It may also be, of course, that the manual worker will ascribe such scarcity to natural rather than to institutional causes, say, to a shortage of land brought on by increase of population, or, like mediaeval merchants and master workmen, to the small number of customers and the meagre purchasing power of these. At all events, whether he thought the cause of the apparent limitations to be institutional or natural, a scarcity consciousness has always been typical of the manual worker, in direct contrast to the consciousness of an abundance of opportunity, which dominates the self-confident business man.

By correlating economic types, as we do here, with an abundance or a scarcity consciousness, respectively, we are enabled to throw a bridge between our own time and earlier periods. The mediaeval craftsman and gild master, notwithstanding his economic "independence," was of the same economic type as the wage earner of today. The gildsman maintained his independence solely because his rudimentary business psychology sufficed for an age when the market was limited to the locality, and the tools of production were primitively simple. Put the average wage earner back into the Thirteenth Century, and he would set up as a master; transfer a gild master into the age of modern business, and he would fall into the ranks of wage labor. While, to be sure, the economic historian was justified in refusing to see any historical continuity between gilds and trade unions, he often overlooked their common fundamental psychology: the psychology of seeking after a livelihood in the face of limited economic opportunity. Just as, to the gildsman, opportunity was visibly limited

to the local market, so, to the industrial wage earner, it is limited to the number of jobs available, almost always fewer than the number of job seekers.

The economic pessimism of the manual group is at the bottom of its characteristic manner of adjusting the relation of the individual to the whole group. It prompts also the attitude of exclusion which manual groups assume towards those regarded as "outsiders." Again the manualist's psychology can best be brought out by contrast with that of the fully developed business man. Basically the business man is an economic individualist, a competitor *par excellence.* If opportunity is plentiful, if the enterprising person can create his own opportunity, what sane object can there be in collectively controlling the extent of the individual's appropriation of opportunity, or in drastically excluding those from other localities? Nor will this type of individual submit to group control, for he is confident of his ability to make good bargains for himself. If, on the contrary, opportunity is believed to be limited, as in the experience of the manual worker, it then becomes the duty of the group to prevent the individual from appropriating more than his rightful share, while at the same time protecting him against oppressive bargains. *The group then asserts its collective ownership over the whole amount of opportunity,* and, having determined who are entitled to claim a share in that opportunity, undertakes to parcel it out fairly, directly or indirectly, among its recognized members, permitting them to avail themselves of such opportunities, job or market, only on the basis of a "common rule." Free competition becomes a sin against one's fellows, antisocial, like a self-indulgent consumption of the stores of a beleaguered city, and obviously detrimental to the individual as well. A collective disposal of opportunity, including the power to keep out undesirables, and a "common rule" in making bargains are as natural to the manual group as *"laissez-faire"* is to the business man.

In practice the same methods employed

n solving the internal problem of a fair apportionment of opportunity among the "legitimate" participants are found also o answer the purpose of securing the argest possible return from the outside classes. After all, inferiority as a bargainer, when the individual acts alone, is ut the other side of opportunity circumscribed. When the gild or the trade union applies the "common rule" as "working ules" (or "rules for the occupancy and enure of opportunity," as we might term hem), which abolish or check competiion for jobs or for patronage of customers, it creates a solid bargaining front against employer or customer, and at the ame time tends to bring about a distriution of the opportunity to earn a livehood, fair to all. Checking the race for mployment opportunity tends to equalize ecurity among the members, and simulaneously safeguards or raises the standrd of life, establishes industrial liberty, rotects future earning power, and inreases leisure. . . .

What relation has this opportunity heory of the labor group psychology to he plans of the socialists, to "workers' ontrol," to the "abolition of wagery," nd so forth?

Socialism, in its many varieties, while orrectly grasping a part of the true psyhology of the worker—his desire for soldarity—overlooks his unwillingness to ecome completely merged with his own lass. Whenever and wherever full "workrs' control" has been tried, by "self-govrning workshops" and like organizations, istory shows that sooner or later the orkers have, consciously or unconciously, opposed the creation of a solidarity exceeding a common control of oportunity and common "working rules," —that is, if the undertaking did not die t birth, or, surviving, experience a conersion, materially prosperous but spirtually degrading, into a capitalist enterrise owned by a few of the "smarter" o-operators. For, the workers, it seems, ill cheerfully submit to an almost miliary union discipline in their struggles against the employer; they will be guided y the union working rules in seeking and

holding jobs; but they will mistrust and obstruct their union leaders who have become shop-bosses under whatever scheme of "workers' control." Perhaps in abstract reasoning, the wage earner might be expected to envisage the whole of the economic organization of society as the ultimate source of his job opportunity; and therefore wish for a complete "workers' control" of industry. Actually, however, the typical wage earner, when he can express himself in and through his trade union free of domination by intellectuals, who are never too bashful to do his thinking for him, seldom dreams of shouldering the risks of management. Ordinarily he traces the origin of his opportunity not much farther back than the point where it materializes in jobs, and will grasp and support only such union policies as will enable or force the employers to offer more jobs, equally available to all fellow craftsmen, and upon improved terms. . . .

America is a significant illustration of how the psychology of economic groups is shaped by economic opportunity. In this country, primarily in the non-slavery states, history has manifested probably the most extensive, if not the only large-scale example of the availability to the manual worker of practically unlimited economic opportunity. This unboundedness of opportunity was the effect of easy access to the natural resources of a rich and unoccupied continent; it lay further in the simplicity of the industrial and business structure of a young community. In consequence, the great mass of American manual producers—which includes farmers, mechanics, small manufacturers, and small business men—developed a competitive psychology which greatly exceeded in intensity the competitive psychology of the very same classes in Europe, and was strongly akin to the typical business men's psychology. Surrounded on all sides by opportunity, in natural resources and in business, the thought could scarcely have occurred that opportunity needed to be rationed, or that anyone had to be kept out, or that the individual competitor needed to be controlled and restricted by his fellows, in the common interest and in the interest of his own protection from oppressive bargains. Let each individual seek his own opportunity to his heart's content, and the outcome can only be good; so ran the accepted social maxim.

Yet, the individualist millennium was far from realization, even in pioneer America. Wealth somehow showed a preference for the coffers of the few rather than for the tills of the "producers." Nevertheless the producing community was not turned away from its individualistic creed, but developed a remedial program based on a characteristic "anti-monopoly" philosophy. The trouble with America was—as the theory went—that access to opportunity was really not free: that, aided by traitorous legislators, a small number of monopolists had succeeded in locking up the legitimate opportunities of the American people. The land speculator robbed the willing producer of his chances for profitable self-employment upon the soil. The money and credit monopolist, the banker, denied to the producer a free enjoyment of credit opportunity, which was really his by right of personal integrity and by right of his toil-created physical property. Thus credit was converted into a means for exploitation, notwithstanding that it was, in the last analysis, the mere product of the producers' confidence in one another's honesty. Similarly, the mercantile monopolist and the manufacturing "trust," aided and abetted by publicly chartered banks and by other special privilege institutions—tariffs, patent rights, public utility franchises, and by a private appropriation of limited natural resources—denied to the honest producer free marketing opportunity, and forced upon him a monopoly price both as buyer and seller. The remedy was "anti-monopoly," namely, to cut away the ground from under the monopolists by destroying, through legislation, their special privileges. Once the monopolist had been forced to restore free access to opportunity, free competition could be relied upon to set up a producers' paradise. It was only monopoly and the monopolist

that needed regulating—not the honest producer in his relation to economic opportunity.

That was the core of all "producer" philosophies in America—from Shay's Rebellion through Jackson, to Bryan and to La Follette. And so powerful was the grip of "anti-monopoly" philosophy upon the labor movement, that nearly three-quarters of a century had to elapse before it could shake loose and arrive at a philosophy of its own—the philosophy of trade unionism. Trade unionism, particularly the trade unionism of the American Federation of Labor, marked a clear shift in the psychology of American labor. It was a shift from an optimistic psychology, reflecting the abundance of opportunity in a partly settled continent, to the more pessimistic trade union psychology, built upon the premise that the wage earner, in a complex industrial structure, is faced by a scarcity of opportunity. The new attitude no longer called for a restoration of free competition, but for control and administration by the union of all job opportunities available to the group. This includes determination by the union of the rules under which the individual was permitted to occupy and hold his proper share of the total group opportunity. When, in the Presidential campaign of 1934, the American labor movement supported Senator La Follette, it was not a return to the former "anti-monopoly" theory, but merely an alliance cemented by the political issues of curtailing the powers of the judiciary and of presenting a united front to reaction. The trade unionism of the American Federation of Labor, far from repeating the traditional "anti-monopoly" clamor against "big business" and for free competition, envisages unionism as the necessary counterbalance to inevitably "big business." The province of the union is therefore, to assert labor's collective mastery over job opportunities and employment bargains, leaving the ownership of the business to the employer, and creating for its members an ever-increasing sphere of economic security and opportunity, equal to that which the craft gild

—those superb manifestations of the manual worker's aspirations and power—were able to guarantee to workingmen's communities of an earlier age. . . .

While it is true that a union can never become strong or stable except by attaching the individual to itself through the tangible benefits accruing to him from its administration of the job opportunities of the group as a whole, neither can it be a union in the full sense of the word unless it has educated the members to put the integrity of the collective "job-territory" above the security of their individual job tenure. Unionism is, in this respect, not unlike patriotism which may and does demand of the citizen the supreme sacrifice, when the integrity of the national territory is at stake. Just as a mere pooling by forty million Frenchmen of their individualistic self-interests will not yet produce a patriotic France, so a bare adding together of the individual job interests of five million wage earners, united in a common organization, will scarcely result in a labor movement. To have a really stable unionism and a really stable labor movement, the individual members must evince a readiness to make sacrifices on behalf of the control by their union of their collective "job-territory," without stopping to count too closely the costs involved to themselves. And like nationalism, unionism is keenly conscious of a "patria irredenta" in the non-union portion of its trade or industry.

But if unionism means an idealistic readiness on the part of the individual to offer, as the need arises, unstinted sacrifices for the group as a whole, what then of "business unionism"? May even such a unionism have an "ideology"? To many, of course, any "ideology" whatsoever in unionism which is merely "business" and which avowedly limits its objective to a mere control of jobs, is entirely and definitely precluded. However, upon closer examination, it would seem that if, by naming the predominant type of American unionism "business unionism," it was meant to bring out that it had no "ideology," then the name was clearly a misnomer. The difficulty arises from a disposition to class as idealistic solely the

professions of idealistic aims—socialism, anarchism, and the like,—but to overlook the unselfconscious idealism in the daily practice of unionism. In truth, unionism, even "business unionism," shows idealism both in aim and in method; only it does so in the thoroughly unsophisticated way of "Tom, Dick, and Harry idealism." All unions sooner or later stress "shop rights," which, to the workingman at the bench, are identical with "liberty" itself,—since, thanks to them, he has no need to kowtow to foreman or boss, as the price of holding his job. And, after all, is not this sort of liberty the only sort which reaches the workman directly and with certainty and that can never get lost *en route*, like the "broader" liberty promised by socialism? For, in practice, that other liberty may never succeed in straining through the many layers of the socialistic hierarchy down to the mere private in industry. Secondly, a union which expects its members to sacrifice for the group on a scale almost commensurate with the sacrifices which patriotism evokes, cannot be without its own respectable ideology. Frequently, therefore, the "materialism" of unionism proves only the one-sidedness of the view of the particular observer.

Yet, granting that even "business unionism" possesses ideology after a fashion, might it not be that, after all, the conception of unionism advanced here could fit only a narrow craft unionism, not a unionism with a wider conception of labor solidarity? True, the more distinct the trade identity of a given group and therefore the clearer the boundaries of its particular "job-territory," the stronger are normally the bonds which tie the members together in a spontaneous solidarity. Yet, on the other hand, the specific area of that common job-territory, or of the common opportunity which a group considers its own, is seldom fixed, but is constantly tending to widen, just as the numerical size and the composition of the group itself is constantly tending to grow. When accumulated technological changes have undermined the partitions between the several grades of labor in an industry and have thus produced a virtually undivided "job-territory" for all employed in it, the function of framing "rules of occupancy and tenure" for the job opportunities included within the now expanded job-territory will sooner or later be taken over by an *industrial* union or by an *amalgamated* union bordering upon the industrial type. And that union, when it will come to face the common enemy, will display a solidarity no less potent than the solidarity of the original craft unions, although as a job administrator the new and expanded union will endeavor to give recognition, so far as it will still remain possible, to the original particularistic job claims.

Nor need a job conscious unionism, with respect to many portentous issues, arrest the growth of its solidarity, short of the outer boundaries of the wage earning class as a whole. Many are the influences affecting union job control: the legal status of unionism, the policies of the government, a favorable public opinion, and others. Thus every union soon discovers that the integrity of its "job-territory," like the integrity of the geographic territory of a nation, is inextricably dependent on numerous wide relationships. And the very consciousness of the scarcity of opportunity, which is basic to labor's thinking, engenders in individual unions, labor's original organic cells, a wish for mutual cohesion, a common class-consciousness, and eventually a readiness to subordinate the interests of the individual cell to the aspirations of the whole labor organism. We know from history that the most craft-conscious bodies that ever existed, the mediaeval gilds, left nothing to be desired so far as solidaristic action against the common overlords was concerned. There is, however, a

practical limitation upon labor's solidarity, and this limitation is a very vital one namely that, in a labor movement which has already gone beyond the emotional stage and acquired a definite *rationale* of its own, an appeal for common class action, be it through a sympathetic strike or through joint political action, will only be likely to evoke the response which is desired if the objective of the proposed common undertaking be kept so close to the core substance of union aspiration that Tom, Dick, and Harry could not fail to identify it as such.

Just as we find job conscious unionism far from devoid of idealism of a kind, so its ultimate industrial vision need not at all be limited to the job itself. In truth such a unionism might easily acquire a lively interest in problems of management without previously undergoing mutation. It is not at all unnatural that a unionism which is intent upon job opportunities should join with management in a joint campaign to reduce the cost of operation and raise efficiency—all for the "conservation" of the current job opportunities. However, to grant so much is far from making the claim that labor might be brought to embrace "efficiency" as its primary concern instead of merely pursuing it secondarily to the primary interest in jobs. Thus it grows out of the preceding that whether one is trying to "improve" labor's "ideology," to broaden its solidarity, or to awaken its interest in "efficiency," one will indeed do well, in order to avoid wasted efforts, to steer close to the fundamental scarcity consciousness of the manual worker, which rules unionism today as it ruled the gild of the past. . . .

Frequently several movements appear at the same period of time that have many common features in their ideology and may overlap extensively in membership. In spite of the individual failures and successes of the specific movements, an increasingly wide acceptance of these common ideological features may be taking place. Often the individual movements can be viewed as expressions of the growth of this broader ideology. Herbert Blumer has referred to these broader shifts as *general movements*. General movements give rise to large umbers of interrelated specific movements and limit the possible success of movements whose ideologies are in opposition to the prevalent general movement.

General movements are not social movements as we have defined them, since hey have no organizational identity apart from their specific movements. The general movement is rather a social trend and preoccupation in mass values which is both reflected in and facilitated by specific social movements.

Edwin Sutherland has shown that the specific movement for treatment of sex offenders as patients rather than as criminals is not an isolated phenomenon in contemporary society. In the following paper he points out that the direction of his movement reflects the prevailing general movement more than it reflects any comparative evaluation of the effectiveness of different programs for dealing with sex offenders.

THE DIFFUSION OF SEXUAL PSYCHOPATH LAWS
Edwin H. Sutherland

This paper is an analysis of the diffusion of sexual psychopath laws from the point of view of collective behavior. Since 1937 twelve states and the District of Columbia have enacted sexual psychopath laws. With minor variations they provide that a person who is diagnosed as a sexual psychopath may be confined for an indefinite period in a state hospital for the insane. This confinement is not ordered by a criminal court as a punishment for crime but by a probate court for the protection of society against persons who are believed to have irresistible sexual impulses.[1]

Implicit in these laws is a series of propositions which have been made explicit in an extensive popular literature, namely, that the present danger to women and children from serious sex crimes is very great, for the number of sex crimes is large and is increasing more rapidly than any other crime; that most sex crimes are committed by "sexual degenerates," "sex fiends," or "sexual psychopaths" and that these persons persist in their sexual crimes throughout life; that they always give warning that they are dangerous by first committing minor offenses; that any psychiatrist can diagnose them with a high degree of precision at an early age, before they have committed

serious sex crimes; and that sexual psychopaths who are diagnosed and identified should be confined as irresponsible persons until they are pronounced by psychiatrists to be completely and permanently cured of their malady.[2]

Most of these propositions can be demonstrated to be false and the others questionable. More particularly, the concept of the "sexual psychopath" is so vague that it cannot be used for judicial and administrative purposes without the danger that the law may injure the society more than do the sex crimes which it is designed to correct. Moreover, the states

[1] In some states conviction of a sex crime is a prerequisite to the operation of this law. Even in this case the significant characteristic of the law is that it takes the criminal out of the realm of ordinary punishment and treats him as a patient with a mental malady.

[2] J. Edgar Hoover, "How Safe Is Your Daughter?" **American Magazine,** CXLIV (July, 1947), 32–33; David G. Wittels, "What Can We Do about Sex Crimes?" **Saturday Evening Post,** CCXXI (December 11, 1948), 30 ff.; C. J. Dutton, "Can We End Sex Crimes?" **Christian Century,** XLIV (December 22, 1937), 1594–95; F. C. Waldrup, "Murder as a Sex Practice," **American Mercury** (February, 1948), 144–58; Charles Harris, "A New Report on Sex Crimes," **Coronet** (October, 1947), 3–9; Howard Whitman, "Terror in Our Cities: No. I, Detroit," **Collier's,** November 19, 1949, pp. 13–15, 64–66.

Reprinted by permission, from The American Journal of Sociology, 56 (Sept., 1950).

which have enacted such laws make little or no use of them. And there is no difference in the trend in rates of serious sex crimes, so far as it can be determined, between the states which enact such laws and adjoining states which do not.[3]

These dangerous and futile laws are being diffused with considerable rapidity in the United States. Michigan first enacted such a law in 1937.[4] Illinois followed in 1938, and California and Minnesota in 1939. Thus four states have had these laws for ten years. In 1943 Vermont passed a sexual psychopath law; in 1945 Ohio; in 1947 Massachusetts, Washington, and Wisconsin; in 1948 the District of Columbia; and in 1949 Indiana, New Hampshire, and New Jersey. They continue to spread, with no indication of abatement. What is the explanation of this diffusion of laws which have little or no merit?

First, these laws are customarily enacted after a state of fear has been aroused in a community by a few serious sex crimes committed in quick succession. This is illustrated in Indiana, where a law was passed following three or four sexual attacks in Indianapolis, with murder in two. Heads of families bought guns and watchdogs, and the supply of locks and chains in the hardware stores of the city was completely exhausted.[5]

The sex murders of children are most effective in producing hysteria. Speaking of New York City in 1937, after four girls had been murdered in connection with sexual attacks, Austin H. MacCormick says:

For a while it was utterly unsafe to speak to a child on the street unless one was well-dressed and well-known in the neighborhood. To try to help a lost child, with tears streaming down its face, to find its way home would in some neighborhoods cause a mob to form and violence to be threatened.[6]

The hysteria produced by child murders is due in part to the fact that the ordinary citizen cannot understand a sex attack on a child. The ordinary citizen can understand fornication or even forcible rape of a woman, but he concludes that a sexual attack on an infant or a girl of six years must be the act of a fiend or maniac. Fear is the greater because the behavior is so incomprehensible.

A protracted man-hunt following a sex attack arouses additional fear. The newspapers report daily on the progress of the chase, and every real or imagined sex attack, from near and far, is given prominence. In the case of Fred Stroble in Los Angeles in November, 1949, three days elapsed between the discovery of the mutilated body of his victim and his capture. A description of the crime and of the suspected criminal was sent to all adjoining cities and counties, and blockades were set up along the Mexican border. Watches were set at hotels, motels, bus stations, railway stations, and saloons. Hundreds of reports came to the police from Los Angeles and from other cities. Timid old men were pulled off streetcars and taken to police stations for identification, and every grandfather was subject to suspicion. The body of a drowned man, recovered from the ocean, was at first reported to be Stroble. The history of Stroble's molestations of other girls was reported. A detailed description of seven other cases of sex murders of girls in Los Angeles since 1924 was published. At the end of the week, twenty-five other cases of molestations of girls in Los Angeles had been reported to the Los Angeles police.[7] After three days it appeared that Stroble had gone to Ocean Park, or the edge of Los Angeles, and had stayed in hotels there. He then returned to Los Angeles with the intention of surrendering to the police. He went into a bar after alighting from a bus and was recog-

---

[3] These appraisals of the sexual psychopath laws have been elaborated in my paper in the **Journal of Criminal Law and Criminology**, XL (January–February, 1950), 534–54.

[4] This law was declared unconstitutional, but a revised law was enacted in 1939.

[5] **Time**, November 24, 1947, pp. 29–30.

[6] "New York's Present Problem," **Mental Hygiene**, XX (January, 1938), 4–5.

[7] "Molestation" is a weasel word and can refer to anything from rape to whistling at a girl.

nized and pointed out to a policeman. The picture of the policeman who made the arrest was published in scores of newspapers over the United States as the "capturer of the sex fiend." After his capture, other details of the case and of related cases kept the community in a state of tension. As soon as the district attorney secured from Stroble an account of the manner of the murder, he went to the assembled reporters and repeated the story, "with beads of sweat standing on his face and neck." The psychiatrist's diagnosis of Stroble was published: he loved this little girl because he was a timid and weak old man, insufficiently aggressive to approach grown women; the murder of the girl was merely an incident due to fear of being caught and punished.

Fear is seldom or never related to statistical trends in sex crimes. New York City's terror in 1937 was at its height in August, although that was not the month when sex crimes reached their peak. The number of sex crimes known to the police of New York City was 175 in April, 211 in May, 159 in August, and 177 in September.[8] Ordinarily, from two to four spectacular sex crimes in a few weeks are sufficient to evoke the phrase "sex crime wave."

Fear is produced more readily in the modern community than it was earlier in our history because of the increased publicity regarding sex crimes. Any spectacular sex crime is picked up by the press associations and is distributed to practically all the newspapers in the nation; in addition, it is often described in news broadcasts. Then weekly and monthly journals publish general articles on sex crimes. All this produces a widespread uneasiness which, given a few local incidents, readily bursts into hysteria.

Although this condition of fear has been found in all the states prior to the enactment of their sexual psychopath laws, it is not a sufficient explanation of the laws. For generations communities have been frightened by sex crimes and have not enacted sexual psychopath laws. In the present generation the states which have not enacted sexual psychopath laws have had similar fears.

A second element in the process of developing sexual psychopath laws is the agitated activity of the community in connection with the fear. The attention of the community is focused on sex crimes, and people in the most varied situations envisage dangers and see the need of and possibility for their control. When a news broadcaster, in connection with the Stroble case, expressed the belief over the radio that something should be done, he received more than two hundred telegrams agreeing with him. The mother of the murdered girl demanded punishment for the daughter of Stroble, who had harbored him without notifying the parents of girls in the neighborhood that he was a dangerous criminal. A woman spoke in condemnation of strip-tease and other lewd shows as stimulating sex fiends and demanded that they be closed. Letters to the editors demanded that sex criminals be castrated; others recommended whipping. The City Council of Los Angeles adopted a resolution demanding that the legislature of the state be called in special session to enact laws which would punish sex crimes more severely and would make sex criminals ineligible for parole. The attorney-general of the state sent a bulletin to all sheriffs and police chiefs urging them to enforce strictly the laws which required registration of all sex criminals. The judiciary committee of the state legislature appointed a subcommittee to study the problem of sex crimes and to make recommendations to a special session of the legislature. The superintendent of city schools urged, among other things, that sex offenders who loitered around the schools should be prosecuted. The grand jury met and started a general investigation of sex crimes. The Juvenile Protective Committee urged an appropriation of $50,000 for medical and clinical treatment of sex offenders, and the County Probation Department energetically requested the authorizing of a psychiatric clinic for the study and super-

---

[8] Citizens' Committee for the Control of Crime in New York, "Sex Crimes in New York City," quoted in **Journal of Criminal Law and Criminology**, XXIX (May, 1938), 143–44.

vision of sex offenders. It was reported that some psychiatrists in the city opposed these suggestions for psychiatric clinics as "socialized medicine" and "statism."

In the meantime, organization developed in other directions. The sheriff's office set up a special detail on sex offenses, with a staff to co-ordinate all police activities on sex offenses in the county. The Parent-Teacher Association sponsored mass meetings, with blanks on which interested persons could enrol as members of an organization which would continue its efforts until effective action for control of sex crimes was taken. At the first mass meeting, attended by about eight hundred people, speakers were scheduled to explain the existing laws and procedures and to suggest programs for improvement. The news of the Stroble crime and of subsequent events was carried over the nation by the press associations and produced national reactions. J. Edgar Hoover was quoted as calling for an all-out war against sex criminals. The Associated Press's science editor wrote a syndicated column on the views of leaders in the nation regarding methods of controlling sex crimes.

The third phase in the development of these sexual psychopath laws has been the appointment of a committee. The committee gathers the many conflicting recommendations of persons and groups of persons, attempts to determine "facts," studies procedures in other states, and makes recommendations, which generally include bills for the legislature. Although the general fear usually subsides within a few days, a committee has the formal duty of following through until positive action is taken. Terror which does not result in a committee is much less likely to result in a law. The appointment of a committee is a conventional method of dealing with any problem. Even during the recent agitations in California and Michigan, which have had sexual psychopath laws for ten years, committees have been appointed to study sex crimes and to make recommendations.

These committees deal with emergencies, and their investigations are relatively superficial. Even so, the community sometimes becomes impatient. Before a committee appointed by the Massachusetts legislature had had time for even a superficial investigation, the impatient legislature enacted a sexual psychopath law. The committee report several months later recommended that the statute which had just been enacted should be repealed on the ground that sex crimes should not be considered apart from the general correctional system of the state.[9] Similarly, the legislature of New Jersey enacted a sexual psychopath law in 1949 and also appointed a committee to investigate sex crimes and to suggest a policy. In New York City, on the other hand, the mayor took certain emergency actions in 1937 and did not appoint a committee until several months after the crisis. This committee made a very thorough study of all sex crimes in New York City in the decade 1930–39 and did not report for two or three years. The result was that New York State did not enact a sexual psychopath law; and, in fact, the committee was divided in its recommendation that such a law should be enacted.

In some states, at the committee stage of the development of a sexual psychopath law, psychiatrists have played an important part. The psychiatrists, more than any others, have been the interest group back of the laws. A committee of psychiatrists and neurologists in Chicago wrote the bill which became the sexual psychopath law of Illinois; the bill was sponsored by the Chicago Bar Association and by the state's attorney of Cook County and was enacted with little opposition in the next session of the state legislature.[10] In Minnesota all of the members of the governor's committee ex-

[9] Massachusetts, "Report of the Commission for Investigation of the Prevalence of Sex Crimes," **House Reports,** Nos. 1169 and 2169, 1948.

[10] W. S. Stewart, "Concerning Proposed Legislation for the Commitment of Sex Offenders," **John Marshall Law Quarterly,** III (March, 1938), 407–21; W. H. Haines, H. R. Hoffman, and H. A. Esser, "Commitments under the Criminal Sexual Psychopath Law in the Criminal Court of Cook County, Illinois," **American Journal of Psychiatry,** CV (November, 1948), 422.

ept one were psychiatrists. In Wisconsin he Milwaukee Neuropsychiatric Society hared in pressing the Milwaukee Crime Commission for the enactment of a law. n Indiana the attorney-general's committee received from the American Psychiatric Association copies of all of the exual psychopath laws which had been nacted in other states.

Such actions by psychiatrists are consistent in some respects with their general views. Most psychiatrists assert that serius sex crimes are the result of mental athology, although few of them would nake such unqualified statements as that ttributed to Dr. A. A. Brill at the time f the panic in New York City in 1937: Sex crimes are committed only by peole of defective mentality. All mental defectives have either actual or potential ex abnormalities." [11] Also, psychiatrists lmost without exception favor the view hat criminals should be treated as patents. Moreover, since the sexual psychopath laws usually specify that the dignosis for the court shall be made by sychiatrists, they have an economic inerest in the extension of this procedure.

While psychiatrists have often played n important part in the promotion of exual psychopath laws, many prominent sychiatrists have been forthright in their pposition to them. They know that the exual psychopath cannot be defined or identified. Probably most of the psychitrists in the nation have been indifferent o legislation; they have exerted themelves neither to promote nor to oppose nactment.

The function of the committee is to rganize information. The committee, lealing with emergency conditions, cusomarily takes the information which is vailable. Much of this has been distribted through popular literature, which ontains the series of propositions outned above. The latter are customarily ccepted without firsthand investigation y the committee and are presented to the legislature and the public as "science." Although these propositions are all false or questionable, they have nevertheless been very effective in the diffusion of the laws. Bills are presented to the legislature with the explanation that these are the most enlightened and effective methods of dealing with the problem of sex crimes and that the states which have sexual psychopath laws have found them effective. Very little discussion occurs in the legislature. When the bill for the District of Columbia was presented in Congress, the only question asked was whether this bill, if enacted, would weaken or strengthen the sex laws; the questioner was satisfied with a categorical reply that the bill would strengthen them. [12]

The law is similarly presented to the public as the most enlightened and effective method of dealing with sex offenders. After the sexual psychopath bill had been drafted in Indiana, the *Indianapolis Star* had the following editorial:

> Indiana today is one step nearer an enlightened approach to the growing menace of sex crimes. A proposed new law to institutionalize sexual psychopathics until pronounced permanently recovered has been drafted by a special state citizens' committee which helped the attorney general's office to study the problem. . . . Such a law should become a realistic, practical answer to the sex crime problem. This type of legislation has succeeded elsewhere and is long overdue in Indiana. [13]

The diffusion of sexual psychopath laws, consequently, has occurred under the following conditions: a state of fear developed, to some extent, by a general, nationwide popular literature and made explicit by a few spectacular sex crimes; a series of scattered and conflicting reactions by many individuals and groups within the community; the appointment of a committee, which in some cases has been guided by psychiatrists, which organizes existing information regarding sex crimes and the precedents for their

[11] Quoted in **Time,** August 23, 1937, pp. 2–44. If the Kinsey Report is trustworthy, ll males, whether defective or not, "have ither actual or potential sex abnormalies."

[12] **Congressional Record,** XCIV (April 26, 1948), 4886.
[13] December 8, 1948.

control and which presents a sexual psychopath law to the legislature and to the public as the most scientific and enlightened method of protecting society against dangerous sex criminals. The organization of information in the name of science and without critical appraisal seems to be more invariably related to the emergence of a sexual psychopath law than is any other part of this genetic process.

The most significant reason for the specific content of the proposals of these committees—treatment of the sex criminal as a patient—is that it is consistent with a general social movement.[14] For a century or more two rival policies have been used in criminal justice. One is the punitive policy; the other is the treatment policy. The treatment policy is evidenced by probation, parole, the indeterminate sentence, the juvenile court, the court clinic, and the facilities in correctional institutions for education, recreation, and religion. The treatment policy has been gaining, and the punitive policy has been losing, ground.

The trend toward treatment and away from punishment is based on cultural changes in the society. The trend away from punishment in criminal justice is consistent with the trend away from punishment in the home, the school, and the church. The trend toward treatment is consistent with a general trend toward scientific procedures in other fields, as illustrated by medicine, with its techniques of diagnosis and with treatment and prevention based on scientific knowledge of the causes of disease. The trend away from punishment toward treatment is not, however, based on a demonstration that treatment is more effective than punishment in protecting society against crime, for no such demonstration is available. Also, the fact that the trend in punishment is consistent with trends in other aspects of culture is not an adequate explanation of the trend in punishment. A general theory of social change must in-clude more than a showing that one par of a culture changes consistently wit other parts of a culture.

Not only has there been a trend towar individualization in treatment of offend ers, but there has been a trend also to ward psychiatric policies. Treatment tend to be organized on the assumption tha the criminal is a socially sick person; de viant traits of personality, regarded a relatively permanent and generic, are re garded as the causes of crime. Since th time of Lombroso, at least, the logic c the typological schools of criminology ha remained constant, while the specific trai used as the explanation of criminal be havior has changed from time to tim The first school held that criminals con stitute a physical type, either epileptoi or degenerate in character; the secon that they are feeble-minded; the thir and current, school holds that crimina are emotionally unstable. All hold tha crime can be caused only by a menta pathology of some type. The profes sionally trained persons other than law yers who are employed in the field o criminal justice, whether as social work ers, psychologists, psychiatrists, or soc ologists, tend toward the belief that emo tional traits are the explanation of crim This conclusion likewise has not bee demonstrated, and the body of evidenc in conflict with the conclusion is increas ing.

A specific aspect of this trend towar treatment of offenders as patients is th provision for psychotic and feeble-minde criminals. When such persons do th things prohibited by criminal law, the may be held to be irresponsible from th legal point of view and may still be or dered to confinement in institutions fc the protection of society. All the state have some provision for psychotic crim inals, and several have provisions fc feeble-minded criminals. In some Eure pean nations the provisions for psychoti and feeble-minded criminals have bee expanded and generalized under the nam of "social security" laws: some have in cluded sexual criminals under their soci security measures, and the latter are th

14 See Herbert Blumer, "Social Movements," chap. xxiii in **New Outline of the Principles of Sociology**, edited by A. M. Lee (New York: Barnes & Noble, 1946).

direct precedents for the sexual psycho-path laws of the United States.

One of the questions in criminal law has been the criterion of responsibility. The courts have generally held that "knowledge of right and wrong" is the most satisfactory criterion. The psychiatrists have generally opposed this; they have argued that 90 per cent of the inmates of state hospitals for the insane can distinguish right from wrong but are, nevertheless, legally irresponsible. The important consideration, they argue, is that the psychotic person has impulses which he cannot control and that "irresistible impulse" should be substituted for "knowledge of right and wrong" as the criterion. The psychiatrists, however, have not been able to make their criterion clear cut for practical purposes.

The trend away from punishment and toward treatment of criminals as patients is to some extent a "paper" trend. Laws are enacted which provide for treatment rather than punishment; but the treatment goes on within a framework of punishment, and in many respects the punitive policies continue, despite changes in legislation. Probation, for instance, is upheld from the constitutional point of view as a suspension of punishment rather than as a method co-ordinate with punishment and is regarded by some persons as effective primarily because of the threat implied in it that punishment will follow violation of probation.

The sexual psychopath laws are consistent with this general social movement toward treatment of criminals as patients. Some laws define sexual psychopaths as patients"; they provide for institutional care similar to that already provided for psychotic and feeble-minded criminals; they substitute the criterion of "irresist-ible impulse" for the criterion of "knowledge of right and wrong"; and they reflect the belief that sex criminals are psychopathic. The consistency with a general social movement provides a part of the explanation of the diffusion of sexual psychopath laws.

In the United States the connection between the enactment of sexual psychopath laws and the development of treatment policies is, at best, vague and loose. This is obvious from a consideration of the distribution of the laws. Three New England states, one Middle Atlantic state, and two Pacific Coast states have passed such laws; but the remainder—half of all the states with sexual psychopath laws —are in the North Central region. These laws, in fact, have been enacted in a solid block of North Central States: Ohio, Indiana, Illinois, Michigan, Wisconsin, and Minnesota. On the other hand, no state in the southern, South Central, or Mountain regions has a sexual psychopath law. These regions also are less committed to treatment policies than are the regions which have sexual psychopath laws. While this association may be found when large regions are compared, it is not found when specific states are compared; New York State, for instance, has had an extensive development of treatment policies but no sexual psychopath law. Similarly, the states which have sexual psychopath laws are not differentiated clearly from states which do not have such laws by any statistical variable which has been discovered: they are not differentiated by the rate of rape, by the racial composition of the population, by the proportion of immigrants in the population, by the sex ratio in the population, or by the extent of industrialization or urbanization.

The concept of a *general movement* is merely a simplified representation of the gradual and cumulative emergence to prominence of certain types of ideas and values during any period of social and economic change. In an example of this type of analysis Rexford G. Tugwell shows how succeeding groups of reformers in the United States came closer to the ultimate philosophy of the New Deal. Nineteenth-century reform movements were largely consonant with the rural rather than the urban mentality. But within the cities there developed movements that came closer and closer to the type of planning that became a central theme in the early Roosevelt administration.

In light of this type of analysis, the New Deal—and other similar movements —become a culmination of many movements. Consequently, the movement draws together many ideological threads, not all of which join in a consistent fashion. Movements within any particular general movement may merge for strategic purposes, or because their respective purposes are in harmony. Thus the abolition movement and the woman suffrage movement were much identified before the Civil War in the United States, because many of their leaders and adherents were moved by a common equalitarian value.

But however ill-defined the official program and identity of any movement they may well become more confused once the movement attains some effec tive power. This is partly because a movement which demonstrates any power promptly attracts those who see it only as a vehicle through which to gain power for themselves. But it is also because the many related movements are likely to ally themselves with any movement that shows real power. The ascendance of the representatives of various movements led to abundant shifts in policy within the New Deal, so that it would be difficult to locate any single consistent ideology that was maintained throughout.

Furthermore, the practical exigencies of enacting the desired reforms place the movement in a different position from that of a movement that is not made responsible for its actions. Extreme programs are compromised and the move ment becomes more conservative as it now has a commitment to preserve its own *status quo.* Priorities among the objectives of the various allied movements also force revisions, as in the early New Deal postponement of strong action on race relations in favor of other reforms.

In short, whether or not a movement has a clearly defined set of values before it comes to power, its access to power is certain to make them unclear.

Representation of the values. There are many ways in which the logic of a movement's program and the ideology which gives it justification may be com municated. Formal declarations, the speeches of persons thought to represent the movement, dramatic actions, and many other devices serve this purpose. But it would be an error to view the program and ideology primarily as cognitive mat ters, to be explained in direct language.

The vital element in the ideology and program is a *sense of value,* a feeling for a certain direction of change. Those who attack particular movements on cognitive grounds constantly point to unworkable details in their programs. Fol lowers are not greatly distressed by a certain amount of this sort of criticism since their conviction is that practical details can be worked out as the plan goes into operation if only the right kind of people who hold the right kind of values are in control. This is to a considerable degree true of movements that have had an important impact on history, as well as of minor "crackpot" movements.

The official spokesmen of movements necessarily share this sense of value and the subordination of details of program. It is not surprising, then, that official representations of a movement's ideology are largely taken up with depicting the movement in terms of values, rather than logical details. It is to be expected that the public representations will be more concerned with the arousal of feeling

ıan with rational exposition. Such concentration on feelings may be the sincere
xpression of the movement, or it may be simply a tactic to exploit irrational
ɪpport.

Following a content analysis of the documents of a series of revolutionary
ıovements in France, Jean Belin-Milleron observes this noncognitive character
f the public representations of movement ideology. He attempts to make the
bservation more precise through a series of generalizations.

SYMBOLIC EXPRESSIONS IN THE COLLECTIVE PSYCHOLOGY
OF POLITICAL CRISES

JEAN BELIN-MILLERON

'he study of popular political texts sup-
ɪies useful information to the social psy-
ɪologist on what can be called the un-
erlying collective consciousness. In fact,
ıere is found in such interesting docu-
ɪents as the addresses and petitions of
ıe revolutions of 1789 and of 1848, as
ɪso in certain testimonies of 1871, a tech-
ique of intensive suggestion which ex-
ɪnds from the well-known *image* of the
ɪsychoanalysts to a sort of grasp of the
ɪoral and social universe through the in-
ɪrmediary of the physical universe. We
hall seek here to discern, in the course
f a concrete study, the kind of symbol-
ɪm into which this political psychology
ɪ translated, by drawing conclusions from
ɪe manipulation of unedited documents.

1. *Symbolic combinations*—When the
ɪasoning contained in the petitions, ad-
ɪresses, journals, hand bills, and tracts of
ɪe revolutions of 1789, 1848, and 1871,
ɪ examined piece by piece, it proves that
ɪertain processes of thought are repeated
ɪith a regularity which allows them to be
ɪnalyzed and classified. We have sepa-
ɪated these processes into 3 groups. From
ɪe start the public mind has linked to-
ɪether juridical and political ideas—"civil
ɪberty," "constitution," "democracy,"—
ɪoral and social notions—"public good,"
civic virtue," "solidarity," all of which

are ideas that have served as symbolic
expressions.

If, as we have done, one prepares a
statistical survey of the values most appreciated by opinion—for example, political and civil liberty, "people," "equality"
—one notes that they are interrelated
by means of intercalary terms and that
they are assimilated to each other, whatever their precise signification or the logical relation in which they figure may be.
Thanks to the practice of symbolic linkage among words, the diverse systems
that have been used by revolutionary
thought have, down to a few terms, the
same symbolic content. It follows that
political notions cease to be abstract and
distinct concepts to become poles of attraction which are measured by the multiple complements which surround them
in the collective mind. Moreover, in concrete use one can no longer consider each
concept as a unity. It is appropriate to
understand, beyond them and with the
same logic, the collection of connected
ideas which is to be interpreted in the
political psychology of a given epoch.
Then one sees the technical concepts *develop* in long chains of ideas and of sentiments which represent symbolic superim-
positions of the social experience upon
space and time.

The study of these experiences can be
approached thanks to what we propose to
call the statistical method of connections.
For each great political notion adopted
as a major idea one uncovers networks
of connected terms. Their collation reveals that certain notions are doubled,

Translated by Ralph H. Turner from
ean Belin-Milleron, "Les Expressions Sym-
oliques dans la Psychologie Collective des
rises Politiques," **Cahiers Internationaux
e Sociologie**, 10 (1951), pp. 158–67. Used
y permission of Aux Editions du Seuil and
he author.

quadrupled, quintupled, or carried to higher powers. The index or frequency of these repetitions indicates the intensity of the symbolic work which has been effected on these words in the collective thought.

A second procedure, necessitated by the first, is that of symbolic *substitutions* which serve to bring about a promotion of ideas, such as those of people and of equality in 1792, 1848, and 1871. Since the chains communicate by means of common terms which they include, it is possible to replace any notion by the ideas which are directly or indirectly linked in the symbolism of the chains. Such is the operation of substitution. To substitute equality in the liberty network is to replace equality by the collection of terms which are linked to it in the revolutionary symbolism. By these "operations," one is led to writings where repetitions are observed again, and consequently to a geometric augmentation of the number of connections and of frequency.

Finally, the comparative examination of the promotion of ideas from one to another of our revolutions shows the existence of a third process, *reinterpretation*. This is explained by the psychological work accomplished through the process we have just studied, but goes beyond it. Let us follow its successive articulations. From the first the public mind has, in 1848 and in 1871, linked the terms bequeathed to it by the French Revolution to a newly appreciated theme. Thus the traditional ideas of "liberty" and "equality" have been linked to the idea of "people" or to the notion of "economic need" in order to introduce the problem of the relations between capital and labor. This elementary process of coupling which serves to bring together two meanings separated in historical time, is at the base of the social reinterpretation of political notions; it is encountered in each line written by the petitioners of 1848. Then, when the newly appreciated political or economic idea introduced through this process occupies opinion sufficiently to render it relatively independent from the ancient political themes, the phenomenon correctly called reinterpretation appears.

The newly received notion—"people," for example—will be promoted by mean of the process of substitution described above. Let us note that in this case substitution will be accompanied by surviv als. As a matter of fact, other terms from the traditional ideology, such as "liberty," will remain linked to the term which ha been promoted in time ("people"), as if in order to preponderate, the latter required the support of an ancient notion which does not offend the habits o thought and can acclimatize a new idea When the idea which must be promoted is finally received, one of two things happens; either the ancient term which ha served it as protector disappears, or th latter undergoes a reinterpretation in it turn. This is what happened when liberty and equality became, in popular writings synonymous with the "right to live."

Finally, and this will be the last aspec of reinterpretation, one witnesses a re turn to the process of multiple linkag which has been defined earlier; the idea advanced are linked among themselves t furnish mutual support. "Equality" is ad joined to "fraternity," the "people," th "revolution," or yet the word "people" i adjoined to the trilogy "revolution," "equality," "welfare." Thus reinterpreta tion, which appears to us as a phenome non of selection of values, is accompanie by a condensation of psychological sig nifications about a small number o strongly symbolic ideas.

The study of these processes gives ris to two observations. On the one han terms are connected, in revolutionar symbolism, between which no universa linkage exists. It follows that the socia psychologist is not dealing with ideas tha have sharp contours, such as those o logicians and jurists, but with themes o varying combinations whose distinctiv trait is the psychological tension whicl propels them. That is to say, political no tions seen throughout the public min are characterized by a deep practical ori entation which can only be judged by in timacy with the most concrete evidence.

In the second place, we assert that a the terms of the liaisons are ambiguou notions, since they are suspended from historical facts which could not have produced them, with implications very different according to whether they are placed in 1790, in 1792–1793, in 1848, or in 1871, and according to whether one observes the requests of the towns or the country, etc. The public mind has experienced this radical uncertainty of the great political words—words which are at the same time moral; also it has sought in certain moments of enthusiasm or of crisis to escape from this ambiguity. For that purpose it has imagined a use of words which is no longer the liaison of ideas, but a *projection* of ideas sometimes in the framework of time and sometimes in the framework of space. Projected in time the ideas we have encountered in chains and reinterpretations are absorbed in the ideas of historical *cycle* and of *progress*. Projected in space, they are materialized. Let us examine first the former process.

2. *Oriented social time*—Time in our texts is simultaneously both oriented and reversible; it is compatible with human intervention in historical events. This is seen as early as in the formula of the "regeneration" employed in 1789, but again in 1848. Regeneration is the reformation of institutions, opening out in the direction of public welfare and using the teachings of the past in view of the future. A forward step, but also a return to history; with its highly symbolic character, this expression possesses a considerable force. Another oriented theme is that of progress, certainly meaningful following 1848 since the appearance of industrialism. After the transformations which have taken place in industry, how can one be astonished, explain the texts, that analogous transformations are produced in the political, social and moral order? "It is true of revolutions as it is of industry: as time moves on, progress is made. It was up to us, as children of the July Revolution, to surpass our fathers of 1830." Two essential ideas are placed in circulation. On the one hand social time, for the collective consciousness, flows in the direction of the future which is that of progress; the principle

again is that of oriented time. On the other hand, political, social, and moral progress is depicted as being commanded by economic transformations. Conforming to the process of the carrying forward of ideas explained above, the term progress is introduced here by the traditional word "liberty," to which the memorials have taken care to connect it.

The idea of a time with fixed direction has introduced a third theme, that of the "new era." A phase of material and moral civilization has begun which will be distinguished from earlier periods by the absence of any future regression. "No revolution will put an end to it"; for that reason it is said that the new order "has no precedent whatever in the history of the world." Sometimes this theme is going to be developed in political and moral actions that we know: "the new era which has just appeared . . . must be for all the French the era of welfare, equality, and liberty." Or it mobilizes liberty and fatherland, the "reign of justice" and the republic, "political liberty" and the "government of the people by themselves," or yet the notions of welfare and humanity, of regeneration and fraternity. Sometimes the "era" is sufficient to itself; there is a condensation of feelings about this theme; one remains within the bounds of the formulae: "new era," "new phase of humanity." All this phraseology supposes that civilization is divided into periods of progress, of stagnation and regression, that is to say that there are "epochs of history," as George Sand wrote in April, 1848. Thence, in our texts, came the sentiment of a historic "destiny" and even a dynamism, in the terms used in the petitions: the parties "depose" their prejudices, men "march, hands clasped, toward this happy age," "the world is marching." This movement of minds, accelerated by universal suffrage, is described as a unique phenomenon, "a first time in history, as an event of civilization which presages the future and earns for the French people the messianic title of "first people of civilization."

Finally, this conception of an oriented and privileged time reacts on the institutions by introducing the political symbol of *Republic*. The Republic, surrounded by the dynamic images of which we have just taken note, will be considered in a perpetual state of becoming for the accomplishment of the privileged time which is that of progress and of the phases of civilization already evoked. This becoming is proclaimed to be perpetual, "in the sense that there will always be the immature in human societies, the ignorant and the feeble." In this both dynamic and symbolic perspective of themes and of political forms, how does one define a government, the provisional government for example? It is a government "to the limit," as the mathematicians would say; it is a political form which "will never wholly exist," say the petitions or the lampoons. Similarly, to define the Republic is impossible; the form is not sufficiently hardened, for it is carried on the arrow of social time, and passes from an inferior phase of humanity to a superior phase. Also one will go as far as to say in a language which is not itself unrelated to that of certain great mystics that the Republic possesses "an unknown character" of which "no history would be able to give the measure." These many formulae show that political notions are very far from the sharp concepts which jurists handle, and that they must be studied above all by the social psychologist who will study them in the context of the privileged time which already appertains to a desired future and which confers on them, as we shall see, a characteristic potentiality.

3. *Symbolic spatialization*—Let us pass to the second factor that we have mentioned, the spatial factor. When they are projected in space, political notions are materialized. This materialization is especially visible in 1848 and 1871. Following are several examples. The idea of revolution is identified with the idea of work, which is materialized: "The revolution," writes one, "has need of work." Moreover the materialization of the revolution takes the form of a "portion 'taken' at the banquet of social life." Or yet socialism is represented by a "beacon suspended over the abyss" which permits attainment of the "promised land." The Republic is identified with the "day" which dissipate the "moral night," or with "the rainbow" which follows the storm. Even a moral notion such as fraternity becomes an object, it is a "jewel." Similarly civic virtue is corporealized as the "stone" which each carries to the common work of reform which, in its turn, is materialized in a "social edifice." For its part the socialization of private property is accompanied by intense materializations: the soil, the "portions," the "shares," the food products reserved to the possessing class such as wine, etc. In the course of the process of spatialization one endeavors on the other hand to encompass social history within the laws of material bodies, such as are enunciated by the physician and the chemist. Thus a lampoon claims to be supported by the work of the chemist J. B. Dumas, at the same time as by the notions of "force" and of "physical attraction" considered as laws of the universe, to affirm by analogy that men in society obey "the passionate attraction" and eight "soul stimuli." Finally, one sees affirmed here and there a mystic materialism which incarnates moral forces in the stars. Thus one will explain that the moon is the principle of evil, of death, and that its influence is, in February 1848, dominant over a world corrupted by an unjust division of wealth. The cosmic element will serve to present the socialization of the soil, but it also utilizes in its technique the liaisons of ideas that we have encountered at the beginning of this article. One will say that justice, economic equality, welfare will be realized only with the preponderance of the very foundation of good which is the sun.

Such is the spatialization through evocation of the inanimate world. But it also exists in the revolutionary symbolism of materializations borrowed from the animate world. In this category appears the theme of the tree. Bringing back a very ancient tradition well known to mythologists, the revolutions of 1789 and of 1848 have planted the trees of liberty, the "oak of liberty," but the oak has ceased to be the sacred plant of immemorial cosmolo gies to become "the social tree." The tree is a symbol because in the collective consciousness there persists a fund of naturalism which is unconscious in the manner of a complex. Then beyond the animate beings the biological theme of life has been used. This word, also endowed with a high symbolic value, is associated with ideas of revolution, of republic, of people, conveying, in the milieu of linkages of political ideas, the echo of a residual naturalism. The dissertations on economic and social questions which we have surveyed have been very often hitched to ideas of nature and of life; it is explained that the factors of life which form the "soul of the world" have tended to be eliminated by money, so much that after the struggle of man against natural forces must begin the struggle of man against the evil forces of society. This serves to signify that social understanding is the logical sequel to the understanding of nature. In the prolongation of the latter is opened the "new world of solidarity," which correlatively to the mastery of the material universe will bring the moral liberation of humanity.

4. *Conclusion: the underlying political consciousness*—In conclusion, let us disentangle the characteristic traits from the course that we have just analyzed. First of all what distinguishes the spontaneous political consciousness is the *orientation* which is manifest in the symbolism of words and of their use. Certainly political terms designate social, economic, and institutional realities, that the sociologist and the historian reveal by monographic studies which must be as localized as possible in space and time, in order to grasp the turns of meaning. But the phraseology which holds our attention comports above all a considerable mobilization of emotions, of evocations whose fascinating imagery informs the social psychologist concerning the *underlying* revolutionary consciousness, that which lies subjacent to the great historical events, to the revolutionary "journeys," to laws and to concilitations. The interest of the popular texts, from which we have just summarized the principal psychological processes, is precisely to restore the core sub-

jacent to this imaginative consciousness. It is a lyrical and fabulous locale, aesthetic and sociocosmological, in which the reality of social conditions, of events and of hopes are amalgamated to form a structure. This structure can be analyzed in terms of connections among words and their frequency, in terms of condensed themes that can be recognized which associate concepts, things, and beings to the implications of the political consciousness. Taken from real life, these testimonies have value as so many projections of an underlying mentality. From the start there is not any symbolism of political liberty, of revolution and of life except as there are "secondary elaborations," we say, borrowing an expression from the psychoanalysts. These elaborations are the connections of ideas, of sentiments and of images which constitute the chains of statements that we have indicated. The words are sometimes added, sometimes substituted one for the other, as to exhaust the *orientation* of the popular consciousness. But in these connections there is only an imperfect identification, which, moreover, is not at all surprising since the logician asserts in other domains that pure reason itself is "inaccessible." Hence, in our findings come these clear "equations," which make of the supplementary and of the intercalary a sort of law of political consciousness. These equations suppose a conception of number not unitary but plural, of combinations which belong to meta mathematics.

Let us go further and substantiate a use of ideas where opposites are together; "equality" is not at all equivalent to the "constitution," since the latter installs a suffrage by fee; political liberty is a notion deemed contradictory when economic liberty of salary is not realized, etc. But there is for each epoch, and in the public mind, coexistence of ideas which can be associated without manifesting their contradictions, so that the underlying collective consciousness reconciles them in the symbolic implications which we have examined and which form as a whole. If the illogic appears, it does so suddenly, when one passes to a different level of the political consciousness, to the stage of evocations of real spatial collections (cosmo-social), with the themes of "work" or of "life." For there the perspective is distorted. The political ideas, by being subordinated to a vision which is no longer exclusively centered on abstract themes, lose a part of the symbolic force which masked the disharmonies and contradictions. Also they fall in the field of rational criticism and the ambiguity appears. This process of combination followed by separation of contraries recalls what one observes in the history of religions when the neophyte inserts his experience in a cosmic group. Like him, the citizen who nourishes political and social themes internally in the course of an experience which is both personal and collective, remakes, beyond the conceptual thought, an original synthesis which can be analyzed thus:

At the base liaisons of concepts with powerful images take place; then a particular combination intervenes on the heterogeneous symbols; finally, a push toward cosmo-social wholes unifies this disordered proliferation about a very few condensers. In the course of these processes the subject, at once both individual and collective, which is that of concrete documents merges with the conceived object, an image or political idea. In every case the states of consciousness are polarized by the theme which they summarize and which they tend to realize more and more completely. Let us translate this phenomenon by saying that the *orientation* of the imaginative political consciousness is accompanied by an integration into spatialized collections which respond to a collective mentality and to a particular technique. In fact, the representation of political ideas or symbolic themes is for the petitioner the representation of something which touches both him and as his social category. It is a matter of a difference of juridical, economic, moral, professional treatment which he allocates to the class or party or to the nationality to which he belongs. What he discerns is a privilege and an injustice. To this positive element are added the elements of a *complex*. In ef-

fect the mentality of the "patriot" of 1789, like that of the worker of 1848, or of the "communard" of 1871, is determined by the long powerlessness in which the institutions and the customs which oppose the expression of his desires have kept him. The texts often supply details which illuminate this aspect of revolutionary mentality, shared by an entire category of men. A man of this type dispatches his project of reform with the conviction that he believes it useful to the common welfare and as an "offering to the nation," while adding that he feels that he "will not be heard." Another, a peasant secularly pressured by the public treasury, petitions by saying that "nothing will change." Others whose mentality is wrought in the pressure of the imperial regime express a deep pessimism which is explained in the last number of *Salut Public*, printed May 23, 1871, in these words: "Work without results, misery without end. No more hope . . ." All these notations do not fail to recall certain avowals which characterize the complexes studied today in psychoanalysis. Let us pass to the structure of the liberators' themes themselves. The revolutionary experiences them as potentials. The themes of liberty, of fraternity, of the people, draw positive or negative solutions, while in another connection each historical event—Federation, invasion, fall of the July monarchy or of the Empire, and also each minor happening—seems to correspond in advance to the interrogations posed by the collective consciousness and to take its place among the implications of potential themes. In this perspective one comprehends more completely the symbolic technique in its role of combining notions and of integration in cosmo-social wholes. This technique represents a mental work undertaken at the same time in reality and in the imaginary. In following the mental work through expansion and contraction of conceptual linkages, one can restore the exploration of the moral world by the underlying collective consciousness. Studies that we follow in the domain of the social psychology of myth have shown us that these processes answer to a more general scheme of the investigations of the collective mentality beneath the clear consciousness.

An ideologist for the French Syndicalist movement, Georges Sorel, makes this noncognitive character of movement values the explicit justification for the myth of the "general strike." Dedicated to a revolutionary socialism and despising "parliamentary socialism" as an insincere surrender to capitalist forces, he urges that all socialist energies be devoted to spreading the doctrine of one general strike which will paralyze all society. Sorel's work is of interest here not because of his particular brand of socialism, but because of his analysis of the noncognitive character of *myth*. Only a brief excerpt is included here to suggest the line of thought developed in his book, *Reflections on Violence.*

THE MYTH OF THE GENERAL STRIKE

Georges Sorel

. . . Syndicalism endeavours to employ methods of expression which throw a full light on things, which put them exactly in the place assigned to them by their nature, and which bring out the whole value of the forces in play. Oppositions, instead of being glozed over, must be thrown into sharp relief if we desire to obtain a clear idea of the Syndicalist movement; the groups which are struggling one against the other must be shown as separate and as compact as possible; in short, the movements of the revolted masses must be represented in such a way that the soul of the revolutionaries may receive a deep and lasting impression.

These results could not be produced in any very certain manner by the use of ordinary language; use must be made of a body of images which, *by intuition alone,* and before any considered analyses are made, is capable of evoking as an undivided whole the mass of sentiments which corresponds to the different manifestations of the war undertaken by Socialism against modern society. The Syndicalists solve this problem perfectly, by concentrating the whole of Socialism in the drama of the general strike; there is

thus no longer any place for the reconciliation of contraries in the equivocations of the professors; everything is clearly mapped out, so that only one interpretation of Socialism is possible. This method has all the advantages which "integral" knowledge has over analysis, according to the doctrine of Bergson; and perhaps it would not be possible to cite another example which would so perfectly demonstrate the value of the famous professor's doctrines.

The possibility of the actual realization of the general strike has been much discussed; it has been stated that the Socialist war could not be decided in one single battle. To the people who think themselves cautious, practical, and scientific the difficulty of setting great masses of the proletariat in motion at the same moment seems prodigious; they have analyzed the difficulties of detail which such an enormous struggle would present . . .

. . . There is no process by which the future can be predicted scientifically, nor even one which enables us to discuss whether one hypothesis about it is better than another; it has been proved by too many memorable examples that the greatest men have committed prodigious errors in thus desiring to make predictions about even the least distant future.

And yet without leaving the present, without reasoning about this future, which

Reprinted in part by permission of The Free Press, from Georges Sorel, **Reflections on Violence,** translated by T. E. Hulme and J. Roth (Glencoe, Illinois: The Free Press, 1950), pp. 139–40, 142–44, 150–51.

seems for ever condemned to escape our reason, we should be unable to act at all. Experience shows that the *framing of a future, in some indeterminate time,* may, when it is done in a certain way, be very effective, and have very few inconveniences; this happens when the anticipations of the future take the form of those myths, which enclose with them, all the strongest inclinations of a people, of a party or of a class, inclinations which recur to the mind with the insistence of instincts in all the circumstances of life; and which give an aspect of complete reality to the hopes of immediate action by which, more easily than by any other method, men can reform their desires, passions, and mental activity. We know, moreover, that these social myths in no way prevent a man profiting by the observations which he makes in the course of his life, and form no obstacle to the pursuit of his normal occupations.

The truth of this may be shown by numerous examples.

The first Christians expected the return of Christ and the total ruin of the pagan world, with the inauguration of the kingdom of the saints, at the end of the first generation. The catastrophe did not come to pass, but Christian thought profited so greatly from the apocalyptic myth that certain contemporary scholars maintain that the whole preaching of Christ referred solely to this one point. The hopes which Luther and Calvin had formed of the religious exaltation of Europe were by no means realized; these fathers of the Reformation very soon seemed men of a past era; for present-day Protestants they belong rather to the Middle Ages than to modern times, and the problems which troubled them most occupy very little place in contemporary Protestantism. Must we for that reason deny the im-

mense result which came from their dreams of Christian renovation? It must be admitted that the real developments of the Revolution did not in any way resemble the enchanting pictures which created the enthusiasm at its first adepts; but without those pictures would the Revolution have been victorious? . . .

The myth must be judged as a means of acting on the present; any attempt to discuss how far it can be taken literally as future history is devoid of sense. *It is the myth in its entirety which is alone important:* its parts are only of interest in so far as they bring out the main idea. . . .

The strike throws a new light on all this; it separates the interests and the different ways of thinking of the two groups of wage-earners—the foremen clerks, engineers, etc., as contrasted with the workmen who alone go on strike—much better than the daily circumstances of life do; it then becomes clear that the administrative group has a natural tendency to become a little aristocracy; for these people, State Socialism would be advantageous, because they would go up one in the social hierarchy.

But all oppositions become extraordinarily clear when conflicts are supposed to be enlarged to the size of the general strike; then all parts of the economico-judicial structure, in so far as the latter is looked upon from the point of view of the class war, reach the summit of their perfection; society is plainly divided into two camps, and only into two, on a field of battle. No philosophical explanation of the facts observed in practical affairs could throw such vivid light on the situation as the extremely simple picture called up by the conception of the general strike.

Chapter 16

Control movements and power orientations

$\mathcal{T}$HE PERSISTENCE, prominence, and power of the membership and of their organization often come to be the effective criteria of success in a social movement. The objective of gaining some power, recognition, or special status for the movement as a whole may be more important than other objectives in directing the movement's course. Programs of societal reform may be sacrificed or modified in the interests of the group's recognition and power. Ideologies may either be flexible so as to fit in with changing strategic considerations or may be designed merely to justify the claims of power and recognition that the group is making.

The simplest instance of such an orientation, a movement devoted to dominating the larger group or society of which it is a part while leaving its value objectives flexible or undefined, we shall call a *control movement*. We shall first discuss the control movement in general, and then examine power-orientations within other types of movements.

While the control movement is the simplest case of dominant power orientations, we shall also discuss two related kinds of movement. First is the movement whose principal objective is to oppose and defeat another movement. To the degree to which defeat of the other movement comes to exceed in importance the values at issue, we shall speak of the *counter-movement* as a power-oriented type. Second, there are movements to sever ties with a dominant group or to achieve some separation or autonomy within the dominant group. When the preoccupation with reducing or eliminating the power of the dominant group by achieving some degree of separation exceeds other objectives in importance, we

361

may speak of the *separatist movement* as another power-oriented type. We shall discuss this latter type, as exemplified in political splinter movements, ethnic and racial minority movements, and sectarian religious movements, at some length.

Control movements. Some of the best-known illustrations of the control movement include many of the national dictatorships, urban movements that culminate in political "machines," "palace" and military "revolutions" such as those frequent in South America, and recurring factional movements for control within established organizations of many sorts. From an examination of these and other examples, it is apparent that such movements may operate in two rather contrasting ways. On the one hand, they may operate like the dictatorships of modern Europe on the basis of an extensive mass support. Many political machines likewise depend upon their ability to "deliver the votes" and function quite openly. On the other hand, some control movements depend upon concealing their activities and even their existence from the mass and achieve control through strategic infiltration and the surprise *coup d'état*.

(1) Control movements of the latter sort which are not dependent upon mass support begins within groups that already possess important power that is limited in scope. Such movements are frequently military revolts in which officials use their control of the armed forces to capture the state machinery as well. Military *coups d'état* are often spectacular when they finally culminate, but comparable movements consisting of an economic elite extending their control to the political sphere, or of a political elite expanding their power, or of a church elite pursuing economic or political domination, may proceed almost unnoticed at the time.

Since such movements are the work of those who already hold some legitimate power, their success normally reflects a strongly embedded cultural tradition that provides justification for such extension of power. Societies in which power is conceived as incorporating a responsibility toward the governed provide less fertile soil for such movements than those in which power is regarded chiefly as a prize. On the other hand, when the possession of certain types of power is defined in the cultural tradition as evidence of superior worth or supernatural sanction, this circumstance facilitates any movement to extend such power to other areas. For example, the Western European tradition of "noblesse oblige"— that nobility implies obligations toward one's inferiors—is an obstacle to the military *coup d'état*. However, the Protestant-Capitalist tradition that the possession of wealth is evidence of superior personal worth facilitates movements among the economic elite for the control of political and even religious power. The latter tradition justifies the control movement in its activities and makes the power-holders in other spheres receptive to influence from the economic elite.

If such elite control movements are to operate in secrecy they must also monopolize the means of mass communication. Thus, control of the press by the economic, military, religious, or political elite facilitates such movements. But elite control movements may also operate successfully in fairly open struggle under certain conditions. A mass conviction that shifts in power "up there" make no difference to the life of the ordinary man provides the background for a non-interventionist spectator attitude. Indeed, those who resist the *coup d'état* may be viewed as unnecessarily prolonging the crisis and delaying return to normal activities. Likewise, an aristocratic tradition that keeps the masses from ever realizing that they might wield some power leads to a "hands off" policy when such elite power struggles are taking place.

(2) With a tradition of popular control and failure to monopolize the agencies of mass communication, the control movement resorts to mass sanction for its activities and attempts to manipulate mass support as one of its weapons. Such movements range from those inspired by elites seeking to extend their power to those originating among groups that lack legitimate power. Two conditions appear to be essential if control movements dependent upon mass support are to develop and succeed. First, there must be some weakness in the established power, frequently produced by a divisive rivalry among the various elites. Second, the masses must lack effective organization through which to determine and register their interests in a continuous manner.

Except when there is no established power, control movements appealing to mass support succeed in large part because of the support they receive from one or more of the established elite groups. In the rivalry among elite groups one faction sees the budding movement as a weapon which can be used against its rivals. The movement acquires access to established power through making bargains with such a faction. Without such access it would be difficult to overcome the inherent advantage of those already in power. The support of Hitler by the wealthy Junkers, for example, provided resources that made the Nazis more than just one of several competing parties. Political machines often receive surreptitious support from ambitious "insiders" among the established elite and from business groups who hope to gain more favorable operating conditions from the machine.

Emil Lederer refers to "the amorphous masses" as the indispensable basis of modern political dictatorship. Large masses of people without respected leadership and stable group affiliation may be unable to assess the promises and claims extravagantly made. Unrepresented and unheard by society's legitimate power-holders, they are susceptible to movements that pretend to some special interest in them. Without effective channels of discussion with other groups they are unable to take note of the contradictory promises made to these other groups.

The pattern of private dealings with groups in power and public gestures to those lacking all regular channels of influence have been characteristic of the political dynasties, such as that of Huey Long in Louisiana, and of the big city political machines. Through frank bargains with minority interest groups and through a ward organization which maintains a personal kind of contact with the otherwise unrepresented individuals, the machine incorporates people into an organization that appears interested in their individual needs. Frequently the most intense personal loyalties are evoked.

The control movement is generally a highly centralized, authoritarian organization, making up for its lack of sanctioned respectability by evidence that it can take decisive and drastic action where established authorities appear to act with indecision and compromise. Frequently, elaborate pathological explanations are offered to account for susceptibility to these control movements. However, in the face of a widespread feeling that (a) conditions could not be much worse than they are, and that (b) there are no real alternatives, nothing is more normal than to cast one's lot with a movement that appears at least capable of drastic action. A widespread attitude of cynicism toward the stated programs of all organizations will conceal ideological differences between the power-oriented and the more value-oriented organizations, so that the apparent ability of a movement to act becomes the foremost consideration.

The conditions conducive to such mass attitudes have been described frequently. In one such discussion, J. O. Hertzler stresses the part played by a disruptive crisis in facilitating dictatorship. His discussion anticipates in certain respects our later treatment of the movement built around a conspicuous leader. However, the dictator is a special type of leader, one who tends to exalt power in his person and to employ his power ruthlessly to maintain his control.

CRISES AND DICTATORSHIPS
J. O. Hertzler

Most nations have had some kind of "one man rule" at some time during their history. Dictatorship has been a common and recurrent form of this type of rule. Among some ancient peoples, a dictator was provided for under certain conditions by the constitution; in the overwhelming proportion of instances, however, the would-be dictator, usually with the assistance of a clique or party, and at the opportune time, seized power which he wielded arbitrarily. In most cases, such dictatorial power has been held in an unorthodox, irregular, illegal, or extralegal manner, by the *post facto* invention of some fiction of regularity or constitutionality, or by belated approval involving some strained constitutional interpretation.

The present writer has examined some thirty-five instances of this latter type of dictatorship selected from ancient Greece and Rome, from Europe since the Middle Ages and up to the World War, from Latin America in the 19th and 20th centuries, and from postwar Europe and the Near East. These various historical and contemporary dictatorships have revealed many peculiar individual variations, as determined by their own particular times, the developmental stage of the country in which they appeared, their unique regional differences, their exceptional men, and the conditions as reflected concretely in their cultural traits and patterns. This

Reprinted by permission of The American Sociological Society, from **The American Sociological Review**, 5 (April, 1940), 157–69.

is what one must expect among all natural phenomena, even those of the same type, regardless of whether they fall within the physical, biological, or social realm. At the same time, it is equally evident from the case analyses of this larger study that dictatorships have many striking and frequently recurring uniformities. Of primary significance in this paper is the fact that dictatorships, regardless of their constitutional or unorthodox nature, are a pattern of control which the logic of circumstances often tends to thrust upon people when certain crisis conditions prevail.

The Crisis Situation. The members of human societies are subjected to a variety of crises to which adjustment must be made. Crises induced by nature and individual life crises have been abundantly treated. More important from the point of view of this paper are the crises which develop from various social processes and have as their precipitating factors such things as financial panic and depression invasion, war, revolution, civil strife, folk depletion, the breakdown of strategic institutions, and so on. These have been important and recurrent throughout history, they have affected social processes and social structures profoundly, but there is available very little competent and comprehensive analysis, either of the processes involved or the group adjustments necessitated by them. An attempt will be made here to synthesize and supplement the fragmentary material now available.

A certain degree of disorder, confusion and inadequate functioning of the social machinery appears to be endemic in all societies. Certainly no group or society functions perfectly. In fact, we must look to Utopias for conceptions of societies perfect in structure and function. However, this endemic disorder and inadequacy does not mean that a crisis situation exists. All societies can absorb a considerable amount of failure and discontent relative to existing institutions and conditions. Most social processes are carried on with fairly satisfactory results, there is no general feeling of unrest or insecurity or dislocation, and there are no demands for radical measures of readjustment or willingness to support them. Like the human body, human societies can and must endure many minor ailments and much tinkering.

While one cannot definitely determine the precise point at which what might be called "normal" disorder and confusion becomes abnormal, it can be said that a society must have a considerable amount of breakdown and inadequacy in its existing machinery to produce a crisis situation. We have a crisis only when we have a striking excess of incapacity, inefficiency, and insecurity of existing rulers and machinery. Furthermore, as LaPiere states,

No circumstance, however unusual, is a crisis unless it is so defined by human beings; that is . . . the individuals involved must either be aware of the danger which is actually present or else must believe that danger is present.

The social crisis is due to the disintegration, the over-rapid expansion of one or more of the strategic parts of the social system. The disintegration may be a gradual accumulation of socially disorganizing occurrences which eventually destroy the old equilibrium. Due to some dramatic event, the people become conscious of the situation. On the other hand, a concatenation of circumstances, due to unexpected internal or external events, may occur with great rapidity and throw the people into a panic. In either case,

whether the incubation of factors has been gradual or fairly sudden, the elements making for social disorganization have precipitated and the trend has reached a climactic stage. The social structure seems to be disorganized; series of problems present themselves which seemingly are insoluble by the old or existing social machinery—at least, in its disorganized state. There is serious disturbance of the habits, customs, values, and working life-patterns of the group. The functional efficiency of existing institutions and the conventional patterns of control are lessened or lost entirely. The old control personnel, deep in its ruts of tradition and established practice, is unable to cope with the situation.

Then the time comes when the group defines the situation as a crisis, tensions heighten to the breaking point, suppressed fears become panic, and everyone is aware of insecurity, but is helpless. The people are projected into the world of the unknown; they are at their wits' end. The ordinary and expected has been replaced by the extraordinary and unexpected. Fear becomes widespread; confusion and disorder reign; morale disintegrates. Many individual crises are induced. Chaos seems to threaten. Problems of survival, group solidarity, and welfare become of paramount importance. The dangers of irrational and precipitate action are greatly increased. The suffering people want escape or release from the crisis situation. Matters cannot be allowed to become worse; they must, if possible, become better. There is a demand for solutions, for order, fixity, and security, and a tangible, even though temporary, program of action. The great majority are willing to pay a price for these.

The Demand for Regimental Behavior. Obviously such unprecedented disorganization cannot be prepared for in the organization of the society. Hence, in a crisis situation, the group finds itself unable to effect a collective solution of the highly complicated problem of reorganization. At the same time, there is the apparent need of concentrating power and control in order to centralize planning and facilitate orderly and constructive procedures. The situation takes on the characteristics of a military emergency. The entire community cannot function as a debating and voting society; it must be organized and marshalled for quick and decisive action. Stern discipline and absolute hierarchy of personnel culminating in a generalissimo is essential. In brief, a system of regimental behavior must be established. A befuddled and fearsome mass in time of crisis is nearly always ready, nay anxious, to give over control to anyone who gives evidence of ability to wield it efficiently. This situation, in turn, both demands and provides the opportunity for a leader or a cohesive minority group which offers a ready-made formula of social procedure and which promises a dynamic attack upon the problems. Hence, in time of crisis, a leader and his aides, either by invitation or by insinuation of themselves into the affair, are often gratefully accepted and permitted to arbitrarily reestablish the routines of social life. In times of disorder and distress, the benefits derived from the ruthlessly forceful organization of strict, unquestioning discipline often more than outweigh the benefits of liberty in the opinion of the people.

Crises Preceding Dictatorship. Practically every dictatorship examined has been preceded· by a period of confusion and emergency which terminated in crisis. In the times preceding the ancient Greek and Sicilian dictatorships, we note class antagonisms, civil war, ever-present threats of barbarian invasions, economic distress, rival cities, widespread violence. Preceding the Romans—Marius, Sulla, Caesar, and Augustus—there was civil war and foreign invasion, unequal distribution of wealth, mongrel and hungry populations, poverty, devastation, piracy and brigandage, expensive, and not often successful wars, rival cliques, sensational intrigue, revolts of gladiators and slaves, riots, conspiracies, and massacres. In the "age of despots" in the fourteenth to the sixteenth centuries, we find eastern and central Europe aflame with the Hussite revolt, the oncoming Turks were threatening Europe, and everywhere there was

unrest and ferment; civil war between Guelf and Ghibelline, between city-states, and between plebeians and aristocracy flourished. The quarter century preceding Cromwell's dictatorship is a story of struggle between king and commons, dissolution of Parliaments, violations of the Petition of Rights, unsuccessful military exploits, religious strife, insurrection in Ireland, strife between king and Parliament, and successive civil war. From a bankrupt treasury, a paralyzed monarchy, an incessantly turbulent nobility, warring religions, a people gaining neither wealth nor liberty, and a state internationally embarrassed, one comes to Richelieu's absolutistic administration. Behind Robespierre and Napoleon Bonaparte, there is the whole train of events which precipitated the French Revolution, and the confusion of the Revolution itself, with its conflict between Jacobins and Cordeliers, Girondists and Constitutionalists; its Reign of Terror, its defeated armies under the Directory, its coalition of powers against France, not to mention increased poverty, recurrent mob rule, and eternal confusion. Louis Napoleon is preceded by a corrupt public service, crushing taxation, economic depression, the revolution of 1848, and much political bungling by Cavaignac and others.

The Latin American dictators almost without exception came into power during crisis or times of emergency—civil war and rampant factionalism, plotting *Juntas*, invasion or threat of invasion revolution, machinations of politicians disorganized national finances, feeble and ephemeral existing governments, warring petty *caciques* and *caudillos*.

The postwar dictators of Europe and the Near East almost without exception capitalized on the chaos and travail—social, economic, and political—of that unhappy period. Most of us have lived through it all. A vast flood of literature far too extensive to attempt listing, ha further informed and misinformed us. Th story need not be retold. However, whil the specific ingredients of the crises pre ceding the different dictatorships, ancient mediaeval and modern, varied consider ably, as did the dictatorships themselves, all reveal certain common types of social disintegration.

In this first stage of dictatorship, we usually find most of the following unsettling factors in operation: (1) economic weakness and dislocation, in the form of depression, inflation, bad harvests, shortages of the necessities of life, impaired standards of living, frightened capitalists and business men hesitant to undertake new enterprises or to continue with the old; (2) international complications, foreign war, the pressure of war, military catastrophe, a prostrating or "mutilated" victory, or the harrowing state of a postwar period; (3) revolution or civil war, or the threat of either, violent class cleavages, hatreds and clashes, and the shaky condition of the ruling classes; (4) the breakdown or serious impairment of political institutions, weak and vacillating rulers, the loss of confidence in the existing governmental agencies, the multiplication of factions and parties, or the political illiteracy or ineptitude of the people as a whole; and (5) personal disorganization, psychological upheaval, moral breakdown, and low morale of considerable numbers of the people.

The close relationship between revolution and dictatorship should be noted particularly. As cases in point, we might mention the dictatorships of Cromwell, Napoleon Bonaparte, Louis Napoleon, numerous Latin-American *caudillos,* the Russian dictatorships, and, to a degree, that of Hitler. During and after a revolution, the moderates, first in control, make many mistakes. One faction after another is in control. The masses may have power but they do not know how to use it. The seat of power shifts back and forth from right to left. Leadership is poor or lacking altogether. Eventually, the hope and confidence which preceded and accompanied the insurrection have evaporated. The people have no more revolt in them. After the revolution has thus misfired, there is bleak suffering, the people are fearful and feel impotent, they want peace and order desperately. In general, the group is on the verge of collapse. The society the individuals have known is disintegrating;

they are confronted by vast incomprehensible menaces. The fear which befalls people in such circumstances is paralyzing; it leaves no room for action. Self-assertive tendencies are inhibited or seem to be entirely futile. Sources of information are inaccessible; programs of action cannot be formed or initiated in any known and tried manner.

In fact, dictatorship practically presupposes a condition of crisis and emergency prior to its establishment. Without crisis the dictatorship would be neither possible nor necessary. If the crisis situation did not exist, it is quite reasonable to assume that the ordinary constitutional governors or administrators would be functioning through the standard and established machinery of control. Everything would be running smoothly; people would not feel distraught or insecure; propagandists would sing in vain their siren song of revolutionary change in institutions and location of power; the people would staunchly resist any extralegal assumption of power.

The Demand for Deliverance. For three hundred years, the Church of England has had in its litany this supplication: "From famine, from battle and murder and from sudden death, from all seditions, privy conspiracy and rebellion, Good Lord deliver us." If the Good Lord seems to be rather remote and otherwise preoccupied in time of crisis, a lesser deliverer is demanded and arranged for, or he is given his opportunity.

At such times, people have temporarily set aside their devotion to their constitutions and their normal political institutions. In order to weather the crisis and restore order and routine, they have deliberately asked a strong and sometimes a wise and experienced man, or small clique, to assume exclusive and dictatorial power. On other occasions, when security was conspicuously impaired, an ambitious man, often a hero—a "man on horseback"—has been able to seize power. In either case, the crisis situation created the demand for a deliverer; in the latter case, crisis was invariably the avenue to dictatorship.

In ancient Greece and Rome, constitutional provision was made for a dictator in time of crisis or emergency. In Thessaly of the fourth century B.C., the office of *tagus* was technically one carrying tyrannical or dictatorial authority to which an outstanding leader, usually a member of the predominant noble family, was elected in order to pursue a foreign war or to deal with some crisis of vital importance. With the passing of the stipulated emergency, he retired to private life.

In the ancient Roman Republic, the "dictator" was a recognized official legally appointed to deal with a crisis so exceptional and so pressing that it could not be dealt with by ordinary governmental agents operating through familiar constitutional forms. These emergencies most frequently grew out of the threat of invasion, civil strife, financial disaster, or administrative deadlock. At such times, the citizens voluntarily surrendered their liberties to a strong man. The Senate decreed a suspension of the ordinary checks and balances of the constitution and the consuls were ordered by the Senate to appoint one person to whom was given absolute power (*imperium*) for the duration of the crisis. It was thus a regular constitutional procedure for exceptional times. The title "dictator" by etymology meant "one who can speak with great, indeed, irresistible, force, one who can command and compel obedience and need not try to persuade." The old Roman motto was, "Let the public safety be the first law."

The office was bestowed in solemn, legal fashion, by means of a special ceremony held in the dead of night. Though the power was absolute, the tenure was temporary. When the task was completed, the constitutional agencies of control and administration were again put into effect. Thus, when Rome's army was threatened with destruction by the Aequians, the Senate immediately appointed the venerable Cincinnatus (519–439 B.C.), a grand old patrician, as dictator. He gathered a Roman army, surrounded and captured the enemy, forced them all beneath the yoke of submission, returned his army to Rome in triumph, laid down his office,

and after a total lapse of sixteen days again enjoyed the retirement of his farm.

During the three centuries, beginning with 501 B.C. when the office was first established, and ending with the last instance of its use in 201 B.C., Rome had eighty-eight dictatorships. These dictators could not retain office beyond the legal term of the consuls by whom they were appointed, nor in any event could they function for more than six months. At the expiration of their term, an accounting of their acts had to be made to the Senate. Thus, while acting extraconstitutionally, they were doing so by constitutional mandate in order to preserve the constitution. This old "constitutional" dictatorship—the original form, incidentally—practically came to an end with the Hannibalic Wars.

The greater portion of the unorthodox unconstitutional, or self-appointed dictators were gratefully accepted by the people as saviors and deliverers. After the Battle of Actium, which brought a century of chaos to a close, the Roman Senate, with the approval of the people accepted Octavius as the revered chief Presently, he was made *imperator* for life and was offered the dictatorship which he refused but which he exercised, nevertheless. After matters in Florence had been going from bad to worse for generations and collapse was impending Cosimo de Medici, one of the city's leading citizens, on October 6, 1434, was hailed by people and government as "the patriot whom the Republic delighted to honor." In 1649, nearly everybody in England was agreed that the one hope for a strong and stable government rested on Oliver Cromwell. When Napoleon Bonaparte had himself made First Consul on the 18th Brumaire, after ten years of turbulence, France was willing to submit its destiny to his mastery. After the bloody days of June, 1848, Louis Napoleon was called back to France. During the next three years, though opposed by the deputies, he was permitted to entrench himself. On December 2, 1852, he was proclaimed emperor, and the people were ready to allow another Napoleon-

n imperial dictator—to do their ruling
or them.

In 1814, Francia of Paraguay was
hosen dictator by the national assembly
nd three years later he was made "per-
etual" dictator. After the Revolution of
877 in Mexico, Porfirio Diaz was the
utocrat, the benevolent tyrant, who or-
anized order out of chaos. On March 1,
920, the Hungarian National Assembly,
fter war and Bolshevism, elected Horthy
s "Protector of the Magyar Republic."
hough Mussolini, like many another dic-
ator, "dressed" the situation in his own
ehalf, the Italians accepted him. Why?
ecause he acted and gave the people to
nderstand that he was halting anarchy
nd establishing order. In December,
923, Kemal Atatürk, who had already
istinguished himself by his brilliant mil-
ary exploits, was elected president and
lowed to set up one of the most notably
onstructive dictatorships of modern
mes. In 1923, Reza Khan of Iran, after
series of order-producing military and
olitical successes, resigned as Secretary
: War. The inhabitants of various prov-
ces and cities rose *en masse* demanding
at he withdraw his resignation, which
: did. Soon he made himself Prime Min-
ter. On December 13, 1925, he was ap-
ointed Reza Shah Pahlevi and the Pah-
vi dynasty became possessor of the
ersian Peacock Throne. It is generally
nceded that the establishment of Primo
: Rivera's dictatorship in Spain on Sep-
mber 13, 1923, met with the approval
the majority of the people, and if sub-
itted to the *Cortes,* it would have been
nstitutionally adopted. When old Gen-
al Josef Pilsudski rode into Warsaw
the morning of May 12, 1926, to stop
hat he called the "suicidal fooling," he
und the bulk of the army, the workers,
e poorer peasantry, and the lower mid-
e classes behind him. Early in 1928,
e thirty-nine year old professor of
ance, Dr. Oliviera Salazar, was invited
the Portuguese capital, and his own
rms for taking over the financial dic-
torship of the country were gladly
anted. When he converted this into a
olitical dictatorship as well in July, 1932,
most no protest was voiced.

Abel's German case histories, covering
the period from the end of the War to
the time when Hitler came into power,
reveal the longing of the people for a
strong man to unify their divided and
chaotic sentiment and action. On January
30, 1933, when Adolf Hitler was appointed Chancellor of the Reich, he was
accepted by the majority of the people
who in turn were receptive to Nazi agitation. When General Metaxas, the Gre-
cian Premier, was faced on August 3,
1936, with the painful necessity of choosing between anarchy and dictatorial control, he decided upon the latter. In general, people of all parties welcomed the
change, accepted his authority with relief, and hoped that he would rule with
an iron will.

In times of social disorganization, such
as have been outlined above, political dictatorship is a form of coercive accommodation in which a reign of concentrated
power is established which inflicts its control upon the whole population. The prospective deliverer is often accepted on his
own terms.

The "Leadership Principle." Closely
related to the above is the underlying significance of leadership *per se* in crisis.
Personalities, as Sims points out, are the
most elemental forces that society knows.
When policies, programs, or established
social machinery fail, people dissolve their
emotional and intellectual tension by falling back upon that ultimate factor, personality. "By the acts of one man society
thus seeks to break the otherwise un-
breakable impasse." Not only are the feelings and desires of the group focused upon
a solution, but the confused, multiple
counsel is silenced by a single authoritative voice and the conflicting procedures
are submerged by a single clearcut, audacious line of action. At such times, people
invariably not only accept but even welcome the imperious "strong man" with
his reassuring self-confidence, his willingness and readiness to make decisions by
his own fiat. Underlying this is the "leadership principle." Loewenstein makes the
observation that

As the "leadership principle" works

automatically by its inherent spell . . . it becomes a sort of abstract force dissociated from its personal embodiment, and the ascendancy of the leader is easily established. [Again] . . . the person of the "leader" or in some cases of the rival "leaders," is less important than the leadership principle itself.

The Messiah or Savior state of mind is almost a universal reaction to a crisis situation. The Jews throughout the last 2500 years have lived in a state of perpetual crisis. During all this time and to this day, they have cherished the idea of a coming Messiah. Applying this principle to the dictator, we note that he frequently becomes an almost mystical symbol of authority, leadership, and national greatness. In various dictatorships, there has been a tendency to look upon the dictator as a Messiah, to develop a ruler cult, and to deify the dictator. In recent years Mussolini, Kemal Atatürk, Pilsudski, Lenin, and Hitler have been discussed among their people as Messiahs, and so accepted by some. Miss Spearman states that,

> The hero-myths which appear in so many parts of the world suggest that the fantasy of a beneficent all-powerful savior is one which arises in the minds of many peoples in face of disaster. [She is of the belief that] The cult of the dictator in the modern state seems to have as its foundation the same impulse or impulses as the deification of the Hellenistic monarchs and of Augustus.

In this connection, Rostovzeff is convinced that the cult of Augustus grew up spontaneously and was not imposed from above. There is much justification for the article published a few years ago with the suggestive title, "Stalin as Ikon." Modern scholars are of the belief that the deification of leaders has not been simply a form of flattery, but has arisen in part from a genuine psychological impulse.

The official propaganda itself of many dictatorships suggests that there is a desire for a powerful and irrepressible ruler. Not only does it not refrain from calling attention to the overwhelming position of the dictator; it actually exaggerates his all-pervading influence, and asserts the joy, the dignity, and the worth of obeying him. Thus do the distraught and humiliated individuals merge themselves with something which is assertive, powerful and reputedly invincible.

This tendency is crystallized in the titles assumed or given—titles which stimulate loyalty, focus allegiance, and make childlike submission a joy as well as a duty. Thus, Caesar was made consul, dictator for life, and Pontifex Maximus; Octavius was made *princeps* and then "Augustus" (the revered); Cosimo de Medici was called "Pater Patriae" after his death; Cromwell was given the title "Lord Protector" for life; Mussolini is "Il Duce" and Hitler is "der Führer"; Kemal Atatürk in 1922 was given the title "Ghazi" (the Victorious) and later "Atatürk" (Chief Turk); in 1929, Gomez of Venezuela was given the ill-deserved title, "E Benemerito" (the Well-Deserving).

Appropriating the Crisis. While there always are ambitious men who seek to grasp personal power, achieving it ordinarily is a rather slow process. Most societies in normal times have regular routines for selecting their leadership. However, in a crisis situation with its unsettled conditions, with the people conditioned to expect anything and ready to follow an imperious, all-promising deliverer, the business of appropriating the crisis by an ambitious and often unscrupulous would-be dictator is greatly facilitated. But even then, the crisis situation does not automatically produce a dictatorship. From the Greek Tyrants to Franco, the greater proportion of the dictatorships have been caused quite as much by the tactics of the would-be dictator and his clique or party as by the crisis conditions. Most dictators, dominated by their "will to be dictator," have deliberately sought power. Furthermore, they have been able cleverly to seize and capitalize existing conditions, manipulate, direct and crystallize them, exaggerate them, or even foment or revive crisis conditions, in order to create a demand for their own particular brand of incisive and arbitrary saviorhood, or to justify it. It is quite conceivable in many cases, notably in the case f Russia, Italy, and Germany among the ¦cent dictatorships, that half the emer¦ency would have disappeared if the 'ould-be dictator had commanded his irieking followers to cease their nefari¦us activities. Significant also is the di¦bolically clever enlistment of hatred gainst a minority which has long served ¦ a traditional scapegoat, or the presen¦tion as a whipping dog of some new *ête noir* within or without the group. his safely channelizes antipathetic emo¦ons and deflects attention from the real ¦sue.

Especially to be emphasized is the fact ¦at the would-be dictator has been aided ¦ developing and appropriating the crisis y small but effective pressure and action ¦oups, often including semiprivate ar¦ies and police. Cromwell's New Model rmy, Napoleon's army groups, the or¦inizations wanting Louis Napoleon, the ¦olsheviks in Russia, the Fascist bands of ¦aly, Pilsudski's "Defensive," the Nazi ¦ands in Germany, and the army cliques ¦ Spain, are but cases in point. Such ¦oups work for the dictatorship and its ¦usative revolution; they direct the crisis ¦ward dictatorship. They are relatively ¦nall, well-organized, single-minded, well¦sciplined, and readily maneuvered. Be¦g dominated by a feeling of "special ¦ction," often fanatically devoted to the ¦ader, and conscious of a definite pur¦ose, they are able to make quick and ¦al decisions, act decisively, push ¦rough to the goal, and "take over" ¦ther easily. They thus make possible the ¦hievement of that "brilliant" initial suc¦ss in "restoring order" which is so im¦ortant.

Furthermore, the would-be dictators ¦ow how to make the "bitter pill" not ¦ly palatable but actually attractive— ¦en eminently desirable. They know that ¦ a crisis situation the sufferers seek re¦ase from their confusion and their sense ¦ being at fault. People cannot permit ¦emselves for long to think of themselves ¦ the latter light; to do so would be to ¦cuse themselves of ineptness, failure, ¦d bungling. Still less can they allow ¦emselves to be considered such by com¦ting peoples. To embrace a bold leader

and accept his flamboyant ideology is a means of compensating for the sense of inferiority and frustration.

By their ideologies, the would-be dic¦tators soothe the distraught people, "cure" their panicky state of mind and feelings of humiliation, flatter and exalt them with great ideals and objectives, and even pro¦vide outlets for their masochistic and sa¦distic tendencies. Throughout the ideolo¦gies, there run such appealing phrases as Napoleon's "Grand Empire," Louis Na¦poleon's "Restoration of the Empire," the Latin-Americans' "Liberation," "Unifica¦tion," *"La Restauracion,"* "Pacification," *"Causa Rehabilitadora,"* the Bolshevik's "Dictatorship of the Proletariat," Beth¦len's "Hungary for the Magyars," Mus¦solini's "The Resurrection of Ancient, United, World-Controlling Rome," Kemal Atatürk's "Modernization of Turkey" and his "Turkey for the Turks," Pilsudski's "Polonization" and "National Reconstruc¦tion," and Hitler's *Gleichschaltung* and his "Chosen people" philosophy.

The final confirmation of the fact that dictatorship usually is seized is evidenced in the almost universal use of the *coup d'état.* Under cover of crisis, while the crowds mill and muddle, the crucial gov¦ernmental and military offices are taken over forcibly, usually with some spectac¦ular and dramatic gesture—Pisistratus seizing the Acropolis, Sulla marching on Rome, Caesar crossing the Rubicon, Cromwell forcibly dissolving Parliament, Napoleon overthrowing the Directory on the 18th Brumaire, Gomez taking posses¦sion of Miraflores Palace, Kemal Atatürk deliberately setting up a new government at Ankara, Mussolini's "March on Rome" (himself in a *wagon lit*), Pilsudski enter¦ing Warsaw and stopping the "fooling," Hitler's dissolution of the Reichstag on February 1, 1933, Metaxas marching the Army into Athens and dissolving Parlia¦ment on August 5, 1936. These men who engineer *coups d'état* are not bothered by theories of democratic equality or legality of action or by policies of moderation; they are ruthless extremists with a com¦plete contempt for the inhibitions and principles which serve other men as ideals.

They are Machiavellians, or as Crane Brinton aptly puts it, they are not philosopher-kings, but philosopher-killers.

In general, dictators are not the kind of men who would be ruling in more normal times. On the whole, whether we like to admit it or not, they are abler than those necessary in more normal times. Many men can fit into a well-organized going concern, but the man who can organize chaos must be a genius of a sort. So these men who appropriate a crisis and become dictator combine in themselves diabolical cleverness, arrogance, the love for intrigue, unscrupulousness, a bent toward strategy, and fanatical idealism, along with hard-shelled realism, and the ability quickly to utilize every advantage. The crisis provides the opportunity for the would-be dictator, but successfully to appropriate it takes great abilities—of a sort.

Conclusion. While crisis or alleged crisis is not the guarantee of dictatorship, it is its only *raison d'être.* No one knows this better than the successful dictator himself. Therefore, he must always act as if an emergency existed. He must and often does manufacture emergencies to justify his own existence, especially in the form of war and war scares, and by his activities as an "institution wrecker," as Max Ascoli puts it. There is also the temptation for him, as for other adminis-

trators and executives, to *assume* that state of emergency always exists; hence there is too much use of the concentration of power principle and the development of what might be called the executive "frame of mind." Translated into Pennsylvania Dutch, this means that dictators come to think of themselves as being "Heavengesent."

When the dictator finds that such an interpretation of the situation is no longer accepted by the people, he has one of three choices: (1) he may try to converhis rule into a dynasty as Augustus anReza Shah Pahlevi succeeded in doing and as Napoleon Bonaparte and LouNapoleon tried to do; or (2) he may arrange to die, in bed, before the emergencpasses, as did Cromwell, Richelieu, LeniiPilsudski, Gomez, and Kemal Atatüror (3) he may leave quickly before th"break" comes, preferably under cover of darkness, for Paris, that haven of ex-abselutists and other dispossessed rulers, did Diaz and several other Latin-Ameican dictators. Otherwise he will suffe(a) forcible detention or exile; or molikely, (b) be the victim of his own favoite device, namely, sudden and viole"liquidation." Why? Because thus far history, when a society has achieved nomality, it has discarded its dictators arset up a system of "checks and balances

Growth of control tendencies. Within any movement there is likely to be fairly continuous struggle between value-orientations and power-orientations. A a consequence, many movements which originate with the promotion of a clear sensed value undergo transformation until the value objectives are extensive subordinated to power objectives. There are three major ways in which such change may occur.

First, a strong belief in the unlimited worth of a movement's objectives ten to provoke the attitude that any means are justified by the ends to be gaine The acquisition of power seems to be a much easier way to accomplish the ai of the movement than the slow process of winning a favorable public and getti constituted authorities to accept the movement program. To some extent, extreme dedication to the movement—an inability to understand how anyo could disagree with its aims except through ignorance or willfulness—is a natu product of highly developed *esprit de corps* and morale. Such an attitude mak the members and leaders impatient with value-toned discussions of what metho are proper and what are not. Even when leaders are inclined to search th consciences regarding strategy, the demands by members for immediate a tangible accomplishments may force decisions in terms of power, irrespective of their consistency with the movement's values. Such compromise of principle probably occurs in every movement to a degree, but frequently it extends far enough that the value-orientations sink into the background of movement decisions.

Second, a movement may be taken over or subverted to power considerations by outsiders who see its potential usefulness to themselves. A movement of any considerable strength immediately has to contend with many efforts to "capture" it for power purposes. But even movements that represent only small minority interests have nuisance value or a potentially crucial influence when major forces are balanced. Consequently opportunists seek to capture the movements and trade concessions of policy for personal gain. It has been noted that many of the small political movements in the United States have lost their distinctive ideologies in this manner. Starting with a fairly radical viewpoint and commanding a small but vigorous body of supporters, the movement becomes important enough to trouble the leaders of the major parties. As skilled opportunists work themselves into key positions, the sharp edge of the radical doctrine becomes blunted until eventually it becomes almost indistinguishable from that of more established groups.

Third, certain kinds of opposition so narrow the range of tactics available to a movement that it has no alternative other than to adopt effective means irrespective of their immediate consonance with the values of the movement. The movement that is regarded as revolutionary by the society in which it operates is in this position, as we have pointed out earlier. If a revolutionary movement is to achieve any appreciable measure of success in the face of restrictive practices, it must develop an extensive strategy and employ tactics that more value-oriented movements avoid. Adherence to a carefully defined strategy must not be weakened by internal division, questions of public acceptability, or matters of sentiment. It is for this reason that some of the clearest and most realistic statements of movement strategy are to be found in revolutionary literature.

The international communist movement, for example, has worked out strategies for organization and for the subversion of other organizations to their purposes in great detail. The pre-eminence of power-orientations within the movement is evidenced by the fact that some of the major splits among Marxist groups have occurred about the strategy of gaining power rather than about differences in values to be promoted. In connection with the Bolshevik revolution of 1917, Lenin is said to have commented: "Seizure of power is the point of the uprising. *Its political task will be clarified after the seizure . . .*"

The revolutionary movement is not simply a form of control movement, however. While power-orientations loom larger in the revolutionary movement than in most value-oriented types, the value-dominance is never entirely displaced in the typical revolutionary group. If it were displaced, we should expect to see successful infiltration followed by conservatization and a move toward respectability. From the standpoint of sheer power considerations the unacceptable ideology should be softened for more general acceptability after the initial strength has been built up among the malcontents. But the communists in the United States operating within labor unions and other organizations in many instances have suffered severe setbacks because of continued promotion of a threatening ideology.

Power and strategic considerations. No movement can progress far withou some deliberate formulation of the strategy for gaining power. The value-orienta tions will dictate the general outlines within which strategy may be formulated If the value lies in some improvement of democratic political processes, the strategy will have to be formulated chiefly in terms of legitimate democratic political process. If the value lies in the attitudes of people, the strategy will have to center about communicating effectively to the masses and eliciting individua demonstrations of loyalty to the new values.

However, whether blueprinted in advance or strictly *ad hoc,* some genera strategy must determine specific tactical decisions in every movement. A genera strategy will deal with such matters as when to invest all its resources in a par ticular move and when to make only token effort. It may be considered good strategy, for example, for a minority political party to invest all its resources i one precinct so as to elect one official rather than to push equally in all area with the probability of getting none elected. Questions of when to compromis and when not to do so will also have to be governed by broad notions of strategy The desirability of coalitions among movements will likewise have to be weighed

Strategy has often been called an "art" rather than a "science." By this state ment it is generally meant that no rigorous set of rules can be devised to deter mine "best" strategy because of the complex variation in situations to which must be applied. At the same time it is supposed that a person through experienc can gain a "sense" of what is good strategy whereby he makes right decision without himself being able to state fully the principles governing his judgmen Whatever truth there may be to such a conception, there have been a few care fully developed statements which are designed as general guides in the strateg of power. The historically famous formulation by Niccolo Machiavelli applie specifically to a group already in possession of power and seeking to retain However, many of Machiavelli's principles can be applied to the attainment power by a movement. Recently a general formulation of power strategy ha been developed in mathematical terms. Although the complete formulation highly technical, a number of efforts have been made to apply portions of it specific practical problems. We shall present one such statement, which relat the theory to the problem of movements engaged in power struggles.

STRATEGY AND SOCIAL POWER: SOME PRELIMINARY FORMULATIONS

GIDEON SJOBERG

Social power [1]—the ability to direct other persons toward one's own goal—is a fundamental element in social organization. This subject is of major import for the modern world with its many groups, all striving to gain special advantages. One

Reprinted by permission of the South-western Social Science Association, from **Southwestern Social Science Quarterly,** 33 (1953), 297–308.

facet of the general problem of power particularly significant: What is the ki of social action, or more specifically t strategy, employed by special inter

[1] The concept, "power," is used here encompass that of authority. Certain the rists have distinguished between power authority, authority being an institution ized form of power. This, however, does appear to be a valid distinction. It seems the writer that social power can only wielded if it is to a degree institutionaliz

oups in achieving and/or maintaining wer in a competitive social order? Little ention has been given to this question. p to now; studies of strategy in social ations have had to rely upon such concts as those formulated by the military corist, von Clausewitz.[2] Although a mber of scholars, Machiavelli, Weber, erriam, Mosca, and more recently Lassell and Bierstedt,[3] among others, have ded measurably to our understanding the problem of power, their treatment strategy is incomplete. Fortunately, rent theoretical developments, especially se of John von Neumann and Oskar orgenstern,[4] although still overlooked many social scientists, offer a basis for plaining the social action of individuals d/or groups under conditions of comtition.

In their book, von Neumann and Mornstern have taken games, e.g., poker

Karl von Clausewitz, **On War,** trans. by J. Matthijs Jolles (New York: Random use, Inc., 1943). Although this book cons a few important concepts, these have t been carefully formulated.

Niccolo Machiavelli, **The Prince,** trans. W. K. Marriott (New York: E. P. Dut- and Co., 1925); H. H. Gerth and C. right Mills (trans. and eds.), **From Max ber: Essays in Sociology** (New York: ford University Press, 1946); Charles ward Merriam, **Political Power** (New rk: McGraw-Hill Book Company, Inc., 4); Gaetano Mosca, **The Ruling Class,** ns. by Hannah D. Kahn (New York: Graw-Hill Book Company, Inc., 1939); rold Lasswell and Abraham Kaplan, **wer and Society** (New Haven: Yale Uni- sity Press, 1950); Robert Bierstedt, "An alysis of Social Power," **American Soci- gical Review,** XV, No. 6 (December, 0), pp. 730–38.

John von Neumann and Oskar Mor- nstern, **Theory of Games and Economic havior** (2nd ed., Princeton: Princeton iversity Press, 1947). For simplified dis- sions of this theory see: J. Marschak, eumann's and Morgenstern's New Ap- ach to Static Economics," **Journal of itical Economy,** LIV, No. 2 (April 1946), 97–115; Kenneth J. Arrow, "Mathemat- Models in the Social Sciences," in Dan- Lerner and Harold D. Lasswell, **The icy Sciences** (Stanford: Stanford Uni- sity Press, 1951), pp. 129–54; John Mc- nald, **Strategy in Poker, Business and r** (New York: W. W. Norton and Com- ıy, Inc., 1950).

and "matching pennies," as prototypes of social situations. They suggest that their theory can be applied to economic rela- tions—especially those of the market place. And although their concepts have not generally been utilized to explain so- cial action in other areas of societal com- petition, these concepts have definite im- port for the analysis of social power.

The von Neumann and Morgenstern study derives the principles of strategy mathematically. Possibly this is the reason that their theory has not received due recognition among social scientists. Also, at the present stage of inquiry such a mathematical treatment of complex so- cial data is impossible. However, a liter- ary rendering of some of the concepts which have been derived for simplified models, and the application of these to specific social situations, should be profit- able. This will be attempted herein. Of course, the ensuing discussion suffers from a number of limitations. In translat- ing these mathematically formulated con- cepts into verbal form a great deal of preciseness and rigor is sacrificed, and many of the nuances of the von Neumann theory have had to be disregarded.[5] Also, as presently constituted, it is essentially a static theory and furthermore is not al- together satisfactory for games where there are three or more players.[6] Finally, it describes an ideal pattern which is only approximated by the actions of persons or groups in a complex society;[7] yet, no theory can do more than this.

Some of the ideas presented in *The Theory of Games,* including the main principles of strategy, are sketched below. Next two case studies are offered; these empirically attest to the feasibility of in- terpreting social action in competitive sit-

[5] Therefore, such refinements as those presented by J. C. C. McKinsey, **Introduc- tion to the Theory of Games** (New York: McGraw-Hill Book Company, Inc., 1952) are not considered in this discussion.

[6] Ibid., pp. 303f, 355ff. Here other limita- tions are discussed.

[7] A number of critics have argued that the von Neumann theory is not particularly applicable to social data. However, some of these writers have used as their yardstick the criterion that a theory should account for all the "facts."

uations according to the von Neumann strategy. For only if a player subscribes to these rules of action can he expect to achieve power against a rational opponent.

A game is defined by the set of rules which describe it. Its component elements are called moves; these are either personal (the choice of the player) or dependent upon chance. The game has a specific duration, after which the spoils of victory are allocated. Von Neumann and Morgenstern describe this game mathematically; the description forms the basis for a set of axioms from which their major concepts are derived. Thus, their axioms are not merely arbitrary definitions but are constructed upon empirical reality: the game.

The authors further simplify the game by introducing the concept of strategy. This is the over-all "plan" of the game (it might also be considered a set of personal moves). In the von Neumann game there are a finite number of strategies; one of these is selected by the participant before the game begins. Now, even a person in a social order must devise some general plan of action prior to the inception of actual competition: a "good" strategy can not be predicated solely on day-to-day reasoning. And although, theoretically, the number of strategies available to an individual in a social situation may be infinite, they are in practice indeed limited. Furthermore, a player in a game, by selecting a strategy in terms of mathematical expectation, is able to account for chance factors.[8] Finally, the von Neumann player is rational. As such he is willing to "maximize" his gain, which is considered in terms of numerical (monetary) utility. In this paper, however, the von Neumann and Morgenstern notion of utility has been interpreted

more broadly, i.e., in terms of social utility.[9]

Essential to the formation of a rational strategy are the concepts of the minimax, randomized strategy, and coalitions. First the minimax. In sharp contrast to certain classical theories of social action, the von Neumann theory rigorously shows that player should not expect to achieve the greatest possible gain. This could only be accomplished in a so-called Robinson Crusoe society where nature alone is exploited. In a competitive social situation with two or more players, no single player controls all the variables. In undertaking to secure optimum satisfaction, a player must, if he acts rationally, take into account the potential strategies of his opponent. Therefore, a "good" strategy which maximizes a player's gain, is one which seeks not the greatest possible gain but an outcome between the maximum and minimum: the minimax. Thus, the advantaged player endeavors to achieve the minimum of the maximum, his opponent the maximum of the minimum. In a game or social situation in which both players possess equally good strategies and where one's loss is another's gain both, if rational, would in the end attain the same value.

To many social scientists, especially those who have been imbued with the twentieth-century belief that the main area of scientific investigation is "irrational action," this emphasis upon rationality may be unacceptable. Yet, significantly, von Neumann and Morgenstern demonstrate that if a player's goal is to acquire gains in a competitive situation he must play rationally; irrational action works to the advantage of the opponent. As will become apparent in the case studies, this applies to competition in the social order as well.

A second, and most unique, contribution introduced by *The Theory of Games* is the concept of mixed or randomized strategy—a pattern of action which is pursued when a player lacks complete

[8] The manner in which individuals in a society view situations involving uncertainty is a difficult problem. The writer doubts that this kind of action is based solely on mathematical expectation. However, the ramifications of this issue can not be considered here. It is sufficient to note that this theory makes provisions for the "chance factors."

[9] Justification for this view is given to degree by von Neumann and Morgenstern themselves, op. cit., pp. 176–78, in their discussion of the Holmes-Moriarty episode.

nformation concerning the past course of he game. Thus, in order to avoid having is strategy detected ". . . a player does ot, as previously, choose his strategy, ut he plays all possible strategies and hooses only the probabilities with which e is going to play them respectively. . . By this device the opponent cannot ossibly find out what the player's strat- gy is going to be . . ." [10] Of course, un- ler certain conditions only a single or 'pure" strategy is feasible; this would be ssigned the probability of one and the ther strategies probabilities of zero.

Just what implications does this con- ept of randomized strategy have for the tudent of power? Obviously, members of society do not sit around choosing robabilities. However, just as in poker, luffing is practiced. The kinds of ruse, ecrecy, or deceit employed will vary ac- ording to the rules of the "game." [11] A erson will engage in this inconsistent be- avior in order to conceal his real inten- ions, or strategy. His actions thus become ess vulnerable to attack, and his oppo- ent is kept "off-balance." [12]

Finally, coalitions are an integral ele- nent of good strategy in many games vith three or more players. The problem f coalitions, however, has many ramifi- ations, only a few of which are men- ioned here. First of all, rational players ealize that they can secure as great a ain and possibly more by cooperating vith others. Therefore, in many competi- ive social situations, just as in games, oalitions arise. But they are inherently nstable and as such can easily be upset. n order to secure a partner, a player nust refrain from demanding too great a hare of the gain: otherwise, the potential artner will seek an alliance with some- ne else and the overdemanding player

will have to "go it" alone. Von Neumann and Morgenstern demonstrate, especially for three-person games, just how stability can be achieved—the so-called "solution." But these "solutions" represent a rather delicate equilibrium and thus appear to be difficult to maintain.

Now that the primary components of good strategy—the minimax, randomized strategy, and coalitions—have been de- scribed, their empirical validity must be determined. The following case studies illustrate the actual operation of these principles in a societal context. Here the players are groups rather than individuals. Although this introduces a complicating factor, it should not perceptibly detract from the results of the analysis.

CASE STUDY NO. 1: The struggle between Robert A. Taft and Dwight D. Eisen- hower for the 1952 Republican Presiden- tial nomination revealed the actual op- eration of strategy in politics. [13] This competition in the political arena had much in common with a game. Rules (both legal and informal) were present according to which the contest was car- ried on. In the struggle to achieve power the two combatants had to secure dele- gates: this corresponds to the monetary reward in, for instance, poker. To attain his end, each candidate had at his com- mand a number of strategies from which to choose. In theory these were infinite, but in practice they were quite limited. Now, no successful politician works out his strategy simply as events unfold; in- stead, every attempt is made by means of an over-all plan to anticipate future de- velopments. But, as in many games, the outcome of a political contest may be in- fluenced by chance occurrences. Even after a strategy has been selected, the pos- sibility exists that it may go awry. Radio commentators and newspaper columnists, in reporting trends within the Republican Convention, frequently prefaced their re-

[10] von Neumann and Morgenstern, op. it., pp. 145–46.
[11] Georg Simmel was a sociologist who ecognized the role of such factors as se- recy in human action. See: Kurt H. Wolff trans. and ed.), **The Sociology of Georg immel** (Glencoe, Ill.: The Free Press, 950), Part 4.
[12] The idea of mixed strategy takes into ccount the element of surprise which was mphasized by von Clausewitz.

[13] Most of this material is rather common knowledge: it can be found in almost any daily newspaper. However, **The New York Times, The Christian Science Monitor,** and **Newsweek** were the writer's principal sources.

marks with the reservation, "uncertainty is ever present in politics."

Without an elaboration of all the historical details, it can be noted that during most of the campaign for the Presidential nomination Taft was the leading candidate. He commanded a favorable position because of a well-organized political machine: much of the Republican Party was from the beginning Taft-controlled. Eisenhower began as a much weaker candidate even considering his important primary victories.

The question arises: What were some of the "mistakes" made by Taft which cost him the nomination? Von Neumann's principle of the minimax is of real importance in understanding this problem. For it appears that if any single action led to Taft's defeat, and, conversely, Eisenhower's victory, it was Taft's failure to conduct his campaign according to the minimax rule. Taft undertook to secure the greatest possible number of delegates in certain Southern states where he had almost complete control of the Republican Party machinery. Particularly at the various state conventions, the Taft organization offered (at least publicly) few concessions to the Eisenhower group, whose source of strength was outside the regular party organization. For example, at the Republican State Convention in Texas the Taft group claimed all the delegates: those supporting Eisenhower were obliged to meet in a "rump convention." This action, however, opened up to the Eisenhower forces a new and effective strategy—something they had lacked up to that time. The Texas situation, in particular, resulted in the leveling of such charges as "steamroller" and "big steal." And this became the overriding issue in the weeks just prior to the National Convention. It was exploited by the Eisenhower faction through the media of both the press and radio to muster opinion and sentiment for their candidate inside and outside the Party. Eisenhower's claim to many of the contested delegates was supported by many newspaper columnists, editors, and radio analysts. And what is more significant, Taft's actions were a

factor in stimulating a great majority c the Republican Governors attending conference at Houston to petition th National Convention to vote for the Ei senhower-sponsored amendment whic stipulated that contested delegates wer not to be allowed to vote on their ow seating. All of this unquestionably serve to gather some wavering delegates int the fold. Thus, it was Taft's own plannin which made it possible for the Eisen hower forces to adopt advantageousl this particular strategy. If Taft had earl compromised on Texas,[14] his oppositio would have had little basis for its charge of "dishonesty." To generalize from thi incident: the very attempt by an organ ized group to secure the greatest possibl gain, an irrational act in von Neumann' terminology, leaves open to the opponer a strategy which would otherwise hav been unavailable if the minimax princip had been observed. Many students of pol itics have noted the role of compromis in political activity, but the von Neu mann theory seems to point up mor sharply just why compromise is essentia even on the part of a rather powerfu group.

Further limitations of Taft's strateg were manifested in the Convention itsel His organization, which dominated th Convention machinery, voted to bar ra dio and television from the Republica National Committee hearings on the sta tus of contested delegates. But this at tempt to exercise monopolistic contro simply lent added support to the Eisen hower strategy. It helped sustain th charge that something was really "wrong with Taft's position.

The second principle—that of the ran domization of strategy—is apparent i most political campaigns, for the partici pants seldom possess complete informa tion about their opponent's intentions an

[14] Taft sought to compromise the issu when the Republican National Committe voted to seat part of the Texas Eisenhowe group. However, by this time the Eisen hower forces would accept no compromise making every effort to exploit their ad vantage. **The New York Times,** July 3, 195? p. 1; July 5, 1952, p. 1.

trength.[15] The Taft-Eisenhower contest was no exception. Bluffing, for example, was evidenced in the claims, many of them exaggerated, which each side advanced during the course of the campaign and in the Convention itself concerning the number of delegates who were pledged to vote for their candidate. But this was only one aspect of more complicated action. For both Taft and Eisenhower appear to have engaged in "double talk" or were indecisive about some key issues. At least a few delegates were uncertain as to their choice of candidate: one stand was designed to appeal to some, another position on the issue to appeal to others. Furthermore, acting and talking in this inconsistent manner served to confuse the opponent and to make a position (which was as a result rather ill-defined) more difficult to assail.

Coalitions also played an important role in determining the final outcome of the campaign. Inasmuch as the Eisenhower forces went into the Convention as the weaker organization (in terms of actual pledged delegate strength), they were compelled to seek out other groups with whom they could combine in a coalition against Taft. By effecting an alliance with the delegations controlled by such weaker candidates as Warren and Stassen and by aligning themselves with Summerfield and Fine, leaders of the large state party organizations of Michigan and Pennsylvania, respectively, the Eisenhower group succeeded in halting Taft's advance.[16] This coalition was able to adopt the so-called "fair play" amendment, which held that contested delegates would not be permitted to vote on their

own seating. And this victory made it possible to seat those contested Southern delegates who were pledged to support Eisenhower: he was thus practically assured of winning the nomination. Therefore, another element in Taft's defeat was his inability to build a coalition which matched that of his opponent. Finally, the rumors just previous to the final balloting pointed to the instability of political coalitions [17]—i.e., Taft was seeking an alliance with Warren and Stassen against Eisenhower, obviously without success.

CASE STUDY NO. 2: The whole process of collective bargaining in union-management relations can be viewed from the standpoint of strategy; at least one writer has commented upon its similarity to the game of poker.[18] For collective bargaining is conducted according to a set of rules, both legal and informal. And the participants are obviously vying for a gain; the desire for monetary reward represents only a part of the general aspiration for social power.

A brief examination of the conflict between the steel companies and the C.I.O. Steelworkers Union in 1952 reveals the workings of strategy, although the actions of the participants were so complex that only rough approximations to the ideal pattern are apparent in certain instances. The history of this struggle extends over a long period of time; the present discussion begins, however, with the March, 1952, recommendations of the Wage Stabilization Board.[19] Among the provisions were a straight wage increase of 12.5 cents an hour retroactive to January 1, 1952, an additional 2.5

[15] The importance of inconsistent action political campaigns has, of course, been observed by other writers. For example, see: Frank R. Kent, **Political Behavior** New York: William Morrow and Co., 28), passim.

[16] This coalition resulted to a large degree from Taft's efforts to secure the greatest number of delegates possible in some Southern states and from his attempt to retain rigid control over the Convention. Taft apparently did not make the necessary concessions to gain the support of the aforementionad groups, something his opponent seemed willing to do.

[17] Other materials on the instability of political enmities as well as coalitions can be found in Kent, op. cit., chap. xxvi. Also, note that even after this rather "bitter" pre-convention campaign, Taft and Eisenhower did cooperate during the Presidential campaign proper.

[18] Hugh G. Lovell, "The Pressure Lever in Mediation," **Industrial and Labor Relations Review**, VI, No. 1 (October, 1952), p. 29.

[19] A convenient summary of some of the principal facts in this case is presented by: Mary K. Hammond, "The Steel Strike of 1952," **Current History**, XXIII (November, 1952), pp. 285-90.

cents increase on July 1, 1952, and 2.5 cents more as of January 1, 1953. In addition, certain fringe benefits were advocated; some of these were to take effect at once, and others were to be granted in 1953. This meant a total gain of about 26.1 cents an hour for the steelworkers by mid-1953. Also recommended was the installation of some kind of union shop.

The Union readily accepted the provisions of the Wage Stabilization Board. The representatives of industry, on the other hand, agreed to accept these terms only if they were assured of a price increase of $12.00 a ton for steel by the Executive Branch of the Government rather than the amount permitted under the existing rule, approximately $3.00. Furthermore, the companies balked at the idea of a union shop.

The two parties to the dispute could not reach an agreement at first, and a 53-day-long strike ensued. Yet, the final solution seems to have been in general accordance with the minimax principle. For although the C.I.O. and the steel companies were rather far apart at the inception of the negotiations over the recommendations of the Wage Stabilization Board, the final settlement was a compromise: it was not the worst and not the best for either group.[20] The steelworkers secured a wage raise of some 16 cents an hour plus 5.4 cents an hour in fringe benefits. In addition, they were granted a modified form of union shop. The industry, on the other hand, was permitted by the Government to increase the price of steel by an average of $5.64 a ton. Now, it seems apparent that neither side could have continued to insist upon its original demands without running the risk of incurring even greater losses. For the Union was continually faced with pressures exerted internally by its own membership who were without adequate funds and externally by other unions who were experiencing work stoppages resulting from the strike. Management underwent similar strains. It experienced a dim-

inution of income and pressures from other industries which were compelled to close their plants because of the strike. And the fear of adverse reactions on the part of "public opinion," [21] from special interest groups such as the military, and particularly from various branches of the Federal Government definitely worked in favor of an approximate minimax settlement. With neither group having a monopoly of the strategies, compromise between the two contestants was essential if they were to continue to receive support from their own membership and from sympathetic groups.

Inconsistent, or randomized, behavior was another integral part of the collective bargaining process. First of all, each side resorted to bluffing, all the while realizing that its original demands concerning the provisions of the new contract would necessarily undergo modification. A concrete example of mixed strategy occurred after the management failed to agree to a compromise formula, especially as it related to the controversial union shop issue. The Union's reaction was to revert immediately to the stand which it originally had maintained.[22] This kind of maneuvering seemingly was designed to keep the opposition uncertain as to the concessions which the Union might finally offer or finally accept.

The importance of coalitions in this dispute has already been alluded to. On one side were aligned the six major steel companies, as well as a number of smaller companies. Opposing them was a coalition of the Executive Branch of the Federal Government and the Steelworker Union. The existence of this coalition was clearly demonstrated by the support given by President Truman to the Union's de-

---

[20] For a summary of some of the important steps in the negotiations process, see: **Newsweek,** XL (August 4, 1952), p. 65.

[21] It was more than a coincidence that the Truman Administration, acting in coalition with the Union, permitted the companies to raise the price of steel just at the time of the Democratic National Convention, thus bringing about a final settlement. Here President Truman seemed concerned lest continuation of the strike lead to a reaction against the Party at the polls.

[22] **The New York Times,** July 22, 195[ ] pp. 1, 21.

ands and also by his reluctance to in-
oke the Taft-Hartley Act. Now, the
resident, working with the Union, at
ne point seized the struck plants. How-
ver, the Judicial Branch of the Govern-
ent declared this illegal. A plausible in-
rpretation of this action in light of the
on Neumann theory is that the Courts,
erving as an umpire, ruled that the Pres-
lent's seizure in this instance was not in
ccordance with "the rules of the game."

In the actual bargaining process, the
Jnion leaders showed a keen awareness
f the instability of coalitions. They at-
empted to pursue the pattern set by the
949 negotiations. At that time, the Un-
on was able to bargain separately with
ne Big Six steel corporations. As a re-
ult, a contract was first signed with Beth-
hem Steel, after which the other com-
anies quickly came to terms. But in 1952
ne major steel corporations were able to
resent a united front,[23] and although the
nal contract evidently grew out of the
egotiations with Bethlehem Steel, the
ther companies were able to restrain
ethlehem from signing until all had
greed upon the contract's provisions. In-
smuch as the coalition of the large steel
orporations held firm, the union shifted
s attention to the smaller companies,
ho, having fewer resources, were more
ulnerable to the strike. By signing con-
acts with a number of these smaller
ompanies, the C.I.O. Union strengthened
s position with the larger corporations
t the bargaining table.

Now, the preceding case studies, it
ould be noted, represent only a few of
ne competitive situations to which this
neory seems applicable. A question might
e raised concerning the role of greatly
isadvantaged players. Their actions, also,
onform largely to those of the "von
Teumann player." For example, third
arties in American politics have often
ecognized the fact that although they
ould not possibly win an election, they
ould by running a candidate threaten to
eprive a major party's candidate of a
ufficient number of votes so as to force
im to compromise his position in the

minority group's favor. Here the goal is
simply the attainment of the maximum of
the minimum. And the application of this
theory is not limited to the kinds of political and economic conflict described
herein.[24] Conflicts among educational and
religious organizations might similarly be
studied. Probably the most important field
deserving of analysis within the framework of strategy is that of international
relations. Throughout the history of conflict among nation-state systems, bluffing
and ruse have constantly been employed;
the contemporary international scene is
no exception. Also, history is replete with
examples of the formation and dissolution of coalitions as various nations have
sought to gain special advantages by joining first with one group and then with
another. And empirical evidence is available pointing to the major role of the
minimax principle in international affairs.
A specific instance of the failure to apply
this rule seems to have been the policy of
the Western Allies who sought the greatest possible gain by demanding from Germany unconditional surrender during
World War II. This act opened up to the
Soviet Union, as well as to special groups
within Germany, the use of strategies in
the post-War years which would otherwise have been ineffective. One result has
been that the United States and its Allies
are finding themselves faced with ever-
growing problems in Europe, particularly
as they relate to Germany.

CONCLUSIONS

The major purpose of this paper has
been to indicate that in the struggle for
social power among special interest
groups in a competitive social order, certain kinds of actions can be observed—
those involving the minimax, randomized

[24] It appears that studies such as David
B. Truman, **The Governmental Process**
(New York: Alfred A. Knopf, 1951), which
analyzes the functioning of special interest
groups and their effects upon political parties and the legislative and the administrative processes, could profit from the utilization of the concepts developed by von
Neumann.

[23] **The New York Times,** July 3, 1952, p. 1.

strategy,[25] and the formation and dissolution of coalitions. A consistency is apparent in competitive action which makes it amenable to scientific analysis. This action is not necessarily irrational as some social scientists have supposed. Neither is it necessarily random, although "chance factors" have not been overlooked in the von Neumann theory.

In the brief survey of the contest for the 1952 Republican Presidential nomination and the 1952 union-management dispute in the steel industry, evidence is offered to verify empirically the hypothesis that the principles of strategy which have been formulated by von Neumann and Morgenstern are useful in interpreting the actions of groups in competitive social situations. Social power is achieved and maintained according to certain rules, the nonobservance of which may well undermine the strength of any organization. No question has been raised concerning the moral rightness of this kind of behavior; this study has merely sought to demonstrate that some recurrent patterns of action are observable in competitive social situations.

It should not be assumed that this theory disregards the role of the ideologies and values adhered to by the contesting groups. Instead, the values are incorporated within the concept, "the rules of the game." And the relative importance of such variables as manpower and "technical skills" is a function of "the rules of the game," or the total social situation. The point made is that no organization—no matter what its ideology, values, manpower or technical skills—can afford to pursue an irrational strategy, for rational

strategy is the mechanism by which power is achieved and maintained, or, in the case of the disadvantaged player, the means by which one's loss is minimized.

If the foregoing analysis is essentially correct, the implications for social theory of von Neumann's and Morgenstern's work are manifold. One of the most far reaching is that this theory is "extra-cultural" in the sense that groups with divergent and even antagonistic value systems and/or goals may have to resort to similar actions in order to attain their different objectives.[26] Up to now, an "extra-cultural" approach to the problem of strategy has been generally lacking in the social sciences. Too often a particular strategy has been considered as merely a function of unique historical events.

Finally, a word about the future. This paper has attempted to suggest some applications of the von Neumann theory for the study of power. However, inasmuch as the theory is still in an early stage of development, certain limitations are apparent. Undoubtedly future mathematical formulations will make this theory even more useful for analyzing social action—e.g., the recent study of so-called noncooperative games suggests such a trend. Therefore, social scientists will be well advised to follow the progress in this field. A direct mathematical treatment of social data along the lines of game theory may not be feasible for a long time to come. However, even a verbal interpretation of the mathematically derived concepts offers a significant advance beyond the various "common-sense" formulations which have been made, and therefore these concepts contribute to an understanding of some problems which have troubled scholars for centuries.

25 A qualification, noted earlier, might be emphasized. There are situations in games where a "pure" or single strategy must be played; this is also true in certain kinds of societal competition. Thus, the rules or the circumstances may demand consistency and penalize inconsistency. This problem requires some intensive investigation.

26 The techniques, tactics, or "means" utilized by a group to carry out its strategy appear to be relative to the cultural situation. In other words, these vary according to the kinds of competition: rational strategy does not.

Counter-movements. Movements evoke varying kinds and degrees of opposition. Probably most unsuccessful movements arouse no organized or active opposition of any kind. Unopposed movements may die through simply being unnoticed, or they may die from the disillusionment or internal dissension among their members. On the other hand, a movement may die from the unanimity of lip service given its program, with the result that no group attaches the program to its primary interests.

Under some circumstances, however, opposition will be focused in a movement with some organization, program, recognized leadership, and membership. The presence of any vested interest group whose prerogatives seem to be threatened by the initial movement is a primary source of *counter-movements*. The likelihood that opposition of vested interests or other groups will be organized into a counter-movement depends on the supposed strength of the initial movement itself. The judgment that a movement is potentially strong may come from a sense that the grievances it represents are real. A counter-movement is more likely to develop against an initial movement combatting widely recognized grievances than against a movement reflecting superficial dissatisfactions.

The public appearance of an initial movement may also determine the strength imputed to it. An official interpretation of the successful drive to enact woman suffrage in the Illinois state legislature attributes the success in part to an underestimate of the strength of the drive, with the result that no effective counter-movement was organized. Regarding Mrs. Sherman Booth, who did the work of contacting legislators, it was remarked that, "She was so obviously helpless that even the bitterest antis did not worry about her."

Movements with conflicting ideologies and programs will inevitably come into opposition. However, only when the effort to defeat or wrest power from the initial movement begins to transcend the original program and ideology in shaping the opposition movement's course may we speak of a counter-movement. In a true counter-movement the ideology and program are adjusted as necessary to support strategic power considerations.

The most important determinant of changes in the ideology of a counter-movement is the increasing success or failure of the initial movement. When the latter is weak, the counter-movement ideology is likely to describe its personnel as traitors, heretics, conspirators—terms that completely outgroup the members and evoke intolerant suppressive activity. When the initial movement is strong, however, the counter-movement cannot afford to attack its members in this manner, but must treat them with some respect and depict them as "well-meaning but misguided," "misled by an insidious minority," victims of propaganda, and the like.

A more fundamental change in counter-movement ideology also takes place with increasing success of the initial movement. The counter-movement begins to adopt popular elements of the initial movement's ideology as its own, attempting thereby to satisfy some of the discontent and also to get the opposed movement identified with only the most extreme portions of its whole program. Where movement and counter-movement are of long standing, it is not infrequent that the counter-movement may eventually come to promote everything that the early adherents of the initial movement sought. At times a movement and counter-movement may become ideologically indistinguishable.

This adoption of the initial movement's ideology by the counter-movement may be illustrated in some degree by the anti-socialized medicine movement. From an early tendency to include many types of health insurance and prepayment medical plans within the despised category of socialized medicine, there has been an increasing espousal of these same programs as the "free enterprise answer to socialized medicine." The definition of the opposed object has been altered, and the counter-movement now champions some of the opposed movement's earlier accomplishments. Similar tendencies can be observed in the anti-New Deal movement and the anti-prohibition movement. It is a far cry from the 1936 campaign of "repeal social security" to the Eisenhower program to expand social security coverage, for example. Likewise, the anti-Prohibitionists' claims to be the true advocates of effective liquor control, assuring the public that they would never allow the pre-Prohibition saloon to return to America, represent ideological absorption from the Prohibition movement.

The ideology of a counter-movement may also have certain distinctive characteristics merely because it is more preoccupied with opposing than with promoting a particular program. Suggestive in this regard is an interesting study by Elizabeth Herzog comparing the kinds of arguments used by the "pros" and the "cons" in response to questions dealing with several issues of interest to the United States government. The most important difference lay in the relative emphasis upon means or ends:

> It was found repeatedly that those who reported in favor of a program or policy tended to speak in terms of the objective: the ends to be served, the needs to be met. The opposition, on the other hand, tended to voice objections to the means proposed, insisting either that these would not achieve the objective or that their concomitants and results would be so bad as to offset any possible gains—or both.*

Whether a similar difference applies to the ideologies of "pro" and counter-movements, and whether the results apply generally or merely to the rather moderate kinds of proposals included in the study, constitute questions for further investigation.

The significant long-range effects of the conflict of movement and counter-movement may lie not so much in the ultimate victory of one or the other in the power struggle but in the effect on societal myth. We speak of myth in a sense similar to that defined by Malinowski, not as a sort of primitive science or recreational speculation, but as a statement of supposed reality which serves "to strengthen tradition and endow it with a greater value . . ." While myth for Malinowski always refers to the supernatural, we may use it more broadly, as dealing with *beliefs concerning fundamental reality which justify prevailing institutions.* Counter-movements depend chiefly on evoking the established myth of the society to oppose change. However, as a counter-movement absorbs elements from the new movement's ideology it must reinterpret the societal mythology into consistency with these additions. It is thus through the agency of the counter-movement that far-reaching changes are incorporated into the society's values without loss of continuity. Thus today the ideas of free enterprise, civil rights, and the republican form of government persist as strong as ever but have been extensively modified from their earlier meanings by the very activities of their staunchest defenders.

* Elizabeth Herzog, "Patterns of Controversy," **Public Opinion Quarterly,** 13 (1949) pp. 39-52.

Chapter 17

Separatist movements

A SEPARATIST movement is a social movement whose activities are devoted to the maintenance or attainment of its separate identity as a group to such a degree that this preoccupation shapes the entire character of the movement. Thus any distinctive ideology tends to become subservient to the strategic concerns of becoming an independent group. The degree of separateness sought may range from mere public recognition and limited autonomy to complete secession or partitioning of the parent group.

Among the more clear-cut examples of separatism are movements for national independence such as the American Revolution or the Confederacy. Such movements are generally not revolutionary in the sense of challenging the major institutions of the parent body. The government of the United States was established largely on the basis of British tradition and common law, and the Confederacy was patterned after the American government. Although the movements' objectives were couched in terms of governmental reform, these objectives were applied only as necessary to justify separation. Dr. Samuel Johnson, for example, wrote a famous essay charging the American colonists with hypocrisy in demanding liberty while they continued to hold slaves. In the same manner the Puritans had come to America earlier to establish religious liberty, but only in the sense of freedom for their own religion while retaining the right to be as intolerant of dissent as they chose.

Examples of separatist movements are also abundantly found in the realm of religion. The term *sect* is characteristically reserved for a relatively small religious movement which sets itself apart from and in opposition to the established religious organization. A small religious movement almost inevitably takes on sectarian characteristics both because the nature of religious inspiration is conducive

385

to a claim that all other religious groups must be in error and because the new group constitutes a threat to the integrity of the established churches.

In addition to sectarian and political independence movements, minority ethnic and racial and minority political party movements have been most extensively studied. However, movements in the realm of ideas and the arts may also acquire separatist characteristics. Personal rivalry between two art leaders, for example, may lead their respective followers to emphasize the opposition in their schools of art to the point that the maintenance of distinctiveness between the two followings becomes their major preoccupation. Or in the realms of ideas, dissenting interpretations and theories give rise to "schools" whose rivalry tends to displace the search for truth as the governing orientation.

We shall treat the separatist movement as a special form of the *power-oriented* movement, and as a complementary type to the control movement. As subtypes of the power-oriented movement, both the control and separatist types are concerned primarily with securing some position of advantage for the group and its members. Characteristically the two tendencies are mixed within any particular movement. Not only does the movement for autonomy easily shift into a movement for dominance, as Louis Wirth has pointed out, but the frustrated control movement readily shifts into a movement for separation. The Confederacy, for example, came as the culmination of a regional battle for domination of the government and economy of the United States. In another instance the population and economic dominance of California was shifting southward during the 1930's while the entrenched political domination remained disproportionately in the hands of Northern Californians. Simultaneously and in close association there developed two movements in Southern California, one for secession and establishment of a forty-ninth state, and the other to wrest political domination away from the North. As the latter movement, aided by further shifts in population dominance and by expansion of Southern California economy, made appreciable gains, the separatist movement gradually disappeared. In a very real sense the control and separatist orientations had been the alternate strategies of a single movement concerned with political control.

Sources of separatism. There are two general sources of separatist movements, depending upon whether the separatist orientation is directed toward a group which was originally a parent body or not. Frequently two (or more) movements acquire separatist characteristics simply because they are in close competition and have rather similar programs. If one such movement has less strength than its competitor and relatively little difference in program, the more powerful movement will tend to absorb the smaller. Interested members and leaders of the weaker body who are committed to the movement itself or to fine points of difference in program will then find their efforts increasingly directed away from their formal objectives and toward resisting merger. With this shift in emphasis the movement acquires more and more separatist characteristics. If two such movements are of nearly equal strength, both may acquire separatist characteristics as they resist two-way merger tendencies.

In the foregoing type of situation, movements that were originally independent bodies become separatist movements in resisting absorption. The second and more commonly recognized source of separatist movements, however, is the splintering of established bodies. In these instances dissent within a *parent body* —a nation, political party, church, social movement, etc.—produces *splinter* movements. A portion of the parent body breaks away and its members attempt to establish a separate identity.

Splintering often reflects a mixture of two broad kinds of conflict of interest. On the one hand there may be conflicts with regard to ideology and values within the parent body, and splintering follows failure to convert the group to the policies of the dissident members. In these cases separatism is usually only the culmination of an unsuccessful reform or control movement within the parent group. On the other hand, splintering may be the work of persons who possess only a "second-class membership" in the larger body. Racial and ethnic minorities and subject peoples generally fall in this group. In many of these instances separatism will have been the initial orientation.

Perhaps the most important differentiation to be made within movements that have splintered from a parent body is based on the extent of original identification with the parent body. Separatist movements may consist of people who have always been rather fully identified with the parent church or state, but have become dissenters on a single issue or as a consequence of recent developments. On the other hand, they may involve a group that has never been identified in their own minds with the parent body.

The movements of subject peoples usually derive from a great historic irreconcilability of interests between the separatist movement and the parent group. However, even in these movements considerable effort must usually be directed to arousing the sense of irreconcilable interests before the more extreme kinds of separation can be demanded. For example, the pan-Slav movement arose among slavic peoples in several nations of eastern Europe who had largely lost their sense of self-identity. Scholars were needed to revive lost languages and lost customs that could serve as symbols about which the sense of separateness might develop.

Ralph Linton has surveyed the various movements for independence among pre-industrial peoples of the world in order to provide a framework for their study. His discussion should be compared with the paper by Louis Wirth on minority movements, as offering another approach to the same class of phenomena. There are perhaps two orienting differences between the two papers. First, Wirth's data concern chiefly ethnic minorities in industrial nations, while Linton deals with pre-industrial peoples subjected to colonial status. Partly as a consequence of the data they use and partly as a reflection of their respective sociological and anthropological approaches, Wirth's analytical scheme revolves about different kinds of power relationships while Linton's distinguishes different kinds of efforts toward the preservation of cultural integrity by the nativistic group.

NATIVISTIC MOVEMENTS
RALPH LINTON

At the time that the centennial meeting of the American Ethnological Society was planned, the writer was invited to

Reprinted by permission of the editors from the **American Anthropologist,** 45 (1943), pp. 230–40.

contribute a paper on nativistic movements in North America. When he attempted to prepare this it soon became evident that there was a need for a systematic analysis of nativistic phenomena in general. Although the Social Science Research Council's Committee on Acculturation [1] had made some progress in this direction much remained to be done. The present paper is an attempt to provide such a systematic analysis and is presented in the hope that its formulations may be modified and expanded by further research.

The first difficulty encountered in the study of nativistic movements was that of delimiting the field. The term "nativistic" has been loosely applied to a rather wide range of phenomena, resembling in this respect many other terms employed by the social sciences. For the writer to determine arbitrarily which of several established usages is to be considered correct and which incorrect is not only presumptuous but also one of the surest ways to promote misunderstanding of the theoretical contributions he hopes to make. The only satisfactory definition under such circumstances is one based upon the common denominators of the meanings which have come to be attached to the term through usage. With this as a guide, we may define a nativistic movement as, "Any conscious, organized attempt on the part of a society's members to revive or perpetuate selected aspects of its culture."

Like all definitions, the above requires amplification to make its implications clear. Its crux lies in the phrase "conscious, organized effort." All societies seek to perpetuate their own cultures, but they usually do this unconsciously and as a part of the normal processes of individual training and socialization. Conscious, organized efforts to perpetuate a culture can arise only when a society becomes conscious that there are cultures other than its own and that the existence of its own culture is threatened. Such consciousness, in turn, is a by-product of close and continuous contact with other societies; an acculturation phenomenon under the definition developed by the above mentioned committee.[2]

The phrase "selected aspects of its culture" also requires elaboration. Nativistic movements concern themselves with particular elements of culture, never with cultures as wholes. This generalization holds true whether we regard cultures as continuums of long duration or follow the usual ethnographic practice of applying the term "a culture" to the content of such a continuum at a particular point in time. The avowed purpose of a nativistic movement may be either to revive the past culture or to perpetuate the current one, but it never really attempts to do either. Any attempt to revive a past phase of culture in its entirety is immediately blocked by the recognition that this phase was, in certain respects, inferior to the present one and by the incompatibility of certain past culture patterns with current conditions. Even the current phase of a culture is never satisfactory at all points and also includes a multitude of elements which seem too trivial to deserve deliberate perpetuation. What really happens in all nativistic movements is that certain current or remembered elements of culture are selected for emphasis and given symbolic value. The more distinctive such elements are with respect to other cultures with which the society is in contact, the greater their potential value as symbols of the society's unique character.

The main considerations involved in this selective process seem to be those of distinctiveness and of the practicability of reviving or perpetuating the element under current conditions. Thus the Ghost Dance laid great stress on the revival of such distinctive elements of Indian culture as games and ceremonial observances, elements which could be revived under agency conditions. At the same time it allowed its adherents to continue the use of cloth, guns, kettles and other objects of European manufacture which were obviously superior to their aboriginal equivalents. In fact, in many cases the converts were assured that when the dead returned

---

[1] R. Redfield, R. Linton, M. J. Herskovits, **A Memorandum for the Study of Acculturation (American Anthropologist,** 38, 1935), pp. 149–52.

[2] "Acculturation comprehends those phenomena which result when groups of individuals having different cultures come into continuous first-hand contact, with subsequent changes in the original culture patterns of either or both groups." Redfield, etc., op. cit.

and the whites were swept away, the houses, cattle and other valuable property of the whites would remain for the Indians to inherit.

All the phenomena to which the term nativistic has been applied have in common these factors of selection of culture elements and deliberate, conscious effort to perpetuate such elements. However, they differ so widely in other respects that they cannot be understood without further analysis. At the outset it is necessary to distinguish between those forms of nativism which involve an attempt to revive extinct or at least moribund elements of culture and those which merely seek to perpetuate current ones. For convenience we will refer to the first of these forms as *revivalistic nativism,* to the second as *perpetuative nativism.* These two forms are not completely exclusive. Thus a revivalistic nativistic movement will be almost certain to include in its selection of elements some of those which are current in the culture although derived from its past. Conversely a perpetuative nativistic movement may include elements which had been consciously revived at an earlier date. However, the emphases of these two forms are distinct. The revivalistic type of nativism can be illustrated by such movements as the Celtic revival in Ireland, with its emphasis on the medieval Irish tradition in literature and its attempt to revive a moribund national language. The perpetuative type of nativism can be illustrated by the conditions existing in some of the Rio Grande Pueblos or in various Indian groups in Guatemala. Such groups are only vaguely conscious of their past culture and make no attempts to revive it, but they have developed elaborate and conscious techniques for the perpetuation of selected aspects of their current culture and are unalterably opposed to assimilation into the alien society which surrounds them.

There is a further necessity for distinguishing between what we may call *magical nativism* and *rational nativism.* It may well be questioned whether any sort of nativistic movement can be regarded as genuinely rational, since all such movements are, to some extent, un-realistic, but at least the movements of the latter order appear rational by contrast with those of the former.

Magical nativistic movements are often spectacular and always troublesome to administrators, facts which explain why they have received so much attention from anthropologists. Such movements are comparable in many respects to the Messianic movements which have arisen in many societies in times of stress. They usually originate with some individual who assumes the role of prophet and is accepted by the people because they wish to believe. They always lean heavily on the supernatural and usually embody apocalyptic and millennial aspects. In such movements moribund elements of culture are not revived for their own sake or in anticipation of practical advantages from the element themselves. Their revival is part of a magical formula designed to modify the society's environment in ways which will be favorable to it. The selection of elements from the past culture as tools for magical manipulation is easily explainable on the basis of their psychological associations. The society's members feel that by behaving as the ancestors did they will, in some usually undefined way, help to recreate the total situation in which the ancestors lived. Perhaps it would be more accurate to say that they are attempting to recreate those aspects of the ancestral situation which appear desirable in retrospect.

Such magical nativistic movements seem to differ from ordinary messianic and millennial movements in only two respects. In the nativistic movements the anticipated millennium is modeled directly on the past, usually with certain additions and modifications, and the symbols which are magically manipulated to bring it about are more or less familiar elements of culture to which new meanings have been attached. In non-nativistic messianic movements, the millennial condition is represented as something new and unique and the symbols manipulated to bring it about tend to be new and unfamiliar. Even in these respects the differences are none too clear. New elements of culture often emerge in connection with magical nativistic movements, as in the case of the distinctive Ghost Dance art. Conversely, messianic movements may lean heavily upon the familiar symbolism of the culture, as in the case of most Christian cults of this type. The basic feature of both messianic cults and magical nativistic movements is that they represent frankly irrational flights from reality. Their differences relate only to the ways in which such flights are implemented and are, from the point of view of their functions, matters of minor importance.

What we have chosen to call rational nativistic movements are a phenomenon of a quite different sort. While such movements resemble the magical ones in their conscious effort to revive or perpetuate selected elements of culture, they have different motivations. What these are can be understood more readily if we reintroduce at this point the distinction previously made between revivalistic and perpetuative nativistic movements. Rational revivalistic nativistic movements are, almost without exception, associated with frustrating situations and are primarily attempts to compensate for the frustrations of the society's members. The elements revived become symbols of a period when the society was free or, in retrospect, happy or great. Their usage is not magical but psychological. By keeping the past in mind, such elements help to reestablish and maintain the self respect of the group's members in the face of adverse conditions. Rational perpetuative nativistic movements, on the other hand, find their main function in the maintenance of social solidarity. The elements selected for perpetuation become symbols of the society's existence as a unique entity. They provide the society's members with a fund of common knowledge and experience which is exclusively their own and which sets them off from the members of other societies. In both types of rational nativistic movement the culture elements selected for symbolic use are chosen realistically and with regard to the possibility of perpetuating them under current conditions.

It must be emphasized that the four forms of nativistic movement just discussed are not absolutes. Purely revivalistic or perpetuative, magical or rational movements form a very small minority of the observed cases. However, these forms represent the polar positions of series within which all or nearly all nativistic movements can be placed. Moreover, it will usually be found that a given nativistic movement lies much closer to one end of such a scale than to the other if it is analyzed in terms of the criteria used to establish the polar positions. If we combine the polar positions in the two series, the result is a fourfold typology of nativistic movements, as follows:

1. Revivalistic-magical
2. Revivalistic-rational
3. Perpetuative-magical
4. Perpetuative-rational

Forms 1, 2, and 4 in this typology recur with great frequency, while form 3 is so rare that the writer has been unable to find any clearly recognizable example of it. The reason for this probably lies in the conditions which are usually responsible for magical nativistic movements. The inception of such movements can be traced almost without exception to conditions of extreme hardship or at least extreme dissatisfaction with the status quo. Since the current culture is associated with such conditions and has failed to ameliorate them, magical efficacy in modifying these conditions can scarcely be ascribed to any of its elements. Nevertheless, a perpetuative-magical movement might very well arise in the case of a society which currently occupies an advantageous position but sees itself threatened with an imminent loss of that position. It is highly probable that if we could canvass the whole range of nativistic movements examples of this type could be found.

An understanding of the various contact situations in which nativistic movements may arise is quite as necessary for the study of these phenomena as is a typology of such movements. There have been many cases of contact in which they have not arisen at all. The reasons for this seem to be so variable and in many cases so obscure that nothing like a satsfactory analysis is possible. The most that we can say is that nativistic movements are unlikely to arise in situations where both societies are satisfied with their current relationship, or where societies which find themselves at a disadvantage can see that their condition is improving. However, such movements may always be initiated by particular individuals or groups who stand to gain by them and, if the prestige of such initiators is high enough, may achieve considerable followings even when there has been little previous dissatisfaction.

Although the immediate causes of nativistic movements are highly variable, most of them have as a common denominator a situation of inequality between the societies in contact. Such inequalities may derive either from the attitudes of the societies involved or from actual situations of dominance and submission. In order to understand the motives for nativistic movements the distinction between these two sources of inequality must be kept clearly in mind. Inequality based on attitudes of superiority and inferiority may exist in the absence of real dominance, although situations of dominance seem to be uniformly accompanied by the development of such attitudes. As regards attitudes of superiority and inferiority, two situations may exist. Each of the groups involved in the contact may consider itself superior or one group may consider itself superior with the other acquiescing in its own inferiority. There seem to be no cases in which each of the groups involved in a contact considers itself inferior. The nearest approach to such a condition is the recognition of mixed inferiority and superiority, i.e., the members of each group regard their own culture as superior in certain respects and inferior in others. Such a condition is especially favorable to the processes of culture exchange and ultimate assimilation of the two groups. It rarely if ever results in the development of nativistic movements.

The type of situation in which each society considers itself superior is well illustrated by the relations between Mexicans and Indians in our own Southwest. In this case factors of practical dominance are ruled out by the presence of a third group, the Anglo-American, which dominates Indian and Mexican alike. Although the two subject groups are in close contact, each of them feels that any assimilation would involve a loss of prestige. The transfer of individuals from one social-cultural continuum to the other is met by equal resistance on both sides and the processes of assimilation never have a chance to get under way. Under such circumstances the life of each of the societies involved becomes a perpetuative-rational nativistic movement. Each group is conscious of its own culture and consciously seeks to perpetuate its distinctive elements. At the same time this consciousness of difference is devoid of envy or frustration and produces no friction. The members of each group pursue their own goals with the aid of their own techniques and, although the situation does not preclude economic rivalries, witness the constant quarrels over water rights, it does preclude social rivalries. It seems that the establishment of such attitudes of mutual social exclusiveness, without hatred or dominance, provides the soundest basis for organizing symbiotic relationships between societies and should be encouraged in all cases where the attitudes of one or both of the groups in contact preclude assimilation.

Contact situations comparable to that just discussed are not infrequent but they seem to be less common than those in which both groups agree on the superiority of one of the parties. It must be repeated that such attitudes are not necessarily linked with conditions of actual dominance. Thus the Japanese during the early period of European contact acquiesced in the European's estimate of his own superiority and borrowed European culture elements eagerly and indiscriminately although maintaining national independence. Again, the disunited German states of the eighteenth century acknowledged the superiority of French culture and were eager for French approval even when no political factors were involved.

When two groups stand in such a mutually recognized relationship of superiority and inferiority, but with no factors of actual dominance involved, the contact will rarely if ever give rise to nativistic movements of the magical type. The relationship cannot produce the extreme stresses which drive the members of a society into such flights from reality. On the other hand, the contact may well give rise to rational nativistic movements, but these will rarely if ever appear during the early contact period. At first the superior group is usually so sure of its position that it feels no reluctance toward borrowing convenient elements from the culture of the inferior one. Conversely, the inferior group borrows eagerly from the superior one and looks forward to full equality with it as soon as the cultural differences have been obliterated. During this period impecunious members of the superior group are likely to turn their prestige to practical advantage by marrying rich members of the inferior one and, for a time, genuine assimilation appears to be under way. In such a situation the nativistic trends will normally appear first in the superior group, which is naturally jealous of its prestige. The movements inaugurated will generally be of the perpetuative-rational type, designed to maintain the status quo, and will include increasing reluctance to borrow elements of culture from the inferior group and the increase of social discrimination against its members and those of the superior group who consort with them.

When such a nativistic movement gets well under way in the superior group, there will usually be a nativistic response from the inferior one. Finding themselves frustrated in their desire for equality, with or without actual assimilation, the inferiors will develop their own nativistic movements, acting on the well known sour grapes principle. However, these movements will be of the revivalistic-rational rather than the perpetuative-rational type. The culture elements selected for emphasis will tend to be drawn from the past rather than the present, since the attitudes of the superior group toward the current culture will have done much to devaluate it. In general, symbolic values will be attached, by preference, to culture elements which were already on the wane at the time of the first contact with the superior group, thus embodying in the movement a denial that the culture of the other group ever was considered superior.

We have already said that attitudes of superiority and inferiority seem to be present in all cases of contact involving actual dominance. Combining these two sets of factors we get the following possible situations for contact groups:

1. Dominant-superior
2. Dominant-inferior
3. Dominated-superior
4. Dominated-inferior

These situations assume agreement on the part of the groups involved not only with respect to dominance, readily demonstrable, but also with respect to attitudes. The frequent lack of such agreement makes it necessary to add a fifth situation, that in which the dominant and dominated group each considers itself superior. The other possible combinations those involving attitudes of inferiority on the part of both dominant and dominated and those involving attitudes of mixed inferiority and superiority on both sides may be ruled out from the present discussion. The first of these possible combinations simply does not occur. The second occurs rather frequently but, as in the cases where it occurs without domination, normally results in assimilation rather than the production of nativistic movements.

The idea that nativistic movements may arise in dominant as well as dominated groups appears strange to us since most of our experience of such movements comes from the contact of Europeans with native peoples. However, we must not forget that Europeans have occupied a singulary favored position in such contacts. Even where the European ettles permanently among a native population, he remains a mere outlier of white society and, thanks to modern means of transportation and communication, can keep close touch with the parent body. This parent body is shielded from contact and assimilation and is thus able to send out to its colonial ruling groups constant increments of individuals who are culturally unmixed. Moreover, the technological superiority of European culture has, until recently, rendered the dominance of colonial groups secure. The nativism of Europeans has, therefore, been largely unconscious and entirely of the perpetuative-rational type. It has manifested itself in such things as the practice of sending children back to Europe to be educated or the Englishman's insistence on dressing for dinner even when alone in a remote outpost of empire. Most dominant groups have been less fortunate. They have found themselves threatened, from the moment of their accession to power, not only by foreign invasion or domestic revolt but also by the insidious processes of assimilation which might, in the long run, destroy their distinctive powers and privileges. This threat was especially menacing when, as in most of the pre-machine age empires, the dominant and dominated groups differed little if at all in physical type. Among such rulers the frustrations which motivate nativistic movements in inferior or dominated groups were replaced by anxieties which produced very much the same results.

Returning to the contact situations previously tabulated, we find that dominant-superior groups tend to initiate perpetuative-rational forms of nativism as soon as they achieve power and to adhere to them with varying intensity as long as they remain in power. Thus the various groups of nomad invaders who conquered China all attempted to maintain much of their distinctive culture and at the height of their power they issued repressive measures directed not only against the Chinese but also against those of their own group who had begun to adopt Chi-

nese culture.[3] It seems probable that revivalist-rational forms of nativism will not arise in a dominant-superior group, at least as regards elements of culture which were moribund at the time of their accession to power, although this form of nativism might develop with respect to culture elements which had fallen into neglect during the period of power. It seems possible also that, under conditions of extreme threat, some form of brief revivalist-magical nativism might arise in such a group, but information that might verify these conjectures is lacking.

The situation in which a dominant group acknowledges its cultural inferiority to the dominated is one which must arise very infrequently. However, examples of it are provided by such cases as that of the Goths at the time of their conquest of Italy. Such a group immediately finds itself caught on the horns of a dilemma. It can remove its feelings of inferiority only by undergoing cultural if not social assimilation with the conquered society, while such assimilation is almost certain to cost it its dominant position. It seems probable that such a society might develop nativistic movements either when its desire for cultural assimilation with the conquered was frustrated or when it found its dominant position seriously threatened, but again information is lacking.

There is abundant information on nativistic movements among dominated groups and in discussing these we stand on firm ground. A dominated group which considers itself superior will normally develop patterns of rational nativism from the moment that it is brought under domination. These patterns may be either revivalist or perpetuative but are most likely to be a combination of both. One of the commonest rationalizations for loss of a dominant position is that it is due to a society's failure to adhere closely enough to its distinctive culture patterns. Very often such nativism will acquire a semi-magical quality founded on the belief that if the group will only

[3] Karl A. Wittfogel and C. S. Feng, **History of Chinese Society, Liao,** ms.

stand firm and maintain its individuality it will once again become dominant. Fully developed magical-revivalist nativism is also very likely to appear in groups of this sort since to the actual deprivations entailed by subjection there are added the frustrations involved by loss of dominance. These frustrations are somewhat mitigated in the cases where the dominant group recognizes the superiority of the dominated group's culture. Such attitudes strengthen the rational nativistic tendencies of the dominated group and diminish the probabilities for magical-revivalist nativism of the more extreme type. Lastly, in cases where the dominant group concurs with the dominated in considering certain aspects of the latter's culture superior but will not grant the superiority of the culture as a whole, this attitude will stimulate the dominated group to focus attention upon such aspects of its culture and endow them with added symbolic value.

A dominated group which considers itself inferior, a condition common among societies of low culture which have recently been brought under European domination, is extremely unlikely to develop any sort of rational nativism during the early period of its subjection. It may, however, develop nativism of the revivalist-magical type if it is subjected to sufficient hardships. The threshold of suffering at which such movements may develop will vary greatly from group to group and will be influenced not only by the degree of hardship but also by the society's patterns of reliance upon the supernatural. A devout society will turn to nativism of this sort long before a skeptical one will. If the hardships arising from subjection are not extreme, the inferior group will usually show great eagerness to ·assume the culture of the dominant society, this eagerness being accompanied by a devaluation of everything pertaining to its own. Nativistic movements tend to arise only when the members of the subject society find that their assumption of the culture of the dominant group is being effectively opposed by it, or that it is not improving their social position. The movements

which originate under these circumstance are practically always rational with a combination of revivalist and perpetua tive elements. In this respect they resem ble the nativistic movements which origi nate in inferior groups which are no subject to domination and there can b little doubt that the primary causes ar the same in both cases. These movement are a response to frustration rather than hardship and would not arise if the highe group were willing to assimilate the lowe one.

Rational nativistic movements ca readily be converted into mechanisms fo aggression. Since the dominated societ has been frustrated in its earlier desire to become acculturated and to achiev social equality, it can frustrate the dom inant society in turn by refusing to accep even those elements of culture which th dominant group is eager to share with i Dominated societies which have acquire these attitudes and developed consciou techniques for preventing further accu turation present one of the most difficu problems for administrators. Passive re sistance requires much less energy tha any of the techniques needed to break down, especially if the culture patterns c the dominant group preclude the use c forcible methods.

One final aspect of nativistic move ments remains to be considered. The gen eralizations so far developed have bee based upon the hypothesis that societie are homogeneous and react as wholes contact situations. Very frequently this not the case, especially in societies whic have a well developed class organizatio In such societies nativistic tendencies wi be strongest in those classes or individua who occupy a favored position and wh feel this position threatened by cultu change. This factor may produce a spl in the society, the favored individuals groups indulging in a rational nativisr either revivalistic or perpetuative, whi those in less favored positions are eag for assimilation. This condition can observed in many immigrant groups America where individuals who enjoye high status in the old European socie attempt to perpetuate the patterns of that society while those who were of low status do their best to become Americanized.

In a rapidly shrinking world the study of nativistic movements, as of acculturation in general, has ceased to be a matter of purely academic interest. As contacts between societies become more frequent and more general, the need for an understanding of the potentialities of such contact situations becomes more urgent. The troubles which they usually involve can be traced, with few exceptions, to two factors: exploitation and frustration. The first of these is the easier to deal with and may well disappear with the spread of modern science and techniques to all parts of the world. The second is more difficult to deal with since its removal entails fundamental changes in attitudes of superiority and inferiority. Without these there would be no bar to the assimilation of societies in contact situations or to the final creation of a world society. However, this seems to be one of those millennial visions mentioned elsewhere in this report. Failing assimilation, the happiest situation which can arise out of the contact of two societies seems to be that in which each society is firmly convinced of its own superiority. Rational revivalistic or perpetuative nativistic movements are the best mechanism which has so far been developed for establishing these attitudes in groups whose members suffer from feelings of inferiority. It would appear, therefore, that they should be encouraged rather than discouraged.

Sectarian movements have more in common with nativistic movements than may be immediately apparent. Behind the issues of theology, faith, and practice about which controversies have raged, many an investigator has noted the dissent of a disadvantaged minority. Certain types of social class subordination provide fertile ground for the growth of religious sects. Like those of nativistic movements, the ideologies tend to be formulated in revivalistic terms, as the rediscovery of the original faith from which the parent church has deviated.

Several decades ago John L. Gillin published a paper which laid down what are still many of the basic principles of sectarian movements. He pointed out that religious sects have their origin in social rather than primarily religious antagonisms. Social heterogeneity and the breakdown of insularity brings diverse groups into contact. Power is unequally distributed, and sects arise in the disadvantaged groups. The religious sects are but part of the effort of those groups who do not possess legitimate power to ". . . organize themselves so as to be able to deal as classes with the upper classes."

Almost every sect of Protestant Christendom has originated in the lower classes as a protest against what they felt was oppression by the superior classes. That their griefs were largely social is shown by their leanings toward apocalyptic hopes of a kingdom in which their wrongs would be righted; and the seriousness of their oppressions is indicated by the fact that they expected it to come suddenly. Their doctrines apart from this are mostly negative, another indication that they arose out of class consciousness.*

In accounting for separatist movements the crux of the matter is not discovering the sources of divergent interests, but in finding out why a sufficient number of persons should organize for separation rather than for some other manner of handling their differences. Difference and long-standing dissent leading to power struggles and persisting minorities are characteristic of any organization. Reform

* John L. Gillin, "A Contribution to the Sociology of Sects," **The American Journal of Sociology,** 16 (Sept., 1910), p. 245. Quoted by permission of the University of Chicago Press.

and control movements which take place entirely within an established group are the source of continuing change in organizational policy and practice. They may be the means of continuing adaptation of the organization to social and cultural change. The struggles may be bitter and chronic without splintering the group.

Three broad types of conditions will determine whether such internal movements become splinter groups. These are (1) the extent of integration of the dissenting group into the parent body; (2) the power of the parent body to enforce its legitimate actions and suppress dissent; and (3) the ability of the parent body to absorb dissent either through changing in response to growing pressures or by encompassing internal variability.

(1) Mere expressing of dissent within an established body is different from the more serious step of relinquishing the privileges and self-identification of membership. Consequently, only those who have been consistently deprived of the normal privileges of membership or have failed to attain an emotionalized self-identification with the group are likely to band together in a separatist movement. This observation sheds light on the economic foundations of religious sectarianism. Questions of faith and practice are constantly being raised and disputed within established churches. But they are raised by persons who may be participating with full equality in church activities, who find in the church a group of people with whom they have a great deal in common in spite of points of disagreement, and who find themselves accepted within the group so long as they do not press their dissent too far. But when the disputants are persons who feel that they are not accepted as first-class members of the church and who feel no deep emotional response to the ceremony and ritual of the organization, it is relatively easy for them to adhere to their point of issue and break away from the parent group. For example, the movement for church reform in England which subsequently became the sectarian movement known as Methodism was built around working-class people who constantly found conceptions of white-collar respectability held against them in the church and experienced only frustration in the reserved expressiveness of the established church ceremony.

V. O. Key, Jr., suggests what may be a special application of this principle in generalizing about the minor political parties which, in the United States, serve as a form of dissent against the two major parties:

> The distribution of minor-party strength suggests a hypothesis about the conditions that permit and discourage minor-party activity. The strength of these parties has been greatest in those western states without strong traditions governing political behavior, with a social system in a state of flux, and with comparatively weak and unstable governing groups. Third-party strength over the entire period of 1864-1936, was at its weakest in the South. Social stratification, political tradition, and the pressure to conform exerted by the governing groups have been very different in the South than in the West. One kind of condition may facilitate the operation of dissenting groups; the other definitely discourages such movements.*

Integration into the established body may be weakened by the availability of a well-established substitute group with which the dissenters may continue to identify while relinquishing identification in the parent body. This principle may be one of the reasons for the sectional basis of many third-party movements

---

* V. O. Key, Jr., **Politics, Parties and Pressure Groups** (New York: Thomas Y. Crowell Co., 1946), p. 291.

ohn D. Hicks has observed that the two major parties must try to command
upport in every section of the United States. "Let a whole section begin to feel
at its interests are being permanently discriminated against by both old parties,
nd the time for a plain-spoken third party, organized mainly along sectional
nes, is about ripe." * Thus the loyalty due one's region can provide a rallying
oint that offsets the loss of identification with an established political party.

Intrinsic to some types of organization is a progressive departure from the
terests of many of the rank and file members. One of these tendencies is for
a organization to lose sight of other issues in its preoccupation with strategy,
ocedural matters, and legalities. Fred E. Haynes regards this tendency in polit-
al parties as a source of third-party movements:

> The two great political parties have had for their principal interests political and
> constitutional reforms, while the group of lesser parties—beginning with the Anti-
> Monopoly and Reform parties of the seventies, continuing with the Greenback and
> Labor parties of the eighties, and ending with the Populist party of the nineties—
> have voiced the protests of people who felt keenly the need of economic and social
> change.**

(2) The power of a parent body to suppress dissent depends upon its posses-
on of values with which the members are unwilling to dispense. Widely diver-
ent elements are maintained within the confines of each major political party in
ne United States because a dissenting group can hardly hope to duplicate the
ntrenched and elaborate political machinery nor to overcome traditional party
yalty of the majority of voters. The Catholic Church has been able to make
ne fear of excommunication and other penalties more effective against separatism
an have most of the Protestant churches.

(3) In spite of the strict insistence on certain core beliefs and practices, the
oman Catholic Church has also exceeded the Protestant denominations in its
bility to permit divergent forms of religious practice, as represented by the
arious *orders,* within the church. Frequently the confidence of the parent body
 its own principles makes for toleration of divergent elements within its memership. Absence of a strong nationalistic tradition and the dominance of dem-
cratic traditions among the controlling elements of a state facilitate the toleration
 minorities within the confines of the state.

Characteristics of separatist movements. Underlying the characteristics of most
 paratist movements is the extent to which the interests and values of the sepa-
 tist members are identified with those of the parent body. Even a subject people
 e likely to have adopted many items from the culture of the dominant group.
 ahatma Gandhi, in his program for Indian independence, encountered some
' his major obstacles in the degree to which his own people were adopting the
 dustrial way of life from the ruling British. In addition to cultural identification,
 ere is likely to have developed a *symbiotic* relationship, such as the dependence
 a trading with the dominant group for luxuries and necessities. Cultural identity
 d symbiotic interdependence are constant obstacles to successful separatism.
Furthermore, the crucial conditions giving rise to separatism are often not
 cognized and seldom are such as to be fully admitted by the movement's

---

* "The Third Party Tradition in American Politics," **Mississippi Valley Historical Re-
ew,** 20 (1933), 27–28.
** Fred E. Haynes, **Third Party Movements Since the Civil War** (Iowa City: The State
istorical Society of Iowa, 1916), p. 470.

members. The economic bases indicated by Gillin, Niebuhr, and others for reli
gious sects cannot be made official values of the movement. In the case of separa
tism from a competing group rather than a parent body the ascendance of grou
commitment over the stated objectives cannot possibly be admitted either to th
public or to the majority of the members. As a consequence of this fact and th
identification with the parent group or competing movement, the separatist move
ment typically exhibits several characteristics.

(1) The values that appear most prominently in the official ideology of th
separatist movement will be selected more on the basis of the fact that the
differentiate the separatist group from the parent body or competing movemen
than because of the members' initial attachment to them. The values becom
important symbolically, as signalizing their opposition to another group. Separa
tist values constitute a medium through which ill-understood conflicts of interes
may be conceptualized by the members to themselves and to the outside world.

The importance of revivalistic values in nativistic movements is further clari
fied in this context. As the native group comes to accept the advantage of th
colonial power's culture in many respects, a sense of dependence and identit
between the two begins to grow which must be contradicted if the movement i
to win and hold vigorous adherents. Gandhi had to *teach* the Indians to valu
their own culture, such as their primitive methods of spinning cloth, which the
were fast relinquishing. The European Slavs had largely forgotten their histori
culture until they were taught to value it by the scholars and leaders of th
pan-Slav movement.

In this connection the negative character of sectarian values mentioned b
Gillin is understandable as indicating focal points of differentiation from parer
churches. Likewise the apparent triviality of the issues of faith and practic
that have been salient in historical religious separations may be comprehendec
The fundamental faith and ritual that the sect retains are the property of th
parent church, so unusual prominence must be accorded traditionally mino
points of interpretation.

(2) The greater the initial identification of the dissident group with the parer
group, the later in the movement's development will the separatist orientatio
become the dominant one. Most separatist movements begin as reform or contr
movements, with only minor overtones of separatism. While more extremis
voices are usually heard from the start, they typically remain minority voice
until enough people become convinced that there is no hope of attaining th
majority of advantages of membership in the parent body. The early stages c
national independence movements, sects, and minor political parties illustrate
this principle.

Similarly, the *degree* of separatism demanded is usually moderate when th
dissident group is closely identified with the parent body. The frustration of suc
limited demands, or the deprivation of important advantages of membership i
the parent body, are likely to lead to demands for more complete separatism.

(3) Separatist movements are among those types that are most likely t
depend upon a charismatic leader for their strength. In the absence of vit;
ideology about which to unite, and lacking the confidence in an established or
ganization, dependence upon the drawing power of a leader with great popula
appeal may be crucial to the movement's existence. V. O. Key, Jr., has pointe

 out the large number of minor-party movements that have been almost one-man affairs. He points to the dependence of the socialist party on personal loyalty to Eugene V. Debs and later Norman Thomas, the Progressive party on Theodore Roosevelt, the Union party of 1936 on Father Charles E. Coughlin, and we might add the Independent Progressive Party in 1948 on Henry A. Wallace. Most of the well known religious sects were clearly identified with a single leader in their truly sectarian period.

(4) The stated values of separatist movements tend to appear trivial or ridiculous to those who have no interest in the conflict. As a consequence, the person who joins a separatist movement is likely to forfeit his social respectability. Fred E. Haynes observes,

> The caricatures of Kansas Populists, as presented by cartoonists of the metropolitan press, are typical of the way in which third parties have been regarded by the majority of Americans. According to this view a man of good sense connects himself with one of the regular parties in preference to throwing away his vote upon a third party candidate. To such a person, representing as he does the more or less prevalent popular view, a third party is made up largely of reformers, cranks, and discredited leaders of the older parties.*

Undoubtedly membership in a movement that is defined in this manner is either rejected by the normally socialized individual in a group or requires him to redefine his more generalized position in relation to the norms of the larger group. As an hypothesis we may suggest that continued membership in a separatist movement provokes a suspiciousness of conventional people and conventional behavior. The individual is forced to build a defensive curtain between himself and conventional citizens to protect himself against their evaluations of his behavior. This he may do by suspecting their motives, their sincerity, and their morals.

(5) Partly as a consequence of the foregoing, the values of separatism tend to be short-lived, either being abandoned by all but a die-hard minority of the original membership or becoming subordinated to a more conventional value-orientation in time. In order that they may persist the movement must be subjected to persecution so that the symbolic intensity of the values is heightened.

The observation by William B. Hesseltine that all successful new political parties in the United States have achieved success very quickly is relevant to the foregoing generalization. One unsuccessful election is often sufficient to convince people that their vote is being wasted or to raise doubts about the social acceptability of their political alignment.

On the other hand, the values of separatism may gradually be displaced by a return to conventionality within the movement itself. The mere fact of bringing some people who have been relatively isolated from meaningful group ties into a satisfying group relationship with the development of morale in pursuit of a collective goal may be a socializing experience. And in more specific ways the personal dedication to a set of values may itself arouse a desire for respectability where little had existed before.

H. Richard Niebuhr, as part of a definitive work on the sociological aspects of religious denominationalism, has pointed out the transmutation that typically occurs in a strong religious sect. In the following selection we have brought to-

* Ibid., p. 1.

gether several major generalizing paragraphs with a portion of Niebuhr's discussion of Quakerism as an illustrative case. The original work covers each of the
important sectarian movements in Christendom, and dwells upon several other
types of division within the church in addition to that based on economic disadvantage. The conversion of Christian values into a form that appealed to many
who had been neglected by the traditional churches resulted in moving the new
adherents out of the socio-economic class that had accounted for their original
response to separatism.

THE CHURCHES OF THE DISINHERITED

H. RICHARD NIEBUHR

One phase of denominationalism is largely
explicable by means of a modified economic interpretation of religious history;
for the divisions of the church have been
occasioned more frequently by the direct
and indirect operation of economic factors than by the influence of any other
major interest of man. Furthermore, it is
evident that economic stratification is often responsible for maintaining divisions
which were originally due to differences
of another sort. Social history demonstrates how a racial class may retain its
solidarity and distinction by becoming an
economic class, and religious history offers examples of churches which were
originally racial in character but maintained their separateness under new conditions because the racial group developed
into an economic entity. It is true, of
course, in this case as in that of others,
that no one element, the religious or the
economic or the racial, operates alone.
Economic classes tend to take on a cultural character and economic differences
between groups result in educational and
psychological distinctions between them.
The interaction of the various factors is
well exemplified in the history of immigrant groups in the United States. These
are distinguished at first by racial or national character, but they are usually also
the lowest groups in the economic and
cultural scale during the first generation

and, therefore, their distinction from
other groups is triply fortified. Their
churches, as a result, are distinguished
economically and culturally as well as ra-
cially from the denominations of previous
immigrants who have risen in the economic scale while losing their specifically
national or racial character.

An exclusively economic interpretation
of denominationalism would, because of
this interaction, be as erroneous as the
exclusively economic interpretation of political history is bound to be. It is quite
unjustifiable, above all, to leave the religious factor itself out of account in dealing with religious movements. Only because the inspiration of such movements
is religious do they develop the tremendous energy they display in history. Yet
an exclusively religious interpretation, especially a doctrinal one, is likely to miss
the point of the whole development even
more completely than does an exclusive
economic explanation. For if religion
supplies the energy, the goal, and the motive of sectarian movements, social factors no less decidedly supply the occasion, and determine the form the religious
dynamic will take. Were spiritual energies
to develop unchecked they would scarcely
issue in the formation of such denominations as now compose Christianity. Religious energies are dammed up, confined
to narrow channels, split into parallel
streams, by the non-religious distinctions
and classifications of Christians. The
source of a religious movement, therefore,
need not be economic for its results to
take on a definitely economic character

Reprinted in part by permission of The
Shoe String Press and the author, from H.
Richard Niebuhr, **The Social Sources of
Denominationalism** (Hamden: The Shoe
String Press, 1954), pp. 26–29, 48–57, 72–76,

On the other hand, economic conditions may supply the occasion for the rise of a new religious movement without determining its religious value. In any case, however, the character of the denomination issuing from the movement is explicable only if the influence of economic factors be taken into consideration.

So regarded, one phase of the history of denominationalism reveals itself as the story of the religiously neglected poor, who fashion a new type of Christianity which corresponds to their distinctive needs, who rise in the economic scale under the influence of religious discipline, and who, in the midst of a freshly acquired cultural respectability, neglect the new poor succeeding them on the lower plane. This pattern recurs with remarkable regularity in the history of Christianity. Anabaptists, Quakers, Methodists, Salvation Army, and more recent sects of like type illustrate this rise and progress of the churches of the disinherited.

Not only the religious revolutions of the poor, however, have left their impress on the denominational history of Christendom. One may also speak with G. K. Chesterton of the revolt of the rich against the poor. Some of the earlier churches of the Reformation received much of their specific character from their alliance with rising commercialism and set forth an interpretation of Christianity conformable with their major economic interests. To this group belong especially the Calvinistic churches, as has been shown by Weber, Cunningham, and Tawney. Other sects, whose origins are not so readily identifiable with economic movements, have preserved their separate character because of the economic status of their members and are distinguished from their sister denominations less by doctrine than by their wealth and the consequent conservatism of ethics and thought. . . .

The stream of religious and political revolt was divided into numerous channels. Until George Fox came there was no leader great enough to define its banks and to give it direction. Like almost all such revolts of the disinherited it almost came to naught because of the lack of an adequate leadership to stop its extravagances and to guide its great dynamic. Crude and sometimes horrible excesses were discovered, to be exploited as the atrocities of the movement by its enemies and to alienate the sympathies of many friends. But in all of its ramifications and divisions there was a certain unity; two characteristics marked the religious social revolt from Diggers and Levellers to Quakers—the doctrine of inner experience as the source of authority and the common hope of Christ's kingdom on earth. These two major common characteristics implied other equally general but less important features, such as the sectarian organization, the rejection of professional clergy, and the dependence on lay preaching, the spiritualist interpretation of Scriptures, the rejection of the monarchy and the less frequent, but not rare, espousal of communism.

In Millenarianism, the special inspiration of Harrison and the Fifth Monarchy men but common to all the sects, the two tendencies toward emotional and individual religious experience and toward ethical and social reconstruction met. "Their prate," says Coke, of the Fifth Monarchy men, "was to make way for Christ's monarchy on earth." This apocalypticism was combined with spiritualist, prophetic fervour. Visions, revelations, and illuminations are the natural accompaniment of such dynamic religious movements which receive fresh stimuli in this direction also from the example of primitive Christianity. Winstanley, the Digger leader, was both mystic and communist. "Not a year since," he wrote, "my heart was filled with sweet thoughts and many things were revealed to me I never read in books nor heard from the mouth of flesh; and when I began to speak of them some people could not hear my words. Then I took my spade and began to dig on St. George's Hill." Or again, "This Spirit of reason (the creative reason which is the divine Logos) is not without a man, but within every man; hence he need not run after others to tell him or to teach him; for this Spirit is his maker, he dwells in him and if his flesh were subject thereunto, he would daily find teaching therefrom, though he dwelt alone and saw the face of no other man." Even the Levellers, political rather than religious party though they were, shared much of the religious character of the sects. The Ranters "made it their business to set up the Light of Nature under the name of Christ in Men, and to dishonour and cry down the church, Scriptures, Ministry, Worship and Ordinances; and called men to hearken to the Christ within them." The Seekers, says the same writer, taught that "the Scriptures were uncertain . . . that our ministry is null and void and without authority." The excesses of the time, Naylor's proclamation of himself as the Christ, the frequent occurrences of prophesying by naked men and women parading through the streets, Fox walking barefoot through the "bloody city of Litchfield"—give evidence also of the spiritualist character of the movement. The Quaker doctrine of the inner light was the final quiet precipitate of this turbid emotionalism. The priesthood of all believers rather than the authority of the Scriptures is the guiding principle here and the assurance of salvation through immediate experience, not through the mediation of priest and sacrament or word, is the goal of religious endeavor.

The second characteristic of the movement was its program of social reformation. Its expectation of the coming of the Kingdom of Christ had its solid foundation in the physical needs of the poor. To quote Winstanley again: "At this very day," he wrote in 1650, "poor people are forced to work for 4d. a day and corn is dear. And the tithing-priest stops their mouth and tells them that 'inward satisfaction of mind' was meant by the declaration, 'The poor shall inherit the earth.' I tell you the Scripture is to be really and materially fulfilled . . . You jeer at the name of Leveller. I tell you Jesus Christ is the Head Leveller." Elsewhere this same benevolent mystic warns the rich "Pharaohs" who have "rich clothing and full bellies," their "honours and ease," that "the day of judgment is begun and that it will reach" them ere long. "The poor people you oppress shall be the sa-

viours of the land. If you will find mercy, let Israel go free; break to pieces the bands of property." Some of the Anabaptists set aside the quietistic principles they had learned from their Dutch teachers and reverted to something like the revolutionary program of their German predecessors at Muenster, although the majority remained quiet in their discontent. The Fifth Monarchy men under Harrison are the stormy petrels of revolution, drawing to themselves "many of the most violent and desperate spirits." "Though they speak great words of the reign of saints and seem to invite none but the holy seed," said an official report, "yet the baits they lay to catch men are the taking away customs, excise, taxes, tithes." Even the early Quakers had their radical wing and this group was the one which seemed to the seventeenth century to represent characteristic Quakerism. "It was learnt, that, though they were never seen with a weapon in their hands, several had been found with pistols under their cloaks. A Quaker took up his position at the doors of Parliament and drew his sword on a group of members. When questioned he replied, that he was inspired by the Holy Spirit to kill every man that sat in the House." But whether by revolutionary activity, or in quiet waiting for the manifestation of the apocalyptic kingdom, or by patient non-resistance, all phases of the movement looked toward social amelioration and sought redress for the wrongs of the poor. With its emotional piety it mated the social radicalism of the gospel and so qualified as a genuine religious movement of the disinherited.

Misunderstood, not so much because of its own excesses as because of the prejudices of those who profited by the existing order—including the clergy—without competent leaders save one, rejected by Cromwell, persecuted and derided, the movement seemed bound to collapse, like that of the Anabaptists in Luther's day. It was saved by George Fox. That typical church of the disinherited which he gathered out of the religiously and economically homeless souls of the day, in which a Winstanley, a Lilburne, a Plockboy

Fifth Monarchy Men, and Anabaptists found refuge, lived because it denied itself the way of violence, overcoming the recklessness of its enemies within. Choosing the way as well as the aim of the gospel it survived the persecution and contempt of Presbyterians, Anglicans and Independents, Republicans and Royalists. It is interesting to note that in the case of the English sects as in that of the German the method of non-resistance was not espoused until efforts toward a violent revolution had been found unavailing in the face of the superior power of the ruling classes, while, at the same time, the ideal of a new social order was abandoned in favor of a sectarian organization of mutual aid and brotherhood. Yet the Quakers, even more than the Anabaptists, continued to represent the social idealism of the churches of the disinherited. Their love of equality, symbolized in the refusal to uncover their heads, and in the use of the familiar "thee" and "thou," their refusal to participate in war, their attitude toward slavery, their production of men like Bellers, whose Christian socialism greatly influenced Robert Owen, their continued support of humanitarian activities, all of these indicate the revolutionary source of the movement and represent an effective continuation of its democratic ethics. But, like the Anabaptists before them, the followers of Fox and Winstanley were prevented from becoming a really inclusive church of the disinherited by the persecutions which isolated them and drove them back upon themselves to form a narrow sect with group loyalty and sectarian consciousness largely taking the place of the larger idealism which inspired the founders. Out of the rejection of the religion of the disinherited a new denomination once more took its rise.

The Quakers, no less than their predecessors among the churches of the poor, soon settled down to an "equable respectability." They accommodated themselves to the social situation and confined their efforts toward social reformation to the work of gaining converts to their faith, to the works of charity and to occasional efforts to influence public opinion on so-

cial questions. A number of factors were responsible for this decline in revolutionary fervor. The effect of persecution has been pointed out. Another important factor in the development of such denominations from revolutionary groups to settled social bodies, content with their place in the scheme of things, is the substitution of a second generation, which holds its convictions as a heritage, for a first generation which had won these convictions painfully and held them at a bitter cost. But most important among the causes of the decline of revolutionary churches into denominations is the influence of economic success. The churches of the poor all become middle-class churches sooner or later and, with their need, lose much of the idealism which grew out of their necessities. There is no doubt of the truth of Max Weber's contention that godliness is conducive to economic success. From the days of Paul at Thessalonica onward, Christianity has not failed to exhort its adherents "that with quietness they work and eat their own bread," while at the same time it has commanded them to abstain from luxury, but, having "food and covering," "therewith to be content." Monastic asceticism, supported by a dualistic view of life, carried the second of these ideas to its extreme, and was rejected by Protestantism, but the Reformers introduced in place of the "extra-worldly" asceticism of the monks an "intra-worldly "asceticism, which regarded work in trade and vocation as the primary duty of life and a service to God; yet they continued to condemn any indulgence in the comforts and luxuries of life as sinful. Restrictions on consumption accompanied by emphasis upon production have their inevitable result in an economic salvation which is far removed from the eternal blessedness sought by the enthusiastic founders of the Protestant sects, but which is not less highly valued by the successful followers of later generations. This process, which is repeated again and again in the history of Christian sects, also took place in the case of the Quakers. In the second and third generations, with the aid of the prosperity prevailing in the days of good Queen Anne, this church of the disinherited became a more or less respectable middle-class church that left the popular movement from which it originated far behind. It continued to hold the tenets of its social program but now as the doctrines of a denomination rather than as the principles of inclusive social reconstruction. In America, especially, the economic rise of the Quakers was speedy and permanent.

Once more, therefore, the poor were without a gospel. The Millenarian hopes which had fired the popular movement of the seventeenth century with enthusiasm were definitely left behind. The ethics of Jesus was dissolved completely into a mild morality of respectability. Eighteenth-century England, ecclesiastical and academic as well as political, feared nothing so much as enthusiasm. Its reaction against the tense emotionalism of Civil War and Revolutionary days, its disillusionments, its lack of vital energies, exhausted as it was by the turbulent passions of religious and political revolt, left it sterile and cold in religion, enamored only with the bleak beauty of mathematically-minded philosophy, or more frequently, indifferent to the claims of any ethical or religious idealism. Lecky, describing the religion of the period, writes, "The sermons of the time were almost always written, and the prevailing taste was cold, polished and fastidious." "As is always the case, the habits prevailing in other spheres at once acted on and were influenced by religion. The selfishness, the corruption, the worship of expediency, the scepticism as to all higher motives that characterized the politicians of the school of Walpole; the heartless cynicism reigning in fashionable life which is so clearly reflected in the letters of Horace Walpole and Chesterfield; the spirit of a brilliant and varied contemporary literature, eminently distinguished for its sobriety of judgment and for its fastidious purity and elegance of expression, but for the most part deficient in depth, in passion, and in imagination, may all be traced in the popular theology. Sobriety and good sense were the qualities most valued in the pulpit, and enthusiasm and extravagance were those which were most dreaded." . . .

The Methodist revival was the last great religious revolution of the disinherited in Christendom. And it was not wholly a popular movement. Perhaps that is one reason why it was the last. It is a striking fact that the revolutionary tendencies of the poor in the nineteenth century were almost completely secular in character, while in preceding eras they were always largely religious in nature. The socialism of 1848 and later years was closely akin in many ways to Anabaptism and Quakerism as well as to Lollardy and the Waldensian revolt. It cherished as these did the hope of an inevitable social renewal which would cast down the mighty from their seats and exalt them of low degree. Like these it provided the oppressed with an emotional escape from the weariness and grime of uneventful and profitless labor. Like these it brought to consciousness the latent sense of social solidarity and endowed the impoverished individual life with the significance of participation in a cosmic event. But for the angels who fought on the side of Baptists and Quakers it substituted economic laws, and in place of the early coming of the Son of Man it anticipated the class struggle and the dictatorship of the proletariat. What were the reasons for this change?

The conditions which preceded the rise of socialism were not dissimilar to those which formed the background of the religious revolutions of previous centuries. There was present the actual exclusion of the poor from churches grown emotionally too cold, ethically too neutral, intellectually too sober, socially too aristocratic to attract the men who suffered under the oppression of monotonous toil, of insufficient livelihood and the sense of social inferiority. There was present also the awakening of the disinherited to the consciousness of their human dignity and worth. But the result was not a religious revolt. On the contrary socialism often assumed the character of an anti-religious movement. Its secularism was doubtless lue to many causes—to the growth of he scientific temper and of nineteenth-entury materialism, to the prevalence of he mechanistic conception of life which ndustrialism fosters, to the determinism •f the Hegelian philosophy in which Marx had been trained, to the bare fact hat the leaders of the movement were ot religious men. But among the causes f this secularism the absence of an effective social idealism within any of the Christian churches was of especial importance. The last previous religious movements among the disinherited, Methodism nd Pietism, had failed to follow in the teps of the Baptists and Quakers. They ad allowed the millenarian hopes to apse; they had substituted for the concept of the kingdom the symbol of eaven; they had been concerned with he redemption of men from the hell beond the grave alone and had held out ttle promise of salvation from the various mundane hells in which the poor suffer for other sins besides their own. So hey had failed to keep alive within the hurch those realistic hopes which had lways been the source of new religious prisings in the centuries before; and they ad joined with the older churches in roclaiming a purely other-worldly hope. n any other century of Christian history his failure to keep alive the promise of ocial amelioration through Christian ethes and by divine miracle might have had ess far-reaching results. In the century of nventions and of industrial production, a time so largely occupied with the resent world and its values, the absence f this social element from the preaching f the gospel was fatal to the religion of he disinherited. It is significant that much f the leadership of the social movement ow came from a group which had been urtured in the ideals of Old Testament rophecy, and which even when it lost s religious faith did not fail to give expression to ideals which had been derived rom that religion. The leadership of the ews in the social revolutions of the nine-

teenth and twentieth centuries had these religious sources; it was the only effective substitute for the Christian leadership which had once been unfailingly available in every crusade for justice but which had died out, perhaps as a result of attrition in a theological and other-worldly church.

The nineteenth century, it is true, did not entirely lack representatives of the naive religious movements. The Salvation Army is an outstanding example of the manner in which a separate conventicle must be formed by the religious poor, who have been excluded from the denominations of their newly enriched brothers. But Booth was neither a Francis nor a Wesley. The movement he inaugurated was not a popular movement of spontaneous character; the very organization of the Army implied a home-mission enterprise rather than a religious and social awakening. Moreover the under-privileged of the modern era have been too greatly alienated from the gospel as well as from Christianity, whether by the silent forces of the industrial environment, or by the strident voices of Marxian apostles, or by the indifferent attitude of churchmen, for the Army to be able to repeat the successes of its victorious predecessors. Other contemporary movements of the religious poor toward the attainment of adequate religious experience and expression come to light in many a gospel tabernacle and evangelistic society and millenarian association. But the mass of the workers remains untouched; there is no effective religious movement among the disinherited today; as a result they are simply outside the pale of organized Christianity. Yet without the spontaneous movement from below, all efforts to re-pristinate the ethical enthusiasm of the early church and to reawaken the Messianic hope are unavailing. The churches which again and again have been recalled to consider a neglected message by the religious revolutions of the unfortunate are so much the poorer because there is no sect of the disinherited today. . . .

(6) Members of a persisting and strong separatist movement are likely to

experience more than ridicule and contempt and become the victims of active
intolerance. A typical sequence is one in which the separatist movement is firs
looked upon with amusement as harmless madness. If it persists it begins to be
viewed more seriously until its significance may be magnified out of all reasonable
proportion and the whole movement be viewed in a sinister light. At this point a
feeling may develop that the unwillingness of the handful of members of a sec
to salute the American flag is a threat to the entire sentiment of patriotism ir
the United States, and expensive legal action will be evoked to enforce the out
ward forms of loyalty.

While limited intolerance may often strengthen the separatist determination
of members and increase alienation from the conventional group, a more com
plete intolerance may either wipe out the movement or force migration. The
Church of Jesus Christ of the Latter Day Saints affords an example of migration
enforced by increasing intolerance. This case is informative because it suggest
that a factor in the extent of intolerance evoked by a separatist movement is the
degree to which separatism encompassed the total lives of the movement's mem
bers. A *segmental* movement, one whose members continue normal social par
ticipation in most respects, is more likely to continue to be regarded as harmles
than a *totalital* movement which governs the entire lives of its members. At the
same time the *totalital* movement almost necessarily requires physical separa
tion from other people if it is to carry on successfully. There are abundant illus
trations of such religious sects which have migrated to achieve isolation, and o
political and economic utopias which have attempted to establish themselves ir
isolation from the surrounding world.

At certain periods of time separatism is more likely to be tolerated than a
other times. In the most general sense, toleration is lowest when the sense o
group identity and the sense of threat to the group are greatest. Wartime is per
haps the best example of such a period. In the following selection we may se
quantitative evidence of the consequence of the wartime atmosphere for the lif
of dissenting political parties.

SMALL POLITICAL PARTIES CASUALTIES OF WAR?

HUGH A. BONE

Minor political parties are on the road to
becoming one of the casualties on the
home front. Since the beginning of international tensions a decade ago they have
found it increasingly difficult to obtain
funds and to secure a place on the ballot.
With the outbreak of the European war
in 1939 their position has been rendered
even more precarious. In the November
1942 elections there were fewer third
party candidates for U.S. senator, repre-

Reprinted in part by permission of The
National Municipal League, from **National
Municipal Review**, 32 (Nov., 1943), pp. 524–
27.

sentative, governor or other statewide of
fices than in 1940—a total of 293 against
375 two years before. Together with ir
dependent nominees they polled in th
Congressional elections of 1942 onl
563,018 votes, or 2 per cent of the tota
This may be compared with the 193
Congressional vote wherein minor partie
cast 1,334,222 or 3.7 per cent of th
votes.

Minor party candidates appeared i
only twenty states in 1942 and there wa
a proportionately greater decline in non
inations for state over federal offices. Th
Communist party put forward only eleve

andidates in 1942 as compared with fifty-ine in 1940 while Socialist nominees ropped from seventy to fifty-one. The rohibitionists showed the smallest drop –from ninety-two to eighty-three. The 'ommunists were unable to muster the ecessary 50,000 votes for their guberna-rial nominee in New York in order to tain a position on the ballot.

Two local parties, however, made a reditable showing in 1942. The Progres-ves in Wisconsin elected a governor and e American Labor party in New York olled well over 400,000 votes for its bernatorial nominee. In many Con-essional districts, however, the party pported Democratic candidates.

REASONS FOR DECLINE

There are many reasons for the decline minor parties. A convenient explana-n is public apathy, an apathy which ected the major parties as well in 1942. ut this hardly explains the difference be-een the Socialist vote of 590,400 in 16 and of 117,000 in 1940, particularly view of the smaller electorate in 1916. Undoubtedly the various Socialist and armer-Labor parties have, in recent ars, lost many former "protest votes" the Democrats because of the social ogram of the New Deal. Many of the forms advocated by minority parties ve seen enactment into federal and ate law during the past decade. As a sult these groups are badly in need of habilitation and revitalization. The post-ar issues now on the horizon will give e lesser parties an opportunity to cham-n new programs of political action.

More serious, however, is the fact that en before the outbreak of war in 1939, e American public was becoming in-easingly suspicious of alien influences, sms," and fifth column activity. There s been a tendency to associate subver-e influences with minor political groups d this in turn has led to agitation to ep their names off the ballot. State leg-atures have resorted to extraordinary vices to make minor party nominations ore difficult.

These have been of three types: (1) financial restrictions, (2) amendment of laws relating to nominating petitions, and (3) prohibition by statute or administrative ruling of "un-American" parties, or those which have "international connections," or advocate the overthrow of government by force and violence. The first two methods were well established before 1939, but since that time they have been extended and made more stringent. The third is largely an outgrowth of unfavorable reaction to the Russo-German pact of 1939.

RESTRICTIONS ON NOMINATIONS

Arkansas requires a fee of fifty cents for each presidential elector in each of the counties of the state. This amounts to $327.50 for the nine presidential electors—an obvious hardship on the smaller parties.

The Maryland General Assembly in 1941 passed a law which provides a means whereby the names of candidates can be placed on the ballot by a certificate of nomination. This law requires a notary signature (usually twenty-five cents) for each name signed on nominating petitions, the number of signers varying according to the importance of the office. Thus, an independent, new, or minor party candidate for a state office would have to pay $500 in addition to the regular filing fees. A full legislative ticket would cost thousands of dollars. Furthermore, the act requires that the names of all signers of such petitions shall be published in the newspapers. In Indiana each signature must also be notarized and a similar rule has been established by administrative order in Maine, New Hampshire, and Vermont.

The most popular method of keeping third parties off the ballot is the requirement of a prohibitive number of signatures together with strict requirements for accepting names. Illinois has one of the most stringent laws in this respect. It requires 25,000 names on a nominating petition for statewide offices with not less than 200 signers from each of fifty counties. This has the effect of excluding both workers' parties whose main support lies in the cities, and farmers' parties whose strength is found almost exclusively in rural areas. This law kept Communist candidates off the ballot both in 1938 and in 1940 though they secured 25,000 signers, mostly in Cook County.

California requires approximately 175,-000 signatures for a nominating petition and Ohio requires 15 per cent of the vote cast in the last election in order for a minority party to place its candidates on the ballot under its own label. The Florida election code makes no provision for independent or new party nominations. Candidates are nominated by primaries and a political party is defined as one having registered as members thereof at least 5 per cent of the state's total registered voters.

Norman Thomas, Socialist leader, attempted in the spring of 1940 to arouse public sentiment against what he termed "petition tricks" designed to work a hardship on his and other minor parties. Among the more cumbersome of the laws he found were those requiring such parties to "file their petitions at an absurdly early date. Among the worst offenders in this respect is California which recently a New Deal legislature made it impossible for a new or minority party to get on the ballot unless by February 15—more than eight months before the election—a petition should be filed containing the signatures of 10 per cent of the vote cast at the last election—a plainly impossible requirement. In Pennsylvania the filing date was April 3, Oklahoma May 3, Michigan May 5, and West Virginia May 13. Kansas, Kentucky, and Nevada are among the other states requiring the filing of petitions at dates before July 1, that is, before the Democratic convention will have been held."

Mr. Thomas also called attention to North Carolina, "Where in 1936 the Attorney-General ruled that each of the necessary 10,000 signers of nominating petitions would be guilty of fraud unless they actually join the Socialist party, not merely desire that the party should get the benefits of a place on the ballot." Minnesota prohibits the collection of signatures

prior to the day of the primary so that small party is allowed less than thir days in which to collect the require 2,000 signatures.

OUTLAWRY OF SUBVERSIVE PARTIES

Prior to 1939 the laws of Arkans Delaware, Indiana, and Tennessee e cluded from their ballots the candidat of parties which advocate the overthro of government by force and violence. I spite of the fact that the Communist par as early as 1938 disavowed the use violence and came out "unqualifiedly fe the right of the majority to direct t destinies of our country," the laws Arkansas and Indiana were invoked deny the Communists an opportunity present a ticket. The California legislatu in 1940 barred from the ballot politic candidates using the word "Communis as a part of their party designation. ruling from the Attorney-General and/ the Secretary of State barred Communis in 1940 from the ballot in Arizon Georgia, Kentucky, and New Mexic Meanwhile in 1940 the official severan of the American Communist party fro the Communist International was cor pleted. Yet between the signing of t Russo-German pact in 1939 and the Ge man attack on Russia in June 1941, ni more states enacted legislation barri Communist candidates from the ball These were Illinois, Kansas, Ohio, O gon, Oklahoma, Texas, Wisconsin, a Wyoming. Arkansas strengthened its e isting laws in this respect. Similar legisl tion was considered but failed of passa in Colorado, Idaho, Massachusetts, a Michigan.

In May 1942 a special committee Pennsylvania, headed by the Governc ruled the Communists off the ballot as party advocating the overthrow of go ernment by force. The Secretary of Sta in Ohio banned the Communist ticket c similar grounds. In the meantime son substance was given to these rulings the decision of Attorney-General Bidd in the case of Harry Bridges to the effe that the Communists advocated the u of force. . . .

Chapter 18

Participation-oriented movements

*T*HE PERPETUATION and size of some movements seem little related to the promotion of any program in the larger society. Either the group has no scheme for reform of the larger order, or the members' allegiance is in no whit affected by failure to win support for their program of reform in the larger society. Such movements we shall call *participation-oriented* movements. By this term we mean to indicate that the major characteristics of the movement center around the satisfactions that members gain from *the mere fact of participation* in the movement itself.

The kinds of satisfaction derived from participation in movements are many, and any separation into types is somewhat arbitrary. However, we shall provisionally divide the participation-oriented movements into the following subtypes: (a) *passive reform,* or those movements whose members occupy themselves with preparing for a state of societal reform that is to come without their active intervention; (b) *personal status* movements, which promise their members the benefits of greater success or recognition within the society or afford them a basis for reinterpreting their own position in the larger society; (c) *limited personal* movements, in which the primary gratification of membership in a somewhat exclusive movement compensates for the frustrations of conventional life without replacing that life. In addition we shall treat two types which fall between the value-oriented and the participation-oriented types, namely, reform movements which retain their strength in spite of a reform program that appears unlikely to be attained, and movements that aim to alter the social order solely through modifying the behavior of a large enough number of its members.

Passive reform movements. The most obvious type of participation-oriented movement is that in which a fantasy reform is substituted for active promotion of reform. In movements of this sort the members decry the existing state of the social order as genuinely as do the members of active reform and revolutionar movements. However, either because they are too small or impotent a group t effect change, or because they fear personal reprisals for active reform effort: or because they cannot visualize a program that would lead to the desire reform, they develop a conviction that the reform is inevitable and requires n assistance from them.

Two concerns dominate the activity of these movements. First, the moveme: cultivates the conviction of inevitable reform against the scepticism of outsider: This is accomplished through creating a powerful in-group sentiment and throug rationalizing their belief. Sometimes the rationale depends upon supernatur: intervention, the coming of a messiah. In other instances a more secular rationa posits an inevitable historical dialectic or unilinear evolution which will culminat in the desired state of society.

Second, the movement prepares its members for a favorable status in the ne order. Practice in the ways of the forthcoming society, personal purificatio: seeking advance favor with the messiah, joining those groups that will have th inherent advantage in the new order—all these techniques permit the believers t gain a headstart over outsiders and assure them the best positions when suc reform occurs.

In a valuable study, Bernard Barber has examined the spread of two wave of messianic movements among American Indian tribes. In particular he poin: out the source of messianic ideology in the pre-existing mythology of the socie: and identifies the circumstances required to transform a cultural myth into vital belief in imminent transformation.

ACCULTURATION AND MESSIANIC MOVEMENTS

Bernard Barber

Robert H. Lowie has recently called our attention again to the problem of messianic movements among the American aborigines. Among the North American Indians, one of the fundamental myths was the belief that a culture-hero would one day appear and lead them to a terrestrial paradise. Under certain conditions, which this paper will describe and analyze, these myths have become the ideological basis for messianic movements. In the messianic movement, the ushering in of the "golden age" by the messiah is announced for the *immediate* future. Twenty such movements had been recorded in the United States alone prior to 1890.

The messianic doctrine is essentially a statement of hope. Through the interve: tion of the Great Spirit or of his emissar the earth will shortly be transformed in: a paradise, enjoyed by both the living ar the resurrected dead. In anticipation the happy return to the golden age, b lievers must immediately return to t: aboriginal mode of life. Traits and cu: toms which are symbolic of foreign i: fluence must be put aside. All members the community—men, women and ch: dren—must participate. Besides reverti: to the early folkways, believers mu adopt special ritual practices until t: millennium arrives. Thus, in the Ame: can Ghost Dance movements ceremoni: bathing and an elaborate dance were t: chief ritual innovations. The doctrine a ways envisages a restoration of earth values. These values will be enjoye however, in a transcendental setting, f: in the age which is foretold there will :

Reprinted by permission of the American Sociological Society, from the **American Sociological Review**, 6 (Oct., 1941), pp. 663–69.

sickness or death; there will be only ernal happiness. The messianic doctrine peaceful. The exclusion of the whites om the golden age is not so much a flection of hostility toward them as a mbolization of the fulfillment of the rmer way of life. The millennium is to established through divine agency; lievers need only watch and pray.

The general sociocultural situation that recipitates a messianic movement has en loosely described as one of "harsh mes." Its specific characteristic is the idespread experience of "deprivation"— e despair caused by inability to obtain hat the culture has defined as the ordiry satisfactions of life. The fantasytuation pictured in the messianic docine attracts adherents chiefly because it cludes those things which formerly proded pleasure in life, the loss of which nstitutes deprivation. The pervasiveness the precipitating cultural crises may be ferred from the broad range of socioltural items to be restored in the golden e. For example, one of the Sioux rticipants in the Ghost Dance expericed a vision of an old-fashioned buffalo nt, genuine in all details. He said that had beheld the scouts dashing back to oclaim the sighting of a herd. Now, the lling off of the buffalo was probably the eatest blow to the Plains Indians. Anher bitter grievance was the exproprian of the Indian lands and the segregan of the tribes on reservations; removal a new geographical setting had more less direct repercussions on every phase the culture. For example, the prophet nohalla promised, among other things, e restoration of the original tribal lands.

Deprivation may arise from the deruction not only of physical objects but so of sociocultural activities. In the original Sioux culture, millions of ffalo furnished an unlimited supply of od. Buffaloes and their by-products ere perhaps the most important comodity in the Sioux economy, being emoyed as articles of exchange, as material r tepees, bedding, war shields, and the ke. In addition, the buffalo was the focal int of many ritual and social activities

of the Sioux. When the buffaloes were destroyed, therefore, the Sioux were deprived not only of food, but also of culturally significant activities. The tribal societies concerned with war and hunting lost their function and atrophied. The arts and techniques surrounding the buffalo hunt, arts and techniques which had once been sources of social status and of pride in "workmanship," were now rendered useless.

The impact of the white culture, besides depriving the Indians of their customary satisfactions, adds to their suffering by introducing the effects of new diseases and intoxicating liquor. In 1889, the Sioux suffered decimating epidemics of measles, grippe, and whooping cough. It is significant that Tenskwatawa prophesied that there would be no smallpox in the golden age. Complaints about the evil influences of firewater were expressed by "Open Door"; by "Handsome Lake," the Iroquois Prophet; by the Delaware Prophet; and by Känakuk, among others.

The messianic movement served to "articulate the spiritual depression" of the Indians. Those groups which faced a cultural impasse were predisposed to accept a doctrine of hope. Correlatively, the tribes that rejected the doctrine were in a state in which the values of their old life still functioned. In a condition of anomie, where there is a disorganization of the "controlling normative structure," most of the members of the group are thrown out of adjustment with significant features of their social environment. The old set of social and cultural norms is undermined by the civilized culture. Expectations are frustrated, there is a "sense of confusion, a loss of orientation," there is no longer a foundation for security. At such a time, messianic prophecies are most likely to be accepted and made the basis of action. Messiahs preach the return to the old order, or rather, to a new order in which the old will be revived. Essentially, their function is to proclaim a *subtle order,* one which will define the ends of action. Their doctrines describe men's former life, meaningful and satisfactory.

The stabilizing function of the messianic movement may be illustrated in specific cases. Investigation of the 1870 and 1890 North American Ghost Dance movements shows that they are correlated with widespread deprivation. The two movements, though they originated in the same tribe, the North Paiute of Nevada, spread over different areas, depending upon the presence or absence of a deprivation situation. A comparison of the two movements makes the relationship clear-cut. The Ghost Dance of 1870 spread only through northern California; the tribes in that area had "suffered as great a disintegration by 1870 . . . as the average tribe of the central United States had undergone by 1890." In 1890, the Ghost Dance once again spread from the North Paiute, but this time not to California. By 1875, the movement there had exhausted itself and was abandoned. All the dancing and adherence to the rules of conduct had failed to bring the golden age. Disillusionment supervened upon the discovery that the movement was an inadequate response. The alternative response seems to have been a despondent and relatively amorphous adaptation. The Indians "had long since given up all hope and wish of the old life and adapted themselves as best they might to the new civilization that engulfed them." The 1890 movement did spread to the Plains tribes because by 1890 their old life had virtually disappeared, and the doctrine of the Ghost Dance was eagerly adopted for the hope that it offered. The radical changes among the Plains tribes in the twenty-year period, 1870–90, may best be traced by examining the history of the Teton Sioux. Up to 1868, they were the least affected by white contact of all the tribes of the Plains area. By 1890, however, they were experiencing an intense deprivation situation, the climax of a trend which had begun twenty years before. Especially severe were the years between 1885–90, when crops failed, many cattle died of disease, and a large part of the population was carried off by epidemics.

Further corroboration of the positive correlation of the messianic movement with extended deprivation has been pre-

sented by Nash. In 1870, the Ghost Danc doctrine was presented to three tribe which had been brought together on th Klamath reservation six years before, th Klamath, the Modoc, and the Paviots(Of the three tribes, the Modoc, who ha experienced the greatest amount of d(privation, participated most intensely. Th Paviotso, who had experienced minim; cultural changes, participated least of al Moreover, Nash found that within th tribes the members participated differ entially, in rough proportion to the d(privation experienced.

A case study of the Navaho furnishe still further support for our thesis. Unt quite recently, the Navaho territory wa relatively isolated; few roads crossed and there were not more than two thou sand white inhabitants. The Navaho ha managed to maintain the essentials c their own culture; their economic life ha remained favorable; and, from 1869 t 1931, they increased in numbers from les than 10,000 to 45,000. In 1864, in retali; tion for their marauding, the Unite States Government rounded up the Nav aho and banished them to the Bosqu Redondo on the Pecos River. This exil was an exception to the fact that in gen eral they had not suffered deprivation They could not adapt to the agricultur; life imposed on them and begged for pe mission to go home. Many died durin epidemics of smallpox, whooping cough chicken pox, and pneumonia. After fou years, they were given sheep, goats, an clothing by the Government and allowe to return to their own country.

The equilibrium of the Navaho cultur was quickly restored. The tribe grew ric in herds and silver. The old way of lif was resumed in its essentials despite th greater emphasis on a pastoral economy The deprivation situation of 1864–68 wa left behind; life was integrated around stable culture pattern. In the winter c 1889–90, when Paiute runners tried t spread the belief in the coming of th Ghost Dance Messiah, their mission wa fruitless. "They preached and prophesie for a considerable time, but the Navah were skeptical, laughed at the prophet nd paid but little attention to their prophecies." There was no social need of a redeemer.

Within the last fifteen years, however, the entire situation of the Navaho tribe has changed. There has been constantly increasing contact with the white culture. Automobiles and railroads have brought tourists. The number of trading stores has increased. The discovery of oil on the reservation has produced rapid changes. Children have been sent to Government schools, far from their homes. Since 1929, the depression has reduced the income from the sale of blankets and silver jewlry. By far the most important difficulty now confronting the Navaho is the problem of overgrazing and soil erosion. To vert disaster, a basic reorganization of the economic activities of the tribe is necessary. Therefore, the Government to meet this *objective* condition, has introuced a soil-erosion and stock-reduction program but it has been completely unsatisfactory to the Navaho. Stock-reduction not only threatens their economic interests, *as they see them,* but undermines the basis of important sentiments and activities in the Navaho society. To destroy in wanton fashion the focus of so many of their day-to-day interests cuts the cultural round from under them.

Thus at present the Navaho are experiencing widespread deprivation. Significantly enough, within the past few years there has been a marked emergence of anti-white sentiment. Revivalistic cults have appeared. There has also been a great increase in recourse to aboriginal ceremonials on all occasions. Long reports of Navaho revivalistic activities were carried recently in *The Farmington Times Rustler,* a weekly published in Farmington, New Mexico. These activities bear a detailed similarity to the Ghost Dance and other American Indian messianic doctrines.

Despite the positive correlation of the messianic movement and deprivation, there is no one-to-one relation between these variables. It is here suggested that the messianic movement is *only one of*

several *alternative responses.* In the other direction, the relationship is more determinate; the messianic movement is comprehensible only as a response to widespread deprivation. The alternative response of armed rebellion and physical violence has already been suggested. The depopulation among the natives of the South Pacific Islands may be viewed as still another response. The moral depression which, it often has been held, is one of the "causes" of the decline of the native races may be construed as a mode of reaction to the loss of an overwhelming number of satisfactions.

The theory of alternative responses may be tentatively checked against another set of data. The Ghost Dance among the Plains tribes lasted little more than a year or two, coming to a sharp end as a result of the suppression of the so-called "Sioux outbreak" with which it adventitiously had become connected in the minds of the whites. The Government agents on the Indian reservations successfully complied with their instructions to exterminate the movement. However, the deprivation of the tribes remained as acute as ever. It is in this context that the Peyote cult emerged and spread among the Indians *as an alternative response.* It became the focus of a marked increase of attention and activity after 1890, thus coming in approximate temporal succession to the Ghost Dance. Completely nonviolent and nonthreatening to the White culture, the Peyote cult has been able to survive in an environment which was radically opposed to the messianic movements.

The general and specific sociocultural matrices of the Peyote cult are the same as those of the messianic movements. The Indians

Fifty years ago, when Peyote first became known to them . . . were experiencing . . . despair and hopelessness over their vanishing culture, over their defeats, over the past grandeur that could not be regained. They were facing a spiritual crisis . . . Some turned to Peyotism, and as time has but intensified the antagonistic forces, more and more have become converted to the new religion which offers a means of escape . . .

The Peyote cult, like the messianic movement, was an "autistic" response, in Lasswell's terms, but the essential element of its doctrine was different. Whereas the Ghost Dance doctrine had graphically described a reversion to the aboriginal state, the Peyote cult crystallized around passive acceptance and resignation in the face of the existing deprivation. It is an alternative response which seems to be better adapted to the existing phase of acculturation.

Thus we have tested the hypotheses that the primitive messianic movement is correlated with the occurrence of widespread deprivation and that it is only one of several alternative responses. There is a need for further studies, especially in regard to the specific sociocultural conditions which produce each of the possible responses.

Personal status movements. In preparing for the imminent better world of messianic promise, the members of passive reform movements are at the same time achieving for themselves a new status in the social order and a new vantage point from which to interpret the flow of events. Hence the orientation toward passive reform cannot be viewed apart from the personal status that participants seek. However, a great many movements serve chiefly to redefine the status of their members within the *existing* social order. They may or may not incorporate a promise of ultimate societal reform, but the altered status of members does not wait upon the achieved reform.

Movements in which the messianic element is only secondary may best be identified by their continuance in full strength when the new order does not occur as predicted or when the new order is prophesied for a far distant or indefinite date in the future. The movements of which Barber writes collapsed when the messianic hope was not realized, and the people were immunized by the experience against further messianic movements. However, many movements with messianic ideology are little affected by such failures, the ideologists proceeding immediately to redefine the time or circumstances of eventual reform.

The circumstances under which a movement may reorient the individual to the present order in a manner that is rewarding independently of societal reform have not been subject to investigation that would afford precise generalizations. In a general way, however, the *personal status* movement must alter crucial frustrating aspects of the individual's life. Individuals who are chiefly lonely or lacking a sense of personal worth may find gratification in the mere fact of active membership in a vital group. By contrast, the problems of the Indians were unchanged by a temporary arousal of enthusiasm within the old tribal group.

There are two broad ways in which a movement may reorient the member to the present society. On the one hand a movement may redefine the individual's value scheme, supplanting his old reference groups with new ones representing new values. Thus the individual discovers that purity of character is a higher value than material success so that he need no longer pursue the latter. Or he finds that the good opinion of the faithful is more to be sought than the plaudits of the misguided multitudes.

On the other hand, a movement may reorient its members in the society through assisting them to attain the types of success already recognized in the society. It may enable them to call upon mystical powers which assure success to their every enterprise, or it may provide resources through which they may vercome such personal deficiencies as alcoholism. In this second broad form he personal status movement does not challenge the existing status system, but ccepts it wholeheartedly.

The first manner of reorienting the individual is commonly found among miority groups, religious movements, and various political, aesthetic, and intellecual movements which remain out of touch with practical considerations of nplementing their schemes. Anton Boisen has attempted to describe how memership in a certain group of religious cults gives the member a new world in vhich to reorient himself. The gratifying small world or "microcosm" of the Holy Roller group replaces the frustrating larger world for these people.

ECONOMIC DISTRESS AND RELIGIOUS EXPERIENCE
A Study of the Holy Rollers
ANTON T. BOISEN

One of the striking phenomena of the period since the depression began is the rapid increase of eccentric forms of religion. Students of religion have been much concerned regarding the extent and the significance of this increase and I have found myself drafted for the task of studying those sects which are known popularly as "holy rollers." A preliminary report has just been completed. It contains some findings which may be of interest to psychiatrists and sociologists as well as to theologians.

The term "holy roller" is applied to certain sects which cultivate an extreme form of mystical religion. They belong to the general group of "holiness" sects, holding in common with them the doctrine that in addition to the experience of "conversion" the true Christian must have also the experience of "sanctification." They speak of this as the "second blessing." As distinct from other holiness sects the holy rollers believe that in order to be saved it is also necessary to be "baptized by the Holy Spirit" in accordance with the account of the Day of Pentecost as given in the Book of Acts. For this reason the word "Pentecostal" frequently appears in their official names. Evidence of this

Reprinted by special permission of The William Alanson White Psychiatric Foundation, Inc., from Anton T. Boisen, "Economic Distress and Religious Experience: A Study of the Holy Rollers," **Psychiatry, 2** (1939), pp. 185–94. Copyrighted by the Foundation.

baptism of the Spirit they find in the phenomenon of "speaking with tongues." Along with this go other abnormal manifestations, such as dancing, jumping, jerking, thrusting up the hands, falling on the floor and even passing into states of unconsciousness. . . .

My findings indicate that the reports on the growth of these sects are not without foundation. They have indeed been vigorously active. The largest of them, which is known as the "Assemblies of God," increased from 11,000 in 1916 to 48,000 in 1926 and 175,000 in 1937. The Pentecostal Assemblies of Jesus Christ, known commonly as the "Jesus Only" Church, is in its present form only four or five years old. It lists for 1935 more than 800 ordained ministers and evangelists. Its membership may be estimated at not less than 30,000. Three bodies which originated in Cleveland, Tennessee, and known respectively as the "Church of God," the "Original Church of God" and the "Tomlinson Church of God," have today an aggregate membership of about 80,000 as compared with 23,000 in 1926. Besides these there are a number of other organizations, some of which are new since 1926. In all cases these cults are recruited from among the underprivileged classes. They are distributed all over the country but appear to be strongest in Texas, California, Oklahoma, Arkansas, Missouri, Indiana, Ohio and Illinois. . . .

Although arising among the underprivileged and rooted in the social and economic injustices of our present-day civilization, the Pentecostal sects concern themselves not at all with the problem of social betterment. They are not seeking to save the world, but to save individuals out of a world which is getting worse and worse. They believe that the second coming of the Lord is near at hand and in their preaching they have much to say about the signs of the times. In any case salvation for them has to do chiefly with the life to come. Thus in the convention of the Church of God in Chattanooga nine of eleven hymns used in their evening service had an other-worldly theme. Among them were the following first lines: "That home of the soul over there," "When we cross the great divide," "Somebody's going to be left behind." At one point a little girl of seven sang, "I'll never feel at home in this world any more." An examination of their hymn-book showed that 75 of their 170 hymns related to the future life.

Doctrinally these groups are rigidly fundamentalistic. The Bible is for them the literally inspired Word of God. Jesus was God, born of a virgin, who died for our sins in order to free us from the wrath to come. Man himself is totally depraved. There is no health in him and no hope of salvation except through conversion and regeneration. . . .

It is important to recognize that the doctrine of holiness, which is common to all these groups, is primarily a matter of religious experience. These people are commonly austere in their piety. They forbid card-playing, dancing, theatre-going and the like, but they are not interested in virtue for its own sake. They are interested rather in that sense of fellowship with the Greater-than-self to which we give the name of mysticism. Their austerity is either just a means toward obtaining and keeping that experience or else an expression of their faith in the potency of the experience. With some it means, "You can't do this thing and that thing and have the Holy Spirit." With others it means, not sinlessness, but a permanent change of heart, a state of grace in which one is freed from the con-

sciousness of wilful transgression in orde to strive for the overcoming of his im perfections. . . .

Among those who belong to holy rolle cults and pass through such experience there are, as we might suppose, some wh become mentally disordered. I have dea with a number of these. For the most par however their experiences may be re garded as constructive. With all the ex cesses that characterize the holy rolle groups, we must give them credit for help ing many individuals to re-organize live that had been quite unsatisfactory and t make a better job of living. In any cas they are helping many of their people t carry on in the face of considerabl difficulties.

The explanation may be found in th social influences which are brought int play. In the case of mental illness we ar dealing with individuals who feel them selves isolated or estranged from thei fellows. In fact the sense of estrangemen due to the presence in the heart of tha which can neither be renounced no acknowledged for fear of condemnatio may be regarded as the basic evil in mos cases of functional mental illness. Menta illness thus furnishes evidence of th social nature of man. We cannot liv apart from our fellows and it is for u death to feel ourselves cut off from tha fellowship to which religious people giv the name of God and which exists for a of us whether we call ourselves religiou or not. Herein we may find the explana tion of the fear, the anxiety, and th destructive force of those experiences t which we give the name of mental di order. Mr. T. on the other hand was n thus isolated. His experience took plac within a social matrix. Not only was h supported by that inner forum which w call conscience but also by the approvin and rejoicing black people who made u the mission. More than that, the exper ence itself followed patterns which wer already established and valued by them.

This explanation will be far fro adequate unless we examine more closel what is involved in the view that man is social being and then go on to consid he significance of the experience of feeling oneself brought face to face with God. That is of course no light task. It may perhaps be sufficient for our purpose to say that the view which seems to me to throw the greatest light upon our problem is that advanced by George H. Mead. His view stated very briefly and incompletely is that the human personality is a social product and is made possible through the use of language. Where in the beehive or ant-hill the social organization is based upon physiological plasticity, the various individuals of the colony co-operating automatically because of the way they are built, the human being co-operates by internalizing the social organization within himself. He does this by learning to respond to symbols which call forth the same response in himself as they do in others. In this way he builds up within himself more or less consistent responses to certain common social symbols and the particular organization of social attitudes which he takes over is his character. The individual's system of values thus depends upon the group which he reflects or represents. They are in other words functions of his social relationships, particularly to those with whom he identifies himself.

A consequence of this view, which Mead himself did not develop, but which seems to me to follow inevitably, is that the idea of God is the symbol under which the group loyalty is commonly raised to the level of the universal and abiding. It stands for that in his social experience which the individual most admires and loves and to which he gives his allegiance and by which he judges himself. The sense of guilt thus becomes the social condemnation which the individual pronounces upon himself on the basis of what he knows of the attitudes of those who have helped to determine his idea of God.

To be brought face to face with God is then the experience of feeling oneself brought into that fellowship which is for the individual all-important. And inasmuch as the entire personality organization and its existing scale of values is a social product and the reflection of a particular social group, so to feel oneself identified with a superior fellowship means inevitably a new social reference. It means also a new conception of oneself and a thorough-going re-organization of values. The emotional impact of the mystical experience is thus a consequence of the social nature of man and of the practical significance of any change in social reference.

It is worth noting at this point that the tendency of a vital religious faith to bring about a thorough-going change of social attitudes is strikingly exemplified in Mr. T. and in his House of Prayer. Where the conventional negro churches in that city were much occupied with the problem of white superiority and were endeavoring to meet it by imitating the whites, the House of Prayer and other groups of its kind were so firmly convinced that they had found the fellowship supremely worth while, that other white persons besides Mr. T. were joining their circle. And white Pentecostal groups frequently welcome negroes. The new basis of fellowship which they had found gives them a new set of social values which transcend and disregard the lines of color and class.

It may now be clear why so much depends upon whether the experience is solitary or whether it is shared and whether God is thought of as approving or disapproving. In the case of the acutely disturbed mental patient God may be thought of as an avenging Judge. Frequently however he is thought of as suffering through the individual's failures and transgressions. It is in the latter case that we are apt to find the cosmic identification so characteristic of the acute disturbances. The idea of being God or Christ which so often appears is to be regarded as a reflection of the solitary character of the experience. In the case of Mr. T. there is the sense of approval rather than of condemnation. This together with the fact that he was one of an actual human fellowship enabled him to keep his mental structure intact.

This principle carries with it some important implications. In the many studies which have been made of the effects of the depression upon the mental health of our people there is rather general agreement that mental illness has not been greatly increased. The increased population in our mental hospitals seems due chiefly to other factors, such as the greater difficulty in hard times of supporting the unproductive members of the family and the greater difficulty in finding work for hospital patients who have improved and who in better times could go back to their jobs. In fact one well-known psychiatrist has even gone so far as to suggest that there are some whose mental difficulties are mitigated when hard times come. His explanation is that their suffering satisfies their need for punishment.

In the light of our findings we are ready to offer an additional explanation. The smallness of the amount of mental illness which can be directly attributed to the depression may be accounted for by the increase in neighborliness which characterizes such periods. Especially during the initial period most of the relief is said to have come from friends and neighbors. This means that the strain was being shared. It follows then that one result of the economic strain is to lessen the sense of isolation and to increase the sense of social solidarity and thus to induce a state of mind favorable to religious experience rather than to mental disorder. The fact that people suffer together through no particular fault of their own leads them, at least in many cases, to seek for some common solution, some common hope, and to find this in religious faith. Through their suffering they are, like the acutely disturbed mental patient, brought face to face with the ultimate issues of life and the great verities with which religion deals come alive. But because the strain is shared their mysticism is generally steadying and constructive.

The first and most obvious solution of this shared economic stress is to be found in the otherworldly emphasis which we have found to be characteristic of these cults. They look to the future life where the injustices of the present earthly existence shall be done away and sorrow shall be turned into joy.

But this hope carries with it certain consequences. The attention is focusse upon the idea of God, and God, accordin to the religion in which they have bee reared, is a God of love and of righteous ness. It becomes necessary to come t terms with this God. This means a attempt to face their frailties and weak nesses. The satisfaction of the need fo punishment which economic distres brings with it may be enough for some but for the group we are considering ope confession is the solution. The problem o sin and salvation is for all these group the central theme. On a recent visit to Pentecostal Church I heard the followin testimony given by a manly looking fellov in the early prime of life: "I know wha it means to be under sin. I know what means to have your conscience gnawing a your heart. I know what it means to b wretched and miserable. I know what means to be delivered and to have th burden lifted and your heart flooded wit joy and hope. I know what it means have God talk to you just as he talked the old prophets. I know you can be le of God and that he can guide you i every little bit of thing. Yes, my friend I can testify that God lives and work today just as much as ever he did." It wa easy to see that this man was speakin straight out of his heart to the hearts many who were present. They wer people who knew what struggle mean people who felt themselves beset wit dangers both within and without. Th message which this man gave in his test mony is the message of the Pentecost churches. They proclaim individual salv tion from sin. They deal with a proble which for multitudes of men and wome is still a matter of life and death.

In comparing themselves with the earl Christians these Pentecostal people a not without justification. They also wei an underprivileged group. Not only we they among the poor people of their tim but they belonged to a subject race. The were under the Roman yoke and they fe it keenly. It is to be recognized furthe more that the early Christians also wei in for emotional excesses. The Penteco tals may be right in believing that the wn "speaking with tongues" is similar to ie "glossolalia" described in the New estament. In both cases we are undoubt- lly dealing with ecstatic utterances hose significance lay in the fact that they eemed to come from an outside source. ut along with these emotional excesses, ie early Christians had insights that went r in advance of their time. They had so wise leadership which was able to rect their enthusiasm into ethical and ractical channels. And out of it came the eat Christian Church.

The history of the Christian Church, as ichard Neibuhr has pointed out, fur- shes many instances in which this proc- ss has been repeated. Little groups of ke-minded persons, nearly always of the ruggling, underprivileged classes, have me together on the basis of some new sion, some vivid sense of the presence of ie divine. Others have been drawn in on e basis of a shared experience. Then adually the voluntary society becomes a urch. The original believers are re- aced by their children and institutional- ation follows. The sacraments become eans of grace rather than symbols of nfession. The creeds become standards ' doctrine rather than confessions of ith. Even religious experience itself nds to become standardized in the form : patterns which have to be induced by sorts of meretricious devices. But in neral the process is one of leveling. The eat, prophetic, forward movements are veled down and conventionalized. The centric and regressive manifestations are veled up and become respectable.

The Pentecostal churches undoubtedly :long in the group of the eccentric and en of the regressive. Their fundamental sumption is highly dangerous. They be- ve that the divine manifests itself in the usual and that the prompting which ems to come from without is authorita- ve. Even though no personality disorgan- ation may result and even though there ay be no commitment to a mental hos- tal, that assumption is a false premise hich is likely to produce all sorts of fficulties in groups as well as in indi- duals.

The tendency to ascribe to a divine source the idea which flashes into the mind is as old as the human race and is not without some justification. Certainly new and creative ideas do come in just this way. So also do ideas that are value- less and ideas that are false and disturb- ing. The difficulty lies in the assumption that the process is the important thing. It is the same fallacy as that of the psychiatrist who gets concerned because his patient hears voices and disregards what the voices say. The old Christian mystics had to learn the lesson that some of the ideas which came darting into their minds could hardly come from God. They assumed that they must come from the devil. Some of us today may need to learn the opposite principle that not every hallucination is necessarily of the devil. In any case we are beginning to learn that the way an idea comes is determined by the way the mind works and that the origin of our ideas is to be found in our desires and wishes. The important ques- tion is therefore not *how* an idea comes but *what* it is. To ascribe an idea to the Holy Spirit is properly to express a judg- ment as to its value. If after grappling earnestly with some difficult and im- portant life problem, the solution comes to us in a sudden flash of insight, the religiously inclined may be justified in believing that it comes from God. To recognize the psychological process is not to pass judgment on the ultimate origin. The answer to that question will be de- termined by the individual philosophy of life with a consideration of value as the safest criterion.

But the Pentecostals go one step fur- ther. Their emphasis is so far removed from content and value that it relates to motor phenomena. To find themselves *doing* things they can't account for is for them the all-sufficient evidence of control by the Holy Spirit. More than that they resort to very questionable devices for inducing these phenomena.

We may also be struck by the fact that even though the Pentecostal sects arise among the underprivileged, their religion does not concern itself with improving the social and economic conditions. There is in their message nothing which goes to the heart of the problems of this sick and suffering world. They are content to let it get worse and worse. They have no social vision, no promise of social salvation except that which is to come miraculously when the Lord returns in glory.

One is also impressed with the diminutive size of the universe which their message depicts. It is only a little larger than that of the private world in which the psychotic lives. It has in it no room for all that we have been finding out about stars and atoms and plants and men. It is merely a tiny world into which they may withdraw and feel themselves secure. Such a religion may be a comfortable one for the older people. Like the delusional system of the paranoic it may give them stability. But it is not a satisfactory answer to the problems with which religion undertakes to deal. It is not conducive to the attitude of reverence nor to the attain-

ment of true perspective. And it is woe fully hard on their children.

And yet I see constructive element With all their regressive features, thes sects are none the less manifestations c nature's power to heal. They are th spontaneous attempts of the common pec ple to deal constructively with the stresse and trials which fall with peculiar severit upon them. Their unconcern with ece nomic and social conditions which the are powerless to change and their turnin to problems for which they are directl responsible is not entirely an unwhole some reaction. Certainly leaders of refor movements have reason to become a quainted with other types who seek attempt to reform the system an escap from the necessity of reforming then selves. In any case these "holy rollers" a bringing to many distressed individua release from the burden of guilt. They a giving them hope and courage an strength to keep going in the face of diff culties. . . .

Hadley Cantril incorporates into a more extensively developed theory of soci movements many principles similar to the foregoing statement by Boisen. H analysis of four movements is a major contribution to the theory of participatio orientations in social movements. His theory appears most clearly as he examin the Kingdom of Father Divine, a Negro cult centered in New York's Harlem an built on the conviction that a Negro known as Reverend Divine is God. Membe ship in the movement is attributed to three kinds of needs which are satisfied fc the participants. (1) Members are assured an *escape from material hardship* through the provision of "food, shelter, peace, security." Belief in miracle cure for physical ailments helps to substantiate the conviction that Father Divine world is the kingdom of heaven on earth in the present. (2) The movement pr vides *meaning—*

> an escape from a tortuous mental confusion caused by complex, conflicting circun stances. He gives meaning to the individual life and to the world. It is perha largely for this reason that one finds in the movement so many "joiners"—peop many of them whites, who have been Baptists, Holy Rollers, Christian Scientis and Theosophists before coming to Father. Their search for a solution to the mea ing of life leads them from one formula to another.*

(3) Finally, the movement *raises the members' status*. Father Divine speaks o against all discrimination, he encourages the self-respect of his followers ar builds the impression of membership in a huge and universally recognized mov ment.

* Hadley Cantril, **The Psychology of Social Movements** (New York: John Wiley & So Inc., 1941), p. 141. Reprinted by permission of John Wiley & Sons, Inc.

Cantril and Boisen employ the same concept of the *microcosm,* as the device through which these participation-gratifications are attained. The movement becomes a small world in itself, commanding the total allegiance of its members and providing a totality of values and gratifications requiring renunciation of the larger world outside. Father's microcosm and the world of reality are completely incompatible:

> One collapses when the other is entered. Compromise is impossible. Behind this fact lies the explanation of Father Divine's following. His children are people who want to escape the world of reality, where their needs are not satisfied, and enter into a new world, where they will have material and psychological comfort.*

While the Oxford Group, more commonly known in the postwar period as Moral Rearmament or "M. R. A.," contrasts as a white middle-class movement, it appears to rest on similar needs. Because of the status of its members, the search for meaning and the concern for future security assume greater relative importance than present deprivation. Whereas a depressed minority such as the Negroes may eschew active reform in favor of a personal status type of movement because of the evident unattainability of reform of the white man's society, the Oxford Group attracts people who fear that reform movements can only make their condition worse and deprive them more surely of their advantaged position which they already feel is threatened:

> Buchmanism [the Oxford Group] has gathered momentum, therefore, essentially because it shows certain bewildered people a way to interpret their personal troubles and the larger social problems of their world without endangering their status. It provides a psychological mechanism whereby they can escape the responsibility of dealing directly with conditions which they realize are not right and just. It attracts to itself people who want to improve these conditions without injuring their own positions and who want to avoid any alignment with existing institutions or ideologies which assume that individual problems cannot be solved without collective action.*

As our discussion has indicated, two aspects of an individual's status are of primary importance for *personal status* movements. Status implies, first, *prestige,* position on the vertical continuum from the least highly regarded to the most highly regarded persons in society. And status also relates the individual to the rest of society, providing a vantage point from which to interpret relevant events and conditions. Members of disadvantaged minorities may seek to escape from a well-defined status that carries both low prestige and an intolerable frame of reference for interpreting the world. Others are susceptible to such movements largely because they have *no* well-defined status, and can neither identify their position relative to others in the society nor determine a vantage point for interpreting events. *Personal status* movements are consequently likely to thrive in periods of social change in areas of acculturation.

The alteration of one's status in movements of this sort is frequently supported symbolically through giving up one's old name and adopting a new one. In the movement popularly called "Voodooism," among Negroes in Detroit and elsewhere, all members are given names that have an Arabian sound. In abundant

* Ibid., p. 137.
* Ibid., p. 184.

other ways the initiation rituals signify that the member is no longer the person he was before joining.

In the present world the acculturation of rural populations to patterns of urban industrial life is a source of much status-disorientation. John B. Holt attributes the rise of "holiness religion" in the southeast United States to this phenomenon. The Assemblies of God, Nazarenes, various Church of God groups, and Pentecostal and Holiness churches flourished in the decades between World Wars I and II among lower-level whites affected by urbanization. The destruction of old rural values and life-ways, the disruption of social ties, and isolation from durable personal ties constitute what Holt calls *culture shock*. This in turn leads to a vigorous religious revivalism, an extreme orthodoxy and rejection of liberal trend in the established churches.*

Improvement of personal status through re-evaluating the conventional value system shades into the cultivation of more satisfactory personal status within the existing scheme, the two frequently being combined in movements recruited from persons who do not have such irremovable determinants of low status as racial characteristics. Movements that promise their members the means to attain what everyone in the society wants generally offer a caricature of the culturally sanctioned means for achieving success. When material success and prestige are linked with religion, movements flourish that offer shortcuts to success through religion and in particular through somewhat less personally exacting forms of religion. When the relation of physical well-being to mental health and personal success is being stressed by legitimate medical authorities, food-faddism thrives in dozens of movements. As psychiatry has achieved respectability and public recognition, movements such as Dianetics promise success by way of techniques patterned after the popular conceptions of psychiatry.

Perhaps even more than in other types of movements, these latter attract thousands of individuals who spend their lives passing from one such movement to another. Typically these movements reach a peak of membership and enthusiasm quite early in their existence when they take on the attributes of a fad, and then gradually drop to a small loyal residue of members as the mass of adherents search for ways of winning quicker and more drastic indications that their lives have been transformed.

These movements are also probably more subject than any other type to exploitation for financial gain. If the founder himself does not see the opportunity for personal enhancement, such movements quickly attract numbers of persons who feel no compunction over fleecing the gullible. An important factor in the demise of many such movements has been the public exposure of corruption and exploitation of members through legal action or publicity. The general acceptance of conventional standards of value in such movements makes the charisma of their leaders more vulnerable to such attack than the charisma of leaders in movements which reject societal standards of success. The martyrdom of the leader in the latter type of movement may strengthen his hold over his followers while the immediate reassurances of loyalty in the former kind of movement are short-lived unless the leader is publicly exonerated.

Typical of these movements was the New Thought cult of the early 20th cen-

* John B. Holt, "Holiness Religion: Cultural Shock and Social Reorganization," American Sociological Review, 5 (1940), pp. 740–47.

tury. For the unpleasant, conventional route to success via hard work, it substituted success by "right thinking." But at the same time it drew its ideology out of the culturally sanctioned traditions of American society, wearing the dress of a religious movement and supporting the doctrine that economic success reflects personal moral worth. The more recent "Dianetics" movement drew upon the currently popular view that success reflects one's psychic adjustment. Through a set of procedures vulgarized from psychoanalysis, the member sought to become "clear," and thus able to deal with life's problems more masterfully.

Limited personal movements. These movements, which provide a substitute or fantasy status for the individual or offer him means to alter his major status in society, are more dramatic but touch directly the lives of fewer people than the many movements that afford more modest escapes or supplements to daily life. Movements of this latter sort shade off into the myriad of voluntary associations which people establish for recreational purposes and which cannot genuinely be referred to as movements.

Limited personal movements, however, spring up about the persistent points of strain induced by the mores and the status structure of a society and respond to any shift in prestige and role of a major status group in the society. Many such movements, for example, are one-sex groups, jealously guarding their privacy and limited prerogatives from invasion by the opposite sex. Probably an important fund of "joiners" for these limited movements is provided by those classes, such as the minor white-collar workers today, who feel themselves losing out in the historical rearrangements of status.

A certain amount of exclusiveness and of mystery are requisites if a movement is to provide a supplementary prestige or some respite from the restraints of ordinary customs. The power of movements such as the lodges that proliferated in the United States during the last century to boost the member's prestige would be nil if each lodge were merely a voluntary grouping of men assembling to engage in amusing rituals. Through elaborate induction ceremonies and ritual requirements for membership the composition is made to appear more exclusive than it really is. Through secrecy and the use of symbolism the rituals of the movement are made to appear more profound than they would otherwise be. In this context, elaborate uniforms and insignia that would otherwise seem ridiculous contribute to the total significance of participation.

The status-enhancing aspects of these movements depend ultimately on the prestige accorded them by outsiders. Membership in a movement like that of Father Divine or any esoteric religious cult may lessen a person's prestige in the larger society, which in turn may drive the participants even more strongly into the folds of the movement. But unlike members of the latter movements, adherents of the *limited personal* movements seek only to supplement rather than to reject conventional valuations. Accordingly, the procedures of these movements must be consonant with conventional values.

During the current century the secret lodges of the 19th century seem to have lost their effectiveness and have declined or been transformed into mere voluntary service and recreational organizations. This decline probably reflects the secularization and disenchantment of mass attitudes and the sophistication which now dubs such activities as childish. Perhaps the emerging movements of the 20th century consist more of revelous and hedonistic behavior, somewhat refined from its first flourish in the myriad of small movements identified with the "roaring twenties." The movements, ranging from "party behavior" with its discrete but limited deviations from the strict sexual mores to the various "free love" groups described by Willard Waller as prevalent escapes from the frustrations of the marriage mores, are the more characteristic personal movements of a secular era. Widespread, open ambivalence toward conventions and mores permits sufficient mass envy of those who are able to defy the mores on occasion to give such groups a prestige-conferring function.

The exclusiveness that all movements of this type require constitutes a problem for the group. A movement that is too exclusive remains unknown, insignificant, and, unless recruited from an established elite, without prestige. Some proselyting is therefore essential. More prestige can be gained from a larger movement because of the very recognition and size of the organization. At the same time, however, the typical member's position in the movement becomes less significant and membership differentiates him from fewer people. This dilemma of exclusiveness versus proselyting induces crises in many of these movements. Such crises should be a valuable focal point for research on the internal dynamics of movements.

One of the pioneers of sociological theory, Georg Simmel, devoted some attention to secrecy as an aspect of established social orders and to secret societies as world-wide phenomena. From his extended discussion we have excerpted several of his important insights concerning secret societies. The excerpts, however, overlap the boundaries of this chapter in at least two important respects. First, Simmel treats institutionalized, secret orders as well as secret movements. Hence, his analysis crosscuts the fields of collective behavior and institutional behavior. Second, many of the secret societies that he discusses are revolutionary movements rather than participation-oriented movements, and hence his observations fit more appropriately in the subsequent treatment of movements forced into power tactics because of their revolutionary character.

THE SOCIOLOGY OF SECRET SOCIETIES

Georg Simmel

. . . Every [secret society] contains a measure of freedom, which is not really provided for in the structure of the surrounding society. Whether the secret society, like the *Vehme,* complements the inadequate judicature of the political area; or whether, as in the case of conspiracies or criminal bands, it is an uprising against the law of that area; or whether, as in the case of the "mysteries," they hold themselves outside of the commands and prohibitions of the greater area—in either case the apartness which characterizes the secret society has the tone of a freedom.

In exercise of this freedom a territory is occupied to which the norms of the surrounding society do not apply.

The nature of the secret society as such is autonomy. It is, however, of a sort which approaches anarchy. Withdrawal from the bonds of unity which procure general coherence very easily has as consequences for the secret society a condition of being without roots, an absence of firm touch with life, and of restraining reservations. The fixedness and detail of the ritual serve in part to counterbalance this deficit.

Here also is manifest how much men need a settled proportion between freedom and law; and, furthermore, in case the relative quantities of the two are not

Reprinted in part by permission of the University of Chicago Press, from **The American Journal of Sociology,** 11 (1906), pp. 441–98.

prescribed for him from a single source, now he attempts to reinforce the given quantum of the one by a quantum of the other derived from any source whatsoever, until such settled proportion is reached. With the ritual the secret society voluntarily imposes upon itself a formal constraint, which is demanded as a complement by its material detachment and self-sufficiency. It is characteristic that, among the Freemasons, it is precisely the Americans—who enjoy the largest political freedom—of whom the severest unity in manner of work, the greatest uniformity of the ritual of all lodges, are demanded; while in Germany—where the otherwise sufficient quantum of bondage leaves little room for a counterdemand in the direction of restrictions upon freedom—more freedom is exercised in the manner in which each individual lodge carries on its work. The often essentially meaningless, schematic constraint of the ritual of the secret society is therefore by no means a contradiction of its freedom bordering on anarchy, its detachment from the norms of the circle which contains it. Just as widespread existence of secret societies is as a rule, a proof of public unfreedom, of a policy of police regulation, of police oppression; so, conversely, ritual regulation of these societies from within proves a freedom and enfranchisement in principle for which the equilibrium of human nature produces the constraint as a counter-influence. . . .

. . . The secret society sets itself as a special society in antithesis with the wider association included within the greater society. This antithesis, whatever its purpose, is at all events intended in the spirit of exclusion. Even the secret society which proposes only to render the whole community a definite service in a completely unselfish spirit, and to dissolve itself after performing the service, obviously regards its temporary detachment from that totality as the unavoidable technique for its purpose. Accordingly, none of the narrower groups which are circumscribed by larger groups are compelled by their sociological constellation to insist so strongly as the secret society upon their formal self-sufficiency. Their

secret encircles them like a boundary, beyond which there is nothing but the materially, or at least formally, antithetic, which therefore shuts up the society within itself as a complete unity.

In the groupings of every other sort, the *content* of the group-life, the actions of the members in the sphere of rights and duties, may so fill up their consciousness that within it the formal fact of socialization under normal conditions plays scarcely any role. The secret society, on the other hand, can on no account permit the definite and emphatic consciousness of its members that they constitute a society to escape from their minds. The always perceptible and always to-be-guarded pathos of the secret lends to the form of union which depends upon the secret, as contrasted with the content, a predominant significance, as compared with other unions.

In the secret society there is complete absence of organic growth, of the character of instinct in accumulation, of all unforced matter of course with respect to belonging together and forming a unity. No matter how irrational, mystical, impressionistic their contents, the way in which they are constructed is always conscious and intentional. Throughout their derivation and life *consciousness of being a society* is permanently accentuated. The secret society is, on that account, the antithesis of all genetic societies, in which the unification is more or less only the expression of the natural growing together of elements whose life has common roots. Its socio-psychological form is invariably that of the teleological combination. This constellation makes it easy to understand that the specifications of form in the construction of secret societies attain to peculiar definiteness, and that their essential sociological traits develop as mere quantitative heightenings of quite general types of relationship.

One of these latter has already been indicated; viz., the characterization and the coherence of the society through closure toward the social environment. To this end the often complicated signs of recognition contribute. Through these the individual offers credentials of membership in the society. Indeed, in the times previous to the general use of writing, such signs were more imperative for this use than later. At present their other sociological uses overtop that of mere identification. . . .

. . . There is separation from others because there is unwillingness to give oneself a character common with that of others, because there is desire to signalize one's own superiority as compared with these others. Everywhere this motive leads to the formation of groups which are obviously in sharp contrast with those formed in pursuit of material purposes. As a consequence of the fact that those who want to distinguish themselves enter into combination, there results an aristocracy which strengthens and, so to speak, expands the self-consciousness of the individuals through the weight of their sum.

That exclusiveness and formation of groups are thus bound together by the aristocracy-building motive gives to the former in many cases from the outset the stamp of the "special" in the sense of value. We may observe, even in school classes, how small, closely attached groups of comrades, through the mere formal fact that they form a special group, come to consider themselves an elite, compared with the rest who are unorganized: while the latter, by their enmity and jealousy, involuntarily recognize that higher value. In these cases secrecy and pretense of secrecy are means of building higher the wall of separation, and therein a reinforcement of the aristocratic nature of the group. . . .

The bar against all external to the circle, which, as universal sociological form-fact, makes use of secrecy as a progressive technique, gains a peculiar coloring through the multiplicity of degrees, through which initiation into the last mysteries of secret societies is wont to occur, and which throw light upon another sociological trait of secret societies. As a rule, a solemn pledge is demanded of the novice that he will hold secret everything which he is about to experience, before even the first stages of acceptance into the society occur. There-

with is the absolute and formal separation which secrecy can effect, put into force. Yet, since under these conditions the essential content or purpose of the order is only gradually accessible to the neophyte—whether the purpose is the complete purification and salvation of the soul through the consecration of the mysteries, or whether it is the absolute abolition of all moral restraint, as with the *Assassins* and other criminal societies—the separation in material respects is otherwise ordered; i.e., it is made more continuous and more relative.

When this method is employed, the initiate is in a condition nearer to that of the outsider. He needs to be tested and educated up to the point of grasping the whole or the center of the association. Thereby, however, a protection is obviously afforded to the latter, an isolation of it from the external world, which goes beyond the protection gained from the entrance oath. Care is taken . . . that the still untried shall also have very little to betray if he would, inasmuch as, within the secret principle which surrounds the society as a whole, graduated secrecy produces at the same time an elastic zone of defense for that which is inmost and essential. . . .

In spite of the actual quantitative delimitation of every real society there is still a considerable number the inner tendency of which is: Whoever is not excluded is included. Within certain political, religious, and class peripheries, everyone is reckoned as of the association who satisfies certain conditions, mostly involuntary, and given along with his existence. Whoever, for example, is born within the territory of a state, unless peculiar circumstances make him an exception, is a member of the highly complex civic society. The member of a given social class is, as a matter of course, included in the conventions and forms of attachment pertaining to the same, if he does not voluntarily or involuntarily make himself an outsider. The extreme is offered by the claim of a church that it really comprehends the totality of the human race, so that only historical accidents, sinful obduracy, or a special divine purpose excludes any persons from the religious community which ideally anticipates even those not in fact within the pale.

Here is, accordingly, a parting of two ways, which evidently signifiy a differentiation in principle of the sociological meaning of societies in general, however they may be confused, and their definiteness toned down in practice. In contrast with the fundamental principle: Whoso is not expressly excluded is included, stands the other: Whoever is not expressly included is excluded. The latter type is presented in the most decisive purity by the secret societies. The unlimited character of their separation, conscious at every step of their development, has, both as cause and as effect, the rule that whoever is not expressly adopted is thereby expressly excluded. The Masonic fraternity could not better support its recently much emphasized assertion that it is not properly a secret order, than through its simultaneously published ideal of including all men, and thus of representing humanity as a whole.

Corresponding with intensification of separateness from the outer world, there is here, as elsewhere, a similar access of coherence within, since these are only the two sides or forms of manifestation of one and the same sociological attitude. A purpose which stimulates formation of a secret union among men as a rule peremptorily excludes such a preponderating portion of the general social environment from participation that the possible and actual participants acquire a scarcity value. These must be handled carefully, because, *ceteris paribus,* it is much more difficult to replace them than is the case in an ordinary society. More than that, every quarrel within the secret society brings with it the danger of betrayal, to avoid which in this case the motive of self-preservation in the individual is likely to co-operate with the motive of the self-preservation of the whole. Finally, with the defection of the secret societies from the environing social syntheses, many occasions of conflict disappear.

Among all the limitations of the in-dividual, those that come from association in secret societies always occupy an exceptional status, in contrast with which the open limitations, domestic and civic, religious and economic, those of class and of friendship, however manifold their content, still have a quite different measure and manner of efficiency. It requires the comparison with secret societies to make clear that the demands of open societies, lying so to speak in one plane, run across each other. As they carry on at the same time an open competitive struggle over the strength and the interest of the individual, within a single one of these spheres, the individuals come into sharp collision, because each of them is at the same time solicited by the interests of other spheres. In secret societies, in view of their sociological isolation, such collisions are very much restricted. The purposes and programs of secret societies require that competitive interests from that plane of the open society should be left outside the door. Since the secret society occupies a plane of its own—few individuals belonging to more than one secret society—it exercises a kind of absolute sovereignty over its members. This control prevents conflicts among them which easily arise in the open type of co-ordination. . . .

Corresponding with the peculiar degree of cohesion within secret societies is the definiteness of their centralization. They furnish examples of an unlimited and blind obedience to leaders, such as occurs elsewhere of course; but it is the more remarkable here, in view of the frequent anarchical and negative character toward all other law. . . .

The sociological character of the individual elements of the secret society, corresponding with this centralized subordination is their individualization. In case the society does not have promotion of the interests of its individual members as its immediate purpose, and, so to speak, does not go outside of itself, but rather uses its members as means to externally located ends and activities—in such case the secret society in turn manifests a heightened degree of self-abnegation, of leveling of individuality, which is already an incident of the social state in general, and with which the secret *society* outweighs the above-emphasized individualizing and differentiating character of the *secrecy*. This begins with the secret orders of the nature peoples, whose appearance and activities are almost always in connection with use of disguises, so that an expert immediately infers that wherever we find the use of disguises among nature peoples, they at least indicate a probability of the existence of secret orders. It is, to be sure, a part of the essence of the secret order that its members conceal themselves, as such. Yet, inasmuch as the given man stands forth and conducts himself quite unequivocally as a member of the secret order, and merely does not disclose which otherwise known individuality is identical with this member, the disappearance of the personality, as such, behind his role in the secret society is most strongly emphasized. In the Irish conspiracy which was organized in America in the seventies under the name Clannagael, the individual members were not designated by their names, but only by numbers. This, of course, was with a view to the practical purpose of secrecy. Nevertheless, it shows to what extent secrecy suppresses individuality.

Among persons who figure only as numbers, who perhaps—as occurs at least in analogous cases—are scarcely known to the other members by their personal names, leadership will proceed with much less consideration, with much more indifference to individual wishes and capacities, than if the union includes each of its members as a personal being. Not less effective in this respect are the extensive role and the severity of the ritual. All of this always signifies that the object mold has become master over the personal in membership and in activity. The hierarchical order admits the individual merely as agent of a definite role; it likewise holds in readiness for each participant a conventional garb, in which his personal contour disappears.

It is merely another name for this effacement of the differentiated personality, when secret societies cultivate a high degree of relative equality among the members. This is so far from being in contradiction of the despotic character of their constitutions that in all sorts of other groupings despotism finds its correlate in the leveling of the ruled. Within the secret society there often exists between the members a fraternal equality which is in sharp and purposeful contrast with their differences in all the other situations of their lives. Typical cases in point appear, on the one hand, in secret societies of a religio-ethical character, which strongly accentuate the element of brotherhood; on the other hand, in societies of an illegal nature. Bismarck speaks in his memoirs of a widely ramified pederastic organization in Berlin, which came under his observation as a young judicial officer; and he emphasizes "the equalizing effect of co-operative practice of the forbidden vice through all social strata."

This depersonalizing, in which the secret society carries to an excessive degree a typical relationship between individual and society, appears finally as the characteristic *irresponsibility*. In this connection, too, physical disguise is the primitive phenomenon. Most of the African secret orders are alike in representing themselves by a man disguised as a forest spirit. He commits at will upon whomsoever he encounters any sort of violence, even to robbery and murder. No responsibility attaches to him for his outrages, and evidently this is due solely to the disguise. That is the somewhat unmanageable form under which such societies cause the personality of their adherents to disappear, and without which the latter would undoubtedly be overtaken by revenge and punishment.

Nevertheless, responsibility is quite as immediately joined with the ego—philosophically, too the whole responsibility problem is merely a detail of the problem of the ego—in the fact that removing the marks of identity of the person has, for the naive understanding in question, the effect of abolishing responsibility. Political finesse makes no less use of this correlation. In the American House of Representatives the real conclusions are reached in the standing committees, and they are almost always ratified by the

House. The transactions of these committees, however, are secret, and the most important portion of legislative activity is thus concealed from public view. This being the case, the political responsibility of the representatives seems to be largely wiped out, since no one can be made responsible for proceedings that cannot be observed. Since the shares of the individual persons in the transactions remain hidden, the acts of committees and of the House seem to be those of a super-individual authority. The irresponsibility is here also the consequence or the symbol of the same intensified sociological de-individualization which goes with the secrecy of group-action. In all directorates, faculties, committees, boards of trustees, etc., whose transactions are secret, the same thing holds. The individual disappears as a person in the anonymous member of the ring, so to speak, and with him the responsibility, which has no hold upon him in his intangible special character.

Finally, this one-sided intensification of universal sociological traits is corroborated by the danger with which the great surrounding circle rightly or wrongly believes itself to be threatened from the secret society. Wherever there is an attempt to realize strong centralization, especially of a political type, special organizations of the elements are abhorred, purely as such, entirely apart from their content and purposes. As mere unities, so to speak, they engage in competition with the central principle. The central power wants to reserve to itself the prerogative of binding the elements together in a form of common unity. . . . This danger from the special organization for the surrounding whole appears at a high potency in the case of the secret society. Men seldom have a calm and rational attitude toward strangers or persons only partially known. The folly which treats the unknown as the non-existent, and the anxious imaginativeness which inflates the unknown at once into gigantic dangers and horrors, are wont to take turns in guiding human actions. Accordingly, the secret society seems to be dangerous simply because it is secret. Since it cannot be surely known that any special organization whatever may not some day turn its legally accumulated powers to some undesired end, and since on that account there is suspicion in principle on the part of central powers toward organizations of subjects, it follows that, in the case of organizations which are secret in principle, the suspicion that their secrecy conceals dangers is all the more natural. . . .

Marginal types of movements. Of those movements which are marginal to the true participation-oriented category, two kinds require special mention. First of these is the ostensibly value-oriented movement whose objectives are so remote as to seem improbable of achievement. A person who is devoted to fostering a particular value in society is likely to back movements that show promise of tangible accomplishments within the fairly immediate future. But mixed with the reform interest there is often a concern with validating the self-conception that one is right in a world that is wrong or that one is good in a world that is evil. To the degree to which membership in any value-oriented movement strengthens such self-conceptions, it is immaterial that the movement should achieve any tangible successes. Indeed it may even be better that the group remain small and exclusive so that its failure to win notable success will highlight more sharply the contrast between the adherents and the rest of society.

Movements of this sort have been largely neglected as subjects for research, so it is only possible to speculate concerning the particular movements that have this character. It appears likely that those of calendar reform and some of the small international language movements must have some of this element to maintain them.

The other marginal type of movement is the proselyting individual reform movement. Movements which not only seek to reform the character of their adherents but have an active program of proselyting in order to make a better society are more than mere participation-oriented movements. To the degree to which a movement, such as some of the pacifist movements, eschew any tactics other than to "pacify the hearts" of individuals, many of the principles governing the relation of tactics to ideology and the relation of the movement to its public will not be applicable. On the other hand, the criterion of substantial success in effecting a societal change will govern the enthusiasm of its adherents. Thus the Oxford Group, by concentrating its program on preventing war through the moral reform of individuals, suffered a temporary setback when World War II reached full scale.

Chapter 19

Participation-orientations

THE ABSENCE of a fixed line between those movements which are directed by a concern for reform and those which are shaped by the rewards of membership itself is well illustrated in the transitions that take place from one to the other. Movements that later became actively reformist have sometimes begun as limited personal types. The first labor unions, for example, were principally fraternal bodies for the care of their members. The Farmers' Alliance, which later developed a vigorous political program, was originally created for "catching horse thieves, rounding up estrays, and purchasing supplies." It is quite possible that any homogeneous group, meeting repeatedly for whatever purpose, might develop a concern for the members' common interests and grievances, which might lead to a reform program.

In some movements the concern over reform is carried by but a small segment of the membership, while the large membership is moderately indifferent to value orientations. But when the activist core depend primarily on pressure tactics to gain their desired reforms, such a docile but dependable membership may be an advantage to them. The fact that they speak as representatives of such a large group enables them to wring concessions from public officers and officials of private organizations, without having to subject their proposals to serious examination within the movement. Hence a movement whose impact on society is that of a value-oriented movement may be actually a small reform movement saddled onto and making use of a large participation-oriented movement.

Even to the most devoted adherents of movement ideology for its own sake, the fact of being a member, the type of role available, and the kind of people with whom one associates as a member all have their influence on the quality of participation. Thus participation-orientations have to do not only with a special class of members who help to round out any movement but also with a facet of each member's contribution to the movement.

Participation proneness. Writers in this field generally take for granted that

431

some kinds of people are more easily recruited to social movements of any kind than are others. However, designations of "participation prone" types are often deficient in several respects. Most analyses of membership types are designed to discredit certain kinds of movements by "proving" that only neurotics, incompetents, and the unscrupulous constitute the bulk of their members. Thus the investigator's biases make his findings inevitable. Analyses also frequently begin with some preconceived theory of personality which is then used to "explain" the social movements, rather than with the circumstances in which a movement operates. Furthermore, statements are usually based upon a few types of movement, and it is seldom clear how extensively they may be generalized. Finally, the same error frequently creeps in as we noted in discussing the crowd. Superficially apparent homogeneity of membership may actually conceal a variety of types of persons who interact to make the movement work.

Two aspects of any movement's relation with its social milieu operate selectively to make certain people more likely than others to become adherents. First is the competition between the activities of the movement and the many conventional activities available to potential members. To become an *adherent*—active in the movement rather than merely a member of a public discussing issues favorable to the movement or a sympathetic member of the mass—the individual chooses activity in the movement *in preference* to other possible activities. Thus the gratifications of movement participation must outweigh the gratifications available to the individual from more conventional activities. Second, each adherent must adjust himself to whatever reaction his associates may have to membership in the movement. In this connection the classification of movements according to respectability is important. Many movements will accordingly draw their recruits disproportionately from those who are least disturbed by such unfavorable evaluations.

The recruits who will choose participation in movements in preference to other activities and who will not be deterred by outsiders' reactions to their membership will be found in some kinds of social roles more than in others. Generally speaking, full integration into family, neighborhood, community, and special interest groups means the acceptance of obligations and the habituation to certain gratifications that will be deterrents to more than passive acquiescence in any new movement. The same extensive ties are a serious obstacle to the acceptance of ridicule or condemnation associated with movements that are not entirely acceptable. A relatively strong attraction to the movement is required to overcome these obstacles. Similarly, participation in a social movement is more likely to provide the personal gratifications of group membership otherwise lacking in the lives of those who are relatively isolated. Kurt Reizler, for example, regards "outcasts" as a major element in the success of contemporary revolutionary movements.

Finally, a frustrating role is important here as in other kinds of collective behavior. Frustration may lead to devaluation of conventional demands and provide the more intense motivation necessary to overcome ordinary obstacles to movement membership. However, frustration by itself is never a guarantee of receptivity to movements. Long-continued frustration characteristically leads to hopelessness which mitigates against participation in the promotion of any reform. Frustration from *recent* losses or the experience of *improving* conditions is more likely to make receptive individuals than long-continued frustration.

There is undoubtedly a basis for participation-proneness beyond simply the role in which a person finds himself. There are probably some personality types that are especially receptive to the appeals of membership in movements, irrespective of their particular values. Thelma McCormack has prepared a cautious review of empirical studies dealing with personality characteristics of radicals. The studies she reports do not deal with known adherents to such movements, but with people who endorse statements found in the ideologies of such movements, and must therefore be interpreted with care. To what degree the techniques reveal adherence to particular values and to what degree merely the willingness to be identified with unconventional groups cannot be determined from the reports. Only to the extent that the evidence deals with the latter can we conclude that her generalizations apply to participation-orientations in particular. There are, however, plausible bases for supposing that willingness to be identified with unconventional groups accounts for the so-called "radical" attitudes as much as does the endorsement of a particular set of values for the larger society.

THE MOTIVATION OF RADICALS

THELMA HERMAN MCCORMACK

I

The analysis of social movements and social change presupposes three categories of data: (1) on the institutional structure or historical period (including events which may act as an impetus) in which the desire for change develops; (2) on the structure and development of social movements for change as well as those opposing it; and (3) on the motivation of those who participate in such movements.

Of these three general categories, the third is the most neglected. Often it is treated as a literary embellishment of the analysis of the first two categories. When it is considered seriously, it is usually done within an outmoded theoretical framework which fails to take cognizance of recent developments in the theory of motivation. It is perhaps an evidence of our democratic faith that we tend to think of the wish for change and social improvement as phenomena which require little explanation. Yet it must be acknowledged that for practical, political, and

Reprinted by permission of the University of Chicago Press, from the **American Journal of Sociology,** 56 (July, 1950), pp. 17–24.

theoretical reasons we cannot take for granted the personality traits of those who devote themselves to reform; nor can we of those who would obstruct it.

We shall consider here studies of the motivation of radicals, persons who advocate institutional change and who would presumably participate in a movement designed to bring it about. Institutional change in this instance will refer to economic reform, because most of the literature is concerned with economic change.

II

American studies of the radical were done for the most part during the 1920's and 1930's.[1] Possibly the general intellectual ferment of the twenties stimulated scientific interest in the problem, and the interest was sustained for practical reasons by the depression of the thirties, after

[1] The definition of "radical" varies from study to study. Usually, the procedure was to give the subjects an opinion questionnaire and to regard one statistical extreme as "radical." In one study this meant those who believed in a graduated income tax; in another, those who believed in complete socialization. Another method, less frequently used, has been to start from self-declaration, subjects being chosen from among the members of radical organizations.

which it declined. It might have persisted but for the war. In any case, it is clear that professional interest in the personality of the radical has declined noticeably in the past decade.

One inevitable and unfortunate consequence of the fact that these studies were done so long ago is that they lack the methodological finesse we have grown to expect in studies of attitudes. Projective techniques, for example, are not used. Often the phrasing of questions is clumsy and naïve. Were such research being done today, it would unquestionably reveal far more about the problem than these earlier studies do.

A second general characteristic is the emphasis on the ideational aspects of the radical's behavior. As attitude studies, they treat the ideology of the radical but do not explore the psychological implications of the more complete political role. For material on the nonverbal routines involved in carrying out the functions of a radical political party, it is necessary to turn to literary sources such as autobiographies, biographies, journalistic accounts, etc.

Finally, the hypothesis that left-wing political attitudes develop in response to economic dislocation—the traditional Marxian approach—is almost entirely disregarded in these studies. In most of them variables, such as income, occupation, and class position, are held constant. Contrary to expectation, the subjects were not usually low-income groups, the "proletariat," but middle- and upper-class college students. If anyone's thinking can be said to have influenced the theoretical orientation of these studies, it is Freud rather than Marx.[2]

[2] In order to find material bearing on the Marxian theory, it is necessary to turn either to European studies or, in the case of American research, to studies of unemployment, that is, studies which specifically investigate the effects of changing economic conditions. An example of the former is Henry De Man, **The Psychology of Socialism**, trans. Eden and Cedar Paul (London: George Allen & Unwin, Ltd., 1928). An example of an American sociological study is E. Wight Bakke, **Citizens without Work** (New Haven: Yale University Press, 1940).

III

1. *The pattern of radicalism.*—For theoretical reasons the first problem to be solved in a psychology of radicalism was whether or not economic liberalism was a generalized attitude, extending to other issues as well as the economic one. If it was generalized and consistent with other attitudes held by the individual, it would then be possible to speak of a personality *pattern*. And researchers would be justified in searching for deeper underlying motives as the key to the individual's behavior.

Gordon Allport in a study of a group of Dartmouth students found evidence of such consistency.[3] In a study done one month prior to the presidential election of 1928, he classified attitudes according to the student's voting intention: Hoover, Smith, or Thomas. Within each group he found that those who were radical on political issues tended to be radical on other social issues as well. The same was true of the conservatives.

In a study of Yale and Dartmouth undergraduates, Moore found what he called "radical" and "conservative" temperaments.[4] Radicals showed greater readiness to break old habits in a mirror drawing test. In a neuromuscular test their reactions were quicker. A card-sorting test indicated that they were more willing to sacrifice accuracy for speed, suggesting a greater willingness to make snap judgments. And on a verbal free association test, the radicals proved slightly more original. Of all these differences, the one which seemed to Moore to stand out most sharply was the radical's "independence in the face of majority influence." Moore concludes: "Despite the enormous preponderance that environment and education may have in determining the particular radicalism of any particular individual, I submit that these environmental differences may be underlaid in very signifi-

[3] Gordon W. Allport, "The Composition of Political Attitudes," **American Journal of Sociology**, XXXV (1929), 220–38.
[4] Henry T. Moore, "Innate Factors in Radicalism and Conservatism," **Journal of Abnormal Psychology**, XX (1925), 234–44.

cant ways by innate differences in type of neuro-muscular machinery." [5]

Generally speaking, Allport's or Moore's findings have been accepted. As noted above, they are a necessary theoretical premise for developing the concept of the radical personality. Evidence of this may be seen in Flugel's recent attempt to develop the psychoanalytic basis for political types in which he quite logically cites the American findings as his point of departure.[6] There is support from clinical work and studies of other attitudes for the notion that attitudes cluster, revealing a common thematic pattern.

There is some evidence, however, from other sources which suggests that political attitudes are less consistent than is usually assumed. Reed found that only 30 per cent in a group of two hundred and fifty-five, which included members of trade-unions and students at labor colleges, were consistent in their attitudes on international, religious, governmental, sex, economic, and race issues.[7] Extreme radicals, he found, however, were more consistent than the conservatives.

When the Moore study was repeated at Vassar College, the results did not confirm Moore's.[8] And, third, historical material often suggests that consistency may be the exception. For example, examining the biographies of Labour MP's, it is typical to find a firm believer in the socialist program who is at the same time the model of bourgeois respectability. Far from being bohemians, they are Sunday-school teachers, teetotalers, and so on, as well as socialists.[9]

Age, education, and class position may account for the discrepancy between the studies of Allport and Moore, on one hand, and Reed's, on the other, although these variables would not explain the Vassar results. In the former studies, the subjects were middle-class college men who often have, for whatever psychological reasons, a need to develop a "philosophy of life" that is both rigid and consistent. With greater maturity, this uncompromising attitude may yield to flexibility and a greater segmentalization of attitudes. It is possible, too, that the type of radicalism which develops in the middle class is different in this respect from the type that develops in low-income groups. These are hypotheses which require further exploration. It is sufficient here to point out the possible error in holding such variables as income constant. Stratefied samples would present a somewhat different picture.

2. *Radicalism as a form of extremism.* —Having once established or accepted a priori the concept of a radical personality, researchers were then able to pursue the radical's motivation in more detail. In one group of studies radicalism is regarded as an example of deviant or extremist behavior, not unlike the extremism at the end of a political continuum. These studies are distinguished by their emphasis on the form of the attitude rather than the content.

D. A. Hartman and Floyd Allport, studying student opinion at Syracuse University, concluded that there were more similarities between the "reactionaries" and the "radicals" than there were between either of these two groups and the "middle-of-the-roaders." [10] Both radicals and reactionaries had greater difficulty than the middle group in accepting established conventions, and both felt less bound by them. Both were more willing to deviate from views held by their parents. And both were more reluctant to answer questions on their attitude toward sex.

Interpreting their findings, the investi-

---

[5] Ibid., p. 244.

[6] J. C. Flugel, **Man, Morals and Society** (London: Duckworth, 1945), pp. 281-301.

[7] Ellery F. Reed, "Does the Individual Tend To Be Consistently a Progressive or a Conservative," **Social Forces,** VI (1927), 49-52.

[8] M. F. Washburn, H. Kepler, N. McBroom, W. Pritchard, and I. Reimer, "The Moore Tests of Radical and Conservative Temperament," **American Journal of Psychology,** XXXVIII (1927), 449-52.

[9] **The Herald Book of Labour Members,** ed. S. V. Bracher (London: Labour Publishing Co., Ltd., 1923).

[10] Floyd H. Allport and D. A. Hartman, "Measurement and Motivation of Atypical Opinion in a Certain Group," **American Political Science Review,** XIX (1925), 735-60.

gators start out with what appears to be a bias in favor of the middle position: "In any issue upon which the mass of people divide into opposing camps, there is some truth upon each side, otherwise so many 'reasonable people' would not be converted to one side or the other. The full truth, therefore, probably lies somewhere between the two extremes." [11]

Assuming that the golden mean is the "reasonable" attitude, it then follows that the extremes are motivated by nonrational factors. "It is suggested that the atypical extremists are actuated in their thinking by partially repressed emotional drives, and that they develop a method for concealing from themselves and others the fact that their opinion is determined rather by wishes than the process of reason." [12]

They do not indicate what these wishes or "partially repressed emotional drives" are. In so far as they account for the apparent differences between radicals and reactionaries, it is along the lines of Jungian psychology, the radical being more inclined toward the introvert, the reactionary toward the extravert. But they regard this difference as secondary: "If extraversion and introversion are simply different ways in which people resolve their mental conflicts, does it follow that the common basis we have found for reactionary and radical is really the existence of conflicts underlying the thinking of each?"

In Rinaldo's *Psychoanalysis of the Reformer* the reformer is defined as anyone who does not accept society as it is— without distinguishing, for example, between the socialist and the militant prohibitionist.[13] According to Rinaldo, the drive to reform society, whatever its social direction, is a frustrated sexual need producing hysteria in the individual, which latter is expressed in the drive to reform society. The adjusted person is the one who accepts the prevailing institutions. Lasswell similarly dismisses the ideologi-

cal differences between attitudes, studying instead the manner in which the attitude is expressed.[14] He compares the "agitator" with the "administrator" rather than the "socialist" with the "conservative."

Two things are significant in these studies. The first is that, in the search for underlying or basic motivation, the differences between right and left are obscured. For purposes of studying social change and the motivation of those who urge it this approach is limited, since it is precisely the difference between those who urge social change and those who are opposed or indifferent to it that needs to be explained.

In the quest for "deeper motivation" there is, so to speak, considerable danger of throwing out the baby with the bath. An example of this may be seen in the Vassar study, in which, when the investigators could not find evidence of a radical temperament, they asked themselves the following question: "Is radical temperament necessarily indicated by radical opinions on public questions?" [15] If the response to public issues does not indicate the radical temperament, then studies of the radical temperament can have no meaning for an understanding of social change.

Second, studies that minimize the differences between conservativism and liberalism may have a negative value. By suggesting what these attitudes have in common, they indicate what properties are extraneous to the particular attitude. This would seem to be, however, a roundabout way of isolating properties unique to the different attitudes.

3. *The radical as a deviant.*—One of the problems in all these studies is whether or not radical behavior is a symptom of maladjustment. Evidence of this approach can be seen in the Allport and Hartman study [16] as well as in Rinaldo's.[17] In both the conclusion was that the radical attitude, in contrast with other

[11] Ibid., p. 740.
[12] Ibid., p. 740.
[13] Joel Rinaldo, **Psychoanalysis of the Reformer** (New York: Lee Publishing Co., 1921).

[14] Harold D. Lasswell, **Psychopathology and Politics** (Chicago: University of Chicago Press, 1930).
[15] Washington et. al., op. cit., p. 455.
[16] Op. cit.
[17] Op. cit.

ypes of political attitudes, indicates a
nore basic personality disturbance. Lass-
vell goes further than any of the others
n spelling out the nature of the disturbance.[18]

Starting with the assumption that politi-
al behavior is a displacement of un-
esolved conflicts originating in infancy,
e seems to regard all political behavior
s unadjusted behavior. Presenting the
ase history of a socialist agitator, he
uggests three themes which find expres-
ion in the doctrinal aspects of the indi-
idual's behavior. (In this respect he
eparts from his avowed purpose of ex-
laining only the "agitation.") A repressed
atred of a brother was inverted into the
hilosophy of brotherly love, an ambiva-
nt attitude toward the subject's father
as reflected in the refusal to accept the
apitalistic system, and latent homosex-
ality made acceptable the socialist theme
f martyrdom.

Lasswell did not state that these three
nemes universally constitute the psycho-
ynamics of the socialist philosophy, nor
id he suggest that this person or any so-
alist is "neurotic" in the strict clinical
nse. His material on the radical's values
as incidental to another purpose and
nnot therefore be considered as his
omplete statement of the problem.

The study is chiefly important for pre-
nting a systematic Freudian approach:
) It assumes that political predisposi-
ons originate in infantile needs and are
etermined long before the individual
counters adult economic experience.[19]
) It assumes a parallelism between
ivate and public experience. Public at-
udes are thought of as projections of
ivate needs. Psychologically speaking,
olitical experience presents the same op-
ortunities to the individual for manipu-

lation and expression as does the area of
face-to-face relationships in childhood.

Equally as important as Lasswell's theoretical contribution is his restatement of
the problem. He rejects the rational-irrational dichotomy; to him, all political attitudes—left, right, and center—are basically nonrational.

Continuing in the Freudian tradition,
Flugel compares the psychoanalytic basis
for attitudes on the "left" with attitudes
on the "right." [20] His hypothesis is that
attitudes on the "left" represent a healthy
emotional adjustment and the triumph of
the demands of the ego over those of the
superego. In contrast with the tradition-
bound conservative, the radical has freed
himself from the force of authority and
convention, that is, from the father image,
and, in so doing, he has taken a step
which is, according to Flugel, necessary
to the mature development of personality.
"In so far as the 'left' aims at an escape
from blind authority," he writes, "and a
social adjustment in the light of conscious
ego functions, it does on the whole correspond to the 'tendencies' of progress."

With an eye perhaps to modern political
realities, Flugel is careful to qualify his
position by pointing out that an extremist
kind of revolt carries its own psychological liabilities. It may, he says, lead to
"an excessive emphasis on destruction
. . . and efforts at restitution and perhaps
to the reinstatement of a father figure in
the form of a dictator." [21]

The notion that radicalism represents a
protest against authority, the child's rebellion against parental authority, finds
some empirical support in Gordon Allport's study.[22] Allport discovered that the
best single index of political attitudes was
a question concerning the individual's own
voting in relation to his father's: those

---

[18] Op. cit.
[19] That Lasswell does not consider these
condary group experiences as important
ay be seen in the vague way in which he
es them. Statements such as **"During
ese exciting troubles,** he became a social-
." or **"As time passed,** he began to dissent
om many of the dogmas of his immediate
cial environment" illustrate the minor
portance which Lasswell gives secondary
oup experience. (Emphasis mine.)

[20] Op. cit., pp. 281–301.
[21] While Flugel allows for the possibility
of an excessive destructiveness, Ernest
Jones regards it as the distinguishing feature of revolutionary behavior. In a revolutionary situation, according to Jones, the
individual symbolically murders his father
(cf. "Evolution and Revolution," **International Journal of Psycho-analysis,** XXII
[1941], 193–208).
[22] Op. cit.

who rejected the voting intention of their fathers were the most radical.

Krout and Stagner addressed themselves directly to the problem of the radical's emotional stability. Using an autobiographical schedule with items selected from personality theory and clinical experience upon members of the Young People's Socialist League and the Young Communist League as the experimental group, they found no marked tendency among radicals toward neuroses. "Our data," they reported, "showed as many symptoms of maladjustment among controls as among radicals." [23]

Although the Krout and Stagner study does not throw light directly on Flugel's specific hypothesis concerning the origin of radical ideas in the struggle to overcome parental authority, it does demonstrate that radicalism is not in itself a symptom of emotional disorder. Their findings suggest, too, the irrelevance of many of the items in a clinical inventory for understanding political behavior. Finally, the Krout and Stagner study is important for methodological reasons; using as subjects members of radical organizations, they introduce a natural field approach.

In working on the problem of the radical's mental hygiene, Diamond used somewhat different tactics.[24] The question he raised was: What effect does radicalism have on the developing personality? His hypothesis was that modern society is conducive to a kind of mass introversion. By providing the individual with a new method for evaluating events and their relation to himself, the radical program lowers the unhealthy tension which the society generates. "The individual who adopts a philosophy of class revolution will thereafter habitually judge events not by their influence upon him, but by their influence upon the larger group with which he has identified himself." The

effect of this should be, he thinks, to encourage the development of extraver tendencies.

Like Krout and Stagner, Diamond too] as subjects the members of radical polit ical parties and of conservative organ izations. After being classified politically they were given extraversion-introversio tests in which they were asked to com pare their present behavior with thei behavior of three years earlier. Result indicated that the change from introver sion to extraversion is most frequen among active Communists and bimoda for college students who favored eithe the Socialist or the Communist party. H concludes that radicalism is a factor i personality development which may b divided into two phases: an increase introversion followed by an increase extraversion.

Some question might be raised abou Diamond's use of the extraversion-intro version typology, and his assumption tha extraversion is in itself a criterion of emc tional health. Much would depend on th ends toward which the extraversion wa directed, whether or not it involved th acceptance of an authoritarian type c social structure.

In spite of some internal difficulties, th Diamond study is important historicall First, as in Krout and Stagner's study, i subjects were persons actively identifie with a radical movement. Second, in con parison with Lasswell's Freudian a; proach, Diamond's allows for greate plasticity in the personality. He assume that personality can be crucially red rected at a relatively late age. Thir Diamond's study opens the way f further investigation of a dynamic rel tionship between the individual's perso ality and the organizations in which l participates.

One study which does not fit into o classification scheme deserves mention b cause of its theoretical importance. The dore Newcomb in a study of Benningt students over four years found that, i college milieu where predominantly liber values are expressed by the faculty, t students are inclined to take over su

---

[23] Maurice H. Krout and Ross Stagner, "Personality Development in Radicals: A Comparative Study," **Sociometry,** II (1939), 31–46.

[24] Solomon Diamond, **A Study of the Influence of Political Radicalism on Personality Development** ("Archives of Psychology," No. 203 [New York, 1936]).

alues.[25] It is possible for students to accept liberal values notwithstanding their earlier acceptance of conservative values at home.

Newcomb's main concern in the study was the role of the community as a mediating agent between personality and the social attitude. The study has, however, several implications for a theory of social change. If his findings are correct that situational factors may influence the political attitude, then two alternatives logically follow: either the personality may undergo significant change during and after adolescence or, within a given personality structure, a range of political attitudes is possible. In the latter case, personality and political attitudes are not so closely connected as previous studies indicate.

Second, Newcomb's study touches upon the other side of Flugel's coin. Radicalism may represent a protest against established values, but it is also a positive identification with other values. Newcomb's study suggests the need for further investigation of the identifications of radicalism. Finally, by demonstrating the situational effect, Newcomb focuses attention on the link between motivation and the historical situation. Assuming a personality predisposition and an objective historical situation in a state of disequilibrium, the individual must at some point be exposed to radical values before accepting them himself. And it is to these smaller groups that the sociologist must look for the actual communication of radical values.

IV

Throughout these studies there are several lines of development. In the earliest phases the radical was seen as a maladjusted irrational creature. Later studies were more sympathetic. In these the radical was seen as no more neurotic than persons who hold other political beliefs. Finally, radicalism was regarded as a superior type of emotional adjustment

25 Theodore M. Newcomb, "Community Roles in Attitude Formation," **American Sociological Review**, VII (1942), 621-30.

when compared with other political attitudes. Whether or not this shift represents changing attitudes on the part of the researchers or a change in the objective situation cannot here be determined.

Institutional factors, too, have been increasingly recognized. Whereas Moore was convinced that environmental factors were only effective if the neuromuscular pattern was present, Krout and Stagner point out that child-rearing practices alone cannot control the development of radicalism and that "certain combinations of developmental factors, socio-economic as well as personal, [may] 'sensitize' the individual to the influence of radical groups or radical theory."

Third, looking at these studies in retrospect, changes in the theory of personality may be observed. In the earlier studies it was assumed that reason dictated one type of political attitude, irrationality another. Later, the rationality-irrationality dichotomy was dropped: all political attitudes were seen as reflections of emotional needs which arose in primary group relationships. More recently, the accent on childhood and infantile determinism has given way to a more flexible conception of personality which allows for basic changes occurring after adolescence and under the impact of secondary groups.

These studies have had, however, moderate success in establishing the concept of a radical personality, in spite of the fact that often there is disagreement on the details. Their chief limitation lies in the eschewal of a sociological context. With few exceptions they are not related to an actual social movement. And in no case are they related to the type of historical situation which generates a radical movement. Possibly the fact that radicalism has been an isolated and scattered phenomenon in American life, never seriously threatening the social structure, would account for the neglect of these sociological and historical dimensions. In contrast with Europeans, American investigators have not had the opportunity to study radicalism except *in vacuo*. In studying radicalism apart from the context of social change, they may have unwittingly studied a selected group of radicals: those whose radicalism stems primarily from inner personal needs rather than from environmental pressure. This type of motivation is frequently found in the early phases of a social movement; or it may be typical of the middle-class radical. Whether or not it is true of the mass in a social movement— those who participate only in a period of marked social and economic upheaval or who come from lower-income groups—is still to be determined. To do this, it is necessary to turn to the social movement as the point of departure, to study the structure of the movement in all its phases of development, its subgroups and division of labor, and its roles. In such an analysis it might be possible to locate not *a* personality pattern common to all the participants but several patterns. We could then evaluate personality studies of the radical more realistically from the point of view of social change.

Out of many speculations and unrigorous case analyses concerning participation-proneness, five interrelated personal characteristics may be cited. These characteristics are not to be viewed as systematic or complete, but as a sampling of the literature.

(1) Imperviousness to certain kinds of social isolation may be necessary, not only for participation in unconventional movements, but for active adherence to movements with a generally favorable public. A sort of *prestige isolation* overtakes any individual who sets himself apart from his fellows by assuming a leadership role or an active role with respect to values that his fellows accept passively. His fellows can no longer joke about their political convictions or make light of their candidate's foibles in the presence of an individual who is committed to a serious and unequivocal support of a particular program of reform. The adherent's serious preoccupation makes his fellows fear that their small talk will not be of interest to him. Ordinary, informal communication is thus inhibited, and relations tend to become stilted. Furthermore, the activist is likely to be the recipient of friendly "kidding" for "going overboard," or of a certain amount of awe and admiration for having more courage and conscientiousness than his fellows, all of which sets him apart from ordinary primary group relations. Only if prestige is more sought than intimate acceptance will the individual be likely to resist these subtle pressures against activism. In the terms of W. I. Thomas, the individual must choose between social recognition (prestige) and personal response (intimate acceptance).

(2) Something of a desire for martyrdom often seems to be a component of movement participation. Hazel Wolf has demonstrated the anticipation of martyrdom shown by many of the prominent figures in the American abolition movement.* From letters and public statements she has shown that many not only expected to be martyred but expressed much morbid satisfaction in looking forward to their ultimate demise. In less active form, rank and file members often pride themselves in belonging to a despised minority. As a way of life the martyrdom attitude does take care of certain adjustments that the individual might otherwise have to make. The fact that he is persecuted explains in advance any personal failures and protects him from the necessity of coming to grips with making effective long-range plans for himself. As a recipient of unfair treatment from society at large the individual feels himself morally freed from the obligations that society might otherwise impose upon him.

* Hazel Wolf, **On Freedom's Altar** (Madison, Wis.: University of Wisconsin Press, 1952)

(3) Authoritarian types are to be found among the adherents of almost any movement with a program of societal reform. These are people who are dissatisfied unless they can impose their will on others. In the classic study by Theodore Adorno and his associates an effort has been made to show that there are several authoritarian personality syndromes that incline people to accept fascist types of ideology.* But the opportunity to dominate masses of people may be provided in the most democratic movements. Even in movements dedicated to strengthening popular control there may be authoritarian satisfactions in forcing the masses to "accept their responsibilities" and in manipulating the intolerance of the masses to bring dissident individuals into conformity.

(4) Many writers have noted the sense of personal inadequacy that drives some people to identify themselves with a movement that is symbolized as strong and uncompromising.

Many writers, particularly those with a psychoanalytic bent, stress a combination of personal weakness and authoritarianism in the same individual. Leon Festinger contends, however, that proselyting activity, often interpreted as a sign of deep commitment to a movement, may also indicate a lack of confidence:

> *If more and more people can be persuaded that the system of belief is correct, then clearly it must, after all, be correct.* Consider the extreme case: if everyone in the whole world believed something there would be no question at all as to the validity of this belief. It is for this reason that we observe the increase in proselyting following disconfirmation. If the proselyting proves successful, then by gathering more adherents and effectively surrounding himself with supporters, the believer reduces dissonance to the point where he can live with it.**

One of the best known analyses centering around the theme of a sense of personal inadequacy is Erich Fromm's treatment of the circumstances of modern society that make for receptivity to movements such as Nazism. Out of the isolation and a sense of powerlessness experienced by many men in modern industry there develops a "sado-masochistic" character structure, one which takes delight in being punished by and subservient to those above him and in turn gains pleasure from mistreating those beneath him. Through yielding up his independence in subservience to an authoritarian movement the individual "escapes from freedom" which he lacks the resources to use, and gains a sense of overwhelming power through identification with the powerful movement and its dictator leader.***

(5) A final characteristic of importance is a tendency to see issues in simple "black and white" terms. Any tendency to see elements of truth in both of two opposing viewpoints interferes with one's enthusiastic participation. In any case, such "broad-mindedness" is likely to bring about ostracism by the more determined converts of the movements.

Interaction of member types. The course of a movement is dependent in part upon the kinds of members it attracts and upon the interaction that takes place between different types of members within the movement. The techniques that can be effectively employed by the movement will be related to membership composition. A movement, for example, that is for the bulk of its members

---

* T. W. Adorno et al., **The Authoritarian Personality** (New York: Harper & Brothers, 1950).

** Leon Festinger et al., **When Prophecy Fails** (Minneapolis: The University of Minnesota Press, 1956), p. 28. Copyright 1956, University of Minnesota.

*** Erich Fromm, **Escape from Freedom** (New York: Farrar and Rinehart, 1941).

merely a participation-oriented movement, will only be able to employ effectively such pressure techniques as lobbying, in which leaders impress decision-makers with the size and strength of the group they represent. For in such a movement the members cannot be counted on to promote the influence of the movement's program actively themselves. As another example, the greater the degree to which considerations such as those outlined in the preceding section account for a large portion of the membership, the more dependent the movement will be on direct power tactics rather than on creating a friendly public. Recruitment of a major portion of membership from the impotent and deviant members of society makes it unlikely that an extensive enough friendly public could be created.

Kinds of membership will affect internal relations and stability. Movements that draw upon the chronically discontented and the determinedly isolated soon become objects for the same reactions as their members had toward the larger social order. Partly because extremist movements of any sort attract many such individuals, their reform objectives are constantly hampered by internal dissension. Movements with a large limited-personal appeal will generally lack support from within for programs that call for extreme changes or for the use of tactics that depart from the conventional.

Interactions among membership types parallel some of those within the crowd. The authoritarians, the martyrs, and the confirmed deviants tend to commit the movement to more extreme positions than those whose adherence to the ideology is not backed by a complete rejection of conventionality. The latter group must then either reject the movement or back the more extreme position forced on it.

Esprit de corps. Whatever the motives of its members, a social movement must weld them into a group with a strong in-group sense and enthusiasm for the "fellowship" or "comradeship" of the movement, and give them determination to continue in the face of obstacles. Herbert Blumer makes a distinction between *esprit de corps* and morale which corresponds in part to the difference between adherence because of the gratifications of participation and adherence to the program and ideology of the movement. Whereas morale gives "persistency and determination to a movement," *esprit de corps* gives "life, enthusiasm, and vigor to a movement." *Esprit de corps* is "The sense which people have of being identified with one another in a common undertaking." In making the distinction Blumer also points out the limitations of a movement too preponderantly built about mere participation-orientations with too little devotion to the values the movement promotes. Except for such marginal motivations as the desire for martyrdom, apparent failures or discrediting of a movement may stop new recruitment and lower the enthusiasm of members. *Esprit de corps* feeds on success while the test of morale is "whether solidarity can be maintained in the face of adversity." *

It is in the development of *esprit de corps* more than anywhere else that the mechanisms of crowd behavior come into play in the social movement. A social movement with a strong *esprit de corps* is in some sense a diffuse crowd, in which enthusiasm has become contagious.

Herbert Blumer suggests three principal techniques through which *esprit de corps* is developed, all of which have appeared in our discussion of the participation-oriented movement. These techniques are, "the development of an ingroup

---

* Herbert Blumer, "Collective Behavior," in **Principles of Sociology,** ed. A. M. Lee (New York: Barnes & Noble, Inc., 1953), pp. 208-10.

utgroup relation, the formation of an informal fellowship association, and the participation in formal ceremonial behavior." Among the devices which are at once ceremonial and foster both fellowship and the ingroup-outgroup relation is the music of a movement. Roland Warren has shown how similar may be the major themes of the songs used by movements with widely divergent ideologies, but confronted with the common task of establishing *esprit de corps* in the movement.

GERMAN *PARTEILIEDER* AND CHRISTIAN HYMNS AS INSTRUMENTS OF SOCIAL CONTROL

ROLAND L. WARREN

National Socialism as a movement has depended from the . beginning on the sustained emotional appeal of a crisis psychology. Stirring speeches, repetition of emotionally toned slogans, breath-taking visual displays, mass meetings, press propaganda, and the appeal to German history, tradition, and legend have all been exploited as instruments for maintaining the necessary morale to support the movement. An important source of emotional support is also furnished by group singing, a fact which has received little attention in the United States, perhaps because group singing in this country does not play as important a role as it does in Germany.

In times of war crisis, it is true, song-writers rise to the occasion by contributing their bit to national defense. There are many significant differences, however, between the fighting songs of the United States and those of National Socialist Germany. Perhaps the greatest difference is that most of the American songs are rag-time or jazz, designed for dancing as well as singing. The National Socialist songs, on the other hand, are designed to be sung, rather than to be listened to or danced to. Many are designed to be sung without accompaniment, and resemble the simplicity of the folk song.

Further, American "morale songs" arise generally during limited emergencies. So it was with the World War I songs, most popular of which was prob-

ably George M. Cohan's "Over There," so it was with depression songs such as "Marching along Together," and so, more recently, with the host of morale songs which stemmed from the success of "God Bless America." A counterpart for "The White Cliffs of Dover" and "Remember Pearl Harbor" cannot be found in the National Socialist songs. The first is too manifestly sentimental, the second too "football-ish." "My Buddy" and "Ich hatt einen Kameraden," both popular in World War days, point the contrast. The former was composed during the war, was a dance tune, and was designed to meet the current market for sentimental war numbers. The latter went back for its tune to 1825, and for its words to Ludwig Uhland, a famous German poet who composed them in 1809. It is more rigorous, and, although equally sentimental, it is almost "marchable" and tells a story.

Indeed, the National Socialist songs are more comparable to Christian church hymns than they are to American war songs. They occupy a place of permanence in the national life, they depend upon the same psychological mechanisms of mass singing, they are highly symbolic, and are inspired by a similar prerogative of eternity. The "Horst Wessel" song is in many respects more similar to "Onward, Christian Soldiers" than it is to "Marching along Together." The last-mentioned shows the characteristic football derivation of most American marching songs, while the first two have in common their broader, slower rhythm,

Reprinted by permission of the American Psychological Association, from the **Journal of Abnormal and Social Psychology,** 38 (1943), pp. 96–100.

their implications of eternity, their appeal to dead heroes, their reference to "the foe," and their urging on to victory. The National Socialist and Christian hymns have a double purpose. Their *primary* function is to arouse the emotions of the singers to a point where they are more sensitive to the impact of the words (sermon, political address) of the speaker. But they also fulfill the *derivative* function of exercising a lasting influence over the attitude of the individual participants after they leave the group.

Interstimulation is the key process which transforms a mere group of people in close physical proximity into a crowd. Psychologists have analyzed the techniques employed by religious leaders in furthering this process. The use of symbols encrusted with emotional meaning, the performance of hallowed rituals, the group recitation of the creed, the singing of hymns—all help in the primary function of breaking down resistances which inhibit the desired responsive attitude in the members of the fold.

Seashore has emphasized the "feeling of freedom, luxury, and expanse" created by the rhythmic qualities of music, tending to neutralize inhibitions and make the individual feel "as if one could lift oneself by one's bootstraps."[1] Pratt has reported the increase in suggestibility brought about by group singing of hymns.[2] The individual, as he repeats the words borne up by the compelling urge of the melody, affirms his faith, and that in a loud voice. Through singing he can say things which it would embarrass him to repeat in his more inhibited moments. And, hearing his own uninhibited confession on the lips of those surrounding him, he is led to an even deeper affirmation of faith in what he is reciting. It was this insight which led William James to speak of "faith in someone else's faith." Common affirmation of faith, supported by rhythm and melody, is an important fac-

tor in "whipping up a crowd," as an evangelist will testify.

The derivative function of hymns is that of conditioning attitudes which will remain with the individual after the group has dispersed. As such, their verbal content can be analyzed in terms of "the control of opinion by significant symbols," as Lasswell has succinctly put it;[3] and consequently many of the better known propaganda techniques apply to these hymns as well as to other instruments of controlled attitude-formation. Propaganda must be considered in its context. To be successful, it must meet the level of interests and prejudices of those whom it is to influence, as well as adjust its appeal to their degree of emotional excitement. Religious leaders have sensed this condition, as evidenced by the care which they use in selecting hymns appropriate to the main theme of the sermon or to the festival which the church is celebrating. The Nazi hymns are also selected according to the "message" to be implanted and the state to which the emotions of the singer are expected to be aroused.

A careful analysis of the hymns included in the National Socialist party songbook indicates that certain clearly discernible appeals occur with unusual frequency.[4] The appeals most frequently employed are to the following motives: loyalty, eternity, dead heroes, self-sacrifice, the leader, freedom, chief symbol, the fatherland, nearness of victory, "everybody's doing it," not too much questioning of goal, enemies, youth, and "all together in the cause." It will be shown

[1] Carl E. Seashore, **Psychology of Music** (New York: McGraw-Hill, 1938), p. 142.
[2] James B. Pratt, **The Religious Consciousness: A Psychological Study** (New York: Macmillan, 1921), p. 172 ff.

[3] Harold D. Lasswell, **Propaganda Technique in the World War** (New York: Knopf, 1927), p. 9.
[4] **Liederbuch der nationalsozialistische deutschen Arbeiterpartei,** herausgegebe vom Kulturamt der Reichspropagandaleitung. Munchen: Franz Eher Nachfolge 1939. Landsknecht and Soldier Songs have been omitted from the following analysis for two related reasons: First, most of these songs have an origin independent of the National Socialist movement, many of them antedating the first World War, and secondly, the Party has had a particularly difficult problem in transforming the army ideologically, so that even those songs of recent origin have little direct reference to the current situation.

elow that the Christian church hymns re replete with substantially the same ype of leading motives.

The National Socialist songs are an excellent example of the efficient adaptation f means to ends in the formation of roup sentiment. This is not to imply that a every case a song fulfilling certain definite functions was made to order for the arty. Indeed, some of the songs antedate ie National Socialist movement. Three eneralizations would appear to be waranted, however: (1) The songs which vere either "pushed" by the Party or ame more naturally to popularity were iose which, as a matter of fact, had high inctional value in strengthening the National Socialist cause. (2) The songs hich were purposely written to bolster arty solidarity employed, as a matter of ict, those techniques of appeal which vere already apparent in the movement nd which were potentially effective in ie social milieu from which the songs rose. (3) As a result, the songs, partly y deliberation, partly by accident, beame an integral part of the total propaanda effort on the home front.

Typical quotations from the party ings are given below under the heading f the leading motive of the appeal. Accompanying each set of quotations are irresponding quotations from a representative Christian hymn book.[5] The comiarison serves to illustrate the similarity appeal, and affords another interesting cample of a remarkable correspondence tween certain appeals used by the hurch and the National Socialist Party.[6]

Loyalty: (17)[7] Though all should

grow disloyal, we shall still remain true. . . . Defiantly waved their flags as they lowered him into the grave, and they swore eternal loyalty for the Hitlercomrade. . . .

Am I a soldier of the cross, a follower of the Lamb? And shall I fear to own His cause, or blush to speak His name? (488) I bind this day to me for ever, by power of faith, Christ's Incarnation. . . . (525)

Eternity: (17) . . . Germany, the proud manor, carries thy countenance, carries thy spirit into all eternities. We shall hold thee, flag . . . high over death's rule into eternity.

Breathe on me, Breath of God, so shall I never die; but live with Thee the perfect life of Thine eternity. (380) . . . To Him that overcometh, a crown of life shall be; He with the King of glory shall reign eternally. (538)

Dead heroes: (15) . . . Marching on before us, with battle-scarred flags, are the dead heroes of the young nation. . . . Comrades shot by Red Front and Reaction march in spirit with us in our rows.

For all the saints, who from their labours rest, who Thee by faith before the world confessed, Thy Name, O Jesus, be for ever blessed, Alleluia. (295) The martyr first, whose eagle eye could pierce beyond the grave; who saw his Master in the sky, and called on Him to save. . . . Who follows in his train? (85)

Self-sacrifice: (23) . . . We are faithfully devoted to Hitler, faithful unto death. . . . Heart that has loved only Germany, heart which is battle never degenerated, heart which gives itself to the people.

Fight on, my soul, till death shall bring thee to thy God. . . . (118) Yea, let Thy cross be borne each day by me; mind not how heavy, if but with Thee. (163)

The leader: (18) . . . we come like a storm, the *Führer* has called. Soon Hitler flags will flutter over every street, the oppression will last only a little while longer.

Jesus calls us; o'er the tumult of our life's wild restless sea, day by day His

[5] A Hymnal: as authorized and approved r use by the General Convention of the rotestant Episcopal Church in the United ates of America in the year of our Lord 16. . . . (New York: Gray, 1916).
[6] In an earlier study, the writer compared scism and the Church from the standint of structure and techniques of apal. See "Fascism and the Church," American Sociological Review, 6 (1941), pp. 45–51.
[7] Under each topic, quotations from Nanal Socialist songs will be given first, and iderneath them quotations from Christian mns. Seventy-six National Socialist songs ire examined for this study. The number parentheses after each topic refers to

the frequency with which the topical motive is employed. The number in parentheses after the quotations from the Christian songs refers to the number of the hymn.

sweet voice soundeth, saying, "Christian, follow Me." (268) Jesus shall reign where'er the sun doth his successive journeys run; His kingdom stretch from shore to shore, till moons shall wax and wane no more. (480)
Freedom: [8] (14) . . . the day of freedom and bread is dawning. . . . Father, in life and death help us to win freedom. . . .
(Such quotations as "Lord make us free!" could be given. No word, however, seems to be the counterpart. Rather, a variety of words and ideas would correspond:)
"Salvation, glory, honour!" I heard the song arise. . . . (542)
Chief symbols: (40) Leader, carry the flag before us into clouds and sun. . . . The flag stretched high, the rows formed close together, S.A. marches with a quiet, firm step. . . .
Onward Christian soldiers, marching as to war, with the Cross of Jesus going on before. . . . Forward into battle see his banners go. (530)
The fatherland: (26) . . . Germany, in flowering beauty you ever rise up anew. Germany, Germany above everything, above everything in the world. . . .
Jerusalem! high tower thy glorious walls. . . . (543) Glorious things of thee are spoken, Sion, city of our God. . . . (468) [9]
Nearness of victory: (11) Soon Hitler flags will flutter over every street, the oppression will last only a little while longer. . . . One day shall come the day of revenge, one day we shall be free. . . .
What rush of alleluias fills all the earth and sky! What ringing of a thousand harps bespeaks the triumph nigh! (541) At last the march shall end; the wearied ones shall rest; the pilgrims find their Father's house, Jerusalem the blest. (537)

8 Offhand, it might be thought that the word "freedom" would be conspicuously absent from these songs. Perhaps the best hint to its meaning in the ideological context of National Socialism can be drawn from Immanuel Kant: ". . . therefore, a free will and a will under moral laws are one and the same thing." But in National Socialism, of course, it is Hitler, not Reason, who dictates the "moral laws."
9 To the same tune as **"Deutschland, Deutschland über alles."**

"Everybody's doing it": (6) . . Millions are already looking to th swastika full of hope. . . . . . . no one can stand idle along the way, ev eryone must come along with us. . .
Onward, then, ye people! Join ou happy throng! Blend with ours you voices in the triumph song! (530 Come, labour on. Who dares stand idl on the harvest plain. . .? (497)
Not too much questioning of goa (2) . . . and no-one is here who i cowardice despairs or tiring, question the way. . . . How stupid to ask, ho small to ask why we are marching!
I do not ask to see the distant scen one step enough for me. (244) Ho blest are they who have not seen an yet whose faith has constant been. . . (555)
Enemies: (18) . . . Day and nig let us guard the flag against all en mies. . . . Judah appears, to win ov the Reich. . . .
Principalities and powers, musterin their unseen array, wait for thy u guarded hours. . . . (128) Christia dost thou see them on the holy groun how the powers of darkness rage th steps around? (126) (Indeed, the Jew come in here, too, for hostile referenc in one hymn:) Have we no tears shed for Him while soldiers scoff an Jews deride? (153)
Youth: (10) . . . We (youths) a the glory of our times. . . . . . . W youths stride through the German lan full of faith facing the sun; we are sacred Spring. . . .
O Thou Whose feet have climbe life's hill, and trod the path of you . . . Thy Name, proclaimed on eve lip, the Master of our schools. (365 . . . In every tongue and nation s (the Church) calls her sons to pra . . . (352)
"All together in the cause": (12 . . . Youth and aged, man for ma embrace the swastika banner. . . Brothers of spade, desk, and hamm silently shake each other's hand.
Bright youth and snow-crowned ag strong men and maidens meek. . . (537) Brother clasps the hand brother, stepping fearless thro' t night. (539) [10]

10 One cannot but recall a simple chi dren's hymn in this connection, which do not limit the in-group to the Aryan rac

The Church hymns come closer to being the American counterpart for the Party hymns than any other group of songs in America. This is not only because they are the only sizable body of songs built around a cause familiar to great numbers of Americans, but because they use a similar technique in their emotional appeal. The similarity can be over-emphasized, however. First, although they employ similar psychological means, their ideological ends are vastly dissimilar. Secondly, and more important for this study, they make appeals on a social psychological level which are employed to a certain degree by all social movements:

"... Yellow, brown and black and white, they are precious in His sight. Jesus loves the little children one and all."

The appeal to enemies to solidify the in-group, the appeal to dead heroes, the sanction of eternity, the employment of symbols, the imminence of victory as a bolster to morale,[11] the rallying around a leader, etc. Thirdly, although the theme has not been fully exploited in this paper, the Party songs, despite their employment of the sanction of eternity, emphasize deeds and this-worldliness, while the Church hymns emphasize faith and the world to come.

[11] Interesting was the use of this technique by Jesus in proclaiming that the kingdom of heaven was at hand. St. Paul and other enthusiasts, as is well known, took this appeal too literally, and much of St. Paul's writings can be understood only in this light.

Member control in crisis situations. From time to time there may arise in a movement, particularly one that is regarded as somewhat unconventional, tests of member loyalty that exceed the usual capabilities of *esprit de corps* and ordinary dedication to the movement's values. Such crises may originate from within or from without the movement. The movement may demand unusual sacrifice from a member, or may demand that he violate his own moral convictions or personal loyalties in the cause of the movement. The demand that he perform violence or sabotage, or that he break with family and friends, will tax a member's loyalty. From outside the movement may come persecution, which can be escaped or at least mitigated by repudiating the movement or by at least assuming a less active role.

Such crises essentially force on the adherent an irrevocable choice between the movement and the outside world. Techniques that lead to repudiation of the outer world in advance of the test, or create partial withdrawal and disillusionment from the outer world, prepare the individual for the ultimate test. A strong discipline that threatens the member who fails the critical test likewise serves to give the faltering member no alternative to carrying out his assigned tasks. Whittaker Chambers describes in his own case the fear that hounds the member who leaves the Communist party, fear for his own life and for the safety of his entire family.

Perhaps the most extreme test is that of martyrdom. While some members find their way into persecuted movements because they find martyrdom congenial, a movement under consistent persecution cannot depend upon such exceptional motivations to maintain its strength. It must develop a systematic program for preparing its members for the imminent possibility of martyrdom. Donald Riddle has shown how the Christians, under persecution by Rome, developed such an elaborate program. In the early stages of Christianity, when persecution was sporadic and frequently more a matter of spontaneous mob action than of institutionalized legal process, there was little opportunity to prepare members systematically for the test. But in later periods the various procedures which Riddle describes were consistently practiced.

THE MARTYRS

Donald W. Riddle

PERSECUTION AND SOCIAL CONTROL

The aspect of the behavior of the martyrs as the result of social control has not yet received adequate attention, though it is of the highest significance. It is obvious that control is a major factor of religion, and the experiences of the martyrs constitute an example of control which is most instructive. Clearly the fate which was suffered by not a few of them was one against which ordinary impulses vehemently rebel. Nevertheless, for certain reasons, and in spite of the usually held points of view, it was not unwillingly accepted. The willingness to undergo suffering is a social attitude which was present as the result of control. It follows that the behavior of the martyrs offers a field for investigation in which much may be learned of the technique of control as it is applied in the religious life, and the sources reflecting their experiences become a veritable laboratory of research. . . .

The elements of the situations which obtained in the best-known cases of Christian martyrdom were simple. The demand on the part of the state in the persecution of Decius, for example, made any subject liable to examination in court. Upon presenting himself, he was faced by a simple alternative: he might confess that he was a Christian, and be remanded for further discipline; or he might deny that he was a Christian, and, upon offering evidence to substantiate his denial, be set at liberty. This procedure reduced the situation to the barest simplicity for both the persecuting and the persecuted groups. . . .

. . . In situations of widespread persecution, or in local situations where one person or a small group was subjected to coercion, the task of the group to which the victims belonged was clearly recognized. So fully was it perceived, indeed, that the terminology which was used to meet it became quite technical. In brief, the task of the Christian group was to secure from those of its adherents who were being tried a confession; while, on the other hand, it was the object of the state to induce them to deny the accusation that they were Christians. . . .

As shall be shown, the Christian groups bent serious effort to assist in the resolution of the doubtful elements in the dilemmas before prospective martyrs. They undertook to prepare such persons as were likely to be examined, so that these would be ready to offer the answer desired by the religious fellowship, hoping thus to inhibit the tendency toward the opposite response. They exerted control even during the conduct of the examination; and after a confession had been made, they frequently found it possible and valuable to keep in touch with the martyr-designate.

The Christian groups accomplished their task by following a specific method. The process was essentially as follows: to secure from its adherents the behavior which was necessary if the movement were to survive, rewards of a sufficiently compelling nature were held forth, so that in the person being examined, or likely to be examined, there would be generated a wish to maintain his present relation. Negative sanction was secured by threatening punishment for failure to do so. The desired goal was repeatedly called to attention by careful visualization. Its realization by others was frequently pictured as a glorious fact. En-

Reprinted in part by permission of the University of Chicago Press and the author, from Donald W. Riddle, **The Martyrs: A Study in Social Control** (Chicago: University of Chicago Press, 1931), Chapters I–IV, passim.

couragement was given by the thought of the participation of others in similar experiences, and it was pointed out that failure or success would be witnessed by one's fellows. In specific detail proper attitudes were suggested, stock answers to the prospective questions were taught, and stereotyped arguments were supplied, together with persuasive evaluations and heroic imagery. The attempt was made to induce in the candidate an emotion of overpowering character, so that he might be carried, if he had been sufficiently prepared, through the harrowing experience with a minimum of exception to the type of behavior which had been found to be desirable.

The facts demonstrate that the method followed by the Christian groups was successful to the point that not a few Christians accepted a fate against which the most basic impulses normally rebel. . . .

THE PREPARATION OF THE MARTYR

The preparation of the martyrs was a process which ranged from extreme informality to specific organization. Of course in the earlier situations technique and method of control had not been acquired, so that it was only in the persecutions proper that the fully worked-out process of control may be seen in operation. The earlier periods are instructive for their evidence of the development of technique.

It was first necessary to induce in the prospective martyr a willingness to undertake the experience, even though he knew it to be unpleasant. The wish for the experience was reinforced by such sanctions as were found to be effective. Rewards for success were suggested with definite imagery, and punishments for failure were pictured with no less specificity. The effect of group contacts was utilized, and from such social influences proper attitudes were engendered and crystallized by powerful indoctrination. All such steps in the process may be seen in the sources which reflect situations of persecution. . . .

It must be understood that not merely a hope of reward was offered but that rewards were assured with exact specifica-tion. What the rewards were may readily be discovered. For one thing, it was important to some of the early Christians that death by martyrdom guaranteed resurrection from among the dead, or, as the Greek rather than Jewish thought-patterns of life after death became current, the immediate and personal immortality of the martyr. . . .

Another value which it was alleged was guaranteed by martyrdom was the forgiveness of sins. Since sin is an ever present problem to the religious person and the religious group, it is no accident that the early Christians saw in martyrdom a means of securing the satisfactory solution of a troublesome question and used this as a sanction to induce the martyr attitude. . . .

Still other values were alleged to be secured by martyrdom. One of these, of much greater significance in the ancient world than in the modern scientific world-view, was the triumph over those demonic powers which were so real to the early Christians. Another was the ability to intercede for one's earthly companions, while others were the authority to judge one's judges and the position of coregent with Christ. . . .

It is also clear that the willingness to undergo punishment for the crime of being a Christian was largely induced by the fear of the consequences of failing to confess. The threat of punishment in the afterworld was urged with co-operative force with the rewards which were at the same time promised. In this matter, again, the sanctions were various, ranging from the exclusion from the religious group to alleged fates of a cosmic consequence. The thought that denial not only would entail the loss of fellowship with the church group but would result in eternal punishment in the afterworld appears to have been of considerable influence in inducing the attitude of willingness to suffer as the result of confession. At any rate, the literature of martyrdom repeatedly suggests the fact. . . .

. . . Specific misfortunes immediately following denial were alleged. Cyprian, for example, related a series of such

(Treatise iii, 24–26). One denier was forthwith stricken dumb. Another was seized by an evil spirit and made to bite out her own tongue, death quickly followed. . . .

Beside the skillful utilization of the sanctions of reward and punishment, the willingness to undergo martyrdom was induced by a second factor, namely, by indoctrination through the use of sacred scriptures. Evidently it was a source of satisfaction to the martyr to reflect that his fate was so fully under the control of God that it had long ago been foretold. The thought that he was one of a noble company was tremendously effective, and he was conscious of his heroic status largely because he found himself to be in a situation similar to those celebrated in sacred story. In the same source were to be found many comforting exhortations, which, if known and heeded, would greatly assist him by pointing out the position gained by exemplary characters of the past, and promising him a like fame. . . .

Indoctrination was effected not only through the use of Scripture but also by the discipline of church customs. It cannot be too forcibly stressed that the conflict of church and state was a conflict of loyalty to groups. The churches were religious societies, exactly as was the state in its attempt to secure religious conformity to approved patterns. To which society should the Christian affirm loyalty? Membership in the Christian group had appealed to him sufficiently to cause him to join it and to remain in fellowship up to the moment of this crisis. Presumably it had not only brought him satisfactions but had also left its mark upon him in teaching him certain manners and habits. Such factors, when perceived in connection with his as yet unbroken fellowship, strongly influenced him. Common worship, the association of the liturgy, particularly of the common liturgical meal, the practical benevolence practiced by the several societies, and all such social features, operated to unite the members into well-knit groups.

The force of such a relation is apparent in the crises through which the churches passed. It is apparent as fellowship was lost through denial. Much distress followed. The sources suggest that many of those who lacked the courage to confess nevertheless, immediately after defection, returned to their group beseeching restoration to fellowship. Many deniers resorted to the confessors in prison to beg "peace" from them. . . .

The effect of the discipline of custom is seen also in the operation of ritual. The withdrawal of the Eucharist, where most particularly dramatic communion was secured, was a serious matter to deniers. Doubtless in this central sacramental feature of the common worship there was considerable magical value for the devotee. But whatever may have been the motive in ascribing value to the rite, the social effect of its customary celebration is undoubted. It is equally obvious that it operated powerfully in the process of control. . . .

. . . There is abundant evidence that willingness to undergo martyrdom depended largely upon the strength of the social contact of the confessor with his church. This appears indubitably from the fact that martyrdom away from the home associations was held by Christian leaders to be less desirable than the public death of a martyr in the sight of his fellows. . . .

THE PRODUCTION OF ATTITUDES

The goal of the church groups, as general practice became typical, was to anticipate whatever event might ensue in the relations between the state and Christians. Uniformity of behavior was desirable; if each witness might be taught to do exactly what his predecessors had done, the possibility of failure to confess would be much reduced. Failure, when it occurred, came when the witness was unprepared, had not undergone the discipline of normative custom, or was faced by some unforeseen circumstance which impaired the uniformity of the course of events. . . .

In the first place, the answers to the question of guilt were centrally important. The witness must admit that he was a

Christian. Consequently, as the acts of the martyrs were published, one sees the skillful use which was made of the court dialogue. By circulating representations of the cases of successful witness, and in them citing the questions asked by the court and the answers given by the confessor, the first necessity, namely, that of suggesting the proper answer to the question of guilt, was met. . . .

There is a hint that a certain posture during the examination was thought to be especially effective. Thus Tertullian: "Then, too, in using such words as these, it (i.e., the soul) looks not to the Capitol, but to the heavens. It knows that there is the throne of the living God, as from him and from thence itself came down" (*Apology* 17).

Certainly it was believed that to make the sign of the cross was efficacious. Tertullian affirms, "We trace upon the forehead the sign" (*On the Crown* 3), and in another place says, "We have faith for our defense, if we are not smitten with distrust also, in immediately making the sign of the cross and adjuring" (*Scorpiace* 1). . . .

The definiteness of these attitudes and the specificity of their functioning were secured by maintaining a degree of fixity of attention upon the end so ardently desired. This prevented the intrusion of unprepared-for eventualities. Control, as is well known, is obtained largely by the focus of attention being fixed upon a given point. The Christian groups maintained, with a high degree of success, such a fixation of attention upon the values which it was thought would lead to the behavior deemed proper. . . .

The discussion of the attitudes which controlled the martyrs necessitates the recognition that in part, at any rate, they were of a psychopathic character. It hardly needs to be said that the experience of martyrdom was one against which ordinary judgment recoils. It will occasion no surprise, then, to find that in cases of martyrdom certain symptoms of a psychosis appear. One finds, for example, a morbid desire for the experience of martyrdom. Even though it may be rationalized that the desire was so keen because of the rewards which were expected to materialize, the affirmation may be offered that the desire was morbid. In the phenomena there appear, too, evidences that there was a morbid pleasure derived from the pains which were endured. Indeed, it seems that martyrdom in the later church occupied the place which in the earlier church was filled by such ecstatic experiences as trance and speaking in tongues. There is a definitely discoverable basis for such phenomena. . . .

THE INFLUENCE OF THE GROUP

. . . True as it was that the readiness with which martyrs endured their bitter experience was the result of preparation, of the production of attitudes, and of the fixation of attention, it is equally true that the crucial moment was that moment when the witness was at the very tribunal. . . . It is easy to suppose that however well prepared one might be, or however strong may have been his resolution to confess, the terror of that moment might, without proper encouragement, undo all that had previously been taught.

Consequently, it is not surprising to find that the Christian groups carried their control to the dramatic point when the witness must confess or deny. Doubtless their practice was learned from bitter experience, for it was early learned that defection had evil influence upon those yet to be examined.

In the first place, Christians who were being examined found that they were not left alone. It was usual for a number of their fellows to be present during the legal process. Naturally this was a factor of importance in the determination of the suspect's conduct. Doubtless it lent encouragement for him to be conscious that friends were present. Of still greater force was the perception that the candidate's own standing was importantly affected by their judgment of his conduct; presently he would be a hero to be praised or an apostate to be reviled. It has been shown that the approval or disapproval of one group or the other would control. The church group took care to exercise all possible influence to impress the candidate that eternal destiny weighted the scale of values in favor of confession, and saw to it that the witness would feel its influence at the critical time. Too, the fact that the general public saw the outcome was of great effect. Not infrequently a denier was greeted by the jeers of the bystanders. . . .

Another aspect of the influence of the group is apparent in the lesson learned by the Christian leaders that successful examples of martyrdom were salutary only when accomplished in the martyr's home surroundings. It was found that when death occurred elsewhere, the loss of effect upon the candidate and upon other Christians was serious. . . .

But the group influence controlling the witness was not alone that of those fellow-Christians who were actually present with him or awaiting him in his familiar surroundings. Fully as powerful in control were the groups whose fellowship was in the realm of the imagination. The martyr was frequently controlled by so intangible a value as this type of imagery. Fellowship with God was a factor. It was made more definite by the thought of fellowship with Christ, especially in view of the fact that Christ was the great proto-martyr. Fellowship with other martyrs who had preceded him in suffering furnished comfort. Altogether the force of such imagined relations possessed influence quite comparable to that of one's immediate friends. The fact was turned to account by the Christian leaders in developing their processes of control in persecution. . . .

It was thus most fortunate for the persecuted Christian that he need not feel himself to be alone in the moment of his crises. Experience in other similar cases proves that resolution flags lowest when the sense of loneliness is the strongest. But the candidate for martyrdom had a large roster of fellows. Standing by were some of the associates of his church group. The officials who were his ecclesiastical superiors were aware of his status. And as his imagination lent itself to flights of comforting fancy, there were the whole line of heroes who before him, through suffering, had been victorious. Scripture

taught him of many famed ones, and the rapidly growing Christian tradition was constantly adding to their number. He was persuaded that, if his courage did not fail, he was ever drawing nearer the apostles. Most dazzling in the whole prospect was the thought that God and Christ were supremely careful of his fate—more so, indeed, than were his earthly friends. Truly, beside the circle of present associates there was indeed a "crowd of heavenly witnesses."

Great as was the force of the influence of the group before and during the martyr's examination, it is of the utmost significance that it was not allowed to end as that crucial moment passed. It was found to be of the highest importance that fully as potent influence was exerted after the legal process was concluded. If the candidate had denied, effort was made to induce him to change his mind and alter his testimony. On the other hand, if he had affirmed his faith and accepted condemnation, the influence of the group was useful after the confession had been made. Attention followed the martyrs-designate while they were languishing in prison. It was a comforting assurance to the confessor that he would enjoy many favors while he possessed that rank. Charity operated in his behalf, so that his physical wants were not neglected. Of even greater importance was the prestige which he enjoyed as a confessor and a prospective martyr. But the matter did not end here; the candidate for martyrdom was assured of still more favorable position after his death. These were considerations which had tremendous influence over candidates. . . .

It became a part of the process of control in persecution to assure those who were liable to martyrdom that after their death they would be made the central figures of cults of veneration which verged upon worship. This assurance appears to have done much to make numbers of candidates the more willing to undergo an otherwise calamitous fate.

Just why the prospect of becoming the center of a cult should assist in building up the attitude of willingness to undertake martyrdom is less easy for the modern than for the ancient to see. But it must be remembered that the early Christians shared the pre-scientific world-view. It may not be amiss to point out that the similarity of the cult of the martyr to the familiar Graeco-Roman hero cults is not without significance. The older conceptions of heroic behavior resulting in apotheosis doubtless paved the way for the rise and ready popularity of the martyr cult of the Christians, who naturally shared common conceptions of the same milieu. . . .

. . . It is not to be thought that martyrs in any significant number could have undergone their fate if they had been abandoned in it by their fellow-Christians. They were able to meet their crisis only because they were members of societies which kept effective the influence of their social bonds. That such influence was operative before and during the time of confession, and even after the confession had been secured, while the confessor lay in prison, or actually, as he fondly supposed, after his faithfulness unto death, accounts for the maintenance of the martyr's courage. In other words, he was enabled to emerge through the painful course of punishment because he was one of a number. He was such a person as he proved to be because of group influences, of which, for this purpose, his Christian fellowship was the most effective. It was because of his integration as one of a group that he was thus controllable. The essential factor in control was the influence, variously applied, of the group.

Chapter 20

The following and leadership

*P*ERHAPS more is written and less known about leadership than almost any other social phenomenon. Perceptions concerning leaders are distorted by the admiration or hatred of the leader. The tremendous importance of the leader in supporting or weakening the accepted values in a society through the prestige of his example makes it difficult for anyone with value-commitments of his own to examine the leader objectively. Furthermore, the very eminence of the leader separates him from others, so that few have the opportunity to know him intimately. Thus his relation to values and the difficulty of getting close to the leader make it unlikely that even accurate factual descriptions of leaders will be available.

A further obstacle to developing accurate conceptions of leadership has been the individualistic bias dominating much serious study. This bias leads the investigator to look for the explanations of leadership solely or principally in the person of the leader. It is often assumed without question that in the absence of a particular person, or of someone else with the same inherent leadership qualities, no leadership would have occurred at a particular point in time. Or the course of history may be construed as a battle between good and bad leadership. These biases have led to reports which list the so-called "traits of leaders." Such lists, of which there are a multitude, may be posed with complete generality, or they may be presented separately for "good" and "bad" leadership. Recent research has produced such lists distinguishing "democratic" from "authoritarian" leaders.

Most of these trait lists may be discounted at once on the grounds that any experienced layman could sit down and make up an equally good list out of his head. Furthermore, the lists usually allow abundant exceptions: many leaders lack many of the characteristics; many nonleaders exhibit most of the traits; and the leader in one situation may not be the leader in another.

454

Without ruling out the ultimate possibility of a useful approach to the person-alities of leaders, we shall start from the opposite pole. If a leader is by definition a person who is followed, then we may commence by examining the character-istics of *followings*. To what degree do the followers of any leader form a col-lectivity? What characteristic patterns of interaction with one another and with the leader do they exhibit? Under what circumstances do followings develop and expand, and under what circumstances do they decline or disappear? What kind of role do the followers create for their leader? With answers to these and related questions already in hand, it should be possible to approach the nature of the leader himself more profitably.

Our present interest is not so much with leadership in general as it is with leadership as an aspect of social movements. While leadership plays a part in every social movement, movements vary tremendously in the extent to which they are conspicuously dependent upon a single leader. Some movements appear to be held together by little other than the loyalty to a single leader and to be given direction largely by his impulses. In other movements the leaders are several and regarded as little more than high grade functionaries. Their scope of decision-making is rigidly limited and the loyalty they command is contingent upon their following the correct "line."

In keeping with our general procedure, we shall examine first the relatively pure case of movements built around and dependent upon a conspicuous leader. These include the simpler case of the *following,* which lacks the full development and societal impact of a true movement, and the *charismatic* movement, a true social movement centered about a leader to whom unusual or supernatural per-sonal qualities are attributed. Then we shall examine the place of various types of leaders within social movements in general.

The leader and leadership do not belong in a particular niche in our scheme of movement orientations. In the full-scale movement all of the orientations con-verge in the role of leader. The leader makes decisions in the realm of values, but more important, he symbolizes to the members and outsiders the value-orienta-tions of the movement. Leadership positions become the focal points in power struggles within and between movements. And the admiration and confidence in a conspicuous leader provide an important kind of participation gratification. The gratification that persons feel in being identified with a respected leader strengthens any movement and may contribute a body of supporters in addition to those concerned with its value objectives.

The following. The *following* is a collectivity made up of persons interacting in some measure to express their admiration of some public figure. Since the activities of the following are limited to expressing in innumerable ways their admiration for their hero, the implications of the following for social change and stability are quite limited. Hence we have referred to the following as a *quasi-movement.* The entire integrity and course of the following are dependent upon the sole fact that members get personal satisfaction out of belonging to a "great man's" following. Hence, to the extent that the following approaches a true movement, it represents an almost pure case of a participation-oriented move-ment.

The most obvious followings are the "fans" who worship some popular hero of the entertainment or sports world. A popular practice of seeking explanations for these followings solely in pre-existing deviant tendencies of the members is

easily adopted by serious writers because the overt behavior is frequently extravagant and the members are adolescents. Accordingly the following is treated as a
reflection of mass personal maladjustment. The swooning, weeping, screaming,
the desire to touch the hero, and other manifestations seem to lend themselves
readily to pathological interpretations. Undoubtedly such interpretations are justified in the case of some of the more extreme participants. But, as we have noted
for crowd behavior, an atmosphere of permissiveness and sanction among the
"normal" people is at least a minimum condition for such extravagant expression
Furthermore, a comparison with more conventional types of followings reveals
widespread similarities. Many of the characteristics of followings about political
leaders or leaders even of scientific thought are basically like those of the fan
clubs of movie stars.

In listing some of these common characteristics, we shall offer illustrations
from two polar types of followings. On the one hand, there is the following made
up chiefly of adolescents whose hero is a popular singer and motion picture idol
such as Frank Sinatra was. On the other hand is a following composed of adult
professionals or business people whose hero is a prominent scientist or business
leader.

(1) The followers develop a definite group sense, communicate extensively
among themselves, and develop symbols and norms whereby the in-group can
be distinguished from the outgroup. The special slang that "fans" adopt, often
taking the favorite phrases of their idols, is approximated by the professional
jargon whereby the followers of particular schools of thought can be identified
The in-group sense not only distinguishes the outgroup but also the less accept
able followers. The unduly boisterous admirers of Sinatra were known as "fiends"
to be distinguished from "fans," and schools of thought differentiate the naive
adherents from those who are sophisticated.

(2) The followers develop a prestige hierarchy among themselves based upon
proximity to the leader and recognition extended by him. Sinatra's fans gained
prestige by seeing him, touching him, or acquiring intimate souvenirs, and they
feared to offend his chief lieutenants. Training under a thought leader, or receiv
ing some attention, or even teaching in the same school, may confer prestige in
an academic following.

(3) Members of a following invariably define their relations to other follow
ings as opposition and rivalry. Sinatra's followers actually enjoyed opportunities
to defend their idol against imagined or real slurs, and they constantly attempted
to detract from other bobby-sox idols and popular singers. Ardent academic fol
lowers devote great pains to proving that the ideas of their leader cannot coexist
with other contemporary schools of thought, and concentrate on discovering the
"underlying fallacies" of other viewpoints.

(4) The members of a following preoccupy themselves with accumulating
every conceivable item of information about their hero, preoccupying themselves
with identifying and interpreting the hero's opinions on various subjects. While
the singer's fans want to know what he eats for breakfast and thinks about the
world situation, academic followers may be more concerned with interpreting
correctly the master's opinion on some subject than they are with the subject
matter itself.

(5) The followers identify with the leader, so that they gloat in his successes
and suffer personally under his setbacks. Sinatra's fans wrote to promote his

nterests and they suffered in his illnesses. Academic followers experience re-
lected prestige when their leader is recognized, and devote much personal energy
o assuring that he is properly recognized by all.

(6) To the followers, the prestige of their leader translates the commonplace
nto the profound and resolves uncertainties by providing a position that they
an adopt. Many of Sinatra's followers attributed omniscience to him and wrote
or personal advice. Academic or business followers quote the most commonplace opinions of their leader as profound contributions and substitute his au-
hority for arguments in resolving moot issues. The academic or business leader,
ike the popular entertainer, constantly finds remarks that he has made lightly
or "off the cuff" taken unduly seriously by his followers.

Besides these and other common characteristics, followings also differ accord-
ng to the image of their leader. On the basis of an extensive survey of popular
heroes, Orrin Klapp has suggested that the major kinds of hero image may be
classified under a few universal hero roles.

THE CREATION OF POPULAR HEROES
Orrin E. Klapp

An age of mass hero worship is an age of instability. The contemporary heroes who are emerging in politics, sports, entertainment, religion, and in every other field in which the public is interested are a focus of social reorientation in a time of rapid change. Max Weber provides a fruitful concept of charismatic leadership which helps to indicate some of the implications of sectarian and revolutionary movements oriented by popular leaders and heroes.

Heroes arise in four general ways: by spontaneous popular recognition and homage; by formal selection, as in the case of canonization and military decoration; by the gradual growth of popular legends; and also as the poetical creations of dramatists, story-tellers, and writers. However heroes emerge, they tend to be recognized by a certain characteristic social behavior of hero worship: they are honored and given special status; they are commemorated by dramas, legends, memorials, relics, and the like; and they frequently receive regular veneration or celebration by organized cults. A hero is defined as a person, real or imaginary,

Reprinted by permission of the University of Chicago Press, from **The American Journal of Sociology**, 54 (Sept., 1948), pp. 35–41.

who evokes the appropriate attitudes and behavior.

The hero in social life is thus essentially more than a person; he is an ideal image, a legend, a symbol. The study of growing hero legends shows us that the fame of a hero is a collective product, being largely a number of popular imputations and interpretations. Once formed, as has been often said, the legend of a hero "lives a life of its own." The creation of a hero from a historical person is therefore visualized as the attachment of certain roles and traits to him through drama, news, publicity, rumor, and other media, so as to show him in a collective interpretation. By far the majority of popular heroes emerge without a deliberate effort having been made to create them; the development of a hero is largely an involuntary collective process.

A hypothetical problem in public relations is (*a*) how to transform a mediocre personality into a personage of heroic stature and great public appeal or (*b*) how to destroy a popular hero by casting him in, or attaching to him, various roles which are especially antiheroic. One might be concerned with such a problem, for instance, in the preparation of a political candidate or in propaganda against the hero of an antagonistic social movement or nation.

This includes specific problems such as the relative importance of the personality features of heroes; precisely what roles to attach to build up or to destroy heroic status; and by what means to attach these roles, e.g., how best to employ publicity and communications media.

A study of popular heroes and hero types in myth and legend [1] provides a basis for the evaluation of certain factors in their creation, namely, (1) the situations in which heroes emerge—principally interest, crisis, and drama; (2) heroic and antiheroic roles; (3) "color"; (4) personal traits; (5) stories and rumors; (6) publicity; and (7) organization of the popular reaction to the hero.

HERO-MAKING SITUATIONS

Heroes arise in areas of life where there is a focus of public interest. These need not be important historical situations but are perhaps better described as events having drama and human interest, such as sports and theatrical performances, as well as battles and political crises. They are situations of suspense or unmet need, such as conflict, competition, effort, or struggle. When an issue is felt to be important and its outcome is, at the same time, in doubt, a favorable situation is created. Practically speaking, a politician who is sensitive to the issues which are temporarily arousing people or who can create crises is in a position to make himself a hero.

HEROIC ROLES

The study of mythical and popular heroes shows the following possible roles: (1) the conquering hero, (2) the Cinderella, (3) the clever hero, (4) the delivering and avenging hero, (5) the benefactor, and (6) the martyr.

The conquering hero as a type is created by roles which give the actuality or the illusion of superhuman power.[2]

The performance of miraculous feats is an outstanding characteristic of folk heroes, such as Beowulf, Siegfried, and Paul Bunyan. In contests the conquering hero is invincible; in feats he is inimitable. Such are Jack Dempsey and Babe Ruth. Also important are tests which show superhuman endurance, skill, bravery, or virtue. Such, for instance, are the stunts which made the late Houdini such a hero as an "escape artist." In practical application, any story, impression, photograph, rumor, or role which can be engineered to emphasize the extraordinary power of the candidate, or his supremacy in any field of endeavor, is likely to help make him a popular hero. Conversely, any sign of weakness will diminish his stature.

If the candidate is a person of youthful or unpromising appearance, the Cinderella or "dark-horse" role may make him a hero. In this role, a hero who apparently hasn't a chance, who perhaps has been ridiculed, rises to success over more favored opponents. Among American popular heroes the cases of Lindbergh and of "Wally" Simpson will be familiar. Lindbergh, arriving to compete in a trans-Atlantic air race at the last moment as an "unknown," created by his unexpected success an unparalleled public impression. A variant of the Cinderella theme is that of the "poor boy who makes good." This is usefully attached to political candidates by publicity writers. Most major American heroes were "poor boys" or "orphans." In another practical context let us take the case of a "rookie" pitcher who has real, but hidden, promise. If it were desired by a professional baseball club to build him up into a hero, it might be useful to publicize him first as a Cinderella-like figure, as an orphan like Babe Ruth or as a boy who has suffered ridicule from other players; then let him shine forth with a brilliant record of victories. Much popular interest might be attracted to this unknown and the basis laid for a popular hero.[3]

---

[1] Orrin E. Klapp, "The Hero as a Social Type" (Ph.D. dissertation, University of Chicago, 1948).

[2] We may note this in the creation of movie heroes who knock out "setups" with the help of sound effects emphasizing the force of their punches.

[3] A third variant of the Cinderella role is that of the "giant-killer," a small person

A role which emphasizes cleverness rather than strength has helped make many American popular heroes, including Abraham Lincoln, Davy Crockett, Will Rogers, and Huey Long. This is found in folklore in the role of Reynard the Fox. A person who bests his rivals by wit, unexpected tricks, or hoaxes is likely to become a great favorite with the people. The clever hero requires the opposition of an opponent of much superior size, power, or pretense. The Eulenspiegel character has the charm of humor as a saving grace which helps to offset any moral defects he may have, for it is well known that the clever hero is frequently a "rogue." But his defeated opponents are fools. In public life, if any person continually and impudently flouts forces which are superior, he may acquire the status of a popular hero even though a lawbreaker.[4] For the appeal of the clever hero is the perennial triumph of "brains over brawn," *la sagesse des petits*. A practical way in which this role might be exploited would be to pit a candidate who has some cleverness against dull opponents whom he can publicly foil with a joke. Much of Lincoln's effectiveness as a stump speaker can be attributed to his resourcefulness vis-à-vis pompous and pretentious opponents.

The delivering hero is one who comes in time of need to save people in danger or distress. The effectiveness of the role depends upon a dramatic climax, in which the plight of the victim becomes as serious as possible before the hero enters. That these situations operate to make heroes in real life is evidenced by the medals given every year for lifesaving. The popularity of military leaders is often based upon this role. Almost any social problem or crisis in politics, sports, or everyday life provides an opportunity for a delivering hero. To make a social problem seem as serious as possible before a political leader takes action to correct it would be one practical way of increasing the popularity of a statesman.

Benefactions also do much to improve the popularity of a public figure. Many American heroes have been kindhearted men who aided the poor and unfortunate. The legends of Franklin, Washington, and Lincoln are full of such stories.[5] Some of Babe Ruth's popularity is due to tales of his visits to sick boys to encourage them and to present them with bats. John D. Rockefeller's reputation was improved by a public relations counsel's advice to give dimes to little boys. Visits to hospitals have become a standard public relations routine for celebrities. It may be noted that some of Al Capone's popularity as a hero centered around his role as a public "benefactor" and the many stories of his "Santa Claus" generosity.

A final role which is of great power in creating heroes is that of the martyr. A theme of self-sacrifice woven into the story of any public figure gives him additional prestige. The strength of martyr cults,[6] as well as the potency of figures such as Lincoln and Gandhi as symbols, rests upon their having suffered death for a cause.[7] Hitler astutely exploited this in the case of Horst Wessel. At times the need of a movement for a martyr may be so great that very unlikely figures become martyr symbols.[8] We may say that any crisis or conflict in which an important cause is involved provides an opportunity for some person to achieve the status of martyr.

"COLOR"

The quality of "color" seems to be in actions or traits which excite popular interest and imagination, giving rise to sto-

---

who unexpectedly defeats a formidable opponent, as in the tale of David and Goliath.

[4] For instance, the bandit leaders Pancho Villa and Jesse James. The appeal of the legendary Robin Hood consisted partly in his continual escapes from the Sheriff of Nottingham.

[5] Native Louisianians still point to the bridges "that Huey built."

[6] See D. W. Riddle, **The Martyrs: A Study in Social Control** (Chicago: University of Chicago Press, 1931).

[7] Note, e.g., the myths of Roland, Siegfried, Achilles, Samson, Cuchulain, Robin Hood, Jesse James.

[8] L. H. Jenks, "The John Brown Myth," **American Mercury**, I (1924), 267-73; note also the Sacco and Vanzetti case.

ries which recount or interpret these features. The term "color" may be applied to public figures who tend to stand out from rivals by virtue of things they do or of striking personal traits.[9] Color has apparently three main functions: (*a*) to excite attention, interest, imagination, and interpretation; (*b*) to set a person apart, rendering him unique or peculiar; and (*c*) to make him unforgettable. There are two ways in which it is exploited by public figures: through actions or roles and through personal traits. In the former case impressive style or virtuosity—sometimes called "grandstanding" or "showmanship" —is of great importance in making performers popular. Musicians frequently play difficult passages not because of their musical merit but because they will show off talents. Dancers and acrobats, similarly, frequently exaggerate the difficulty of certain acts in order to draw applause from the crowd. The other type of color, that of personal traits, is found in distinctive features, mannerisms, and dress; for instance, in Hitler's mustache or General Patton's pearl-handled pistols. We conclude that color in the form of eccentricities, affectations, and the like help in creating heroes, regardless of their other significance, because they excite interest, give people something to talk about, and make a distinct impression on the memory. We must note, however, that there are many heroes who lack personal color.[10] Color by itself is not sufficient to make a hero unless a heroic role is played and the right combination of other factors achieved.

9 "Color" in athletics usually means a peculiar style or idiosyncrasy which serves to attract and excite interest in a player. Both Babe Ruth and Jack Dempsey had "natural color." Another meaning of the term "color" is supplied from the field of literature: being a quality of vivacity or picturesqueness which makes localities or characters stand out as unique places or personalities.

10 It has frequently been observed, for instance, that General Pershing, the most popular hero of World War I, was almost totally devoid of personal color. Similarly, St. Therese of Lisieux was a nun lacking in personal traits or actions which would make her conspicuous.

PERSONAL TRAITS OF HEROES

What part do personal traits play in the making of heroes? In general, personal traits are relatively unimportant, for the emergence of a hero is a matter of popular selection. If a personal trait cannot be perceived, it is of little value in the creation of the public impression which is the essence of the hero. The public, indeed, is usually ignorant of its heroes.[11] There are several reasons for this: First, at the time of emergence of a hero the public usually has little opportunity for making direct observations; second, actions have a permanent advantage over traits in commanding interest and attention; third, the public usually infers the traits of a hero from the thing he has done. Therefore, we may say that roles rather than traits make heroes and that personal traits are subordinate to roles. The conclusion that personal traits are relatively unimportant in creating heroes is consistent with a symbolic theory of the hero: even the best-known public figures are to a large extent legend.[12] Distance builds the "great man." Regardless of what inherent qualities a candidate may have, if he plays a suitable public role he can become a hero. Carlyle was wrong when he said hero worship is the "reverence and obedience done to men really great and wise."

Several ways, however, may be noted in which actual personal qualities help to create the role of the hero. First, the trait which the public is able to perceive should be consistent with the role. For instance when an effort was made to beautify Jack Dempsey for the movies, there was a popular outcry among his fans that they preferred him to remain ugly and look his part as a fighter. Second, a feature, such

11 It cannot perceive their actual traits. All it knows about them is their public roles. The demand for biographies, information, anecdotes, etc., is a testimony of the public's ignorance of its heroes.

12 See R. P. Basler, **The Lincoln Legend** (Boston: Houghton Mifflin Co., 1935); Cameron Rogers, **The Legend of Calvin Coolidge** (Garden City, N. Y.: Doubleday, Doran & Co., 1928).

physique, has a value for suggesting to the public the kind of role the person will play. For instance, broad shoulders predispose a man to the part of the conquering hero. It was said that General Pershing's "strong jaw" lent him an appearance of power. Practically speaking, it easier to cast a small, witty person as a clever hero, a young person as a Cinderella, or a person with a kind countenance as a martyr.[13] Third, where the performance of a role is dependent upon the actual possession of a personal trait, we may say that inherent qualities help to make the hero. For instance, much of Babe Ruth's batting power was attributed to an actual superiority of physique, eyesight, and muscular co-ordination, as established by psychological tests. On the other hand, the opportunities for illusion and legend-building are so tremendous that there is no constellation of personal traits which would keep a person from becoming a hero if a heroic role were played, and there are no personal traits per se which can make a hero unless a heroic role is played or attributed to the person in the public mind.

STORIES AND RUMORS

The remark of an actress that "it is better to have someone talk about you, even if they say ill things, than not to talk about you at all" is valid in the case of popular heroes. The conceptions of heroic and antiheroic roles provide a framework within which deliberately to initiate legends. In addition to heroic roles, anecdotes regarding personal idiosyncrasies and preferences will do much to "humanize" a hero, particularly if he is little known personally.[14] Will Rogers' "wise-

cracks," which depicted him as a clever hero and homespun wit, were repeated throughout the nation. Finally, deliberate fabrication of stories, for example, dime novels, proved to be effective in the case of Buffalo Bill.[15]

PUBLICITY

Any means of placing a figure before the public eye will help to make him a hero. However, the importance of mere publicity has been greatly exaggerated.[16] Heroes emerge typically without deliberate publicity,[17] and many persons in the limelight fail to become heroes. A good example of the failure to make heroes through publicity is provided by inept publicity stunts, such as aerial weddings, flagpole sitting, and dives off the Brooklyn Bridge, which attract attention but fail to arouse hero worship. In the age of mass communications, however, heroes can be more arbitrarily manufactured and more quickly and widely diffused, once a formula for making heroes is found.

ORGANIZING THE POPULAR REACTION TO THE HERO

Finally, some contribution can be made to the creation of a popular hero by organizing the popular reaction to him. Souvenir-collecting, fan-letter writing, and popular homage can be organized in vari-

[13] The exceptions to this are almost as numerous as the rule: Napoleon was a little man who played the conquering hero. Good looks or even a "baby face" can hardly be considered an insuperable obstacle to creating the role of a "killer." While attractive features may be of value in inclining people to like a candidate, some of the least prepossessing persons have become popular heroes. Will Rogers used to remark that he had "the ugliest face in the films." Note also Al Capone.

[14] For instance, the fact that General Pershing stopped to talk to a little boy was

avidly seized upon by the public. Humanizing stories, incidentally, will do much to destroy the character of a villain.

[15] R. J. Walsh and M. S. Salsbury, **The Making of Buffalo Bill** (Indianapolis: Bobbs-Merrill Co., 1928).

[16] "Today, more than ever before, belief in 'the hero' is a synthetic product. Whoever controls the microphones and printing presses can make or unmake belief overnight. . . . Particularly today, any 'front' man can be built up into a 'hero'" (Sidney Hook, **The Hero in History** [New York: John Day Co., 1943], pp. 10, 153).

[17] The case of Sergeant York provides an instance. The rumor of his exploit spread through the Army and finally forced cognizance from headquarters, at which time reporters and photographers picked up the story and disseminated it to the nation. Deliberate agitation, however, served crucially to bring heroes to the attention of the public in the case of Sacco and Vanzetti.

ous ways. Babe Ruth clubs were started among American boys by a candy company. Likewise the autographing of balls and bats by Babe Ruth became a standard public relations technique. Similarly Lindbergh clubs, Rudolph Valentino associations, and Sinatra clubs have been formed. In the latter case, juvenile "swooners" have been encouraged and organized in their behavior by deliberately planted claques. Huey Long's organization was nation-wide and showed signs of becoming a major political party. It is not desired, however, to overemphasize the degree to which popular reaction to a hero can be deliberately stimulated. The success of these efforts depends largely upon a good deal of prior enthusiasm.

ANTIHEROIC ROLES

A difficult problem is presented in the effort to destroy a hero. In general, it may be said that the longer a hero has been in existence, the more developed his legend, the harder it is to destroy him. Certainly it is hard to shake the popular faith in a hero once established.[18] People are loyal to their heroes and usually defend them. Mere truth does not suffice to undermine this loyalty, as the debunkers of Lincoln have found out. There are certain crises in the formation of hero legends which can be exploited to destroy a hero, and there are certain roles or traits which are antiheroic. These are (1) weakness, (2) treachery, (3) persecution, and (4) the character of the clown or fool.

Where the hero is of the "conquering" type, a demonstrated weakness, such as cowardice or defeat in a contest, may serve to destroy the myth of his invincibility. This is evidenced in the case of Al Capone, who after his conviction for income-tax evasion lost much of his glamour. Until then it was popularly thought

that he could "fix" any judge and evade any law.

The hero may also "step down" to another champion. Yet, a "fair and honorable" defeat does not serve to tarnish the reputation of a hero, as is seen in the cases of the boxing heroes John L. Sullivan and Jack Dempsey. If, in his defeat there has been the possibility of unfairness or treachery, this will be made the occasion for casting him as a martyr. Thus, at the time of Dempsey's defeat by Gene Tunney, a "long count" by a referee provided a basis for a claim of unfairness and Dempsey's popularity rose, while Tunney acquired the temporary character of a villain. Similarly, if the hero is overcome by overwhelming forces, as Davy Crockett or Hitler, it is likely that he will be cast as a martyr. Finally, if the hero is assassinated, as in the case of Huey Long, it may be that he will acquire elevated status. Thus, the defeat of a hero unless clearly a result of his own cowardice or weakness, may serve to strengthen rather than to weaken his image.

Any public occasion in which a person is forced to make a stand against a popular person or cause may cast him in an antiheroic role. Thus, in 1940, Lindbergh although he had the status of a hero, took a position of apparent support to Germany and endangered his popularity. In the eyes of many he was almost a traitor. We may say that the "Judas" role [19] is particularly applicable to persons who contend against popular causes or defeat unfairly established popular heroes. Thus, John Wilkes Booth, far from acquiring the status of a champion of the South (which he was in his own eyes) by the assassination of Lincoln, became a detested villain.

Whenever a public figure comes in conflict with a person of inferior power who has some degree of public sympathy, he runs the danger of being defined as a persecutor.[20] The rival, if ruthlessly dealt

18 This is evidenced in the inability of people to believe that the hero has died, as demonstrated by the legends of "sleeping heroes" (e.g., Arthur, Frederick Barbarossa) who will return in time of need. See H. R. Trevor-Roper, "The Last Days of Hitler," **Life,** March 17, 1947; G. E. Simpson and J. B. Cineas, "Folk Tales of Haitian Heroes," **Journal of American Folklore,** LIV (1941), 183–84.

19 The traitor role is found throughout folklore in villains who betray heroes Hagen, Ganelon, Mordred, Robert For Delilah.

20 In folklore this role is embodied in Herod, Pontius Pilate, Goliath, who persecute heroes.

with or persecuted, may become a victim, or even a martyr if identified with a popular cause. Thus, the famous slapping incident in the career of General George S. Patton during the recent war did much to dim the glory of what otherwise might have been a spectacular popular hero. The role of the "bully" is also found in an incident in the early career of Jack Dempsey, which had much to do with a temporary unpopularity. In his fight with Georges Carpentier, a French war hero, in 1921, Dempsey found himself characterized as a "slacker" who had failed to register for the draft. His brutal victory over Carpentier was pictured in the press as a martyrdom for a valiant but outmatched fighter. Dempsey's victory was greeted with hardly a cheer from the public at the ringside. He found himself more unpopular after the knockout than before, bearing the double stigma of a "coward" and "draft-dodger" and of the bully who persecutes righteousness.

Clearly it is dangerous for a potential hero to gain ruthless victories over weaker figures, especially if his own status is insecure. The only time that a hero can persecute ruthlessly is when his opponent has been defined indisputably as a traitor, as in the case of J. Edgar Hoover's pursuit of "public enemies" and Hitler's persecution of the Jews.

One of the most effective roles for depreciating a public figure is that of the "clown" or "fool." Roles portraying ineptness or stupidity,[21] particularly ludicrous defeats at the hands of apparently lesser rivals, will give a personage this character. A victory of a clever hero usually "makes a fool of" somebody. An example is an episode in the early career of General Pershing. Prior to the World War, Pershing was delegated to head a punitive expedition into Mexico, in pursuit of the bandit, Pancho Villa. Much publicity was given to the campaign in the press, and week after week there came reports of how Pancho Villa, the clever hero of Mexico, had outwitted and "escaped" time and again from the formidable American force which had been sent to "get him dead or alive." The situation became ludicrous, and the Wilson administration as well as Pershing narrowly escaped embarrassment by the recalling of the expedition from Mexico to attend to more urgent matters, namely, the war with Germany. Villa never was caught, and he remained the hero of Mexico. It happened that Pershing's next role as deliverer of the Allies overshadowed his previous near-fiasco, and he became a great American popular hero. Much of the strategy of political campaigns, of course, is concerned with making a fool of the rival candidate. And no one who has been thoroughly made a fool in the public eye has much chance to become a hero.

The study of popular heroes suggests that heroes, villains, and fools are among certain basic social symbols. The popular mind is structured with regard to the categories by which it defines persons and situations. When a person becomes defined as a hero, he is potentially a very attractive and powerful leader. These basic roles by which persons are defined constitute primitive images which, while they are not inherited archetypes as Jung suggested but probably are based on universal human experiences, provide a key to collective psychology. The masses react in terms of certain standard definitions which can be appreciated by everybody. In this way large numbers of people can be quickly mobilized into certain collective emotions, whether of hero worship or of generosity, humor, vengeance, or hate.

[21] Chamberlain, after Munich, lingered between two antiheroic roles: the fool and the traitor.

The charismatic movement. The idea of the charismatic leader we owe to Max Weber.* The charismatic leader is one to whom his followers attribute 'charisma.''

* H. H. Gerth and C. W. Mills, **From Max Weber** (New York: Oxford University Press, 1946), pp. 245-52.

The term "charisma" will be applied to a certain quality of an individual personality by virtue of which he is set apart from ordinary men and treated as endowed with supernatural, superhuman, or at least specifically exceptional powers or qualities. These are such as are not accessible to the ordinary person, but are regarded as of divine origin or as exemplary, and on the basis of them the individual concerned is treated as a leader.

The leaders to whom we have been referring are possessed of charisma in the eyes of their followers. The difference between these and the leaders of full-scale charismatic movements lies in (a) the compartmentalization of the former group's spheres of competence and (b) the recognition of the latter group's charisma by a group of persons who are in a position to influence the course of events importantly. The heroic image of the popular entertainer or the scientific leader is safest while he remains in his "proper" sphere. Frequently efforts are made to manipulate the following of a popular figure through linking the leader with a political or social reform program. Recently, motion picture idols have campaigned actively for their favorite candidates for public office. While it is difficult to assess the impact of such efforts when several followings are arrayed on opposing sides, some persons actually come to choose their idols on the basis of their political alignments. But even when the followers take very seriously the political views of their idols, the followers are often adolescents or other persons who are not in a position to carry through a movement to influence effectively the course of events.

A movement takes on certain characteristics by virtue of being built around a charismatic leader. The nature and basis of adherence will affect the "texture" of the movement. The personal following of the charismatic leader provides a highly flexible body of adherents who will give enthusiastic support without questioning unexplained changes or ideological inconsistencies in the movement program. The confidence in the exceptional personal qualities of the leader also contributes an intense and unwavering quality of support which may be lacking in movements without a charismatic leader.

In a strictly value-oriented movement uncomplicated by a charismatic leader the recurring problems of maintaining active support within the movement are likely to revolve about varied interpretations of the movement's values and the necessary value compromises to power considerations. While these problems are lessened when there is strong devotion to the leader, the specific problem of maintaining the charisma of the leader becomes crucial in this type of movement. A movement with a well-worked-out program of reform may suffer an irremediable setback because the popular image of the leader is discredited. It may not even be essential that he is discredited as a person; it may be sufficient merely to demonstrate that he is no more than a capable and conscientious mortal.

The decision-making process in the charismatic movement has an effect upon the stability of the movement objective. The concentration of decision in the person of the charismatic leader frees the movement from the inconsistencies of program due to shifting power structure within the movement. But the decision process is also freed from the stabilizing effect of internal criticism and discussion, so that personal inconsistencies and idiosyncrasies enter disproportionately into program determination.

There is a major tendency in every charismatic movement for the leader, by irtue of his elevated position, to be protectively isolated from normal criticism. A man can seldom maintain a balanced perspective regarding himself when his xposure to evaluations by others is highly selective. The public worship and he expressed admiration of those close to him are likely to generate in the eader an exaggerated conception of his own capabilities. Such an exaggerated onception leads further to arrogance, dependence on his own hunches rather han a careful weighing of viewpoints, and intolerance of all opposition. Thus he personal and impulsive element in decision-making increases, the dispropor- ionate influence of personal favorites becomes greater, and the probability of trategic blunders that will wreck the movement is magnified.

Hans Gerth has demonstrated in the case of the Nazi movement how charis- natic dominance led to a certain kind of internal organization.* Crucial to the ntire organization was the "inner circle," consisting of top officials who were iersonally favored by Hitler. There was no defined route nor any set of pre- cribed qualifications for gaining or losing membership in the inner circle. Jembers were not assigned to specific offices with defined responsibilities and uthority. Instead each member received a vague commission from the Führer nd sought to extend his power at the expense of others among the inner circle. 'Purges" resulted when individuals or factions within the inner circle fell from avor. Under the circumstances, members were in constant fear of loss of favor. Exaggerated attention to such expressions of homage as the "Heil Hitler" salute nd fantastic praise of the leader were constant means of attempting to insure he member's continuing position. Thus key control of the movement was based ot on qualifications to lead but upon, "the changing personality preferences of he leader and . . . the power which the individual member may secure through nstitutional entrenchment and factional support by powerful 'friends.' "

The leader as symbol. Up to this point we have been discussing the single onspicuous leader in a movement, and treating him as if all the leadership "func- ions" were vested in the person of a single leader. However, there are many eaders in every movement, some of whom are conspicuous and some of whom ire completely unknown to the bulk of the movement's adherents. Furthermore, he term leadership implies several different kinds of roles that are essential to a movement but that are often vested in specialized personalities.

These leadership functions may be initially divided into two: those of *symbol* und of *decision-maker*. The leader as symbol is one whose own activities are of ess significance to the course of a movement than the image of him that the nembers hold. As a symbol he represents to them some important aspect of the novement—its ideology, its struggle, its assurance of success, or the kind of ieople who constitute the in-group. In contrast, the leader as decision-maker is ine who actually helps to determine the course of the movement by his own ireferences and activities, and by the effectiveness with which he promotes his iwn inclinations. In this section we shall discuss the leader as symbol, and in he following we shall consider his position as a decision-maker.

The leader may serve as a very general symbol to the movement, or he may iymbolize only one specialized feature. The charismatic leader has the former |uality of symbolizing the entire character and objectives of the movement and he struggle from which it emerges. For this reason the charismatic movement

* Hans Gerth, "The Nazi Party: Its Leadership and Composition," **American Journal** if **Sociology,** 44 (1940), pp. 517–41.

normally demands a leader who is somewhat apart from the conventional authority. Leaders who are known to be capable, who are widely respected and unquestioningly entrusted with major institutional decisions, may be abandoned in favor of unproven leaders when a movement begins to develop. The leader who symbolizes some revolt against convention by his uncultured manner, who symbolizes personal struggle in his own life, who symbolizes the personal independence and power of impulsive action, will strike a more responsive chord than the competent conventional leader among those who have become somewhat dissatisfied with the established order.

In an even more specific way the charismatic leaders of different movements and different eras may symbolize the predominant personal struggles of the group to whom a particular movement appeals, or the predominant struggles of an era. Erik H. Erikson has offered an interesting set of speculations concerning the imagery surrounding Adolf Hitler and its relation to the struggles of German youth within a highly patriarchal family system. John M. Mecklin has examined the *saint* as a leader of charismatic movements specific to certain historical eras. He has attempted to show how the saint rose to prominence in the Middle Ages as he symbolized one of the basic conflicts of that era, and was replaced by a different kind of charismatic leader as an era with new preoccupations succeeded the Middle Ages. The symbol of the saint won devotion in a way that leaders symbolizing nationalistic striving or class striving have done in more recent times.

THE PASSING OF THE SAINT
John M. Mecklin

. . . Summing up the early Christian ideal of the saint we may say that it was based upon religious sanctions arising primarily from a personal attitude to God, loyalty to whom was the source of moral effort and the basis of brotherly cooperation and sympathy. The *mise en scene* of the final act of the drama was otherworldly. In the glow of enthusiasm for the expected consummation all questions as to rights, all distinctions as to property, social position, or political power disappeared. The saint then had no place for any moral values that emerge through conflicting interests or are accentuated through courageous assertion of personal rights. He had no appreciation of a social order that is kept at the highest pitch of vitality and capacity for progress through rational direction and control of contend-

Reprinted in part by permission of the University of Chicago Press, from **The American Journal of Sociology,** 60 (May, 1955), Part Two, pp. 38–53 (first published, ibid., 1919).

ing forces. He recognized no rights or honors that are not the free gifts of the divine grace and therefore he had no immediate interest in the achievement nor in the maintenance of social justice. He was indifferent to existing conditions because he was fully convinced that the Kingdom of God and his righteousness would only be possible with the coming of a new heaven and a new earth.

This ideal which was so effective within the small group of early Christians did not suffice to meet the demands of the rapidly expanding faith that finally triumphed under Constantine. The very qualities that gave the apostolic group a most effective basis for solidarity carried the seeds of subsequent conflict and disintegration. An uncompromising and transcendental ethic based upon the expectation of the speedy end of the world with the resulting discrediting of property political life, and even of family ties doubtless proved a powerful means of eliciting the spirit of sacrifice and the no blest feelings of group loyalty and of comradeship but it did not provide a satisfactory basis for a permanent social order. . . .

It was inevitable then with the access of Christianity to world-power and with the rise of a new social order in the Middle Ages that the conception of the saint should undergo extensive modifications. The ideal of the saint as preached by Paul, Ignatius, or Tertullian would have destroyed rather than furthered the social equilibrium demanded by the age of Aquinas. For the fundamental idea of early Christian saintliness, and perhaps its greatest weakness, lies in its pronounced dualism. It implies a sharp distinction between the worldly and the otherworldly, the natural and the supernatural. Indeed the moral dynamic of the primitive Christian saintliness lay in the frank acknowledgement of this dualism both in theory and practice. The existing social order was justified only as an instrument of moral discipline, or as the dark and imperfect background which served to accentuate the glory and transcendent beauty of the things that "do not yet appear." This is the fundamental idea of Augustine's great work the "City of God" which is the classic statement of the Christian philosophy of society and of history.

With the increasing identification of Christianity, at least in its institutional forms, with society, the social values began to assert themselves. Hence the Middle Ages faced the problem of formulating the ideal of the saint which would conserve the moral idealism and the spiritual dynamic of the primitive otherworldly attitude and at the same time make a place for the values represented by society and its institutions. The solution which in time the Middle Ages worked out of this twofold problem of preserving the spiritual function of the saint and at the same time of making him an integral and necessary part of the social order arouses the profoundest admiration. That solution is still imperfectly perpetuated by the Roman Catholic church but with a strange and almost pathetic disregard for its lack of harmony with the changed conditions of modern life.

The unity of the mediaeval world-view, especially as it was formulated by Thomas Aquinas, does not always appear on the surface of things. To be sure we have in the church a great politico-religious institution dominating apparently every phase of life. The church was the source of absolute authority and truth, the divine institution equipped with sacramental forms for the dispensation of supernatural power in grace and salvation. Subordinated to this supreme authority though vitally related to it as parts of one organic whole, we have the classes and groups of society and the still lower levels of animate and inanimate nature. The cement by which mediaeval thinkers united these heterogeneous elements was found in the *lex naturae* of the Stoics, the teachings of the Bible, the tradition of the Fathers, and the philosophy of Aristotle. The result was indeed a wonderfully symmetrical structure in which all the various gradations of values embodied in physical nature and society were arranged in one logical whole, reaching their culmination and final interpretation in the spiritual sovereignty of a world-church.

Side by side with this idea of a world-church, however, and often antagonistic to its secularizing tendencies we find another conception of society, drawn directly from the gospels, which is constantly being emphasized from century to century. The dominating note here was ascetic or *Weltverneinung,* and the typical form through which it found expression was monasticism. The monastic orders with their ever-recurring efforts for reform were the logical continuation of the otherworldly saintliness of early Christianity. The monastic sects insisted that religion is primarily a subjective relation between the individual and God independent of the objective guarantees of the ecclesiastical forms. From the point of view of secularized Christianity the source of moral and spiritual energy lay in an institution which is superior to the life of the individual, and is the depository of absolute truth and supernatural spiritual power. For the ascetic, moral perfection was a personal matter and dependent upon ceaseless watchfulness; hence one cannot be content with a lesser degree of moral perfection nor may he relax his personal efforts in reliance upon cunningly devised and ecclesiastically sanctioned machinery for the manufacture of morality. Moral relativity from the secular point of view was a constituent element of the *status quo* in that it permitted the varying grades of moral perfection and the hierarchical constitution of society. For the ascetic sin was not to be tolerated because it permitted a stable social equilibrium but it must be eradicated and a new social order created after the evangelical ideal. On the one hand we have a secularized moral ideal based upon the principle of relativity and thereby permitting the introduction of some sort of unity into the conflicting elements of society. On the other hand stands an uncompromising, otherworldly ethic of superlatives that characterized the New Testament saint. The conflict was already foreshadowed in the differences between the love-inspired communism of the Jerusalem circle and the Pauline suggestions toward an accommodation to the existing social conditions. How did the Middle Ages solve the problem?

In the first place it should be observed that in spite of its constant criticism of secular Christianity the ascetic group never broke with the church. No saintly ideals ever flourished in the Middle Ages that did not receive the sanction and enjoy the sympathy and support of ecclesiastical authority. There seemed to be a profound realization of the fact on the part of both the would-be sectarian and the church that saintliness could never endure as an end in and of itself. It could only hope to survive by being made the servant of the social order. The otherworldly ideals of Peter Damiani, of Saint Bernard, of Saint Francis of Assisi, never soared beyond the authority of the pope and the magic supernaturalism of the holy sacraments. With tragic regularity the revolutionary heaven-storming idealism of the saintly ascetic returned with broken wing to the fold of the church convinced that nowhere else was its ideal possible

of realization. We have thus the paradoxical situation that the moral enthusiasm born of otherworldliness is skilfully utilized to further the power of a secularized church. The Monk of Wittenberg finally broke away from the charmed circle of the Holy Catholic church.

The social significance of the saint depended upon this spiritual and moral solidarity the guarantee of which was found in the supreme authority of the church. On the other hand the secret of the spiritual power of the saint was dependent upon his keeping himself separate from a social order given over to sin. Here then we have an interesting paradox. The saintly ideal demands aloofness from the world and its utter renunciation and condemnation and yet any social justification for the saint implies his essential spiritual solidarity with the world. If the measure of moral perfection is separation from the world then a perfect saint, for all practical purposes, unless it be for immediate translation, is useless. The reason for this lies in the fact that his goal, his entelechy as Aristotle would say, lies in another and a transcendental world. His social value, which of course must be measured in terms of his usefulness, decreases then as he nears maturity. This is equivalent to saying that the moral ideal stultifies itself in its attainment. But as we have seen the social solidarity secured to the mediaeval society through the all encircling arm of the church never allowed the saint to break with the social order and thus cease to be socially valuable. The antagonism between the saint and his environment which was necessary to his role as spiritual leader was always subordinated to the good of society as a whole. There was always in the background of the social consciousness of both saint and laity the feeling of common spiritual interests and common ideals. In the saints, therefore, the characteristic products of the religious and moral life of the Middle Ages, we have as Froude has said "the heroic patterns of a form of human life which each Christian within his own limits was endeavoring to realize."

The Middle Ages were most favorabl

o the life of the saint because of the exceeding simplicity of their social structure. The saint flourishes only in a simple society. The emotional intensity, the mystical absorption, the unshaken spiritual loyalty, the singleness of purpose so characteristic of the saint are difficult or even impossible of attainment where the complexities and the contrarities of life are constantly pressing in upon the soul. "The lives of the saints," as James has remarked, "are a history of successive renunciations of complication, one form of contact with the outer life being dropped after another to save the purity of the inner tone." The flight from the distractions of simple mediaeval society to the seclusion of the monastery was the result therefore of the psychological necessities of the saintly ideal. The entire life of the saint in his retreat was shaped so as still further to simplify the problem. No psychologist could have more successfully regulated the mental conditions necessary to the attainment of the saintly ideal of mystical contemplative love of God than Saint Benedict has done in his famous *regula*. Even then we constantly hear complaints of interruptions from the world. "Affairs," writes Hildebert, a monk of the twelfth century, "the enemy of my spirit, come upon me, they claim me for their own, they thieve the private hour of prayer, they defraud the services of the sanctuary, they irritate me with their stings by day and infest my sleep; and what I can hardly speak of without tears, the creeping, furtive memory of disputes follows me miserable to the altar's sacraments."

It is probable, all things considered, that the Middle Ages came nearer socializing the saint than any other period of history. Certainly there has never been a time before or since when saintly enthusiasm was so thoroughly exploited in the service of the whole social order. This specialization in spiritual matters would hardly have been possible apart from the patriarchal régime of the Middle Ages. The community was composed of definite classes and social groups with clearly determined status. Each class was, however,

indispensable to the welfare of the whole and found its justification in the service of the community. Upon the laity devolved the duty of providing the economic support for society and of propagating the race. The saint or "athlete of God" could not by virtue of his own vows of poverty and chastity share in these social duties. Men looked to him, however, to point them by word and act to a higher life; he was the center of spiritual inspiration, of social and moral reform, of intellectual leadership. Furthermore, he assumed, though on a smaller scale, the vicarious functions of the great head of the church. His sufferings and intercessions and also his superior merit were looked upon as most valuable social assets by the other members of the community to be utilized by them in case of need since they were forced by the logic of circumstances to live on a lower moral plane. The liberality of mediaeval society toward the spiritual orders, resulting in the rise of luxury and abuses which became their undoing, was in reality a pious and well-intentioned tribute to holiness and was prompted by a very deep and sincere realization of the social value of the saint. For the saint, to be sure, the living of one's life in actual society was a most perilous venture. Nothing but the strong hand of Hildebrand kept the fiery reformer, Peter Damiani, at his work. Even then, with his heart set on the seclusion of fair Monte Cassino, Damiani could write, "He errs, Father, errs indeed, who imagines he can be a monk and at the same time zealously serve the Curia. Ill he bargains, who presumes to desert the cloister, that he may take up the warfare of the world." Anselm, deeply immersed in the metaphysical problem of finding a final and comprehensive proof for the existence of God, was chosen abbot of the monastery of Bec. He flung himself in tears at the feet of his brother monks and besought them, though in vain, not to imperil his immortal soul with this burden of worldly cares. All the saints, whether it was the politician Hildebrand, the stern preacher of righteousness Bernard of Clairvaux, or the lovable mystic Francis of Assisi, viewed the *vita contemplativa* as the supreme ideal of life.

In spite of the large moral good sense of the church which insisted that the saint place his spiritual powers at the service of the community it was inevitable that the inherent self-contradictions in the saintly ideal should emerge in the course of time. The loss of healthful social contacts soon produced a distortion of the moral perspective. The imaginative absorption in the love of God, though charmingly beautiful, tended to destroy personality and produced the "theopathic" type such as Saint Francis. Constant introspective analysis of the processes of the soul-life induced grotesque exaggerations of the personal sense such as appear in the "voluble egotism" and the "stereotyped humility" of Saint Theresa. The unnatural separation of the individual from the social activities for which nature had fitted him caused strange perversions of powerful human instincts. Saint Louis was forced to shun all female society including that of his mother. Often religion degenerated in the case of neurotic females into an "endless amatory flirtation" with the deity. Finally this ideal placed its sanction upon a cowardly flight to the monastery where, embosomed in its innocuous calm, the saint might selfishly seek the peace of soul he was not strong enough to win surrounded by the full tide of life. Only the worldly wisdom of the church saved the saint from the gaunt and unlovely logic of his moral ideal. Having in her power the oracles of truth and the ultimate sanctions of conduct she forced the saint to abandon his impossible dualism and to recognize the spiritual ties that bound nature, man, and God together in one whole. She thus provided for the saint even against his will a vast and indispensable arena for the development of his powers. The moral energy often aroused by ecclesiastical excesses was thus appropriated by the church and skilfully utilized in strengthening her hold upon the world.

It was in this wise that the saint, even in spite of himself, became the symbol and the interpreter of the essential spiritual solidarity of mediaeval society. For the effective interpretation of this solidarity, which must be felt rather than grasped by reason, a peculiar temperamental equipment was necessary. Mere religiousness did not make the saint. "It is not unlikely," writes Joly, "that the saints . . are gifted, in matters concerning conscience and the spiritual life, with a delicate sensitiveness to which the ordinary run of men are strangers." There can be little doubt that the striking vitality and charm of the mediaeval as contrasted with the Protestant idea of the saint is due to the recognition in the former of the human side. The Protestant saint i elected by divine grace; in a certain sense he is not responsible for his saintliness it is thrust upon him. The mediaeval saint was born. Benedict XIV in laying down regulations for canonization was careful to stipulate that in addition to the "heroic virtues" of faith, hope, and love ther should be an equipment of "natural virtues" such as courage, justice, sympathy and the like.

The delicate sensitiveness of the saint to the deeper spiritual values of his age when joined with the ascetic mode of life easily led to the belief that he enjoyed supernatural power. The miracle became practically the sign manual of sainthood But it would be a great mistake to imagine that the mediaeval crop of marvelous tales of some 25,000 saints that have been gathered by the Bollandist editors i mainly significant as illustrating the credulity and superstitions of men. Gregory' *Lives of the Saints,* one of the earliest of the collections, illustrates their purpose They sought to show that the saint is th special receptacle of divine grace. He i a symbol of universal values. He bodie forth in life and thought the eternal plan The divine grace he represents and no the mere accidents of its expression is th important thing. The chronicler is bent upon making the life of the saint tell striking story of God's truth and love Hence miracles abound. No saint's life was complete without them. Sprung from the pious needs of an uncritical age these beautiful legends flourished for a thousand years. To the modern, however, the are interesting mainly as the naïve and charming record of an age of faith or as valuable material for the study of man's moral and religious nature. "They are exotics not from another climate but from another age; the breath of scorn fell on them and having no root in the hearts and beliefs of men any more, but only in the sentimentalities of make-beliefs, they withered and sank."

The unique position of the saint in the social order and the atmosphere of the supernatural that surrounded him proved in the end a handicap to his role as a moral leader. Because his person and all that concerned him were sacrosanct he became a law unto himself. This is strikingly illustrated in the curious perversion of moral standards attributed to the saints. Instances of saintly conduct abound which, according to more modern ethical ideals, are thoroughly reprehensible. Saint Verona, while the guest of a priest, made free use of his stores to provide for the wants of a neighboring leper colony. On being accused by a servant of stealing wine for the lepers the saint asserted that the jars contained water for the bathing of her patients. Upon examination the priest found that a miracle had been wrought and that the contents of the jars had been changed from wine to water. He at once fell at the saint's feet and begged absolution while the poor servant was stricken blind and afterward became the father of a family of defectives. The questionable morality of such stories is of far greater significance than the matter of their historical verity. They indicate that the sacrosanct character of the saint because of its unnaturalness tended to defeat the moral value of the saint's life. is of the very essence of immorality that the individual will should become a law unto itself . . .

As compared with the red-blooded saint of the Middle Ages the saint of Protestantism appears somewhat tenuous and unreal. Baxter has given us in his *Christian Directory*, in pious and repetitious prolixity, directions extending even to the smallest details for the ordering of the saint's life according to Calvinistic theology. But the Puritan saint even as portrayed by the gentle Baxter is singularly unattractive. We admire his stern moral strength but "he hath no form nor comeliness, and when we see him there is no beauty that we should desire him." The reason is not far to seek. For the saint of Calvinistic theology and of Protestantism in general is essentially a theological creation. He lives and moves and has his being for the most part in a realm of metaphysical values. The holiness he enjoys is primarily artificial in character. It is not his creation but is the result of a juridical pronouncement of infinite justice. His life in the community and the exercise of the civic virtues possess no intrinsic value of their own; they belong to the things that are "added"; they merely supplement the tale of his predestined moral worth.

. . . The mediaeval saint found his *raison d'etre* in moral and spiritual endowments which enabled him to perform a most necessary role in the community. To be sure Baxter's *Christian Directory* abounds as we have said in practical directions to the saint for the discharge of social duties. His congregation of Kidderminster weavers were enjoined to be obedient to authority, diligent, honest and thrifty in business. They were even exhorted to "become rich for the glory of God," an injunction which in time became entirely superfluous, for it has been pointed out that the beginnings of capitalism in England are to be traced to the thrifty manufacturing middle class most thoroughly impregnated with the Puritan ethic of industry and ascetic simplicity. But it remained true that the measure of values for the saint after Baxter's own heart lay not in the community he served but in an eternal and predestined moral order untouched by striving human wills. The saint was not the product of social needs; he was coined by a mysterious and eternal fiat of the divine will. The world of moiling and bargaining humanity was merely the dark foil that served to bring to light the implications of this remote impounding of the moral values of the universe.

It is evident that Baxter's conception of

the saint depended upon the ability of men to vitalize in thought and life the stupendous fabric of Calvinistic theology which was the most logical interpretation of Protestantism. But the decay of this stern theology was inevitable. It could not hold its own against the growing values of the secular order. There is today no more interesting and at the same time melancholy evidence of the spiritual *élan* of the Protestantism of the sixteenth and seventeenth centuries than this vast theological framework, once instinct with the breath of life, now almost as pulseless and inert as the bones of a dinosaur.

With the inevitable secularization of the moral and spiritual values, the Protestant conception of the saint was faced with a dilemma which we can state something after this fashion. The saint is dependent upon the institutional setting of the church with its traditions of thought and worship for the social discipline necessary to the development of the saintly character. But as the church becomes more and more departmental and the center of gravity for moral and spiritual values is transferred to the community the saint himself tends to become departmental, traditional, and conventional and ceases to play the role of moral and spiritual leadership characteristic of the saint of the Middle Ages. Here we have the explanation of the growing sense of unreality, not to say of antipathy, the modern world associates with the saint. There is apparently little or no place for him in the modern social order. This is unconsciously reflected in the thought of religious leaders themselves. "For the rest," writes a representative of liberal Protestantism, "that shining company seems to have retreated into the far distance behind the great fissure of the Reformation, and not all the efforts of hagiologists have made them real. They can hardly come to us, and our imagination can but feebly penetrate to their vanished world, so vast is our divergence from their thought, not simply as to this or that doctrine, but in our whole attitude, insight, and outlook upon life."

It is hardly an exaggeration to say that the idea of the saint, like many other traditions of the Middle Ages, has been shipwrecked upon the ineradicable individualism of Protestantism. The saint lived on, to be sure, enjoying a tenuous, metaphysical existence, thanks to John Calvin's heroic attempt to coerce the realm of spiritual values in the strait-jacket of his logic. But a "bloodless ballot" of theological categories was at best a poor and ineffective substitute for the warm, pervasive, and beneficent solidarity of mediaeval society. Not theology so much as the type of institutional life at Geneva, in Puritan England, Scotland, and New England, gave reality to Baxter's conception of the saint. With the triumph of sectarianism, the logical implication of Protestant individualism, the very heterogeneousness of the saintly complexion destroyed the social significance of the saint. It is no accident that we must seek our modern saints, those who most nearly fulfill the role of Anselm or Bernard or Damiani, in men and women that for the most part are not identified with institutional Christianity. It is our Lincolns, our Florence Nightingales, our Booker T Washingtons, that seem after all to have caught and interpreted the universal human values of the age.

The symbol that a leader represents is partly a product of his own personal characteristics, partly a creation of the promoters of the movement, and largely a projection by the followers. The appeal of the symbol, and the desire to discover the successful resolution of their own struggles embodied in a person of high prestige, create a potential following of persons who are most ready to supply the gaps in the leader image and to overlook contradictions. Some apparent success, recognition, or personal strength is a necessary condition for such large scale projection to take place. Many outstanding charismatic leaders have failed miserably and been mere objects of ridicule in their first efforts at leadership. At a time when they had not yet validated their claim to charisma, the process of imputing to them the qualities of the symbol did not automatically take place. But once sufficiently startling success or personal power can be demonstrated, the symbol-imputation process snowballs.

Besides the danger of revealing personal weakness or lack of self-confidence and unwavering decision, the chief danger to the leader symbol is its violation because of the practical demands imposed by the movement. The prophet who only preaches and is never faced with the practical necessity for implementing his ideas encounters less danger here than the leader with a genuine program of reform to carry out. The latter will be faced with the advantages of compromise, of "deals" with vested interests and established conventional leaders, of obvious errors of judgment and programs which do not work as they are intended to. But even the sheer prophet must cope with jealousy and power struggles within high movement echelons, and heresy and schism within the following.

Two mechanisms help to protect the inviolability of the leader symbol from these dangers. One of these is the self-protecting character of the symbolizing process itself, which makes for selective perception and a special valuation on the actions of the symbolized person. The followers do not see the faults of the leader, they refuse to believe them and attribute the accounts to the malice of others. And the very actions which are despised in the unsuccessful are admired in charismatic leaders. Intolerance in a lesser person becomes resolute action in the leader; inconsistency and wavering in the lesser person become inspired leadership.

The other mechanism is the delegation to subordinates of the more practical tasks and the assignment to them of responsibility for actions which might compromise the leader symbol. It has even been suggested that every great leader has to have someone to "do his dirty work" for him so that his own image remains unbesmirched. As the movement gains by tactics or compromises which may violate its pure value-orientations, the leader is conceived as succeeding in spite of these defections and suffering for the frailties of his followers. In extreme cases the lieutenant can be sacrificed as a scapegoat to an unpopular decision or notorious failure.

In addition to the generalized-symbol leaders there are the many types of specialized symbols which play important but segmental roles in the success of a movement. These specialized images may be crucial at certain stages in the development of a movement or in dealing with some groups of adherents. There is probably an unlimited number of different symbol types which may play parts in maintaining the support and strength of a movement. But unlike the charismatic leader who symbolizes the movement in general these specialized symbols are only effective at certain junctures. At the wrong time in movement development, or in dealing with the wrong population, they may be totally ineffectual, if not damaging, to the movement. We shall make no effort to discuss these specialized symbols in general. Instead we shall illustrate with one of the more prominent types, the *martyr*.

The function of the martyr symbol appears to be chiefly to strengthen the determination of those who are already adherents and to marshall active support from those who are giving passive support or are ambivalent about the movement. This function of winning those on the borderline and reinforcing those within the movement is accomplished by two effects of the martyr symbol. First, the image of the martyr arouses indignation against the opponents of the movement. The suspicion that the movement concerns a disagreement among reasonable men is dissipated if it can be shown that the opponents will "stop at nothing" to resist the movement. The martyr should be outnumbered, never given a chance, betrayed, and killed in an unnecessarily brutal way. Indignation, demand for retributive justice, and the conviction that the movement's opponents are persons outside the moral order help to win support.

Second, the image of the martyr symbolizes true and unwavering devotion to the cause, and thereby evokes guilt and shame in the half-hearted adherents. The member is reminded of his own delinquent support by contrast to the martyr and may even feel that the martyr would not have died except for his and other people's indifference.

While the martyr may sometimes be personally worthy of the badge, he is often merely a fool who has been a constant embarrassment to movement leaders and whose demise takes place in a foolhardy and profitless undertaking. Or he may be merely a chance victim. In either case, however, his image is quickly translated into that of the true martyr. The martyr image is more likely to be created in the early than the late phases of a movement. The extreme sacrifice and the posing of irreconcilable oppositions is more in keeping with the melodrama and enthusiasm of a movement's early stages than with the more practical and either self-confident or defeatist spirit of the later stages.

The leader as decision-maker. There are many kinds of decisions that must be made within a movement, and to varying degrees these become vested in different leaders. Many different classifications of these types of leaders have been attempted. Crane Brinton, for example, suggests four:

> I suggest very tentatively that the entrepreneurship of revolution or other radical change requires at least four kinds of skills not often possessed by one man. First, there is the discovery, the invention, of basic ideas, or better yet, theories. Second, there is the devising of suitable methods of spreading these ideas, getting them accepted, influencing men to act upon them—in short, the task of the propagandist and advertiser. These two functions, that of the theorist and that of the propagandist, are usually in real life very closely intertwined—a classical example is Karl Marx—but I hope you will agree with me that we ought to make an effort to distinguish them in analysis. . . . Third, there is the task of creating and holding the personal loyalty of the followers. This is the function for which the terms orator, symbol, priest, hero are not quite adequate. It is in fact a very complex function, and one which we do not understand very well, though we can recognize success at it in men like Robespierre and Hitler. Fourth, there is the manipulator in the narrow sense, the man in the smoke-filled room, the man who deals not with the masses, but personally and directly with the few important men at the top.*

Earlier, Rex D. Hopper has called our attention to a popular classification of leader types according to their predominance at successive stages in development of the movement. Beginning with the agitator, the succession is to the prophet and reformer, then to the statesman, and finally to the administrator-executive. The succession reflects a steady increase in preoccupation with the administration

* Quoted by permission of the New York University Press from Crane Brinton, "The Manipulation of Economic Unrest," **The Tasks of Economic History**, Supplement VIII (1948), pp. 25-26.

of the movement itself and with tactics for implementing objectives, and an increasing separation between the functions of symbol and decision-maker.

The popular identification of the movement with the conspicuous leader tends to obscure questions concerning the consonance between decisions by leaders and the decisions which in fact guide the movement. And yet in many different ways the actual course of a movement may not correspond to the personal decisions of any of its leaders. We may illustrate this observation with three prominent kinds of discrepancy which are often noted.

First, there is usually a somewhat continuous conflict between those leaders who are more value-oriented and those more concerned with the power and organization of the movement itself. At different stages the decisions may run more in the direction of one group than of the other, but the conflict and compromise between points of view are continuous and give rise to *de facto* decisions which do not correspond precisely to the personal inclinations of either type of leader.

Second, a movement is frequently precipitated into an extreme position which its personally more moderate leaders then find themselves committed to defend and promote. Extreme declarations or actions by minor leaders and others publicly identified with the movement operate in two ways to render moderate positions untenable. On the one hand they anger the opposition and make them less receptive to negotiation and compromise. And on the other hand, as symbols to the adherents, they become rallying points within the movement for extreme action. An incident symbolized as martyrdom likewise precipitates more extreme positions. Many famous leaders have been like George Washington, who at first favored compromise within the framework of the British Empire, and reluctantly moved into leadership of the revolutionary movement which had been precipitated by the actions of others. Lucretia Mott and Susan B. Anthony, who became major leaders in the American woman suffrage movement, were among those not originally in sympathy with women's unseemly departure from their historic status.

Third, the ideologist or prophet who formulates the ideals of the movement frequently suffers disillusionment over the translation of his ideas into the less visionary frames of reference of the movement personnel. Such distortion may occur through the necessary mixing of ideal- and self-interest within the movement. Labor movement ideologists, for example, frequently hold a broader idea of labor movement objectives as being concerned with the promotion of general community welfare, in contrast to membership who apply the more immediate self-interest criteria to policy statements. Within the C.I.O. the leadership have encountered reluctance and occasionally open revolt in their efforts to make equalitarian race relations an objective on a par with improved wages and working conditions.

John Milton provides an instructive example of an ideologist whose absolute ideals led him to reject movement after movement, shifting his own position from that of a moderate reformist to more and more extreme positions as he became disillusioned with all attempts to implement moderate ideas. The end result was to alienate him from all the independence movements of his time and to create a personal disillusionment which led him to adopt essentially aristocratic patterns of thought that contradicted his lifelong dedication to equality and freedom.

The person and scope of the leader. After examining the characteristics of the following, the creation of the charismatic image, and the functions of leaders as symbols and decision-makers, we return to the question of who the person is that steps into one of these roles. The most general answer that can be given to this question is to suggest that each occasion makes its own demands of the leader, and these demands are seldom identical from one situation to another. This conception is neatly summarized by Clarence Marsh Case in what he refers to as the "conjuncture" theory of leadership.

LEADERSHIP AND CONJUNCTURE: A SOCIOLOGICAL HYPOTHESIS

CLARENCE MARSH CASE

Certain talk about "teaching leadership," current at times in educational circles, led the writer to question whether there is actually any such thing as leadership traits in general; or anything else sufficiently abstract and universal about leadership to render the *teaching* of it at all possible. In other words, is not leadership simply one fleeting aspect of a changing social or human situation? Does not leadership itself disappear along with other aspects, such as *followership,* as the situation changes. Indeed, was it not just these shifting relations which, taken together, made up the situation itself in its sum and substance? At the outset leadership seemed to be more truly a matter of social situation than of personality traits, but gradually there came into view a third factor, namely the event. The falling together, or conjuncture, of these three factors produces leadership, or more accurately, the act of leading, according to the hypothesis herein proposed.

The word "conjuncture" was suggested by its use in the field of economics, as may be most briefly shown by the following quotation from Alfred Marshall.

This term is a familiar one in German economics, and meets a need which is much felt in English economics. For "opportunity" and "environment," the only available substitutes for it, are sometimes rather misleading. By

conjunctur, says Wagner, "we understand the sum total of the technical, economic, social and legal conditions . . . which determine the demand for and supply of goods and therefore their exchange value. . . ." [1]

Paraphrasing this, we see in conjuncture, as used in the present paper, the sum total of the personal, social, and historical conditions which determine the demand for and supply of leadership in human interaction. The three factors are defined as follows for the purpose of this hypothesis.

Personality traits represent the more abiding aspects of leadership although they themselves are conceived of as in process of change and development. Among them we may mention those "characteristics of the person which affect his social status and efficiency: (a) physical traits. . . .; (b) temperament; (c) character; (d) social expression. . . .; (e) prestige. . . .; (f) the individual's conception of his role." These are so listed by Park and Burgess.[2] To them let us add Floyd H. Allport's "Traits of Personality" [3] among which appear such rather permanent traits as Perceptual Ability, Emotional Breadth, Insight, and Drive.

The *social situation,* already treated in its relation to leadership by Emory S.

Reprinted by permission of The University of Southern California Press, from Clarence Marsh Case, "Leadership and Conjuncture: A Sociological Hypothesis," **Sociology and Social Research,** 17 (July-August, 1933), pp. 510–13.

[1] **Principles of Economics** (New York, 1907), p. 125.

[2] Cf., **Introduction to the Science of Sociology** (Chicago, 1921), p. 70.

[3] Cf., **Social Psychology** (Boston, 1924), p. 103.

ogardus,[4] was originally defined by
Thomas and Znaniecki[5] as involving
three kinds of data." They say:

(1) The objective conditions under
which the individual or society has to
act, that is, the totality of values—economic, social, religious, intellectual,
etc.—which at the given moment affect directly or indirectly the conscious
status of the individual or the group.

(2) The pre-existing attitudes of the
individual or the group which at the
given moment have an actual influence
upon his behavior.

(3) The definition of the situation,
that is, the more or less clear conception of the conditions and consciousness of the attitudes.

The person, with his traits, facing a
constellation of social values and attitudes in other persons, thus gives us two
of our factors. The third is *the event*. At
this point we have to point out that these
three factors are not mutually exclusive,
since the definition of the situation by the
person in itself constitutes part of the social situation but is also included under
the individual's conception of his role,
which we have accepted above as a personal trait. The same overlapping appears
when we consider the event, which seems
at first glance to be an aspect of the social
situation. This, to be sure, it is, but a
quite special aspect. An event is a form
of change just as a social situation is a
process of many changes in itself. Moreover the growth of personality is a process of mental integration and disintegration in large part. So it appears that all
our factors are aspects or forms of
change. Yet this need not disconcert us,
since leadership, the very thing we are
seeking to factor, is itself a form of
change, a process of society, of interaction between the person and his associates, or with the group as a whole.

An *event* is, as historians have always
regarded it, a significant or outstanding
change. It is part and parcel of the stuff

that the world is made of, namely activity
and change, but it receives, and deserves,
a special name. The reason for this may
be shown by the following quotation from
Frederick J. Teggart wherein he holds:

> The current acceptance of "events"
> as important in and for themselves will
> give place to the concept of events as
> the active element in change; events
> will be conceived, not as the expression
> of the will-acts of individuals, but as
> "intrusions," of whatever sort, affect-
> ing conditions in which the processes
> manifested in "fixity" have been opera-
> tive without disturbance.

He goes on to say:

> The identification of "events" as "in-
> trusions" is a matter of some impor-
> tance. To reach an understanding of
> "how things work" in the course of
> time, we may envisage the facts of ex-
> perience as arranged conceptually in a
> series of concentric circles. Outermost,
> we would have the stellar universe,
> within this, the physical earth, within
> this, the world of organic life; within
> this, again, the world of organic life;
> within this, again, the world of human
> activities; within this, the larger group,
> or nation; within this, the local com-
> munity; and finally, within this, the in-
> dividual. In such a series it is obvious
> that change in any outer circle will
> affect all that lies within it. We may,
> then, define an "event" as an intrusion,
> from any wider circle, into any circle
> or condition which may be the object
> of present interest.[6]

The sentence last quoted is our ground
for regarding, in the present theory of
leadership as conjuncture, any intrusive
change, no matter how trivial or private,
as an event if it disrupts the smooth flow
of routinary change, of static, recurrent
social process, within the field of interest
or leadership under consideration at the
moment. For no sociologist needs to be
told that leadership of an alley gang is
just as valid a case as leadership of the
allied nations, although not, of course, so
important for human affairs.

The present hypothesis is that the con-

---

[4] Cf., **Sociology and Social Research,** XIV
Nov.–Dec., 1931).

[5] Cf., **The Polish Peasant in Europe and
America,** I (New York: Alfred A. Knopf,
1927), p. 68.

[6] Cf., **Theory of History,** by Frederick J.
Teggart (New Haven, 1925), pp. 148–49,

juncture, or falling together, of personality traits, social situation, and event determines leadership from hour to hour in

the relations of obscure persons, an from time to time in the affairs of th world. . . .

The situation prescribes some specific characteristics for the leader. And ye we cannot escape the observation that there are some people who turn up a leaders in a variety of situations. Our study of leadership traits is made mor difficult because institutional leadership positions tend to protect and support th authority of persons who do not possess qualities of spontaneous leadership. Th leaders of social movements are less well protected and their own effectivenes should therefore play a larger part. On the other hand, the leader of a movemer is in a situation unlike that of the leader in a small face-to-face group. His direc personal contacts are with but a few persons in key positions and his relation with the bulk of membership personnel are through intermediaries and his publi personality. Thus the effective primary group leader may lack the public persor ality and a person who is rather unimpressive and even disliked in primary rela tions may become a tremendously effective charismatic leader.

But the leader personality is more than just what he brings to the situatior it includes the personal transformations he undergoes after he begins carryin out the leader role. The image that the following creates demands his cor formity. The selective communication that he receives modifies his perspective The sense of his role and the routine imposed upon him require extensive adjust ment. J. E. Hulett, Jr., has supplied an instructive account of the manner in whic Elizabeth Kenny evolved from the Australian bush nurse putting forward a nove technique for treating paralyzed victims of poliomyelitis to the "Sister Kenny who was the charismatic leader of a world-wide movement against the asserte blindness and selfishness of the established medical profession. For example Hulett notes that:

> One of the ways in which a cult leader responds to the leadership situation is t undergo an evolution of ideas regarding the theoretical basis for the movemen This leader's conception of her role has evolved from that of a simple pragmati to that of the astute hypothesist. Whereas at first she merely applied a pragmat discovery to the treatment of the disease, she now has developed a whole "ne concept" of the disease which she describes as "the direct opposite" of the concep previously held by medical world.*

The characteristics, then, that distinguish the leaders of movements may n be altogether apparent in the individual before he assumes leadership, but ma exist largely in the capacity to respond to his role and his public image in a effective way.

A final question that arises from the preceding discussion concerns the scop of the leader's effectiveness. To the degree to which the leader is an individua who is precipitated into a leadership position by a unique historical conjunctur and whose effective retention of leadership depends upon supporting the imag which his followers create and upon making decisions in keeping with trends i the movement, it may appear that the leader is merely a puppet. It may appea

* Reprinted by permission of the American Sociological Society and the author fro J. E. Hulett, Jr., "The Kenny Healing Cult: Preliminary Analysis of Leadership a Patterns of Interaction," **American Sociological Review,** 10 (1945), p. 366,

that he is nothing but the passive agent through which the determinism of history takes place.

While the issue of such total determinism may not be ultimately resolvable by empirical evidence, one of the clearest and most considered statements on the issue has been made by Sidney Hook. Although events may normally allow the leader little real discretion, there are certain moments in history in which real alternatives do exist, such that the decision of a person in power can determine which of these alternatives will be followed. Decisions made at these junctures may be merely those of persons who happen to be in power and have little conception of the significance of their decision. But occasionally decisions are made in such situations by true "heroes" or "event-making men" who understand the significance of the situation confronting them and act accordingly. Sidney Hook argues that the events in Russia in 1917 created such a situation and that Lenin, as an event-making man, took command and made and effectively implemented the decisions that determined that world history should follow one path rather than some alternative path. In an historically-determined crisis there were potentially several courses that could have been taken, and the decisions of Lenin therefore became crucial.

Chapter 21

End-products of social movements

A SOCIAL movement cannot continue as such indefinitely. Unlike institutionalized associations marked by stability, the social movement is by definition dynamic. When it loses this characteristic it ceases to be a social movement and either disappears or becomes a different social form. In the present discussion we shall be concerned with the process through which a movement changes form as it passes from its dynamic proselyting period.

What transitions take place in a movement will depend upon the effects that the movement has on the environing social order and on the effects that that social order has on the movement. For example, the terminal form of a value-oriented movement that has effectively modified the social structure is likely to be quite different from that of a movement of little consequence. Hence, an examination of the reciprocal interaction between movement and social order is an essential part of the study of the terminal forms of social movements.

Institutionalization. The very success of a movement, in the sense of increased membership and power, leads to a transformation. Increased size threatens to remove control of the movement from any set group and render control and policies entirely capricious. Consequently those in control will seek to regularize procedures to support their own power and policies and those on the periphery will demand responsibility and predictability. The very fact of continuing existence will translate earlier spontaneous patterns into embryonic traditions governing behavior within the movement. Hence out of the demands of both leadership and membership and from the mere fact of repeated association any movement tends to become rigid with time.

Some movements tend not merely toward stability but also toward institutionalization. A movement is institutionalized when it has reached a high degree of stability internally and been accorded a recognized position within the larger

480

society. Institutionalization occurs when the movement is viewed as having some continuing function to perform in the larger society, as it is accepted as a desirable or unavoidable adjunct to the existing institutional arrangements.

Through institutionalization the environing society imposes additional stability upon the movement. A key aspect of institutionalization is the establishment of patterns for dealing with the group. An indispensable condition for such dealings is responsibility, the assurance that authentic decisions will not be negated by unpredictable shifts in leadership or in the loyalties of members. The dealings that recognized agencies of the larger society have with the movement serve to accord prestige to those representatives of the movement with whom they choose to deal. Thus the prestige structure built up within the movement tends to be modified so as to fit better the prestige structure of the society and the requirements of stable, responsible commitments.

A particularly important aspect of institutionalization is the recognition of certain areas of competence and of certain functions as constituting the legitimate scope of the movement. Thus, by calling in labor leaders to testify in public hearings or to participate in conferences as spokesmen for the interests of labor, the society grants the labor union this special area of competence. By the same action institutionalization may restrict the scope of a movement that has tended toward a self-definition of universalized competence. Religious movements that may pretend to judicial and economic functions relinquish these as they become institutionalized within a society whose governmental and economic institutions are already well established.

Institutionalization is imposed not only in the process of dealing with the environing society but also through the acquisition of a stabilized body of adherents with stabilized expectations. Members come to be dependent upon participation in the movement for certain gratifications. Not only does the movement satisfy some pre-existing needs of its members, but participation tends to create needs that can only be satisfied through continuing predictable participation. The institution seems to fill a fixed space in the life scheme of the people.

As it becomes institutionalized, the movement tends to diversify the gratifications of participation. It tends to multiply and diversify activities so as to provide gratifications for all kinds of people. The church establishes the young people's social, and sponsors various recreational groups. The political machine organizes boys' clubs and charity programs.

Particularly important in this multiplication of gratifications is the addition of societal prestige. Participation and prominence in the movement now become a recognized route to prestige in the larger society. So long as the movement is not accorded institutional status, active members gain prestige thereby only in the eyes of persons who look favorably upon the movement. But as the entire organization is recognized in the society, prestige within the group is translated into prestige in the society.

As diversification of participation-gratifications takes place, and as persons are increasingly attracted to the movement in order to attain society-wide prestige, conventional motivations and patterns of behavior displace the distinctive and deviant in the movement. Ideologies are toned down so as to be acceptable to a wider range of people and so as not to undercut the prestige that participants gain.

All types of movements may take on this institutionalized character. A value-oriented movement may become a national safety organization, a national health organization, a national women's organization, etc. Religious cults tend in the same direction, as has been indicated earlier in the selection by H. Richard Niebuhr. Those religious groups which have passed to the stage of institutionalization are referred to as "denominations" or "churches." Earl Brewer suggests some criteria for differentiating the two extreme types as they apply to a religious movement, and tests the types specifically on the Methodist movement.

SECT AND CHURCH IN METHODISM

EARL D. C. BREWER

The sociology of religion may be defined as the scientific study of religion as a social institution, including its interrelationships with other social institutions and other aspects of society and culture.[1] This definition not only differentiates it from other approaches to religious phenomena [2] but makes it cognate with other special sociologies dealing with major social institutions, e.g., family, state, economic organization, education, recreation. The sociology of religion would be dependent upon general sociology, then, for both its theory and methods. Special dependence would attach to that part of general sociology which centers upon social institutions which B. Malinowski regarded as "the legitimate isolate of cultural analysis," [3] and which Talcott Parsons called "the logical focus of sociology." [4] Such theoretical dependence should be mutual since investigations in a given social institution might be expected to have implications for other social institutions if not, indeed, for modification and amplification of general theory. This affinity of the sociology of religion for other special sociologies dealing with social institutions does not, of course, mean that it is not intimately related to and dependent upon other fields of sociology, e.g., community, race, ecology, regionalism, social change, population, social stratification, as well as social psychology and sociology of knowledge.

Most definitions of the concept, "social institution," fall between the rather

specific use of Znaniecki in limiting the term to "such official, impersonally patterned functions and statuses of members of any organized social group . . ." [5] and the more general view of Panunzio that social institutions may be regarded as "those systems of concepts, usages, associations, and instruments which, arising from the experiences of mankind, order and regulate the activities of human beings which are necessary to the satisfaction of basic needs. They are the basic systems of human activities, having considerable permanence, universality, and inter-penetrative independence." [6]

Regardless of the level of generality involved or the specific aspects emphasized, most sociologists and anthropologists who make extensive use of the concept "social

[1] For other definitions and efforts to delimit the field see L. L. Bernard (ed.), **The Fields and Methods of Sociology** (New York: Farrar and Rinehart, 1934), p. 165; Joachim Wach, **Sociology of Religion** (Chicago: University of Chicago Press, 1944), p. 374; Arthur L. Swift, Jr., **New Frontiers of Religion** (New York: The Macmillan Co., 1938), p. vii.

[2] Joachim Wach, op. cit., pp. 1–17.

[3] Bronislaw Malinowski, **A Scientific Theory of Culture** (Chapel Hill: University of North Carolina Press, 1944), p. 51.

[4] Talcott Parsons, "The Position of Sociological Theory," **American Sociological Review,** 13 (April 1948), p. 161.

[5] Florian Znaniecki, "Social Organization and Institutions," in Georges Gurvitch and W. E. Moore (eds.), **Twentieth Century Sociology** (New York: Philosophical Library, 1945), p. 211.

[6] Constantine Panunzio, **Major Social Institutions** (New York: Macmillan Co., 1939) p. 27.

Reprinted by permission of the editors, from **Social Forces,** 30 (May, 1952), pp. 400–408.

institutions"[7] devise categories or type-parts as analytical tools.

These may be summarized and applied to a specific religious body or institution, to use the term in a restricted sense. Thus, a religious institution may be said to be composed of conceptual and ideological elements; usages, ritual and behavioral patterns; associational and organizational elements; and material and instrumental aspects which channelize the activities of human beings toward the satisfaction of basic needs, in this case, commonly recognized as religious. The conceptual and ideological elements would include the manner in which the particular institution conceptualizes the field of religion; works out its evaluational system; rationalizes its own origin, development, and mission; defines its attitude toward and relationships with other religious institutions, other social institutions, and other aspects of society. The usages, rituals, and behavioral patterns include all customs, ceremonials, rituals and other patterned ways of behavior expected of groups or of individuals in those aspects of their behavior related to the institution. The associational or organizational elements include the groups which compose the institutional structure, such as members and leaders occupying various statuses and playing numerous roles, perhaps in terms of institutional offices. The material or instrumental category includes such items as physical property, financial status, and such symbolic traits as language and the cross—in a word, all material and symbolic instruments used by the institution. This scheme deals with the internal structure of an institution. The character of many of these categories will naturally depend upon the functional relationships sustained by the particular structural units

to the total institution. In addition, its position in the social structure, the geographic distribution, the relationships with other institutions of the same system, with all other social institutions as well as with other aspects of culture and society—all these factors are of importance in a structural-functional analysis of a given institution.

The use of this concept with its type-parts as a research tool for handling raw data descriptive of the institution-ways of one or more religious bodies would result in only a rough and static classification of the descriptive material. For a conceptual scheme to have dynamic elements and to be structured in a manner adequate to house correctly framed working hypotheses regarding sequential patterns of change in religious bodies, including the interrelationships between such changes and social change in general, these categories from social institutional theory would need to be related to a typology of religious bodies drawn from studies in the sociology of religion and to constructed types of societies with which to treat societal change.

From Max Weber, especially his student, Ernst Troeltsch, to Howard Becker and his student, Milton Yinger, there has been repeated use of the terms "sect" and "church" to designate "distinct sociological types" of religious bodies.[8] The cumulative results of this theoretical endeavor may be related to the structural categories of social institutions to arrive at a preliminary statement of a constructed sect-type and church-type of religious institution.

A. THE EXTREME SECT-TYPE is, internally, polarized about a small, primary group with face-to-face relationships, with

[7] For examples, see William Graham Sumner, **Folkways** (Boston: Ginn and Co., 1906), p. 53; F. Stuart Chapin, **Contemporary American Institutions** (New York: Harpers, 1935), p. 412; J. O. Hertzler, **Social Institutions** (Lincoln, Nebraska: University of Nebraska Press, 1946, revised); B. Malinowski, op. cit., pp. 52-53; John Gillin, **The Ways of Men** (New York: D. Appleton-Century Co., 1948), p. 492; Constantine Panunzio, op. cit., p. 27.

[8] See Earl D. C. Brewer, Methodism in Changing American Society (unpublished Ph.D. dissertation, University of North Carolina, 1950), for a brief review of this theoretic work which, in addition to these persons, deals with the contributions of John M. Mecklin, Liston Pope, F. H. Giddings, Richard Neibuhr, R. E. Park and E. W. Burgess, R. L. Sutherland and J. L. Woodward, Ellsworth Faris, J. Wach, Reinhold Niebuhr, H. W. Reed, Forest Weller, and A. W. Eister.

relatively undifferentiated leadership of a charismatic character which roots its authority in direct religious experiences and contact with Christ as Head of the Church; and, externally, withdraws into small groups, sets up conflict patterns with secular institutions, and attempts to substitute its own internal religious fellowship for wider socialization.

1. The sect-type, *in its conceptual and ideological type-part,* arises in revolt against, and commonly breaks away from, a church-type religious institution. It appeals to the New Testament and the Primitive Church as ideals with emphasis on religious equality and brotherly love; poverty, and frugality; radical individualism in religious experience; redemption through subjective experience rather than through objective grace; and personal achievement in ethics and religion. There is general criticism of sacramentalism, official spiritual guides and theologians, and the various so-called excesses of the church-type institution. Christ is considered the head of the fellowship of believers. It renounces the idea of dominating the "world" and confines itself to domination of the selected few. There is general hostility or indifference toward the "world," toward ruling classes and state authority, and dislike of technical law and of the oath. There is concern with utopian patterns of thought and a resurgence of biblical eschatology as the only form of universalism.

2. *In its associational and organizational type-part,* the sect-type is a personal fellowship of small, voluntary, select, and exclusive groups. Adult baptism and conversion are the methods of gaining membership-character. Members are drawn largely from the lower classes of the society. Membership is maintained by the quality of religious life and may be discontinued by personal decision or by dismissal for failure to maintain the standards of the group. Typical characteristics of primary face-to-face groups are exhibited in the statuses and roles of members and leaders. These groups prefer isolation to compromise with larger aspects of society. They are dispersed and irregularly distributed as "culture pockets."

The leaders are unprofessional, untrained, and arise largely from the group itself. They possess charisma of the person rather than of the office and are legitimatized by a sense of personal call. There is little or no overhead, hierarchical organization beyond the local group.

3. *In the category of usages, ritual, and behavioral patterns,* the sect-type is at war with many folkways and mores of the general culture and tends to replace these with strict norms and patterns of behavior for its membership. Membership is dependent upon observance of such patterns of behavior, many of which relate to areas not commonly regarded as religious. Patterns of worship and other ceremonials are simple, austere, and casual with large participation by the full membership of the group. Behavior patterns are characteristically those of small primary groups.

4. The sect-type, *in the material and instrumental aspects,* is characterized by poverty. Meetings of groups may be in homes or in simple, inexpensive meeting houses with meager equipment. There is little use of distinctive symbolic instruments. The leadership is either without pay or with very nominal income. Financial contributions are irregular, small in amount per capita, and on a free will basis. Few, if any, philanthropic, welfare, educational, and service agencies of a formal nature are supported. Mutual aid and other such communal sharing is done on a small primary group basis.

B. THE EXTREME CHURCH-TYPE is, internally, polarized about a large, widespread membership with emphasis upon objective institutionalization of the means of grace and salvation, ministered through a hierarchical priesthood, whose bureaucratically differentiated legal-traditionalistic leadership is validated by historical succession from the Founder of Christianity; and is, externally, ideally co-terminous with society, accommodates itself to secular institutions, compromises and attempts to dominate and control them.

1. The church-type, *in the conceptual and ideological type-part,* arises out of an elaboration of an earlier sect-type religious institution in an effort to conserve

gains and to adjust to a more complicated situation. It roots back in Jewish priestly elements, the compromises of the early disciples, and the conservative elements in Paul. It appeals to Jesus as Man-God working in history, to the validity of the Christian tradition, and to apostolic authority expressed in the institutional church. Emphasis is upon the objective validity of the institution as a means of grace and salvation and the necessity to dominate the entire area of influence, to wipe out or absorb all opposing religious movements, and to accommodate to and control all secular institutions. Elaboration of conceptual or doctrinal structure, a deep sense of history, a tendency to rationalize and justify institutional existence, and primary concern with ideological, as opposed to utopian, modes of thought characterize the church-type. It is conservative and exhibits a success complex.

2. *In its associational and organizational category,* the church-type is made up of members from all classes and geographic areas of the society. It is thus widespread and inclusive, if not co-extensive with the given society. Persons are born into a relationship with the church-type organizations and infant baptism and confirmation are stages in passing into full membership. Membership-character is maintained by formal relationships to institutional procedures and may be discontinued at death or through excommunication for institutional reasons. The leadership is professional and specialized. It possesses charisma of the office and statuses and roles are organized into a bureaucratic hierarchy. It develops into the legal-rational and/or traditionalistic types of elaborate organizational structure.

3. The church-type, *in the area of usages, ritual and behavioral patterns,* generally accepts the folkways, mores and morals of prevailing groups of the general culture. It attempts to re-interpret alien patterns in keeping with its own interests and to adjust its own patterns to absorb them. Elaborate rituals and ceremonials are developed for all the major experiences of individual and group life. In spe-

cifically religious behavior, e.g., worship and sacramental rites, large responsibility is delegated to the priesthood. Performances become extremely elaborate, professional, colorful.

4. *In its material and instrumental elements,* the church-type institution is wealthy. Church buildings tend toward the cathedral type with ample, if not ornate, appointments and equipment. It is rich in symbolic instruments. Ownership of vast properties characterize the church-type. The income is from property and taxes or tithes on a compulsory or semi-compulsory basis. The professional leadership is well paid. Widespread philanthropic, welfare, educational, and service agencies of a formal character are supported.

Assuming continua connecting these polar types, it would be possible to analyze data descriptive of a given religious body with respect to placement along such continua. The same procedure would hold for the comparative placements of several religious bodies at a given time or of a single body at different periods in its institutional life. Conceptually, to the extent to which religious institution-ways of a given body approximated the constructed sect-type (or church-type) in their structural-functional manifestations they would be termed sect-ways (or church-ways) and the organization exhibiting them a sect-type (or a church-type) religious institution.

This typology has been useful as a conceptual scheme within which certain propositions regarding religious institutional change could be tested. For example, attention has been focused upon The Methodist Episcopal Church and the pattern of change occurring in it from the decade of organization, 1780–1790, to the decade of unification with other Methodist bodies, 1930–1940. The general hypothesis was that it had moved from the sect-type toward the church-type of religious institution during this period. The conceptual scheme proved fruitful in furnishing the elements necessary for the deduction of working sub-hypotheses, the necessary guidance regarding the types of data needed to test the hypothesis, the categories for classifying such descriptive material, and, finally, the tools for a dynamic analysis of the data in terms of the major hypothesis itself. The study involved an examination of the major primary records deposited by The Methodist Episcopal Church with special attention to the reconstruction of the structural-functional characteristics of the body at four points in the one hundred fifty year period. In addition to "vertical probings" of the terminal decades, two intermediate decades at fifty year intervals (1830–1840 and 1880–1890) were used.

Limiting attention to the terminal periods only, a very brief summary of the data will indicate the extent to which Methodism approximated the sect-type in 1780–1790 and the church-type in 1930–1940. The first summarization of material is for Methodism during the decade of organization.

1. In the beginning, American Methodism was largely a transplantation of English Methodism. This was certainly true ideologically. The early Methodist movement in England had arisen in revolt against the church-type Church of England. There was an appeal to New Testament Christianity and the Primitive Church, yet early Methodism accepted many of the elements of Christian tradition as introduced by Wesley in modification of the patterns of the Church of England. The American Church conceived its mission in Wesleyan terms: "To reform the Continent and to spread scriptural holiness over these lands." The term "scriptural holiness" involved a highly personalized conception of salvation, rationalized the God-man relationship in Armenian terms, with the expectancy of a highly emotionalized process of repentance, salvation, sanctification and Christian perfection. Religious achievement was measured in terms of the "witness of the spirit" and of personal effort in morals and economics. At the same time, there was emphasis upon social reform in terms of bringing criticism to bear upon selected social problems, such as slavery. Social salvation involved essentially the salvation of persons from

society. Early persecution of Methodism in America forced a measure of withdrawal from and conflict with society. However, there was general support of the Federal Government, endorsement of private property, and organization and support of schools and orphanages. Thus, there was limited accommodation to, and to some extent, criticism of prevailing political and economic institution-ways. Ideologically, then, Methodism was basically sect-type in the beginning although it never freed itself of some church-type traits inherited from the Church of England.

2. In the area of groups and organizations, Methodism was small in membership and scattered along the eastern seaboard. Its congregations were relatively isolated from the rest of society, with a sharp differentiation between members and nonmembers. Its membership was drawn predominantly from the lower classes of early American society. A religious experience of salvation was necessary for church membership, though the children of members might secure infant baptism. Membership character was continued by approximating through personal effort the moral standards demanded by the group. Discipline and expulsion of members for behavior deviations were frequent. Methodists were held together in primary groups with intimate sharing of experiences in class meetings and bands. Mutual aid was practiced in religious, social and economic affairs. The local societies or congregations were generalized groups of the total membership with subdivisions into classes and bands for more intimate relationships. These local congregations or groups of laymen had a conference of preachers superimposed upon them. This clerical group possessed, in embryonic form, the basis of the professional ministry structured along specialized bureaucratic hierarchical lines. Thus, the organization of laymen was along sect-type lines, while the conference of preachers was a church-type inheritance from the Church of England.

The chief dividing line in the status-roles and institutional offices separated laymen and clergymen. A generalized role of class leader was differentiated among lay members. Ordained preachers gave full-time service to a circuit or a group of societies on an itinerating basis. Between the visits of these traveling preachers local activities were carried on largely by lay leadership. The preachers were not required to pass educational standards in the beginning but were constantly urged to read and sell books. There was great emphasis on "the call of the Holy Ghost to preach," but in addition, the candidate had to be voted into the conference of preachers before receiving permission to preach. Thus, the basic charisma of the person had to be supplemented by charisma of the office.

3. In the area of usages, ritual and behavior patterns, some of the strongest sect-type characteristics were exhibited. Personal behavior prescriptions were handed down by Wesley against excesses in food, clothing, and shelter. Prohibitions against all recreational activities, slave-holding, drinking, quarreling, taking advantage of a brother in economic affairs, and so on, were imposed. There were positive prescriptions for simple, honest, hard-working personal character traits with emphasis upon mutual aid and support. There was recommended a formal liturgy for Sunday services and ritual forms for such ceremonies as marriage, burial, baptism, Lord's Supper, and ordination. These were modified from the Church of England. The formal liturgy was rejected and the ritual forms greatly simplified before acceptance in American Methodism. The emphasis was upon informal worship and preaching services, with simple revivalistic songs. Thus, in this area, too, there was the interplay of dominant sect-ways with the formal church-ways inherited from the Church of England.

4. In its material aspects, early American Methodism approximated the sect-type almost completely. The lower class people who gave allegiance to Methodism were poor and the societies were characterized by relative poverty, with dependence upon irregular "freewill" offerings for the support of full-time preachers and missionary and other connectional enterprises. Preachers received a common income, which was hardly sufficient to meet actual expenses. There were emotional appeals for collections. The Church was from the beginning involved in the printing business. The local societies met in homes, brush arbors, simple chapels, and in the open fields. The chapels had little equipment and few comforts. There was decided opposition to rented pews, cushions, crosses, stained-glass windows and other so-called excesses characteristic of the church-type religious institution. In this area, the young religious body approximated most closely the sect-type, yet it was through its involvement in the printing business and in other economic enterprises that rationalism entered earliest into the ordering of the bureaucratic structure of the religious institution.

One hundred and fifty years later both Methodism and American Society exhibited characteristics differing greatly from those of the early days of the Republic. To mention only the population changes, the United States had increased from nearly four millions to more than one hundred thirty-one millions of people, while Methodism had grown from fifty thousand to over seven million in membership. These changes in population and in church membership were associated with other structural-functional modifications in American Society and in Methodism. Confining attention to the Methodist Episcopal Church, a summary of its institutional characteristics points to a movement away from the sect-type and toward the church-type.

1. During the decade before Unification the ideology of the Methodist Episcopal Church involved a conception of its own mission in terms of maintaining itself as a dominant religious body and in reforming society in keeping with a liberal theological interpretation of religion, with special emphasis upon the social gospel. Salvation was rationalized as a progressive growth in grace, symbolized by membership in the Church. Religious achievement was measured in terms of church attendance and financial support

of the work of the church. There was selective accommodation to the dominant folkways and mores of American society. There was acceptance of the basic societal values and participation in major social institutional activities. For example, in 1936 the Methodist Episcopal Church identified itself with democracy as completely as ever the Roman Catholic Church did with feudalism during the Medieval Period. It was in sect-type conflict with specific activities, such as legalized liquor, drinking, and gambling. Nevertheless, its social ethics dealt directly with social problems and institution-ways, as well as with personal behavior patterns. There was a growing appreciation of the traditions of Christianity, especially the Protestant branch of it, and an increasing appeal to and use of the institution-ways of all Christian bodies, for example, the hymnody. There was new concern with its own history and traditions. Ideologically, then, Methodism had definitely moved toward the church-type, although there were remnants of the sect-type as seen in conflict patterns with certain folkways and mores.

2. In the area of groups and organizations, the membership of Methodism was spread geographically over the entire United States, although it made up less than five percent of the total population. There was little differentiation between members and non-members. Methodist churches were not persecuted by or withdrawn from the rest of society. The total membership was drawn from all classes of society but given local congregations might be made up predominantly of members from one class. Church membership was based on a formal statement of faith, infant baptism, a training program in the meaning of church membership, and a decision to join the church. Active membership character was maintained by attendance upon services or financial contributions or both. Discipline and expulsion of members were rare, and then more often for failure to support the institution than for personal deviation and behavior. Personal relationships of members tended to become secondary and formal, especially in cities where

members often were not personally acquainted. Specialized groups of members emphasized fellowship meetings to overcome this contractual type of inter-personal relationships. A variety of specialized boards, committees, and groups existed in the local church. These were related to an interlocking hierarchy of organizations above the local church level. A complex set of conferences and other administrative units formed a complex hierarchy in the church at large. Thus, in its groups and organizations, Methodism had moved from the relatively simple local societies and conference of preachers to a highly differentiated bureaucracy.

In keeping with the differentiation in types of groups, specialized lay leadership roles emerged, such as Sunday School teachers, stewards, trustees, chairmen of committees, and secretaries. Many activities of the church were carried on by this specialized lay leadership. Full-time ordained and professionally trained ministers had responsibility for the major functions of the church, although a local ministry was continued. The call to preach received less emphasis than educational standards in determining status in annual conferences. The charisma of the person was thus weakened at the expense of charisma of the office, with emphasis upon structuralization of clerical authority along traditional and legal-rational lines. These specialized lay and clerical status-roles were structured in a complex hierarchy of offices within the bureaucratic religious institution.

3. In the area of usages and behavior patterns, there was growing acceptance of prevailing folkways and mores of society with exceptions in such personal behavior as prohibitions against drinking alcoholic beverages for all Methodists and against the use of tobacco on the part of ministers. There was basic acceptance of and accommodation to various social institutional areas as organized in American Society, with criticisms in terms of particular deviations from Methodist ideology. An example is found in the accommodation to recreation-ways but with

criticism of gambling. Also, there was accommodation to divorce but prohibition against remarriage of divorced persons by Methodist clergy, except under certain circumstances. Generally, there was more attention to institution-ways than to personal behavior patterns. There was increased formality in worship and preaching services with a hymnody representing all types of Christian music, including chants and anthems. There were much more elaborate forms for various ritual performances, although in some cases the meaning of the ceremonies had been changed in keeping with liberal theology. There was a large increase in the number of life situations for which ceremonials were prescribed. This was seen in the development of a Methodist *Book of Worship* or "Prayer Book" and the increased emphasis in professional training on the correct performance of worship and ceremonials. It is obvious that in this area Methodism was becoming more increasingly church-type, although with a holdover of certain sect-type tendencies.

4. Just as in the beginning the poverty of Methodism made it sect-type in its material aspects, so after one hundred and fifty years, it was in this area that it had achieved perhaps its most striking approximation of the church-type religious institution. Methodism had a larger stake in the economic life of America with income, buildings, and equipment in the billion dollar class. Its income was derived through fairly systematic contributions from members and from investments. There was support of orphanages, homes for the aged, settlement work, hospitals, educational institutions, and so on. Economic rationalism permeated this involvement in the economic order, including financial plans from the local church through all conferences and organizations. Ministers were better and more systematically paid than one hundred and fifty years earlier. Also, instead of mutual income arrangements, each individual congregation paid its own minister, an accommodation to individual enterprise economics. Church buildings were as elaborate as a local congregation could afford. In large cities, these attained ca-

thedral proportions, with adequate space for fellowship and educational activities and with elaborate furnishing and equipment. Increasing use of the cross, vestments, and other symbols of traditional Christianity moved Methodism toward the church-type.

It is obvious from this brief summary of the data that Methodism was basically sect-type in 1780–1790 and that it had moved toward church-type characteristics by 1930–1940. Including the intermediate periods under analysis, a rough approximation of this total movement is shown in Figure 1. A warning should be made against interpreting this figure in terms of a calibrated scale measuring quantified data. The level of typological construction used in the conceptual scheme of this study would obviously support only an interpretive judgment as to the extent of movement along this continuum. That judgment is that such a movement has taken place at an accelerating rate, and the figure is simply a graphic way of summarizing that fact. This leads to a further point about a position on this continuum. What does it mean to say that Methodism was nearer one end of it than the other? The conclusion has already been reached that at any given period the religious body actually exhibited characteristics drawn from each end of the continuum. If the sect-type traits tend to dominate the church-type elements in the structural-functional characteristics, as was true in

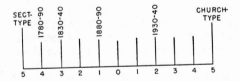

Fig. 1. *Approximation of the position of the Methodist Episcopal Church along the sect-church continuum in stated decades at 50-year intervals, 1780–1790 to 1930–1940.*

[**Source:** Based on Earl D. C. Brewer, Methodism in Changing American Society (unpublished Ph.D. dissertation, Chapel Hill: University of North Carolina, 1950), pp. 587–650.]

1780–1790, the position on the continuum would be near the sect-type end and would reflect the relative dominance of the sect-type over the church-type characteristics, in the judgment of the investigator. Other positions along the line would represent the same process.

A modification of this hypothesis is now possible. The Methodist Episcopal Church began with a heavy dominance of sect-type over church-type traits and has moved along the sect-church continuum to a point where there is a moderate dominance of church-type over sect-type characteristics. This movement has taken place at a slightly accelerated rate and may be expected to continue, following the unification of this religious body with two other branches of Methodism to form The Methodist Church. The extent of the movement is limited, however, by the dissenting tradition and the emergence of the denomination-type of religious body characteristic of this tradition in American society.

A second major problem of the sociology of religion has to do with the interrelationships between the changing patterns within religious institutions and the changes in society as a whole. This requires a conceptual scheme adequate to deal with societal change. In this particular study a typology of social change as constructed by Howard W. Odum was employed. It is built around the ideal types of folk culture and state civilization, the assumption of a trend from the first toward the second, of the interaction between the two, and of the possibility of an equilibrium or balance between them.[9] Using this as an organizing framework the assumption was made that American society had started at the folk-cultural level and had moved toward the characteristics of a state civilization. Broad descriptive historical materials were collected, under this assumption, dealing with settlement and population character-

istics, agriculture and industry, state and government, and, in briefer fashion, with other basic social institutions, such as the family, education, and recreation. Summarizing the conclusions of this work, it was found that the European settlement of America did not approximate the folk cultural level as closely as the earlier Mongolian settlement and that it had, with an accelerated tempo, moved toward the characteristics of the state civilizational type, though stabilizing at the present at a point short of the totalitarianism demanded by the extremes of the constructed type.[10]

Finally, it was possible to deal with the interrelationships between religion and society within the schema of this study. Such questions as: To what extent are these constructed types culture bound, especially the sect-church typology, to European societies with state churches? What is the interrelationship, if any, between these two typologies: the one dealing with social change in general and the other concerned with religious institutional change? Would it be possible to relate folk culture and the sect-type religious institution in such a manner as to say that the latter is a sub-unit of the former? Would it be possible to do the same for the state civilizational type of society and the church-type of religious body? What significance, if any, do these considerations have for understanding the relationships between religion and other aspects of changing American Society?

Without detailing the results of such theoretical considerations,[11] the summary conclusion may be reached that the sect-church typology with appropriate modifications is useful in a scientific analysis of religious institutional data in American Society. Furthermore, the limited level of state civilization reached in America and the movement of religious groups toward the denomination-type along the sect-church continuum reflect reciprocal interactive causal factors making of the civ-

---

[9] For a statement of this typology of social change see Howard W. Odum, Notes on the Changing Structure of Contemporary Society (unpublished paper, Department of Sociology, University of North Carolina, 1948).

[10] For the details see Earl D. C. Brewer, op. cit., pp. 66–208.

[11] For these details see Ibid., pp. 651–703.

ilization a multi-group society with a causally structured culture exhibiting a wide range of alternative patterns. It may be concluded, then, that there is a rough "correlation" between the denomination-type of religious institution and the level of state civilization reached in the United States. Secondary and segmental interaction patterns structured in a bureaucracy tend to develop within the religious institution as in other aspects of state civilization and accommodative relationships with other social institutions are characteristic of this level of the church-type. This stage of American Society in its movement toward the characteristics of the state civilization is oriented more toward the "secular" than the "sacred" constructed type in ideology and structure.[12] These "secular" characteristics are naturally reflected in the religious institutions, especially those of the denomination-type. Liberalism in theology, economic rationalism, legalistic bureaucracy, and segmented and secondary relationships are examples of this tendency. These developments are subversive of the older and more "sacred" and sect-type institution-ways and have called up the "fundamentalistic" reaction to such "modernistic" secularism. It is likely, however, that the extreme church-type religious institution would dictate a prescribed faith in much the same way that an extreme state civilization would be totalitarian in its scope and demands. Thus, there appears to be mutual tolerance and support in the level of state civilization reached by the state and government and the level of church-type reached by Methodism and other dominantly denomination-type religious bodies in the United States.

Yet the sect-type religious organization can only partially be identified with folk culture. Religion in folk societies tends to conform to and sanction prevailing folkways and mores which is a church-type adaptative trait. If, however, the term "folk" is used in Odum's sense as representing a ". . . universal, societal constant in a world of variables . . .,"[13] then the sect-type group possesses kinship with it when used to describe an ever-present and essential primary group aspect of every religious institution. This sect-element is present in the most elaborate and complex church-type institutions. In Medieval Catholicism, for example, this sectness was expressed in monastic orders and societies sanctioned by the Church and often representing the dynamic, growing edge of it. Too, there were groups during this period which had revolted from the Church and maintained themselves as persecuted sects fermenting the Protestant Reformation and the dissenting tradition. In a sense, then, sect-forces furnish the dynamic and sect-forms the structure for the "remnant" element in a decaying religion and the "revival" element in a growing religion. Although this statement should be considered in the nature of a conclusion in need of further study it would, if confirmed, tend to identify this aspect of the sect-type with the folk element in society. It is probable that these phenomena represent "folk forces" operating through religious institutions. If this be true it would help to explain the "cultural lag" between religious institutions and other social institutions. Indeed, it would make possible a tentative interpretation of the sect in terms of the folk and thus generalize the theoretical structure at this point. It would tend to confirm Odum's use of religious phenomena in his search for folk elements in society.

[12] Howard Becker, "Sacred and Secular Societies," **Social Forces**, XXVIII (May 1950), 361-76.

[13] Howard W. Odum, **Understanding Society** (New York: The Macmillan Company, 1947), p. 13.

An influential movement may become institutionalized without surviving as an independent organization. The movement may be accorded a place within an existing organization or it may take control of an existing organization. It has often been suggested that the organizational strength of the Roman Catholic Church lies in this ability to institutionalize dissident movements as orders within the Church and in other ways. The stability of political parties in the United States undoubtedly rests largely on the fact that party composition and control constantly shift as various political movements gain ascendancy. The campaign manager for a victorious nominee becomes chairman of the national committee of the party, and the various local clubs set up to back a particular nominee turn into regular party clubs. The political party incorporates the movement with its channels of communication and influence, its leadership, its ritual, and its membership.

Occasionally such institutional absorption may be incomplete. The movement leaders may be accorded positions of power within the established organization but the movement channels of influence may not be included. The movement is then left outside of the institutional framework but leaderless.

Movement decline. Even with decline in many aspects, movements of any consequence tend to persist for fairly long periods. Typically a movement that undergoes a serious loss of program, power, or membership, passes through a period of transformation leading to restabilization, following which it may persist without further serious decline for an extended period.

Various conditions operate to keep a movement alive in spite of apparent failure. For one thing, leaders and functionaries within the movement have an interest in maintaining even an ineffectual movement as a source of income and prestige. The prestige may not be recognized outside the movement, but to the degree to which the individual has made the movement his reference group, he is dependent upon intra-movement prestige for support of his own self-esteem.

The participation-gratifications of membership perpetuate a movement after the chances of promoting its reforms become negligible. It is a matter of considerable interest that some people cling to a declining movement for the participation-gratifications it gives them rather than leaving it for another movement. Certainly many of these personal satisfactions would seem to be gained more adequately in a movement that has the appearance of success and prosperity than in one on the decline. A determinant of such continued adherence is probably the extent of involvement and commitment of members. Involvement that is quite segmental, leaving the individual in effective contact with the world outside the movement, keeps the member in touch with the evaluation of failure which outsiders apply to the movement. Also, when involvement is segmental a break with the movement requires readjustment in only parts of one's life-arrangements. However, the person who is totally involved may be able through isolation to join with the in-group denial of failure. Furthermore, he will be giving up his only social anchoring for an uncertain new one by making a change. Furthermore, to a person who has acquired a position of any prestige in a movement, there is some loss until a new prestige can be built up within a different movement. There are also merits in the stability and intimacy of a movement whose membership groups are small and have not changed very much for some time. There is interpersonal security in such a situation that is lacking in a large growing movement. Finally, the newer movement may be looked down upon by members of the old movement as consisting of an inferior class or "quality" of people. Particularly if the older movement has been characterized by some restraint and gentility, the newer movements may espouse more openly power tactics and their members be regarded as uncouth by members of the old group.

As the interests of leaders and the involvements of members keep a movement in existence, it must necessarily be shaped by these newly dominant factors. Since the criterion of success through promoting some value in the larger society is no longer relevant, other criteria of success must come to dominate the movement. Occasionally a movement will stabilize around a power orientation because of the crucial influence that any such small but dependable minority can exercise in a balanced-power situation. More commonly, however, the restabilization takes place as a participation-orientation. The movement achieves a form that assures continuance of participation-gratifications to a small but loyal group of adherents whose attention to the formal objectives of the movement becomes merely token. Sheldon L. Messinger, in a careful examination of the condition of the Townsend movement in California, discusses this reorientation and also calls our attention to some of the aspects of rigidification that have taken place.

ORGANIZATIONAL TRANSFORMATION:
A CASE STUDY OF A DECLINING SOCIAL MOVEMENT

SHELDON L. MESSINGER †

It is generally recognized that the organized arms of value-oriented social movements [1] may remain intact long after the movements themselves have lost general impetus. While it is to be expected that these structures will adapt to their changed circumstances, little attention has as yet been given to either the process or product of this adaptation. This paper reports a study of certain organizational consequences of the decline of the Townsend Movement.

THE TOWNSEND MISSION
AND THE END OF RECRUITMENT

While the old age pension movement

Reprinted by permission of the American Sociological Society, from the **American Sociological Review**, 20 (Jan., 1955), pp. 3–10.

† Revised version of paper read at the annual meeting of the American Sociological Society, September, 1954. Acknowledgement is gratefully made to the Institute of Industrial Relations, University of California, Berkeley, for financial assistance in carrying out the research during the early months of 1953; to Mr. P. Leonard Jacobs and Mr. Leonard Syme, for suggestions regarding the ordering and interpretation of the data; and to Mr. John C. Cuneo, California State Organizer, Townsend Plan, Inc., for the cooperation which he and his staff extended to the writer.

seems to be gaining impetus in the United States, the Townsend Movement has all but vanished. To understand this seeming paradox it is necessary to examine the Townsend mission. This has been, and continues to be, not simply national pensions for the aged, but national pensions for the aged *as a mechanism for alleviating or preventing economic dislocation.* The mission is a blending of issues born of the 1930s, and the continued identification of Townsendites with it aids in understanding the movement's decline and the nature of its remaining structure.

Two sorts of data support this characterization of the Townsend mission, as well as the continued identification of the Organization with it.

First, the Townsend Plan,[2] major sub-

[1] "Value-oriented social movements" is a phrasing suggested to the writer by Ralph H. Turner. It refers to social movements fundamentally oriented toward rendering some change in the social structure and of sufficient force to develop organization.

[2] That version which received the widest publicity may be found in the pamphlet **Old Age Revolving Pensions, A National Plan . . . Proposed by Dr. F. E. Townsend**, Long Beach, California: Old Age Revolving Pensions, Ltd., 1934. For a more recent version see **Townsend National Weekly**, August 1,

ject of most Townsend pronouncements, has maintained features directly linking pensions to economic reconstruction. Its provision requiring that the pension be spent within thirty days is intended to provide jobs by keeping money in circulation. Its stipulation that prospective recipients must cease work to become eligible is designed to combat "technological unemployment." [3] These are the key to Townsend claims that theirs is not "just another pension plan." Further, leaders justify changes in other features of the Plan as occasioned by the aim of economic reconstruction. For example, the famous "200 dollars a month," from the first a legislative impediment, was formally discarded in all forms in 1943. Informally it is still mentioned as "essential to the Plan" in the sense that at least this much is requisite to "keep the economy going." Other changeable features, justified in all their forms as necessary to economic reconstruction, include the means of financing and designation of those to receive the pension.

Second, the Organization aside from the Plan has continued to link the pension and depression issues. In 1936, a year after passage of national social security legislation, the Organization changed its name from "Old Age Revolving Pensions, Ltd." to "Townsend National Recovery Plan, Inc.," emphasizing that its mission was far from complete. Not until 1948 did the less anachronous "Townsend Plan, Inc." become the organizational style. The *Townsend National Weekly,* official newspaper of the Organization, has become since 1941 a veritable compendium of "signs" pointing to "impending" economic disaster. Throughout World War II and the post-war boom, Townsendites continued to circulate tracts stressing that their Organization aimed at "a program to bring about full industrial production

for the Nation . . . [and] make jobs for the jobless." [4]

While such aims may again gain currency, it is suggested that under the changed conditions following the end of the depression the Townsend mission was deprived of relevance. Continued identification with this mission has constituted a serious block to Townsend membership maintenance and to the recruitment of new Townsendites. Combined with the short life-expectancies of old Townsendites, this has meant a rapid depletion of the Organization's ranks (see Table 1). [5] In this situation, other "single-minded" old age groups, working to modify existing state aid legislation, have developed to absorb the membership which might earlier have gone to the Townsendites. It is in this context that the Townsend Organization has been transformed.

ORGANIZATIONAL TRANSFORMATION

The Tendency to Deflection. Townsend

---

[3] See, e.g., **Do You Really Know the Townsend Plan?,** n.p.: Townsend Press, n.d., a pamphlet published during World War II and still circulated.

1953. (These and other pamphlets, letters, and newspapers cited here may be found in the Townsend Archives, Library, University of California, Los Angeles.)

[4] **Why I Am For the Townsend Plan,** Cleveland, Ohio: Townsend Press, n.d.

[5] Since the age-sex composition of the Townsend membership is not available, it is not possible to gauge with any accuracy the loss of membership due to death and that due to dropping out. However, the large yearly membership declines following 1939 (when yearly figures first became available) indicate that major losses came from dropouts. See Abraham Holtzman, "The Townsend Movement: A Study in Old Age Pressure Politics," unpublished doctoral dissertation, Harvard University, Cambridge, Mass., 1952, p. 267, for yearly Townsend membership figures 1939–1951.

The long-run personnel problem is, of course, effective recruitment. The considered opinion of Townsend leaders and members is that remaining Townsendites are all "old-timers." In personal contacts with over one hundred California Townsendites, the writer found no variation in this conjecture and met only one person who had joined the Organization since 1948. The growth of such structures as George McLain's California Institute of Social Welfare, since 1941 the major old age pressure-group on the California scene, is an additional indication of what has happened to Townsend recruitment. Of McLain's 60–70,000 members in 1953, less than one per cent had ever belonged to the Townsend Organization. (According to a questionnaire administered by the Institute of Industrial Relations, University of California, Berkeley.)

leaders have attempted to cope with the challenge to their social base. In the process, they have been constrained to direct action in ways deflecting the Organization from its central mission.

The first indication of this tendency came in early 1940 when California Townsendites were urged to aid in qualifying an initiative readjusting state aid legislation.[6] While the campaign was brief and the initiative was not qualified, the event is noteworthy since before this time

TABLE 1. NATIONAL AND CALIFORNIA TOWN-SEND MEMBERSHIP DECLINE, 1936–1951 *

	National Membership	Per Cent Drop	California Membership	Per Cent Drop
1936	2,250,000		330,000	
1951	56,656	97.5	6,839	97.9

* Sources: National and California membership figures for 1936 from U. S. House of Representatives, Select Committee Investigating Old Age Pension Organizations pursuant to H. Res. 443, **Hearings**, 74th Cong., 2nd Sess., Washington, D.C.: 1936 (hereafter: **Hearings: H. Res. 443)**, pp. 41–42, 208. National membership for 1951 from Holtzman, loc. cit. California membership figure for 1951 compiled from records in the Townsend Archives.

national leaders had actively campaigned against any proposal at the state level.[7] Further, they had always carefully disassociated themselves from state "aid" proposals. The "pension," on a national level and not involving indigence requirements, was the proper Townsend goal.

Leadership purposes in supporting this proposal are not far to seek. Urging his lieutenants to support the measure, the California leader said: "Even if we should fail [to qualify it], it is believed we can secure enough publicity and good will to

6 The text of the proposal is given in full in **Townsend National Weekly,** California Edition, April 13, 1940. Its major aim was to block state recovery measures directed at old age aid recipients. For evidence that the tendency to deflection, detailed here only for the California case, was general throughout the Organization see Holtzman, op. cit., 512 ff.

7 See Holtzman, op. cit., p. 510 ff.

justify the effort. We think we can enlist many to join our ranks as a result of this campaign." [8]

In 1943, California Townsendites entered a full-blown campaign for state old age pensions.[9] The nature of this measure permitted it to be presented by both national [10] and state leaders as a "first step" toward the national Townsend Plan. Thus, while only a state-wide proposal with a dollar demand geared to existing state aid legislation (60 dollars was asked), both the "compulsory spending" and "cease work" features of the national Plan were intact. Further, indigence requirements were absent, meaning effectively the end of a state "aid" program and the institution of "pensions" if the measure passed.[11]

The initiative was qualified and placed before the voters in November 1944. It was defeated by over a million votes.[12]

By 1947 membership was at a new low, recruitment at a dead halt, and George McLain's old age pressure-group successfully competing for the allegiance of the

8 Letter from John C. Cuneo, National Representative [for California], Townsend National Recovery Plan, Inc. (hereafter: TNRP, Inc.), to Members of the [California] State Advisory Board, Modesto, California: n.d. (mim.).

9 The proposal may be found in State of California, Secretary of State, **Proposed Amendments to Constitution, General Election, 1944** (hereafter: **Proposed Amendments: 1944),** Sacramento, California: State Printing Office, 1944, p. 11.

10 Holtzman (op. cit., p. 516) reports that national headquarters contributed over 69,-000 dollars to the California campaign. Further, speakers were provided and the **Townsend National Weekly** covered the campaign in detail.

11 In George McLain's opinion it also meant the end of grants-in-aid under Federal Social Security Legislation, as he took pains to point out in his "Argument Against Initiative Proposition No. 11," **Proposed Amendments: 1944,** p. 12. He added: "The proposed law would pension rich and poor alike, thereby lessening the value of the dollar in the hands of the needy—an unjust and vicious proposal." Compare this with later Townsendite handling of McLain issues, below.

12 State of California, Secretary of State, **Statement of Vote, General Election, 1944,** Sacramento, California State Printing Office, 1944, p. 29.

California aged. Aware of the challenge, the California leader proposed a new local effort to national headquarters by saying:

[Even] Dr. Townsend [who is generally opposed to local efforts] has consistently said that "we *must* put on an initiative in California . . . even if we know we will fail before we start. . . ." [This] for the reason that GM [George McLain] has announced that he, too, is going to sponsor a constitutional amendment proposing practically the same objectives. . . . If we fail to present . . . [a local] program, it is only natural that a large number of our own members will be inclined to support him in his efforts. . . . Many people have lost hope and interest in any national program becoming a reality in the near future.[13]

By no stretch of the imagination could the new measure proposed by state leaders be identified as a "little Townsend Plan." [14] First, unlike the 1943–1944 proposal, it was specifically drawn within the framework of existing state legislation for old age assistance and indigence requirements were present.[15] Second, both the all-important "compulsory spending" and "cease work" provisions of the Plan were absent. Townsend propaganda could no longer claim that their measure would effect any significant change in the economic structure.[16]

National leaders at first opposed making a new localized proposal on the grounds that another defeat would do the Movement's national position no good.[17] In August 1947, conceding to California's pressures, they suggested that campaign funds should be raised *outside* the Organization.[18] As late as October 1947, in the midst of efforts to raise money in California for the promotion of the initiative, national leaders carried out two mass meetings in the state to collect funds for national headquarters over the unanswered objections of the California leader.[19]

By June 1948 it was clear that Townsendites had not qualified their initiative, but that McLain had qualified his. State leaders remained as silent as possible in the face of this proposal with "practically the same objectives" and tried to refocus membership attention on national issues.[20]

The passage of McLain's constitutional amendment at the polls was quickly followed by a move for repeal. When the repeal initiative qualified, California Townsend leaders faced a serious dilemma. They could not support repeal, for the advantages brought to the aged by McLain's amendment were patent—e.g., a raise in monthly grant, the end of "rela-

[13] Letter from John C. Cuneo, California State Organizer, TNRP, Inc., to Robert C. Townsend (son of Dr. F. E. Townsend and de facto head of the Organization), Treasurer, TNRP, Inc., Modesto, California: August 14, 1947.

[14] The initiative, which may be found in the Townsend Archives, proposed raising state aid to 75 dollars per month, reduction of recipients' age to 60 years, and institution of a one per cent "gross income tax" to finance the measure.

[15] It is clear from the **Minutes** of [the Townsend California] State Council Meeting at Los Angeles, California, July 26 to 27, 1947, p. 2, that California strategists felt a lesson of the 1943–1944 campaign to have been that the closer to existing legislation, the more chance of success.

[16] About this time, Townsend state leaders began to talk about instituting the "fundamental principles" of the Plan. This euphemism has since spread to the national level. In the 1947–1948 campaign the "gross income tax" was offered as "the fundamental principle."

[17] Letter from Robert C. Townsend, Treasurer, TNRP, Inc. to John C. Cuneo, California State Organizer, TNRP, Inc., Cleveland, Ohio: July 17, 1947.

[18] Letter from Robert C. Townsend, Treasurer, TNRP, Inc. to John C. Cuneo, California State Organizer, TNRP, Inc., Cleveland, Ohio: August 14, 1947.

[19] It should be noted that during the October national call the California leader advised members to raise money for it outside the Organization! See **California Club Bulletin,** Modesto, California: September 6, 1947.

[20] Of particular interest in this connection is the **California Club Bulletin,** Modesto, California: June 10, 1948, immediately following notification of the failure of the initiative to qualify for the ballot. State leaders also indirectly recommended a "no" vote on the McLain initiative through an issue-endorsing group of which they were members. See **News Letter** of the California Legislative Conference, San Francisco, California: n.d. Probably sent October 1948.

ive's responsibility." Nor could they fight epeal, lest an issue now entirely identi- ied with McLain absorb all their mem- »ership's attention and funds. To meet he situation, California leaders tried to traddle the fence by proposing measures o the legislature to supplant McLain's.[21] National leadership, on the other hand, nsisted that the Townsend Organization tay clear of the battle, on the belated grounds that it was for national, not state, pensions. In July 1949, with a repeal measure on the ballot, the California eader wrote the following to national leadquarters:

> We [California leaders] thought that [some anti-repeal statement] was nec- essary as many of our members are supporting McLain financially and at- tending his meetings, to do what they can to hold the gains they have re- ceived. . . . [Now, in view of your po- sition] . . . it seems all we can do is drift; let McLain get the money and our members and let things take their course and keep trying to focus atten- tion of the Washington, D.C. work.[22]

As late as 1953, the crisis continued. Too weak to promote state legislation di- ectly, state leadership fluctuated between 'preserving gains" made by others, "pre- 'enting setbacks," all within the frame- work of state aid legislation, and focusing attention on national issues. But now, for tate leaders, the national issue, above all, s simply success. Late in 1952 the Cali- ornia leader wrote:

> I realize that we have always felt that it was necessary to stick to our

"full program," but if the Republicans will not now accept it "in full," it seems to me that we should try to take the lead with a bill *they will accept* and get something during the next session. . . . I feel that if we don't do something along this line, we can expect McLain to capitalize on the situation and we will lose more and more of our few supporters.[23]

What we have seen here is a tendency to deflection from central aims on the part of Townsend leaders. At the national level, this tendency has been largely checked through a clearer appreciation of the "drift of things" by national leaders themselves. For this drift could only even- tuate in the break-up of the national Or- ganization. At the state level, leaders have tended to exchange identity for security in their search for a viable mission. But here, the pressure from national leader- ship, plus the successful capturing of vital issues by competing groups,[24] have served to hold state leaders within the Organiza- tion and to the Townsend mission.

The Tendency to Salesmanship. Loss of mass support has brought increasing financial difficulty to the Townsend Or- ganization.[25] Adaptation to this circum- stance has transformed Townsend leader- follower relations in such a way as to make recruit interest in the Townsend mission increasingly problematical.

Aside from advertising in the *Town- send National Weekly*,[26] early Townsend

21 At least this was their declared intent; t is not clear whether action was taken. The California leader was driven to state is intentions by "the continued statements y Geo. H. McLain . . . inferring that Townsend Plan leaders and I in particular, re uniting with 'reactionary groups' to try o repeal [the McLain amendment] . . . THE TRUTH IS your leaders are on the ob doing everything possible to see that he major gains made . . . ARE PRE- SERVED." Intro-organizational Bulletin, Modesto, California: January 22, 1949.
22 Letter from John C. Cuneo, California State Organizer, Townsend Plan, Inc. (here- fter: TP, Inc.) to Robert C. Townsend, Treasurer, TP, Inc., Modesto, California: July 28, 1949.

23 Letter from John C. Cuneo, California State Organizer, TP, Inc. to Robert C. Townsend, Treasurer, TP, Inc., Modesto, California: November 8, 1952.
24 This should be taken to include the identification of the Townsend Organization with its traditional mission (i.e., national pensions for economic reconstruction) by relevant publics. It is not a simple matter to escape an identity long and actively sought. Such escape is even more difficult when competing leaderships continually remind potential members of past failures.
25 See Holtzman, op. cit., pp. 313-18, 549- 50, for 1934-1951 income figures.
26 While income from this source was large in the early days of the Organization, it also seems that in those days this rev- enue went into the pockets of Dr. Town- send and the "co-founder" of the Organiza- tion, Robert E. Clements. See **Hearings: H.**

income came largely from the small contributions of individual members. Propaganda materials were sold in large quantities, and royalties accrued from such items as Townsend auto-stickers, buttons, and license-plate holders. It is to be noted that all of these devices *assume commitment on the part of contributors* to the Townsend Organization and its mission.

By 1939, however, members were being urged to purchase *consumable* items bearing the Townsend name. This year saw a Townsend candy bar, then "Townsend Old Fashioned Horehound Drops." In 1940, a Townsend coffee was announced. A little later a "Townsend Club Toilet Soap" and a "Townsend Club Granulated Soap" appeared. In all of these enterprises the Organization merely lent its name; funds, if received, accrued from royalties. The change from auto-stickers, etc., was small but significant because purchase of these new items did not assume commitment to the Organization or its Plan. Townsendites were urged to ask for these items at their usual shopping places, thus, to encourage store owners to stock them. The Organization had yet to become a distributor itself. This was to come.[27]

Beginning in 1943, a series of health foods was offered to members. Of these, "Dr. Townsend's Vitamins and Minerals" soon became the major item. At first distributed only from national headquarters, by 1951 state offices had become distribution points, and Club members were selling pills on commission. In this year, the pills provided one-fifth of the total national income. Intra-organizational communications of all kinds reveal in this period a striking shift from programmatic matters to concern with promoting this product. Perhaps even more significant for the long run, advertising of the pills has come to leave the Organization and

its Plan unmentioned. The most elaborate piece yet prepared (1953) is simply titled "Vitamins and Minerals by Francis E. Townsend, M.D." Its message is entirely one of "health" and "price." Headquarters for the pills is identified as "Dr. Townsend's Vitamins and Minerals" rather than the earlier "Townsend Plan, Inc." Besides this, national radio advertising has been considered, and discussions of this matter have placed promotion of the Plan aside.

This type of money-raising activity is to be clearly differentiated from that of earlier days. Townsend leaders have come to purvey items whose purchase assumes no commitment to the Townsend mission. The pills, especially, are amenable for presentation to others, *once to be seen as potential Townsendites*, without invoking any discussion of the Organization and its aims.

The transformation of leadership activities from the presentation of a program to the purveying of products can be traced in the present approach to recruitment as well. In May 1952, discussing a proposal to offer a 50 per cent commission to members who brought in new recruits, Dr. Townsend said:

> We have innumerable people in our clubs who can be taught to sell. Let's push them into learning by making it necessary to do so if they wish to remain members of a club. After they have learned *what* to do, I believe they will continue to do—with a fifty per cent bait as inducement.[28]

In October of the same year, national headquarters distributed a "training manual" designed to "double the readership of *Townsend National Weekly* and the membership of each Townsend club." [29] The striking quality of this "manual" is that it makes clear that Townsend leaders *no longer even seek active support a*

Res. 443, passim., on this point. Such revenues are, of course, dependent on mass circulation, and presently the newspaper carries little advertising.

[27] Mention of these early items may be found in **California Club Bulletins** for 1939–1940. Apparently none were successful; they are gone without a trace in 1953.

[28] Letter from Dr. F. E. Townsend, President, TP, Inc. to Mildred Atwood, Secretary to John C. Cuneo, Los Angeles, California: May 19, 1952.

[29] **The Busy Bee Program,** n.p.: n.d. The "program" was part of a contest with prizes for those enlisting the most new members and readers.

large. The issue has become simply support in itself. Members are told:

Many big business organizations give their salesmen sales manuals written from long experience in the technique of winning friends to a product. We've done the same for you. . . . Whether you're building a model boat or being a BUSY BEE, tools and technique are the secret of success.[30]

How to extract the "cost" in manageable installments is outlined; little is said about the urgency or value of the mission at hand. The total impression received is that the best salesman is he who receives money with the least pain to the customer. And this is no doubt correct. For Townsend leaders no longer seek "converts" so much as "customers."

The Tendency to "Pure" Recreation. Membership activity at the level of the Clubs [31] provides a final example of the transformation of the Townsend Organization.

Townsend Club "business meetings" are remarkably similar in both form and content. Similarity of form has been encouraged by the various *Townsend Club Manuals,* each containing a procedural outline, plus local leadership unpracticed in organizational ways. Whatever variation is found in content is largely accounted for by the make-up of the Club membership. Clubs with a preponderance of highly religious members substitute 'sings" for card playing. Aside from formalities, Club meetings are given to discussions of plans for social activities such as are discussed below. The usual meeting is attended by less than fifteen persons, lasts a half an hour, and is adjourned. But no one leaves. More likely than not,

five or ten more people enter. Card tables are set up, and what seems to the writer to be the "real" business of the evening begins: recreation. This latter may last for several hours.[32]

This pattern may even be formalized. Examination of Club minutes often revealed that at some time in the past a motion had carried to limit the "business meeting" to an hour or less. Not all members agree that this is the proper order of things. Almost every Club has its "vocal Townsendite," a member always ready to take the floor and present the Organizational mission. Precisely toward these members such motions had been directed. The "vocal Townsendite," once perhaps a Club president, had become an outcast in his own Club. If in any executive role, he can ordinarily be found on the membership committee—a position nobody seemed to want, for obvious reasons. And even here he may remain under fire: many members feel that the membership committees misrepresent Club aims by "selling the Plan too hard," *i.e.,* presenting its realization as imminent ("even now").

Not only are membership social activities built right into Club meetings, but some Clubs have additional "pot-luck nights" or "weekly dances" specifically designed to attract non-members. These activities would seem to furnish ideal occasions for recruitment and the distribution of Townsend propaganda. The evidence in hand suggests that once they did, but no more. Several Club leaders informed the writer that propagandizing would only lower participation, thus reduce sorely needed funds. As public interest in the Plan has flagged, there has been a related change in the nature of Townsend social activities. They have become from the viewpoint of Townsend Club

---

30 Ibid.

31 The Clubs, established early in the history of the Organization, have always played an important role for Townsend leaders as nuclei for education, recruitment, and fund-raising. From 1100 Clubs in California in 1936, only 123 were left in 1952. They have shown a steady decrease in average membership, as well as numbers, since 1939 (the first year for which yearly records are available). E.g., in 1939 there were 91.3 members per California Club; in 1952, 45.0. (These figures are derived from records in the Townsend Archives.)

32 At one large Los Angeles Club, far along in the transformation process described here, the meeting at 11 a.m. finds less than ten persons present. By 1 p.m., when card playing begins, there are ordinarily over 50 persons present. A check indicated that less than one-third of these had ever been members of the Townsend Organization.

leaders purely fund-raising devices. In turn these activities have become, from the viewpoint of non-member participants, purely social.

The "vocal Townsendite" may object to this. In one Los Angeles Club a member insisted that the *Townsend National Weekly* be sold at social events and recruiting attempts made. This same member, then Club president, was the occasion of so much dissension in Club ranks that he was not reelected—which is unusual in Club histories. The next (and 1953) president, while mildly unhappy that many who attend Club social functions "don't know what we stand for," seems more distressed by any falling-off of attendance at these affairs. Further, he regards social groups (*e.g.*, public park dance clubs) as his "most serious competition," not the McLain Organization.

This phenomenon is not far different from that of the Townsend pills. The object of these affairs, as with the pills, is to raise money. This is best done, now, on a "business" basis. The business at hand, in this instance, is providing recreation. And to this business local Townsend leaders apply themselves.

SUMMARY AND CONCLUSIONS: THE PROCESS AND PRODUCT OF ADAPTATION TO DECLINE

In the ascendant phases, when social forces press for reconstruction and changes are still in the offing, the concern of leaders and members of social movements alike is with those things that must be done to translate discontent into effective and concerted action. An evident condition of this orientation is discontent itself. In turn, this discontent must be supplied or renewed by social forces which, it must be believed, can be ameliorated by banding together. These provide the dynamic of value-oriented social movements, as well as the characteristic missions with which their organized arms become identified.

When the movements themselves lose impetus through a shift in the constellation of social forces, their organized arms are deprived of conditions necessary to sustain them in their original form. But organizations are not necessarily dissolved by the abatement of the forces initially conjoining to produce them. They may gain a certain degree of autonomy from their bases and continue to exist. We will expect, however, that the abatement of the particular constellation of social forces giving rise to the movement will have important consequences for the remaining structure. The most general of these is, perhaps, increasing lack of public concern for the organizational mission. This is reflected in the ending of public discussion of the issues which the organization represents or, perhaps better put, with these issues in the frame of reference that they are placed by organizational representatives. Within the organization the abatement of social forces spells dropping membership and, more serious in the long run, the end of effective recruitment. This latter may be reinforced by the development of alternative organizational structures competing for the same potential membership. The end of recruitment is quickly transformed into financial difficulty. Where the organization has been geared to financial support from its own adherents, this last consequence will be especially crucial.

The organized arms of declining social movements will tend to adapt to these changed conditions in characteristic ways. We can broadly describe this adaptation by asserting that the dominating orientation of leaders and members shifts *from the implementation of the values the organization is taken to represent* (by leaders, members, and public alike), *to maintaining the organizational structure as such,* even at the loss of the organization's central mission.[33] To this end, leaders will be constrained to direct action toward new issues or in new ways which will attenuate the organization's identification with the particular set of aims held to be central to it. In this process, the locus of

[33] We do not mean to indicate that leaders do not at all times perform maintenance functions. The crucial issues are what they must do, under changed conditions, to accomplish this and the explicitness with which the function is carried out.

ssue-selection will tend to move outside he organization, to alternative leaderhips who highlight the growing irrele-*ance to most of the traditional central *iission. Presumably, a new mission may *e found.[34] Where this is not the case, eaders will be forced to search out new *neans of financing as the traditional mode

[34] This seems unlikely. It would seem to nvolve, as a minimum, a shift in the or-*anization's core membership, highly iden-ified with the central mission; as well as * shift in perspective that most leaderships *eem unable to make. Further, the identi-*cation of the organization with its tradi-ional mission by prospective members is *lmost assured by the actions of alternative eaders competing for this same social base.

of appeal and reap falls on fewer and deafer ears. In this process, members, and especially potential members, will cease to be regarded as "converts" and will come to be seen as "customers." Finally, membership activities, initiated in a context of declining public interest to support a faltering organization, will work to turn what were once the incidental rewards of participation into its only meaning. This last, by altering the basis for whatever recruitment may take place, would seem to insure that the organization, if it continues to exist, will be changed from a value-implementing agency to a recreation facility. In sum, the organizational character will stand transformed.

Conservatization. Well before a value-oriented movement reaches institutionalization or decline, the relation between the movement's values and those of the ociety at large has an effect on the course of the movement. In spite of its attack *n some or many current conditions, any movement itself arises out of the pre-*ailing societal values. No matter how sweeping may be its condemnation of *ocietal values, it necessarily sanctions its demand for modification of some so-ietal values by reference to others. All movements, therefore, have a conservatiz-ng link to conventional values.

In this sense movements develop out of two kinds of conditions. Either pre-ailing circumstances and the value structure are out of coordination with one *nother, or potential conflicts among values in the society are brought into the *pen. In either instance the demand of the movement is for a modified emphasis *n values, increasing the importance of one value at the expense of another value. *A movement for Fair Employment Practices, for example, advances the value of *qual opportunity at the expense of the value of freedom from interference in unning one's own business.

The conservatizing linkage to conventional values has some effect on the pro-*ram that is advocated for promoting the value-change. Every culture includes * set of folk-prescriptions for dealing with recognized problems. Since few values licit complete conformity, society must constantly cope with the problems arising *rom minor value-failures. Hence each culture will include prescriptions covering *lmost any kind of value-failure. These folk prescriptions, however, are pallia-*ves that keep problems under control, quarantine disorders to prevent their pread, or conceal instances of successful deviation. Such palliatives depend, for *heir effectiveness, upon the fact that the problems are of but limited incidence *n the society, and that the normal operation of the society is such as to keep the *roblems at a minimum. They depend also on the fact that they are relatively eldom used. For example, imprisonment undoubtedly is of some value in con-*rolling crime so long as the normal operations of society promote law-abiding *ehavior most of the time and only a small minority of the population are ever mprisoned.

Most social movements advocate a program that consists of making more extensive and vigorous use of the folk-prescriptions for dealing with a given problem. Most popular movements for the reduction of crime, for example, advocate better law enforcement, improved crime detection, and stiffer penalties. Movements may also call for extension of the folk-prescriptions into new areas of application. Thus the standard means of controlling crime are advocated for dealing with heretical or unpatriotic thinking, the weakening of traditional morals, or racial discrimination.

Movements of this sort may work when an aroused public can make important contributions to the problem's solution. But when the problem in question is being created in the normal operation of the society so that more fundamental changes are essential, such movements may actually resist change. They may channel off much of the protest and potential reform activity into ineffectual work. They may postpone the day of reckoning by controlling or concealing some of the symptoms without touching underlying conditions. Because of their unrealized linkage with the conventional folk-prescriptions, they may help to resist change while appearing to be the vanguard demanding change. Kingsley Davis contends that the mental hygiene movement at one time illustrated this conservatization through the retention of traditional folk-prescriptions for dealing with a problem that had acquired new forms and new dimensions.*

In stressing the conservatizing tendencies within a key movement such as mental hygiene we should not overlook the fact that the movement itself is subject to constant influence from other movements. A pattern such as the following is not infrequent: A movement depending upon traditional folk-prescriptions gains ascendance and partial institutionalization. Among competing movements it acquires a privileged position because its very restriction to folk-prescriptions makes it respectable and acceptable to persons of established prestige. Because of its key position, the movement becomes the focal point of efforts by other movements concerned with the same problem. By "infiltration," by attempted control, or by the influence of continued discussion, the movements whose proposals are more radical gradually modify the program of the key movement. As the key movement is won over, its established respectability enables it to promote the programs of the more radical movements much more effectively than they could do by acting directly upon the established organizations of society. Thus, an essentially conservative movement may come to be a vehicle for change in the same way that a counter-movement, by successive strategic revisions of program, actually promotes the changes it officially opposes.

Revolution. The revolutionary movement is one that claims to reject the folk-prescriptions for bringing about change and openly repudiates, or is forced to repudiate, claims to respectability within the established order. As we have pointed out earlier, however, the degree of change advocated may not indicate the degree of change that a movement actually brings about. An apparently conservative movement may set in motion a series of changes with extensive ramifications. Or what appears to be a demand for major changes may turn out to alter nothing but the superficial forms or the occupants of established positions. It has even been argued that the very natures of the revolutionary movement and of the process of "successful" revolt undercut any program of change so that no

---

* Kingsley Davis, "Mental Hygiene and the Class Structure," **Psychiatry,** 1 (1938), pp. 55–65.

thoroughgoing change can be effected. Without endorsing the contention in so strong a form, we can, however, note some of the influences in this direction.

Because it is not respectable, the revolutionary movement is denied access to the conventional techniques for winning adherents, for appealing to a public, for gaining the support of key persons, etc. Consequently, as we have suggested earlier, the revolutionary movement must resort to the use of more blatant power techniques. But the greater the degree to which such techniques are used, the more chance is there that the values of the movement will be compromised in the process. A revolutionary movement that aims to improve the position of minorities, for example, may be forced to block palliative programs that reduce protest and to disregard the stated desires of those minority members themselves who do not realize that fundamental change is required to eliminate inequality. Thus constant disregard of the minority's immediate interests and the view that the movement knows better what is good for the minority than the latter do themselves may develop into an actual hostility toward the minority. Eventually, the interests of the minority may be served only as a reward for supporting the movement.

Denied access to influence through the legitimate structure, the revolutionary movement must eventually establish its own government to bring about desired reforms. Movements that are not revolutionary usually accomplish their desired reforms by influencing those who exercise legitimate authority. Or if they actually take power themselves, they exercise authority through existing machinery. But the "successful" revolution follows a period of attack on the legitimacy of the existing order and of encouraging people to disobey its dictates. Often law and order themselves have been defined as obstacles to progress. When the revolutionary movement has overcome the existing order, it encounters the new problem of restoring respect for the legitimacy of an order—the new order. There is considerable urgency in this respect, since the underlying economic structure and communications system will have been disrupted in revolution. Not only must these functions be restored quickly but attempts at counter-revolution or further revolt from competing movements must be blocked. Under these circumstances a revolution is likely to be followed by a period during which the revolutionary regime resorts to techniques reminiscent of the old regime to maintain its control and restore minimum order.

During this period, the problem of power tends to predominate over the problem of societal reform in the preoccupations of the revolutionaries. From their standpoint, the ultimate possibilities of accomplishing long-range reform depend on successfully maintaining control and civil order in the short run. But the reforms may also be stifled from a long-range standpoint. The movement may lose popular support since it appears to have repudiated all of its former idealism, and the loss of popular support will force even more exclusive concern with the retention of power. Internal control of the movement may shift to those who have the skills most needed at the moment, including the human insensitivities necessary to subjugate the populace. Once these leaders are in control, the reformers may never again have crucial influence. Furthermore, the practical difficulties of instituting reforms and of gaining popular support for reforms believed to be in the people's interests, the increasing preoccupation with details of administering reforms rather than with the broad outlines of the reforms themselves, cause the reformers to think in terms of an ever longer time span for successful achievement.

One of the striking features of this period of consolidation of power is internal dissension within the victorious movement. Internal dissension which is minor in a movement ·not yet in power becomes serious when the movement acquires power. In the precarious state of initial control, any internal dissent makes the movement vulnerable to attack, and suggests the possibility of defection to one of the competing groups or to the counter-revolution. Consequently, more severe efforts are likely to be made within the movement to suppress dissenting elements. The more repressive policy toward internal disagreement in turn breeds fear and mutual suspicion among the movement leadership.

The power-consolidation period is one that introduces new points of disagreement within the movement. Persons who have agreed on the broad outlines of movement objectives disagree on the immediate techniques of implementation. Especially crucial as a source of dissension are likely to be the compromises of program that are made in the establishment of control. Sincere disagreements on the extent of compromise necessary become the points of violent personal antagonism. And finally, now that the movement has recognized prestige and effective power to bestow on individuals, personal rivalries are likely to come to a head.

These problems of consolidating power over the society and of suppressing internal dissension give rise to a period known dramatically as the "reign of terror." The bloodshed of these periods has been extensively depicted in the popular accounts of the French and Russian revolutions. Likewise, the succession of leaders, each deposed and guillotined, is a well-known feature of the French Revolution.

Recent discussions place less emphasis on the outcome of the struggle of any particular movement for revolution and relate the ultimate outcome of revolutionary transformations to shifts in the class system. One aspect of social change is the shifting concentration of society's wealth and informal power among the classes. While these shifts are taking place, legitimate power resists change, so that there develops a discrepancy between formalized power and the functioning of the social and economic order. Ultimately, revolution may be the means whereby the artificially maintained formal authority is deposed and the class that economic and social conditions have made ascendant acquires formal control commensurate with its functioning ascendancy. Thus the end-result of a revolutionary movement will depend upon the degree to which the changes it demands serve to bring the formal prestige and power structure into closer coordination with actual societal functioning.

Two points deserve emphasis in relation to the foregoing statement. First, revolutions are not engineered by the depressed classes. Revolutions may gain in numerical strength and in extreme forms of collective behavior from such groups, but the successful movement brings to control those whose power has already been growing in the society. And second, the revolution must be examined as shift in power. The values promoted in the revolution relate to the outlook of the class whose ascendancy is taking place.

The latter observation calls our attention to a formula concerning the effectiveness of revolution which stresses the convergence of value-change and power shift. Robert Binkley illustrates such a formula, referring to revolutions at wide dispersed times and places. The general formula may be applicable to other movements than the merely revolutionary. The convergence of value-change and power-shift may be the circumstance that is crucial to the long-range effectiveness of reforms instituted by any movement.

AN ANATOMY OF REVOLUTION

ROBERT C. BINKLEY

When friends and enemies of the Roosevelt administration united in calling it revolutionary, the word revolution entered the vocabulary of American politics in a new way, for which no adequate preparation has yet been made. However hard the political campaign speeches may strain at parallels, they cannot successfully portray contemporary America as a mirror of Soviet Russia or Fascist Italy. The epithet "Tory" fails to establish a resemblance of present events to those of 1776. If the New Deal is a revolution, it belongs to a species hitherto unnoted by the American political observer, who might profitably extend his catalogue of types to include some specimens of the less familiar varieties.

The idea of revolution comes to us as a political conception from the Greek experience in city government, where it was associated with the turning of the wheel of Fortune, which brought one party up and sent another down. The nineteenth century, with the example of the French Revolution so manifestly before it, used the word to describe great institutional changes. Moreover, in connection with a Darwinian thought-pattern we have come to use the word to designate a certain tempo of change: revolution is rapid, evolution is slow.

We expect to find all three of these elements in a revolution: displacement of power, important institutional changes, and a tempo of crisis. How far does the Roosevelt administration show these characteristics? How great is the real displacement of power in America, and how profound the institutional change? Has the change been as sudden as it seems, or have we merely come to see that gradual and continuous developments are now approaching a configuration that we had not previously happened to notice?

We are still willing to call a change a revolution though it lack some of these elements, and the Roosevelt revolution may be of such a class. The industrial revolution, for instance, involved a displacement of power, but took place gradually; the average Latin-American revolution is a sudden and violent displacement, but is not accompanied by important institutional changes. That it is also possible to have a revolution without any displacement of power is illustrated in the history of the Frankish Kingdom of the eighth century.

The school books used to tell the story of the long-haired Merovingian Kings of the Franks who in some way became "weak," and ceased to rule actively. They were the "do-nothing" kings. The Mayors of the Palace, on the contrary, exhibited strong masculine characteristics, and revelled in activity. So it came about that Pepin the Short, Mayor of the Palace and father of Charlemagne, with the approval of the Pope, displaced the Merovingian line and set himself up as King of the Franks. It used to be implied that there was nothing in this interesting espisode that could not have been prevented by feeding the Merovingian kings more spinach and cod liver oil.

There is another way of understanding the story. The Frankish kingdom of that day was a backwoods area in which the principal form of property was land; there were few cities and very little money economy. In this area a Germanic tribal

Reprinted by permission of the University of Virginia, from Robert C. Binkley, "An Anatomy of Revolution," **The Virginia Quarterly Review,** 10 (Oct., 1934), pp. 502-14.

king had fallen heir to the relics of a Roman administrative apparatus which he did not understand, and made an alliance with the Church, which served him as a broker in his relations with God, demons, and people.

Whether because of the absence of an adequate political training, or because the decline of the cities rendered government of the Roman type impossible, it came about that the Frankish kings could no longer protect life and property in their realm. Then there developed, partly out of the old Frankish institution of *mainbour,* or sworn companionship, and partly out of the relics of Roman landholding institutions, a system that came to constitute a secondary government parallel to the Frankish state. This extensive *mainbour* system bore a certain resemblance to the structures of modern racketeering or machine politics. The little man who needed protection would get it by becoming the pledged follower of a magnate who would accept him. He might surrender his land to the leader, receiving it back on dependent terms corresponding to his pledged allegiance. The protector could procure from the king a royal letter of immunity exempting him from royal jurisdiction.

The system lent itself like the corporate organization of modern business to the creation of widely ramified mergers. The family that succeeded in becoming the head of the most extensive combination of all—a kind of consolidated land trust incorporating all the chief magnates of the kingdom with their followings—was the family of Pepin of Heristal, whose family fortune had been built up by marriage and by graft in the service of the king. His place was analogous to that which might have come to the House of Morgan if the elder Morgan had been able to carry out the plans of trust formation attributed to him, while adding the resources of a political boss and gangster chief to his repertory.

From such a strong position, the Mayor of the Palace was naturally tempted to strike for the crown. One of them tried it, but failed because the superstitious reverence of the Franks for the Merovingian line made it seem to them impossible that a member of another family could occupy the throne. Seven hundred years before this time the keen Roman observer, Tacitus, had noted that the Germanic tribal kings were always chosen from the blood royal. A king of the authentic blood seemed a necessity, if for no other reason than for the sake of the calendar, in order that the year might be dated correctly from his reign. This reverence for past traditions was good enough in ordinary times, but in 732 came a crisis in the kingdom—the Moorish invasion.

In the presence of this crisis the Frankish king was unable to raise an army, but Charles Martel, Mayor of the Palace, called upon all his sworn followers, then seized the church lands and gave them out to bring still more followers to his standard. With this army he beat off the Moors in the Battle of Tours. Thereafter it was evident that the sworn following of the Mayor of the Palace was a more effective organization than the traditional government of the king. But it was still necessary to overcome the resistance of tradition to a formal change. This was accomplished by using the authority of the Church against the vestiges of tribal legitimacy. The Pope authorized Pepin the Short, son of Charles Martel, to assume the tribal crown.

There was no shifting of power. The same men, the same families, continued to do the same things in the same way, but the two kinds of government were combined as one. Charlemagne ruled not only as King of the Franks but also as the head of a great body of sworn followers who had taken his pledge.

Modern man also lives under two regimes, to one of which he renders patriotism and loyalty, while to the other he looks for his livelihood. It has often been suggested that the business organization of modern society is becoming more important than its political organization, and that the leaders of business are more powerful than political leaders. Such suggestions encounter resistance in the tradition of popular sovereignty, which rejects Big

Business dictatorship in government as an evil. Perhaps this traditional attitude, like the feeling of the Franks for their royal family, might have weakened in time of crisis, and the public might even have allowed itself to be sacrificed to business leadership as the Frankish churches and monasteries were sacrificed when Charles Martel seized their lands. But the American magnates did not go out to meet the crisis, nor win their Battle of Tours.

American business, therefore, is not in a position to have the merging of business and government legitimated under its own control. It is still possible that the future may bring a development resembling that of the Frankish kingdom, if the N.R.A., as a legalized continuation of the trust movement, should leave the same people doing the same thing that they did before, in the same way, excepting that they will be metamorphosed into code authorities with legal powers, just as the Mayors of the Palace were changed into Kings.

II

Another kind of revolution was engineered by the young Emperor Meiji of Japan in the year 1867. This revolution took place in the presence of a crisis arising out of contact with foreign powers. It put an end simultaneously to the three peculiarities of the Japanese political system: dual government, feudalism, and isolation.

Dual government was the name given to that system by which the Emperor, descendant of the prehistoric tribal leader of the race, continued to be titular ruler while the Shogun governed the country. The powers of the Shogun dated from the mediaeval era, when his office of military commander eclipsed in practical importance the office of the Emperor. It was as if the Frankish Mayors of the Palace had continued as governors acting in the name of the Merovingian kings. When Perry visited Japan he thought the Shogun was the Emperor. He heard that somewhere in the back country there was some kind of a pope who was highly venerated and who lived in august poverty, but the man with whom he made his treaty was the Shogun.

The Shogun's government was feudal; he had his sworn followers, the Daimyo or heads of the great families, who were committed to hereditary loyalty to his rule. They held the strategic points throughout the Empire. There were also some great clans who were, traditionally and by hereditary transmission, legally hostile to the Shogun. From them he exacted a strict obedience. He made them come up once a year to his capital in Yedo (now Tokio), and leave hostages with him when they went back to their estates.

The third peculiarity of the Japanese system, the policy of isolation, dated from the seventeenth century. Western missionaries entering Japan at that time had exercised bad judgment by getting on the wrong side in one of the civil wars. As a result all foreigners were excluded, and Japanese were forbidden to travel abroad. Only one tiny door was left open at Nagasaki, where Dutch traders were permitted to bring in one ship a year. That was the Japanese regime that lasted from the seventeenth to the nineteenth century: Shogunate, feudal system, and isolation.

In the first half of the nineteenth century there developed in Japan internal pressure against this system. A cultural renaissance was taking place, a revolt against Chinese culture and a new interest in the antiquities of Japan. There was a revival of the native Shinto cult as against the imported Buddhist religion. The historians, responding to this interest, propagated the knowledge that the legitimate ruler of Japan was not the great Shogun at Yedo but the Emperor in his obscurity at Kioto. This historical school received support from the younger branches of the Shogun's own family, just as the French revolutionary philosophy had an adherent in the Duke of Orleans, of the younger branch of the royal family of France.

There was another cultural movement that seemed to threaten the established order. It was a philosophical school that followed the teachings of the Chinese philosopher, Wan Yang Ming—a pragmatist. Whereas the official doctrine of the Japanese state insisted upon the implicit obedience of the retainer to his lord, the pragmatists taught that action should be governed by circumstances. The gesture that illustrated the meaning of the teaching of the new school was the act of an official who opened the granaries without proper authority on the ground that the people were hungry. The doctrine seemed as dangerous to a feudal Japan as communism seems to modern Japan. These ferments were at work, wholly unconnected with outside influences.

When Commodore Perry arrived, he completed the destruction of the equilibrium of the regime, for his treaty, signed by the Shogun, ended the three-centuries policy of isolation. This gave the hereditary hostile clans an issue to be used against the Shogunate. They contended that the treaty was invalid because a decision of such importance would require the ratification of the Emperor. The doctrine of the historical school provided ammunition for these Imperial legitimists. Their samurai, rallying to the slogan "honor the Emperor, expel the barbarian," attacked foreigners in the streets.

European states in the nineteenth century did not tolerate such treatment of their nationals; the British government sent a fleet to punish the clan of Satsuma whose samurai had attacked an Englishman, Richardson, on the highway. Thus internal dissension threatened to cause foreign conquest.

The Emperor saved the situation by ratifying the treaties that the Shogun had signed, and then a new Shogun, coming into office in 1866, resigned his powers into the Emperor's hands. That was a year of marvels; for when the Shogun resigned his powers he was followed by all the great Daimyo, who surrendered their powers as well. In a great burst of generosity and patriotism the whole people rallied around the Imperial throne.

The young Emperor, ably advised by a brain trust of samurai, reorganized Japan as a modern state with a centralized administration. Many of those who had surrendered feudal powers received back new authority as officials of the Imperial bureaucracy. Those of the samurai who

had been administrators in feudal Japan became the prefects and subprefects of the new regime; the others were "liquidated" as a class.

It seemed in the spring of 1933 that the Shogunate of American business was almost ready to end dual government, and the Daimyo of finance and industry were prepared to surrender their powers into the hands of an Emperor—especially if they were pretty sure to receive them back and become prefects of their economic provinces. But that period of generous gestures seems to be ending, so that another possibility opens. It may come about that business and government may come into chronic opposition to each other, like Empire and Papacy, State and Church, in mediaeval Europe.

III

The conflict of Empire and Papacy grew out of that eleventh-century revolution known as the struggle over investiture. The situation of that time was one that might have been described as "too much Church in feudalism" by one party, and by the other as "too much feudalism in the Church." In fact, Church and feudal society were interlocked like business and government today.

The bishops in some places, especially in the German kingdom, had worked with the kings, and the kings had helped to build up the bishops as a counterweight to the great dukes and margraves. The oath of fealty and the ceremony of investiture were the cement of the whole system—like credit and contract in our modern society.

Church office under these circumstances, so closely tied up with feudal government, tended to become a kind of property, just as the management and directorship of a modern corporation tends to become a kind of property. The Church had its recognized functions in the society of the time, as business has its recognized functions today. It appeared that this feudalizing of the Church interfered with the function of the Church as the religious organ of society. The Archbishop of Narbonne, for instance, simply bought his office and then exploited it for all he could make, selling bishoprics right and left and even seizing the Church plate. He cleaned out his Archdiocese as a crooked management cleans out a corporation. Then he was ready to buy another church office and start again.

Such scandals as this constituted the grievance that led to a reform movement. The reform program was drawn from the traditions of the Church, nourished in the monasteries, and propagated with evangelical zeal throughout Christendom at the time of the crisis. The propagandists of reform, knowing the psychological value of simplicity in a program, had three main points and stuck to them: there must be no more buying and selling of Church office, no more marriage of the clergy (so that office would not be inherited), and no more investiture in Church office by other than Churchmen. These articles of the reform program led to elaborations of the doctrine of papal supremacy over Christendom. This was the doctrinal ferment in the midst of which Pope Gregory VII railroaded the reform program through a Church Council.

The reform decrees were a challenge to vested interests everywhere. They meant that the Church would pull itself out from its feudal connections, taking its property with it. It was as if the American Congress should pass a law providing that the managers of business corporations should no longer be designated by the stockholders through a board of directors, but should be appointed by the government, or as if the magnates of business should be given the right to appoint all public office holders.

Henry IV, German King and Emperor-elect, whose predecessors had made such heavy grants of property in building up the German bishoprics, resisted the step that seemed to be depriving him of his control over his own possessions. To break his resistance the Pope made use of a weapon more powerful in the eleventh century than the control of credit or currency is in the twentieth—he absolved all German subjects from their oath of fealty, thus dissolving the cement of German political society.

The conflict that followed was never brought to a clear-cut decision. It lasted until both these great all-embracing authorities in Europe, Papacy and Empire, had dragged each other down, depriving Europe of that unitary political structure which the League of Nations has not been able to restore, and leaving Christendom a prey to the tragic consequence of unrestrained nationalism.

If business and government should come to be set against each other in chronic conflict, each using its ultimate weapons, such as sabotage and expropriation, which of the two institutions would prevail, or would they destroy each other?

IV

The French and Russian revolutions of 1789 and 1917 exhibit the standard revolutionary characteristics of class displacement, rapid tempo, and comprehensive institutional change. They illustrate also the physiology of the revolutionary process. As a starting point in the process there were certain concrete grievances of French and Russian peasant and middle class, comparable to the grievances of unemployment and low farm income in America.

The grievances were discussed in an atmosphere full of conflicting doctrines. The teaching of the historical and pragmatic schools in Japan, the writings on papal and imperial power at the time of the investiture dispute, the philosophy of popular sovereignty and laissez faire on the eve of the French Revolution, the various hybrids of socialism and democracy prior to the Russian revolution, and the babel of technocrats and economic planners in early 1933, stand as comparable symptoms of impending change.

Then comes the crisis. It may be a danger from outside the society or a growing strain within it. French public credit collapsed in 1788; the food shortage hit Petrograd in February, 1917; and the bank crisis ushered in the New Deal.

Along with the crisis, it is to be expected that the most generous gestures will be made on all sides, in an atmosphere of highest optimism. The good will that marked the first few months of Roosevelt's administration was more than the normal honeymoon period of an incoming president; it was more like the spirit in which the representatives of the French nobility renounced the feudal rights of their class on the night of August 4th, 1789; it was more nearly comparable to the fervor with which the Japanese feudality surrendered their powers to the Emperor, or the joyous cooperation of classes in Petrograd in the hopeful spring of 1917. This spirit seems to be a psychological opiate that anaesthetizes a social parturition. When the effects have passed away, it will be seen that some new doctrines or catchwords from among those that were in the air before the crisis have assumed the character of obvious truths, while some of the older truths appear hopelessly discredited and out of date. A grievance, a ferment of doctrines, a crisis, and a moment of generous co-operation—and after that—what next?

In observing the course of a revolution the next thing to watch for is the vesting of new interests. In France the peasants get their land, the speculators and other middle-class owners buy into the sequestered estates of nobility and church. It will not be easy to displace them. In Russia the peasant seizes the adjacent lands of the proprietor; the proprietor can never come back. The subordinate group leaders of the modern Fascist type of party install themselves in their bailiwicks as little dictators, maintaining their dictatorships by fostering the cult of the Dictator. It will not be easy to squeeze them from their places. What new interests are becoming vested under the New Deal?

Throughout the country union labor is demanding seniority rights, which have the effect of transforming a job into a kind of personal property like the French peasant's farm. On one railroad an employee even now is granted the right to trade jobs with an employee of the same class in another city, provided each takes the other's seniority rating. Since there is

nothing to prevent money payments in connection with such an exchange, seniority becomes a kind of property, convertible like other property into money.

Business under the N.R.A. is acquiring a valuable right to exclude or limit competition. Let there be no doubt of the property value of this right. It was sought by many kinds of business before the N.R.A. at the risk of costly violations of law—either of anti-trust laws, in the case of big business, or of the common criminal law, in the case of racketeered small business. Another illustration of the property character of these rights to limit competition comes from the history of the decline of the guilds. In some countries, such as Prussia, the possessors of guild rights were compensated with a money payment when their businesses were opened to free competition. Such is the quality of the vested interest that the business man may secure under the New Deal.

The third and most conspicuous type of vested interest is that of the unemployed relief client in a system of relief or made work. When the Civil Works Administration was rapidly demobilized in the Spring it was evident that a property conception of the right of an unemployed man to a C.W.A. job was rapidly forming. If the right to a job, as a vested interest of the working class, is guaranteed by the government, much of the ensuing course of development of the New Deal is thereby determined.

The extent of these new vested interests, of employees, employers, and unemployed, is the measure of the revolutionary quality of the New Deal. If the class that has the most valuable of these new rights turns out to be the same class that had the best position under the old deal, it will mean that the Roosevelt revolution, like the Carolingian revolution of the eighth century, is not displacing one class with another, but only changing the forms by which power is exercised.

If no new vested interests appear, then it is certain that there is no comprehensive and permanent institutional change. The great upheaval of the spirit that accompanied America's entry into the World War could collapse like a bubble and leave nothing behind it, because there were no vested interests tied up with it. No one was committed by a situation into which he had been placed by Wilsonian idealism to fight tooth and nail for the Wilsonian program. The prohibition system was transitory for the same reason. It created no vested interest of any social importance or decisive political power. The forces maintaining prohibition at the end were of the same kind as those which had brought in the system in the beginning, namely a group of people who entertained prohibitionist sentiments. The bootleggers and snoopers were the only groups whose living depended on the continuance of prohibition, and it proved easy to push them aside.

The New Deal cannot live permanently on favorable sentiments and opinions. Unless it creates powerful vested interests committed to its maintenance, or legitimates the powers of some existing interests, it will be in 1937 what the Wilsonian crusade was in 1920; it will prove that it was not a revolution at all.

Part 5

SOCIAL CONSEQUENCES
OF COLLECTIVE BEHAVIOR

Chapter 22

Collective behavior, social change, and social stability

$\mathcal{C}$OLLECTIVE behavior can be studied from several vantage points. It is possible to focus upon individual motivations as they find expression through crowds, publics, and social movements. This approach, which is properly the psychological study of group phenomena, has been de-emphasized throughout our discussion. Instead, we have examined collectivities as groups, characterized by structure and processes. Thus we have explored the composition of collectivities, the changes that take place within them, their internal organization, their expansion and contraction and success and failure. It is also appropriate to examine collective behavior from a third standpoint. Collectivities can be studied from the vantage point of the society in which they exist. We can ask what their effects are upon the larger society of which they are a part. We have already, for example, traced the development, the denouement, and the quiescence of a crowd. There remains the question of what lasting effect this crowd has had upon the course of the larger society.

Looking first at the on-going social order, we observe that it has many parts. Each of these parts is geared in with the other parts so that it contributes in some way to the operation of the whole society. The contributions that any part makes to the whole are known as its *functions*. Since collectivities may be a part of the whole social order, we shall ask whether they serve any functions. In particular, we shall ask whether collective behavior plays any part in the maintenance of stability or the promotion of change in society.

Most of the answers have been supplied in the preceding discussions. The chief purpose here will be to bring together the scattered observations that

515

describe the effect of collective behavior on society. While the entire subject matter of collective behavior is deficient in precise empirical demonstration, the analysis of the long-term effects of collective behavior lacks even more. Our discussion can be regarded as little more than a series of considered speculations, in which we present those conclusions that can find some justification in theory or considerable circumstantial evidence, and that appear to be worthy of further study and effort at empirical test.

EFFECTIVENESS OF COLLECTIVE BEHAVIOR

Viewpoints differ initially concerning whether collective behavior has any real effect on the course of events or whether it is merely the impotent shadow of events that are taking place or already past. From one standpoint change and persistence are shaped by historical causes which make themselves felt through the decisions of persons in responsible positions. Collective behavior is then merely the purposeless arousal and debate among those who have no real part in this decision process.

This viewpoint does not eliminate collective behavior altogether as a factor in social change or persistence, but it does reduce it to an inconsequential by-product which may hamper the orderly processes of change. While collective behavior does not alter the major processes of change, it does materially affect the state of organization or disorganization in the society. Collective behavior becomes a sort of collective mental illness which impedes the organized processes of the society. Both change and persistence will occur with less societal discomfort if the incidence of collective behavior can be reduced.

Although collective behavior contributes to disorganization in society, it is assumed not to be an inevitable accompaniment of societal operation or change. Instead, collective behavior is attributed to some defectiveness in popular understanding of the normal operations of society or of some mental aberration of the people themselves. Different writers have proposed different procedures for correcting this destructive product of collective behavior. Some have contended that culture is a thin veneer that keeps under control primordial savage impulses that find destructive release in collective behavior. To these thinkers the damaging phenomena of collective behavior are inevitable whenever the discipline of the masses by centralized authority is relaxed. To other writers, such as E. D. Martin, the false thinking that creates collective behavior can be corrected through education or mass psychotherapy.

At the other extreme much practical political policy rests on the assumption that social change originates in collective behavior. Those who have a vested interest in an established order fear collective behavior. They fear that "rabble-rousers" will stir up discontent among a satisfied population, who will then demand changes that would not otherwise have occurred to them. Implicit in such thinking is the assumption that collective behavior may arise quite in the absence of any real grievances on the part of its participants. Once collective behavior has reached sufficient proportions, as shown in powerful movements, frequent eruptions of crowd behavior, and active publics, it may be impossible to control. It then brings about changes that would not otherwise have taken place, and a potentially stable and satisfying social order is overthrown or altered.

SOURCES OF WIDESPREAD COLLECTIVE BEHAVIOR

Theories of inherent change. An adequate determination of the place of collective behavior in change and persistence cannot be made without a careful examination of the relative incidence of collective behavior at various intervals. Records are not available even during current times that would enable us to approximate a quantitative study of the occurrence of collective behavior. We must depend upon the selective reports and rough impressions given to us by historians. Consequently, we can arrive at only loosely substantiated guesses in our attempt to relate collective behavior to social change. Such guesses have already been made by several of the writers who offer broad theories of social change.

Theories of large-scale change in society fall into two categories, those which find the impulse and direction of change to inhere in the cultural sequence itself and those which attribute change to external events. In the first category are the theories of continuous cycles. Among the best known theories of continuous cyclical change is that of Pitirim Sorokin. Sorokin holds that there is an inherent tendency for culture to oscillate between sensate and ideational saturation. A sensate culture is one dominated by naturalism, reliance on reason and mechanical contrivance, and realism. An ideational culture is one marked by mysticism, dependence on sentiment and religion, and symbolism. Each type bears within itself the seeds of its own destruction. As it approaches complete dominance by sensate forms or by ideational forms the culture runs out of opportunities for further development in the same direction, so change can only reverse itself. The most recent peak of ideational culture occurred during the Middle Ages. Twentieth century United States has already witnessed the peak of sensate dominance and counter-trends are now well in evidence.

Accompanying the cycle of sensate and ideational dominance is another cycle of increasing and declining societal integration. The peaks of integration occur slightly before the peaks of sensate and ideational dominance, society functioning most smoothly while there is still opportunity for development and elaboration of the dominant tendency. As complete saturation of either sensate or ideational tendencies approaches, integration in the society declines, discontent and disorder increase, and widespread collective behavior supplants much of the established institutional behavior. Thus the general conditions of dissatisfaction with the established culture which are the breeding ground for collective behavior occur as the opportunities for creative activity become limited by the exhaustion of one of the major cultural themes. Collective behavior expresses itself in the exploratory behavior through which the swing toward the opposite cultural pole is established.

According to this viewpoint collective behavior is an important agency of change. However, it is the *mechanism* through which predetermined change takes place rather than the originator of change. The content of collective behavior, i.e., the kinds of values that will be expressed, are predetermined by the imminent cultural change.

Whether Sorokin's complete theory of change is accepted or not, certain portions of it may have merit in themselves. The suggestion that any given cultural emphasis has within it only certain limited possibilities for development offers one generalized explanation for cultural change. As these possibilities are ex-

hausted, activity within the traditional cultural framework becomes less rewarding, so that discontent develops. Out of the discontent comes collective behavior,
collective exploratory activity through which a variety of directions are tested.
Out of this testing process emerges a new dominant cultural direction, whereupon
the collective behavior subsides in part and is conventionalized and institutionalized in part to make up a considerable portion of the new cultural machinery.

Another type of theory that makes change inherent in the nature of sociocultural process proposes a "dialectic" in place of cyclical change. In the various
versions of dialectical theory the culture is first dominated by one scheme of
values, one kind of socio-economic system, etc. The dominant system gives rise
to its opposite, and there then ensues a struggle between the two. Out of the
struggle both systems are destroyed but there arises a new system which reconciles the crucial elements from the original pair of opposites. Expressed in terms
of ideologies, the process has been described as a *thesis* giving rise to its *antithesis,* and the struggle between the two producing the *synthesis.* In the inexora-
ble historical process the synthesis becomes the new thesis which generates its
antithesis as a new dialectical sequence takes place.

The philosopher Hegel is identified with the fullest formulation of historical
process in terms of a dialectic of ideologies. But the application of dialectical
theory by Karl Marx is of greatest interest in the discussion of collective behavior. Marx proposes a sequence of continuing, self-inducing change, centering
about the distribution of social power as derived from economic processes. All
history is a record of struggle between those who have power and those who do
not have power. Each class is supplanted by a class over which it formerly exercised control. Each new ruling class produces a new suppressed class which develops under domination of the former. The suppressed class eventually overthrows
the ruling class and a new dialectic begins.

The dialectical pattern is not entirely uniform throughout history, however.
During past turns of the sequence, subordinate classes have gradually risen to
power and displaced the dominant group. The bourgeoisie who are the present ruling class differ from earlier ruling classes in having dispossessed those
below them. Consequently, the current or capitalistic era has been marked by a
new tendency in history, a tendency toward greater and greater extremes of difference between the rulers and the ruled. As this discrepancy becomes greater,
the bourgeoisie become fewer and fewer in number with corporations larger and
monopolies more general, and the consciousness of being an oppressed class
becomes stronger and more widespread in the rest of the society. The developing
sense of class solidarity leads to varied forms of collective behavior, which will
culminate in revolution and overthrow of the ruling class.

In Marxian theory the place of collective behavior is clearest for the contemporary period. Collective behavior accompanies the development of class consciousness and is its expression. It results from the extreme inequity arising out
of the prevailing economic system. To what extent collective behavior is a part
of the more gradual process through which a ruling class is dispossessed is not
so clearly indicated. It is clear, however, that in Marxian theory collective behavior on a widespread scale is an expression of the opposition between the rulers
and the ruled (as determined by their economic position) and its extensiveness
and intensity are functions of the degree of discrepancy in economic condition
between the two classes.

We have neither presented an adequate account of Marxian thought regarding social change nor shall we attempt its thorough evaluation. Events have not supported well the application to capitalism, though it is still possible to interpret changes which are taking place as an application of the dialectical principle. Many historical periods of extensive collective behavior can be plausibly interpreted as the process of working out a new order from the conflict between ruling classes and ruled. Contrary to the Marxian supposition, there is evidence that leads us to believe that large-scale and concerted collective behavior directed toward overthrow of the ruling group may be more likely to develop under improving conditions and when the distribution of economic goods is not extremely inequitable than under opposite conditions. Extremely inequitable conditions appear in history to be more generally associated with apathy and resignation in the submerged classes. However, the experience of steadily losing advantages that a class has formerly had is likely to bring about vigorous protest activity.

Breakdown of culture and social organization. There are many hypotheses of a less ambitious sort than the cyclical and dialectical theories, hypotheses that merely specify the conditions that characteristically give rise to change and associated collective behavior. Earlier (Chapter 2) we have discussed certain conditions likely to set the stage for collective behavior. These include the breakdown of a system of formal or informal social control, value-conflicts, frustration, and the failure of communication. Theories that place collective behavior in the context of social change go one step behind these conditions. They indicate the broad kinds of circumstances that are likely to create on a society-wide scale such conditions as control-failure or weakening of communication, which latter will in turn give rise to widespread collective behavior. In the context of social change we may look at the conditions specified earlier as the intervening variables between the broad instigating conditions of change in a society and the development of widespread collective behavior. The breakdown of normal communication patterns, for example, is an intervening cause between the events that set change in motion and the emergence of collective behavior.

If we describe the immediate conditions giving rise to collective behavior as states of *culture* and of *social organization,* our problem may be defined as locating the general conditions that initiate change in the culture or the social organization. Widespread collective behavior arises out of the inadequacy of culture on the one hand and out of the failure of the social organization to operate on the other hand.

Culture, as a set of established ways of acting and thinking, ceases to provide directives through which people can express their impulses. Conditions of life create problems or give rise to impulses for which culture cannot provide avenues of solution or modes of expression. The social organization, as the established pattern of interactions among people, ceases to operate in such a way as to get the group's business done. Communication breaks down at essential points. Confidence in the basis for the established division of labor weakens. The control agencies of the society cease to function adequately.

Organization and culture are but two sides of the same phenomena. The going social system may be described in terms of its established behaviors and values as culture, or in terms of the system of relations among people and groups through which the culture is expressed. Any event that seriously disrupts the one must necessarily also unbalance the other. If established cultural values are seriously challenged, then the system of social relations cannot endure without change. If events alter the power among groups in society or change communication networks, a change in the culture must follow to bring the established ways of thinking and feeling into harmony with the organization.

Let us consider first the sources of change in the culture, the basis for questioning the established values and ways of looking at things. The best documented source of challenges to the existing culture is extensive and intimate culture contact. The kind of contact that gives people an opportunity to view a different culture at least partially from the inside gives them a new perspective from which they observe their own culture. The outside culture is like an observation post from which, for the first time, they can look at their own culture in other ways than through the eyes of their culture itself. Culture contact means in part some borrowing of perspectives from the other culture. Such borrowing, however, may not be as important as is sometimes supposed. When individual traits are adopted from another culture, they are likely to be modified in the process into consistency with borrower's culture.

More important than the borrowing is the discovery that there is a vantage point from which one's own values no longer appear unquestionable axioms but as merely one among alternative systems of value. Thus it is not so much the particular culture with which culture contact takes place as it is the *attitude* toward one's own culture that is induced by any serious culture contact. The new attitude creates a receptiveness toward ideas from the other culture, and permits the development of new ideas and values from an examination of the adequacy of one's own culture. Culture contact gives rise not only to borrowing but to new ideas concerning the necessity for change in the established order and the directions in which such change should go.

In addition to this external source of cultural change, there are also probably internal sources. We have already noted Sorokin's view and the dialectical theories. These latter theories must remain hypothetical since the evidence to support them is tenuous and verification difficult. Somewhat more convincing is the thesis that culture, under favorable conditions, develops in the direction of increasing man's control and understanding of both his natural and social environment. To a considerable degree man's cultural values and ideas are a function of the kind of understanding he has of the world around him and the kinds of control he is able to exercise over it. For example, a set of values attuned to a world of semi-isolated small communities becomes untenable in a world that has developed the technical means for rapid transportation and communication on a world-wide basis. Man's conception of himself is built upon what he believes he can and cannot do. As his powers increase his self-conception changes. And the values that he espouses reflect his own self-conception. A change in self-conception leads to the discovery of new kinds of values that seem natural and obvious under the altered self-conception. Developments in technology and in the natural and social sciences seem to have this quality of opening up new self-conceptions and accordingly creating new value perspectives.

Sources of change in the social organization are many. Any drastic change in population or population trends will alter the power structure in abundant ways. Increase or decrease in population growth changes the rates of upward mobility within the class system. It demands adjustments in economic activity. It alters the balance between supply and demand. The established organization ceases to serve people's wants in the manner to which they are accustomed.

Widespread and lasting catastrophe taxes a social order. Studies of disasters that are limited in their scope show that, while much of the established order remains in abeyance immediately after the catastrophe, it tends to be restored and in full operation soon after. Spontaneous forms of social organization that arise immediately do not contradict or change the established order but merely fill the gap until it can be set in full operation again. Furthermore, catastrophe may be envisioned within the existing social order so that the populace are prepared to accept its inconveniences without doubting the basic adequacy of the established system. Such is generally the case in modern wars. Each nation prepares its populace to accept and deal with a considerable amount of bombing, and results indicate that intensive bombing over an extended period of time does not necessarily break confidence in the existing order. Hope by some that concentrated bombing of civilian populations would lead the enemy to revolt against their own leadership turned out to be unfounded.

But when catastrophe is of long duration, widespread, and contradicts the assumptions of the established order, pressures multiply for a change in the system. Thus, when bombing can no longer be accepted as a necessary condition to be tolerated while the armies are steadily moving toward victory, collective opposition to the established order may develop. The epidemics of the plague that scourged entire areas of Europe during the Middle Ages left the social order completely ineffectual in many instances, and gave rise to the dancing manias, pogroms, and other types of collective behavior.

Extensive movements of population have often resulted in disruption and challenge to the established order and a period of widespread collective behavior. The two periods when race riots against Negroes were most widespread in the United States during the current century were associated with the wartime migration of Negroes to the North and their movement into new areas of industrial employment. The tolerance of Negroes that had prevailed was based upon their limited numbers and the maintenance of distance. The order of interracial relations broke down as the implicit premises upon which it had operated were violated. Frontier communities that have grown rapidly generally lack a clearly defined order with effective means for exercising social control and bases for agreement on the working system of social stratification.

Population movement need not disrupt the social order, however. In the first instance cited above the population movement altered the social composition of the populace and involved some redistribution of privileges and alteration of social distance patterns. In the second instance the problem is that of establishing a social order where none exists and where the motives that have brought people together attract disproportionately those who see no immediate gain in a stable social system. A nomadic people, on the other hand, carry their social order with them and possess a social order that is adapted to movement. Population movements such as the migration of the Pilgrims to America also bring their own social order with them. Having an organization from the start, migrating by families rather than by detached individuals, and moving into a sparsely settled area, they were able to cope with problems that developed in an orderly fashion. Nineteenth and 20th century immigrants to the large cities of the United States taxed the social order in certain respects, but the development of collective behavior was limited. The expansion of industry in the United States provided places for the immigrants in the social system. The conflict between old and new social systems for the immigrants made for considerable disorganization in the immigrant communities and weakened in some respects the systems of communication and control in the American community. But the control systems in the larger community were strong enough to prevent the eruption of discontent into collective behavior except sporadically.

The social order is dependent upon the functioning of the subsistence or economic system. While no simple economic determinism can be justified, a minimum effectiveness in the operation of the economic system is essential if the entire social order is to continue to operate. Hence, any disturbance in the economic realm is likely to be reflected in challenge to the social order. Periods of economic depression in modern society witness the rise of social movements and crowd activity, and heightened activity in publics. Drought or other conditions which reduce the food supply may have such an effect in primitive societies if the events are not defined as a punishment requiring even closer conformity in the future.

Over a more extended period, changes in the mode of subsistence or developments in technology and other conditions which alter the economic system have the effect of changing the established distribution of power in society. The traditional order tends to perpetuate the old distribution of power after its economic supports have weakened and the bases for transfer of power to a different class have been established. A struggle then develops between the old and the new, until the traditional order has been destroyed, its defenders have given up attempts to restore it, and the new distribution of power has become recognized. A traditional ruling class may hold onto power that has lost its economic supports because theirs is the only power that is recognized as legitimate by the general populace. The class with newly-achieved power must turn its economic control into social power by acquiring popular recognition. Its attempts, resistance by the ruling group, and the entry of other interests which can take advantage of the breakdown of traditional controls give rise to widespread collective behavior.

Finally, a social order may become rigidified so that it ceases to adjust to ordinary changes and to cope adequately with ordinary discontent. Among various writers who have stressed this tendency in social organization is Vilfredo Pareto in his theory of the circulation of the elite. He proposes that in a normally functioning social order the elites, or those who exercise the legitimate power constantly replenish their numbers by bringing in outstanding individuals from the lower classes. In this manner new ideas are being constantly brought into the elites, the quality of the elites is kept high, and potential leadership for the lower classes is removed. Sometimes, however, this circulation process is interrupted the elites merely perpetuate themselves from within, and upward movement from the lower classes is blocked. When this happens not only do the elite become decadent, but individuals who might otherwise have been absorbed into the elite now become the leaders of the subordinate classes. They help to focus discontent and eventually to lead movements for the overthrow of the traditional elite. Thus a period of heightened collective behavior develops when the normal circulation of elites is interrupted.

THE FUNCTION OF COLLECTIVE BEHAVIOR IN CHANGE

New perspectives and social change. Whatever the combination of sources of change, a period of heightened collective behavior depends upon the widespread arousal of both discontent and a sense of expanding horizons. The latter is particularly the product of cultural contact or rapid growth of technology. Most collective behavior depends as fully upon the striking awareness of new possibilities as upon dissatisfaction. The expanding horizons supply the ideas in terms of which publics may conceive issues, and social movements may formulate ideologies.

There appear to have been periods in history when increasing discontent occurred without exposure to new ideas, leading to limited development of certain kinds of collective behavior. A sort of hypersensitiveness may prevail which increases susceptibility to crowd behavior without providing ideological rallying points to sustain collective behavior and give it continuity. Tendencies to panic are heightened, expressive crowd behavior readily develops beyond the boundaries of conventional behavior, and acting crowds develop to the point of violence with a minimum of provocation. Power struggles based upon the changing distribution of effective power take place, but the resulting control movements operate from an elite rather than a mass base. The only types of movements with any mass appeal are participation-oriented movements, often providing a type of security by revivalist emphases.

When developments imminent within the culture or the new perspectives brought in from the contact between cultures are added to discontent, however, people begin to see the current situation in light of possible directions of change. The awareness of better conditions as a concrete possibility develops. Familiar conditions within the society can now be reconceptualized in the terms supplied by a new or different cultural framework. Discontent, instead of being vague and unfocused, is now identified, usually in a variety of ways. And as it is identified various courses of action are suggested for coping with the supposed sources of discontent.

The function of specific forms of collective behavior. It is under these conditions —widespread discontent *and* the availability of new cultural perspectives that suggest new possibilities for coping with discontent—that collective behavior ramifies and becomes crucial to the life of the society. Out of the unrest there begin to spring up loosely conceived publics, made possible by the definitions of issues. The publics at this point are extremely volatile, short-lived, and small in size. The publics are many, corresponding with a prevalent variety of ways of defining issues. If collective behavior is sustained, the number of publics declines, their size increases as publics combine, and a few of the ways of defining issues survive while the rest disappear.

At times, situations arise which can be quickly defined in the terms established in the prevalent publics, and which are felt to embody most critically and urgently the essence of the issue. These incidents give rise to acting crowd behavior. The crowd action may come from either direction, in support of traditional culture values and patterns of social organization against dangerous new ideas, or in support of one of the newer viewpoints. The pattern of lynchings in the United States represented crystallization of the viewpoint of those who resisted the changes that had been occurring in the interracial social organization. The incidents bringing about lynchings most frequently were depicted as such ultimate breakdown of the caste system as sexual attack on a white woman by a Negro man. Epitomizing the feared condition in its ultimate form, the incident conveyed a sense of urgency which combined with a lack of confidence in legal procedures to demand drastic and extreme action. Crowd actions against the traditional social order often arise when repressive action is taken against the newer ideas and attacks on the existing order. The repression of discussion or of efforts to change the traditional structure epitomize to the discontented the ultimate evils of the traditional order. Thus a sense of urgency provokes the demand for immediate and drastic action.

The acting crowds of such a period have a much more focused significance than the crowd activities of an era of widespread discontent without new perspectives. During the latter periods crowd activities are likely to define their object as a limited grievance or to take expressive form with the pleasurable sensations of activity entirely different from the conventional standing as ends in themselves. Thus, religious expressive crowds such as the frontier revivals very quickly become dominated by overtones of revelry contrasting with the sombre quality of frontier life and with license to violate the prevalent mores in symbolic or actual sexual excitement and other unconventional behavior. Or the pogroms—mob violence against Jewish communities—of certain periods in Europe were episodes of mass brutality unconnected with any broad definition of issues and conception of long-range changes to be brought about.

But when new cultural perspectives have been applied to contemporary discontents in the formation of publics, crowd activity gets defined in the terms provided by some prevalent public. Not only is the crowd activity the expression derived from a pre-existing public, but the crowd action itself becomes a focal point for subsequent consideration of publics. On the one hand the crowd may go sufficiently far in its behavior—further than its particular faction of the public is prepared to defend—that there is a revulsion and opposing factions of the public are strengthened. Thus in the United States when labor strikes turn into crowd violence, the pro-labor factions in publics usually lose support. And lynchings became progressively more embarrassing to those who sought to preserve the interracial caste patterns. On the other hand, crowd action may unify the members of public factions and may supply them with leaders and heroes. The crowd action itself may become an important symbol, serving as a continuing rallying point to bring about more vigorous support. The unpredictable events in the course of the crowd action may change somewhat the emphasis in the public or modify the definition of the issue. But most of all, the crowd action, by precipitating an issue that is only being discussed in the public, tends to draw more sharply the lines between opposing factions in the public, to restructure the issues in more irreconcilable terms.

Thus it is hardly possible to speak of the consequence of crowd behavior taken by itself. Its significance depends first upon whether it springs out of a well-established public, and second upon how the publics conceive the crowd after it has subsided.

Against this background LeBon's suggestion that crowds serve to destroy the old order in preparation for the emergence of a new one may be considered. As we have seen, crowds may be directed toward preserving the *status quo ante* as well as toward destroying it. These efforts may boomerang, but in other instances they may help to preserve the existing structure. The importance of LeBon's observation is perhaps clearest in the periods when discontent is not complemented by novel perspectives. During such periods the activities of crowds are generally feared by officials of the established order since they represent behavior outside of conventional controls. While the crowds are in operation spontaneous leadership takes over and outcomes are unpredictable. In such activity the populace discovers the possibilities and pleasures of escaping the controls of the established social order. People realize that they are conforming largely because they have to rather than because they spontaneously desire to do so. The excitement of following new, though temporary, leaders helps to disenchant them concerning the established leaders. By contrast to the even slightly charismatic crowd leaders, the established leaders are made to appear both prosaic and remote.

The net result of this development is to weaken spontaneous and willing adherence to the established order. The established order itself is not likely to be destroyed from below on this basis alone, since no new ideas and values are present to direct and sustain collective behavior. But people will be readier to hear new ideas and readier to apply them if they become available.

From the publics in a period of heightened collective behavior there emerge not only crowds but social movements. While power-oriented movements with an elite base and participation-oriented movements are found in unsettled periods, the value-oriented movements come into prominence when culture contact or cultural development has brought new perspectives into play. Value-oriented movements are the more stable groupings that develop from the interaction within publics and the attempt to define discontent. The emerging movements partly reflect the definitions of issues that already prevail and partly supply their own modified definitions to the publics. Idiosyncrasies of a charismatic leader, tactical considerations, and response to heterogeneous membership are among the many influences leading a social movement to establish its own somewhat unique definition of the issue.

The tentative process. This entire development in which crowds and social movements operate within the context of changing publics may be regarded as the tentative process within which new directions of culture and social organization are worked out. The process of working out a dominant major direction of change or of settling on a limited number of contending positions whose dialectic will be a continuing feature of change involves two major groups of developments.

First are the processes centering about the defining of issues and values. To a certain degree accepted statements of values and issues emerge through discussion, as affected by crowd activity and promotion by value-oriented movements. But more generally shifts in values occur obliquely. Changes in the prevalent definitions of issues permit realignments without complete reversals in values among individuals. Similarly, change occurs only partially through clear-cut victories by particular movements. Of more consequence for long-term change is the absorption by contending movements of important parts of the most successful movements' values. Victories of particular movements may be ephemeral. Reactions against overly successful movements set in for a variety of reasons, often creating apparent swings between rival viewpoints. For these reasons the interplay of contending movements might have little consequence for long-range directions of change except that the value-orientations of each of the movements undergoes change. Thus certain issues come to be settled, not by admitted agreement, but by moving on to new issues. The value of state support for the aged was established in the United States through acceptance of this principle by the countermovements which effectively defeated the major old-age pension movements of the 1930's. The value of social security became firmly established when the movement which had unsuccessfully opposed it began concentrating its opposition on other matters.

But second, the emerging directions of change may be equally shaped by struggles and alignments to which value questions are secondary. Some movements arise almost exclusively about the efforts of groups to gain control for its own sake. Control movements also develop when the commitment of value-oriented movements to their own persistence and power becomes stronger than their dedication to the values they originally promoted. And movements committed to their own existence may remain after issues to which their values apply have been relegated to the past. Certain value-oriented movements may lose out or gain more than others in the struggle with control movements. Certain values may gain or be discredited by being adopted for tactical purposes by control movements. Separatist movements may draw support away from a major value orientation.

In part these two directions represent the mechanisms of change in culture and social organization respectively. Values are conceptualized as part of the culture. Value-orientations represent direct proposals for alteration of the culture. Issues within publics constitute questions of the relative emphasis or the nature of application of values in the culture. Power-orientations, on the other hand, concern social organization. Successful redistribution of power leads to reorganization, with implications for modification of the cultural values bound to accompany the changes.

From the preceding discussion we may summarize the relation of collective behavior to change in the following manner. (1) A certain amount of isolated and sporadic collective behavior characterizes the most stable society and has no important implications for change. It is simply a response to events which fall outside the limits with which the established order and culture are prepared to cope. (2) Widespread collective behavior over a period of time is probably not a sufficient condition to bring about social and cultural change, though it probably always makes the social order more susceptible to change when the necessary ideas and values can be supplied. (3) Widespread collective behavior becomes the major vehicle of change when contact between diverse cultures or developments within the culture supply novel values about which collective behavior can become focused. (4) Collective behavior then becomes the medium through which tentative directions of change are tested until one major direction prevails. (5) Thus collective behavior is an integral part of the process of social and cultural change. It appears probable that broad potential directions of change are predetermined in the very developments of culture and society that originally give rise to the collective behavior, so that the latter is more a process of discovery than of determination. But it is also plausible that details of change and selection among limited alternatives may actually be determined in the collective behavior processes, within a range of broadly predetermined directions.

THE FUNCTION OF COLLECTIVE BEHAVIOR IN STABILITY

As we observe collective behavior in change, we are forced to note that what are the new ideas of one period become the conservative values in a stable era that follows. The change from a new and radical value to an accepted value that exemplifies the respectable base for a stable order is a gradual one. And the accompanying reduction in the incidence of widespread collective behavior is similarly gradual. But the change is only in part a reduction of collective behavior. It is equally the preservation and transformation of a certain amount of collective behavior, turned now to the purpose of preserving what are coming to be the established patterns. Thus a certain amount of collective behavior is institutionalized, so that it is evoked under conventionalized situations and proceeds within conventionally understood bounds. The processes of the conventionalized crowd, the conventionalized public, and the institutionalized movement, as already discussed, come into play in support of the existing order.

Culturally allowable issues—matters on which there can be disagreement without challenging the fundamental consensus of culture—are resolved through publics under varying degrees of conventionalization. Some may follow the highly formalized procedures of an election. Others, less formalized, may be constrained to approximate the procedures of an election. Despite varying degrees of formalization, these conventionalized publics are alike in preventing differences of opinion from unduly disrupting the stable order.

The particular services of conventionalized crowds are two. First, the acting crowd may arise within a conventionalized framework to maintain a major value in the culture when the social order is temporarily failing to do so. Vigilante committees which have operated in California and elsewhere have frequently maintained a highly conventionalized pattern, carefully imitating the procedures of an institutionalized court of law. In California the vigilante committee arose in the mid-nineteenth century when the *forms* of standard American legal procedure had been extended to the new state, but the system itself had not begun to operate properly. The work of the committee hastened the translation of the forms of government into a functioning government.

The acting crowd within a conventional framework is perhaps the exception. But the conventional expressive crowd appears to be a constant accompaniment of any stable social order. The service of the conventional crowd is to revivify the social order, to combat the tendency of the social order to degenerate into an uninspired enactment of daily routines without imagination or sense of purpose. Frequently the established order demands of individuals a marshalling of energy and enthusiasm or courage not required in performance of routine responsibilities. The conventionalized expressive crowd is employed to arouse the necessary enthusiasm or courage. The disregard of personal safety demanded of the Iroquois warrior entering battle is cultivated through an expressive crowd experience which is part of the ritual preceding battle. Through this experience the individual warrior acquires a vital sense of group support and group pressure which permits him to enter battle. The same principle may be employed in preparing an athletic team for exceptional effort, in a political rally to make people overcome their conventional reserve about knocking on doors to campaign for a favorite candidate, or in the religious service to prepare people to overcome normal cautiousness in giving their money to a worthy cause.

But even in the performance of more routine tasks, people require a vigorous sense of group identity or morale and a conviction that imbues key values with a religious quality. Conventional expressive crowds are used to establish moods and reinforce convictions that are likely to be lost in daily routine. Thus a sense of purpose and worth in routine activities and a basis for aspiration are supplied.

In a stable order, social movements tend to be absorbed into established institutions, to become institutionalized themselves as some churches and political parties have done, or to disappear. Society-wide value-oriented movements are not a characteristic feature of a stable system. Power struggles with a limited elite base may produce small movements of which the majority of the populace are unaware and whose success will make little difference to the course of the society. Participation-oriented movements may offer special satisfactions to minority elements in the society, thus serving as palliatives against the inequities that might otherwise focus discontent against the social order itself. Within conventional bounds, these limited control movements and participation-oriented movements permit occasional redistributions of power and provide substitute satisfactions for frustrated elements, thus assisting in maintaining the social order.

Value-oriented movements are not altogether lacking in a stable order. The significant fact is rather their conventionalization within established institutions. There will be movements dealing with religious values, but these will develop and contend within the institutionalized denominations, rather than outside of them. Instead of making mass appeals, they will pursue their particular interpretation of faith by trying to convince key elements within the denomination. Similarly, political movements will exist, but will operate primarily within established political parties. Insofar as movements accept these institutional boundaries to their actions and limit their tactics to those which are acceptable to the established institutions, they operate as conventionalized movements supporting the general social structure and the culture.

Institutionalization may be an effort to maintain certain useful features of a social movement without retaining the movement as a whole. Max Weber's classic discussion of the "routinization of charisma" deals with this type of process. The true charismatic leader is a product of his following: he only acquires charisma as he acquires a vigorous following who then create and give social support to a superhuman image of their leader. The tremendous trust and devotion toward the charismatic leader is an asset to any social order. Consequently there is an attempt to invest various offices of authority with charisma. Through ritual and myth the king acquires in the eyes of his subjects some of the superhuman qualities of a genuine charismatic leader with a following devoted to his person rather than to his office. To the degree to which such charisma can be carried over from the personal leader of one of the movements crucial in bringing about change to his successors who maintain the changed order through their institutionalized office, the order can command greater devotion and more spontaneous conformity from the populace than would otherwise be the case. Thus, from Jesus Christ, charisma is passed to his hand-picked disciples, from whom charisma is further passed through the institutional office to the entire line of Roman Catholic Popes. Or the personal charisma of the revolutionary leader, Lenin, is transmitted via his office to his successor, Josef Stalin.

A final feature of all types of collective behavior during periods of stability is their alleged "safety valve" function. According to this often expressed view, collective behavior is a means of releasing accumulated tensions, letting people express their discontents so as to get them out of their systems. Frequently a stable social order is characterized by occasional or even regular incidents of crowd activity which either attacks the established order or contradicts the established values. These episodes are followed by acquiescence, as if the steam of rebellion had indeed been expended.

There is, however, another way of viewing these episodes. One cannot fully evaluate his own thoughts until he has expressed them in words. One cannot see one's own potential actions in perspective until he has overtly engaged in them. During these episodic manifestations of collective behavior people say openly those things they have vaguely felt and they behave in ways they have only expressed in private fantasy. Just as a man may discover when he writes it down that his "great idea" is commonplace, so the words and actions may be revealed to be quite disappointing. Or a person who is basically committed to a particular social system or set of values more strongly than he realizes suddenly discovers the strength of his commitment when he witnesses or participates in an attack on them.

From this standpoint such episodic collective behavior is not a process of dispelling tensions by expressing them or achieving catharsis. It is rather a process of *testing* the group's commitment to their value system by discovering what it is like to have them attacked. The enactment of the role of the attacker of values evokes the response role of defending the values. In the process of becoming involved in both types of roles the actors discover where their profounder identification lies. By this occasional testing of loyalties and convictions, conventionalized crowd behavior might contribute to stability of the social order.

Thus, in summary, collective behavior has a place both in change and in stability. In stability it helps to maintain a certain fluidity which resists tendencies toward total inflexibility in the social structure. And it helps to maintain some of the vitality and vigor and religious devotion to values that characterize periods of change. While institutional behavior is associated with man's submission to essential routines, collective behavior is associated with his ideals. The institutionalization of collective behavior helps to weld these two aspects of life together.

Suggested additional readings

PART I: *The nature and emergence of collective behavior*

Gustave LeBon, *The Crowd: A Study of the Popular Mind*. London: T. F. Unwin, 1897. In spite of its obvious deficiencies from the standpoint of modern theory, this is one of the most significant landmarks in the development of the field of collective behavior.

E. A. Ross, *Social Psychology*. New York: The Macmillan Co., 1908. Strongly reflecting the influence of Gabriel Tarde, Ross presents one of the earliest systematic theories of collective behavior.

Herbert Blumer, "Collective Behavior," in A. M. Lee, ed., *Principles of Sociology*. New York: Barnes & Noble, Inc., 1951. Though very brief, this section has for many years been the standard treatment of collective behavior from the approach of social psychology.

K. G. J. C. Knowles, "Strike-Proneness and Its Determinants," *American Journal of Sociology*, 60 (1954), 213–29. Knowles presents evidence that social unrest finds expression in industrial strikes only if the workers have some social cohesion and a tradition of common action.

Lynn White, Jr., "The Spared Wolves," *Saturday Review*, 23 (Nov. 13, 1954), 32–33. Witchcraft among the Navajos is analyzed as a phenomenon arising out of a condition of inadequacy of normative integration.

E. L. Quarantelli, "The Nature and Conditions of Panic," *American Journal of Sociology*, 60 (1954), 267–75. The writer describes the feelings and perceptions of the individual that are likely to lead to panic.

Bradford B. Hudson, "Anxiety in Response to the Unfamiliar," *Journal of Social Issues*, 10 (1954), 53–60. This is an experimental study of response both to the perception of threat and to unstructured environmental stimuli, suggesting that both may arouse anxiety.

E. Paul Torrance, "The Behavior of Small Groups Under the Stress Conditions of Survival," *American Sociological Review*, 19 (1954), 751–55. Shows the effects

531

on behavior of an unstructured situation, as represented in the plight of Air Force bomber crews forced to "bail out."

PART 2: *The crowd*

John R. P. French, "Organized and Unorganized Groups Under Fear and Frustration," in Kurt Lewin *et al., Authority and Frustration.* Iowa City: University of Iowa Press, 1944. This research report should be read for its demonstration of the effects of pre-sensitization and the existence of established communication channels in facilitating social contagion.

E. A. Schuler and Vernon Parenton, "A Recent Epidemic of Hysteria in a Louisiana High School," *Journal of Social Psychology,* 17 (1943), 221–35. A modern "dancing mania" is described, with a detailed analysis of the subjective factors predisposing individuals to be susceptible to social contagion.

Donald Johnson, "The Phantom Anesthetist of Mattoon," *Journal of Abnormal and Social Psychology,* 40 (1945), 175–86. Shows the importance of the media of mass communication in the milling process in modern society.

J. Prasad, "The Psychology of Rumour: A Study Relating to the Great Earthquake of 1934," *British Journal of Psychology,* 26 (1935), 1–15. Contains a detailed analysis of the many rumors that arose following a catastrophe, but should be read especially for the illustration of rumors that arise to validate a strong emotion.

Guy E. Swanson, "A Preliminary Laboratory Study of the Acting Crowd," *American Sociological Review,* 18 (1953), 522–33. In one of the very few attempts to study crowd behavior in the laboratory, Swanson focuses on the form of crowd in which behavior aims at manipulating the external environment.

Paul B. Foreman, "Panic Theory," *Sociology and Social Research,* 37 (1953), 295–304. On the basis of 54 historical cases, the author reviews theories of panic and develops propositions as to the nature of panic and the conditions under which it is likely to develop.

Norman Polansky, R. Lippit, and F. Redl, "An Investigation of Behavioral Contagion in Groups," *Human Relations,* 3 (1950), 319–48; and Daniel Glasser, Polansky, and Lippit, "A Laboratory Study of Behavioral Contagion," *Ibid.,* 4 (1951), 115–42. These two studies demonstrate clearly how the actions of impulsive group members may reduce the forces inhibiting other group members from acting.

John E. Coxe, "The New Orleans Mafia Incident," *Louisiana Historical Quarterly,* 20 (1937), 1067–1106. This account of a little-known lynching shows the participation of "respectable" elements, deliberate instigation in the early stages of crowd development, and the shift of control and leadership from one element in the crowd to another.

Joseph Abrahams and L. W. McCorkle, "Analysis of a Prison Disturbance," *Journal of Abnormal and Social Psychology,* 42 (1947), 330–41. This study contains excellent descriptions of milling and of the use of techniques of crowd control, but has particular relevance to interaction in the crowd. It illustrates the participation and influence of individuals whose inhibitions are already down.

Edward Shils and Michael Young, "The Meaning of the Coronation," *Sociological Review,* 1 (New Series, 1953), 63–81. Discusses the coronation rites in England as a collective experience of the people, with the Monarch serving as a symbol of moral consensus in a political democracy.

J. E. Weckler and T. E. Hall, *The Police and Minority Groups.* Chicago: The International City Managers Association, 1944. This handbook is particularly good because of the concrete examples of crowd termination and control that it contains.

Joe Jordan, "Lynchers Don't Like Lead," *Atlantic Monthly,* 177 (Feb., 1946), 103–108. This very readable account of a near-lynching gives an hour-by-hour account of the development of a crowd to the point at which it was ready to act, and then shows how this action was prevented by an effective show of force.

PART 3: *The diffuse collectivity*

Leo Bogart, "Adult Talk About Newspaper Comics," *American Journal of Sociology,* 61 (1955), 26–30; and "Fan Mail for the Philharmonic," *Public Opinion Quarterly,* 13 (1949), 423–34. These two papers describe two kinds of responses to mass communication, through strictly mass behavior by writing letters and through carrying the content into casual daily conversation.

Bernard Berelson, "What 'Missing the Newspaper' Means," in Paul F. Lazarsfeld and Frank N. Stanton, eds., *Communications Research, 1948–49.* New York: Harper & Brothers, 1949. Interviews with persons deprived of a daily paper by a newspaper strike indicate the various uses to which the newspaper is put.

Herbert Blumer, "Moulding of Mass Behavior Through the Motion Picture," *Publications of the American Sociological Society,* 29 (1935), 115–27. A particularly careful statement of the characteristics of the mass appears in this article.

Elizabeth H. Zerner, "Rumors in Paris Newspapers," *Public Opinion Quarterly,* 10 (Fall, 1946), 382–91. Through content analysis of thirty newspapers the author shows how editorial bias affected the treatment of rumors concerning Stalin's death.

Martin Millspaugh, "Trial by Mass Media?" *Public Opinion Quarterly,* 13 (Summer, 1949), 328–29. This is a brief report on a case in which biased newspaper reporting was judged to have made it impossible to locate an impartial jury.

W. Lloyd Warner and William E. Henry, "The Radio Day-Time Serial: A Symbolic Analysis," *Genetic Psychology Monographs,* 37 (1948), 3–71. The entire paper should be read for the evidence supporting the conclusions.

N. W. Posthumus, "The Tulip Mania in Holland in the Years 1636 and 1637," *Journal of Economic and Business History,* 1 (1929), 434–66; and Homer B. Vanderblue, "The Florida Land Boom," *Journal of Land and Public Utility Economics,* 3 (1927), 113–31, 252–69. Economists document two famous speculative booms.

Herbert Blumer, "Morale," in W. F. Ogburn, ed., *American Society in Wartime.* Chicago: University of Chicago Press, 1943. Blumer contrasts American morale during World War II with other types of morale.

George Katona, *Psychological Analysis of Economic Behavior.* New York: McGraw-Hill Book Company, Inc., 1951, Chapters 12 and 13. The place of crowd phenomena in the business cycle is discussed in considerable detail.

Arnold M. Rose, "Rumor in the Stock Market," *Public Opinion Quarterly,* 15 (Fall, 1951), 461–86. A sociologist describes collective behavior in financial speculation.

Edward Sapir, "Fashion," *Encyclopedia of the Social Sciences.* New York: The Macmillan Company, 1931, Vol. 6, 139–44. This is one of the most comprehensive, concise statements about fashion to be found.

W. Godfrey Cobliner, "Feminine Fashion as an Aspect of Group Psychology," *Journal of Social Psychology,* 31 (1950), 283–89; and Paul M. Gregory, "An Economic Interpretation of Women's Fashions," *Southern Economic Journal,*

14 (1947), 148–62. Two rather different aspects of fashion are presented in examinations of prestige competition and special economic interests respectively.

Walter Lippmann, *Public Opinion*. New York: Penguin Books, 1946 (first published by The Macmillan Company, 1922); and *The Phantom Public: A Sequel to "Public Opinion."* New York: The Macmillan Company, 1930. Lippmann's penetrating exposition of the obstacles to the achievement of sustained effective publics on a nationwide basis in modern society has provided the axioms from which later analyses have begun.

Lindsay Rogers, *The Pollsters: Public Opinion, Politics, and Democratic Leadership*. New York: Alfred A. Knopf, Inc., 1949. The suitability of polling techniques to the understanding of modern public opinion is discussed.

Julian L. Woodward and Elmo Roper, "The Effective Public for Plant-Community Public Relations Efforts," *Public Opinion Quarterly*, 15 (Winter, 1951–52), 624–34. The practical significance of the idea of a specialized public is emphasized here.

Lynn M. Case, "French Opinion and Napoleon III's Decision After Sadowa," *Public Opinion Quarterly*, 13 (Fall, 1949), 441–61. Napoleon III's efforts to establish valid ways of assessing public opinion are discussed.

Nelson N. Foote and Clyde W. Hart, "Public Opinion and Collective Behavior," in Muzafer Sherif and M. O. Wilson, eds., *Group Relations at the Crossroads*. New York: Harper & Brothers, 1953. The writers argue that hypotheses should be derived from a genetic model of public opinion process rather than a static definition, and outline such a model.

Tom Harrisson, "What is Public Opinion?" *Political Quarterly*, 11 (1940), 368–83. Apparently sudden swings of public opinion are attributed in this article to cumulating shifts in private opinion.

Herbert Goldhamer, "Public Opinion and Personality," *American Journal of Sociology*, 55 (1950), 346–54. Goldhamer discusses the relationship between individual psychological states and public opinion.

Francis E. Merrill and Carroll D. Clark, "Money Market as a Special Public," *American Journal of Sociology*, 39 (1934), 626–36. A "special public" is equated with a segmental interest group.

Floyd Hunter, *Community Power Structure: A Study of Decision Makers*. Chapel Hill: University of North Carolina Press, 1953. This type of realistic assessment of the points at which effective decisions are made is an indispensable precursor to the analysis of public opinion.

Elihu Katz and Paul F. Lazarsfeld, *Personal Influence: The Part Played by People in the Flow of Mass Communication*. Glencoe, Ill.: The Free Press, 1955. The place of opinion leaders within networks of informal contact is examined in a variety of opinion spheres.

Selden C. Menefee, "Propaganda and Symbol Manipulation," in Society for the Psychological Study of Social Issues, *Industrial Conflict: A Psychological Interpretation*. New York: Cordon Company, 1939. A general statement on propaganda is given special application to the industrial situation.

Robert K. Merton, *Mass Persuasion: The Social Psychology of a War Bond Drive*. New York: Harper & Brothers, 1946. Using interviews and thematic content analysis, the writer examines the effectiveness of the Kate Smith radio "marathon" in the sale of war bonds.

Harold D. Lasswell and Dorothy Blumenstock, *World Revolutionary Propaganda: A Chicago Study*. New York: Alfred A. Knopf, Inc., 1939. The workings of communist groups, especially during the depression years, is described.

Leo Lowenthal and Norbert Guterman, *Prophets of Deceit: A Study of the Techniques of the American Agitator.* New York: Harper & Brothers, 1949. Recent agitation is examined, using the term to designate efforts toward bigotry and disruption.

Talcott Parsons, "Propaganda and Social Control," *Psychiatry,* 5 (1942), 551–72. Parsons develops a detailed analogy between the role of the physician vis-a-vis the patient and the role of the morale-building propagandist in wartime.

James E. Foster, "The Group in Terms of Propaganda," *American Sociological Review,* 2 (1937), 247–52. The effectiveness of propaganda is related to patterns of multiple group membership.

Herbert M. Brattner, "The Committee for the Nation: A Case History in Monetary Propaganda," *Journal of Political Economy,* 49 (1941), 531–53. The techniques, organization, and effectiveness of a small group working to influence monetary policy are examined.

PART 4: *The social movement*

Rudolf Heberle, *Social Movements: An Introduction to Political Sociology.* New York: Appleton-Century-Crofts, Inc., 1951. Although slanted toward political organization rather than collective behavior, this book is the most adequate sociological treatment of social movements available.

Hadley Cantril, *The Psychology of Social Movements.* New York: John Wiley & Sons, 1941. A psychological framework for examining social movements is carefully developed in the first chapters and then applied in several informative case analyses.

Theodore Abel, "The Pattern of a Successful Political Movement," *American Sociological Review,* 2 (1937), 347–52. Abel uses the Nazi movement to illustrate what he asserts are the essential conditions for success of a movement.

Seymour M. Lipset, *Agrarian Socialism.* Berkeley: University of California Press, 1950. This is an outstanding sociological case study of a single social movement.

Thomas H. Greer, *American Social Reform Movements: Their Pattern Since 1865.* (Englewood Cliffs, N.J.: Prentice-Hall, Inc., 1949). This book contains a series of concise historical accounts of major movements, with a concluding chapter presenting the "problems" with which the value-oriented movement (our term) must deal.

Carl C. Taylor, *The Farmer's Movement.* New York: American Book Company, 1952. An authentic history of value-oriented movements concerned with the interests of farmers.

Daniel Bell, ed., *The New American Right.* New York: Criterion Books, 1955. The recent movement reflected in McCarthyism is examined by a number of social scientists.

James H. Tufts, "Liberal Movements in the United States—Their Methods and Aims," *International Journal of Ethics,* 46 (1936), 253–75. Six movements are compared as to their effectiveness and the means they employ.

Talcott Parsons, "The Role of Ideas in Social Action," *American Sociological Review,* 3 (1938), 652–64. Drawing upon Max Weber, Parsons argues that ideas not subject to empirical verification have played an important part in shaping action.

Alfred Cobban, "An Age of Revolutionary Wars: An Historical Parallel," *Review of Politics,* 13 (1951), 131–41; and Henri Peyre, "The Influence of Eighteenth Century Ideas on the French Revolution," trans. Arthur L. Kurth, *Journal of the*

History of Ideas, 10 (1949), 63–87. Two authors discuss specific ideas and their importance in the French Revolution and the movements that led to it.

Luther S. Cressman, "Ritual, the Conserver," *American Journal of Sociology*, 35 (1930), 564–72. The crucial importance of ritual in building belief and faith is examined with special reference to the Catholic Church.

Georges Sorel, *Reflections on Violence*, trans. T. E. Hulme and J. Roth. Glencoe, Ill.: The Free Press, 1950. The rationale of the general strike as an essential myth is presented among a series of bitter attacks on the moderate socialists.

Franz Neumann, *Behemoth*, New York: Oxford University Press, 1944. The Nazi ideology is analyzed as a tool for gaining control of state machinery rather than as the expression of any particular political theory.

Emil Lederer, *The State of the Masses: The Threat of the Classless Society*. New York: W. W. Norton & Company, 1940. The rise of totalitarian movements in recent times is examined against the background of a society in which organization gives way to the mass.

Kurt Riezler, "On the Psychology of Modern Revolution," *Social Research*, 10 (1943), 320–36. Modern revolutions are interpreted as movements for centralized control, fostered by the misguided support of "outcasts, fools, and experts."

Philip Selznick, *The Organizational Weapon: A Study of Bolshevik Strategy and Tactics*. New York: McGraw-Hill Book Company, Inc., 1952. Selznick offers a systematic sociological analysis of the ways in which Communists have made use of organizations to further their control and influence.

Will Maslow, "F.E.P.C.—A Case History in Parliamentary Maneuver," *University of Chicago Law Review*, 13 (1946), 407–44. This is a detailed account of maneuvers used by proponents and opponents of F.E.P.C. in Congress.

Alfred McClung Lee, "Techniques of Social Reform: An Analysis of the New Prohibition Drive," *American Sociological Review*, 9 (1944), 65–77. Lee juxtaposes the appeals of the prohibitionists and their opponents, providing an informative case in the interaction between contending movements.

Sarah McCulloh Lemon, "The Ideology of the 'Dixiecrat' Movement," *Social Forces*, 30 (1951), 162–71. A recent third-party movement is analyzed as a countermovement, its ideology described and related to the problems of regional power.

Elizabeth G. Herzog, "Patterns of Controversy," *Public Opinion Quarterly*, 13 (Spring, 1949), 39–52. From a content analysis of public statements the author suggests that there may be some characteristics that distinguish "pro" ideologies from "con" ideologies, irrespective of the issue.

Fred E. Haynes, *Third Party Movements Since the Civil War*. Iowa City: State Historical Society of Iowa, 1916; William B. Hesseltine, *The Rise and Fall of Third Parties: From Anti-Masonry to Wallace*. Washington: Public Affairs Press, 1948 and John D. Hicks, "The Third Party Tradition in American Politics," *Mississippi Valley Historical Review*, 20 (1933), 3–28. Here are three historical reviews and analyses of attempts by third parties to break the power monopoly of the two principal American political parties.

Robert J. Alexander, "Splinter Groups in American Radical Politics," *Social Research* 20 (Autumn, 1953), 282–310. This paper reviews the many separatist movements within the larger socialist group.

John L. Gillin, "A Contribution to the Sociology of Sects," *American Journal of Sociology*, 16 (1910), 236–52. This early paper is still one of the best concise statements of the socioeconomic origins of dissident religious sects.

H. Richard Niebuhr, *The Social Sources of Denominationalism*. Hamden, Conn.: The Shoe String Press, 1954 (first published New York, 1929). This book is th classic in sociological analysis of religious sects and of the transformations accompanying their development.

Nels Anderson, *Desert Saints*. Chicago: University of Chicago Press, 1942. This book is an account of one of the United States' most successful separatist movements.

Charles Samuel Braden, *These Also Believe: A Study of Modern American Cults and Minority Religious Movements*. New York: The Macmillan Company, 1949. Brief but careful descriptions of several recent fringe religious movements are presented.

John B. Holt, "Holiness Religion: Cultural Shock and Social Reorganization," *American Sociological Review*, 5 (1940), 740–47. Holiness churches are interpreted as responses to the disturbing effects of urbanization.

Erdmann D. Beynon, "The Voodoo-Cult Among Negro Migrants in Detroit," *American Journal of Sociology*, 43 (1938), 894–907. A Detroit Negro group exemplifies the characteristics of a passive reform movement.

Florence Hawley, "The Keresan Holy Rollers: An Adaptation to American Individualism," *Social Forces*, 26 (1948), 272–80. The unusual case of a Pueblo family joining a Negro "Holy Roller" group is explained as an attempted solution of the personal problems of acculturation.

George Barton Cutten, *Speaking with Tongues: Historically and Psychologically Considered*. New Haven: Yale University Press, 1927. This is a general inquiry into the appearance of a particular kind of symbolic behavior in religious movements.

Alfred W. Griswold, "New Thought: A Cult of Success," *American Journal of Sociology*, 40 (1934), 309–18. New Thought exemplifies the personal-status type of movement, with its conviction that right thinking insures financial success.

Norman R. F. Maier, "The Role of Frustration in Social Movements," *Psychological Review*, 49 (1942), 586–99. Frustration as a determinant of susceptibility to any type of social movement is given empirical support.

Arnold M. Rose, *Union Solidarity: The Internal Cohesion of a Labor Union*. Minneapolis: University of Minnesota Press, 1952. Interviews with four hundred unionists provide clues to the correlates of loyalty.

Joel Seidman, Jack London, and Bernard Karsh, "Why Workers Join Unions," *Annals of the American Academy of Political and Social Science*, 274 (1951), 75–84. Motives quite unrelated to the avowed purpose of labor unions play an important part in determining membership.

Charles P. Loomis and J. Allen Beegle, "The Spread of German Nazism in Rural Areas," *American Sociological Review*, 11 (1946), 724–34. On the basis of the Nazi vote in 1926 and 1932, susceptibility to Nazism is shown to be related to the breakdown of social solidarity.

E. J. Kahn, Jr., *The Voice*. New York: Harper & Brothers, 1947. This popular account of the singer Frank Sinatra's early career and the antics of his teen-age following appeared first in the *New Yorker* magazine.

Verne F. Ray, "The Kolaskin Cult: A Prophet Movement of 1870 in Northeastern Washington," *American Anthropologist*, 38 (1936), 67–75. The author presents the case history of a charismatic leader among a group of American Indians.

Fillmore H. Sanford, "Public Orientation to Roosevelt," *Public Opinion Quarterly*, 15 (Summer, 1951), 189–216. The public response to a modern charismatic leader is documented by quantitative method.

Hans Gerth, "The Nazi Party: Its Leadership and Composition," *American Journal of Sociology*, 45 (1940), 517–41. The internal dynamics of the Nazi movement are examined in relation to their charismatic orientation.

John M. Mecklin, *The Passing of the Saint*. Chicago: University of Chicago Press, 1941. This book traces the development of the saint type from the Early Christian period through the Middle Ages and to its decline in modern times.

Hazel Catherine Wolf, *On Freedom's Altar: The Martyr Complex in the Abolition Movement*. Madison: University of Wisconsin Press, 1952. The major martyrs who played a part in the movement toward abolition of slavery are described, along with the influence of their martyrdom.

John P. Roche and Stephen Sachs, "The Bureaucrat and the Enthusiast: An Exploration of the Leadership of Social Movements," *Western Political Quarterly*, 8 (1955), 248–61. The difference between two types of leaders is illustrated through the British Labor Party.

J. E. Hulett, Jr., "The Kenny Healing Cult: Preliminary Analysis of Leadership and Patterns of Interaction," *American Sociological Review*, 10 (1945), 364–72. Here is a valuable sociological examination of a recent international movement.

Sidney Hook, *The Hero in History: A Study in Limitation and Possibility*. New York: The John Day Company, 1943. Hook's treatment of the perplexing problem of whether the great man is the tool or manipulator of events has become a classic.

Grace E. Chaffee, "The Isolated Religious Sect as an Object for Social Research," *American Journal of Sociology*, 35 (1930), 618–30. The trend of the isolated sect toward assimilation is explored.

Joseph R. Gusfield, "Social Structure and Moral Reform: A Study of the Woman's Christian Temperance Union," *American Journal of Sociology*, 61 (1955), 221–32. The W.C.T.U. is shown to have changed from a middle-class movement to one of indignation against prevalent middle-class patterns.

Kingsley Davis, "Mental Hygiene and the Class Structure," *Psychiatry*, 1 (1938), 55–65. Davis argues that a conservatizing tendency had vitiated the intended accomplishments of the mental hygiene movement.

Lyford P. Edwards, *The Natural History of Revolution*. Chicago: University of Chicago Press, 1927; and Crane Brinton, *The Anatomy of Revolution*, Revised edition. Englewood Cliffs, N.J.: Prentice-Hall, Inc., 1952. These two studies search for the typical sequence of events in revolution, drawing upon the major revolutions of modern times.

PART 5: *Social consequences of collective behavior*

Brooks Adams, *The Law of Civilization and Decay*. New York: Vintage Books, 1955 (first published, 1896). Adams speculates regarding a cyclical theory of social order.

Robert Hunter, *Revolution: Why, How, When?* New York: Harper & Brothers, 1940. Hunter presents a cyclical theory of alternating revolution and counter-revolution.

Sidney A. Reeve, *The Natural Laws of Social Convulsion*. New York: E. P. Dutton & Co., 1933. Following a review of the French Revolution, Reeve proposes a series of "laws" of social convulsion.

Howard Becker, "Unrest, Culture Contact, and Release During the Middle Ages and the Renaissance," *Southwestern Social Science Quarterly*, 12 (1931), 143–55. Becker examines the place of widespread collective behavior in the culture contact and change of the late middle ages.

Lowell Juilliard Carr, "Disaster and the Sequence-Pattern Concept of Social Change," *American Journal of Sociology*, 38 (1932), 207–18. The writer proposes a formalized sequence in reaction to catastrophic change.

William H. Form and Charles P. Loomis, "The Persistence and Emergence of Social and Cultural Systems in Disasters," *American Sociological Review,* 21 (1956), 180–85. Reviewing the evidence from recent disaster studies, the authors point out the persistence of social order and the quick rise of a spontaneous disaster system.

Arnold Whitridge, "1848: The Year of Revolution," *Foreign Affairs,* 26 (1948), 264–75. An effort is made to assess the net consequences of the year's disturbances for long-range historical development.

E. Dekany, "Une Forme 'Elementaire' de la Vie Sociale: Le Public," *Revue Internationale de Sociologie,* 44 (1936), 263–77. Dekany proposes an interesting distinction between the public and certain other forms of collective behavior on the basis of their social functions.

Author Index

Subject Index

543